THE SOUTHERN WALL OF THE
TEMPLE MOUNT AND
ITS CORNERS:
PAST, PRESENT AND FUTURE

Ancient Jerusalem Publications (AJP) Series

III

Series Editor: Efrat Bocher

Managing Editor: Myrna Pollak

Volume Editor: Michal Sinowitz

Art Director: Alina Yoffe-Pikovsky

Graphic Designer: Noa Evron

Assistant Editor: Hannah Rozenblat

Modern color photographs of the Southern Temple Mount by Shai Halevi

THE SOUTHERN WALL OF THE TEMPLE MOUNT AND ITS CORNERS: PAST, PRESENT AND FUTURE

YUVAL BARUCH, RONNY REICH, MORAN HAGBI AND JOE UZIEL

ANCIENT JERUSALEM PUBLICATIONS III

Contributions by

Donald T. Ariel, Yotam Asscher, Uri Basson, Yaakov Billig, Elisabetta Boaretto, Efrat Bocher, Ofer Cohen, Dror Czitron, Benjamin J. Dolinka, Shimon Gibson, Yael Gorin-Rosen, Yael Kalman, Dafna Langgut, Hélène Machline, Nimrod Marom, Yossi Nagar, Dvory Namdar, Orit Peleg-Barkat, Johanna Regev, Helena Roth, Débora Sandhaus, Lidar Sapir-Hen, Moshe Sharon, Meidad Shor, Abra Spiciarich, Svetlana Tarkhanova, Dorit Tsipshtein, Yonathan Tzahor, Yosef Vaknin, Filip Vukosavović, Tamar Winter, Ayala Zilberstein, and Aliza Van Zuiden

EISENBRAUNS
University Park, Pennsylvania

ANCIENT JERUSALEM PUBLICATIONS
Jerusalem

ISRAEL ANTIQUITIES AUTHORITY PUBLICATIONS
Jerusalem

Library of Congress Cataloging-in-Publication Data

Names: Baruch, Yuval, 1963– editor. | Reich, Ronny, editor. | Hagbi, Moran, editor. | Uziel, Joe, editor.

Title: The Southern Wall of the Temple Mount and its corners : past, present and future / [edited by] Yuval Baruch, Ronny Reich, Moran Hagbi and Joe Uziel ; contributions by Donald T. Ariel [and others].

Description: University Park, Pennsylvania : Eisenbrauns ; Jerusalem : Ancient Jerusalem Publications ; Israel Antiquities Authority Publications, [2023].

Summary: "Presents final reports of three excavations at the Southern Wall of the Temple Mount in Jerusalem and its two corners. Examines the architecture, art, inscriptions, cemeteries, and conservation projects in these parts of the ancient compound"—Provided by publisher.

Identifiers: LCCN 2023030596 | ISBN 9781646022632 (hardback)

Subjects: LCSH: Southern Wall (Jerusalem)—Antiquities. | Excavations (Archaeology)—Jerusalem. | Temple Mount (Jerusalem)—Antiquities. | Jerusalem—Antiquities.

Classification: LCC GN780.32.M4 F76 2023

LC record available at https://lccn.loc.gov/2023030670

Printed in the United States of America

Published by The Pennsylvania State University Press,

University Park, PA 16802-1003

Eisenbrauns is an imprint of The Pennsylvania State University Press.

The Pennsylvania State University Press is a member of the Association of University Presses.

It is the policy of The Pennsylvania State University Press to use acid-free paper. Publications on uncoated stock satisfy the minimum requirements of American National Standard for Information Sciences—Permanence of Paper for Printed Library Material, ANSI Z39.48–1992.

ISBN 978-1-64602-263-2

This book and the research it presents could not have been done without the generous support of Nelson Shaller.

———————————

The Ancient Jerusalem Research Center was established in coordination with the Jerusalem Region of the Israel Antiquities Authority and the Ir David Foundation (EL-AD), which is dedicated to the excavation, preservation, examination and scientific publication of the discoveries in the City of David and the landscape of Ancient Jerusalem. The Ancient Jerusalem Publication Series was made possible through the generosity of the Ir David Foundation.

CONTENTS

Our Authors	*Affiliation*	*Email*
Yuval Baruch	*Israel Antiquities Authority, University of Haifa*	*yuval@israntique.org.il*
Ronny Reich	*University of Haifa, Israel Exploration Society*	*ronny@research.haifa.ac.il*
Moran Hagbi	*Israel Antiquities Authority*	*moranhb@gmail.com*
Joe Uziel	*Israel Antiquities Authority*	*joeuziel@gmail.com*
Donald T. Ariel	*Israel Antiquities Authority*	*dtariel@gmail.com*
Yotam Asscher	*Israel Antiquities Authority*	*yotama@israntique.org.il*
Uri Basson	*GeoSense Ltd and University of Haifa*	*ubasson@gmail.com*
Yaakov Billig	*Israel Antiquities Authority*	*billig@israntique.org.il*
Elisabetta Boaretto	*Weizmann Institute of Science*	*elisabetta.boaretto@weizmann.ac.il*
Efrat Bocher	*Bar Ilan University, the Ancient Jerusalem Research Center*	*efrat@ajri.org.il*
Ofer Cohen	*Israel Antiquities Authority*	*Ofer@yad.co.il*
Dror Czitron	*Israel Antiquities Authority*	*drorz@israntique.org.il*
Benjamin J. Dolinka	*Israel Antiquities Authority*	*sherd_boy@hotmail.com*
Shimon Gibson	*University of North Carolina at Charlotte*	*shimgib@gmail.com*
Yael Gorin-Rosen	*Israel Antiquities Authority*	*gorin@israntique.org.il*
Yael Kalman	*Israel Antiquities Authority*	*yaelk@israntique.org.il*
Dafna Langgut	*Tel Aviv University*	*langgut@tauex.tau.ac.il*
Hélène Machline	*Israel Antiquities Authority*	*helenemachline@gmail.com*
Nimrod Marom	*University of Haifa*	*nmarom@marsci.haifa.ac.il*
Yossi Nagar	*Israel Antiquities Authority*	*yossi@israntique.org.il*
Dvory Namdar	*Volcani Agricultural Research Center, Hebrew University of Jerusalem*	*dvoran@volcani.agri.gov.il*
Orit Peleg-Barkat	*Hebrew University of Jerusalem*	*orit.peleg@mail.huji.ac.il*
Débora Sandhaus	*Israel Antiquities Authority*	*debby.reen@gmail.com*
Lidar Sapir-Hen	*Tel Aviv University*	*lidarsap@tauex.tau.ac.il*
Johanna Regev	*Weizmann Institute of Science*	*johanna.regev@gmail.com*
Helena Roth	*Tel Aviv University*	*helenaroth@mail.tau.ac.il*
Moshe Sharon	*Hebrew University of Jerusalem*	*moshe.sharon@mail.huji.ac.il*
Meidad Shor	*Israel Antiquities Authority*	*meidad@israntique.org.il*
Abra Spiciarich	*Tel Aviv University*	*abra.spiciarich@gmail.com*
Svetlana Tarkhanova	*Israel Antiquities Authority*	*svetlanat@israntique.org.il*
Dorit Tsipshtein	*Israel Antiquities Authority*	*dorit.pilnick@gmail.com*
Yonathan Tzahor	*Israel Antiquities Authority*	*tzahory@gmail.com*
Yosef Vaknin	*Israel Antiquities Authority*	*yossiv@israntique.org.il*
Filip Vukosavović	*Ancient Jerusalem Research Center*	*filiprvm@gmail.com*
Tamar Winter	*Israel Antiquities Authority*	*winter@israntique.org.il*
Ayala Zilberstein	*Israel Antiquities Authority, Tel Aviv University*	*ayalaz@israntique.org.il*
Aliza Van Zuiden	*Israel Antiquities Authority*	*alizavanz@gmail.com*

PREFACE

This book is the third in the Ancient Jerusalem Publications (AJP) series of books published by the Center for the Study of Ancient Jerusalem, as part of the publications of the Israel Antiquities Authority (IAA), in consultation with the EL-AD Foundation, which runs the City of David National Park and other ancient Jerusalem sites. The AJP series is a platform for studies focusing on the archaeological excavations conducted in ancient Jerusalem, a geographical space that includes, in addition to the "Old City," the areas surrounding the city wall and especially the southern parts of the ancient city: the "Ophel" area, the Ridge of the City of David and the southern slopes of Mount Zion.

The first two books published in this series detailed excavation reports presenting the results of the excavations conducted in various areas on the City of David Hill. In contrast, this volume, which focuses on the Southern Wall of the Temple Mount compound and its two corners, includes, in addition to excavation reports, chapters on the preservation and conservation of the Temple Mount walls.

This book presents multidisciplinary archaeological reports, which make up an ongoing study that began in the mid-1990s, when the excavations were renewed in the area south of the Southern Wall. This enterprise is part of the initiative and vision of the founder and first director of the IAA, the late Amir Drori, as part of a government plan to mark the 3000th anniversary since King David chose Jerusalem as his capital.

In preparing this book for press, we wished to cover a variety of topics, research methods and periods. Our approach was based on our understanding that the archaeology of Jerusalem is multi-layered and multi-faceted, especially when dealing with the Temple Mount compound and its history.

In addition to the archaeological research, intensive conservation operations were conducted in recent years on the walls of the Temple Mount itself. The excavations and conservation operations were conducted from the outset by teams of archaeologists and conservators on behalf of the IAA, alongside researchers from various fields and various institutions. Discussions on the preservation of the walls of the Temple Mount would assist in analyzing what was achieved in the past. It would also help to understand what is being done at the present and to assess the magnitude of the challenge that awaits us in the future in preserving the architectural aspects of the Temple Mount walls.

Many contributed to the writing and publication of this book: the authors of the various chapters, members of the academic committee: Prof. Israel Finkelstein, Prof. Shimon Gibson, Prof. Andrea Berlin, Prof. Yuval Gadot, Dr. Zvi Greenhut and Dr. Joe Uziel, who each contributed of their time and broad knowledge. Above all, our thanks and appreciation go to the Ancient Jerusalem Publications editorial team, led by Efrat Bocher, the series editor and the spirit behind the editorial concept of the book's pages; the managing editor, Myrna Pollak, whose careful supervision assured the publication of an aesthetic and high-level research work; to Michal Sinowitz for her diligent attention to the written word and for good advice; to Alina Yoffe-Pikovsky for her masterful reproductions and elegant cover; to Noa Evron for her attractive design and layout and eternal patience; to Hannah Rozenblat for her diligence in preparing the references; to Shai Halevi for his wonderful photographs of the modern City of David; and to Nahshon Szanton for his editorial input.

We are grateful to all the persons who assisted in the various excavations presented in this volume, mainly from the IAA, who are mentioned by name in the relevant chapters. Without their dedicated work in the field and in the labs, this volume would have never materialized.

Sincere thanks to our friends at the Pennsylvania State University Press, our partners in publishing and distributing the book. In addition, we thank Michael Baruchi, the administrator and budget manager of the Center for the Study of Ancient Jerusalem, and many others who have not been mentioned here by name but whose contributions, both in advice and in action, were of great importance.

The authors and editors thank all the institutions that have assisted us in our efforts to make this book a reality, in particular the photo archive and the publications department of the Israel Antiquities Authority.

The Ancient Jerusalem Research Center aims to promote archaeological research in Jerusalem and publish the results of the excavations. The center was established as a joint venture of the Israel Antiquities Authority and the Ir David Foundation (EL-AD). We would like to thank the Israel Antiquities Authority directors Israel Hasson (2015–2021), who helped and supported the establishment of the center without reservation, and the current director Eli Eskosido. We also wish to thank the EL-AD Foundation: David Be'eri, CEO; Uriya Dasberg, the Development VP and Doron Spielman, for their support of this unique project and for their great assistance in the success of its goals.

Yuval Baruch and Ronny Reich
June 2023

PART I:

THE SOUTHERN WALL:

ITS

HISTORICAL, ARCHAEOLOGICAL

AND

GEOGRAPHICAL FRAMEWORK

CHAPTER 1

INTRODUCTION

Yuval Baruch and Ronny Reich

There is probably no site in the world more frustrating to the modern archaeologist than the Temple Mount of the Hellenistic and Early Roman (Second Temple) period in Jerusalem. Though the rich history of millennia sits meters, at times only centimeters, from the surface, containing data that could in some cases rewrite history, religious and political activists prevent the archaeological community from excavating within the compound. This situation will remain unchanged in the foreseeable future and archaeologists will be forced to contain their frustration. Even so, archaeologists are a stiff-necked lot, and a substantial amount of research has been and is nevertheless being conducted on the subject. In addition to itself being an example of such research, this book brings together several examples of this kind of research (Fig. 1.1).

A brief introduction to place the ancient Temple Mount in its historical and geographical/urban framework is in order.

In the ancient world, building temples repeatedly on the same spot was a well-known phenomenon. This stemmed from the sanctity ascribed to a place (see, for example, Mazar 1992). The Temple Mount in Jerusalem is a case in point. It was considered the sacred ground where the spirit of the God of Israel dwelt and where His Temple was built. It became a religious tradition that continued uninterruptedly for three millennia. This is undoubtedly due to two factors: first, Judaism is a monotheistic faith, and second, the biblical edict that the Temple, as the house of God, is the only place where sacrificial worship is permitted. This was reinforced by King Josiah's religious reform in the 7th century BCE (2 Kings 22:1–11; 23:1–30) when worship in Jerusalem was centralized, and it was intensified with the rise of the Hasmonean House to power in Judea in the middle of the 2nd century BCE (Rappaport 2004).

In his 18th regnal year (22 BCE), King Herod the Great, already known for his megalomaniacal architectural feats around the country, began a sacred expansion project of the area of the House of God, the Temple Mount in Jerusalem (*Ant.* 15.380). The project would last past his lifetime and would be completed by his heirs. The walls of the Temple Mount represent the final stage in the development of this sacred compound. Some of the remains from the previous phase of Herod's endeavor are evident in the Eastern Wall of the compound (Ritmeyer 2006: 102–105). All other details of the former architectural history are highly speculative, as the Herodian expansion covered everything. It is probable that many details preceding this expansion project, including the original topography, exist below the surface, but as stated above, archaeological excavation is barred.

The Herodian Temple Mount in Jerusalem is one of the largest construction projects in the Land of Israel up to the modern era, and the Temple was possibly the largest religious edifice of its time. The size is evident in the compound's dimensions, the size of the ashlars used, the time required for its construction and the size of the various architectural elements—bridges, gates, staircases, paved streets, etc. (Segal 2013: 266). It should be noted that throughout the period of the compound's expansion works, daily worship continued in the Temple and in the area nearby, which attracted tens of thousands of people in peak times during the main Jewish festivals. The expansion of the

Figure 1.1: Aerial view of the Herodian Temple Mount. Source: Bavarian State Archive, photo taken between September 1917 and September 1918 (Dalman, G. 1925. *Hundert Deutsche Fliegerbilder aus Palästina*. Gütersloh).

Temple Mount most probably affected the entire plan of the city of Jerusalem as a whole, and the daily routine within it.

Since the beginning of archaeological research in the middle of the 19th century, scholars have wanted to dig inside the premises of the Temple Mount and, as this has been prohibited by the local authorities, they turned their attention to documenting the walls of the Temple Mount and conducting minor-scale excavations (see Chapter 2). With the unification of the city in 1967 and up to today, large-scale archaeological excavations have been taking place outside the sacred compound.[1] These excavations have been adjacent to the Western and Southern Walls, that is, in relation to half of the circumference of the Temple Mount, which extends to 1547 m, circumscribing an area of 141.28 *dunam* (which is 14.13 hectares). These excavations and studies, some of which appear in this book, revealed a great deal of information about the construction of the walls themselves (see Chapters 4 and 16). It is hoped that additional methods of remote sensing will be developed to attain data that cannot be obtained through traditional archaeological methods, to enhance our knowledge of this extraordinary site.

This book deals with the Southern Wall as well as the southern segment of the Western Wall of the Temple Mount compound. It is one of four walls that formed the *temenos* or sacred enclosure of the Second Jewish Temple and may well have been the central structure of the complex. Two main

---

[1] *Hadashot Arkheologiyot Online,* on the Israel Antiquities Authority webpage, reports on all excavations carried out in Israel since 2004.

gateways to the compound were located on this wall—the Double Gate and the Triple Gate—both of which the Mishnah (*Middot* 1:3; 2:2) describes as main entrances through which the majority of pilgrims ascended to the Temple on the three main pilgrimage festivals and through which sacrificial animals were led to the altar. In addition to these gates, two more gates had been planned close to the corners of the compound: one near the southwestern corner (above Robinson's Arch), leading directly to the Royal Portico, and another near the southeastern corner of the compound (Fig. 1.2; see Chapters 5, 27, 28).

No visuals or plans of the Temple Mount's construction project have come down to us from antiquity and conjectures of the size of the sacred enclosure by historians, theologians and even archaeologists over the past 150 years have gone in numerous directions (see, for example, Ritmeyer 2006, with extensive bibliography on pp. 402–411). Our opinion is that the sacred space, at the size it attained during the days of King Herod the Great, must have included the architectural envelope that surrounds the Temple Mount proper and that the system of entrances, gateways and roads leading to the compound, as well as the outer faces of the compound walls, were all part of the sacred enclosure. The chapters in this book present the archaeological evidence of the excavations cited, follow-up research and our analysis.

The main objective of the present volume is to publish the results of various excavations that have been conducted in different locations along the walls. Moreover, we attempt to expand the view regarding the Southern Wall and the area close by, while widely referring to its physical aspects, and by doing so, assess the architectural changes that have occurred in the Southern Wall from the late Second Temple (Early Roman) period through to the end of the Early Islamic period.

This book is divided into five parts:

Figure 1.2: Robinson's Arch prior to Mazar's excavations.

Following this introduction, Part I presents a sweeping historical survey (Chapter 2) of archaeological activities carried out in this area over the past 150 years; it then offers a detailed topography (Chapter 3) of the area adjacent to the Southern Wall.

Part II presents three excavations reports: Excavations near the Southeastern Corner (Chapters 4–15); Excavations West of the Southwestern Corner (Chapters 16–25); and Excavations of an Early Islamic Cemetery (Chapter 26).

Part III offers several ongoing studies, some in breakthrough archaeoscientific fields that take our research on a quantum leap from the past into the future. Chapter 32 tracks the thickness of the Temple Mount walls with GPR imaging; and Chapter 34 describes a ^{14}C study of organic remains that enable precision dating of the Temple Mount walls. Other studies focus on architectural design (Chapter 27), inscriptions (Chapters 29–31) and scriptural decoration (Chapter 28).

As of the early 2000s, various large-scale conservation projects were carried out in different locations along the Southern Wall and its corners. The results of these projects are presented in Part IV. Advanced engineering, geophysical, chemical and physical examinations and thorough documentation technologies accompanied these projects.

Beyond their contribution to the improvement of the Temple Mount walls' physical condition, conservation projects have actually enabled the integration of advanced documentation methods. These methods have led to an up-to-date mapping of the walls' sections in the area of Robinson's Arch, including laser scanning and three-dimensional photogrammetric mapping of the arch's structure. This mapping became our basis for renewed research of issues relating to Robinson's Arch and to sections of the walls near it. We see this conservation project with a view to the future. We must study the past but we must also keep it safe for future generations.

Part V summarizes the entire volume.

REFERENCES

Baruch, Y. and Reich, R. 2016. Excavations near the Triple Gate of the Temple Mount, Jerusalem. ʿAtiqot 85: 37–95 (Hebrew).

Ben-Dov, M. 1982. *In the Shadow of the Temple: The Discovery of Ancient Jerusalem.* Jerusalem.

Mazar, A. 1992. Temples of the Middle and Late Bronze Ages and the Iron Age. In: Kempinski, A. and Reich, R., eds. *The Architecture of Ancient Israel, from Prehistoric to the Persian Period.* Jerusalem: 161–187.

Mazar, E. and Mazar, B. 1989. *Excavations in the South of the Temple Mount: The Ophel of Biblical Jerusalem* (Qedem 29). Jerusalem.

Rappaport, U. 2004. *The First Book of Maccabees, Introduction, Hebrew Translation and Commentary.* Jerusalem: 50–55 (Hebrew).

Reich, R. and Billig, Y. 2000. Excavations near the Temple Mount and Robinson's Arch, 1994–1996; Appendix: A Group of Theater Seats from Jerusalem. In: Geva, H., ed. *Ancient Jerusalem Revealed, Reprinted and Expanded Edition.* Jerusalem: 340–352.

Reich, R. and Billig, Y. 2003. Another Flavian Latin Inscription from the Excavations near the Temple Mount, Jerusalem. ʿAtiqot 44: 243–247.

Reich, R. and Shukron, E. 2011. Excavations in Jerusalem Beneath the Paved Street and in the Sewage Channel next to Robinson's Arch. Qadmoniot 142: 66–73 (Hebrew).

Segal, A. 2013. *Temples and Sanctuaries in the Roman East: Religious Architecture in Syria Iudaea/Palaestina and Provincia Arabia.* Oxford.

Warren, C. 1884. *Plans, Elevations, Sections, etc. Shewing the Results of the Excavations at Jerusalem, 1867–70, Executed for the Committee of the Palestine Exploration Fund.* London.

CHAPTER 2

HISTORY OF RESEARCH AND DOCUMENTATION ALONG THE SOUTHERN WALL OF THE TEMPLE MOUNT/ḤARAM AŠ-ŠARĪF: FROM FREDERICK CATHERWOOD TO CONRAD SCHICK

Shimon Gibson

The Temple Mount (known in Arabic as the Ḥaram aš-Šarīf) is a prominent and majestic component of urban Jerusalem, situated on the east side of the Old City, incorporating beneath it biblical Mount Moriah, and topographically perched above the deep Kidron ravine, with the massif of the Mount of Olives looming opposite it. The rest of the city is spread out on several hills, to the north, west and south, comprising large and small domed houses, public buildings, church steeples and minarets. However, the Temple Mount stands apart, and this is the way it has always been—connected while at the same time almost *always* a separate component of that city. It is a very large trapezoidal enclosure (485 × 280 m), with an interior area covering 14.5 hectares (36 acres), comprising open spaces, shrines (notably, the prominent Dome of the Rock, with its golden cupola, enshrining the *as-Sakhra*, centered on a separate platform/plaza of its own), mosques (Al-Aqṣà Mosque, to the south), and a scattering of smaller monuments, cenotaphs, trees, steps and paved areas.

Historically, this area was never intended to be interwoven completely into the general urban fabric of the city, though substantial efforts to make this happen were attempted by builders much later, firstly under the Fāṭimids (10th–11th centuries CE) and then later in the Mamluk period (13th–15th centuries CE), particularly along the western side, through the construction of large buildings, schools and hospices situated above elevated substructures, with the intention of linking the enclosure's interior to the street levels in the rest of the city (Burgoyne 1987). In pre-medieval and earlier periods, however, this platform/*temenos* was purposefully disconnected from the rest of the city, almost like a citadel, with the demarcation of the sacred and profane clearly reinforced by very high and massively built enclosure walls of ashlars with pilasters surrounding the rectangular interior of the platform on three of its sides, except to the north, which had a high rocky scarp (surmounted today by the Umariyya School).

Altogether, the Temple Mount had a visibly well-demarcated and elevated platform/*temenos*. Throughout ancient times (Iron Age to Early Roman periods) this sacred space, known in Hebrew as *Har HaBayit* (cf. Micah 3:12), was largely impenetrable to most visitors, except to pilgrims/worshippers who were permitted to approach the area at times proscribed in sacred Israelite/Jewish calendars and for religious festivities. Those entering were obliged to subscribe to the degrees of accessibility laid down for the different internal parts of the *temenos* (some marked out with physical barriers and fences), and admittance was permitted based on rank and status and prevalent custom, and movement within the compound was constrained by strict and effective prohibitions (Goodman 2005; Branham 2006).

Visitors, pilgrims and explorers, on reaching Jerusalem in the early 19th century, frequently commented upon the Temple Mount as the most conspicuous and monumental part of the city. Effectively, the closest most visitors got to see the interior of the esplanade in its entirety was from viewing areas on the much higher Mount of Olives to the east. Many, however, were able to approach fairly freely some parts of the external Temple Mount walls, remarking particularly on the Western Wall (described in the literature of the 19th century as the "Wailing Wall"), where Jews could be seen to worship, and on the Eastern Wall with its Golden Gate, as seen from the external Muslim cemetery. Reference was also made to the ancient, drafted masonry, which was particularly visible in the Southern Wall, as well as on the remnants of its gates, and on the Aqṣà Mosque looming above it. This chapter will deal specifically with the exploration of the Southern Temple Mount Wall from Catherwood to Schick[1] (Fig. 2.1).

1833–1862: CATHERWOOD TO PIEROTTI

The interior of the Ḥaram aš-Šarīf compound was largely out of bounds to Westerners in the early 19th century. However, owing to the liberal policies of Mehmet Ali, Pasha of Egypt, a few travelers eventually did manage to penetrate the closed-off compound itself. In 1833, Frederick Catherwood, better known for his explorations in South America, covertly gained access to the Temple Mount, and importantly succeeded in making the first accurate general map of the compound importantly succeeded in making the first accurate general map of the compound, showing that the Western Wall of the Ḥaram aš-Šarīf was on one continuous line and not as previously thought.[2] He also succeeded in making architectural drawings of the principal buildings, the Golden Gate, the interior of the Double Gate,[3] and the subterranean Solomon's Stables.[4] It was not an easy task, but Catherwood was determined. He wrote: "The success of my first attempt, induced me to make a second visit the following day. I determined to take in my *camera lucida* and sit down and make a drawing; a proceeding certain to attract the attention of the most indifferent and expose me to dangerous consequences."[5]

---

[1] My thanks to Yuval Baruch for kindly suggesting that I contribute a chapter to this book. I am very grateful to Felicity Cobbing, Executive Secretary and Curator, and to Avantika Clark, Collections Assistant, for providing me with access to archival materials preserved at the Palestine Exploration Fund (PEF) in London. Additional thanks go to Mareike Grosser for her assistance during the production of this paper.

[2] Van de Velde confirmed in 1851/1852 that Catherwood's depiction of the western line of the Temple Mount enclosure wall as a straight line was indeed accurate, whereas earlier mapping efforts had got it wrong (Van de Velde 1854: 252).

[3] The Double Gate was first rediscovered and drawn in 1841 by William Tipping, who was a well-known artist from England (Stewart 1854: 262).

[4] Robert Richardson was one of the earliest scholars given admittance to the underground vaults of the so-called Solomon's Stables (now known as the Marwani Prayer Hall) (Richardson 1822: 309–311). On the history of the exploration of this place: Gibson and Jacobson 1996: 268–279. An examination of the piers of these vaults, which I made during a personal visit in December 1995, indicates they were mostly constructed out of drafted ashlars in secondary use, and so are likely to be Ismaili Fāṭimid in date, at least in its latest phase. It should be pointed out, however, that the masonry at the foundation level of the piers was not visible, and therefore they may very well have had their origins in the Umayyad period. Recently, it has been suggested that this expanded complex was originally a mosque built at the time of Caliph Muʿawiya ibn Abi Sufyan between 640–660 CE (St. Laurent and Awwad 2013).

[5] Catherwood's memoir is included in Bartlett's *Walks About the City and Environs of Jerusalem*: 148–165. The camera lucida mentioned by Catherwood was invented by the English chemist, William Hyde Wollaston, in 1807, and was the preferred instrument using a prism for making architectural drawings, since it projected the scene in front of the artist onto the drawing paper simultaneously and allowed for an accuracy that was difficult to obtain while using only the naked eye. Catherwood reportedly undertook detailed mapping and surveying operations along the Temple Mount walls as well (Bartlett 1844: 160–161). Unfortunately, he did not publish a full report on his results, and he died in an accident in 1854. Catherwood's plan of the Ḥaram aš-Šarīf was reproduced by the publisher John Weale in July 1847, and it shows a remarkable amount of detail concerning the layout of the Aqṣà Mosque and Solomon's Stables. On Catherwood's life: von Hagen 1950.

Figure 2.1: Panorama of the Temple Mount seen from the southeast. Hand-tinted photograph by the Matson Company, ca. 1900 (courtesy of the Gibson Picture Archive).

The name of the American philologist and biblical historian Edward Robinson will forever be attached to a prominent ancient arch jutting out from the southern end of the Western Temple Mount Wall in Jerusalem, which in the 1st century CE served as part of a flight of steps leading from the Royal Stoa to the paved plaza in the Tyropoeon Valley below. It has been assumed by many—even in recent articles and guidebooks—that the reason this ancient monument was named after him was because he must have been the first to see it. But this is not the case: indeed, the background story is clearly given by Goren in a final chapter of his book on Robinson's 1838 journey to the Holy Land (Goren 2020: 245–274). Frederick Catherwood was the first to properly record the arch in 1833 and to him goes that honor, and Robinson was not its discoverer (Gibson 2021: 222–243; even Warren got it wrong: Warren 1876: 69). The facts associated with the study of the arch led at that time to a bitter dispute between Robinson and another scholar named Stephen Olin on the matter of scholarly precedence in regard to the recognition of the significance of the arch.[6]

Robinson was impressed by the Southern Wall, noting in his first account that the Old City wall approached it from the south, subdividing the area in front of it into two patches of ground, with the rectangular area on the west serving in 1838 as a "ploughed field," and he mentions that it was said to be ground belonging to the Aqṣà Mosque (Robinson 1874: 281–306)[7] (Figs. 2.2–2.3). He noted that the Southern Wall had a visible height of some 18 m and that he was able to distinguish two main sets of masonry: eight courses of large ashlars of "early" date, followed above these by 24 courses of smaller stones of "modern" date (i.e., medieval or later), and that in the central part

---

[6]   Robinson was by no means the only one of his period to examine and record impressions concerning the antiquity of the Temple Mount walls and its masonry, and in the footnotes of his publications he refers to some of this earlier scholarship. The historian George Williams, for instance, was one such scholar who had noted in 1842 the great antiquity of the external walls of the Ḥaram aš-Šarīf and the enormous size of some of its visible drafted stones which he ascribed to "Hebrew masons" (Williams 1849: 101, 314–320).

[7]   On deliberations concerning the length of the Southern Wall: Robinson 1856: 176.

Figure 2.2: The southwestern angle of the Temple Mount, with the Zāwiya el-Khatiniyya complex on the right. Gelatin print by an American photographer from 1927 (courtesy of the Gibson Picture Archive).

Figure 2.3: The southwestern angle of the Temple Mount, with the Zāwiya el-Khatiniyya complex on the right, in 2013 (author's photograph).

of this wall he saw the blocked Double Gate with a subterranean passage behind it (Robinson 1874: 304–305).[8] Later, following his 1852 trip, Robinson also described the blocked-up Single Gate and the Triple Gate (Robinson 1856: 175–176, 192–193). Robinson was quite an astute observer of ancient architecture and in conducting his first analysis of the structural components of the Southern Wall, he noted that "the line between these lower antique portions and the modern ones above them, is very irregular, though it is also very distinct. The former, in some parts, are much higher than the others; and occasionally the breaches in them are filled out with later patchwork. Sometimes too the whole wall is modern" (Robinson 1874: 286).[9] He was particularly interested, however, in the earlier "antique" drafted stonework (i.e., Herodian), which he incorrectly thought should be attributed to the time of King Solomon, and this led him to make a closer examination of the southeast corner of the Temple Mount enclosure, where the ancient masonry was particularly conspicuous, noting that sizes of drafted ashlars there reached lengths of 5 m and heights of 1.2 m. At the southwest corner he indicated by comparison that he saw one ashlar block with a total length nearing 9.5 m and with a height close to 2 m. Another important aspect of Robinson's work was his recognition of the fashion by which the ashlars in the lower parts of the wall had been hewn with marginal drafting.

One other point worth mentioning is Robinson's suggested chronology for the Temple Mount stonework. He believed the large ashlar-built foundations of the wall had to belong to the period of King Solomon and on stylistic grounds he thought the masonry certainly predated "Seleucid" (i.e., Hellenistic) or Roman architecture. His examination of the monumental arch (later known as "Robinson's Arch") along the Western Wall near the southwest angle helped confirm him in this dating, since he believed it was part of a bridge across the Tyropoeon Valley that had to be antecedent to the days of Herod the Great. Herod, he believed, concentrated his building work solely on the actual Temple and adjoining porticoes. Importantly, his overall conclusion was that the area of the ancient Solomonic Temple Mount "was identical on its western, eastern, and southern sides, with the present enclosure of the Haram."

Research at the Temple Mount was also made by James Thomas Barclay, an American Campbellite Christian, who resided in Jerusalem from 1850 to 1857. He was able to gain access to the Ḥaram aš-Šarīf at a time when repairs were being done to the Dome of the Rock and other buildings at the Ḥaram aš-Šarīf (Barclay 1858: xv, 477–478, 485). Although he encountered difficulties "from the fanatical demonstration of the guard" while taking measurements at the Ḥaram aš-Šarīf, the exceptional access that he was provided did allow him to study the subterranean Solomon's Stables, the passageway of the Triple Gate, which he believed was used to provide access for sacrificial animals in the Second Temple period (Barclay 1858: 488),[10] and a blocked gateway in the Western Wall (Barclay's Gate) (Barclay 1858: 488–490; Jacobson and Gibson 1997). In terms of measurements, Barclay tabulated the length of the Southern Wall as it had been given by previous explorers and

---

8   Robinson ascribed the Double Gate to the time of Herod, though also conceding it had later been rebuilt as well, and in this regard, he relied heavily on drawings prepared by Catherwood. Robinson managed to access the medieval building complex (ez Zāwiya el-Khatiniyya/Khunthaniya/Khatnyya/Khatuniy) lying in front of the earlier Double Gate during his 1852 visit, but "the interior however was too dark to distinguish anything accurately" (Robinson 1856: 164). Catherwood described the Khatiniyya in 1833: "The mass of buildings projecting at the back [of Aqṣà], beyond the wall of the great enclosure, are merely offices connected with the mosque" (Bartlett 1844: 156).

9   For further comments on the significance of the masonry along the southern Ḥaram aš-Šarīf wall: Robinson 1856: 220–221.

10   Baruch and Reich (2016; see Chapter 27) recently made a convincing case that there was a ramp supported on vaults that led from the southeast angle of the Temple Mount to the Triple Gate, and that it was from there that during the 1st century CE animals (cows and sheep) were led into the Temple area for sacrifice.

compared this with his own measurements (916 feet = 279.19 m) which were undertaken, as he put it, based on "trigonometrical principals." He described the inaccuracies concerning the previous measurements of this wall as follows: "These discrepancies are much to be regretted, but by no means to be censured, for such is the nature of the ground, and such the difficulties arising from impenetrable copses of cactus, interposing buildings, and accumulations of rubbish, that error is unavoidable" (Barclay 1858: 485).

The external enclosure walls of the Temple Mount were also carefully examined by Louis Félicien Joseph Caignart de Saulcy during visits he made to Jerusalem in 1850–1851, preparing detailed drawings of the drafted masonry along the Eastern enclosure Wall, the small arch seen near the southeast corner, and elevations of the Triple and Double Gates along the Southern enclosure Wall (de Saulcy 1853: Pls. XXIII–XXIV) (Fig. 2.4).

In 1857–1861, the Italian engineer Ermete Pierotti, acting on behalf of the governor Surraya Pasha as an "honorary architect," was also able to access the Temple Mount. In his *Jerusalem Explored*, Pierotti indicates that he had been given a privileged opportunity to check the subterranean Temple Mount, since (he boasted) no one previously "has examined the ground, no one has carried on careful and systematic investigations there; all have been content to speak of what appeared above the soil, and were consequently ignorant of the objects of far greater interest below" (Pierotti 1864: 46). He noted that he had "penetrated into the subterranean works, sought out and classified the conduits and ascertained their course, constructed plans" (Pierotti 1864: 46). Pierotti's work has largely been undervalued by scholars, even though his maps of the Ḥaram aš-Šarīf are very detailed and he did succeed in gaining access to many subterranean chambers and tunnels that had previously

Figure 2.4: The Southern Wall of the Temple Mount, with the Zāwiya el-Khatiniyya complex on the left, and the Aqṣà Mosque behind. Note the blocked gate with a semicircular arch on the left. Calotype by Maxime Du Camp, August 1850 (public domain image).

been closed to foreign visitors. The fact he did not receive full recognition for his achievements is partly because his scholarly integrity was subsequently impugned and severely undermined by PEF explorer Charles W. Wilson and architectural historian James Fergusson, probably spurred on by the biblical historian George Grove, in several ferocious reviews that they wrote about his published work, using language veering toward xenophobia. At one point Grove even accused Pierotti of plagiarism in a letter he wrote to *The Times* newspaper (March 7, 1864). Thomas George Bonney, the translator of Pierotti's book *Jerusalem Explored* from Italian into English, defiantly took up the cudgel to defend Pierotti against the animosity of his critics (Bonney 1864; Williams 1864).[11]

Pierotti's book on the Temple Mount is arguably one of the most important and useful resources for current scholarship on the subject, notwithstanding the harsh criticisms made of him by his contemporaries. The large-scale maps of the Ḥaram aš-Šarīf he produced are admittedly some of the best that were available at that time to Western scholars, until the mapping by the Ordnance Survey of Jerusalem team in 1864–1865 (see below). Some of the features appearing on his maps have to be examined critically, however, but they should not be dismissed out of hand.[12] While the biography of Pierotti is replete with colorful and shady stories—including that of his being discharged from the Piedmontese military because of financial irregularities—none of this should affect our estimation of his Temple Mount achievements and the accuracy of his map-making operations.[13] Pierotti's overall contribution to the study of Jerusalem is important for modern scholarship, notwithstanding certain flaws, and for this reason a thorough reassessment of his explorations at the Temple Mount has long been overdue.

Pierotti identified four main chronological phases in the ancient masonry of the Temple Mount walls: Solomonic to Nehemiah, Herodian, Crusader, and Ottoman. The Southern Wall he described as "solid and magnificent" in appearance, noting the Triple Gate,[14] which he thought must be Roman,

---

[11] Bonney (1864) in his vigorous defense of Pierotti wrote: "After living on terms of intimacy with him for more than a year and attending him through a dangerous and well-nigh fatal illness, I feel bound to say that I have always regarded him all that a Christian gentleman should be." In a letter to George Williams, Pierotti complained concerning those he believed had been afflicting him and the "cross" he was forced to bear: "I have carried it 16 years & especially 9 years—from the moment I began to study upon Palestine" (handwritten letter in French from Pierotti to Williams, of November 30, 1864, in the author's collection).

[12] A number of the underground cisterns on Pierotti's map of the Temple Mount are depicted with oval or roughly rounded plans. They look like approximations, and they are markedly different from the plans meticulously recorded by later explorers, notably by Wilson and Schick. In stark contrast to this, the very large cistern on the south side of the Temple Mount (Bir Buhayr, "The Small Sea," Cistern No. 3), situated below the paved area directly in front of the Aqṣà Mosque, was carefully mapped by Pierotti, as one can see from his published plan (Gibson and Jacobson 1996: 36, and Fig. 15).

[13] For an English translation of the final verdict on "desertion and embezzlement" with an exact wording of the judicial sentence bestowed upon Pierotti by the Italian court of justice: PEF Archives/JER/8/1. See also: Legouas 2013: 231–250.

[14] On the history of the exploration of the Triple Gate and the passage extending behind it: Burgoyne 1992: 110–111; Gibson and Jacobson 1996: 259–268. In December 1995, I made an examination of the masonry of the western side wall of the passage leading from the Triple Gate and compared it with the elevation drawing made by Warren in February 1869 (PEF Archives/JER/WAR/62/10: Gibson and Jacobson 1996: Fig. 123). The drawing made by Warren matches up quite well except that the line of bedrock there is not as angular as he has shown it. There does not appear to be any pre-Umayyad masonry in the side walls of this passage that I could see, and the walls built of smaller blocks on either side at the southern end of the passage bond quite nicely with the segmental arches behind the external chamfered semicircular arches. This work might be attributed to the Fāṭimid Caliph al-Ẓahir, perhaps immediately after the earthquake of 1033.

the Double Gate,[15] which he associated with the building works of the Byzantine emperor Justinian, and the Single Gate, which he attributed to the time of the Franks. Interestingly, Pierotti undertook excavations at three locations along the Southern Wall: at the southwestern angle, where he was able to detect three phases of masonry in the wall, at the southeastern angle, where he purportedly found the counter pier for the arch impost seen near the southern end of the wall, and also in front of the Double Gate, reaching in his digging down to the bottom foundation of the wall (Pierotti 1864: 66, 70).[16] He described the most ancient phase of the wall near the southeast angle as having been built of masonry "of large size and rusticated; only the grooves here are small, and the whole surface of the block is well smoothed; they also are perfectly fitted together without mortar, but clamps of iron or soldering plugs of lead are used; as I was able to ascertain when a small part was repaired" (Pierotti 1864: 67).

A major study of the outer masonry walls of the Ḥaram aš-Šarīf was subsequently made by the Marquis Melchior de Vogüé during his second visit to Jerusalem in 1862. His monumental volume was entitled *Le Temple de Jérusalem* (1864) and it included a methodical analysis of the visible sections of the ancient drafted masonry of the Temple Mount walls. He argued—correctly, as it turns out—that the earlier parts of the enclosure walls must date back to the Second Temple period (de Vogüé 1864, with a discussion of the masonry of the outer walls of the Ḥaram aš-Šarīf on pp. 4–7, the Triple Gate on p. 11, Ills. 8–9, and the Double Gate on p. 12, Ill. 10). This is important because so many of his predecessors (e.g., Robinson) had claimed the most ancient segments of drafted ashlar masonry to be of Solomonic date.

1864–1870: WILSON TO WARREN

A concern in certain circles in the West early on in the 19th century regarding the problem of water and sewerage in the city of Jerusalem ultimately led to an English expedition being sent out to the Middle East in 1864 by the British Ordnance Survey, under the guidance of its director-general, Sir Henry James, with the goal of producing a comprehensive map of the city as an essential first step to finding a solution for improving the sanitation of the city (Gibson 2011). This concern was also the reason for earlier work done in the city by the engineer John Whitty, but his accomplishments fell short owing to the lack of a satisfactory surveyed map of Jerusalem and vicinity (Amit and Gibson 2014). Hence, with the help of a substantial financial grant provided by the English benefactress Angela Burdett-Coutts (usually stated to be a grant of £500, but the actual cost turned out to be much more) (Gibson 2001), Captain Charles W. Wilson of the Royal Engineers found himself entrusted with the work. He was accompanied in these endeavors by a team of professional military-trained surveyors and a photographer, James McDonald, who produced a series of excellent albumen photographs (Gibson 1997: 236–237).

The Ordnance Survey of Jerusalem was eventually commenced in the winter of 1864–1865, and the result was a series of surveyed maps of the city and its vicinity, as well as plans of individual building complexes in the Old City (notably the Citadel, Mount Zion and the Church of the Holy Sepulchre), and importantly it also included a very detailed map of the Temple Mount showing all the buildings and other features, visible below and above ground. This included accurate plans

---

[15] On the history of the exploration of the Double Gate and the passage ("Aqṣà al-Qādima") extending behind it: Gibson and Jacobson 1996: 235–259.

[16] Wilson reported that neither he nor Warren was able to locate the supposed foundational pier for this arch near the southeast angle of the Temple Mount (Wilson 1880: 48).

of subterranean cisterns, chambers and conduits (Gibson and Jacobson 1996).[17] A large-format, two-volume album on the results of the Ordnance Survey work was eventually published (Wilson 1866). Many scholars subsequently used the Ordnance Survey maps quite extensively to further their research, including General Charles G. Gordon (of Khartoum), who in March 1883 prepared a detailed topographical map of Jerusalem, and Conrad Schick, who, until close to the time of his death in 1901, was constantly making updated versions of the city map.

Wilson paid great attention to the external stonework of the Temple Mount walls, though he was certainly not the first scholar to do so, while taking measurements and making sure there were comprehensive photographs made of various parts of the wall as well (Wilson 1866: 14–15, Photographs Nos. 11–14, Pls. X–XII) (Fig. 2.5). In his paper entitled "The Masonry of the Haram Wall," Wilson undertook an analysis of the various constructional stages of the Temple Mount walls based on his own survey work in Jerusalem, but also incorporating into it considerable data derived from Charles Warren's unpublished work (Wilson 1880, with remarks on the Southern enclosure Wall on p. 51; Warren 1880; Conder 1880; for the scholarly dispute that arose between Wilson and Warren, see: Gibson 2021). He noted in his structural analysis that at the southwest angle the "ancient masonry" seen in-situ could be traced for some 15 m on either side. Altogether, Wilson reached the conclusion that at this spot there were "five periods of construction, which probably succeeded each other in the following order: the large stones with marginal drafts; the large stones plain dressed; the medium sized stones plain dressed; the small stones with marginal drafts and projecting faces; and the very small stones plain dressed, and mixed masonry" (Wilson 1880: 10). He went on to say that the faces of the lowest six foundation courses at this same location, based on Warren's subsequent work, consisted of "rough picked" or "carelessly dressed" ashlars (see also: Warren 1876: 63; these same lower foundation courses have recently been investigated at the southwest angle: Reich and Baruch 2017).

The Ordnance Survey of Jerusalem conducted by Wilson was a great success and ultimately it led in 1865 to the establishment of the Palestine Exploration Fund (PEF), not long after his return to London, and this new learned society was supported by public subscription and had royal patronage. These were exciting days, and the Fund from the outset decided to dedicate itself to the study of ancient Jerusalem and the Temple Mount. Indeed, the illustrious excavator of ancient Nineveh in Mesopotamia, the explorer Henry Layard, who was one of the people present at the founding meeting of the PEF, suggested that the scientific exploration of Jerusalem should be the primary goal of this new Society, remarking that "we know scarcely anything of the Jews from existing monuments and remains. A few large stones and foundations, discovered at Jerusalem in casual excavations, are all we can point to with certainty" (Gibson 2011). But all of this was to change. The Temple Mount was now seen to be the only place in Jerusalem where substantial excavations might possibly be made, since buildings and houses largely covered the rest of the Old City, with a few exceptions. At that time, in the 1860s, it had still not been realized that the southwestern hill of Jerusalem (i.e., the low hill south of the Temple Mount, referred to today as the "City of David") was where the oldest (biblical) part of the city was situated. The achievements made by Wilson and his Royal Engineer colleagues in Jerusalem, as well as the subsequent founding of the PEF, created such a stir among scholars and the public in England that it eventually led to Lieutenant Charles Warren being sent out to Jerusalem in 1867 to conduct excavations, and his primary goal was the Temple Mount.

---

[17] Wilson also usefully computed the water capacity of 12 of the cisterns on the Temple Mount, but he apparently never published this data; see: PEF archives/JER/WIL/18/16.

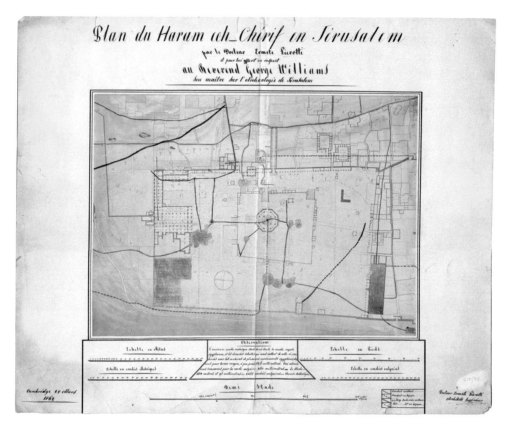

Figure 2.5: Map of the system of conduits on the Temple Mount by Pierotti from 1862. PEF/MAP/6/5/34 (courtesy of the Palestine Exploration Fund).

Warren's contribution to the study of the Temple Mount was remarkable. His work lasted from 1867 until 1870 and resulted in a new detailed map of the Temple Mount, as well as carefully drawn and scaled elevations of the stonework of the outer face of the enclosure walls, including the Southern Wall (Fig. 2.6). His team included the photographer Sgt. Henry Phillips R.E. Within the Ḥaram aš-Šarīf, new measurements were made of several of the subterranean features and cisterns, the gates and passages leading into the Temple Mount from the south and west, and the Antonia rock scarp and the Birket Israil pool to the north. Warren's work was also documented in a number of watercolors prepared by William ("Crimean") Simpson, and some of them were published as steel engravings in popular newspapers, such as *The Illustrated London News* (Simpson n.d.) (Fig. 2.7). While investigating a complex of structures near Wilson's Arch to the west of the Ḥaram aš-Šarīf, Warren came across a subterranean chamber with a central column which he named the "Masonic Hall" (on Warren and freemasonry in Jerusalem in the 19th century: Gibson, Shapira and Chapman 2013: 194; on recent excavations at Warren's Masonic Hall: Onn, Weksler-Bdolah and Patrich 2019) (Fig. 2.8).

These achievements were made notwithstanding frustrations Warren had had with local Ottoman Turkish authorities, principally the Governor Nazif Pacha, whom he thought particularly intransigent, even though the Ottoman vizier at Constantinople had never actually promised to give him a permit to dig on the uppermost part of the Temple Mount. In a letter of May 12, 1868, addressed to the British Consul N.T. Moore, Warren wrote that "Nazif Pacha is acknowledged by his own creed to be a fanatic, and it is quite hopeless and too expensive for Europeans to try

Figure 2.6: The southeastern angle of the Temple Mount. Albumen print by
Sgt. James McDonald, 1864/65 (courtesy of the Gibson Picture Archive).

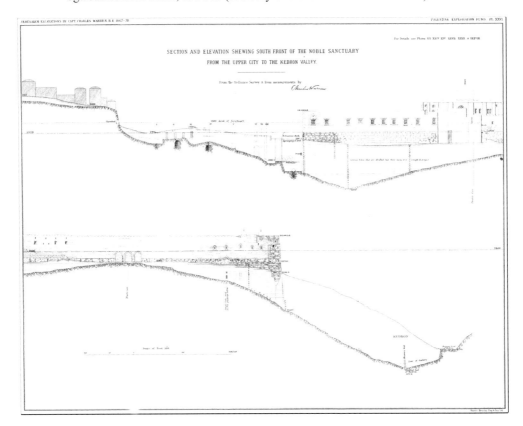

Figure 2.7: Charles Warren's southern elevation of the Temple Mount shown in two parts (Warren
1884: Plate XXVI).

Fig. 2.8: Inside the shaft excavated by Warren near the southeastern angle of the Temple Mount, with markings visible on the drafted stones. Watercolor by William Simpson, 1870 (courtesy of the Palestine Exploration Fund).

and bring him round to look with indifference on our digging in the Ḥaram aš-Šarīf area so long as his own Government does not attempt to cause him to alter his views" (Eliav 1997: 237). The inhabitants of the city also had mixed attitudes toward his work. Warren was frustrated that he could not excavate within the Ḥaram aš-Šarīf itself, which he saw as a major drawback since the Temple Mount had been the primary target of the PEF investigations. Instead, he proceeded to concentrate his efforts on recording the lower external ashlar walls of the Temple Mount, by excavating deep vertical (and lower horizontal) mining shafts (shored up with wooden planking) sunk through debris and soil at different locations from the outside (Fig. 2.9). Warren wrote in 1867: "I have been taking many visitors over the works lately, and I can see that they do not at all realise what is going on until after they have been slung down some of the shafts and squeezed through a few of the holes."[18] Warren's explorations showed that the lower parts of the Temple Mount walls, particularly at the southwest and southeast angles, were preserved to a much greater depth than had previously been thought by Robinson and others (Fig. 2.10). Along the length of the Southern Wall Warren detected the "Great Course." On the north side of the southeast angle, at a distance of 33 m, Warren recorded a vertical joint in the ashlar drafted masonry, with the segment to the north representing the corner of an earlier platform, with further extensions of this ancient

---

[18]   PEF Archives/letter from Warren (no accession number).

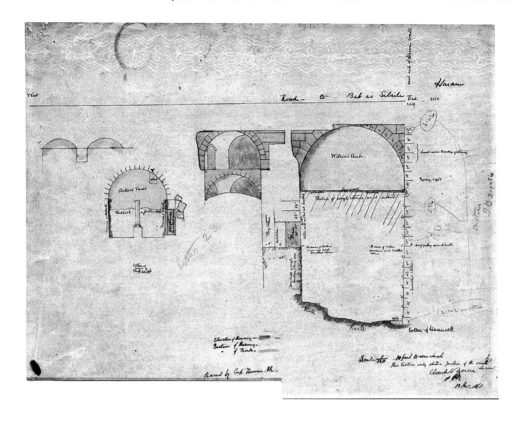

Figure 2.9: Wilson's Arch and the Masonic Hall to its west in an elevation drawing by Warren from 1869 (courtesy of the Palestine Exploration Fund).

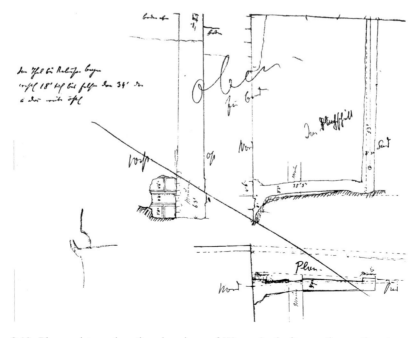

Figure 2.10: Plan and two elevation drawings of Warren's shaft near the southeastern angle of the Temple Mount (north is toward the left of the plan). Drawing by Conrad Schick, ca. 1870 (courtesy of the DEIAHL).

East Wall seen beyond the Golden Gate.[19] At one point, close to the southeast corner, Warren noted markings and letters on the face of some of the foundation stones of the smooth-faced drafted masonry[20] (Figs. 2.11–2.12). In 1925, Warren described his work in Jerusalem: "My work during three years in Palestine consisted chiefly of excavations in the Holy City…. At first money failed to flow into our coffers, and for months we were at our wits' end as to how to survive the crisis. The [PEF] Committee sent me S.O.S. messages, 'Get results and we will send you money,' and I retorted, 'Send me money and I will get you results'" (Gibson 2011).

Warren's success in his work would not have been possible without the help of his trusty companion and right-hand man, Sgt. Henry Birtles R.E., who, on taking charge of much of the logistical difficulties relating to the mining operations, was undoubtedly the unsung hero of the Jerusalem excavations (see also the tunneling work he did at Bir Ayyub [Gibson 2014a]). Warren admitted that without Birtles the success of his excavations would not have been the same. A remarkable unpublished document written by Warren recounts Birtles's accomplishments and shows how essential he was to ensure the success of the work at the Temple Mount. Warren wrote: "I found his assistance invaluable and attribute our immunity from loss of life among our workmen to the care with which he carried out all instructions given to him."[21] While digging beneath Robinson's Arch at the southwest angle of the Temple Mount, Warren and Birtles had to resort to the extreme action of blasting the fallen ashlars and voussoirs to gain access to the lower areas and to the level of the Herodian pavement (Morrison 1871: 101). Importantly, Warren believed that Robinson's Arch served to support a stairway down into the Tyropoeon Valley below, and that it was not part of a viaduct-bridge as was commonly believed at that time (Gibson 2021)[22] (Fig. 2.13). Warren also thought there must have been a ramp extending at a lower level to the west from the flight of steps.[23] On returning to England, Warren published a popular book (1876), but there was a delay in the full publication of the accumulated data, which was further complicated by a dispute in 1880 on plagiarism and interpretation with Wilson, who was a key figure on the executive committee of the

---

[19] The date of the masonry to the north and south of this "vertical joint" has been much debated. While it is generally accepted that the southern stretch with smooth-faced drafted masonry must be "Herodian," the date of the earlier masonry with the protruding bosses seen to the north is less certain (Burgoyne 2000: 483). Laperrousaz (1973) suggested the latter wall might date back to the time of Solomon, but this is highly unlikely. Many believe it should be dated to the Late Hellenistic/Hasmonean period: Wightman 1995; Ritmeyer 2006: 102–105, 213–214. I myself have suggested that the northern segment should be dated to the building activities of Herod the Great, with the southern segment to the time of one of Herod's successors in the early 1st century CE, so as to accommodate the construction of the eastern end of the Royal Stoa (Gibson 2021: 228). This means, of course, that King Herod never got to see the Royal Stoa in its completed form, which is what I believe to be the case (see further discussion in Peleg-Barkat 2017: 91–92). On the evidence from the southwestern angle of the Ḥaram concerning the date of the southern expansion of the Temple Mount: Weksler-Bdolah, S. *et al.* 2015; Reich and Baruch 2017.

[20] The ancient markings (painted and incised) on the stones were discovered by Warren and identified as mason's or quarry marks (Morrison 1871: 139–143), with a later commentary on the same by Wilson (1880: 53). Another different version of the same markings was published by a visitor to his excavations (Morris 1870: 201). See recent comments on the possible significance of these markings: Reich and Baruch 2016; idem 2019.

[21] PEF Archives/letter from Warren to Walter Besant (no accession number).

[22] Warren scribbled on one of his sketches that he had cut a horizontal gallery along the southern side of the main pier of Robinson's Arch in search of ancient inscriptions: PEF Archives/JER/WAR/62/3.

[23] Compare Warren's drawing (our Fig. 2.13) with the reconstruction of the Robinson's Arch complex recently proposed by E. Mazar (2020: 48).

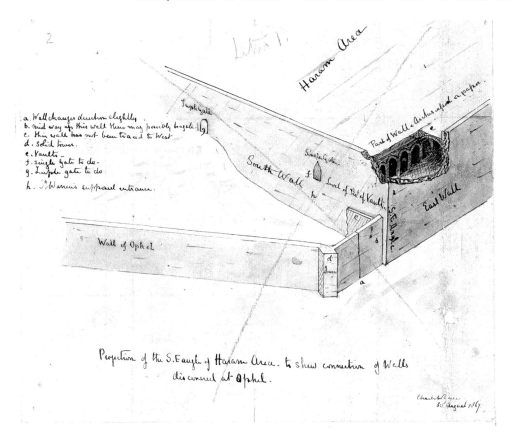

Figure 2.11: Drawing of the southeastern angle of the Temple Mount by Warren from 1869. PEF/JER/WAR/62/1 (courtesy of the Palestine Exploration Fund).

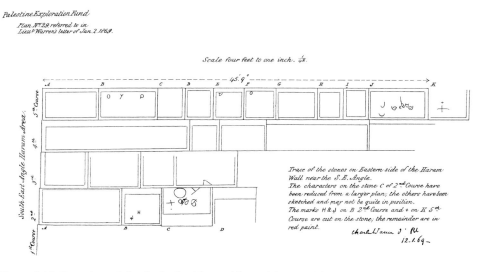

Figure 2.12: Drawing of the drafted ashlars with markings and letters near the base of the wall at the southeastern angle of the Temple Mount. Sketch by Warren from 1869 (courtesy of the Palestine Exploration Fund).

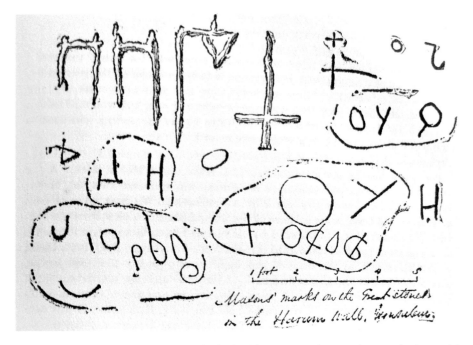

Figure 2.13: Markings and letters on drafted ashlars as seen by Morris near the base of the enclosure wall at the southeastern angle of the Temple Mount (Morris 1870: 201).

PEF at that time.[24] The final publication came out in 1884 and it consisted of a large format portfolio with 50 maps, plans and drawings (Warren 1884).

Warren was the first to address the particulars of the masonry and gates of the Southern Wall of the Temple Mount in some detail (Morrison 1871: 118–134). He excavated vertical shafts down to the foundations of the wall at quite a few locations, uncovering the original Temple Mount wall foundations with marginal-drafted ashlars, remarking that "the faces were not all finely dressed, and that they are *in-situ* … the portion of the wall to the west of the Double Gate appears less ancient than the remainder" (Morrison 1871: 119). Importantly, he determined that the level of the thresholds of the Single and Triple Gates (2375 ¼ feet = 724.00 m and 2379 ¾ feet = 725.14 m respectively) were more or less at the same level as the earthen floor inside Solomon's Stables (2375 ¼ feet = 724.00 m) (Morrison 1871: 134), suggesting that they undoubtedly had to have been functioning *at the same time* as the complex of arches behind the southern Ḥaram aš-Šarīf wall.[25] He also reached the conclusion that masonry evident above the level of these gates was "comparatively modern," by

---

[24] For the full story of this dispute: Gibson 2021. In a letter from 1888 to Thomas Hayter Lewis, who was a well-known professor of architecture at that time, Wilson wrote: "I have the greatest admiration for Warren's excavations but for want of funds, they were far from complete (the east wall [of the Temple Mount] has not been seen below ground except at the N.E. and S.E. angles); and a careful study of Warren's drawings and descriptions of the masonry has led me to form a different opinion of their age" (PEF Archives/LEW/7).

[25] It may very well be that in the Fāṭimid period (10th–11th centuries) the Triple Gate served not just as the entrance to a passageway leading to the Ḥaram interior, but also as the principal southern entrance to Solomon's Stables (Marwani Musalla), at which time the northern nine-arched entrance to the Stables complex, which had been there since Umayyad times, was largely blocked. The Single Gate might also originally date from the Fāṭimid period, though it was very likely rebuilt by the Franks. See further discussion: St. Laurent and Awwad 2013: 26; idem 2016: 445–448.

which he probably meant post-Byzantine, i.e., Islamic/medieval. In front of the Triple Gate Warren detected signs of stone paving (Fig. 2.14), with evidence for steps leading up to it from the south,[26] and beneath it were rock-cut passages that had also been explored by Louis Félicien Joseph Caignart de Saulcy.[27] The Double Gate was blocked in front and to its south by the ez Zāwiya el-Khatiniyya vaults, but Warren in his mapping operations showed that the gate led to an ascending vaulted passage leading to the upper Ḥaram aš-Šarīf surface and beneath the Aqṣà Mosque, and added further information to the work already done by Wilson (Figs. 2.15–2.17).

1869–1901: CONDER TO SCHICK

In the early 1870s, the Ottoman authorities decided to give the Ḥaram aš-Šarīf a facelift, with much repair and building work subsequently conducted there. This provided explorers with an opportunity to look at the interiors of upstanding buildings and to investigate their subterranean chambers. The scholars who took part in this work included Charles Clermont-Ganneau, Henry Palmer, Charles Francis Tyrwhitt-Drake, Claude Reignier Conder, Horatio Herbert Kitchener, Conrad Schick and James E. Hanauer.[28] Tyrwhitt-Drake in 1869 took a photograph of monumental steps (perhaps of Second Temple date), situated on the south side of the internal platform, which were later dismantled (Jacobson and Gibson 1995) (Figs. 2.18–2.19). Henry Palmer at the same time was tracing inscriptions (some in squared Hebrew) visible at the Golden Gate and near the Triple Gate (on the Hebrew inscriptions at the Triple Gate and further bibliography: Mazar 2011: 220, Fig. 6.2.11; Gibson 2021: 229–230) (Fig. 2.20). Conder's work, conducted during the early 1870s, at the time of the Survey of Western Palestine (SWP), was focused particularly on establishing the rock levels of the underlying Mount Moriah visible within the enclosure, and on making a detailed map of *as-Sakhra*.[29] Conder's map of the Ḥaram aš-Šarīf and the rock levels he observed there, dating from October 26, 1878, was eventually published in a paper he wrote about the Temple (Conder 1879: 25–60, Pl. 3).

Concerning the segments of drafted masonry of the Temple Mount enclosure seen in Warren's shafts, Conder wrote:

> Nothing short of a complete examination of the Ḥaram walls by galleries extending their whole length would suffice to prove definitely the continuity of their structure, and even if such proof were obtained the objection might be raised that the masonry was not *in-situ*. However puzzling the minor differences in masonry may be, and however difficult it may be to explain the reasons for straight joints or sudden changes in the finish of the stones, certain important indications will be acknowledged as controlling any conjectures on the subject (Conder 1880: 96).

[26] Warren's observations concerning these steps are important because only indirect evidence has survived today (Baruch and Reich 2016: 91).

[27] De Saulcy records a vertical shaft that was seen descending from the level of the (Herodian) pavement to one of the underground rock-cut passages: Caignart de Saulcy 1865, with a map and elevation on p. 9; Warren 1884: Pl. XXV; for a detailed analysis of the series of rock-cut passages investigated below the Triple Gate, see Gibson and Jacobson 1996: 199–203 (No. 14), Figs. 89–91.

[28] An important photograph in the PEF archives of the Dome of the Rock taken by Kitchener in 1877 shows wooden scaffolding and the exterior stonework of the building *after* the covering tiles had been removed by the Ottoman authorities in 1874.

[29] PEF archives/Conder, map dated October 5, 1872; cf. the map in Dalman 1912: 110, Fig. 7.

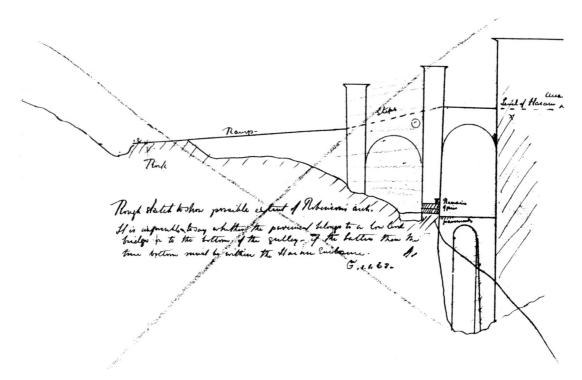

Figure 2.14: A reconstruction elevation by Warren of Robinson's Arch from 1869. PEF/Archives/JER/WAR/62 (courtesy of the Palestine Exploration Fund).

Fig. 2.15: The Triple Gate in the Southern Wall of the Temple Mount. Note that remnants of ancient stone paving are still visible in front of the right-hand jamb of the eastern doorway. Gelatin print by an American photographer, 1927 (courtesy of the Gibson Picture Archive).

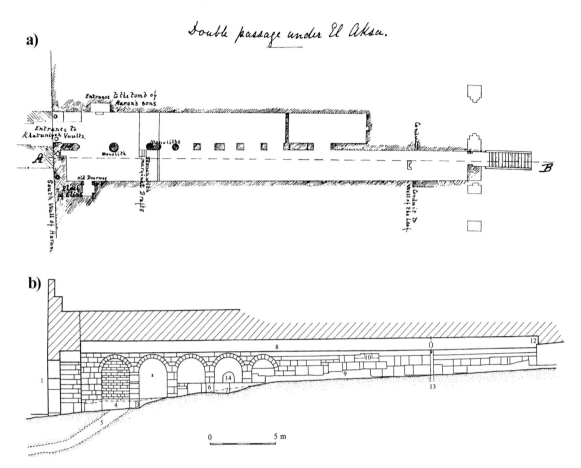

Figure 2.16: (a) Plan by Wilson of the passage leading from the Double Gate northward: PEF/JER/WIL/36/8. (b) Rendering of Warren's elevation drawing of the Western Wall of the passage: PEF/JER/WAR/62/10 (courtesy of the Palestine Exploration Fund).

He then went on to state what he thought these indications might be. In collaboration with Warren, Conder edited the Jerusalem volume of the SWP memoir, and it included quite a lot about new discoveries at the Ḥaram aš-Šarīf and its near vicinity (Warren and Conder 1884: 217–225, and 277–278 for a table of the rock levels). An important discovery attributed to Conder was the detection of pilasters *in-situ* belonging to the enclosure of the Temple Mount wall at its northwest corner (Conder 1877; Bahat 2013). Since the time of Warren's excavations beneath Robinson's Arch (Warren 1876: 314–315), the assumption has been that the fallen voussoirs, drafted ashlars and pilaster fragments, seen heaped particularly along the southern end of the Western Temple Mount Wall and near the southwest angle, are the direct result of damage wrought by the Roman legions following the conquest of the city in 70 CE.[30]

---

[30]   In my opinion, the overall height of these piles of massive fallen stones, looming in places almost to first-floor levels in the immediate proximity of Late Roman buildings (a bathhouse and a bakery), makes this a highly unlikely scenario. It is suggested, therefore, that this collapse of pilasters and ashlar masonry occurred at the time of a major earthquake that ravaged the city in 363 CE (Gibson 2014b; idem, 2016: 177–188).

Figure 2.17: View of the interior of the Double Gate looking south, in photographs taken in the 1930s (a), and in 2009 (b) (courtesy of the Israel Antiquities Authority; Murph Brown).

Conrad Schick is one of the most important scholars to contribute to the study of the Temple Mount (Gibson 2000). He is probably one of the very few who was able to complete a large-scale and methodical examination of *all* of its subterranean features and cisterns, and where possible even the underlying rock topography of Mount Moriah as well. As a resident of Jerusalem, Schick corresponded frequently with Wilson but had a general dislike for Warren.[31] In August 1872, SWP explorer Tyrwhitt-Drake wrote a letter to the PEF concerning Schick's surveying skills and on how his abilities might be used to further their mapping interests at the Ḥaram aš-Šarīf: "I think he [Schick] is a man who ought to be encouraged in every way. I had a good deal of talk with him about the Haram when I was last in Jerusalem & I believe that much might be done if he got leave from the T[urkish] Govt to make plans."[32] Schick's fieldwork eventually resulted in

---

[31]   Writing on December 15, 1871, Schick stated that Warren hardly ever made use of his surveying skills even though they were always on offer, except, as he put it, "in a few and exceptional cases" (PEF Archives/Schick/2). A set of Warren's maps annotated in Schick's handwriting, with corrections and alternative renditions of features found in the Temple Mount works, exists in the archives of the Deutsches Evangelisches Institut in Jerusalem. I am grateful to Gunnar Lehmann, Acting Director of DEIAHL in 1993, for providing me with a set of copies from their archives.

[32]   (PEF Archives/WS/Dra/84). Tyrwhitt-Drake went on to say that since local Ottoman officials were "ignorant" concerning surveying procedures, he thought it might even be possible to "hoodwink" them to gain access to the Bir el-Erwah situated beneath the Dome of the Rock, and that he was certain the local sheikh could be bribed with money. This is exactly what happened 39 years later when Captain Montagu Parker attempted to bribe local officials but with disastrous results (Gibson 2023).

Figure 2.18: View of the interior of the Double Gate looking north. Lantern slide by the Vester Company, ca. 1900 (courtesy of the Gibson Picture Archive).

Figure 2.19: View of the southern side of the interior platform of the Dome of the Rock, looking northwest. Note the remains of a flight of ancient steps on the right. Photograph by Tyrwhitt-Drake from 1869 (courtesy of the Palestine Exploration Fund).

Figure 2.20: View of the southern side of the interior platform with the Dome of the Rock, looking north. Note the remains of a long flight of ancient steps on the right. Albumen print from ca. 1870 (courtesy of the Gibson Picture Archive).

the mapping of many of the upstanding structures within the enclosure, and this work greatly facilitated his eventual preparation of a series of large-scale wooden models, which were intended to include "the whole Haram with the mountain, the substructures, cisterns, and all underground buildings, as well as those above ground."[33] Schick's research on the cisterns of the Ḥaram aš-Šarīf included the study of several disused ancient cisterns that he observed being restored and put back into use (Schick 1896: 87; see also Hanauer 1910: 201–211). He also noted several cisterns that he was unable to enter and record, as well as areas of terraced soil and debris which he believed covered over ruined vaulted chambers. While all the known subterranean features of the Temple Mount have been cataloged (Gibson and Jacobson 1994), it is highly likely that there are many more to be discovered including vaulted structures, rock-hewn chambers, cisterns, ditches, passages and conduits.

Schick's work at the Ḥaram aš-Šarīf began in the 1860s and lasted until shortly before his death in 1901, and most of his findings were conveyed to the PEF in the form of letters and reports, though not everything he sent to them was published. Schick's reports were heavily edited ahead of their publication in the PEF's *Quarterly Statement*, and they included a lot of (supposed) incidental and miscellaneous information, which was cut out, lending added importance for researchers to examine the unedited archival versions of his papers (Gibson 2000; Gurevich 2019). This is the case regarding his work at Solomon's Stables and on the remnants of a very early monumental arch seen inside (Schick 1891; PEF Archives/Schick/28; Gibson and Jacobson 1996: 227–279, Fig. 91: 9), which is of uncertain date, though it is undoubtedly pre-Fāṭimid (Figs. 2.21–2.22). Schick mentions in a letter from February 15, 1895 that the floor of Solomon's Stables had been leveled and that the accumulated rubbish from within had been brought outside and spread on the

---

[33]   Letter to Wilson (PEF Archives/Schick/3; Gibson 2000; Goren and Rubin 1996).

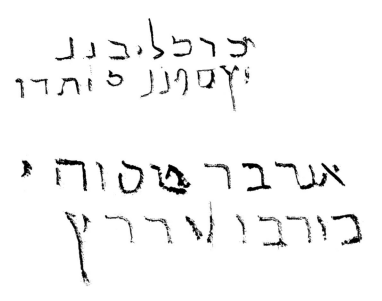

Figure 2.21: Hebrew inscriptions recorded by Henry Palmer at the Triple
Gate in 1869. PEF/PAL/25/2 (courtesy of the Palestine Exploration Fund).

Figure 2.22: The remains of a monumental arch in the area of Solomon's
Stables. Lantern slide, ca. 1891 (courtesy of the Gibson Picture Archive).

surface, thus making it almost a meter higher[34] (Fig. 2.23). Some of these soil and rubble deposits mentioned by Schick are likely to be the same as those extracted with mechanical equipment in 1999–2000 and conveyed outside the city at the time of the preparation of the northern entrance to the Marwani Prayer Hall in the area of Solomon's Stables (Baruch 2007; Barkay and Dvira [Zweig] 2007; Seligman 2007).

One letter sent by Schick to the PEF in London, dated April 12, 1873, contains numerous observations regarding ancient features seen and measured in different parts of the Ḥaram aš-Šarīf, including a wall of hewn stones, the top of which was traced above ground, probably representing the northwest angle of the subterranean Solomon's Stables complex. He also noted briefly a segment of masonry (1.82 m thick) that had a doorway, situated about 70 m to the south of the Golden Gate, and inside the Temple Mount. This wall ran approximately 3 m west of the Eastern Ḥaram aš-Šarīf Wall and parallel to it. It should not be confused with another doorway, most likely medieval, which was located in the eastern Ḥaram aš-Šarīf wall, and much further south (Mantell 1882; Clermont-Ganneau 1899: 133). Importantly, Schick's doorway is located on a direct line with the east side of the Dome of the Rock, but he did not say anything further as to its possible date or function. One would like to associate this doorway with the elusive Shushan (Susa) Gate from the 1st century CE, but it is much more likely to be a structural part of an Umayyad walkway which extended between the Golden Gate and the northern entrance to the Solomon's Stables complex (Gibson 2021: 237, Fig. 17).

Schick made a detailed study of the southern Ḥaram aš-Šarīf wall and more specifically its gates.[35] This led him to map the interesting set of buildings fronting the Double Gate, known as ez Zāwiya el-Khatiniyya or Khunthaniya (referred to by Mujīr al-Dīn as the "Khanthaniyya Zāwiya"), which consists of a series of vaulted chambers (Figs. 2.24, 2.28). These buildings were first examined in some detail by Titus Tobler in 1846, but the description he provided is somewhat confusing (Tobler 1853: I, 490–494).[36] General mapping of the building complex appears on the early maps of Catherwood and Pierotti, but the place only came to be properly mapped in November 1891 by Schick (PEF Archives/Schick/41/2; Schick 1892: 19–24; see also de Vogüé's map from his first trip

---

[34] PEF Archives/Schick: letter in box labeled "QS 1892–1899." The full quotation is as follows: "The much rubbish in the substructions [of] the so called 'horse stables of Solomon'—is brought up and spread out on the surface of the area, by which it became in the southern regions there the surface about 3 feet higher—and the bottom of the stables are leveled; in the southern wall, over the Triple Gate and elsewhere are windows broken in, so all the substructions are now airy, well lighted and dry." Clearance of earth and debris was undertaken earlier by the Muslim authorities over a period of a few months up to April 1891, and some of these fills were also spread eastward within the actual Stables, thereby burying the lower part of the Single Gate and obscuring the tethering holds seen at the corners of the piers.

[35] James E. Hanauer in a letter to the PEF of December 16, 1902, shortly after Schick's death, wrote: "The Rev. C.J. Wilson, M.A. of the Church Missionary Society, took a photograph of the monolithic column in the porch of the Double Gate. The negative proving a good one he kindly allowed me to take prints from it as I had told him that it was a relic of great interest and probably of Herodian date, though the late Dr. Schick used to think it might even be Solomonic" (PEF Archives/HAN/2/56–58). This photograph was reproduced in Gibson and Jacobson 1996: 255, Fig. 117.

[36] It appears Tobler accessed the Khatiniyya building complex from the west, entering through a door (No. 7), passing into a vaulted chamber (8), climbing through a hole into another chamber (No. 4), then climbing down through an opening into yet another chamber (No. 13), before then turning to the north and reaching the western portal of the Double Gate and its passage beyond. The numbers mentioned here refer to my Fig. 2.28. See also the description by Revd. George Octavius Wray following a visit he made to this place in 1863, where he mentions seeing slabs of white marble which might be of Crusader date (Wray 1891).

to Jerusalem: de Vogüé 1860: Pl. XX; and the map made by Kemalletin in 1924: Yavuz 1996: 154, Fig. 7; for more recent mapping of the interior chambers: Hawari 2007: 45–48, Fig. 2.2) (Fig. 2.25). Interestingly, Schick appears to have seen an area of paving in his digging operations in front of the Double Gate and to its east (No. 15), which he referred to on his plan as a "terrace" and estimated at 14 × 18 feet (= 4.27 × 5.48 m). This area seems to match the paved area at the top of the steps leading up to the Double Gate on its eastern side, as it was uncovered in B. Mazar's excavations from the

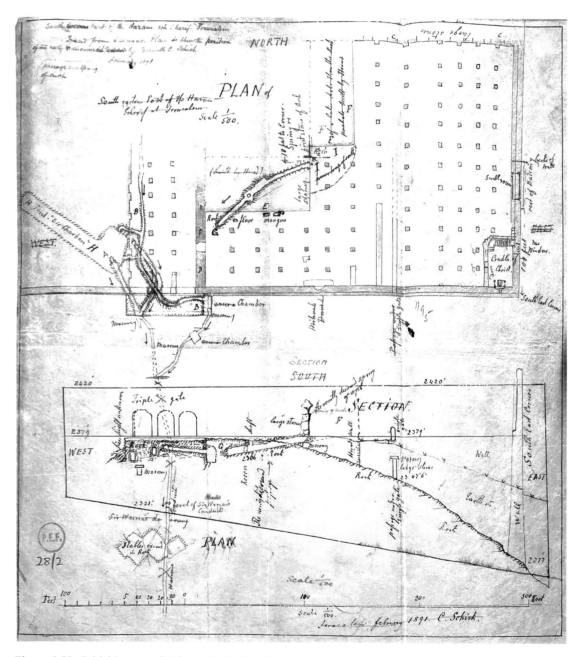

Figure 2.23: Schick's map of Solomon's Stables from February 1891, showing various features including the position of the ancient arch (center, top) seen in Fig. 2.22. PEF/DA/SCHICK/28/2 (courtesy of the Palestine Exploration Fund).

Figure 2.24: A view of Solomon's Stables after the clearing and leveling activities of April 1891 had been completed. Lantern slide by Underwood & Underwood, ca. 1900 (courtesy of the Gibson Picture Archive).

1970s (Fig. 2.26). Two blocked doorways (Nos. 18–19), presumably originally having semicircular arches, were recorded by B. Mazar's team in the east wall of the chamber in front of the Double Gate (E. Mazar 2002: 110–111).

More importantly, Schick was able to record the remains of a substantial "ancient" wall approximately 2.90 m thick (Fig. 2: 28: No. 16, in blue), running north within this block of buildings before forming a right angle, and this is undoubtedly part of the eastern wall and the northeastern corner of Umayyad Building II, which was later partly excavated by Kathleen M. Kenyon and Roland de Vaux, and then substantially by B. Mazar (Fig. 2.26). There is an interesting chronological conclusion to be made from all of this: the northwest angle of the Umayyad Building II must have still been visible as a substantial *free-standing wall* (albeit partly ruined) at the time of the construction of the adjacent vaults of the Khatiniyya gateway complex under Fāṭimid rule (10th–11th centuries). This fits in well with the material evidence obtained from Kenyon's Site J that Building II survived the earthquake of 749 CE and that it continued in use under the Abbasids until the 9th century, at which point it began to be looted for its stone (Prag 2008: 157–160; idem 2018: 85–88; contra St. Laurent and Awwad 2013: 26–27). The Khatiniyya gateway complex probably saw major renovations, following the earthquake of 1033, and at the same time Caliph al-Ẓahir was initiating substantial building work at the Aqṣà Mosque (Pruitt 2017: 45).

Figure 2.25: View of the Zāwiya el-Khatiniyya building complex with Mazar's excavations in the foreground, from May 1977 (courtesy of the Gibson Picture Archive).

Indeed, it appears quite certain that the southern wall of the Ḥaram aš-Šarīf served as the main southern fortification wall on the southeast side of the city under Fāṭimid and then under Crusader rule, with a gateway complex built in front of the earlier Double Gate (Boas 2001: 66–68) (Fig. 2.28). Part of a city wall (2.80 m thick) was traced by B. Mazar extending from the southwest corner of the Ḥaram to the west for 20 m, reaching the eastern jamb of a gate or postern (perhaps representing the original "Gate of the Tannery" mentioned in Crusader sources), but its continuation is unknown. The date of this wall could not be ascertained on stratigraphic grounds, but B. Mazar attributed it to the time of Crusader rule.[37] Not much is known about this wall, except

---

[37] B. Mazar dated this defense wall to the time of Crusader rule, with a suggested construction date of ca. 1182 (B. Mazar 1971: 24. Pl. 11; idem 1975: 279). For a picture of this fortification wall taken in November 1969 before it was dismantled: Gibson *et al.* 2016.

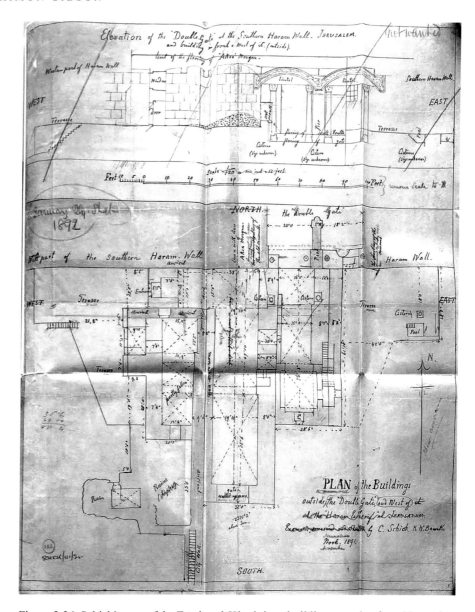

Figure 2.26: Schick's map of the Zāwiya el-Khatiniyya building complex from November 1891. PEF/DA/SCHICK/41/2 (courtesy of the Palestine Exploration Fund).

that it was built out of reused stones; indeed, it was dismantled very early on in the excavation. Adjacent to the wall were trench-cut graves.[38] In my opinion, this wall was originally a Fāṭimid

---

[38] In my opinion, it is quite possible these graves post-date the medieval wall. However, Billig and Reich, based on their excavations, say the foundations of this wall had to have cut through the area of graves, which they identified as Seljūk from 1070–1098 CE (Billig and Reich 1997: 21). However, the exact stratigraphic relationship between the graves and the actual wall is still unclear since it was dismantled down to its foundations at the time of B. Mazar's earlier excavations at this spot. Mazar has suggested dating the graves to 1071, but did not provide further details (Mazar 1971: 24). A map of the graves as seen below Robinson's Arch, based on data provided by Meir Ben-Dov, who was the field archaeologist at the time of Mazar's work, has been published in Abed Rabo's thesis (2012: 420, Fig. 51).

Figure 2.27: The Double Gate and the East Wall of the Zāwiya el-Khatiniyya building complex, with Mazar's excavation of the Herodian steps in the foreground. Photograph by Magen Broshi, ca. 1975 (courtesy of the Gibson Picture Archive).

fortification, which was reused by the Crusaders; the large tower-gate situated about 15 m to the west of the Dung Gate may also be from this period, though it was undoubtedly in use at the time of the Ayyûbids (Boas 2001: 59–62).[39]

---

[39] This may have been the "Iron Gate" which was referred to in ca. 1170 by John of Würzburg (163) as situated at the southern end of the Valley Street (presumably the street excavated by Weksler-Bdolah in the Western Wall Plaza area) and to the east of St. Peter in Chains ("St. Peter ad Vincula"), which was located on the southern side of the Jewish Quarter, and this street eventually led out of the gate toward the eastern slope of Mount Zion (Wilkinson 1988: 268). Wightman suggested that the eastern section of the southern Fāṭimid wall may have run eastward from the Dung Gate over the ruined southern walls of Umayyad Building II (Wightman 1993: 238). I agree that this is certainly feasible when considering the remarkable state of preservation of Building II in the 10th–11th centuries CE. However, see the discussion in Prag 2008: 286–287.

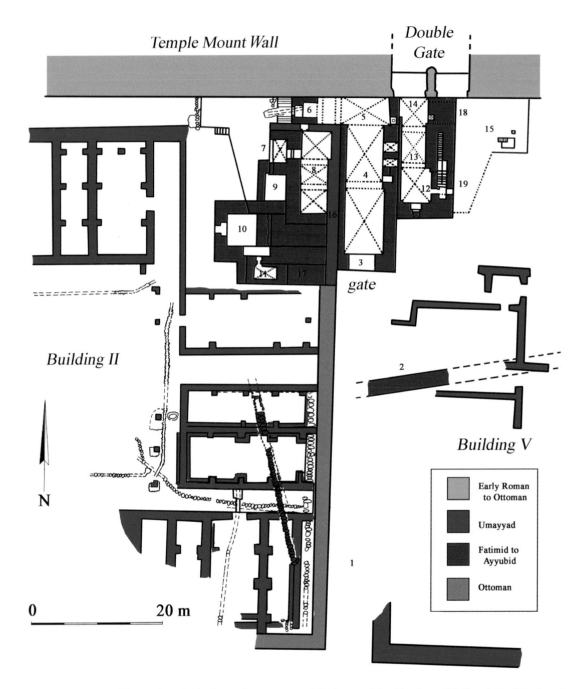

Figure 2.28: Map of the archaeological remains uncovered in front of the Southern Wall and the Zāwiya el-Khatiniyya building complex. 1: street between Umayyad Buildings II and V, leading to gate; 2: segment of Fāṭimid or Crusader outer wall uncovered by B. Mazar; 3: blocked gate; 4–5: vaulted chambers; 6: gate or postern(?); 7: gate; 8: vaulted chambers; 9–10: chambers uncovered in B. Mazar's excavations; 11: small vaulted chamber; 12: door to flight of steps ascending to an upper level; 13–14: vaulted chambers in front of the Double Gate; 15: Schick's terrace and a stepped tank; 16: Schick's "ancient wall" belonging to Umayyad Building II; 17: blocked chamber; 18–19: blocked gates. Drawing based on maps published by Schick (1892); Mazar (2002); and Prag (2008) (drawing by the author based on computerized analysis made by W. Stumpff).

The Khatiniyya gateway complex situated halfway along the southern Ḥaram wall was evidently completely rebuilt and refurbished by the Knights Templar in order to facilitate access to the Temple Mount from the south. Part of an outer wall (with two squared turrets?) was uncovered in B. Mazar's excavations just southeast of the gateway complex and it ran roughly parallel with the southern Ḥaram enclosure wall.[40] At some point in the east, it turned northward to join the southeast corner of the Ḥaram, or perhaps toward the Single Gate.[41] The exact date of this wall is uncertain and it could be either Fāṭimid/Seljūk or Crusader; Ben-Dov assumed it to be Ayyūbid. However, it seems more likely this wall was an integral part of the defensive outwork established by the Templars "to guard their homes and palace [i.e., the Aqṣà Mosque]," as we hear from the German monk Theoderic (ca. 1173) (Theo. XIX: Wilkinson 1988: 295). The entire Khatiniyya gateway, however, was undoubtedly refurbished at the time of Ṣalāḥ al-Dīn in 1191 (Hawari 2007: 45).

LATER ACCOMPLISHMENTS

As a postscript to the accomplishments of the explorations of the 19th century, one should mention the archaeological work undertaken in the immediate aftermath of the 1927 earthquake. It inflicted severe damage on several historic buildings in Jerusalem, including those at the Ḥaram aš-Šarīf, and notably the Aqṣà Mosque, which suffered devastating structural impairment. This led to archaeological work by Robert W. Hamilton beneath the floors of the Aqṣà Mosque in 1938–1942 (Hamilton 1949; Bagatti 1979; Gibson 1999). His mapping efforts included the study of wall foundations and the structural layout of the mosque itself (Fig. 2.30). Beneath the floors of the mosque, Hamilton uncovered sparse patches of a decorated mosaic floor. Although some have attributed this floor to the Byzantine period, it is more likely to be of Umayyad date (Baruch *et al.* 2018: 13–14; Di Cesare 2020). He also found a carved stone depicting a centaur of Late Roman date, built into later flooring (Dvira 2008). According to Hamilton, nothing was found in his excavations that had any bearing on earlier periods; he stated that there was "a notable absence of all traces of monumental building of the Jewish period" (Hamilton 1949: 65), despite the fact that he did excavate the remains of an earlier plastered stepped installation, which has subsequently been identified as a Jewish ritual bath (*miqweh*) from the Early Roman period (Gibson and Jacobson 1996: 56–57; Dvira 2008: 2–3, Figs. 2–3). In two soundings made near the center of the mosque, Hamilton excavated down to a layer of packed and consolidated stones, situated 1.37 m above the vaulted passageway leading from the Double Gate, but he largely ignored the results of Warren's work beneath the mosque (Hamilton 1949: Fig. 30; PEF Archives/Schick/41/2; Gibson and Jacobson 1996: 194, Fig. 88). Indeed, the inevitable chronological conclusion must be that the vaulting of the

---

[40] Not much is known about this defense wall other than it is probably Fāṭimid or Crusader in date. It is certainly post-Umayyad/Abbasid. For further information: Ben-Dov 1983: 70–71, the aerial view on p. 70 indicates that a stretch of some 50 m of wall was exposed, but the map on p. 71: No. 7, seems to be a reconstruction. This wall was eventually completely dismantled and therefore cannot be seen today. See also further comments on the wall in Boas 2001: 47–48; Glücksmann and Kool 1995: Fig. 1: W, Plan 2. Ben-Dov assumes an Ayyūbid date for this wall, but evidence for this was not given (Ben-Dov 1983: 70).

[41] Ben-Dov thought the wall would have had to meet at the Southern Ḥaram Wall next to the Single Gate (Ben-Dov 1983: 70), and the contour of the overlying terrace wall—still visible in photographs of the 20th century (see Fig. 2.1)—may support this. On the history of the passage beneath the Single Gate (Gibson and Jacobson 1996: 204–208). In December 1995 I examined the blocked Single Gate from inside and ascertained that it did indeed have an elliptical arch made out of small voussoir blocks.

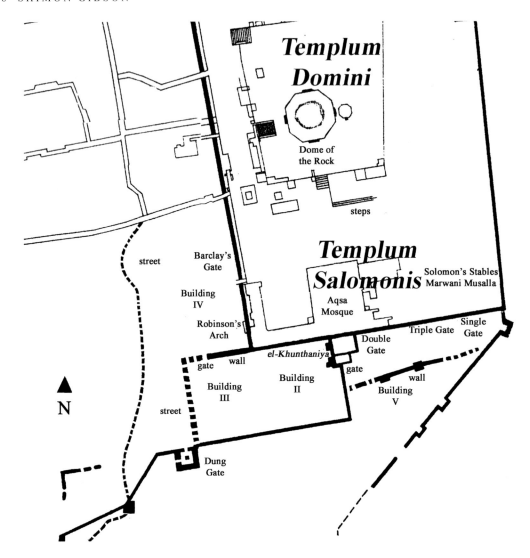

Figure 2.29: Map of the southeastern part of Jerusalem under Fāṭimid, Crusader and Ayyûbid rule, showing the archaeological features mentioned in this paper (drawing by the author).

earlier subterranean passage was visible (or had been rebuilt) at the time of the construction of the earliest phase of the Aqṣà Mosque.[42]

CONCLUSIONS

The hidden interior of the Temple Mount in Jerusalem, dating back to pre-Islamic times, is still largely unknown and unexplored territory, and a sustained campaign of scientific archaeological excavations has never been attempted within the precinct walls in modern

---

[42] The subterranean features on the inner side of the Southern Ḥaram Wall (notably chambers, passages, conduits and cisterns) must have had an impact on the overall planning of the layout of the earliest building of the Aqṣà Mosque (as is shown in our Fig. 2.30), but strangely these features are ignored in a recently published study (Di Cesare: 2017).

times, notwithstanding the significance of this place (Gonen 2003; Reiter and Seligman 2009; Al-Jubeh 2009; Saposnik 2015). This paper has dealt specifically with explorations conducted along the Southern Wall of the Temple Mount/Ḥaram aš-Šarīf during the course of the 19th century, examining in particular the monumental work conducted there by Catherwood, Robinson, Barclay, de Saulcy, Pierotti, de Vogüé, Wilson, Warren, Conder and Schick. Additional investigations continued apace into the 20th century (Avni and Seligman 2001) with Hamilton's work at the Aqṣà Mosque, with Kenyon's work at Sites G and J, and with the large-scale archaeological excavations that were conducted in the 1970s along the entire length of the Southern Wall by Benjamin Mazar (Fig. 2.31). The Southern Wall was the subject of an important detailed architectural investigation by Leen Ritmeyer (2006: 60–101). Structural analysis of the various types of drafted masonry along the Southern Wall, using a process of orthophotography to create drawn "maps" of the wall, was undertaken by Eilat Mazar in a

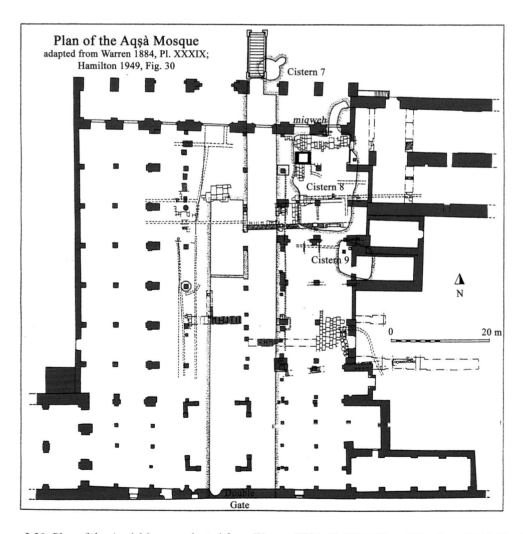

Figure 2.30: Plan of the Aqṣà Mosque adapted from Warren (1884: Pl. XXXIX) and Hamilton (1949: Fig. 30), showing the underlying passage extending to the north from the Double Gate and Cisterns 7, 8 and 9. The blue portions indicate the top of the vaulting above the Double Gate passageway as seen by Hamilton (drawing by the author).

Figure 2.31: B. Mazar's excavations adjacent to the southwestern angle of the Temple Mount, in a color transparency taken in 1981, looking toward the east (courtesy of the Gibson Picture Archive).

project that lasted from 2002 to 2004 (Mazar 2011).[43] It should be noted that there have been many more archaeological discoveries at various locations adjacent to the Southern Wall, and some of these are the subject of the chapters in this volume.

REFERENCES

Abed Rabo, O. 2012. *Jerusalem during the Fāṭimid and Seljûk Periods: Archaeological and Historical Aspects* (Ph.D. dissertation, Hebrew University of Jerusalem). Jerusalem (Hebrew with English summary).

Amit, D. and Gibson, S. 2014. Water to Jerusalem; The Route and Date of the Upper and Lower Level Aqueducts. In: Ohlig, C. and Tsuk, T., eds. *Cura Aquarum in Israel II: Water in Antiquity. Proceedings of the 15th International Conference on the History of Water Management and Hydraulic Engineering in the Mediterranean Region, Israel 14–20 October 2012.* Siegburg: 9–41.

Avni, G. and Seligman, J. 2001. *The Temple Mount 1917–2001: Documentation, Research and Inspection of Antiquities.* Jerusalem.

Bagatti, B. 1979. *Recherches sur le site du Temple de Jérusalem (Ier–VIIe siècle).* Jerusalem.

Bahat, D. 2013. *The Jerusalem Western Wall Tunnel.* Jerusalem.

Barclay, J.T. 1858. *The City of the Great King; or, Jerusalem as It Was, as It Is, and as It Is to Be.* Philadelphia.

Barkay, G. and Dvira (Zweig), Z. 2007. New Data in the Sifting Project of Soil from the Temple Mount: Second Preliminary Report. In: Meiron, E., ed. *City of David: Studies of Ancient Jerusalem.* Jerusalem: 8: 27–68.

Bartlett, W.H. 1844. *Walks About the City and Environs of Jerusalem.* London.

---

[43]   For a modern assessment of the drafted masonry of all the Temple Mount walls: Mazar 2011. One should also note an earlier study by Burgoyne dealing with the structural analysis of masonry types apparent at the southern end of the Western Ḥaram Wall (1987: 263, Fig. 22.5; cf. Hawari 2007: 60–61, Fig. 5.6). Burgoyne also made a study of the masonry along the East Wall of the Temple Mount, in which he posits the importance of conducting methodological structural analysis of the other enclosure walls of the Temple Mount (Burgoyne 2000).

Baruch, Y. 2007. Report on the Archaeological Finds in the Soil Debris Removed from the Temple Mount in Jerusalem, 1999, 2000. ʿAtiqot 56: 55–64 (Hebrew).

Baruch, Y. and Reich, R. 2016. Excavations near the Triple Gate of the Temple Mount, Jerusalem. ʿAtiqot 85: 37–95 (Hebrew).

Baruch, Y., Reich, R. and Sandhaus, D. 2018. A Decade of Archaeological Exploration on the Temple Mount. Tel Aviv 45: 3–22.

Ben-Dov, M. 1983. Jerusalem's Fortifications: The City Walls, the Gates, and the Temple Mount. Tel Aviv (Hebrew).

Billig, Y. and Reich, R. 1997. A New Explanation Regarding the Inscription, 'Your Heart Will Rejoice…' on the Western Wall. In: Faust, A. and Baruch, E., eds. New Studies on Jerusalem 3. Ramat Gan: 18–24 (Hebrew).

Boas, A. 2001. Jerusalem in the Time of the Crusades. London.

Bonney, T.G. 1864. The Holy Places at Jerusalem, or Fergusson's Theories and Pierotti's Discoveries. London.

Branham, J.R. 2006. Penetrating the Sacred: Breaches and Barriers in the Jerusalem Temple. In: Gerstel, S.E.J., ed. Thresholds of the Sacred: Architectural, Art Historical, Liturgical, and Theological Perspectives on Religious Screens, East and West. Harvard: 6–24.

Burgoyne, M.H. 1987. Mamluk Jerusalem: An Architectural Study. Buckhurst Hill.

Burgoyne, M.H. 1992. The Gates of the Ḥaram al-Sharīf. In: Raby, J. and Johns, J., eds. Bayt al-Maqdis, ʿAbd al-Malik's Jerusalem. Oxford: 105–125.

Burgoyne, M.H. 2000. The East Wall of the Ḥaram aš-Šarīf: A Note on Its Archaeological Potential. In: Auld, S. and Hillenbrand, R., eds. Ottoman Jerusalem. The Living City, 1517–1917. London: 479–491.

Clermont-Ganneau, C. 1899. Archaeological Researches in Palestine, 1873–1874, Vol. 1. London.

Conder, C.R. 1877. Age of the Temple Wall: Pilasters of the West Haram Wall. Palestine Exploration Fund Quarterly Statement 9: 135–137.

Conder, C.R. 1879. The High Sanctuary at Jerusalem. Transactions of the Royal Institute of British Architects: 25–60.

Conder, C.R. 1880. Notes on Colonel Wilson's Paper on the Masonry of the Haram Wall. Palestine Exploration Fund Quarterly Statement 12(2): 91–97.

Dalman, G. 1912. Neu Petra-Forschungen der Helige Felsen von Jerusalem. Leipzig.

Di Cesare, M. 2017. A qibla mušarriqa for the First al-Aqṣà Mosque? A New Stratigraphic, Planimetric, and Chronological Reading of Hamilton's Excavation, and Some Considerations on the Introduction of the Concave miḥrab. Annali, Sezione Orientale 77: 66–96.

Di Cesare, M. 2020. The Mosaic Pavements Beneath the Floor of al-Aqṣa Mosque. In: Guidetti, F. and Meinecke, K., eds. A Globalised Visual Culture? Towards a Geography of Late Antique Art. Oxford: 289–317.

Dvira (Zweig), Y.S. 2008. New Information from Various Excavations on the Temple Mount During the Past One Hundred Years. In: Baruch, E. and Faust, A., eds. New Studies on Jerusalem 14. Ramat Gan: 293–355 (Hebrew).

Eliav, M. 1997. Britain and the Holy Land, 1838–1914. Jerusalem.

Gibson, S. 1997. The Holy Land in the Sights of Explorer's Cameras. In: Ben-Arieh, Y. and Davis, M., eds. Jerusalem in the Mind of the Western World, 1800–1948. With Eyes Toward Zion-V. Westport: 235–248.

Gibson, S. 1999. British Archaeological Institutions in Mandatory Palestine, 1917–1948. Palestine Exploration Quarterly 131(2): 115–143.

Gibson, S. 2000. Conrad Schick (1822–1901), the Palestine Exploration Fund and an "Archaic Hebrew" Inscription from Jerusalem. Palestine Exploration Quarterly 132(2): 113–122.

Gibson, S. 2001. The Ordnance Survey and the Palestine Exploration Fund. In: Tishbi, A., ed. Holy Land in Maps, Israel Museum Catalogue 459. Jerusalem: 158–159.

Gibson, S. 2011. British Archaeological Work in Jerusalem Between 1865–1967: An Assessment. In: Galor, K. and Avni, G., eds. Unearthing Jerusalem: 150 Years of Archaeological Research in the Holy City. Winona Lake: 23–57.

Gibson, S. 2014a. Charles Warren's Kidron Valley Tunnels, Bir Ayyub, and the Location of Biblical En Rogel. In: Van der Steen, E., Boertien, J. and Mulder-Hymans, N., eds. Exploring the Narrative. Jerusalem and Jordan in the Bronze and Iron Ages. London: 351–393.

Gibson, S. 2014b. The Pilaster Enclosure Wall of the Temple Mount in Jerusalem. In: Baruch, E. and Faust, A., eds. *New Studies on Jerusalem* 20. Ramat Gan: 17–39 (Hebrew).

Gibson, S. 2016. The Date of the Pilaster Wall in the Chapel of Alexander Nevsky. In: Vieweger, D. and Gibson, S., eds. *The Archaeology and History of the Church of the Redeemer and the Muristan in Jerusalem.* Oxford: 177–188.

Gibson, S. 2021. Archival Notes on Robinson's Arch at the Temple Mount/Haram al-Sharif in Jerusalem. *Palestine Exploration Quarterly* 153(3): 222–243.

Gibson, S. 2023. An Iron Age Stone Toilet Seat (the "Throne of Solomon") from Captain Montagu Brownlee Parker's 1909–1911 Excavations in Jerusalem. *Palestine Exploration Quarterly* 155(1). doi.org/10.1080/0031 0328.2022.2111492.

Gibson, S. and Jacobson, D.M. 1994. The Oldest Datable Chambers on the Temple Mount. *Biblical Archaeologist* 57: 150–160.

Gibson, S. and Jacobson, D.M. 1996. *Below the Temple Mount in Jerusalem. A Sourcebook on the Cisterns, Subterranean Chambers and Conduits of the Haram al-Sharif* (BAR International Series 637). Oxford.

Gibson, S., Lewis, R.Y. and Tabor, J. 2016. New Finds from the 11th to 13th Centuries Along the Southern City Wall of Mount Zion. In: Stiebel, G.D., Uziel, J., Cytryn-Silverman, K., Re'em, A. and Gadot, Y., eds. *New Studies in the Archaeology of Jerusalem and Its Region* 10. Jerusalem: 39–55 (Hebrew).

Gibson, S., Shapira, Y. and Chapman, R.L. 2013. *Tourists, Travellers and Hotels in Nineteenth-Century Jerusalem* (PEF Annual 11). Oxford.

Glücksmann, G. and Kool, R. 1995. Crusader Period Finds from the Temple Mount Excavations in Jerusalem. ʿAtiqot 26: 87–104.

Gonen, R. 2003. *Contested Holiness. Jewish: Muslim and Christian Perspectives on the Temple Mount in Jerusalem.* New Jersey.

Goodman, M. 2005. The Temple in First Century CE Judaism. In: Day, J., ed. *Temple and Worship in Biblical Israel.* London.

Goren, H. 2020. *"The Loss of a Minute Is Just so Much a Loss of Life": Edward Robinson and Eli Smith in the Holy Land* (Studia Traditionis Theologie 39). Turnhout.

Goren, H. and Rubin, R. 1996. Conrad Schick's Models of Jerusalem and Its Monuments. *Palestine Exploration Quarterly* 128(2): 103–124.

Gurevich, D. 2019. Digging in the Archives: Methodological Guidelines on Conrad Schick's Documents at the PEF and the Study of Archaeology. *Strata* 37: 141–162.

von Hagen, V.W. 1950. *Frederick Catherwood, Architect.* New York.

Hamilton, R.W. 1949. *The Structural History of the Aqṣà Mosque: A Record of Archaeological Gleanings from the Repairs of 1938–1942.* London.

Hanauer, J.E. 1910. *Walks about Jerusalem.* London.

Hawari, M.K. 2007. *Ayyubid Jerusalem (1187–1250): An Architectural and Archaeological Study* (BAR International Series 1628). Oxford.

Jacobson, D.M. and Gibson, S. 1995. A Monumental Stairway on the Temple Mount. *Israel Exploration Journal* 45: 162–170.

Jacobson, D.M. and Gibson, S. 1997. The Original Form of Barclay's Gate. *Palestine Exploration Quarterly* 129(2): 138–149.

Al-Jubeh, N. 2009. 1917 to the Present: Basic Changes, but Not Dramatic: Al-Haram al-Sharif in the Aftermath of 1967. In: Grabar, O. and Kedar, B.Y., eds. *Where Heaven and Earth Meet.* Jerusalem: 274–299.

Laperrousaz, E.M. 1973. A-t-on dégagé l'angle sud-eat du "Temple de Salomon"? *Syria* 50 (3–4): 355–392.

Legouas, J.Y. 2013. Saving Captain Pierotti? *Palestine Exploration Quarterly* 145(3): 231–250.

Mantell, A.M. 1882. Jerusalem. Newly-Opened Gate in the East Wall of the Haram. *Palestine Exploration Fund Quarterly Statement* 14(3): 169–170.

Mazar, B. 1971. *The Excavations in the Old City of Jerusalem near the Temple Mount: Preliminary Report of the Second and Third Seasons, 1969–1970.* Jerusalem.

Mazar, B. 1975. *The Mountain of the Lord.* New York.

Mazar, E. 2002. *The Complete Guide to the Temple Mount Excavations.* Jerusalem.

Mazar, E. 2011. *The Walls of the Temple Mount.* Jerusalem.

Mazar, E. 2020. *Over the Crossroads of Time: Jerusalem's Temple Mount Monumental Staircases as Revealed in Benjamin Mazar's Excavations (1968–1978).* Jerusalem.

Morris, R. 1870. *Youthful Explorers in Bible Lands.* Chicago.

Morrison, W. 1871. *The Recovery of Jerusalem: A Narrative of Exploration and Discovery in the City and Holy Land, by Capt. Wilson, R.E., Capt. Warren, R.E., &c.* London.

Onn, A., Weksler-Bdolah, S. and Patrich, J. 2019. A Herodian Triclinium with Fountain on the Road Ascending to the Temple Mount from the West. In: Geva, H., ed. *Ancient Jerusalem Revealed: Archaeological Discoveries, 1998–2018.* Jerusalem: 123–135.

Peleg-Barkat, O. 2017. *The Temple Mount Excavations in Jerusalem 1968–1978 Directed by Benjamin Mazar, Final Reports,* Vol. 5: *Herodian Architectural Decoration and King Herod's Royal Portico* (Qedem 57). Jerusalem.

Pierotti, E. 1864. *Jerusalem Explored: Being a Description of the Ancient and Modern City*, Vol. 1. London.

Prag, K. 2008. *Excavations by K.M. Kenyon in Jerusalem 1961–1967,* Vol. 5: *Discoveries in Hellenistic to Ottoman Jerusalem.* Oxford.

Prag, K. 2018. *Re-Excavating Jerusalem: Archival Archaeology* (The Schweich Lectures of the British Academy). Oxford.

Pruitt, J. 2017. The Fatimid Holy City: Rebuilding Jerusalem in the Eleventh Century. *The Medieval Globe* 3(2): 35–56.

Reich, R. and Baruch, Y. 2016. Notes Archéologiques. The Meaning of the Inscribed Stones at the Corners of the Herodian Temple Mount. *Revue Biblique* 123(1): 118–124.

Reich, R. and Baruch, Y. 2017. On Expansion of the Temple Mount in the Late Second Temple Period. *Cathedra* 164: 7–24 (Hebrew).

Reich, R. and Baruch, Y. 2019. The Herodian Temple Mount in Jerusalem: A Few Remarks on Its Construction and Appearance. In: Eisenberg, M. and Ovadiah, A., eds. *Cornucopia: Studies in Honor of Arthur Segal.* Rome: 157–169.

Reiter, Y. and Seligman, J. 2009. 1917 to the Present: Al-Haram al-Sharif / Temple Mount (Har Ha-Bayit) and the Western Wall. In: Grabar, O. and Kedar, B.Y., eds. *Where Heaven and Earth Meet.* Jerusalem: 231–273.

Richardson, R. 1822. *Travels Along the Mediterranean and Parts Adjacent*, Vol. 2. London.

Ritmeyer, L. 2006. *The Quest: Revealing the Temple Mount in Jerusalem.* Jerusalem.

Robinson, E. 1874. *Biblical Researches in Palestine, and in the Adjacent Regions: A Journal of Travels in the year 1838. By E. Robinson and E. Smith,* Vol. 1. Boston.

Robinson, E. 1856. *Later Biblical Researches in Palestine, and in the Adjacent Regions: A Journal of Travels in the Year 1852. By E. Robinson, E. Smith, and Others,* Vol. 2. Boston.

Saposnik, A.B. 2015. Wailing Walls and Iron Walls: The Western Wall as Sacred Symbol in Zionist National Iconography. *American Historical Review* 120(5): 1653–1681.

de Saulcy, L.F.J.C. 1853. *Voyage de la mer morte et dans les terres bibliques*: *Atlas.* Paris.

de Saulcy, L.F.J.C. 1865. *Voyage en Terre Sainte*, Vol. 2. Paris.

Schick, C. 1891. Reports from Jerusalem: The Newly-Discovered Arch in "Solomon's Stables." *Palestine Exploration Fund Quarterly Statement* 23(3): 200–201.

Schick, C. 1892. Letters from Baurath C. Schick: November 10th, 1891: The Buildings South of the "Double Gate." *Palestine Exploration Fund Quarterly Statement* 24(1): 19–24.

Schick, C. 1896. *Beit el Makdas oder der alte Tempelplatz zu Jerusalem; wie er jetzt ist: Mit einem Anhang.* Jerusalem.

Seligman, J. 2007. Solomon's Stables, The Temple Mount, Jerusalem: The Events Concerning the Destruction of Antiquities 1999–2001. ʿAtiqot 56: 33–53 (Hebrew).

Simpson, W. no date. *Underground Jerusalem: Descriptive Catalogue of the Above Collection of Water-Colour Drawings.* The Pall Mall Gallery. London.

Stewart, R.W. 1854. *The Tent and the Khan: A Journey to Sinai and Palestine.* Edinburgh.

St. Laurent, B. and Awwad, I. 2013. The Marwani Musalla in Jerusalem: New Findings. *Jerusalem Quarterly* 54: 7–30. http://vc.bridgew.edu/art_fac/8.

St. Laurent, B. and Awwad, I. 2016. Archaeology & Preservation of Early Islamic Jerusalem: Revealing the 7th Century Mosque on the Haram Al-Sharif. In: Stucky, R.A., Kaelin, O. and Mathys, H.P., eds. *Proceedings of the 9th International Congress on the Archaeology of the Ancient Near East, 9–13 June 2014, Basel*, Vol. 2. Wiesbaden: 441–153.

Tobler, T. 1853. *Topographie von Jerusalem und seinen Umgebungen*, Vol. 1. Berlin.

Van de Velde, C.W.M. 1854. *Narrative of a Journey Through Syria and Palestine in 1851 and 1852*, Vol. 2. Edinburgh.

de Vogüé, M. 1860. *Les Églises de la Terre Sainte*. Paris.

de Vogüé, M. 1864. *Le Temple de Jérusalem. Monographie du Haram-Ech-Chérif suivie d'un essai sur la topographie de la ville-sainte*. Paris.

Warren, C. 1876. *Underground Jerusalem: An Account of the Principal Difficulties Encountered in Its Exploration and the Results Obtained.* London.

Warren, C. 1880. Notes on Colonel Wilson's Paper on the Masonry of the Haram Wall. *Palestine Exploration Fund Quarterly Statement* 12(2): 159–166.

Warren, C. 1884. *Plans, Elevations, Sections, etc. Shewing the Results of the Excavations at Jerusalem, 1867–70, Executed for the Committee of the Palestine Exploration Fund.* London.

Warren, C. and Conder, C.R. 1884. *The Survey of Western Palestine: Jerusalem.* London.

Weksler-Bdolah, S. 2015. The Enlargement of the Herodian Temple Mount: An Archaeological Perspective. In: Ben-Arieh, Y., ed. *Study of Jerusalem Through the Ages.* Jerusalem: 19–72 (Hebrew).

Wightman, G.J. 1993. *The Walls of Jerusalem from the Canaanites to the Mamluks* (Mediterranean Archaeology Supplement 4). Sydney.

Wightman, G.J. 1995. Ben Sira 50:2 and the Hellenistic Temple Enclosure in Jerusalem. In: Bourke, S. and Descoeudres, J.P., eds. *Trade, Contact, and the Movement of Peoples in the Eastern Mediterranean: Studies in Honour of J. Basil Hennessy* (Mediterranean Archaeology Supplement 3). Sydney: 275–283.

Wilkinson, J. 1988. *Jerusalem Pilgrimage 1099–1185.* London.

Williams, G. 1849. *The Holy City: Historical, Topographical, and Antiquarian Notices of Jerusalem.* London.

Williams, G. 1864. *Dr Pierotti and His Assailants; or a Defence of "Jerusalem Explored."* London.

Wilson, C.W. 1865. *Ordnance Survey of Jerusalem.* London.

Wilson, C.W. 1880. The Masonry of the Haram Wall. *Palestine Exploration Fund Quarterly Statement* 12(1): 9–65.

Wray, G.O. 1891. Southern Projection from the Masjed al Aksa, Jerusalem. *Palestine Exploration Fund Quarterly Statement* 23(4): 320–322.

Yavuz, Y. 1996. The Restoration Project of the Masjid al-Aqsa by Mirmar Kemalettin (1922–26). *Muqarnas* 13: 149–164.

CHAPTER 3

TOPOGRAPHY

Yuval Baruch and Ronny Reich

The current Temple Mount complex occupies most of the northern part of ancient Jerusalem's Eastern Hill (Figs. 3.1–3.2). The settlement, which centuries later would come to be known as the City of David, was founded in the southern part of the hill, close to a spring. In the second millennium BCE, it became a city (Reich 2021: 3–20) and continued to evolve across the millennia. The northern part of the hill, which is also its higher part, was dedicated as a holy site and was consecrated for the erection of cultic edifices. This is mentioned in the Bible in relation to the activities of Kings David and Solomon (2 Sam 7; 1 Kings 5:17–19; 6:1–38; 8:15–21; 1 Chron 28–29) and was most probably the case in Canaanite periods that preceded the second millennium. On the early biblical cultic edifices and facilities (altar, tent, tabernacle, temple) there is no extant archaeological information. Evidence for Canaanite impact on the natural topography of the area is also lacking.

Archaeological evidence of the the earlier days of the Second Temple era, which covers the Persian and Early Hellenistic periods, is also lacking. While there are numerous historical, i.e., textual, references, archaeological data on the subject are scant. There is only one section of the Eastern Wall of the Temple Mound that represents parts of the pre-Herodian Wall (Ritmeyer 2006: 102–105). This in itself is sufficient evidence to point to grand-scale architecture and provides some details on measurements and directions, but it gives no indications of any plan and topography. It was to this Hasmonean holy precinct that King Herod related when in his 18th regnal year he initiated his major expansion project (22 BCE) (*Ant.* 15.380).

Unlike the compound's predecessor, which had been square in outline, the Herodian Temple Mount consisted of a vast, almost trapezoidal platform. The early researchers of the city (Pierotti [1864], Wilson [1865], Warren [1884], Schick [1887, 1896] and Kümmel [1906]) measured and took levels of bedrock exposed in its cisterns and (Fig. 3.3) created reasonably detailed topographical maps of the area. Their work is summed up by Gibson and Jacobson (1996) (see Chapter 2). Between the many levels registered on the map in Fig. 3.2, it has been possible to reconstruct the topography of the area by means of interpolation.

The Herodian compound, located amid three valleys, occupies the larger part of the highest northern area of the Eastern Hill. The Kidron Valley is to the east; adjoining it from the northwest is the Beth Zetha Valley, which crosses under the northeastern corner of the Temple Mount. On the west, it is delimited by the valley, or brook, that crosses the city lengthwise, from north to south. This is referred to in the Bible as the *naḥal* (נחל; Neh 2:15). In the Second Temple period, it was known as the Tyropoeon Valley (*War* 5.140). The builders of the southwestern corner of the Herodian Temple Mount did not take the topography of the Tyropoeon Valley into consideration when they planned the southwestern corner of the Temple Mount. They set the southwestern corner on the west bank of the valley, which is the eastern slope of the Upper City, thus damming the Tyropoeon Valley (Fig. 3.4d). They did the same with the northeastern corner, which dammed the Beth Zetha Valley.

The data at hand shows that the Herodian compound was built almost without regard for topography, consequently ignoring the massive engineering challenges caused by those conditions.

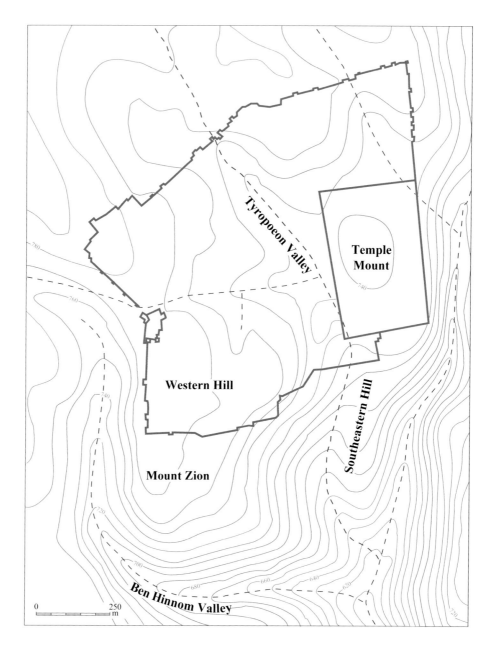

Figure 3.1: Schematic map of ancient Jerusalem, showing main topographical features.

Nearby construction in various periods did take the topography into consideration; some structures, like the buildings from the late Iron Age uncovered farther to the south by E. Mazar (Mazar 2015: 459–474), were built in stepped terraces directly on the rock surface. Other structures, such as the Umayyad buildings, overcame the gradient by raising floors to a considerable height and supporting them with massive walls. Still others, such as the monumental staircase leading to the Double Gate, cut deeply into the rock. Also noteworthy are drainage channels, particularly those cut into the rock, which took advantage of the slope southward, to provide drainage for the Temple Mount in that direction (Ben-Dov 1971).

Figure 3.2: Map after Kümmel 1906, part.

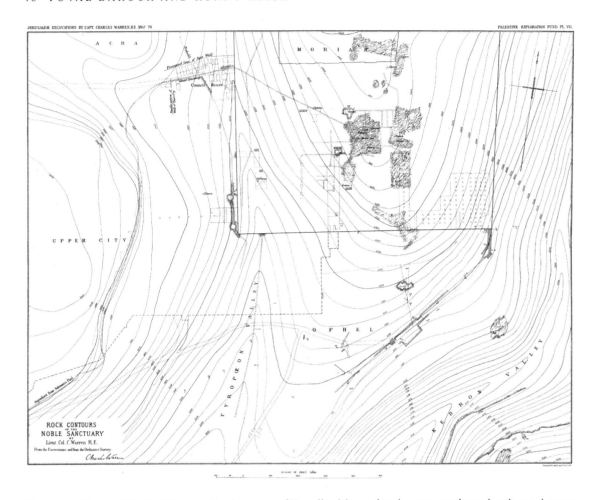

Figure 3.3: Warren 1884: Pl. VII (part). Southern part of Herodian Mount showing topography and rock-cut cisterns.

DOCUMENTATION OF THE TOPOGRAPHY

Undoubtedly, Herod's expansion to the south of the Temple Mount complex radically reshaped the topography of the Ophel area, which occupies the center of the Eastern Hill. Warren and Conder (1884: 274–292; Warren 1884) provided the most important data pertaining to the shape of the rock in the area on which the Southern Wall of the Temple Mount and its two southern corners were situated (Fig. 3.4a). In the cross-sections which face west (Fig. 3.4b), it seems that in the region of the Ophel the topography slopes southward in a relatively gentle gradient. However, on the east–west cross-section (Figs. 3.4c, 3.4d) the bedrock slopes eastward dramatically (30°) toward the Kidron Valley bed.

The Tyropoeon Valley bed is located some 30 m east of the southwestern corner of the Temple Mount (Warren 1884: Pl. 27). Here the slope ascending eastward toward the Double Gate is ca. 15° and the slope ascending westward toward the Upper City is ca. 20° (Fig. 3.5).

The eastern doorjamb of the Triple Gate is located at the summit of the hill on this east–west axis, at about 726 m asl. The southeastern corner of the Herodian enclosure is about 86 m to the east of this point, and the rock level at the corner is at 695.85 m asl. This means that at a distance of 86 m the bedrock drops some 30 m.

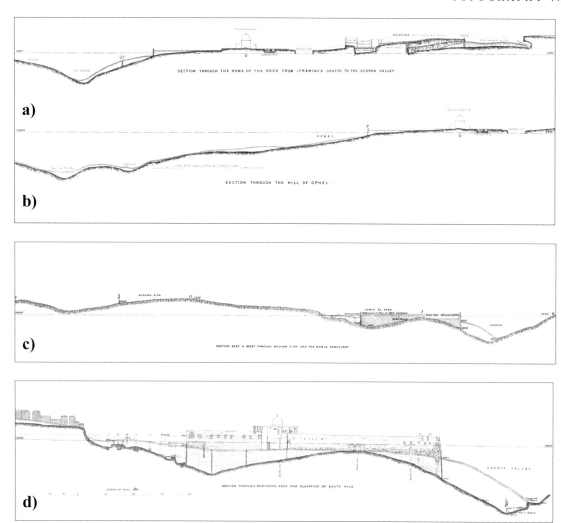

Figure 3.4: (a) Warren 1884: Pl. IX, Sections T–O (b) Warren 1884: Pl. IX, Sections D–Q (c) Warren 1884: Pl. VIII, Sections F–K (d) Warren 1884: Pl. X, Sections A–B.

The southwestern corner of the Herodian enclosure is ca. 100 m from the western doorjamb of the Double Gate. The corner is located ca. 30 m to the west of the Tyropoeon riverbed on the lower part of the slope ascending to the Upper City. As the Tyropoeon riverbed was blocked by the southwestern corner of the Temple Mount, it had to be replaced by an artificial aqueduct. In order to solve the problem of the rainwater runoff in the Tyropoeon Valley, a large drainage channel was cut in the bedrock as a local replacement of the riverbed, bypassing the southwestern corner. That said, in specific areas, special care was given to reshaping the rock (see below).

Parts of the foundation of the Southern Wall were planned and constructed in conjunction with the three monumental staircases that led to the Double Gate, the Triple Gate and the ramp that abutted the eastern part of the wall that ascended to the eastern opening of the Triple Gate. This fact enhances the importance of the gates.

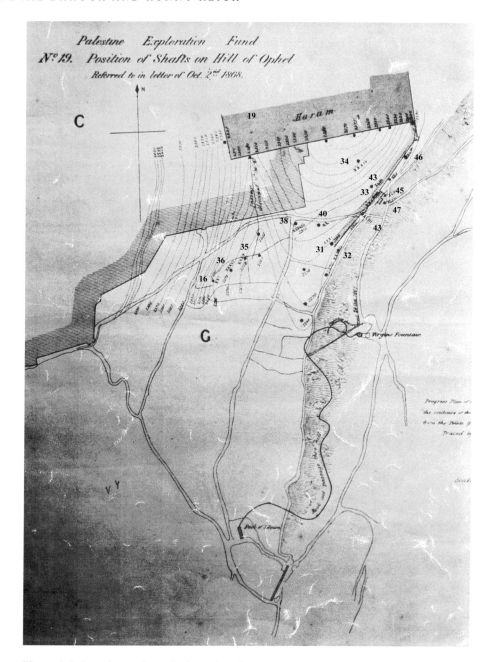

Figure 3.5: Location and numbering of shafts dug by Warren to the south of the Temple Mount in order to locate bedrock and measure its level for the topographical map.

The length of the Southern Wall is 279.01 m (Reidinger 2004: 9). The topography along the wall will be described in three sections, as follows:

1. The highest point of the bedrock—between the Double Gate and the Triple Gate (length ca. 66 m) (Fig. 2.7).

2. The bedrock from the Triple Gate to the southeastern corner (length ca. 87 m) (Fig. 3.6).

3. The bedrock from the Double Gate to the southwestern corner (length ca. 100 m) (Fig. 3.7).

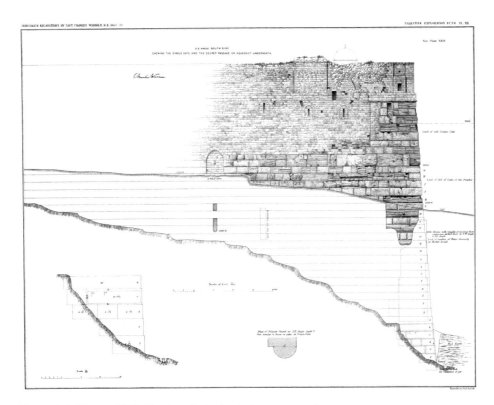

Figure 3.6: Warren 1884: Pl. XX. The bedrock from the Triple Gate to the southeastern corner.

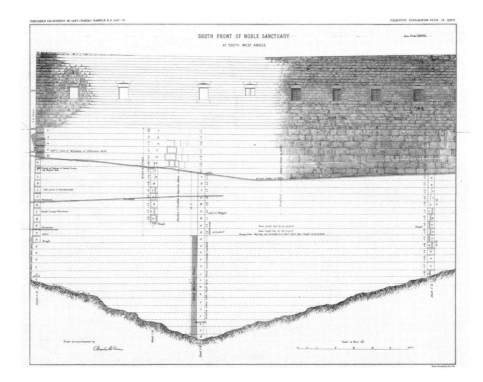

Figure 3.7: Warren 1884: Pl. XXVII. The bedrock from the Double Gate to the southwestern corner.

THE BEDROCK BETWEEN THE DOUBLE GATE AND THE TRIPLE GATE

The bedrock between the entrances to the Herodian Temple Mount was cut and shaped into a flat surface (average level 724.80 m asl), which served as an entrance plaza. This rock was turned into a ca. 3.5 × 66 m wide plaza by adding large, rectangular flagstones (Figs. 3.7–3.8). We assume that the plaza continued for a few meters to the west of the Double Gate, merged into the Stepped Street and ascended toward the southwestern corner of the Temple Mount enclosure.

Two monumental staircases spanned from the Double and Triple Gates southward. A spacious staircase was constructed, partially cut from the rock and partially built, along the width of both openings of the Double Gate (Figs. 3.9–3.10). This was unearthed by B. Mazar and M. Ben-Dov (Mazar 1975). Another flattened, rock-cut plaza was unearthed at the south of the staircase, at its lower end. A second monumental staircase led to the Triple Gate. Only the substructure of this staircase has been preserved (Figs. 3.11–3.12).

THE BEDROCK FROM THE TRIPLE GATE TO THE SOUTHEASTERN CORNER

This section includes two segments: one where the bedrock was cut as part of the construction of the wall and a ramp abutting it, and a second part without consideration to the topography.

As part of the construction of the Southern Wall, in the first segment extending from the Triple Gate to the southeastern corner of the Temple Mount, a significant effort was invested in cutting the bedrock into steps (Fig. 3.13).

The quarrying of the rock—from the gate's doorjamb to approximately 70 m to the east—lowered the rock and shaped it for the placement of the foundations of the wall. This process attests to the planning of the Herodian enclosure before the laying of the ashlars began. This includes the planning of the ramp on the southeastern side, which was built adjacent to the Temple Mount (Fig. 5.17). The ramp's foundations were divided into a series of 14 rock-cut compartments that supported

Figure 3.8: Plaza paved with rectangular flagstones (photo by A. Schick).

Figure 3.9: Staircase leading to the Double Gate, looking north (photo by S. Halevi).

Figure 3.10: Staircases leading to the Double Gate (top staircase) and to the Triple Gate (lower staircase), looking northwest (photo by A. Schick).

barrel-shaped vaults, which in turn supported the ramp. Five additional compartments to the east were constructed entirely of stone on bedrock.

In this segment, the stones of the Southern Wall's foundation were placed in quarried trenches. It seems that in this short segment, due to the steep topographical gradient, the engineers chose not to reshape the bedrock, as they did farther to the west toward the gates area.

According to Warren (1884: Pls. 10 [third cross-section], 19, 20, 26), it is obvious that the southwestern corner of the Temple Mount was constructed without any consideration for the topography.

Figure 3.11: Substructure of the staircase that once led from the south toward the Triple Gate, looking north.

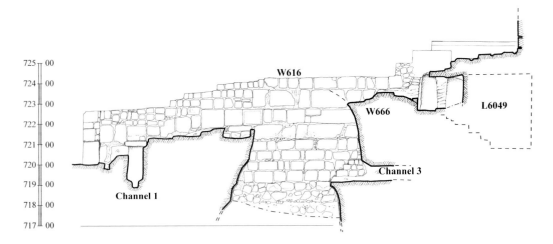

Figure 3.12: Cross-section through the rock-cut part of the substructure which supported the staircase leading from the south toward the Triple Gate, looking west.

Figure 3.13: The Southern Wall of the Temple Mount founded on steps cut into the bedrock, looking west (photo by Yuval Baruch).

THE BEDROCK FROM THE DOUBLE GATE TO THE SOUTHWESTERN CORNER

It should be borne in mind that the Temple Mount walls we see today are the result of the vast expansion of an older Temple Mount enclosure project initiated by Herod. This extension was carried out north, south and west of the old *temenos*. As part of the expansion of the Temple Mount complex to the west, its southwestern corner was located on the western bank of the Tyropoeon Valley, some 30 m west of the valley riverbed. According to Warren (2,279 feet = 694.6 m asl, see Fig. 3.4d)—the Temple Mount's foundations descend 17 courses below the level of the Herodian Street in the Tyropoeon Valley, which stretches along the Western Wall, compared to 6–7 courses below the street, down to the foundation near the southwestern corner (709.0 m asl).

Mazar and Ben-Dov's excavation showed that the bedrock here, i.e., on the eastern slope of the Tyropoeon Valley, retained its original appearance save for the cutting of a foundation trench into which the foundation course was inserted (Mazar 1971: Fig. 5). According to Mazar, in order to overcome this significant topographical hindrance and create a convenient leveled surface on which to lay the Stepped Street ascending from the southwestern corner toward the Double Gate in the Southern Wall, a series of square compartments was constructed abutting the wall. The walls of those compartments descended as far down as the bedrock and the compartments were filled with debris. This created a raised platform that, in fact, covered the entire valley (on the results of the excavation of several of the compartments along the Western Wall from its southwestern corner northward, see Chapter 16).

A construction project of walls the magnitude of the Temple Mount must inevitably be founded on bedrock. The planners and builders affixed the foundations of the walls to bedrock in various ways. In the east, they extended the existing wall, which had been constructed generations earlier, southward. In the west, they moved the wall rather bluntly to the western bank of the Tyropoeon Valley with little consideration for topography. In the south, they adapted the bedrock to the foundations of the wall.

REFERENCES

Finkelstein, I., Koch, I. and Lipschits, O. 2011. The Mound on the Mount. *Journal of Hebrew Scriptures* 11: 2–24. https://doi.org/10.5508/jhs.2011.v11.a12.

Gibson, S. and Jacobson, D.M. 1996. *Below the Temple Mount in Jerusalem: A Sourcebook on the Cisterns, Subterranean Chambers and Conduits of the Haram al-Sharif* (BAR International Series 637). Oxford.

Knauf, E.A. 2000. Jerusalem in the Late Bronze and Early Iron Ages: A Proposal. *Tel Aviv* 27: 75–90.

Kümmel, A. 1906. *Materialien zur Topographie des Alten Jerusalem: Begleittext zu der Karte der Materialien zur Topographie des Alten Jerusalem.* Halle.

Mazar, B. 1971. *The Excavations in the Old City of Jerusalem near the Temple Mount: Preliminary Report of the Second and Third Seasons, 1969–1970.* Jerusalem.

Mazar, B. 1975. *Mountain of the Lord: Excavating in Jerusalem.* Jerusalem.

Mazar, E. 2015. *The Ophel Excavations to the South of the Temple Mount 2009–2013: Final Reports*, Vol. 1. Jerusalem.

Pierotti, E. 1864. *Jerusalem Explored: Being a Description of the Ancient and Modern City*, 2 vols. London.

Reich, R. 2021. A Moment in which to Be Born. In: Reich, R. and Shukron, E., eds. *Excavations in the City of David, Jerusalem (1995–2010): Areas A, J, F, H, D and L, Final Report* (Ancient Jerusalem Publications Series 1). University Park and Jerusalem.

Reidinger, E.F. 2004. The Temple Mount Platform in Jerusalem from Solomon to Herod: An Archaeological Re-Examination. *Assaph* 9: 1–64.

Schick, C. 1887. *Beit el Makdas oder der alte Tempelplatz zu Jerusalem, wie er jetzt ist: Mit einem Anhang.* Jerusalem.

Schick, C. 1896. *Die Stiftshütte, der Tempel in Jerusalem und der Tempelplatz der Jetztzeit.* Berlin.

Warren, C. 1884. *Plans, Elevations, Sections, etc. Shewing the Results of the Excavations at Jerusalem, 1867–70, Executed for the Committee of the Palestine Exploration Fund.* London.

Warren, C. and Conder, C.R. 1884. *The Survey of Western Palestine: Jerusalem.* London.

Wilson, C.W. 1865. *Ordnance Survey of Jerusalem.* London.

PART II:
EXCAVATIONS

Part IIa:
Excavations near the Southeastern Corner

CHAPTER 4

EXCAVATION NEAR THE SOUTHEASTERN CORNER— AREAS A AND B

Yuval Baruch and Ronny Reich

This excavation near the southeastern corner of the Temple Mount followed the previous Baruch and Reich dig (2016)[1] near the Triple Gate (sometimes called the Eastern Hulda Gate).[2] Both excavations were a preparatory stage for the reconstruction works of the monumental staircase built to the south and in front of the Triple Gate (Figs. 4.1–4.2).

LOCATION

The excavation was on two relatively small areas abutting the extramural face of the Southern Wall of the Herodian Temple Mount (Figs. 4.3–4.4):

- Area A (16 × 11.5 m) was excavated ca. 45 m east of the Triple Gate.
- Area B (15 × 11 m) was excavated ca. 16 m farther to the east of Area A, abutting the western face of the Ophel Wall.

The main feature of our excavation exposed in this area was a series of 19 compartments, numbered C1–C19, constructed along the Southern Wall of the Temple Mount, starting in the west near the Triple Gate and continuing eastward to the southeastern corner (Fig. 4.3).

The excavation near the southeastern corner of the Temple Mount is almost the last area to be excavated at the Southern Temple Mount Wall. In the western area (Area A), the excavation succeeded in digging down to bedrock; in the eastern area (Area B), however, the excavation was halted at Square B1 705.05 m asl and will be resumed in the future on undisturbed deposits. The excavation surveyors and draftsmen documented in detail the exposed lower parts of the Herodian Temple Mount wall, between the Triple Gate and southeastern corner of the Temple Mount.

OBJECTIVES

The objectives of the excavation were as follows:

1. To study the architectural features of the southeast corner of the Temple Mount complex and the wall segment between the Triple Gate and the southeastern corner.

---

[1] The excavation, on behalf of the Israel Antiquities Authority (Permit No. A-3242), was directed in 1999–2000 by the authors, with the assistance of G. Kotovski (area supervisor), A. Abu Gharbiya (administrator), T. Kornfeld, M. Kunin and W. Esman (surveyors), C. Amit (photography), E. Kamaiski (pottery restoration), N. Mai (drafting), E. Altmark and R. Vinitzky (metal cleaning, the Metal Conservation Laboratory, IAA), N. Zeevi, K. Hirsch (pottery drawing), S. Kweller (architectural reconstruction). We owe special thanks to Dèbora Sandhaus for organizing and collecting the excavation data.

[2] The gates in the Southern Wall of the earlier, pre-Herodian Temple Mount are referred to in the Mishnah (*Middot* 1:3) as the "Hulda Gates." The gate on the west is the Double Gate and the gate on the east is the Triple Gate.

2.   To study the development in the area in the period before and after the sack of Jerusalem and the Temple complex in the year 70 CE.

3.   To investigate the series of weathered spots along the Southern Wall in a section that extends from the Triple Gate to the southeast corner of the complex.

4.   To probe the connection point between the Ophel Wall and the southeastern corner of the Temple Mount complex.

ARCHITECTURE AND STRATIGRAPHY

AREA A

As described in Table 4.1, five strata were discerned in Area A (Figs. 4.4–4.5). Our primary aim here was to clean the area from the accumulation of previous excavations and to document it anew. The excavation covers an area that is ca. 16 × 11.5 m in size. The entire area of vaulted Compartments C10, C11, C12 southward and up to the large edifice of the Byzantine period, located 9.5 m from the Temple Mount, at the southeastern corner was buried beneath a thick layer of earthen fill (see also Chapter 5).

The fills reach the Southern Wall of the Temple Mount as a result of B. Mazar's excavations along the wall, which reached the bedrock (Mazar 2003, Figs. 4.6, 4.7, 4.8).

Stratum V: Iron IIC

The earliest remains in this area are three architectural units which include two hewn and plastered installations (A, B) and a hewn and leveled stone surface (C). Note that only Unit C is dated by

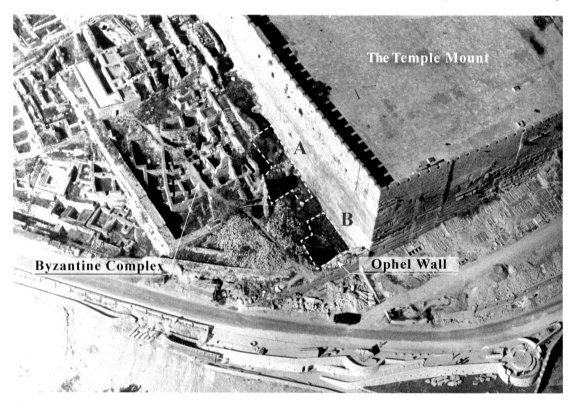

Figure 4.1: Aerial view of the area prior to excavation, showing the Temple Mount's southeastern corner, looking northwest. Note excavation Areas A and B (photo courtesy of IAA).

pottery sherds to the Iron IIC, while Units A and B are dated to the same period due to their stratigraphic and architectonic relations to Unit C. The plan of the three units is partial since Unit C was damaged by late construction activity. Units A and B extend beyond the excavation boundary. The units are separated by Walls 653 and 654 (Figs. 4.5–4.6). The date of the various remains is based partly on stratigraphic considerations and partly on artifacts, mainly pottery from Loci 6136 and 6081, associated with the remains of Unit C (see Chapter 6). These rock cuttings, walls and stones cover an area of ca. 35 sq m.

The lower parts of Walls 654 and 653 are rock-cut, while the upper parts are built of roughly cut stones. The extension of these architectural units to the south is not clear, because the foundation

Figure 4.2: Area prior to excavation, looking west (photo by Y. Baruch).

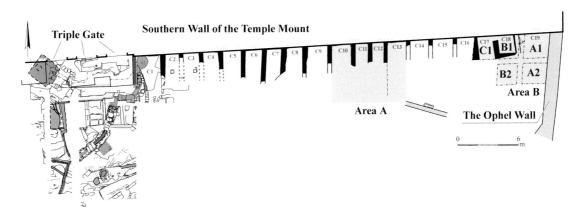

Figure 4.3: General plan of excavation areas, from the Triple Gate to the southeast corner of the Temple Mount.

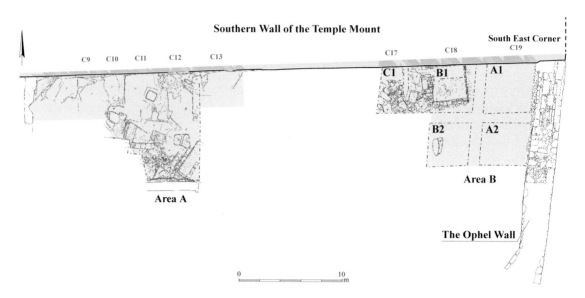

Figure 4.4: Excavation Areas A and B.

Table 4.1: Area A, Excavated Strata and Main Remains

Stratum	Period (years)	Main remains
V	Iron IIC (late 7th–early 6th centuries BCE)	Rock cuttings, walls, occupation traces
IV	Pre-Herodian (second half of 1st century BCE)	Rock-cut installations (miqwaʾot), walls and water channels
III	Herodian to sack of Jerusalem (1st century BCE–70 CE)	Extension southward of Temple Mount; traces of monumental staircase, ramp along wall, miqwaʾot, large yard south of ramp
II	Late Roman (2nd–4th centuries CE)	Remains of monumental staircase and ramp, floors, drainage channels, rich assemblage of bricks, roof tiles, pipes and bathhouse tubuli imprinted by Tenth Roman Legion
I	Late Byzantine (6th–7th centuries CE)*	Extensive construction, dwellings

* If there were any remains that postdate the Byzantine period in this area, they were totally removed during the Jordanian occupation (Ritmeyer 2006: 100–101) and later by the previous excavators. These were monumental remains of the Umayyad period and later fortifications, which ran to the southeastern corner of the Temple Mount.

of Wall 652 of a later date (Byzantine) was built over it. These seem to have taken a southeast-to-northwest orientation, which is oblique to the orientation of the nearby, later, Herodian Temple Mount's Southern Wall. The rock cuttings in Unit A, only the northwestern part of which was exposed, are ca. 0.8 m deep; the lower part is rock-cut and the upper part is built. It is plastered with beige-colored non-hydraulic plaster. The northwestern face of Wall 653 is almost 3.3 m long and 1.3 m high. The lower part is cut in bedrock and the upper part is constructed of rough stones with mortar and small stones in the joints as binders. These remains were covered by a series of earthen deposits containing mainly rubble and pottery sherds of the Early Roman period (Loci 6079, 6086, 6091, 6096, 6107; Figs. 4.5–4.6).

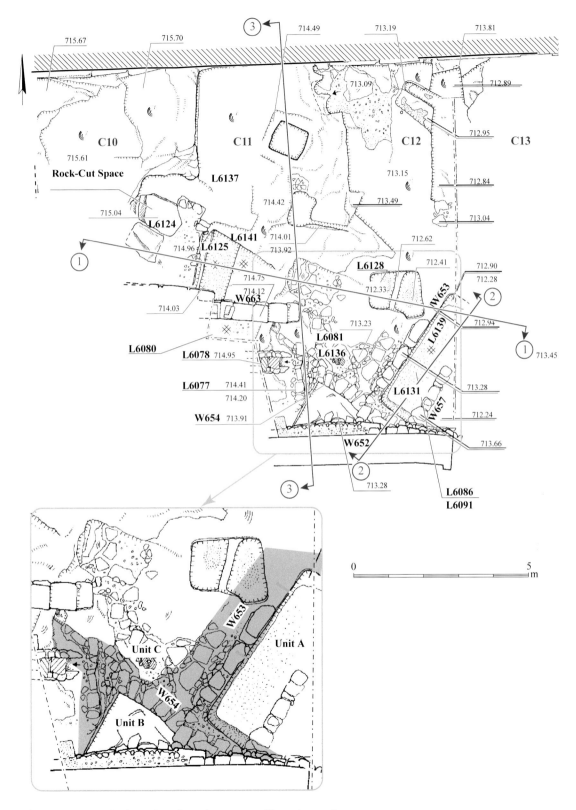

Figure 4.5: Area A plan. Note the enlargement of Iron Age units.

Wall 657 was constructed of rough stones on the floor of Unit A (Fig. 4.5). The wall was constructed on the plastered floor of the installation (Locus 6139); therefore, it probably postdates the units discussed here. However, as this wall was found covered with earth containing pottery

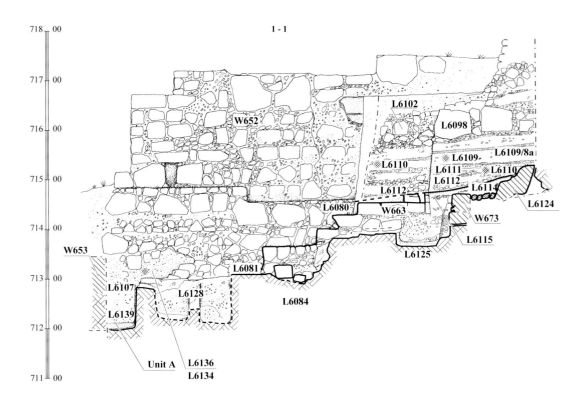

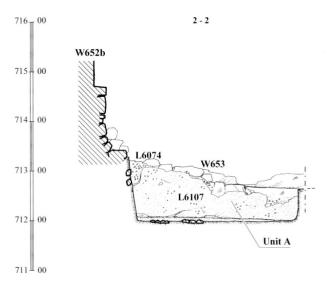

Figure 4.6: Area A, Section 1, looking south (see note 5); and Section 2, looking west.

sherds of the Second Temple period, it seems to be a later repair of Unit A and it is not clear what it was used for and in what period.

Unit C is a rock-cut surface in the area between the plastered installations, filled with small- to middle-sized fieldstones (Locus 6134), serving as a foundation to a floor of crushed limestone

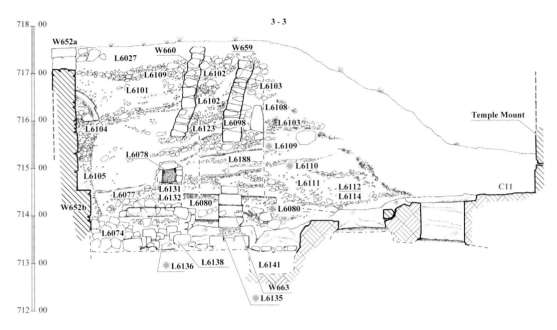

Figure 4.7: Area A, Section 3, looking west.

Figure 4.8: Area A, looking south (photo by Y. Baruch).

(Locus 6136), fragmentarily preserved (Fig. 4.9) (3 × 2.5 m). The floor was covered with a layer of fieldstones (0.4 m thick; Locus 6081). On it, there was a thin layer of earth that contained organic material and several fragments of pottery jars, including a late Iron Age jar handle with a rosette seal impression (see Chapter 6).

It seems possible that the rock-cut space located under Compartment C10 (Locus 6124) dates to pre-Herodian times. Its rock-cut opening was found partially blocked by two large stones (Figs. 4.5–4.6), and by the wall of *Miqweh* 6125. The wall appears to have antedated the *miqweh* and cannot be dated. However, in light of the remains unearthed in the area, it most likely could be dated to Stratum V.

In summary, it seems that the fragmentary remains described are part of a late Iron Age architectural complex of which several rock cuttings and a patch of floor were preserved. We have no suggestions for their function or for a reconstruction. We must remain content with saying that the area was occupied in this period. The dating of Units A–C to Iron IIC is based on the pottery sherds that were found *in-situ* in Unit C (Loci 6081 and 6136), including a storage jar with the handle imprinted by a rosette stamp impression.

Stratum IV: Pre-Herodian

In this report, we have divided the ancient Roman period into two: the defined pre-Herodian period, dating up to the expansion of the Temple Mount complex, and the Herodian period, which deals with architectural finds built in direct relation to the walls of the complex. This division, even though not reflected in ceramic typology changes, is based on the recognition that the Temple Mount expansion project resulted in a change in the orientation of the area.

In other words, because the topography of the northern part of the eastern hill sloped at this point from the northwest to the southeast in the direction of the Kidron River, the various buildings of the pre-Rhodian phase were carved and built in relation to this topography.

Figure 4.9: Area A, Unit C, Locus 6136, Iron Age (photo by Y. Baruch).

Moreover, as the topography changed drastically in the Herodian period, the remains from the pre-Herodian period are certainly identifiable, both because of their different orientation and because they are either covered or are cut by the Herodian remains.

The remains in Stratum IV pertain to the pre-Herodian period prior to the operations undertaken to enlarge the Temple Mount (Figs. 4.5–4.7). These fragmented remains are mainly two rock-cut installations (Loci 6125, 6128) and a water channel (Locus 6077); they represent activity of a domestic nature that took place in this area prior to the expansion (Figs. 4.5, 4.7, 4.14, 4.15).

A short section of a water channel, Locus 6077, from north to south, from which only the western wall was preserved to a length of 1.6 m, was built in a slightly curved arc. The wall of the channel was built of medium-sized stones that are roughly hewn and bonded with grayish clay material, on which there is a remnant of gray plaster. The channel was built on top of a level of stones and fills that covered the Iron Age installation system. This side of the channel was sealed with a fill of earth and stones (Locus 6133) on which the Locus 6080 floor was built; both date to the early Roman period. The north side of the channel probably relates to a grayish plaster level Locus 6135 (floor?).

Installation Locus 6125 is located ca. 4.5 m south of the Temple Mount Wall, opposite Compartments 10–11 (Figs. 4.11, 4.12). It is a small installation in which the lower part is cut into the bedrock. Its

Figure 4.10: Area A, Unit A, Iron Age (photo by Y. Baruch).

2-m-long outline is trapezoidal and it is between 1 and 2 m wide. We identified one step and the bottom of the installation. It might have been the lower remains of a *miqweh*. The western wall of the installation (Wall 673) is what survived of the upper parts. Its walls were constructed of crudely shaped ashlars and were plastered with gray hydraulic plaster. The southern part of the installation ran under Herodian Wall 663 (Stratum III), meaning that it went out of use before the wall was constructed.

Installation Locus 6128 (Figs. 4.5, 4.6, 4.13) was excavated by a previous expedition. We re-cleared the installation and the surrounding rock surface. A layer of earth, which eroded after a previous excavation, contained a few early Roman pottery sherds. It had an irregular outline (ca. 1.3 × 1.6 m). A low rock partition (0.2 m) divided it into two parts: the northern was 1.05 m deep, the southern was 0.6 m deep. We can suggest that Locus 6128 served as a kind of household installation.

Stratum III: Herodian

The most significant action during this period and in the history of ancient Jerusalem, in general, was the construction of the Temple Mount complex in its expanded format. This enterprise included not only the erection of retaining walls (one of which is the Southern Wall along which the present dig was carried out) and the construction of the buildings on the Mount itself, but also a system of roads leading to the Mount from all around the city, a gathering plaza and a system of magnificent gates leading in and out of the complex. All of these will be discussed in detail below. In this section, we will focus on the results of the excavations in which we also uncovered some of the remains associated with this impressive construction operation.

The main item we found in Stratum III was Wall 663 (Figs. 4.5–4.8, 4.11, 4.14, 4.15), constructed ca. 6.2 m south of and parallel to the Temple Mount Wall. We followed Wall 663 northward for ca.

Figure 4.11: Area A, *miqweh*, Locus 6125, looking west. Note two large stones blocking the open rock-cut space Locus 6124 (photo by Y. Baruch).

2.8 m, up to the point where it was buried under unexcavated earthen fills, indicating that the wall was longer than what we exposed. Of the section that we unearthed, only two to three courses were preserved. These courses were made of carefully worked ashlars that had been placed one on top of the other and bonded with light lime-based material. Over this structure was a stone threshold broken into two parts. We are not sure if this wall was originally built higher than what we exposed

Figure 4.12: Area A, *miqweh,* Locus 6125, view from above (photo by C. Amit).

Figure 4.13: Area A, rock-cut installation Locus 6128, view from above (photo by C. Amit).

but we believe that it served as a foundation for a wall or fence, on which a railing or a low partition was built. This construction would have bordered an open space on the south, located south of the compartment system below the sloping street (opposite Compartment 11). The wall itself would have been built into the plastered installation of Stratum IV (Locus 6125), the *miqweh*.

Figure 4.14: Area A, part of Water Channel Locus 6077, looking south (photo by Y. Baruch).

Figure 4.15: Area A, Drainage Channel Locus 6078, and floor Locus 6080 from an earlier Roman period, looking west (photo by C. Amit).

A level floor made of crushed limestone, Locus 6080 from the south, Locus 6114 from the north, abuts Wall 663 (Figs. 4.5–4.8, 4.15). The limestone floors were built at the same level as the top of the wall (714.76 m asl) but did not cover the broken threshold. These floors were laid on top of an accumulation of earth and stone fills, which packed several rock cuttings and installations, including the *miqweh* (Locus 6125) into which the wall was built. As stated above, these facilities were probably installed prior to the expansion of the Temple Mount, and it appears that the earthen fill that covered them was intended for leveling the area. A thick soil level was discerned in this accumulation (Locus 6115, Fig. 4.6). Many artifacts were found inside this soil layer—mainly pottery sherds and stone vessel fragments, typical of the late Second Temple period, as well as ashes (see Chapter 7). The latter apparently represents the remains of hearths and stoves that were dismantled from buildings and were used as construction fill.

Inevitably, these fragmentary remains are insufficient to reconstruct the appearance of the entire area in the period in question. However, it seems that the filling and leveling of the area in front of the compartments, at least south of Compartments 9–12, created a fairly broad open space between the Southern Wall of the Temple Mount and Wall 663. This space (for example, 714.49 m asl in C11) may have served as a narrow street that ran at the foot of the ramp, which was constructed above the series of compartments (see Chapters 5 and 27).

Stratum II: Late Roman

Stratum II dates to the Late Roman period, representing human activity in this area near the southeastern corner of the Temple Mount, but without any architectural remains.

Two phases have been documented in Area A: IIa—A floor made of crushed limestone (Locus 6110) on a base of earth and rubble (Locus 6111); IIb—A hard-trodden floor (Locus 6109), level earthen fills (Loci 6131 and 6132) and a drainage channel (Locus 6078).

Locus 6078, which is a channel, runs in a north–south direction (Figs. 4.5, 4.7, 4.14, 4.15). A segment of ca. 1.6 m of its length was exposed, and its western wall was preserved. It was built of crude stones and part of its bottom was made of hard-trodden earth on a makeup of small stones. On its inner face traces of hydraulic gray plaster were barely preserved, indicating that it was most probably a drainage channel. No potsherds were found in the section we made at the northern end of the channel, so its dating is based on stratigraphic considerations.

Phase IIa: A floor or surface was excavated (Locus 6110) without any architectural association, made of crushed limestone (at average level 715.30 m, 3 cm thick).[3] The floor (Locus 6110) was laid over a light brown earthen fill (ca. 0.8 m thick) and small stones (Locus 6111), which contained pottery sherds from the middle of the 1st–2nd century CE, including a rich assemblage of fragmented bricks, roof tiles, pipes and bathhouse *tubuli* imprinted with the stamp of the Tenth Roman Legion *Fretensis*. This leveled surface seems to have been used as a flat open space in front of the rock-cut compartments (Fig. 4.8). Although the ramp was probably destroyed in the 70 CE destruction, some of the compartments, especially those with their lower parts cut into the rock, continued to be used. Their purpose, however, is as yet unknown.

Phase IIb: Locus 6109, a hard-trodden floor. The surface was raised to 715.90 m. The level of this floor resembles the floor of Compartment 11 under the ramp. A drainage channel had been constructed (Locus 6078, upper width 0.3 m, inner depth 0.25 m), with a square cross-section, which runs from west to east (Figs. 4.6, 4.7, 4.15) under floor Locus 6109, with earthen fills, in the

---

[3] In Fig. 4.6 the floor appears level, while in Fig. 4.7 the floor slants from north to south.

southern part of the section (Fig. 4.7).[4] The square drainage channel was constructed over earthen fills and small stones which served as its foundation (Loci 6131, 6132), from which pottery sherds of the 2nd–3rd century CE were extracted. The walls of the channel were made of roughly cut stones. The channel floor was made of hard-trodden earth and was covered with flat stones. In our limited excavation, we did not find any plaster on the walls and therefore it seems that it was a drainage channel or sewer.

Stratum I: Late Byzantine

South of the excavated area, a large late Byzantine architectural complex was constructed that included rooms and courtyards. It had been excavated previously and described by E. Mazar (2015: 78–85) and by Gordon (2007: 201–215, Fig. 18.3, No. 16). An alley supported by a wall was built north of the building, on an east–west course.

The complex is elaborate and covers an area of ca. 500 sq m. The structures were well preserved. Despite some massive dismantling in the 1980s by the previous excavators, one can still follow some of its architectural features (Mazar 2003). The building's floor plan comprises, at floor level, about 30 rooms and inner courtyards. Some of the rooms are interconnected. To the northeast, the building opens through an impressive portal decorated with a cross. To the west, there is a narrow door that leads into an expanse that has a wing appended to it from the west. Additional rooms adjoin the trapezoidal complex from the south and northeast. The floors of these rooms are occasionally covered with white tesserae with simple patterns, flagstones and even terracotta tiles. Some of the rooms contain various installations, including constructed and portable ovens and water basins. Gordon (2007: unit No. 16 on his map, Fig. 18.3) suggested that this building served as a hospice for pilgrims, as part of the establishment and organization of a new late Byzantine quarter south of the Temple Mount.

Some of the walls, such as Wall 652, which borders the area of our excavation and which we studied and documented, indicate that the structure probably had two floors that were supported by a series of masonry arches (Figs. 4.5, 4.6, 4.8, 4.14).

In our excavation, we dug a foundation trench (Loci 6104, 6105) in the earthen levels which ran onto the northern face of Northeast Wall 652 of the appended wing (Figs. 4.5–4.7).

Wall 652 was preserved to a considerable height of 7.8 m. Its outer, northern face was plastered with rough grayish plaster. The outer, northern face was made of large and medium-sized stones, including some taken from the destruction of the Herodian stone collapse. The wall is comprised of two parts: a lower (Wall 652b) and an upper part (Wall 652a). The lower part of the wall belonged to the first floor of the building and was thicker (0.8 m) than the upper part (0.5 m). The second story of the building contained a funnel-shaped window (0.6 × 0.3 m), set at about 1.2 m above the second-story floor (Fig. 4.17).

Prior to the construction of Wall 652, a foundation trench was dug (Loci 6101, 6104, 6105) down to the layer of large stones (Locus 6074), which were used as a foundation for the wall (Fig. 4.7). This layer was uncovered before we excavated the foundation wall. It was dug to a depth of ca. 2.6 m below the surface, before the construction of the Byzantine edifice (at about the level of 716.85 m). The foundation trench has a funnel-shaped cross-section with a wide top

---

4   For objective reasons related to the state of Area A as it remained after the previous excavations, Section 4.6 was excavated not in a straight line but as a three-dimensional graded section, where each segment of the section stood on its own and actually presented three views in three different positions relative to the viewer, with the right side away from the observer (see Fig. 4.8).

(up to 1.2 m on the northern side) and is bounded on the north by a terrace (Wall 659), while the lower part of the trench is quite narrow (0.12 m). The upper part (Locus 6104) was filled with brownish gravel while the lower part of the foundation trench (Locus 6105) was filled with grayish earth. Only a few indicative pottery sherds, dating to the late Byzantine period, were found in the fill.

After the construction of the wall and the filling of the foundation trench, the upper part was sealed off with a thick plaster layer that gave it a convex profile with a reddish hue due to the crushed pottery contained in it (Reich 2004: 130. Locus 6101; Fig. 4.7). This is a technique meant to protect the outer wall from infiltration of rainwater and moisture, especially when parts of the walls are buried in the ground and covered. The construction along the wall has two parts: a core made of binding material, clay and stones; and an outer, watertight layer made of hydraulic plaster (0.1 m thick). The presence of this constructional element points to the existence of an open space north of the Byzantine edifice. The width of this open space is about 3.5 m and it is bound on the north by supporting Wall 659 (0.9 m thick at its base, 0.55 m at its head, and preserved to a height of 1.9 m), which can be followed for some 4.8 m from our excavation area to the north. This supporting wall was constructed of stones, without any binding material. The lowest stone courses—made of larger stones (Wall 659)—were founded on a hard layer (Locus 6109) and later supported a thick layer made of gravel and small stones (Locus 6108), containing pottery sherds from the Late Roman period. We do not rule out the possibility that the upper, narrower part of the wall was a later addition (Fig. 4.7).

Undoubtedly, Wall 659 was built as a retaining wall along an alley parallel to the southeast appended wing of the Byzantine structure. In a later phase, still in the Byzantine period, the alley was narrowed and its level raised. Now it was bound from the south by Wall 660. This wall slants. It is made of stone fragments in secondary use. Its northern side supports an intentional fill of earth and gravel (Loci 6102, 6123) which raised the alley level. The fills between these walls contained pottery sherds dating to the late Byzantine period.

It seems that a fill of the foundation trench of Wall 652a abuts the lower part of Wall 660 from the south. This can indicate that the lower part of the wall is an earlier wall (Fig. 4.7).

Area B

This area abuts the southeastern corner of the Temple Mount and the Ophel Wall to the east. Our intention at first was to excavate five squares; eventually, however, we excavated two extensively and excavated the other three superficially (Figs. 4.1, 4.3, 4.4).

Our goal near the southeastern corner of the complex was to examine the continuation of the compartments' structure. We wanted to see if the ramp from the Triple Gate, which, in our opinion, was supported by the row of compartments, sloped down to the east to a point where, according to our estimation, the ramp ended. In addition, we examined the archaeological features of the meeting point between the Ophel Wall and the southeastern corner of the Temple Mount complex.

We discerned three archaeological strata in this area, and they are well in line with the stratigraphic division discussed in Area A (Figs. 4.16–4.20).

Stratum III—Herodian (Late 1st Century BCE–Beginning of 1st Century CE)

In two squares (Squares B1 and C1), we excavated down to bedrock. The main features uncovered were two compartments (Nos. 17, 18. Their inner size is ca. 3.1 × 3.1 m). These compartments abut

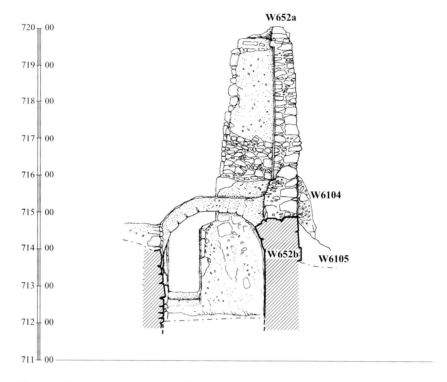

Figure 4.16: Byzantine structure, Wall 652, cross-section, looking west. Excavated by M. Ben-Dov. Wall 652a and 652b excavated by Baruch and Reich.

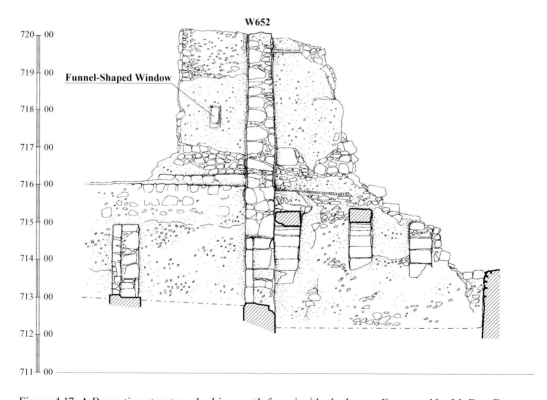

Figure 4.17: A Byzantine structure, looking north from inside the house. Excavated by M. Ben-Dov.

Table 4.2: Area B, Excavated Strata and Main Remains

Stratum	Period (years)	Main remains
III	Herodian (late 1st century BCE–beginning of 1st century CE)	Construction of Southern Wall of Temple Mount and adjacent ramp
II	Late Roman period (2nd–4th centuries CE)	Thick layer of earthen fills and stone-cutting waste, many pottery sherds including terracotta pipes for water and air (*tubuli*), and numerous mud bricks
I	Byzantine period (6th–7th centuries CE)	Thin layer of earthen fills and small stones

the Southern Wall of the Temple Mount, continuing the line of compartments in the section between the Triple Gate and the excavation area discussed here. Compartments Nos. 17 and 19 were found intentionally filled with earth, as will be described below (Figs. 4.18–4.19).

The walls of the compartments are partly cut in rock and partly constructed of ashlars. Compartments Nos. 1–13, excavated by our predecessors, all had hewn rock walls and flat, leveled rock floors (except for Compartment No. 1). However, here the rock bottom was quite bulky and leveled out with a layer of hard, compacted earth. Locus 6130 is the lowest of the layers (Fig. 4.18).

Compartments 17 and 18 had a common built wall (Wall 662, 0.95 m thick, 2.5 m long, 2.15 m high), made of seven courses of roughly-cut stones of varying sizes, with small stones in between. One large stone with a flattened upper face (0.85 × 0.6 × 0.25 m)—entirely different from the other stones in the wall—was set on the top of the wall, on its western side. Next to it, to the east, was a square stone in which a circular cup mark was cut (0.1 m in diameter; 0.07 m deep) that may have been used to hold some object (Figs. 4.21–4.22).

At 3.1 m west of Common Wall 662, rock-cut Wall 668, 4 m long and at least 1 m wide, was exposed. The wall was preserved to a height of more than 1 m above the rock surface (Fig. 4.23). The upper part of the wall was hewn as a flat surface, and at the top a circular cup mark was cut (0.1 m diameter, 0.1 m deep), similar in size and opposite the abovementioned cup mark in Wall 662. This wall represents the easternmost rock-hewn compartment of this series. Wall 656 stands east of Wall 662, common to both compartments and at a similar distance from it. Like Wall 662, it was built with eight courses of roughly cut stones and abuts the Southern Wall of the Temple Mount. Its estimated thickness is 1 m, its length is 3.3 m, and it was preserved to a height of at least 2.7 m. A thin layer of crushed limestone was found on top of the wall.

Compartment No. 18 was bounded by Wall 661, which was also constructed in the same building technique as the other walls in the compartment and built at the same time. It was exposed mainly in Square B1, with one difference: in this wall, the stones that face the space of the compartment were elongated and placed as headers (Figs. 4.18, 4.22). However, on the southern side of Square C1, which was found covered with a thick stone layer from the Late Roman period (Loci 9088, 6093), no remains of a wall were unearthed (Fig. 4.23). In addition, Wall 668 (the rock-cut wall), which forms the western wall of Compartment No. 17, was about 0.8 m longer than the compartment's inner space. There may be implicit evidence here that Compartment No. 17 was open to the south or, alternatively, that in this area the compartment system included another, additional, architectural element.

In our estimation, once the compartments were constructed, their lower part was packed with intentional fills, presumably to create a level surface on top of the unleveled rock, while the upper part was kept open and empty. In Square B1, below the earthen fill of the Late Roman period, we

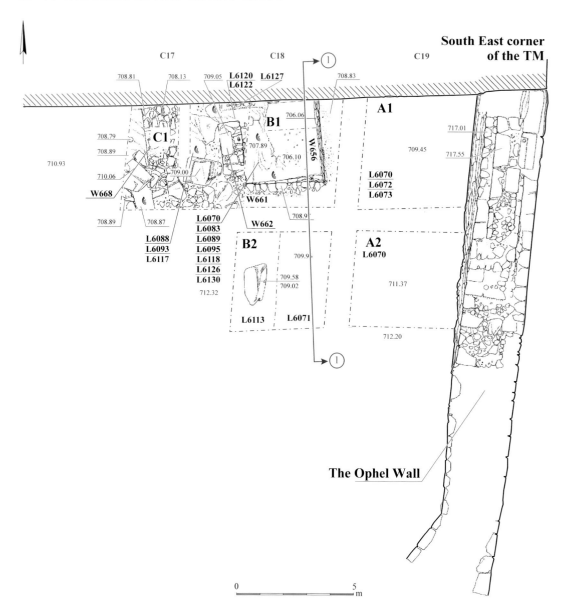

Figure 4.18: Area B, general plan.

excavated three layers of fills (Loci 6118, 6126, 6130; Figs. 4.18, 4.24). Based on the pottery analysis, these three layers of fills date to the end of the Early Roman period (see Chapter 7). These fills did not cover the entire height of the compartment's inner space but only its lower part.

A similar fill (Locus 6120), which is also dated to the Early Roman period, was excavated and documented in the gap between Wall 662 and the Southern Wall of the Temple Mount. In contrast to Square B1, here, a thin layer of crushed limestone (Locus 6122) was documented under Locus 6120—placed above a thin layer of fill. It is possible that this level is a floor surface that represents the floor level of both compartments. As noted above, the northern part of Wall 662 did not reach the Southern Wall of the Temple Mount, creating a gap of about half a meter between the two walls, perhaps to allow free passage between those two compartments (Fig. 4.18).

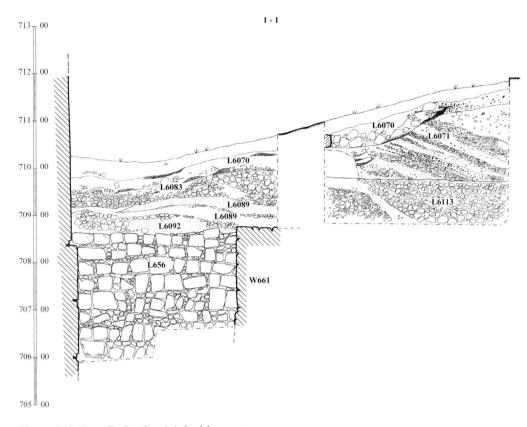

Figure 4.19: Area B, Section 1-1, looking east.

Figure 4.20: Area B, general view, looking west (photo by Y. Baruch).

Figure 4.21: Area B, Wall 662, looking north (photo by
C. Amit).

After excavating the fills in this gap (Loci 6120, 6122), we found that the fill layer covered part of
a rock in which a foundation trench had been cut (Locus 6127, 1.8 m long, 0.3–0.2 m wide). This is
a small part of the foundation trench of the Southern Wall in which two stones of the Southern Wall
itself were placed. After the stones were set in the trench, the latter was filled with smaller stones
bound together with a grayish binding material. For conservation reasons of this special find, we
chose not to excavate (Figs. 4.18, 4.25).[5] It turned out that, in contrast to the archaeological evidence
revealed in the other hewn compartments to the west (Nos. 1–13), the rock surface in C1 and B1
was not worked or hewn and remained in its natural form. It was found that the height differences
between the western and eastern parts of Compartment No. 18 are almost 1.6 m, which required
leveling, by means of a compacted earthen fill.

In Squares B1 and C1, two compartments were exposed that abut the Southern Wall of the Temple
Mount. The compartment in Square B1 (No. 18) does not open southward like all the other rock-cut
compartments. It is interconnected with Compartment No. 17 by a narrow opening set in Wall 662.
We do not have sufficient information to enable a full reconstruction of Compartment No. 17 in
Square C1. These two compartments are doubtlessly a direct continuation of the series of rock-cut
compartments exposed to the west.

---

[5]   For reasons of safety and time we excavated only part of the compartments down to bedrock.

Figure 4.22: Area B, Wall 662, looking west (photo by C. Amit).

Figure 4.23: Area B, Walls 662 and 668, looking north (photo by C. Amit).

Figure 4.24: Area B. Fills, Loci 6118, 6126, 6130 (photo by Y. Baruch).

Stratum II: Late Roman Period

In the Late Roman period, dating to the 2nd–3rd centuries CE, massive operations of filling and leveling the surface were carried out near the southeastern corner of the Temple Mount complex, as will be described below.

Several building stones were found scattered on the surface before the beginning of our excavation. Some of the stones originated from the Herodian compound walls themselves and some probably belonged to other buildings that were on the Temple Mount platform or part of the buildings at its foot. In contrast to the archaeological situation at the foot of Robinson's Arch to the west of the Temple Mount, where a ca. 3 m high layer of stone collapse remained *in-situ*, no such stone collapse was found near the southeastern corner of the complex. A reason for this absence was the reuse of the stones for new structures, or as raw material for filling the area and leveling it. And indeed, an analysis of this leveling revealed that this operation was begun by filling the area and leveling it with stones, some of them, as mentioned, taken from the Temple Mount Wall, and some originating from the walls of the compartments discussed above (Fig. 4.23). (See further suggestions in the discussion below.) This included decorated stones that were found broken and partially preserved (Chapter 8). The earth accumulation between the stones included many potsherds dating to the Late Roman period.

This layer of stones, ca. 1 m thick, was excavated and documented in Compartment No. 17 (Square C1, Locus 6093, as well as Square B2, Locus 6113), although with considerably fewer stones. No such layer was found in Square B1, and we have no explanation for this (Figs. 4.18–4.19). The layer was, however, clearly visible in the southern section of Square C1 and therefore extended southward

Figure 4.25: Gap between Wall 662 and the Southern Wall
of the Temple Mount, looking west. Note the rock-cut
foundation trench (photo by C. Amit).

beyond the excavation's limit. In Square C1, the stone layer covers the walls of Compartment No. 17 and is placed on top of the leveling layer of the compartment from the time of its occupation. In this regard, we note that most of the stones used in the fills were construction stones that we believe were incorporated into the compartment walls, but there were also some construction stones that were originally incorporated in the walls of the Temple Mount.

As mentioned above, in our opinion this layer of stones is in fact the result of the use of stones as raw material for leveling the surface, an action that we believe was taken only in the Late Roman period when people reverted to using the area near the southeastern corner of the Temple Mount. Still, even if the stones may not be defined as a layer of collapse *in-situ*, this finding is direct evidence of the period of the destruction of the Temple and its consequences.

Above this layer of stones, we found an earthen fill layer (Locus 6088; Fig. 4.18). These layers, which were purposely piled one on top of the other, were discerned in all the excavation squares, leveling the area and covering the architectural remains from the previous strata. This is undoubtedly an extensive engineering operation that ended in the area near the southeastern corner of the Temple Mount. The Southern Wall of the Temple Mount bound this flat surface on the north and a segment of the Ophel Wall bound it on the east.

The Lower Layer

The lower fill is a thick layer of trodden earth compacted with rough gravel material: in the northern part of Square C1, this layer (Locus 6088, 0.6 m to 1.3 m thick) covered the former layer of stones (Locus 6093); in the northwestern part of the square, this layer of fill was laid directly on top of Wall 668 and covered it completely (Fig. 4.18). In Square B1 the level of fill (Locus 6095, up to 1.3 m thick) was laid on the upper layer of the Early Roman period (Locus 6118). These two loci included a large amount of pottery and tiles from the 2nd and 3rd centuries CE (Late Roman period; see Chapters 7 and 8).

The Upper Layer

The upper layer of the fills (Squares A1, A2, Locus 6072; B2, Loci 6113, 6071; B1, Locus 6083; C1, Locus 6093) is a layer of quarrying waste and gravel mixed with earthen fills (0.5–1.5 m thick), intentionally laid with a slant to the north. This slanting layer of gravel material was laid above the horizontal layer from the Early Roman period below (Figs. 4.18, 4.19, 4.24).

The outstanding element in these layers of gravel material is chiseling waste, which points to construction operations of buildings in the close vicinity. In our opinion, the use of gravel material for filling and leveling of open spaces was due, among other things, to its porous quality, allowing optimal water infiltration. This is also the reason why the trodden filling layer below is tighter. These layers included many Late Roman pottery sherds dating from the 2nd and 3rd centuries CE, including a rich assemblage of fragmented bricks, roof tiles, pipes and bathhouse *tubuli* imprinted with the stamp of the Tenth Roman Legion *Fretensis* (see Chapters 7 and 9).

Stratum I: The Byzantine Period

After the removal of a layer of modern garden soil that covered the area, a ca. 0.3-m-thick layer of earth with small stones was excavated (Locus 6070, designated to Squares A1, A2, B1, C1), containing many potsherds, the latter dating to the late Byzantine period (see Chapter 7). The fact that this was the first archaeological stratum that we encountered strengthens our opinion that the excavators who preceded us removed layers of earth that probably contained remnants post-dating the late Byzantine period (Figs. 4.18, 4.19).

Two squares (A1, A2) were excavated at the eastern edge, where the Ophel Wall abuts the southeastern corner of the Temple Mount. The excavation deepened just slightly below the surface (0.9 m deep, Loci 6072, 6073) into an earthen fill with small stones. This layer of earth abuts the ashlar courses of the Ophel Wall on the western side and the Southern Wall of the Temple Mount to the north. Based on the pottery, this layer could be dated to the late Byzantine period (see Chapter 7).

THE OPHEL WALL

The so-called Ophel Wall, which abuts the southeastern corner of the Temple Mount, runs southward for a distance of 182 m. In the segment that we explored, the topmost part is 2.4 m thick, and it widens slightly toward the wall's bottom, reaching a width of 3 m at the point where our dig ceased (Figs. 4.1, 4.3, 4.4, 4.18, 4.26).

This segment of the wall was first excavated by Warren, who pointed out that the wall is made of cut ashlars constructed over a foundation of rubble, which is built directly above a thick layer of soil, as detailed in Table 4.3. On the western face of the northern segment, two distinct constructional phases can be discerned: the original phase made of ashlars, and a later repair made of roughly hewn stones and fragments of stones in secondary use. This repair is not recorded on the eastern extramural face of the wall, which is made of large, nicely cut ashlars, not described by Warren (Fig. 4.27).

At a distance of ca. 25.80 m from the Temple Mount's corner, the Ophel Wall makes an obtuse angle. Studying this spot on an aerial photo gives the impression that we face an architectural anomaly that requires further study. At this point, Warren excavated a large tower (Warren and Conder 1884: Pl. V, No. 4), which measures 7.1 × 2.2 m.

We cleaned the top of the wall. A stone threshold made of hard limestone was exposed 1.8 m south of the Temple Mount. The segment that survived is 1.45 m long and 0.7 m wide. It was set at 717.55 m asl. In front of the threshold, to the west of the Ophel Wall, several flattened stones were exposed. The threshold is set back from the line of the wall by ca. 0.3 m. According to the door sockets, the doors opened westward (Fig. 4.18).

As mentioned above, two squares (A1 and A2) were excavated at the point where the Ophel Wall abuts the southeastern corner of the Temple Mount. The excavation descended a short distance

The Ophel Wall

The Second Wall

The Tower

Figure 4.26: Aerial view, looking south. Note the Ophel Wall, which we identified as two different walls and a tower (photo courtesy of IAA).

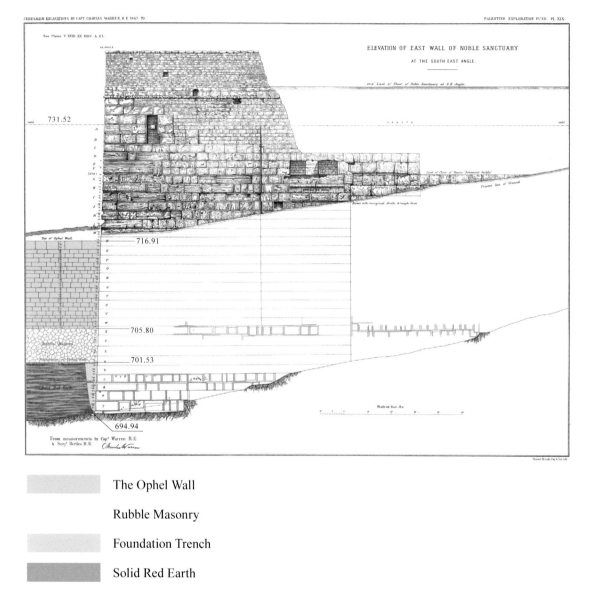

The Ophel Wall

Rubble Masonry

Foundation Trench

Solid Red Earth

Figure 4.27: The Ophel Wall by Warren (1884: Pl. XIX).

(0.9 m, Locus 6070). It turned out that the upper earthen fills dated to the end of the Byzantine period (see above). In Squares A1 and A2, the excavation was halted at the Byzantine layers. However, in the excavation squares to the west (Squares B1 and C1), we dug earthen fills dating mainly to the Late Roman period (for example, Loci 6083, 6088, 6089). Based on these findings, we do not rule out the possibility that the entire area was filled in and leveled in the Late Roman period, up to the Ophel Wall.

In other words, the possibility exists that a section of the wall, which abuts to the southern corner of the Temple Mount complex, is, in fact, the remains of the wall or a building that preceded the Byzantine Ophel Wall. Moreover, earlier in this discussion we also raised the possibility that the foundations of the Ophel Wall, the part built of fieldstones and rubble, is perhaps a continuation of the compartment system built along the Southern Wall from the Triple Gate to the east.

Table 4.3: The Ophel Wall—Warren's Description

Construction stage	Warren's description	Type of stone	Elevation*	Temple Mount courses
Upper part	Course of large stones (1.2 m in height)	*Meleke*	716.91 705.80	N–O
Main wall	Square ashlar stones, probably in secondary use	*Meleke*	705.80 701.53	O–X
Lower part (or foundation of Ophel Wall)	Rubble irregular stone		701.53 694.94	X–A

* Converted from Warren system to metric system

It is reasonable to assume that the Ophel Wall is related to the Byzantine city wall constructed in the Ophel area by the Empress Eudocia (443–460 CE, Wightman 1993: 215; Mazar 2007: 181–200; Mazar and Lang 2015: 339–341) and probably remained in use also in the Early Islamic period. Nevertheless, at the point where the Ophel Wall abuts the southeastern corner of the Temple Mount, our excavation has yielded new archaeological data permitting a reassessment of the dating of this ca. 20 m segment of the wall.

As we have shown above in Stratum II, the earthen fills covering the ashlar courses of the Temple Mount Wall from its southern side (half of Course S and Course T) are dated to the Late Roman period. These fills, which in our estimation cover 3 m of the height of the ashlar-constructed wall (the bottom of the ashlar wall that is equal to the height of the Temple Mount's Course U), were purposely done in order to create a leveled, open plaza.

This datum allows us to suggest that at least this particular segment of the wall, the line of which dates primarily to the Byzantine period, makes use of a part of an earlier structure, possibly even a wall from the Late Roman period. As we suggested above, this ashlar segment itself is founded on the remains of a Herodian wall built of coarsely hewn stones and rubble. This may also explain the architectural anomaly—i.e., the change of line in the wall's course.

In addition, at the southern edge of this segment and at a distance of ca. 20 m southeast of the Temple Mount corner, a tower documented by Warren was found. It is generally accepted that this is a tower in the Byzantine city wall, the so-called Wall of Eudocia. This tower may have also been part of a gatehouse that had already been constructed in the Late Roman period and reused in the Byzantine period. Later on, when the Wall of Eudocia was constructed, the Byzantine masons incorporated the remains of the earlier wall into the tower or southern gatehouse.

REFERENCES

Baruch, Y. and Reich, R. 2016. Excavations near the Triple Gate of the Temple Mount, Jerusalem. ʿAtiqot 85: 37–95 (Hebrew).

Gordon, B. 2007. The Byzantine Quarter South of the Temple Mount Enclosure. In: Mazar, E., ed. *The Temple Mount Excavations in Jerusalem 1968–1978 Directed by Benjamin Mazar, Final Reports*, Vol. 3: *The Byzantine Period* (Qedem 46). Jerusalem: 201–215.

Mazar, B. 1971. The Excavations in the Old City of Jerusalem near the Temple Mount—Second Preliminary Report, 1969–70 Seasons. *Eretz-Israel* 10: 1–35 (Hebrew).

Mazar, E. 2003. *The Temple Mount Excavations in Jerusalem 1968–1978 Directed by Benjamin Mazar, Final Reports*, Vol. 2: *The Byzantine and Early Islamic Periods* (Qedem 43). Jerusalem.

Mazar, E. 2007. *The Temple Mount Excavations in Jerusalem 1968–1978 Directed by Benjamin Mazar, Final Reports*, Vol. 3: *The Byzantine Period* (Qedem 46). Jerusalem.

Mazar, E. 2015. *The Ophel Excavations to the South of the Temple Mount 2009–2013: Final Reports*, Vol. 1. Jerusalem.

Mazar, E. and Lang, T. 2015. The Byzantine Wall. In: Mazar, E., ed. *The Ophel Excavations to the South of the Temple Mount 2009–2013: Final Reports*, Vol. 1. Jerusalem: 337–354.

Reich, R. 2004. Raymond Weill's Excavations in the City of David (1913–1914)—A Reassessment. In: Shanks, E., ed. *The City of David, Revisiting Early Excavations*. Washington, D.C.: 123–152.

Reich, R. and Shukron, E. 2011. Excavations in Jerusalem Beneath the Paved Street and in the Sewage Channel next to Robinson's Arch. *Qadmoniot* 142: 66–73 (Hebrew).

Ritmeyer, L. 2006. *The Quest: Revealing the Temple Mount in Jerusalem*. Jerusalem.

Warren, C. 1884. *Plans, Elevations, Sections, etc. Shewing the Results of the Excavations at Jerusalem, 1867–70, Executed for the Committee of the Palestine Exploration Fund*. London.

Warren, C. and Conder, C.R. 1884. *The Survey of Western Palestine: Jerusalem*. London.

Wightman, G.J. 1993. *The Walls of Jerusalem from the Canaanites to the Mamluks* (Mediterranean Archaeology Supplement 4). Sydney.

CHAPTER 5

THE ROADS LEADING TO THE TEMPLE MOUNT
FROM THE SOUTH

Yuval Baruch and Ronny Reich

As part of the Herodian monumental development of the area south of the Temple Mount, a street was constructed that ran along the entire course of the Southern Wall. Segments of this street were exposed by the Mazar and Ben-Dov excavations in the 1970s (Mazar 1971: Pl. 2). It was some 280 m long and can roughly be divided into three parts, all of which are clearly diverse in nature and function: The western sector runs from the central street of the Tyropoeon Valley and the southwestern corner of the Temple Mount to the Double Gate; the eastern sector spans from the Triple Gate to the southeastern corner of the Temple Mount; and the central sector occupies the area between the Double and the Triple Gates. As the current report pertains to the eastern sector of the street, and that is also the main subject under discussion, we begin our discourse there (Fig. 5.1).

THE EASTERN SECTOR: A SERIES OF VAULTS

The Herodian masonry on the face of the eastern sector of the Southern Wall of the Temple Mount is dappled with a series of deep weathering effects that have rounded upper arch-like edges. According to Ritmeyer (2006: 100), he, in 1973, as a member of the B. Mazar expedition, was the first to observe this phenomenon. Based on this evidence, he concluded that along the eastern part of the Southern Wall a series of vaulted cubicles had been constructed (Fig. 5.2, Compartments 1–16). According to Ritmeyer this series of vaults carried a paved, stepped street. This is the eastern continuation of the stepped street which was partially exposed by B. Mazar next to the southwestern corner of the Temple Mount (Mazar 1971: Pl. 2). From the vaults proper almost nothing is extant, save for the constructed and rock-cut foundations of most compartments. Only two arched stones of the vault above Compartment No. 1 survived *in-situ*, directly under the eastern doorjamb of the Triple Gate (Table 5.1, Fig. 5.3). No fallen parts of the vaults, flagstones or steps of the street carried by them have been retrieved by any of the excavations thus far.

In two squares (Squares B1 and C1), the excavation reached down to bedrock. This exposed two compartments (Nos. 17–18; Fig. 4.18) that abut the southern wall of the Temple Mount. The detailed description of the various findings in this area is given in the stratigraphic report (Chapter 4). These compartments continue the line of compartments (Nos. 1–16) excavated by our predecessors between the Triple Gate and the excavation area discussed here. Compartments Nos. 17 and 19 were found intentionally filled with earth. The walls of the compartments are partly cut in rock and partly constructed of ashlars. Compartments 17 and 18 had a common built wall (Wall 662) between them.

Compartment No. 18 does not open southward, like all the other rock-cut compartments. It is interconnected with Compartment No. 17 by a narrow opening set in Wall 662. We do not have sufficient information to enable a full reconstruction of Compartment No. 17 in Square C1.

Figure 5.1: The row of stains along the Southern Wall (before the excavations), general view looking east (photo by Y. Baruch).

Figure 5.2: General view along the rock-cut compartments and of the stains in the Western Wall, looking west (photo by Y. Baruch).

Figure 5.3: Compartment 1, the western ashlar wall of the compartment and the beginning of the vault built adjacent to the Southern Wall (view to the north beyond, photo by Y. Baruch).

The wall, which is the western wall of Compartment No. 17, was somewhat longer than the compartment's inner space. This might point to the fact that Compartment No. 17 was open to the south or perhaps that in this area the compartment system included another, additional, architectural element, which might have continued southward, close to the southeastern corner of the Temple Mount.

We believe that, once the compartments were constructed, their lower part was packed with intentional fills, presumably to create a level surface on top of the unleveled rock, while the upper part was kept open and empty.

In total, this series included at least 19 compartments. The uniqueness of this architectural system exposed in Squares B1 and C1 is that the compartments are entirely constructed, while the other compartments are rock-cut at their lower parts. We estimate that the transition from the architectural method of rock-cut compartments to constructed compartments is the outcome of the engineering adaptation of the architecture to the natural topography. It should be noted, based on Warren's research and our excavations (see Chapter 3), that in this area the bedrock surface drops dramatically to the east. Consequently, the most appropriate solution to this topographical challenge was the construction of compartments in stone.

This method of stone-built compartments is not unique to this area. It is known in other locations around the Temple Mount walls. An excavation of a similar system was documented under the street that runs along the Western Wall and Robinson's Arch (Reich and Shukron 2011; see Chapter 26), as well as in B. Mazar's excavations (1971: 5–10) along the western part of the Southern Wall. Mazar interpreted these compartments differently from our current proposal.[1] In both instances, the compartments' inner measurements are ca. 3.1 × 3.1 m and the construction methods are similar to the ones described above, indicating that these measurements were an architectural standard. Yet

---

[1] Currently (2022–2023), excavations are being conducted at the southwestern corner of the Temple Mount by Y. Baruch, H. Machline and N. Rom, in which similar compartments, filled with earth layers, are being exposed.

Table 5.1: Compartments

Compartment no.	Description of weathering	Remarks	Fig.
1	Stains with circular upper outline seen on wall on Course H* and lower rim of Course G	Compartment cut in bedrock. Eastern and Western Walls constructed of ashlars. On west side springer stones of vault survived	5.3–5.4
2	Large stains on Course H	Bottom of compartment not excavated	
3	No stains on Herodian wall. On lower part of stone in Course H curved incised line at location of expected intrados of vault	Bottom of compartment not excavated	
4	No particular weathering signs		
5	Clear weathering signs on Course I, with upper curved outline		5.5
6	Clear weathering signs on Course J, with curved incised outline		
7	No traces of weathering on Herodian stone. Horizontal line incised on stone of Course K		
8	Clear weathering signs with curved outline on Course K and lower part of Course J		5.6–5.7
9	Clear weathering signs with upper curved outline on Course K		5.7
10	Clear weathering signs with upper curved outline on lower part of Course K and Course L		
11	Clear weathering signs on western side on upper edge of Course L		5.8–5.9
12	Clear weathering signs on western side in middle of Course L		5.10
13	No traces of weathering on Herodian stone		
14	Stains on stone on Courses M and N. On these courses also a small square hole, indicating that this part of wall was inside a closed space	Rounded edge of stain or weathering is not clear	
15	Circular stain visible on Course N and lower part of Course M		5.11
16	Stone in Course N hollowed to a round cavity	Probably the last compartment to the east, as bedrock falls considerably	5.11
17	See excavation Area B (Chapter 4): the western wall of the compartment is rock-cut		

Compartment no.	Description of weathering	Remarks	Fig.
18	See excavation Area B (Chapter 4): compartment walls built of reused stones		
19	See excavation Area B (Chapter 4): not excavated; presumed to be as Compartment 18. Includes the Ophel Wall foundations		

* Numerals of courses according to Warren (Warren and Conder 1884: 120).

Figure 5.4: Compartment 1, the eastern ashlar wall of the compartment built on top of earlier quarries (photo by Y. Baruch)..

there is one difference between them: in our interpretation, the rock-cut compartments were open, and their space had a purpose, while the built compartments did not have openings and were filled in with hard-trodden earthen fills used to support the road paving which was laid right on top of them.

Although we do not possess any data that enables us to assess the nature of the architectural system, if there ever was one, east of Compartment No. 18 in Warren's excavations near the southeastern corner of the Temple Mount, stone courses were documented on which the Ophel Wall was based. These abut Temple Mount Courses X, Y, Z (Warren 1884: Pl. XIX), defined by Warren as "rubble masonry." Apparently, this is a wall built of fragments of stone, perhaps similar to the walls described above. Such a technique of construction on courses of hewn stones is indeed unique to this section of the Ophel Wall, that is, the portion adjoining the Temple Mount wall. It was not recorded in other sections where the Ophel Wall was excavated. It is therefore possible that this segment, recorded by Warren and named by him Rubble Masonry and Foundation of Ophel Wall, is in fact a direct continuation of the above-described series of compartments. In fact, it is a direct continuation of the series of compartments installed along the Southern Wall, from the Triple Gate eastward, and later continued to be used as a foundation for the wall above it.

Figure 5.5: Compartment 5, its lower part cut in bedrock. On the right, a hewn rock wall common to Compartments 5 and 6 (photo by Y. Baruch).

Figure 5.6: Compartment 8, its lower part cut in bedrock. On the right, a hewn rock wall common to Compartments 8 and 9 (photo by Y. Baruch).

Figure 5.7: Compartments 8 and 9 and the hewn rock wall between them. At the top of the wall a circular cup mark was carved (photo by Y. Baruch).

Figure 5.8: Compartment 11, with clearly visible rounded outline. On the right is a hewn rock wall common to Compartments 11 and 12 (photo by Y. Baruch).

Figure 5.9: Compartments 11 and 12, their lower part cut in the bedrock. There is no partition wall between them (photo by Y. Baruch).

THE WEATHERED EFFECT ON THE SOUTHERN WALL

B. Mazar's expedition observed a peculiar series of arched stains of weathered stone on the Southern Wall of the Temple Mount (Ben-Dov 1982: 109; Ritmeyer 2006: 63, 100). It was assumed that this effect was the result of the fires inflicted on the Temple Mount area when it was sacked by the Romans in 70 CE.

Several geological studies on material from the Second Temple destruction layers pointed to groups of stones with the impact of high temperatures that reached up to ca. 800 °C (Shimron, Deutsch and Peleg-Barkat 2004; Shimron and Peleg-Barkat 2010; Peleg-Barkat 2017: 34–37). It should be stressed that stones affected by fire do not show a weathering effect similar to the ones observed on the Southern Wall. And yet the conclusion that the stains were the result of fire is reasonable; the only question was when precisely the fire occurred (Figs. 5.12–15).

Ritmeyer (2006: 100, box) attributed what he called the "gray effect" on the Southern Wall to the fires set by the Romans as described by Flavius Josephus (*War* 6.353–355). In his opinion, the fire had an extremely destructive effect on the stone vaults, causing them to disintegrate and collapse, and the entire stone-paved street carried by them to collapse with them.

Figure 5.10: Compartment 12. In the lower right corner is the beginning of a low partition wall that it shares with Compartment 13 (photo by Y. Baruch).

Figure 5.11: Compartments 15, 16 and 17 (photo by Y. Baruch).

Figure 5.12: Southern Wall, Compartment 1. Note the springer of the stone vault and the weathered effect (photo by Y. Baruch).

Figure 5.13: Southern Wall of Temple Mount. Compartment numbers 4, 5, 6. Weathered effect on the Southern Wall with an arched upper margin (photo by Y. Baruch).

It should be noted that such a fire would have left considerable charred wood, or other charred organic material such as soot, on the floors of these vaulted compartments. However, neither our predecessors nor our own excavations in Compartments Nos. 11 and 12 found any traces of soot or other charred material. It is therefore highly questionable if these effects on the Southern Wall were indeed caused by fire. It should be noted that traces of such weathering were found in the shops that abut the Western Wall of the Temple Mount, under Robinson's Arch (Reich and Billig 2000: 346), and no traces of charred wood or soot were found anywhere in the excavations. It should be emphasized that charred wood, and particularly soot, is a material that does not decompose and disappear. Its remains are visible, for example, in the contemporary burnt houses

Figure 5.14: Southern Wall of Temple Mount, Compartment numbers 9, 10, 11. Weathered effect on the Southern Wall with an arched upper margin (photo by Y. Baruch).

Figure 5.15: Southern Wall of Temple Mount, Compartment numbers 5 and 6. Note the weathered effect on the Southern Wall (photo by Y. Baruch).

excavated in the Upper City in which a considerable amount of charred wood and soot are extant (Avigad 1983: Figs. 132–140; Geva 2010: 65–66) as well as in several places along the sloping Stepped Street along the Tyropoeon Valley from the late Second Temple period (Szanton, Shor and Hagbi 2017).

A comparison between the weathered Southern Wall within the vaulted compartments with collapsed stones from the Western Temple Mount Wall at Robinson's Arch is of interest. Among the collapsed stones, some were observed with a finely chiseled face (lacking the marginal drafting that characterizes the outer face of the wall). These stones seem to be part of the inner face of the Temple Mount walls. Upon these, the effect of fire can be clearly seen, expressed in a certain change of color and fine cracking of the stone, reaching several millimeters into it. As stated above, this phenomenon was observed and studied from the chemical aspect (Shimron, Deutsch and Peleg-Barkat 2004; Shimron and Peleg-Barkat 2010). The weathering on the Southern Wall within the compartments is considerably more extensive (with 5–10 cm thick splinters missing). Such an effect seems to require a very long burning process, or alternatively, a different reason.

There is always the possibility that the destruction of the paved road on the vaults was a consequence of the Roman war in 70 CE, or of the aftermath, while the weathering of the wall was caused by the function of these compartments over a period of several decades prior to the destruction. They might have been in use, for instance, as holding pens for livestock, for storing materials with a corrosive effect on limestone, as crafts workshops, etc., all of which might have caused this effect. Additional proof for this suggestion is provided by Compartments Nos. 7, 13 and perhaps also 17, in which the original face of the Herodian wall survived intact, with no signs of the said weathering, as they housed, for a long time, different types of commodities or were the venues for different types of human activities. This question warrants additional study of the residues left on the weathered wall.

There are about ten weathered and charred stains with an upper semicircular outline on the Southern Wall (in Compartments Nos. 1, 5, 6, 8, 9, 10, 11, 12, 15, 16). In addition, there are similar stains with an unclear upper edge (Compartments Nos. 2, 14). One of the objectives of the excavation was to document the lower part of the Southern Wall, from the Triple Gate to the southeastern corner (Fig. 5.16). From an examination of this part of the wall, from the drawing as well as from the site itself, the following important conclusion emerges:

The apexes of the weathered semicircular stains create a straight line that slopes downward in an easterly direction. We assume that the vaults over the compartments were made of stones ca. 50 cm thick, with a ca. 20 cm thick street paving. In a reconstruction, the line of the street forms a straight line with a uniform moderate fall (gradient). From the eastern doorjamb of the Triple Gate, which is at 726.0 m asl, the sloping street descends toward the southeastern corner (which is ca. 82.5 m away, and at 715.0 m asl). Along this length, the street descends ca. 11 m (a fall of ca. 7.5°) (Fig. 5.16).

To conclude, contrary to former reconstructions that suggested a stepped street similar and symmetrical to the western part of this Southern Wall (Ritmeyer 2006: 61, 66, 90, 97, 101, 232), we see the eastern part of the southern street along the Temple Mount Wall as a sloping ramp. We assume that these former reconstructions were prepared with little forethought, but in symmetric accordance with the western sector (Ritmeyer 2006: 100–101; Amit 2009: 24; the virtual reality at the Davidson Center near the Temple Mount, cf. www.archpark.org.il/virtual10.shtml). The western sector of the street not only contained flights of steps but was not founded on stone vaults like its eastern continuation.

TRANSPORTING SACRIFICIAL ANIMALS VIA THE TRIPLE GATE RAMP

The Temple Mount in the late Second Temple period (1st century BCE to 1st century CE, up until the sacking of the city by Rome) was a crowded place, particularly during the three pilgrimage festivals (Pesach, Shavuʿot and Sukkot), in which it was frequented daily by several tens of thousands of people (Geva 2007; Reich 2014). The entrance and exit of the pilgrims were regulated by an elaborate system of streets, gates, staircases and bridges, supplemented by regulations and behavioral habits of the crowds (e.g., Mishnah *Middot* 2:2; *Pesachim* 5:5–10).

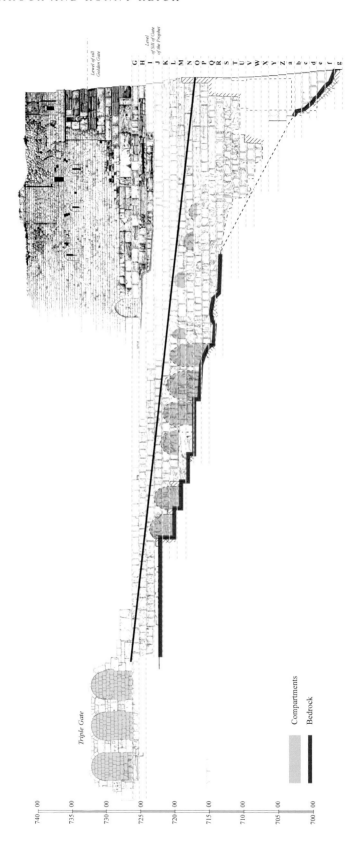

Figure 5.16: Southern Wall of Temple Mount. Weathered effect indicated by blue color. Note the upper semicircular ending of the weathered areas and the slanting straight line from west to east indicating the reconstructed ramp.

Scholars have paid less attention to the action of bringing large numbers of sheep and cattle up to the Temple Mount for sacrifice.[2] The numbers culminated at the *Pessah* offering, which was sacrificed in a ratio of one sheep per three-generation household. From a simple formula, it is clear that if at Passover the city housed several tens of thousands of residents and pilgrims, representing several thousands of households, then a similar order of magnitude of sheep (several thousand) were sacrificed on the Temple Mount. This action was carried out in an organized way (Mishnah *Pesachim* 5:5–10; Safrai 1965: 181–189). Had it not been so, it would not have been possible to slaughter thousands of sheep in one afternoon before the festival began at sundown.

Nowadays, the Samaritans sacrifice ca. 35 sheep on their Pesach feast on Mt. Garizim. This is the number of sheep required for a congregation amounting to several hundreds. A community of several tens of thousands, as the inhabitants of Jerusalem together with the pilgrims, a similar ratio would have been required, amounting to several thousand sheep (Reich and Baruch 2014: 180, note 7).

Assuming that we are dealing with ca. 5000 sheep, how and from where were so many animals led onto the Temple Mount? Herding animals on a stepped street was no easy task; herding cattle there, given their hoof formations, would have been practically impossible. Sheep were somewhat easier. At the time under discussion, public entrance to the Temple Mount was possible from the streets encircling the holy precinct through Robinson's Arch, Barclay's Gate, Warren's Gate on the Western Wall, and the Double and Triple Gates on the Southern Wall, or through a bridge at Wilson's Arch and Gate, directly from the Upper City. The bridge that led directly to the Temple Mount could have provided a direct access route for the animals. However, this bridge led from the Upper City, and it is unlikely that animals would have been led daily through the alleys that crossed the affluent residential area, let alone that large herds would have crossed it days before the holiday.

We suggest that the eastern sector of the southern street, which was a stairless ramp with a moderate gradient, was used as the access lane for leading the animals to the Temple Mount. This suggestion is supported by the following: (1) It is the area most remote from the residential areas of the city, as well as from the areas where crowds gathered; (2) The Triple Gate is wide and has three adjacent openings. In this respect, it is the only one of its kind in the Temple Mount walls. This is in contrast to the Double Gate located to its west, which was closer to the main street of Jerusalem and was certainly used by larger crowds of people, and to the other gates in the Western Wall. The Triple Gate, located farther from the main street, saw less traffic (Fig. 5.17). This means that its larger size was not planned in order to accommodate large groups of people, but rather for herds of sheep.

We suggest that two of the western openings of the Triple Gate were used by worshippers to ascend the Temple Mount. The western openings led to wide staircases which ascended from the south (Baruch and Reich 2016). The sacrificial animals were led in on the ramp ascending from the east. The ramp was constructed on the series of vaults discussed here.[3]

Humans and animals gathered together in the large space in the basements of the Temple Mount known as "Solomon's Stables." Separation began as humans went up from the north to the Temple Mount's large esplanade, while the animals remained in the basement for some time.

Some scholars maintain that in the late Second Temple period, and perhaps even earlier, sheep were gathered north of the Temple Mount, and perhaps they were led to the Temple Mount from

---

2   Although Barclay (1857: 488) has already suggested that the Triple Gate was used for bringing in animals for sacrifice.

3   Architectural parallels for a specific ramp for animals leading into a holy precinct are rare. One can find a ramp that is entirely within the holy precinct in the Bel Temple in Palmyra of the Late Roman period (Segal 2013: 104, Fig. 54: E).

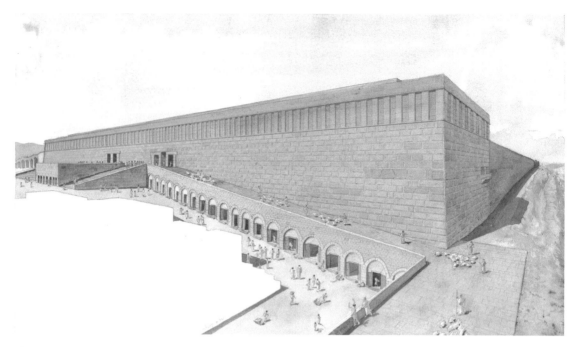

Figure 5.17: Southern Wall of the Temple Mount. Reconstruction of the ramp built over a series of vaulted compartments, used to convey sacrificial animals onto the Temple Mount (reconstruction R. Reich and Y. Baruch. Art: S. Kweller).

there (e.g., Avi-Yonah 1956a: 161). There is scholarly consensus that the "Sheep Pool" *(Piscina Probatica)* should be identified with the pool known as Beth Hisda (Bethesda)/Bethsaida (Gurevitch 2014: 119–123). John (5:2–4) mentions that the Probatica pool was located near a gate with a similar name.

It is possible that parallel to the infrastructure built to the south of the Temple Mount, to facilitate the herding of animals to the Temple Mount and housing them within, as suggested here, a similar infrastructure existed in the northern sector of the Temple Mount as well. The difficulty in conveying large numbers of sheep from the north is in the absence of a large subterranean space in this part of the Temple Mount. It is well known that the approach to the eastern part of the Northern Wall of the Temple Mount was blocked by the Pool of Israel and the western part was blocked by the Antonia Fortress, thus leaving limited space for housing animals (Fig. 5.18).

THE ROUTE OF THE YOM KIPPUR SCAPEGOAT AND THE RED HEIFER

Apart from the large numbers of sacrificial animals that were led onto the Temple Mount, two animals were led down, alive. These were, on very rare occasions, the Red Heifer (Mishnah *Parah* 3:5), and the scapegoat, on Yom Kippur (Mishnah *Yoma* 6:4).

The Red Heifer was sacrificed on the mount east of Jerusalem; its ashes were mingled with water from the Gihon Spring and were used for purification purposes. The scapegoat was led to the desert and pushed over a high cliff, carrying the sins of the Jewish people with it.

The Mishnaic description of the gates to the Temple Mount (Mishnah *Middot* 1:3) represents the reality that preceded King Herod. Josephus's descriptions, however, relate to the Temple Mount after it was enlarged by Herod, and he writes of new gates added and others eliminated

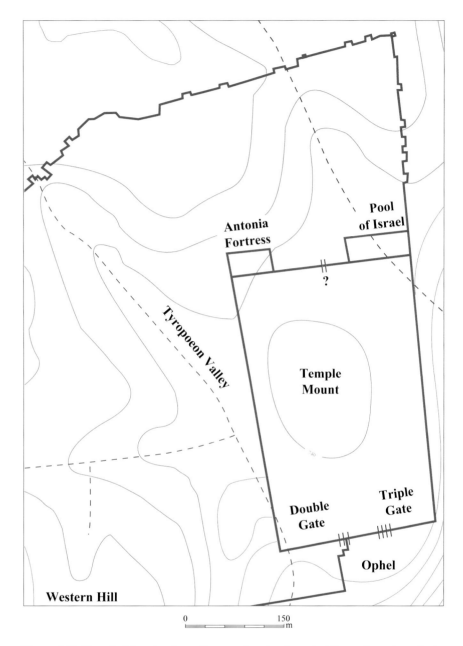

Figure 5.18: Temple Mount, schematic map showing layout at its northern boundaries.

or transferred to different locations. Among the gates mentioned in the Mishnah is the Shushan Gate, which is discussed in relation to the Red Heifer, as the gate through which it exited the holy precinct. Josephus does not write about the Red Heifer and its manner of departure from the Temple Mount. Scholars have suggested that the Red Heifer was led directly from the inner court (*Azara*) eastward, through the eastern gate (Shushan Gate) and from there over a ramp, as mentioned in the Mishnah (*Para* 3:6). Some scholars reconstructed this ramp as a bridge crossing the Kidron Valley. One view saw this as a descending ramp (Avi-Yonah 1956b: 415); another reconstructed it as a horizontal bridge (Lurie 1980: 267; Ritmeyer 2006: 112–113), like the viaduct of a modern highway. One should remember that such a level bridge had to rise 55–60 m above the Kidron, a height that is inconceivable.

This was the case in the pre-Herodian Temple Mount. We suggest that later the ramp on vaults at the Southern Wall was used to lead the Red Heifer out. This is corroborated by the vaults mentioned in the Mishnah (*Para* 3:6). Leading the Red Heifer out was a delicate and cumbersome procedure since if the cow in any small way became injured, it would have been disqualified from sacrifice. The eastern sector of the road along the Southern Wall provided the safest and easiest way to exit the Temple Mount, down the external part of the southeastern corner. To this one should add that this road or ramp is currently the only paved road known to rest upon a series of vaults, which were meant to create a route that is at the same time pure and not defiled from any unknown subterranean tomb, as described in Mishnah *Parah* 3:6.

The sacrifice of the Red Heifer was a rare event, as the rabbinic literature mentions only seven occasions during the late Second Temple period when it occurred (Mishnah *Parah* 3:5). Moreover, the saying in Mishnah *Shekalim* 4:2 puts the expanses of the Red Heifer ramp in one line with the aqueduct, city wall and towers—as all come from the Temple's treasury.

As for the path of the Red Heifer, from the southeastern corner and further on, we have no data yet that reconstructs it toward *Har HaMishcha* (which may be part of or the entire Mount of Olives), as this area has not yet been excavated. We have no indication where this site was located on the mount east of Jerusalem. The most likely path for the Red Heifer would have been one with a moderate slope. A path due north from the corner between the Eastern Wall and the Kidron Valley—one that crossed close to the Tomb of Mariamne—would be a good possibility. As Ben-Eliyahu (2003: 185) suggested, there might have been a short and low bridge that crossed the valley at this spot.

The Yom Kippur Scapegoat (Mishnah *Yoma* 6:3–4) also left the Temple Mount alive. It was said that a special ramp was constructed so that the returning Babylonian exiles would be unable to pluck hairs from the scapegoat's fur as it exited the mount. That meant that the path used by the scapegoat had to be separated from those used by pilgrims. The descending ramp along the Southern Wall was ideal for this purpose. Since a goat is easier to lead than a heifer, the priest leading the goat to its destination had a less difficult task to deal with; there was no need to ensure that it would not be injured. As for the part of the path beyond the southeastern corner, it seems it turned southward. Avi-Yonah (1956b: 415) suggested that the ramp for the scapegoat was on the Eastern Wall, close to the southeastern corner. There was a gate here, as attested by the stump of an arch that emerges from the Eastern Wall. However, Warren's excavations demonstrated that no arch with a staircase or ramp had been constructed after all (Reich and Baruch 2014: 183–188).

ROADS, PLAZAS, STAIRCASES AND GATES

In Chapter 3, we reviewed the topographic conditions and discussed the challenges faced by the engineers of Herod's Temple Mount expansion project, especially the expansion to the south, the erection of the complex's walls and the construction of a system of roads leading to the gates in the Southern Wall, i.e., the Double Gate and the Triple Gate. The discussion below is based on the fact that the height of the threshold of the gates is 725.85 m asl on average and therefore forms the reference point of the road system leading to the gates.

Four roads and two main staircases led to the gates of the Southern Wall. They all converged in a narrow plaza located between the gates.

PLAZA BETWEEN THE GATES

The strip of land that served as an open plaza in front of the gates and as a connecting road between them was hewn and shaped as a long, narrow, flat surface. It is 6.45 m wide (in front of the Double Gate) and 65.2 m long. It begins in the east, near the Triple Gate's doorjamb; then the plaza merges with the sloping ramp rising from the east toward the Triple Gate. From here the plaza extends westward, up to the Double Gate, and perhaps even west of it (the area is obstructed by the *al-Hatuniya* building). The bedrock was shaped, among other things, in order to enable this area to be paved with large stone slabs of varying sizes. These were placed on top of an orderly fill of stones and bonding material (Baruch and Reich 2016: 45–47). These paving stones are similar in size to the stones used for paving the Stepped Street that leads up northward from the Siloam Pool, as well as the stones used for paving the street at the foot of Robinson's Arch (Reich and Billig 2000: 343–345).

MONUMENTAL STAIRCASES LEADING TO THE GATES

Two monumental staircases led from south to north and were perpendicular to the gates. It is difficult to know how these staircases were demarcated on each side, but the discovery of *miqwaʾot* between the two staircases indicates that there was a structure in which these *miqwaʾot*, whose walls did not survive, were located. In front of the staircases from the south, two plazas were leveled out. They have undergone many changes since the days of the Second Temple, and we therefore have no additional data available about the original construction (Ritmeyer 2006: 65–66, 75–80; Baruch and Reich 2016).

THE STAIRCASE IN FRONT OF THE DOUBLE GATE (FIG. 5.19)[4]

This staircase was primarily rock-cut and was constructed as part of the rock-shaping operation that preceded the expansion phase of the Temple Mount complex to the south. The 32 steps are arranged at a fixed sequence of 12 pairs, with alternating narrow and wide treads; at the top and the bottom of the staircase are a series of four narrow stairs, indicating that the staircase had a completely symmetrical architectural rhythm. In places where the rock was damaged, the steps were completed with thick stone slabs of varying lengths.

THE STAIRCASE IN FRONT OF THE TRIPLE GATE (FIG. 5.20)

This staircase, which did not survive, led directly to the front of the Triple Gate and, according to our reconstruction, was narrower than the gate and was built over a wide barrel vault. This rock-cut system was divided into two more or less equal areas, which included a rock-hewn partition wall in between. A rock-cut shelf at the top of the northern wall of the rock-hewn system forms the springer of the vault.

FROM THE DOUBLE GATE TO THE SOUTHWEST CORNER

The data regarding the rock level in this section of the Southern Wall is based on Warren's measurements. Warren reconstructed the line of the rock as descending sharply from the Double Gate area to the west, down to the Tyropoeon Valley bed. The height difference between the Double Gate threshold (ca. 726 m asl) and the valley bed (ca. 698 m asl) is ca. 28 m. At this point, i.e., at the base of the Tyropoeon

---

[4] See Mazar and Cornfeld 1975: 142–143; and Ben-Dov 1982: 108–113.

Figure 5.19: The staircase in front of the Double Gate, looking northwest.

Figure 5.20: The remains of a rock-cut vault that supported the staircase leading to the Triple Gate, looking northwest. Note the curving of the rock, indicated by an arrow (photo by Y. Baruch).

Valley, the foundations of the Temple Mount complex are as low as 16 stone courses below the level of the street paved at this location, i.e., ca. 20 m above the base of the valley bed. As stated above, these topographic conditions posed an engineering challenge for the builders of the walls themselves as well as for the constructors of the street paved along this section of the Southern Wall.

ROAD DESCRIPTION

The western part of the road built along the Southern Wall was excavated by B. Mazar (1971: 5–10, Fig. X: 2; E. Mazar 2020: 42–44). This section of the road was constructed as a stepped street with a regular cadence of three steps: two steps with a relatively narrow tread (height 0.22 m, width 0.36 m) and a relatively wide step or landing (1.66 m). Some of the stairs were constructed from a single block.

The B. Mazar excavations revealed only a short section of the road (7.4 m wide), which starts at a distance of 5.65 m from the southwestern corner of the Temple Mount complex and continues with a paved plaza that meets and merges with the paved street along the Western Wall of the Temple Mount, below Robinson's Arch (the "Herodian Street").

From the south, the stepped road is built adjacent to a paved surface, which was probably a large gathering area. Rectangular curbstones were placed between the stepped road and the plaza (Fig. 5.21).

Under the stepped street, adjacent to the Southern Wall and near the southwestern corner of the Temple Mount complex, the Mazar expedition uncovered a row of sealed compartments (along this section, a total of 24 compartment pairs [not all of which have been excavated] were recorded). The sealed compartments were deliberately filled in with earth that dates to the 1st century CE. The Reich and Shukron excavations (2011) uncovered another compartment system below the Herodian Street, and Hagbi and Uziel (Chapter 16) later exposed them farther to the south.

It is now clear to us that the sealed compartments near the southwestern corner of the Temple Mount complex are similar to the system of built and sealed compartments uncovered near the southeastern corner and discussed at length in Chapter 4 (Compartments 17–19), and as noted above by Reich and Shukron, and later by Uziel and Hagbi. The similarity between the compartments in each of the areas is reflected both in their measurements (3.1 × 3.1 m on average), in the nature of the construction, their use of small, reusable building blocks and fragments, and in the nature of the earth that filled the compartments to capacity. As stated above, similar to the compartment system exposed and documented near the southeastern corner of the Temple Mount complex (Chapter 4), the compartment walls exposed by B. Mazar were also built of reused building stones and stone fragments. Here, too, they were placed on the bedrock and followed the topography, that is, the eastern bank of the Tyropoeon Valley.

After construction of the compartments was completed, they were filled with earth, and the surface above them was used to pave the stepped road. It should be noted that the rock-hewn compartments below the sloping street are different, and they were constructed as open and accessible compartments.

CONCLUSIONS

The Southern Wall of the Herodian Temple Mount is one of the four walls of the sacred precinct, and it can be estimated that in terms of importance, during the days of the Second Temple it had the status of primacy. The importance of the Southern Wall stemmed primarily from the two main gates to the compound—the Double Gate and the Triple Gate, located in the center of the Southern Wall. In the Mishnah, they were called "Hulda Gates" and were described as the entrance gates through which most pilgrims ascended to the Temple. As stated, "The two Hulda gates on the south

Figure 5.21: Stepped street along the Southern Wall, close to the southwestern corner, looking east (photo by Y. Baruch).

that served for the coming in and for the going out" (Mishnah *Middot* 3:1). This source reflects, among others, the way the crowds flowed on their way to the Temple Mount and how they were regulated (crowd control). We suggest that the Triple Gate (the eastern entrance) was also the route for conveying the sacrificial animals into the basement of the Temple Mount.

It is accepted that the Double Gate and the Triple Gate replaced the "Hulda Gates" mentioned in the Mishnah and represent the pre-Herodian compound.

In the direction of the Triple Gate, there are two monumental staircases. A sloping ramp ascends from the east, constructed on top of a series of compartments, and continues west. These compartments opened to the south and were used for various functions (storage, workshops, etc.). From the southwestern corner of the Temple Mount complex, a stepped road ascended to the Double Gate. This was constructed on a system of rock-based compartments filled to capacity with earth and debris. The finds retrieved from these fills date to the 1st century BCE. This line of compartments is similar to the one excavated under the "Herodian Street" at the foot of Robinson's Arch.

REFERENCES

Amit, D. 2009. *Model of Jerusalem in the Second Temple Period.* The Israel Museum. Jerusalem.

Avigad, N. 1983. *Discovering Jerusalem.* Nashville.

Avi-Yonah, M. 1956a. Archaeology and Topography. In: Avi-Yonah, M., ed. *Sepher Yerushalayim (The Book of Jerusalem).* Jerusalem and Tel Aviv: 305–319 (Hebrew).

Avi-Yonah, M. 1956b. The Second Temple. In: Avi-Yonah, M., ed. *Sepher Yerushalayim (The Book of Jerusalem).* Jerusalem and Tel Aviv: 392–418 (Hebrew).

Barclay, J.T. 1857. *The City of the Great King; or, Jerusalem as It Was, as It Is, and as It Is to Be.* Philadelphia.

Baruch, Y. and Reich, R. 2016. Excavations near the Triple Gate of the Temple Mount, Jerusalem. *ʿAtiqot* 85: 37–95 (Hebrew).

Ben-Dov, M. 1982. *In the Shadow of the Temple: The Discovery of Ancient Jerusalem.* Jerusalem.

Ben-Eliyahu, E. 2003. The Ramp of the Red Heifer. *Cathedra* 107: 183–186 (Hebrew).

Geva, H. 2007. Estimating Jerusalem's Population in Antiquity: A Minimalist's View. *Eretz-Israel* 28: 50–65 (Hebrew).

Geva, H. 2010. Early Roman Pottery. In: Geva, H., ed. *Jewish Quarter Excavations in the Old City of Jerusalem, Conducted by Nahman Avigad, 1969–1982,* Vol. 4: *The Burnt House of Area B and Other Studies, Final Report.* Jerusalem: 118–153.

Gurevitch, D. 2014. *Unroofed Water Pools in Jerusalem in the Late Second Temple Period* (Ph.D. dissertation, University of Haifa). Haifa.

Lurie, B.Z. 1980. The Red Heifer Ramp. In: Lurie, B.Z., ed. *Jerusalem Chapters—Studies on the Antiquities and Inhabitants of Jerusalem.* Jerusalem: 260–267 (Hebrew).

Mazar, B. 1971. The Excavations in the Old City of Jerusalem near the Temple Mount—Second Preliminary Report, 1969–70 Seasons. *Eretz-Israel* 10: 1–35 (Hebrew).

Mazar, B. and Cornfeld, G. 1975. *The Mountain of the Lord.* New York.

Mazar, E. 2020. *Over the Crossroads of Time: Jerusalem's Temple Mount Monumental Staircase as Revealed in Benjamin Mazar's Excavations (1968–1978).* Jerusalem.

Peleg-Barkat, O. 2017. *The Temple Mount Excavations in Jerusalem 1968–1978 Directed by Benjamin Mazar, Final Reports,* Vol. 5: *Herodian Architectural Decoration and King Herod's Royal Portico* (Qedem 57). Jerusalem.

Reich, R. 2014. A Note on the Population Size of Jerusalem in the Second Temple Period. *Revue Biblique* 121(2): 298–305.

Reich, R. and Baruch, Y. 2014. Conducting Animals for Sacrifice to and from the Herodian Temple Mount, and the Gates Close to Its South-Eastern Corner. In: Stiebel, G.D., Peleg-Barkat, O., Ben-Ami, D. and Gadot, Y., eds. *New Studies in the Archaeology of Jerusalem and Its Region* 8. Jerusalem: 176–189 (Hebrew).

Reich, R. and Billig, Y. 2000. Excavations near the Temple Mount and Robinson's Arch, 1994–1996; Appendix: A Group of Theater Seats from Jerusalem. In: Geva, H., ed. *Ancient Jerusalem Revealed, Reprinted and Expanded Edition.* Jerusalem: 340–352.

Reich, R. and Shukron, E. 2011. Excavations at Robinson's Arch 2011: From the Paved Street to Natural Rock. In: Baruch, E., Levi-Reifer, A. and Faust, A., eds. *New Studies on Jerusalem* 17. Ramat Gan: 219–238 (Hebrew, with English abstract 56–57).

Ritmeyer, L. 2006. *The Quest: Revealing the Temple Mount in Jerusalem.* Jerusalem.

Safrai, S. 1965. *Pilgrimage at the Time of the Second Temple.* Tel Aviv.

Segal, A. 2013. *Temples and Sanctuaries in the Roman East: Religious Architecture in Syria, Iudaea/Palaestina and Provincia Arabia.* Oxford.

Shimron, A., Deutsch, Y. and Peleg-Barkat, O. 2004. The 70 CE Temple Mount Conflagration: First Scientific Evidence. In: Baruch, E. and Faust, A., eds. *New Studies on Jerusalem* 10. Ramat Gan: 19–33.

Shimron, A. and Peleg-Barkat, O. 2010. New Evidence of the Royal Stoa and Roman Flames. *Biblical Archaeology Review* 36(2): 57–62.

Szanton, N., Shor, M. and Hagbi, M. 2017. "We Have Returned to the Cisterns"—The Lower City of Jerusalem at the Second Temple Period. In: Meiron, E., ed. *City of David: Studies of Ancient Jerusalem* 12. Jerusalem: 87–103 (Hebrew).

Warren, C. and Conder, C.R. 1884. *The Survey of Western Palestine: Jerusalem.* London.

CHAPTER 6

IRON AGE POTTERY FOUND NEAR THE SOUTHEASTERN CORNER OF THE TEMPLE MOUNT

Efrat Bocher

LOCUS 6136—FILL ABOVE LOWEST FLOOR IN AREA A (FIG. 6.1)

A pottery assemblage that dates to the end of the Iron Age was exposed in Unit C above a layer of fieldstones (Locus 6081) that covered a floor composed of crushed limestone (Locus 6136; see Fig. 4.9). The assemblage includes a complete storage jar with a stamped rosette, bowls, stands, jugs and a krater.

BOWLS (FIG. 6.1: 1–2)

Large, open and deep bowls with thick walls and thick out-folded rims. The surface of the inside shows evidence of wheel burnish. The bowls resemble mortar bowls, but unlike them, they are composed of a reddish-brown material and are not light in color. No parallel mortar bowls of reddish-brown material were found in the City of David.

KRATER (FIG. 6.1: 3)

Large krater with softly-carinated, thick-walled body and folded rim. The krater is of reddish-brown ware with a thick gray core. This type of large krater (Type B9: Yezerski and Mazar 2015: 247–248) was also found at the summit of the City of David in Area C, Stratum 8 (Uziel, Dan-Goor and Szanton 2019: Fig. 4.4.1).

JUG (FIG. 6.1: 4)

Jug with long wide neck and simple straight rim that flares slightly outward. The jug is made of light brown clay. This type of jug was common in Area E, Stratum 12, Type J2 (De Groot and Bernick-Greenberg 2012: 76, Fig 4.4.11).

JAR (FIG. 6.1: 5)

Almost complete storage jar with slightly rounded shoulder and elongated body. The handle bears a rosette stamp impression with eight petals. The jar resembles Type IIA8 of Koch and Lipschits (2013). This type is found in settlement strata in Judea of the middle 7th and early 6th centuries BCE (Sergi, Karasik, Gadot and Lipschits 2012: 64–92; Koch and Lipschits 2013: 55–78; Lipschits 2021: 61–67).

STANDS (FIG. 6.1: 6–7)

Two types of stands were found. The first (Fig. 6.1: 6) is wide with a relatively thin and short rim that bends outward and forms a sharp triangular cross. This type is more common in the 6th–5th centuries BCE. This type is well known at Ramat Raḥel III (Gadot, Freud, Tal and

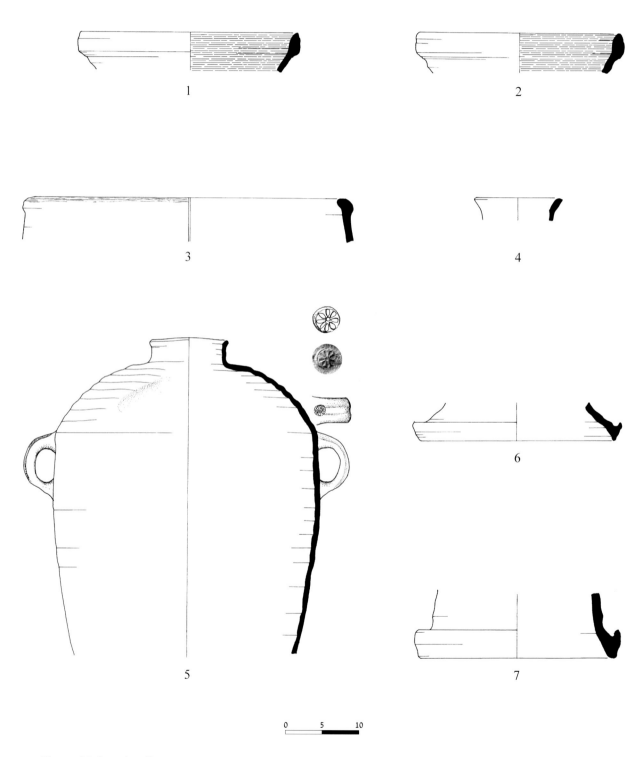

Figure 6.1: Iron Age Pottery.

Figure 6.1: Iron Age Pottery

Description	Locus	Reg. No.	Type	Fig. No.
Reddish-brown material with gray core and white grits	6136	60622\20	Bowl	1
Reddish-brown material with gray core and white grits	6134	60622\5	Bowl	2
Light pink material with gray core and white grits	6136	60611\4	Krater	3
Very worn sherd, gray-brown material with very coarse and large black and white grits	6136	60611\5	Jug	4
Reddish-brown material with a rosette stamp impression on the jar handle.	6081	6088	Jar	5
Brown material with coarse and large white grits	6136	60611\1	Stand	6
Brown material with coarse and large white grits	6136	60611\7	Stand	7

Taxel 2016: Fig 8.19: 3); the summit of the City of David, Layer 10–2 (Yezerski and Mazar 2015: Fig 5.14: 208).

The second (Fig. 6.1: 7) is a large and long stand with a thick wall and a thick, sharp rim. This type is more common during the 8th–7th centuries BCE. It is well known at Ramat Raḥel III, Type ST1 (Freud 2016; Gadot, Freud, Tal and Taxel 2016: Fig. 8.17: 20, 22; Fig. 8.19: 6–7; Fig 8.23: 13); Givʿati Parking Lot, Phase XIA (Ben-Ami 2013: Fig. 3.8: 7); the summit of the City of David, Layer 10–2 (Yezerski and Mazar 2015: Fig. 5.14: 205).

SUMMARY

All the vessel types from this assemblage correspond to the common repertoire typical of the 8th to 6th centuries BCE. The storage jars, the bowls and the stands narrow the range of the date of this pottery group to the late 7th and the beginning of the 6th centuries BCE.

REFERENCES

Ben-Ami, D. 2013. The Iron Age Pottery. In: Ben-Ami, D., ed. *Jerusalem: Excavations in the Tyropoeon Valley (Givʿati Parking Lot)*, Vol. 1 (IAA Reports 52). Jerusalem: 63–82.

De Groot, A. and Bernick-Greenberg, H. 2012. The Pottery of Strata 12–10 (Iron Age IIB). In: De Groot, A. and Bernick-Greenberg, H., eds. *Excavations at the City of David 1978–1985, Directed by Yigal Shiloh,* Vol. 7B: *Area E: The Finds* (Qedem 54). Jerusalem: 57–198.

Freud, L. 2016. Pottery of the Iron Age: Typology and Summary. In: Lipschits, O., Gadot, Y. and Freud, L., eds. *Ramat Raḥel III: Final Publication of Yohanan Aharoni's Excavations (1954, 1959–1962),* Vol. 1 (Monograph Series of the Institute of Archaeology of Tel Aviv University 35). Tel Aviv and Winona Lake: 254–265.

Gadot, Y., Freud, L., Tal, O. and Taxel, I. 2016. Sub-Sector ACS1: Courtyard 380 (Squares Q–W\15–20). In: Lipschits, O., Gadot, Y. and Freud, L., eds. *Ramat Raḥel III: Final Publication of Yohanan Aharoni's Excavations (1954, 1959–1962),* Vol. 1 (Monograph Series of the Institute of Archaeology of Tel Aviv University 35). Tel Aviv and Winona Lake: 97–129.

Koch, I. and Lipschits, O. 2013. The Rosette Stamped Jar Handle System and the Kingdom of Judah at the End of the First Temple Period. *Zeitschrift des Deutschen Palästina-Vereins* 129: 55–78.

Lipschits, O. 2021. *Age of Empires: The History and Administration of Judah in the 8th–2nd Centuries BCE in Light of Storage-Jar Stamp Impressions* (Mosaics: Studies on Ancient Israel 2). Tel Aviv and University Park.

Sergi, O., Karasik, A., Gadot, Y. and Lipschits, O. 2012. The Royal Judahite Storage Jar: A Computer-Generated Typology and Its Archaeological and Historical Implications. *Tel Aviv* 39: 64–92.

Uziel, J., Dan-Goor, S. and Szanton, N. 2019. The Development of Pottery in Iron Age Jerusalem. In: Ben-Shlomo, D., ed. *The Iron Age Pottery of Jerusalem: A Typological and Technological Study* (Ariel University Institute of Archaeology Monograph Series No. 2). Ariel: 59–102.

Yezerski, I. and Mazar, E. 2015. Iron Age III Pottery. In: Mazar, E., ed. *The Summit of the City of David Excavations 2005–2008: Final Reports,* Vol. 1: *Area G.* Jerusalem: 243–298.

CHAPTER 7

EARLY ROMAN–BYZANTINE POTTERY FOUND NEAR THE SOUTHEASTERN CORNER OF THE TEMPLE MOUNT

Dèbora Sandhaus

The following report analyzes the pottery recovered from the southeastern corner of the Temple Mount excavations. The pottery was collected and sorted in the field; the subsequent study included an overview of indicative sherds and a selection of the representative forms included in the plates. The discussion is organized according to assemblages that represent the critical loci in each square. Not all the items are described in the figures. The discussion does, however, include all the indicative forms found in the loci (unillustrated sherds are noted).

Pottery from Jerusalem is well defined and broadly known and this provided us with the primary basis for dating the assemblages and establishing the chronological frame. Our figure tables include pottery reports with parallel material bodies within Jerusalem. These reports include those from the excavations in the Jewish Quarter (Geva 2003, 2010; Geva and Rosenthal-Heginbottom 2003; Geva and Hershkovitz 2006; Magness 2006); Area E in the City of David (Berlin 2012); the Givʿati Parking Lot (Balouka 2013; Sandhaus 2013; Tchekhanovets 2013; Shalev et al. 2021); the Eastern Cardo (Rosenthal-Heginbottom 2019); the Convention Center pottery workshop in the Binyanei Haʾuma (Berlin 2005; Magness 2005; Rosenthal-Heginbottom 2005); Wilson's Arch (Uziel, Lieberman and Solomon 2019); the Western Wall Plaza excavations (Rosenthal-Heginbottom 2011); and Shuafat (Terem 2016). In addition, research reports such as Masada (Bar-Nathan 2002) and Jericho (Bar-Nathan 2006) and comprehensive pottery studies, such as those by Magness (1993) and Berlin (2015), and other publications on specific related topics were consulted.

POTTERY FROM AREA A

Loci 6080, 6114 and 6115—Dismantling of Miqweh Locus 6125 Floor (Fig. 7.1: 1–7)

During the dismantling of the floor of the *miqweh*, two layers were identified: the upper layer was composed of pieces of chalk (Locus 6080 and Locus 6114). The lower layer was made of coarse gravel (Locus 6115).

Pottery sherds dating from the Second Temple period were found across the upper layer of the floor makeup of the *miqweh*. The pottery assemblage is characteristic of the 1st century CE. Sherds included those of cooking pots with a triangular grooved rim (Fig. 7.2: 1), storage jars with slightly thickened rims and a ridge at the bottom of the neck (Fig. 7.2: 2), the fragment of an amphora (Fig. 7.2: 3), and flasks with twisted handles (Fig. 7.2: 4).

Amphorae with a rounded, thickened rim such as the one found within *Miqweh* 6125 seem to continue the tradition of Koan amphorae (Ariel 2021: 554–560). However, the specimen discussed here has handles with cylindrical sections, a feature unknown among the Koan amphorae.[1]

---

[1] According to Rosenthal-Heginbottom (personal comment), similar amphorae, probably of local manufacture, appear in Roman assemblages from unpublished excavations in Jerusalem.

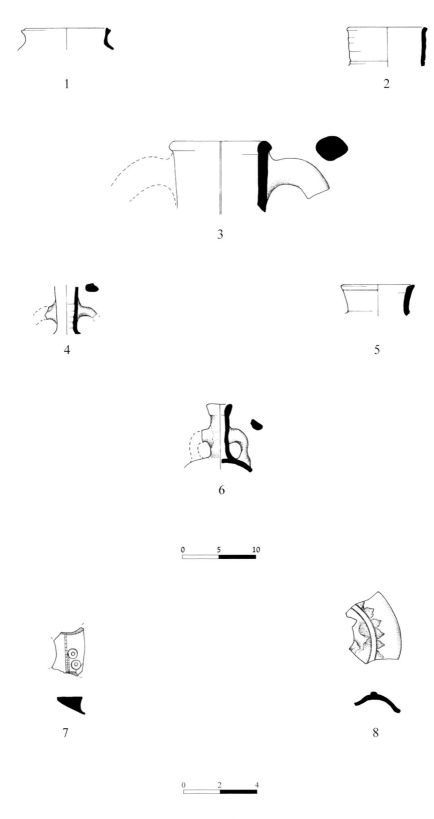

Figure 7.1: Pottery from Area A, Loci 6080, 6114, 6115 and 6131.

Figure 7.1: Pottery from Area A, Loci 6080, 6114, 6115 and 6131

No.	Locus	Reg. No.	Vessel Form	Description	Parallels
1	6080	60608/7	Cooking pot	Dark gray fabric	Same as Fig. 3: 3–4
2	6080	60608/1	Storage jar	Pink fabric	**Jerusalem**: Jewish Quarter: Geva and Rosenthal-Heginbottom 2003: 177–178; Pl. 6.9: 1–2 (1st century BCE–1st century CE). Geva 2010: 122: Pl. 4.2: 1–4 (characteristic of 1st century CE) **Jericho**: Bar-Nathan 2002:33–34, Pl. 6: 40–41 (Type J-SJ7B1, from the end of the 1st century BCE to 1st. century CE) **Masada**: Bar-Nathan 2006: 55, Pl.5: 22 (Type M-SJ7B1, 28/26 BCE–73/74 (115) CE
3	6114	60486/2	Amphora	Pink fabric, numerous grits	
4	6080	60608/3	Flask	Pinkish-buff fabric, red and light gray core	**Jerusalem**: Jewish Quarter: Geva and Rosenthal-Heginbottom 2003: 183, Pl. 6.1: 44–46; 6.5: 16–19; 6.9: 9–10 (1st century BCE–1st century CE). Geva 2010: Pl. 4.3: 12–13 (context dated to 70 CE).
5	6115	60589/1	Storage jar	Pink fabric, pale brown core	**Jerusalem**: Jewish Quarter: Geva and Rosenthal-Heginbottom 2003: 177–178; 6.5: 2 (late 1st century BCE–early 1st century CE). Geva 2010: 122: Pl.4.2: 1–4 (characteristic of 1st century CE) **Masada**: Bar-Nathan 2006: 55–56, Pl. 5:27 (Type M-SJ7B2, from 1st century–first third of 2nd century CE)
6	6115	60523/3	Flask	Reddish-yellow fabric, very pale brown interior/ exterior	Same as No. 5
7	6115	60523/11	Lamp	Reddish-yellow fabric	**Jerusalem**: Jewish Quarter, Rosenthal-Heginbottom 2003: 219, Pls. 6.9: 44; 6.12: 18 (1st century–middle of 2nd century CE). Geva 2010: Pl. 4.7: 1 (1st century CE) **Masada**: Barag and Hershkovitz 1994: 43–53, types CI–VI, nos. 38–39 (1st century CE until at least 70 CE)
8	6131	60625/10	Lamp	Buff fabric, black exterior slip	Loeschcke Type VIII; imitating Broneer XXV. **Jerusalem**: Convention Center: Magness 2005: 101, Fig. 32: 8–9 (second third of 1st century–3rd century CE); Hershkovitz 2005: 290–293, Fig. 11: 5–7 (from the end of the 1st century–3rd century CE, context: 1st–2nd century CE) The Eastern Cardo: Rosenthal-Heginbottom 2019: 115–117; cat. nos. 805–806 (70–3rd century CE)

The lower layer (Locus 6115) contained sherds of storage jars with simple rims (Fig. 7.1: 5), flasks with twisted handles (Fig. 7.2: 6), and fragments of knife-pared lamps (Fig. 7.1: 7), some of which are decorated with a band of concentric circles on the nozzle. The three indicative vessel forms are most common in assemblages of the 1st century CE. The storage jar and the lamp continue to appear at the beginning of the 2nd century CE. However, the flasks are rare in contexts later than 70 CE.

Based on the pottery analysis from the makeup of the *miqweh*, we can conclude that the *miqweh* was not built *before* the 1st century CE and should most likely be attributed to the Herodian period.

LOCUS 6131—FOUNDATION FILL BELOW DRAINAGE CHANNEL 6078 (FIG. 7.1: 8)

The fill of Locus 6131, set immediately below Drainage Channel 6078, functioned as its foundation. This fill yielded sherds of cooking pots with a triangular rim like the one illustrated in Fig. 7.1: 1 and a simple bowl (not illustrated) together with a discus lamp (Fig. 7.1: 8) decorated with palmettes on the shoulders. The appearance of the discus lamp suggests a Legionary date for the channel since this type first appears at the end of the 1st and continues to the 3rd century CE (for a detailed discussion, see Rosenthal-Heginbottom 2019: 115–116). Although it is not possible to identify the entire design on the discus of the lamp because the lamp is incomplete, an animal standing on its hind legs is discernible.

LOCI 6091 AND 6096—LOWER FILL INSIDE THE HEWN AND PLASTERED INSTALLATION BELOW LOCUS 6086 AND ABOVE LOCUS 6107 (FIG. 7.2)

The fill includes a large number of pottery sherds and animal bones. The pottery assemblage comprises cooking vessels, storage jars, jugs, juglets and flasks. Scattered among the pottery are two complete vessels, a storage jar (Fig. 7.2: 9) and a jug (Fig. 7.2: 10).

The cooking vessels included carinated casseroles with triangular rims, two strap handles attached from rim to shoulder (Fig. 7.2: 1–2), cooking pots with triangular rims and one groove on top (Fig. 7.2: 3–4), and cooking jugs with triangular pointed rims (Fig. 7.2: 5). The storage jars comprise two main types: the first has a long neck and a ridge at the junction point with the shoulder (Fig. 7.2: 6–7), and the second type is characterized by a thickened rim and a ridge at the bottom of the neck (Fig. 7.2: 8–9). A complete jug with a funnel rim (Fig. 7.2: 10), flasks with twisted handles (Fig. 7.2: 11–12) and sherds of juglets with cup-rim (Fig. 7.2: 13) were also found in this assemblage.

Based on the analysis of the pottery of these loci, it can be concluded that the assemblage is typical of the 1st century CE in Jerusalem and can be associated with the Herodian period. However, it should be noted that while most of these vessel types continue to appear in the 2nd century CE, the lack of typical 2nd century CE forms and tiles reinforces a date within the 1st century CE for the lower fill inside the *miqweh*.

LOCI 6079 AND 6086—UPPER FILL INSIDE HEWN AND PLASTERED INSTALLATION ABOVE LOCUS 6091 AND 6096 (FIG. 7.3: 1–12)

Most of the pottery sherds accumulated within the upper fill include sherds that date from the 1st century CE, with some of them dating from the late 1st to the 2nd centuries CE. The earlier material, dated to the 1st century CE, includes sherds of simple hemispherical bowls (Fig. 7.3: 1–2), cooking pots with a triangular rim (Fig. 7.3: 3), cooking jugs (Fig. 7.3: 4) with a triangular rim, funnel-rim jugs (Fig. 7.3: 5), flasks (Fig. 7.3: 6) and a fusiform unguentarium (Fig. 7.3: 7). The latest datable pottery types were represented by: a bowl with an out-folded rim (Fig. 7.3: 2); a storage jar with a thickened triangular rim slightly pulled downward, a short neck and a marked ridge at the bottom of the neck (Fig. 7.3: 8) that was trendy in Legionary pottery assemblages; a storage jar with a triangular rim pulled aside at the edge (Fig. 7.3: 9); and a knife-pared lamp (Fig. 7.3: 10). As these vessel forms are typical of the middle of the 1st/beginning of the 2nd centuries CE, we suggest a date from that time range for this assemblage.

LOCUS 6123—FILL INSIDE FOUNDATION TRENCH OF WALL 652 (NOT ILLUSTRATED)

A few rims were scattered about from the foundation trench of Wall 652. They included an arched rim basin and a bag-shaped storage jar with a rim folded toward the inner side and a ridge at the bottom of the neck. Both types are well-known forms in Jerusalem in Byzantine contexts from the late 3rd/4th to the 6th centuries CE (Magness 1993: 204–205, 224). We can conclude that Wall 652 was built not before the Byzantine period, and most likely during this period.

LOCUS 6108—DEBRIS LOCUS 6108 SUPPORTED BY WALL 659 (NOT ILLUSTRATED)

The pottery from Locus 6108 includes ledge-rim bowls, ridged casseroles with a sharp rim and two horizontal handles, storage jars with a thickened rim and a ridge at the bottom of the neck, and jugs with either an out-folded or a funnel rim. The vessel forms suggest a date for accumulating the layer from the middle of the 1st to the 2nd centuries CE.

LOCUS 6109—DEBRIS BELOW WATER CHANNEL LOCUS 6077, INCLUDING TWO POSSIBLE PACKED EARTH FLOORS ABOVE THE CHALK FLOOR—LOCUS 6110 (FIG. 7.3: 11–12)

The pottery assemblage found beneath Locus 6109 comprises much pottery, including bowls, storage jars, amphorae and lamps dating from the mid-1st to the 2nd century CE. Among these forms are large deep bowls with shelf rims (not illustrated; Bar-Nathan 2006: Type M-KR2, Pls. 23–24, nos. 4–21; Magness 1993: 202), storage jars with ledge rims and a ridge at the bottom of the neck (not illustrated; Bar-Nathan 2006: 62–64, Type M-SJ13, Pls. 12–13) and amphorae with out-flaring rims and a bud-like section and two cylindrical handles attached from the rim to the shoulders (Fig. 7.3: 11). This amphora type, which resembles Early Imperial amphorae, was probably produced in southern Spain (Keay 1984: 151–153; Type XVI A, Fig. 58.3). The amphorae are dated to the beginning of the 2nd or 3rd centuries CE (Keay 1984: 151, 155).

Finally, lamps in the assemblage include a knife-pared lamp and the base of a lamp made in buff clay and covered with a black slip, probably belonging to a discus lamp (Fig. 7.3: 12).

POTTERY FROM AREA B

LOCI 6126 AND 6130—PACKED FILLS SURFACE OF COMPARTMENT 18 (NOT ILLUSTRATED)

These fills contain a large amount of pottery, mostly dating from the late Iron Age, although later Hellenistic sherds were also present. However, a few sherds dating from the late 1st century BCE to 70 CE provide the chronological anchor date for this assemblage (not illustrated). Among the sherds are very thin bowls with traces of painted decoration and a small sherd of the nozzle from a knife-pared lamp (not illustrated), which provide the latest date between the end of the 1st century BCE and 135 CE (see Barag and Hershkovitz 1994: 24–53; Sussman 2008: 219–220; Magness 2009: 80–81; Rosenthal-Heginbottom 2016: 431–432; Rosenthal-Heginbottom 2019: 121).

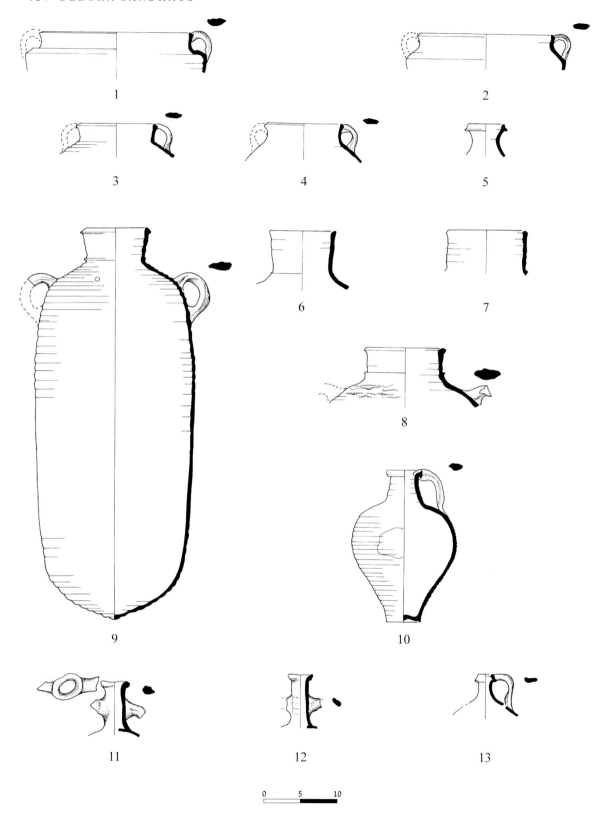

Figure 7.2: Pottery from Area A, Loci 6091 and 6096.

Figure 7.2: Pottery from Area A, Loci 6091 and 6096

No.	Locus	Reg. No.	Vessel Form	Description	Parallels
1	6096	60544/6	Casserole	Red fabric, dark gray core	**Jerusalem**: Jewish Quarter, Burnt house: Geva 2010: 126, Pl. 4.5: 13 (Stratum 2, 1st century CE up to 70 CE assemblage) **Masada**: Bar-Nathan 2006: 164–166, Pl. 30, nos. 51–55, Type CS1A (from last third of 1st century BCE–first 3rd of 2nd century CE)
2	6091	60399/6	Casserole	Red fabric	Same as no. 1
3	6096	60544/4	Cooking pot	Red fabric, calcite inclusions	**Jerusalem**: Jewish Quarter: Area A: Geva and Rosenthal-Heginbottom 2003, Pls. 6.5: 38; 6.9: 17–18; 6.10: 12 (Strata 5–4) Area E: Geva and Hershkovitz 2006: Pls. 4.13: 16 (Stratum 2). Burnt house: Geva 2010:125–126, Pl. 4.5:1–8, Cooking Pot Type 1 (Stratum 2, 1st century CE up to 70 CE assemblage). **Masada**: Bar-Nathan 2006: 154–158, Pls. 27–28, Nos. 6–25, Type CP1B (from last third of 1st century BCE to first third of 2nd century CE)
4	6091	60419/1	Cooking pot	Red fabric, dark gray core	Same as No. 3
5	6091	60609/1	Cooking jug	Red fabric, dark gray core	**Jerusalem**: Jewish Quarter: Area A: Geva and Rosenthal–Heginbottom 2003: 181, Pls. 6.5: 42 (Stratum 5, the type is dated to the 1st century BCE–1st century CE). Givat Ram, Hershkovitz 1987: 315–316, Fig. 1: 19–20 (72 CE up to 2nd century CE) Convention Center: Berlin 2005: 39, Fig. 6: 3–7 (ceramic phases 2–4–late 1st century BCE to 70 CE); Rosenthal-Heginbottom 2005: 266, no. 143 (late Second Temple period); Hershkovitz 2005: 286, Fig. 1: 19–20 (1st century BCE to 2nd CE) **Masada**: Bar-Nathan 2006:174–175, Pl. 31:87, (Type M-CJ1B, from last third of 1st century BCE to first third of 2nd century CE)
6	6091	60410/1	Storage jar	Pink fabric	**Masada**: Bar-Nathan 2006:55–56, Pl. 5:27 (Type M-SJ7B2, from 1st century to first third of 2nd century CE)
7	6091	60420/1	Storage jar	Pink fabric, dark gray core	**Jerusalem**: Jewish Quarter: Area A: Geva and Rosenthal-Heginbottom 2003:178, Pls. 6.9:4; 6.10:5 (Strata 4–5, typical of 1st century CE) **Masada**: Bar-Nathan 2006:55, Pl.5:22 (Type M-SJ7B1, 28/26 BCE–73/74 (115) CE
8	6091	60393/1	Storage jar	Reddish-yellow fabric	**Jerusalem**: Jewish Quarter: Area A: Geva and Rosenthal-Heginbottom 2003: 178, Pl. 6.9: 5 (typical of 1st century CE) Burnt house: Geva 2010: 122 (Type 2, typical of 1st century CE) **Masada**: Bar-Nathan 2006:62, Pl. 11 (Type M-SJ12, from 1st century CE to first third of 2nd century CE)

No.	Locus	Reg. No.	Vessel Form	Description	Parallels
9	6091	60420/5	Storage jar	Reddish-yellow fabric	**Jerusalem**: Jewish Quarter: Area A: Geva and Rosenthal-Heginbottom 2003: Pl. 6.10 (Stratum 4a, typical of 1st century CE) **Masada**: Bar-Nathan 2006: 57, Pl. 8: 41 (Type M-SJ8, from 1st century CE to first third of 2nd century CE)
10	6096	60544/5	Jug	Pinkish-buff fabric, gray core	**Jerusalem**: Jewish Quarter: Area A: Geva and Rosenthal-Heginbottom 2003: 127–128, Pls. 6.9: 8 (Stratum 4, 1st century BCE–1st century CE) Area E: Geva and Hershkovitz 2006: 105, Pl.4.10: 6 (Stratum 3, last quarter of 1st century BCE) Area B, Burnt house: Geva 2010: 123, Pl.4.3: 3 (Type 2, Stratum 2, 1st century CE) **Masada**: Bar-Nathan 2006: 104, Pl. 19: 17–18 (Type M-JG5C, from mid–1st century CE to first third of 2nd century CE)
11	6091	60399/3	Flask	Pink fabric, light gray core	**Jerusalem**: Jewish Quarter: Geva and Rosenthal-Heginbottom 2003: 183, Pl. 6.1: 44–46; 6.5: 16–19; 6.9: 9–10 (1st century BCE–1st century CE); Geva 2010: Pl. 4.3: 12–13 (context dated to 70 CE)
12	6091	60399/5	Flask	Buff fabric, red core, large calcite inclusions	Same as No. 15
13	6091	60420/2	Juglet	Light gray fabric, pinkish-gray core	**Jerusalem**: Jewish Quarter: Area A: Geva and Rosenthal-Heginbottom 2003: 185, Pls. 6.2: 3–4, 6.5: 20; 6.9: 12 (1st century CE) Area E: Geva and Hershkovitz 2006: Pls. 4.412–14; 4.11: 1–5; 4.13: 5–6 (1st century CE) Area B, Burnt house: Geva 2010: 124, Pl. 4.3: 8–9 (Type 2 (1st century CE) **Masada**: Bar-Nathan 2006: 190–193, Pl. 33: 6, Type M-JT1A (from 1st century BCE to first third of 2nd century CE)

LOCUS 6095 AND LOCUS 6118—DEBRIS CANCELING WALL 668 (FIG. 7.4)

Many sherds common to the 2nd to 1st centuries BCE were collected from these loci, with the majority representing the late 2nd and 1st centuries BCE. However, the latest pottery sherds date to the Early Roman period (i.e., late 1st century BCE–70 CE).

Among the earliest types dating to the 2nd century BCE are sherds of local hemispherical bowls that imitate Greek prototypes (Fig. 7.4: 1), cooking pots with thick walls and straight necks that end in simple rims (Fig. 7.4: 2) and storage jars with very thickened rims with a square section (Fig. 7.4: 3). The most abundant types in the debris are attributed to the Hasmonaean period (mid/late 2nd–first half of 1st century BCE), including mostly storage jars, either with high collared (Fig. 7.4: 4) or out-folded rims (Fig. 7.4 :5).

The vessels that are later in date range chronologically from the late 1st century BCE to 70 CE, though some of the types are typical of the late 1st century BCE and are rare after that. This later assemblage is comprised of casseroles with ridged rims and rounded bodies (Fig. 7.4: 6), storage jars with long collared rims (Fig. 7.4: 7–8), juglets with cup-rims (Fig. 7.4: 9) and several sherds of

EARLY ROMAN–BYZANTINE POTTERY NEAR THE SOUTHEASTERN CORNER 127

unguentaria (Fig. 7.4: 10–11). Based on the analysis of the pottery, it is clear that the debris covering and canceling Wall 668 should be dated to either the Herodian period or later. The stratigraphy analysis associates the debris sealing Wall 668 with a Late Roman activity. It is possible that the debris including sherds dating to the Hasmonean and Herodian periods was brought from somewhere in the vicinity to be used as debris material.

Loci 6071 and 6113—Debris (Fig. 7.5)

This assemblage represents homogeneous debris from below the surface which includes a large amount of pottery and tiles. The pottery collection contained many sherds that are mostly dated to the 2nd/3rd centuries CE. Sherds from earlier periods—Iron Age, Hasmonaean and Early Roman— were also scattered about. Some of the tiles bear inscriptions of the Tenth Roman Legion.

The sherds that dated from the 2nd and 3rd centuries CE included fragments from six different discus lamps (not illustrated), bowls with a simple rim (Fig. 7.5: 1), bowls with a ridge below the rim on the exterior (Fig. 7.5: 2), medium to large sized bowls with rilled rims (Fig. 7.5: 3–4), kraters or table amphorae with overhanging rims (not illustrated), a few casseroles with ridged bodies, horizontal loop handles and sharp beveled rims (Fig. 7.5: 5–6), cooking pots with a high neck and ridged rim (Fig. 7.5: 7) or with grooved handles (Fig. 7.5: 8), an amphora with rounded rim and oval sectioned handle (Fig. 7.5: 9), a wide variety of storage jars (Fig. 7.5: 10–12), ridged beakers with stump bases (Fig. 7.5: 14–16) and a miniature vessel (Fig. 7.5: 17).

Residual sherds of storage jars and bowls from the Iron Age and bowls and cooking pots from the Early Roman period were included in the fill.

Bowls with an offset rim (Fig. 7.5: 2) are known from assemblages attributed to the Tenth Roman Legion at the Jerusalem Convention Center report (Magness 2005: Fig. 2: 5) and are attested in the Crowne Plaza excavations (Rosenthal-Heginbottom forthcoming) and the Cardo excavation (Rosenthal-Heginbottom 2019: 16). Rosenthal-Heginbottom (personal comment) suggested that they might be lids rather than bowls.

Rilled-rim bowls (Fig. 7.5: 6–4) of various sizes are well known in Jerusalem and the nearby region. The sizes of these bowls range from medium to large and they were made from different wares. Initially, they were ascribed to the late 3rd/4th to 6th centuries CE (Magness 1993: 202–209). Following evidence revealed from the Convention Center excavations, their first appearance was down-dated to around 200 CE (Magness 2005: 105; Rosenthal-Heginbottom 2005). Recently, Rosenthal-Heginbottom suggested, based on her study of the Crowne Plaza and the Cardo pottery assemblages, that these bowls first appeared in the last quarter of the 1st century CE (2019: 272).

The casseroles with horizontal handles and sharp-cut rims (Fig. 7.5: 5–6) were traditionally attributed to the Late Roman, Byzantine and Early Islamic periods. More recently, however, scholars have suggested that their first appearance should be placed in the 2nd century CE. They appear in small quantities in 2nd-century assemblages. However, by the late 2nd and 3rd centuries, they became more common (based on personal assessment of the pottery from the Givʿati Parking Lot excavations and the pottery workshop in the Nuseiba neighborhood ascribed to the late 2nd/3rd century CE).

The same is true for the cooking pots with high necks and grooved rims (Fig. 7.5: 7). They appear in small quantities in assemblages attributed to the Tenth Roman Legion (Rosenthal-Heginbottom 2005: 261) but are most common during the 3rd and the early 4th century CE (based on personal assessment based of Givʿati's plot finds and Nuseiba's neighborhood). Cooking pots with ridged handles are typical of Legionary Roman assemblages (Rosenthal-Heginbottom 2005: 261).

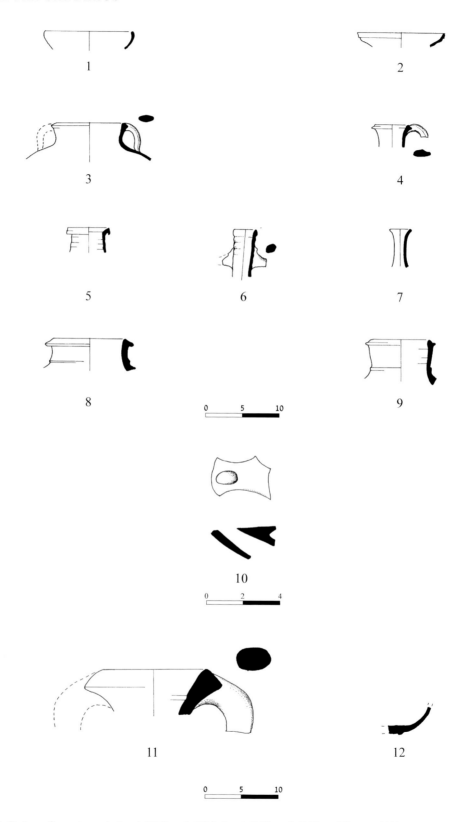

Figure 7.3: Pottery from Area A, Loci 6079 and 6086, Loci 6108 and 6109 and Locus 6111.

Figure 7.3: Pottery from Area A, Loci 6079 and 6086, Loci 6108 and 6109 and Locus 6111

No.	Locus	Reg. No.	Vessel Form	Description	Parallels
1	6079	60355/33	Bowl	Red fabric	**Jerusalem**: Convention Center: Rosenthal-Heginbottom 2005: 248, No. 57 (phase 2: last third of 1st century BCE–70 CE)
2	6079	60355/36	Bowl	Pink fabric, light red interior; fine fabric	**Jerusalem**: Convention Center: Magness 2005: 75, Fig. 2: 7 (2nd century CE)
3	6079	60355/31	Cooking pot	Yellowish-red fabric, reddish-yellow interior/exterior	**Jerusalem**: Convention Center: Rosenthal-Heginbottom 2005: 243, Nos. 19 and 20 (phase 2: last third of 1st century BCE–70 CE)
4	6079	60355/8	Cooking jug	Red fabric, dark gray core	**Jerusalem**: Convention Center: Rosenthal-Heginbottom 2005: 245, no. 33 (1st century BCE–1st century CE)
8	6079	60355/3	Jar	Pinkish-gray exterior, pink interior, light gray core	**Jerusalem**: Convention Center: Hershkovitz 2005: Fig. 1: 3 (1st–2nd century CE) The Eastern Cardo: Rosenthal-Heginbottom 2019: Fig. 3.1: 5, cat. No. 122–124, group 1 (75–125 CE context)
9	6079	60355/34	Jar	Pink fabric, light gray core	**Jerusalem**: Jewish Quarter: Geva and Rosenthal-Heginbottom 2003: 177–178, Pl. 6.5: 7 (1st–2nd century CE) The Eastern Cardo: Rosenthal-Heginbottom 2019: Fig. 3.1: 5, cat. No. 123, group 1 (75–125 CE context)
5	6079	60355/32	Jug	Pink fabric, calcite inclusions	Same as Fig. 1: 13
6	6086	60380/1	Flask	Red fabric fired to pink on interior and exterior	Same as Fig. 1: 15–16
7	6079	60355/38	Unguentarium	Reddish-yellow fabric	**Jerusalem**: Jewish Quarter: Geva and Rosenthal-Heginbottom 2003: 185, Pl. 6.5: 25 (end of 1st century BCE–1st century CE)
10	6079	60355/37	Lamp	Light reddish-brown fabric	**Masada**: Barag and Hershkovitz 1994: 24–35, Fig. 11: 77 Type C VI (last quarter of 1st century BCE–early 2nd century CE)
11	6109	60463/2	Amphora	Pale red fabric	Spain: Keay 1984: 151–153; Type XVI A, Fig. 58: 3 (beginning of 2nd–3rd century CE)
12	6109	60463/1	Lamp	Pale red fabric, black slip	

Jugs with grooved handles are seen as typical of military productions (Magness 2005: 104–108; Rosenthal-Heginbottom 2019: 3, 4, 18–19, 281).

The amphorae with an almond-section rim (Fig. 7.5: 9) seem to be a local development imitating those of the Dressel 2–4 types. These amphorae are present in Jerusalem in the 1st through 2nd/3rd centuries CE contexts.

Storage jars with ridges at the bottom already appeared in the late 1st century BCE (Fig. 7.5: 10). Storage jars with a ledge rim and ridge at the base of the neck are standard in the 1st through the early 2nd centuries CE, although they first appear in the late 1st century BCE (Fig. 7.5: 11). Storage jars with short necks, thickened rims and a ridge are well known from the late 1st through the 3rd

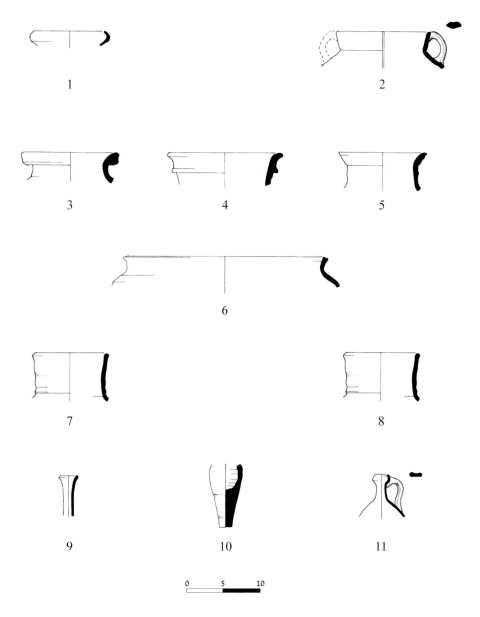

Figure 7.4: Pottery from Area B, Loci 6095 and 6118.

Figure 7.4: Pottery from Area B, Loci 6095 and 6118

No.	Locus	Reg. No.	Vessel Form	Description	Parallels
1	6095	60537/4	Bowl	Gray fabric	**Jerusalem**: Jewish Quarter: Geva 2003: 143, Pl. 5.3: 27, 28 (most common in 3rd–2nd century BCE, beginning of 1st century BCE)
2	6095	60537/3	Cooking pot	Pinkish-gray fabric	**Jerusalem**: Jewish Quarter: Geva 2003: Fig. 5.2: CP7, Pl. 5.4: 30 (end of 2nd–1st century BCE); Convention center: Berlin 2005: 35–36, Fig. 3 (1st century BCE)
3	6118	60618/1	Storage jar	Pink fabric, light-gray core	**Jerusalem**: Jewish Quarter: Geva 2003: 121–125, Fig. 5.1, SJ3a (2nd–early 1st century BCE, see parallels there); Convention Center: Berlin 2005: 30, Fig. 1: 7–8 (2nd–early 1st century BCE)
4	6095	60537/7	Storage jar	Pale-red fabric, pink interior, and exterior	**Jerusalem**: Jewish Quarter: Geva 2003: 122, Fig. 5.1: SJ1a (2nd–early 1st century BCE); Convention Center: Berlin 2005: 30, Fig. 1: 2 (2nd–early 1st century BCE)
5	6095	60501/1	Storage jar	Pinkish-gray fabric, light gray core	**Jerusalem**: Jewish Quarter: Geva 2003: 124–125, Fig. 5.1: SJ4 (late 2nd but most typical in 1st century BCE); Convention Center: Berlin 2005: Fig. 1: 6 (2nd–early 1st century BCE)
6	6118	60557/10	Casserole	Red fabric	**Jerusalem**: Convention Center: Berlin 2005: 39–40, Fig. 7 (1st century CE–70 CE) **Jericho**: Bar-Nathan 2002: 74–75, Pl. 13: 164–165, Type J-CS3 (late 1st century BCE (?)–1st century CE)
7	6095	60501/2	Storage jar	Light red fabric, pink exterior	Same as Fig. 7.4
8	6095	60537/5	Storage jar	Pink fabric, calcite inclusions	Same as Fig. 7.4
9	6118	60557/8	Juglet	Pink fabric	Same as Fig. 7.14
10	6118	60557/7	Unguentarium	Pink fabric	**Jerusalem**: Jewish Quarter: Geva and Rosenthal-Heginbottom 2003: 185, Pl. 6.5: 25 (end of 1st BCE–1st century CE)
11	6095	60537/6	Unguentarium	Pink fabric, dark gray core	-

and even 4th centuries CE, although they are most common in assemblages of the 2nd and 3rd centuries CE (Fig. 7.5: 12).

Ridged juglets with stump bases are usually dated to the 3rd–8th centuries CE (Magness 1993: 246, Form 6A). Despite that, they are known to appear in northern assemblages where they date from the late 2nd and 3rd centuries CE (Sandhaus and Balouka 2015: 189–190; Fig. 4.6: 8).

Miniature vessels, or pyxides, referred to at Masada (Bar-Nathan 2006: 36–39), are known from the Hellenistic and Early Roman periods. They appear in the late 1st century BCE to the 1st century CE assemblages in the Jerusalem area (Fig. 7.5: 17).

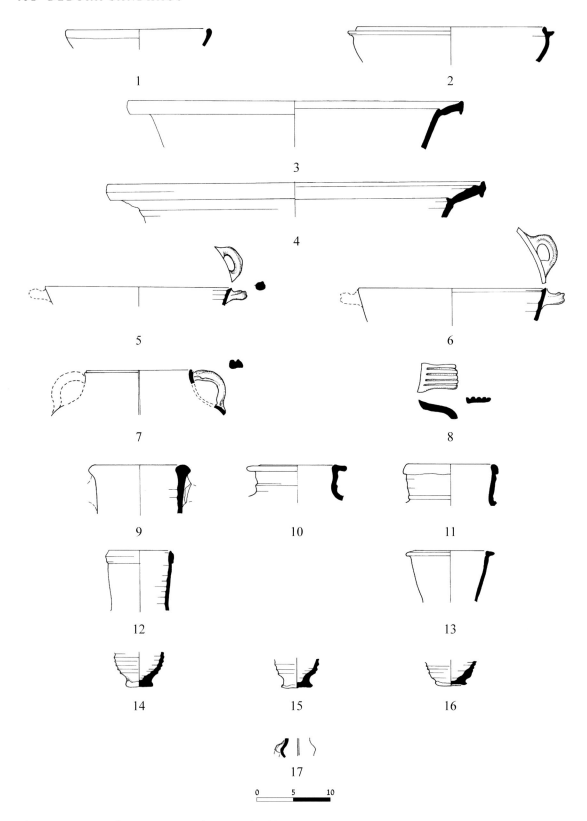

Figure 7.5: Pottery from Area B, Loci 6071 and 6113.

Figure 7.5: Pottery from Area B, Loci 6071 and 6113

No.	Locus	Reg. No.	Vessel Form	Description	Parallels
1	6113	60468/2	Bowl	Pinkish-buff fabric, red slip	**Jerusalem**: The Eastern Cardo: Rosenthal-Heginbottom 2019: 285: cat. No. 171; Fig. 3.11: 3 (typical of Late Second Temple period continuing after 70 CE)
2	6071	60329/3	Bowl	Pink fabric, light gray core	**Jerusalem**: Convention Center: Magness 2005: 275–277; Fig. 2: 5; Crowne Plaza (Rosenthal-Heginbottom forthcoming) The Eastern Cardo: Rosenthal-Heginbottom 2019: 16, cat. No. 57; group 2f; the Roman dump (75–125 CE context)
3	6113	60486/5	Bowl	Reddish-yellow fabric, buff interior/exterior	**Jerusalem**: Magness 1993: 203–204; 2005: 95; Fig. 27: 4–8 ; Rilled rim basins (late 3rd/early 4th–6th century CE; redated to no later than the 2nd century CE instead of late 3rd century CE **Jerusalem**: Jewish Quarter: Magness 2006: 184, Pl. 7.1: 9 (ca. 200–continuing to the 6th century CE)
4	6113	60486/6	Large bowls	Reddish-yellow fabric, reddish-gray core	**Jerusalem**: Convention Center: Magness 2005: 95; Fig. 27: 8 (2nd–3rd century CE)
5	6113	60468/7	Casserole	Red fabric, reddish-gray interior, and exterior	**Jerusalem**: Convention Center: Magness 2005: 91; Fig. 19: 8 (2nd–3rd century CE) The Eastern Cardo: Rosenthal-Heginbottom 2019: 90–91, 234–235, cat. No. 681; Figs. 3.11: 31; 3.15: 1, groups 3 and 4b, preparatory work for the construction of the cardo (first quarter of the 2nd century CE context); Givᶜati's plot (first half of 4th century CE); Nuseiba's neighborhood (3rd–4th century CE)
6	6071	60364/2	Casserole	Red fabric, dark gray core	Same as Fig. 7.5: 5
7	6113	60485/2	Cooking pot	Light reddish-brown fabric, dark reddish-gray interior and exterior	**Jerusalem**: Convention Plot: Rosenthal-Heginbottom 2005: 252, No. 85 (early 2nd century CE) The Eastern Cardo: Rosenthal-Heginbottom 2019: 86, cat. Nos. 617–618; Fig. 3.16: 8, 24; group 4b (first quarter of 2nd century CE context); Givᶜati's plot Sandhaus forthcoming (first half of 4th century CE); Nuseiba's neighborhood (3rd–4th century CE, general assessment)
8	6071	60367/2	Grooved cooking pot handle	Red fabric, light gray core	**Jerusalem**: Convention Center: Rosenthal-Heginbottom 2005: 261, No. 122 (70–300 CE)
9	6071	60306/1	Amphora	Pinkish-buff fabric	

No.	Locus	Reg. No.	Vessel Form	Description	Parallels
10	6071	60356/1	Storage jar	Pink fabric, calcite inclusions	**Jerusalem**: Jewish Quarter: Geva 2010: 122, Fig. 4.2: 9 (1st century CE) The Eastern Cardo: Rosenthal-Heginbottom 2019: 80–81, cat. no. 591–594; Fig. 3.12: 39; group 4b (75–125 CE context) **Masada**: Bar-Nathan 2006: 62–64, Type M-SJ13, Pl. 12: 64 (last third of 1st century BCE–1st century CE) and Bar-Nathan and Eisenstadt 2013: 14, Pl. 1.19: 703 (1st–2nd century CE)
11	6071	60364/4	Storage jar	Light reddish-brown fabric, pinkish-white exterior	**Jerusalem**: Magness 2006: 185, Pl. 7.1: 22; see references there (late 1st/2nd–4th century CE) The Eastern Cardo: Rosenthal-Heginbottom 2019: 78–80, (75–125 CE context); cat. No. 577; Figs. 3.11: 14; 3.12: 1–2; 3.13: 9; 3.14: 9
12	6113	60467/3	Storage jar/ jug	Pale red fabric, calcite inclusions	**Jerusalem**: Magness 1993: 222, Form 2 (3rd–4th century CE) The Eastern Cardo: Fig. 3.13: 7; group 4b (first quarter of 2nd century CE context); Nuseiba's neighborhood (3rd–4th century CE, personal assessment); Givʿati's plot (3rd–early 4th century CE, personal assessment) **Masada**: Bar-Nathan 2006: 74–75, Type M-SJ24, Pl. 16: 99 (1st century CE–early 2nd century CE, noted by the author that the majority was found in Garrison camp 2)
13	6071	60297/1	Jug	Reddish-yellow fabric, pinkish-gray exterior	**Jerusalem**: The Eastern Cardo: cat. No. 555; Fig. 3.15: 16 (first half of 2nd century CE context) Crowne Plaza: Rosenthal-Heginbottom forthcoming (2nd century CE)
14	6071	60356/2	Juglet base	Red fabric, pink interior, and exterior, calcite inclusions	**Jerusalem**: Magness 1993: 246, Form 6A (late 3rd–6th century CE) The Eastern Cardo: Rosenthal-Heginbottom 2019: Cat. nos. 300–303 Beth-Sheʾan: Sandhaus forthcoming (2nd–3rd century CE)
15	6071	60323/2	Juglet base	Yellowish-red fabric, reddish-yellow exterior	Same as Fig. 7.5: 14
16	6071	60358/1	Juglet base	Reddish-yellow fabric, calcite inclusions	Same as Fig.7.5: 14
17	6071	60492/2	Miniature vessel	Pink fabric, red exterior slip	Geva 2010: 125, Pl. 4.4: 15; references there (1st century CE context) **Masada**: Bar-Nathan 2006: 36–39, Pl. 35 (last third of 1st century BCE–1st century CE)

LOCI 6088 AND 6093—COLLAPSE OF STONES (FIGS. 7.6–7)

Many pottery sherds and tiles were found inside the debris (Locus 6088) of the massive collapse of stones. During the excavations, another layer of debris, one with fewer stones, was identified below this collapse (Locus 6093). The ceramic assemblages from both loci are associated with the dismantling of an early Tenth Legion structure by the 3rd or early 4th century CE. The collections from the two assemblages differ in character but not in chronology. The material from Locus 6088 is varied and included table service, preparation vessels (e.g., bowls and deep bowls) and storage vessels (e.g., amphorae and storage jars). The assemblage from Locus 6093 included cooking ware that was absent from the upper level and almost no storage vessels.

The best parallel assemblages are from the Western Wall Plaza—the bakery (Rosenthal-Heginbottom 2011), Wilson's Arch excavations (Uziel, Lieberman and Solomon 2019), the Nuseiba neighborhood (in preparation) and the Givʿati Parking Lot (Sandhaus forthcoming). The rich pottery assemblage exhibits a great variety of vessel forms: bowls with relatively thin walls and ledge rim (Fig. 7.6: 1) and rouletted bowls decorated with a red slip of the modeled rim type (Fig. 7.6: 2–3). A variety of large, deep bowls (Fig. 7.6: 4–6) with rilled rims, made in coarse ware similar to that of the tiles, are common in the assemblage.

Initially, rouletted bowls were ascribed to the late 3rd/4th to 6th centuries CE. Lately, their first appearance was down-dated to around 200 CE following the results from the Convention Center excavations (Magness 2005: 103–105; 2006: 184–185; Rosenthal-Heginbottom 2005: nos. 79, 80, 154; Rosenthal-Heginbottom 2011: 210–213). Rosenthal-Heginbottom has suggested that these bowls appeared even earlier in the late 2nd century CE. This is based on her study of the Crowne Plaza and the Cardo pottery assemblages (Rosenthal-Heginbottom 2019: 273). Deep rilled-rim bowls with remarked grooved rims are one of the hallmarks of Legionary pottery assemblages (Magness 2005: Figs. 27: 3–8; 42: 4–6; Rosenthal-Heginbottom 2019: 273; for discussion, see there and above). In the debris, flat-bottomed pans, locally produced and resembling their Pompeian ware counterparts, are also present (Fig. 7.6: 7). These pans appear in the Convention Center excavations as ascribed to the Roman Legion repertoire of vessels common from the 2nd to 3rd centuries CE (Magness 2005: 89–90; Rosenthal-Heginbottom 2019: 47–49; see further discussion there). These local pans are also known in the Givʿati Parking Lot mansion assemblages dating to the early 4th century CE (Sandhaus forthcoming).

The imported amphorae include the Spanish amphorae with out-flaring rims, a bud-like section and two cylindrical handles attached from the rim to the shoulders (Fig. 7.6: 8–9), and two pinched handles (Fig. 7.6: 10, one exemplar not illustrated) characteristic of the south coast of Anatolia amphorae dating from the 1st to the 4th centuries CE (Leonard and Demesticha 2004: 198, Fig. 13; Lund 2000: 569). The specific pinched handle uncovered in the Hulda Gate excavations corresponds to those typical of the 1st and 2nd centuries CE. The latest examples have distorted, almost un-pinched handles (Lund 2000: 571).

Storage jars with a thickened elongated rim (Fig. 7.6: 11), typical of the 2nd to 4th centuries CE, are frequent within the fill. They are not illustrated. Small stands of many forms are included in the assemblage. In addition, fragments of discus (Fig. 7.6: 12) and knife-pared (not illustrated) lamps are present in the assemblage.

The contents of the lower debris (Locus 6093, Fig. 7.7) consists mostly of pottery from the 2nd to 4th centuries CE, with a limited amount of residual Hasmonaean pottery. The presence of large numbers of Roman Legion tiles ascribed to no later than the 2nd century CE and the appearance of rouletted and rilled-rim bowls narrowed the date of the assemblage to the 2nd century CE.

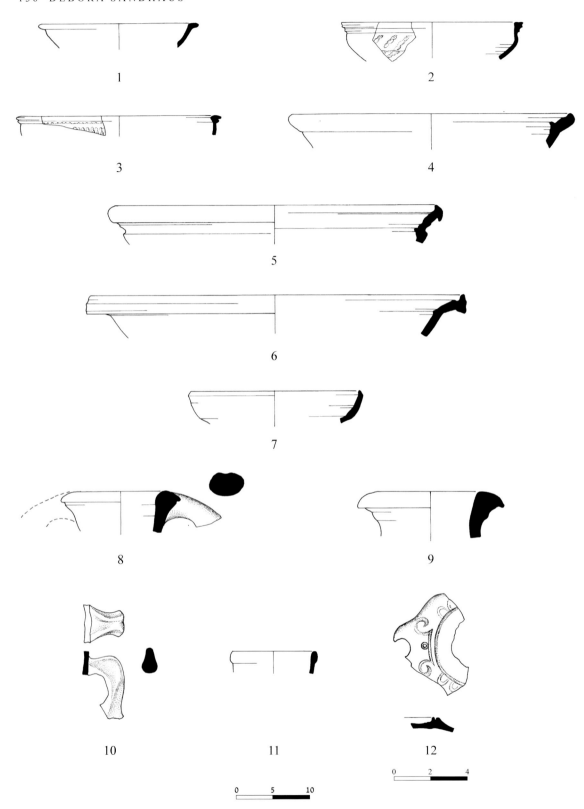

Fig. 7.6: Pottery from Area C, Locus 6088.

Figure 7.6: Pottery from Area C, Locus 6088

No.	Locus	Reg. No.	Vessel Form	Description	Parallels
1	6088	60370/2	Bowl	Pink fabric	**Jerusalem**: Crowne Plaza: Rosenthal-Heginbottom forthcoming (2nd century CE)
2	6088	60414/5	Bowl	Weak red fabric	**Jerusalem**: Magness 1993: 185–187, Rouletted Bowls Form 1 (late 3rd/early 4th through 5th century CE (Magness 2005: 103–105; 200–first half of 6th century CE) Convention Center: Magness 2005: 103–105 (200 CE to 3rd century CE); Rosenthal-Heginbottom 2005: Nos. 79, 80, 154 Crowne Plaza: Rosenthal-Heginbottom forthcoming (2nd century CE) The Western Wall Plaza: Rosenthal-Heginbottom 2011: Fig. 9.5: 58–62 Wilson's Arch: Uziel, Lieberman and Solomon 2019: Figs. 10a: 4; 11a: 1–2; 12a: 1–2 (Stratum 5b dated to late 3rd century CE and Stratum 4 dated to the late 4th century CE) Givᶜati Parking Lot: Sandhaus forthcoming (early 4th century CE)
3	6088	60370/1	Bowl	Reddish-yellow fabric, dark gray core	Same as Fig. 7.6: 2
4	6088	60371/6	Large bowl	Red fabric, pink interior, and exterior	**Jerusalem**: Magness Rilled-rim bowls; The Convention Center (Magness 2005: Figs. 27: 3–8; 42: 4–6; Rosenthal-Heginbottom 2005: 273) The Eastern Cardo: Rosenthal-Heginbottom 2019: Figs. 3.11: 11; 3.13: 25 (75–125 CE) The Western Wall Plaza: Rosenthal-Heginbottom 2011: Fig. 9.6: 71 Wilson's Arch: Uziel, Lieberman and Solomon 2019: Fig. 12a: 5 (Stratum 4 dated to the late 4th century CE). Givᶜati Parking Lot: Sandhaus forthcoming (early 4th century CE)
5	6088	60414/1	Large bowl	Reddish-yellow fabric	Wilson's Arch: Uziel, Lieberman and Solomon 2019: Fig. 10a: 9 (Stratum 5b dated to late 3rd century CE) Givᶜati Parking Lot: Sandhaus forthcoming (early 4th century CE)
6	6088	60414/4	Large bowl	Reddish-yellow fabric	Same as Fig. 7.7: 4

No.	Locus	Reg. No.	Vessel Form	Description	Parallels
7	6088	60441/3	Pan	Reddish-yellow fabric	**Jerusalem**: Convention Center: Magness 2005: 87–90 (second third of 1st century–3rd century CE) Crowne Plaza: Rosenthal-Heginbottom forthcoming (2nd century CE) The Eastern Cardo: Rosenthal-Heginbottom 2019: 47–48; cat. no. 323–330 Roman Dump (75–125 CE) The Western Wall Plaza: Rosenthal-Heginbottom 2011: Fig. 9.5: 51–52 Givʿati Parking Lot: Sandhaus forthcoming (early 4th century CE)
8	6088	60391/1	Amphora	Reddish-yellow fabric, pink interior, and exterior, biotite mica inclusions	Spain: Keay 1984: 151–153; Type XVI A, Fig. 58: 3 (beginning of 2nd–early 4th century CE) The Western Wall Plaza: Rosenthal-Heginbottom 2011: Fig. 9.6: 80–81 (3rd century CE)
9	6088	60389/1	Amphora	Pink fabric	Same as Fig. 7.6: 8
10	6088	60441/13	Amphora handle	Reddish-yellow fabric with calcite inclusions	Leonard and Demesticha 2004: 198 (1st–4th century CE); Lund 2000: 565–578; Givʿati Parking Lot: Sandhaus forthcoming (early 4th century CE)
11	6088	60370/4	Storage jar	Pinkish-gray fabric	**Jerusalem**: Magness 1993: 222, Form 2 (3rd–4th century CE); Nuseiba's neighborhood (3rd–4th century CE, personal assessment); Givʿati plot Sandhaus forthcoming (early 4th century CE) **Masada**: Bar-Nathan 2006: 74–75, Type M-SJ24, Pl. 16: 99 (1st–early 2nd century CE)
12	6088	60442/1	Lamp	Red fabric	Round Lamp with decorated discus: Rosenthal and Sivan 1978: 85–90 (second half of 1st century CE–3rd century CE) Hershkovitz 2005: Fig. 11: 5 (end of 1st to 3rd century CE) **Jerusalem**: The Eastern Cardo: Rosenthal-Heginbottom 2019: 115–116; Cat. No. 803); Western Wall Plaza: Rosenthal-Heginbottom 2011: Fig. 9.1: 12 (3rd century CE); Givʿati Parking Lot: Sandhaus forthcoming (early 4th century CE)

The bulk of the pottery includes rouletted bowls with different variations in the rim treatment, modeled, simple or ledge rims (Fig. 7.7: 1–5), deep bowls with a grooved rim (Fig. 7.7: 6–7), cooking pots with a groove on top of the rim (Fig. 7.7: 8), storage jars with thickened rim, long neck and a ridge at the bottom of the neck (Fig. 7.7: 11) and a jug with a groove on the interior (Fig. 7.7: 12).

Large pieces of a cauldron decorated with incised bands of lines (Fig. 7.7: 8) were also found within the debris, as were sherds of discus lamps (Fig. 7.7: 13).

Based on the pottery analysis, it can be concluded that the debris within the collapsed stones must be dated from the late 2nd to early 4th century CE.

SUMMARY

The pottery from the southeastern corner of the Temple Mount excavations includes vessels that range from the late Iron Age to the 2nd century CE, thus reflecting the different occupational sequences at the site. This report described the assemblages associated with the activity during the Herodian period (1st century CE until 70 CE), that of the Tenth Roman Legion (late 1st–2nd century CE), that of those who dismantled the previous building (3rd–early 4th century CE) and that of the Byzantine period.

The Herodian Period (1st Century CE Until 70 CE)

The *miqweh* was built before the 1st century CE and is most likely associated with the Herodian period. Results of the pottery analysis of the makeup of the floor sealing the installation (Loci 6080, 6114 and 6115) indicate that it went out of use during the 1st century CE. This is based on the finding that by the middle of the 1st century–beginning of the 2nd century CE (probably at 70 CE) the pottery from Channel 6077—which perhaps channeled water to the *miqweh*—yielded pottery dated to that period. This conclusion is supported by analysis of the fill from inside the pool (Locus 6086 and Locus 6107), dated to the late 1st/ early 2nd centuries CE.

Tenth Legion Activity (Late 1st–Beginning of 2nd Century CE)

The chalk floor Locus 6110. The pottery originated above the chalk floor Locus 6110, and below the Byzantine structures, yielding mostly types dating from the late 1st and the beginning of the 2nd century CE. However, sherds of indicative kinds, such as the Spanish amphora found above the floor and the duck figurine (see Chapter 10) located below the floor, point to a date in the 2nd century CE. The fact that no roof tiles were found, nor any of the typical large rilled-rim and rouletted bowls of the 2nd century, although possibly circumstantial, seems to suggest a date from the beginning of the 2nd century (see Chapter 9).

Late Roman Period (3rd–Early 4th Century CE)

The assemblage of Late Roman fills from Area B finds its closest parallels in the assemblage from the Givʿati Parking Lot and Nuseiba workshop, dating to the 3rd and early 4th centuries CE. Most of the forms fit a date between the 2nd and the early 4th centuries CE. However, the presence of remarked rilled-rim bowls, rouletted bowls and cooking pots with remarked rims suggests a rather later date in the 2nd century CE and it seems more likely to associate it to the 3rd–early 4th centuries CE. The presence of stamped tiles can be understood as a pre-activity that was dismantled by the 3rd–early 4th centuries CE.

The Byzantine Period (Unillustrated)

The foundation trench of Wall 652 and the fills attached to Walls 659 and 660 included pottery dating from the 4th to the 6th century CE.

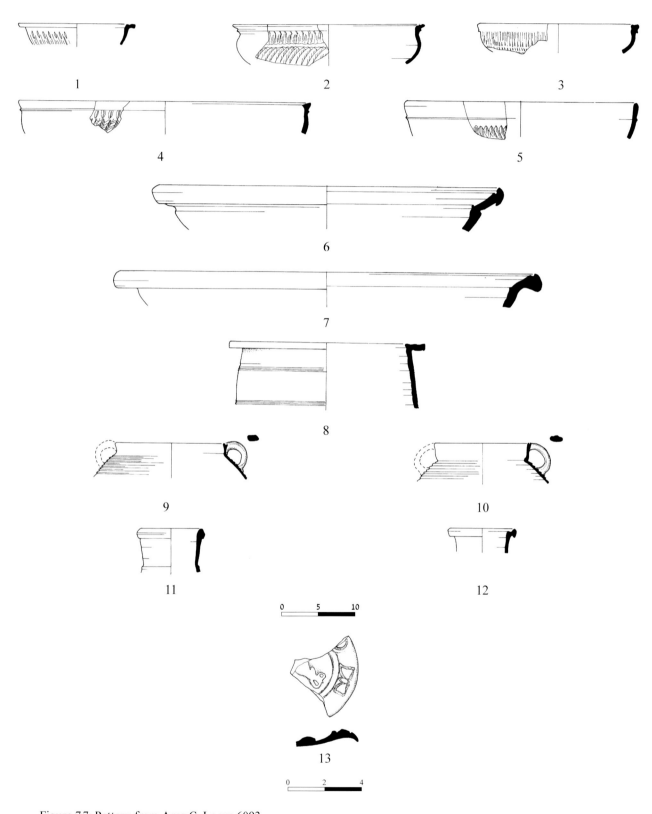

Figure 7.7: Pottery from Area C, Locus 6093.

Figure 7.7: Pottery from Area C, Locus 6093

No.	Locus	Reg. No.	Vessel Form	Description	Parallels
1		60552/2	Bowl	Reddish-yellow fabric	**Jerusalem**: Magness 1993: 189–191, Rouletted Bowls Form 3B (first half of 6th to mid-6th century CE; redated by Magness 2005: 104 to no later than the 2nd century CE instead of late 3rd century CE); Nuseiba's neighborhood (3rd–4th century CE, personal assessment); Givᶜati Parking Lot: Sandhaus forthcoming (early 4th century CE)
2		60539/10	Bowl	Pinkish-gray fabric	Same as Fig. 7.6: 2
3		60506/4	Bowl	Reddish-yellow fabric, dark gray core/interior	Same as Fig. 7.6: 2
4		60592/1	Bowl	Pink fabric, red interior, reddish-gray exterior	Same as Fig. 7.6: 2
5		60488/3	Bowl	Reddish-yellow fabric	**Jerusalem**: Magness 1993: 189–191, Rouletted Bowls Form 3C (late 6th–7th century CE); Wilson's Arch: Uziel, Lieberman and Solomon 2019: Fig. 10a: 5 (Stratum 5b dated to late 3rd century CE); Nuseiba's neighborhood (3rd–4th century CE, personal assessment); Givᶜati Parking Lot: Sandhaus forthcoming (early 4th century CE)
6		60516/2	Large bowl	Pink fabric, calcite inclusions	Same as Fig. 7.6: 6
7		60506/7	Large bowl	Pink fabric, light gray core	Same as Fig. 7.6: 6
8		60539/4	Basin	Reddish-yellow fabric, pink exterior, calcite inclusions	**Jerusalem**: Magness 1993: 206–207, Arched rim basins Form 2A, No. 11 (6th to early 7th–8th century CE, with a few pre-6th c. examples); Crowne Plaza: Rosenthal-Heginbottom forthcoming (2nd century CE); Wilson's Arch: Uziel, Lieberman and Solomon 2019: Fig. 11b: 10 (Stratum 5 dated to late 3rd century CE)
9		60539/5	Cooking pot	Gray fabric	**Jerusalem**: Givᶜati Parking Lot: Sandhaus forthcoming (early 4th century CE); Nuseiba's neighborhood (3rd–4th century CE, personal assessment)
10		60506/6	Cooking pot	Yellowish-red fabric	Same as Fig. 7.7: 9
11		60552/3	Storage jar	Reddish-yellow fabric, light gray core	**Jerusalem**: Magness 1993: 222–223, Form 3, No. 4 (2nd–4th century CE); Crowne Plaza: Rosenthal-Heginbottom forthcoming (2nd century CE)
12		60473/7	Jug	Reddish-yellow fabric, light gray core	Magness 2005: Fig. 7: 9 (context dated to 2nd century CE)
13		60553/1	Lamp	Reddish-yellow fabric, red exterior slip	Same as Fig. 7.6: 12; Givᶜati Parking Lot: Sandhaus forthcoming (early 4th century CE)

ACKNOWLEDGMENT

I wish to thank Binyamin Dolinka for his assistance with the preparation of the figures and tables, the translation of the Greek inscription on the "Candlestick Lamp," and a preliminary draft of the paper.

REFERENCES

Ariel, D.T. 2021. Stamped Amphora Handles. In: Reich, R. and Shukron, E., eds. *Excavations in the City of David, Jerusalem (1995–2010): Areas A, J, F, H, D and L, Final Report* (AJP Series 1). University Park and Jerusalem: 529–562.

Balouka, M. 2013. Roman Pottery. In: Meyers, E.M. and Meyers, C.L., eds. *The Pottery from Ancient Sepphoris*. Winona Lake.

Barag, D. and Hershkovitz, M. 1994. Lamps from Masada. In: Aviram, J., Foerster, G. and Netzer, E., eds. *Masada IV: The Yigael Yadin Excavations 1963–1965, Final Reports*. Jerusalem: 7–106.

Bar-Nathan, R. 2002. *Hasmonean and Herodian Palaces at Jericho* III: *Final Reports of the 1973–1987 Excavations,* Vol. 3: *The Pottery*. Jerusalem.

Bar-Nathan, R. 2006. *Masada VII: The Yigael Yadin Excavations 1963–1965, Final Reports: The Pottery of Masada*. Jerusalem.

Bar-Nathan, R. and Eisenstadt, I. 2013. The Ceramic Corpus from the Roman Estate at Jericho: Late 1st–Early 2nd Centuries CE. In: Bar-Nathan, R. and Gaertner, J., eds. *Hasmonean and Herodian Palaces at Jericho: Final Reports of the 1973–1987 Excavations,* Vol. 5: *The Finds from Jericho and Cypros*. Jerusalem: 3–84.

Berlin, A. 2005. Pottery and Pottery Production in the Second Temple Period. In: Arubas, B. and Goldfus, H., eds. *Excavations on the Site of the Jerusalem International Convention Center (Binyanei Haʾuma): A Settlement of the Late First to Second Temple Period, the Tenth Legion's Kilnworks, and a Byzantine Monastic Complex; The Pottery and Other Small Finds* (JRA Supplementary Series 60). Jerusalem: 29–60.

Berlin, A. 2012. The Pottery of Stata 8–7 (The Hellenistic Pottery). In: De Groot, A. and Bernick-Greenberg, H., eds. *Excavations at the City of David 1978–1985, Directed by Yigal Shiloh,* Vol. 7B: *Area E: The Finds* (Qedem 54). Jerusalem: 5–30.

Berlin, A. 2015. The Hellenistic Period. In: Gitin, S., ed. *The Ancient Pottery of Israel and Its Neighbors from the Iron Age through the Hellenistic Period*. Jerusalem: 629–672.

Geva, H. 2003. Hellenistic Pottery from Areas W and X-2. In: Geva, H., ed. *Jewish Quarter Excavations in the Old City of Jerusalem, Conducted by Nahman Avigad, 1969–1982,* Vol. 2: *The Finds from Areas A, W, and X-2, Final Report*. Jerusalem: 113–175.

Geva, H. 2010. Early Roman Pottery. In: Geva, H., ed. *Jewish Quarter Excavations in the Old City of Jerusalem, Conducted by Nahman Avigad, 1969–1982,* Vol. 4: *The Burnt House of Area B and Other Studies, Final Report*. Jerusalem: 118–153.

Geva, H. and Hershkovitz, M. 2006. Local Pottery of the Hellenistic and Early Roman Periods. In: Geva, H., ed. *Jewish Quarter Excavations in the Old City of Jerusalem, Conducted by Nahman Avigad, 1969–1982,* Vol. 3: *Area E and Other Studies, Final Report*. Jerusalem: 94–143.

Geva, H. and Rosenthal-Heginbottom, R. 2003. Local Pottery from Area A. In: Geva, H., ed. *Jewish Quarter Excavations in the Old City of Jerusalem, Conducted by Nahman Avigad, 1969–1982,* Vol. 2: *The Finds from Areas A, W, and X-2, Final Report*. Jerusalem: 176–191.

Hershkovitz, M. 2005. Pottery of the Late 1st and 2nd Century AD from the 1949 Excavations. In: Arubas, B. and Goldfus, H., eds. *Excavations on the Site of the Jerusalem International Convention Center (Binyanei Haʾuma): A Settlement of the Late First to Second Temple Period, the Tenth Legion's Kilnworks, and a Byzantine Monastic Complex; The Pottery and Other Small Finds* (JRA Supplementary Series 60). Jerusalem: 283–296.

Keay, S.J. 1984. *Late Roman Amphorae in the Western Mediterranean, A Typology and Economic Study: The Catalan Evidence* (BAR International Series 196). Oxford.

Leonard, J.R. and Demesticha, S. 2004. Fundamental Links in the Economic Chain: Local Ports and International Trade in Roman and Early Christian Periods. In: Eiring, J. and Lund, J., eds. *Transport Amphorae and Trade in the Eastern Mediterranean: Acts of the International Colloquium at the Danish Institute at Athens, 26–29.9.2002.* Athens: 189–202.

Loffreda, S. 1990. The Greek Inscriptions on the Byzantine Lamps from the Holy Land. In: Bottini, G., ed. *Christian Archaeology in the Holy Land: New Discoveries.* Jerusalem: 475–500.

Lund, J. 2000. The "Pinched Handle" Transport Amphorae as Evidence of the Wine Trade of Roman Cyprus. In: Iōannidēs, G.K., Chatzēstyllēs, S.A. and Theocharidēs, I.P., eds. *Third International Congress of Cypriot Studies. Nicosia, 16–20.4.1996.* Nicosia, Cyprus: 565–578.

Magness, J. 1993. *Jerusalem Ceramic Chronology, Circa 200–800 CE.* Sheffield.

Magness, J. 2005. The Roman Legionary Pottery. In: Arubas, B. and Goldfus, H., eds. *Excavations on the Site of the Jerusalem International Convention Center (Binyanei Haʾuma): A Settlement of the Late First to Second Temple Period, the Tenth Legion's Kilnworks, and a Byzantine Monastic Complex; The Pottery and Other Small Finds* (JRA Supplementary Series 60). Jerusalem: 69–194.

Magness, J. 2006. Late Roman and Byzantine Pottery. In: Geva, H., ed. *Jewish Quarter Excavations in the Old City of Jerusalem, Conducted by Nahman Avigad, 1969–1982,* Vol. 3: *Area E and Other Studies, Final Report.* Jerusalem: 184–191.

Magness, J. 2009. The Pottery from the 1995 Excavations in Camp F at Masada. *BASOR* 353: 75–107.

Rosenthal-Heginbottom, R. 2005. The 1968 Excavations. In: Arubas, B. and Goldfus, H., eds. *Excavations on the Site of the Jerusalem International Convention Center (Binyanei Haʾuma): A Settlement of the Late First to Second Temple Period, the Tenth Legion's Kilnworks, and a Byzantine Monastic Complex; The Pottery and Other Small Finds* (JRA Supplementary Series 60). Jerusalem: 229–282.

Rosenthal-Heginbottom, R. 2011. The Pottery Assemblage from Locus 6032. In: Mazar, E., ed. *The Temple Mount Excavations in Jerusalem 1968–1978 Directed by Benjamin Mazar, Final Reports,* Vol. 4: *The Tenth Legion in Aelia Capitolina* (Qedem 52). Jerusalem: 195–228.

Rosenthal-Heginbottom, R. 2016. Innovation and Stagnation in the Judean Lamp Production in the Late Second Temple Period (150 BCE–70 CE). In: Japp, S. and Kögler, P., eds. *Traditions and Innovations: Tracking the Development of Pottery from the Late Classical to the Early Imperial Periods.* Vienna: 429–442.

Rosenthal-Heginbottom, R. 2019. *Jerusalem: Western Wall Plaza Excavations,* Vol. 2: *The Pottery from the Eastern Cardo* (IAA Reports 64). Jerusalem.

Rosenthal-Heginbottom, R. Forthcoming. The Pottery from Strata V–III. In: Beʾeri, R., Levi, D. and Sandhaus, D., eds. *Excavations at the Site of the Jerusalem International Convention Center (Binyane Haʾuma – Crowne Plaza Hotel) 2009–2010,* Vol. 2: *The Ceramic and the Epigraphic Evidence.* Jerusalem.

Sandhaus, D. 2013. The Hellenistic Pottery. In: Ben-Ami., D., ed. *Jerusalem: Excavations in the Tyropoeon Valley (Giʾvati Parking Lot),* Vol. 1 (IAA Reports 52). Jerusalem: 83–108.

Sandhaus, D. Forthcoming. The Pottery. In Ben-Ami, D. and Tchekhanovets, Y., eds. *Jerusalem: Excavations in the Tyropoeon Valley (Givʿati Parking Lot),* Vol. 3 (IAA Reports). Jerusalem.

Sandhaus, D. and Balouka, M. 2015. The Pottery. In Mazor, G. and Atrash, W., eds. *Beth Sheʾan III: Nysa-Scythopolis: The Southern and Severan Theaters,* Part 1: *The Stratigraphy and Finds* (IAA Reports 58/1). Jerusalem: 189–206.

Shalev, Y., Bocher, E., Roth, H., Sandhaus, D., Shalom, N. and Gadot, Y. 2021. Jerusalem in the Early Hellenistic Period: New Evidence for Its Nature and Location. In: Berlin, A. and Kosmin, P.J., eds. *The Middle Maccabees, Archaeology, History, and the Rise of the Hasmonean Kingdom.* Atlanta: 17–36.

Sussman, V. 2008. The Oil Lamps. In: Patrich, J., ed. *Archaeological Excavations at Caesarea Maritima; Areas CC, KK and NN, Final Reports,* Vol. 1: *The Objects.* Jerusalem: 207–300.

Tchekhanovets, Y. 2013. The Early Roman Pottery. In: Ben-Ami, D., ed. *Jerusalem: Excavations in the Tyropoeon Valley (Giʾvati Parking Lot),* Vol. 1 (IAA Reports 52). Jerusalem: 109–150.

Terem, S.V. 2016. *Jerusalem and Judaea in the First and Early Second Century C.E.: Continuity and Change in the Ceramic Culture* (Ph.D. dissertation, Bar-Ilan University). Ramat Gan (Hebrew).

Uziel, J., Lieberman, T. and Solomon, A. 2019. The Excavations Beneath Wilson's Arch: New Light on Roman Period Jerusalem. *Tel Aviv* 46(2): 237–266.

CHAPTER 8

ARCHITECTURAL FRAGMENTS FOUND NEAR THE SOUTHEASTERN CORNER OF THE TEMPLE MOUNT

Orit Peleg-Barkat

In the year 2000, during the second season of the Baruch and Reich excavations at the Triple Gate and at the foot of the southeastern corner of the Temple Mount, several hard limestone (*mizzi hilu* and *meleke*) and marble items of architectural decoration were found. Most of the fragments date from the late Second Temple period, while a few are later, probably from the Byzantine or Umayyad periods. The late Second Temple period fragments include three column drums (Fig. 8.1: 1–3), four fragments from three different types of cornices (Fig. 8.2: 4–7), seven fragments of soffits, probably from decorated ceilings (Fig. 8.3: 8–15), three ashlars with drafted margins from pilasters (Fig. 8.4: 16) and four fragments of molded doorframes (Fig. 8.5: 19–22). The Byzantine/Umayyad period items include fragments of a column drum, the lower part of a small marble column shaft (Fig. 8.6: 24), a chancel screen post and a chancel screen panel (Fig. 8.6: 25).

Unfortunately, none of the architectural fragments was found *in-situ*. Most were found in fills, although several items were retrieved from topsoil. Even so, it is possible to reconstruct the original architectural context for some. It can be suggested that the three ashlars from built pilasters originally adorned the upper story of the Royal Portico—the *Stoa Basileios*—constructed, according to Flavius Josephus, by Herod at the southern flank of the Temple Mount complex (see below). The column drums and one of the cornices might have also originated from this edifice.

The late Second Temple period architectural fragments found in 2000 join about 20 similar fragments that were found during the first season of excavations and were published by the excavators (Baruch and Reich 2016: 69–82). Many of these fragments were found incorporated in secondary use in Wall 615, which bounds Umayyad Building V on the east. They included a column base, several column drums, a fragment of a large Corinthian capital, two Doric frieze fragments, fragments from several types of cornices, as well as fragments from decorated soffits and doorframes.

More than 450 architectural decoration fragments were retrieved from a much larger area south and southwest of the Temple Mount during the B. Mazar excavations in 1968–1978 (Peleg-Barkat 2017: 25–90). The assemblage of architectural decoration elements from this dig, combined with the findings from the Baruch and Reich excavations, is one of the most important and richest assemblages discovered to date in Second Temple period Judea. It provides a glimpse into the grandeur of architectural decoration on the Temple Mount and nearby vicinity during the Herodian period and displays the work of the finest artisans in Jerusalem at that time. The assemblage of the architectural decoration fragments includes a wide variety of shapes and a richness of designs. The source of these fragments is several structures built on the Temple Mount and at its foot to the south and southwest, in particular the Royal Portico, the western and eastern porticoes of the Temple Mount, the Triple Gate and

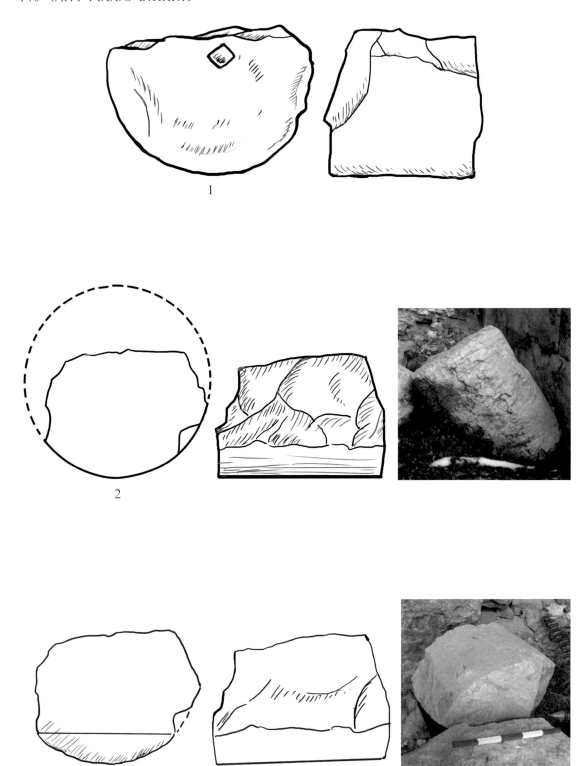

Figure 8.1: Column drums.

Figure 8.1: Column Drums

No.	Registration no.	Locus	Description H: height; D: diameter; L: length; W: width	Fig.
1	60634	Topsoil	Column drum, hard limestone (*mizzi hilu*), slightly reddish; more than half of circumference survived, curved face polished, flat side comb chiseled; H. 0.65 m; D. ~1.0 m; irregular square socket on flat side 8 × 9 cm, 1.5 cm deep	Fig. 8.1: 1
2	70/3 #6	Topsoil	Column drum, hard limestone (*mizzi hilu*), slightly reddish; original face of column severely obliterated and weathered, flat side comb chiseled, central socket not preserved; H. 0.90 m; D. 1.02 m	Fig. 8.1: 2
3	60633	Topsoil	Column drum, hard limestone (*mizzi hilu*), slightly reddish; ca. half of circumference survived, curved face polished, flat side not preserved; H. 0.90 m; D. ~1.0 m. Traces of square protrusion (8 × 8 cm) on curved polished face, obliterated but not polished away	Fig. 8.1: 3

Robinson's Arch. In accordance with the scale of the structures, the architectural fragments found also vary in size. They include Attic bases of columns with small diameters of ca. 1 m and of 45 cm; column drums with diameters of 1 m; a heart-shaped column drum of the 45 cm diameter series; 60 cm and 35 cm Doric capitals; 1 m and 45 cm Ionic capitals; various types of Corinthian capitals of two sizes (most fragments belong to columns with a diameter of 1 m); four types of Doric friezes, one with an Ionic architrave carved below; one type of Doric cornice; three types of modillion cornices; many decorated ceilings; and various types of doorframes (Peleg-Barkat 2007: 275–323, 2017: 25–90).

The following typological discussion examines the style and composition of the architectural fragments retrieved during the second season of the excavations at the Triple Gate and at the foot of the southeastern corner of the Temple Mount according to type, technical aspects of the decoration and *comparanda*.

DISCUSSION

Column Drums (Fig. 8.1: 1–3)

Three column drums were found, diameter ca. 1 m, all made from the same type of stone (*mizzi hilu*) (Fig. 8.1: 13). Their curved face is polished, while the flat sides show marks of multi-toothed chisels. An irregular square socket is carved in the center of one of the flat sides of one of the column drums (Fig. 8.1: 1). This socket was either used to hold the tenons between the drums or to hold the drum while it was prepared on the lathe or while raised to its position in the column. A protruding knob is apparent on the curved face of one of the column drum fragments (Fig. 8.1: 3). Similar unchiseled clamps (in the shape of small square knobs) are discernible on several other column drums from Herodian Jerusalem, as well as at several other sites in Judea (see below). These protuberances cast a shadow that changed direction throughout the day and thus broke the monotony of the colonnades. Similar clamps on building stones are still visible in the walls of the Temple Mount and the Cave of the Patriarchs in Hebron (Schiller 1967: 13). In the Classical period, such clamps were sometimes left unchiseled in the rear walls of buildings, for example, in the Propylea on the Athenian Acropolis (5th century BCE; Brouskari 1997: Fig. 56). In 1st century BCE Italy, however, it seems that these clamps were considered quite fashionable, as is suggested by several frescoes in Rome and in Campania that show numerous such clamps left on columns and pilasters (e.g., in the House of the Griffins on the Palatine in Rome and in the Villa of P. Fannius Synistor in Boscoreale; Ling 1991: Figs. 21, 27). Examples of column drums with similar knobs exist in the Western Wall tunnels, in the Upper City, in the Siloam Pool and in the tomb of Queen Helena of Adiabene. Outside Jerusalem, similar examples appear in the peristyle at the mountain palace-fortress at Herodium, at Beth She'an/Scythopolis, at Ḥorvat 'Eleq in Ramat Hanadiv and at the oval plaza in Jerash (Mazor and Bar-Nathan 1998: 8–10, Fig. 7; Peleg-Barkat 2007: 268, Figs. 168, 341–346, Nos. 1017, 1021).

The use of stone-carved column drums on the Herodian Temple Mount and its vicinity corresponds with the characteristic technique of erecting columns in Second Temple period Judea, as well as most Hellenistic constructions (Peleg-Barkat 2007: 139–140).[1] Together with the column drums retrieved during the first season of excavations and those collected by the Mazar expedition, there is a total of 12 column drums with diameters of approximately 1 m. Most of these drums were found in the vicinity of the Triple Gate. It has been suggested by the excavators (Baruch and Reich 2016: 73), as well as by this author, that the drums belong to the 162 columns that stood, according to Josephus (*Ant.* 15.414), in the Royal Portico and collapsed in the turbulent events of the seizure of the Temple Mount , along with the upper portion of the Southern Wall by the Roman soldiers in 70 CE (Peleg-Barkat 2011: 41–45; 2017: 100–101).

CORNICES

Several types of cornices were found during the second season of excavations at the Triple Gate and at the foot of the southeastern corner of the Temple Mount. Two fragments (Type A; Fig. 8.2: 4–5) belong to the upper member of a modillion cornice. Another fragment (Type B; Fig. 8.2: 6) is part of a flat modillion of a unique modillion cornice type, many fragments of which were found during the first season of the excavations, as well as by B. Mazar. The fourth fragment (Type C; Fig. 8.2: 7) is a rather unusual cornice, decorated on two sides and which apparently originated in an entrance, a niche, or an orthostat.

Type A

Two fragments (Fig. 8.2: 4–5) were apparently part of the same or a similar cornice of the modillion cornice type. One fragment (Fig. 8.2: 5) relates to the soffit of the cornice, decorated with modillions and coffers. The modillions are relatively flat (projecting 1.7–3.4 cm) and are almost square (12–14 cm in width and 10–11 cm in length). They have an undecorated *cyma reversa* profile and their surface is carved with a symmetrical and rather flat leaf with multiple

---

[1] One exception to this rule can be seen in the Northern Wing of Herod's Third Palace in Jericho (in Triclinium B70 and Courtyards B64 and B55), where the columns were constructed of small, brick-shaped sandstone blocks carved in a manner similar to *opus quadratum*. This peculiar construction technique of the columns in Jericho, unparalleled at other Herodian sites, apparently resulted from the employment of Roman artisans (Peleg and Rozenberg 2008: 487). Although Josephus mentions the presence of monolithic columns in Herodian buildings, for example, in the Northern Palace at Masada (*War* 5.190), or in the porticoes of the Temple Mount in Jerusalem (*War* 7.290), no such columns have been found to date, except for the rather narrow columns encircling the tholos on the Mausoleum discovered at Herodium (Peleg-Barkat and Chachy 2015).

leaflets. Simple discs fill the coffers' width (5.5–6 cm) and even overlap the edges of the *cyma reversa* frame. The stone surfaces are well polished. The second fragment (Fig. 8.2: 4) relates to the top part of the original cornice and consists of two moldings—an ovolo and above it a *cyma recta* profile. The ovolo is decorated with eggs and darts (in the shape of a simple pointed leaf),[2] while the *cyma recta* profile is very poorly preserved and its decoration cannot be reconstructed.

Fragments of similar cornices were found along the Southern Wall by the B. Mazar expedition (Peleg-Barkat 2007: 305–306, Figs. 629–631, 2017: Nos. 1151–1161). The coffers of these cornices are sometimes decorated with disks and in other cases with simple six-petaled rosettes (Peleg-Barkat 2017: Figs. II. 65–72).[3] The leaf carved on the modillions has no parallels in the local contemporary architecture; the modillion cornices found in Herod's palaces and in his other construction projects, as well as in wealthy dwellings and contemporary tombs, are carved with rectangular or S-shaped modillions that were left undecorated (Peleg-Barkat 2007: 151–152; Figs. 267–274, 491–503).[4] Although acanthus leaves regularly decorated modillions of Corinthian cornices throughout the Mediterranean during the 2nd and 3rd centuries CE (including in Late Roman and Byzantine Palestine; Turnheim 1996: 126), they are absent in the earlier examples. Thus, for example, they do not appear on the Late Republic and Early Augustan cornices in Rome (such as the Temple of Divus Julius, the Temple of Saturn and the Regia in the Forum Romanum). The earliest surviving example of modillions carved with an acanthus leaf appears in the Arch of Augustus in Rimini, built in 27 BCE. Later it appears on many Augustan buildings in Rome, such as the Temple of Apollo Sosianus,

---

[2] Ovolo moldings from cornices decorated with eggs and darts were found during B. Mazar's excavations at the foot of the Southern Wall (Peleg-Barkat 2017: Nos. 1155, 1179–1183), in the Upper City of Jerusalem (Avigad 1989: 38; Reich 2003: Pl. 8.7: 9–10), at the *opus reticulatum* building on Haneviim Street in Jerusalem (Netzer and Ben-Arieh 1983: Fig. 6:1) and in the Herodian palaces of Jericho (Netzer 2001: Fig. 427). In these examples, the darts are depicted in the same fashion as on Fragment No. 4. This is in contrast to the arrowhead-shaped darts on a cornice from Qumran (Humbert 1999: Fig. 4) and on the Ionic capitals from the Tomb of Zachariah in Jerusalem (Avigad 1954: Fig. 47). Another type of ovolo with egg and bud pattern can be seen on the echinus of the large Ionic capitals found in the Upper City of Jerusalem (Avigad 1983: 181). Nevertheless, there are common characteristics to all these Herodian examples—the apsidal shape of the eggs and the fact that their casings do not open to the sides but follow closely the outlines of the eggs. From the Flavian dynasty onward, there is a much more accentuated carving of the casing of the eggs that leaves a wide depression between the egg and its casing (Kähler 1939: 70–71).

[3] This feature of the motif exceeding from the framed panel allocated to it and having it cover the frame also appears in a large number of soffit fragments from B. Mazar excavations in this area and perhaps can be distinguished as a mark of a particular workshop.

[4] A large fragment from the upper part of a cornice consisting of a similar corona and above it an ovolo molding and a decorated *cyma recta* was found in Archelais in the Jordan Valley (Hizmi 1992: Fig. 14). Another example of this type of cornice was carved into the bedrock decorating the façade of a Second Temple period tomb in Shmuel Hanavi Street in Jerusalem (Macalister 1902: 119). Cornices with similar moldings, but with modillions left in a blocked-out state, decorated the Tomb of the Kings in Jerusalem (Vincent and Steve 1954: 358, Fig. 101A, Pl. 95, upper left, Pl. 96, upper and center left), the Tomb of the House of Herod (Vincent and Steve 1954: Pl. LXXXVI: 1) and the *opus reticulatum* building on Haneviim Street (Schick 1879: Pl. 3). Similar fragments were found in the Upper City of Jerusalem (Reich 2003: Pl. 8.7: 9) and in Herodium (Corbo 1989: Pl. 93; Peleg-Barkat and Chachy 2015). A much cruder cornice with dentils and soffit with blocked-out modillions and coffers decorated with rosettes was found in Jericho in the lower wing of Herod's Second Palace (Netzer 2001: Fig. 296). Stucco modillion-cornices were common at contemporary sites, usually with blocked-out consoles, and were found at Caldarium 104 at Masada (Foerster 1995: 58–59, Figs. 81–82), in Jericho (Peleg and Rozenberg 2008: 493, Ill. 666) and at Cypros (Netzer 1975: 59).

built in ca. 20 BCE. Gradually, the decoration on the modillions becomes more elaborate, as can be seen in the Temple of Mars Ultor in the Forum of Augustus and in the Temple of Concordia in the Forum Romanum, dated to the beginning of the 1st century CE (Strong 1963: 80–84, Pl. VIII). From this time onward, decoration of modillions with an acanthus leaf becomes common, until eventually it becomes the norm. The fact that the Herodian cornice, whose fragments were retrieved near the Triple Gate, is decorated with a leaf on its modillions is testimony to the degree to which the Jerusalemite architects and masons were attuned to the new fashions and architectural trends of Augustan Rome and to how quickly they adopted them in their local constructions.

Type B:

One fragment seems to relate to another type of modillion cornice that is unique to this area south of the Temple Mount (Fig. 8.2: 6). This type is characterized by an exceptionally deep soffit that includes an additional ornamented strip behind the flat modillions, decorated with laurel

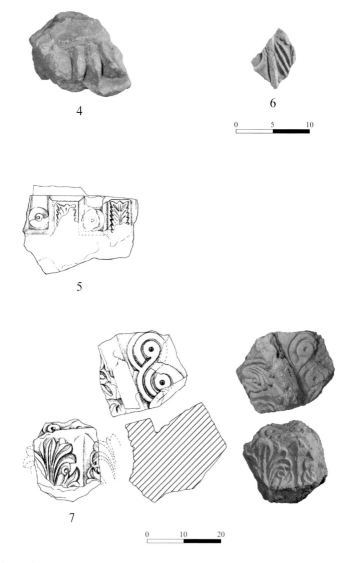

Figure 8.2: Molded cornices.

Figure 8.2: Molded Cornices

No.	Registration no.	Locus	Description H: height; D: diameter; L: length; W: width	Fig.
4	60449	6100	Fragment of a molded cornice, hard limestone (*mizzi hilu*), slightly yellowish. Preserved profiles of ovolo and *cyma recta*. Ovolo molding decorated with eggs and darts. One dart and two eggs partially preserved. Measurements: H. 30 cm; L. 23 cm; W. 20 cm	Fig. 8.2: 4
5	60701	Topsoil	Fragment from soffit of molded cornice, hard limestone (*mizzi hilu*). Two modillions and two coffers have survived. Modillions are rather flat and decorated with leaf, while each coffer adorned by disk. Measurements: H. 22.5 cm; L. 33 cm; W. 7.5 cm	Fig. 8.2: 5
6	60385	6089	Fragment from flat modillion that decorated soffit of large cornice, hard limestone (*mizzi hilu*). Decorated with olive branch and another floral design too fragmentarily preserved to be identified. Olive branch bordered on one side by simple fillet, 1.2 cm wide. Measurements: H. 8 cm; L. 6 cm; W. 1.7 cm	Fig. 8.2: 6
7	60700	Topsoil	Fragment from top sima of cornice, decorated on two sides, hard limestone (*mizzi hilu*). One face decorated with fillet border and three-band guilloche. Another face has *cyma recta* profile and decorated alternately with palmettes and long narrow leaves. Measurements: H. 20 cm; L. 20.5 cm; W. 16 cm	Fig. 8.2: 7

leaves and other floral designs instead of acanthus leaves. The fragment belongs to the soffit of the cornice. The blocked-out façade of this type of cornice is preserved on a large fragment, retrieved during the first season of excavations, and published by Baruch and Reich (2001: 89; Baruch and Reich 2016: 73–74; Fig. 43). Several other fragments were found by the expedition headed by B. Mazar (Peleg-Barkat 2007: Nos. 1169–1177, 2017: Fig. II.75). The modillion cornice fragment that was found in the second season discussed here (Fig. 8.2: 6) probably relates to a flat modillion from the soffit of such a large cornice. It is decorated with a simplified flat laurel garland, only two leaves and two berries of which are partially preserved. The modillion is bordered by a narrow fillet (1.2 cm); on the other side of the fillet one can discern the decorated coffer that cannot be reconstructed due to its poor state of preservation. The modillion projects only ca. 2 cm in relation to the coffer. A similar flat modillion decorated with a laurel garland adorns the large cornice fragment found during the first season of the excavations (Baruch and Reich 2001: 89, 2016: Fig. 43). Another cornice of this type is incorporated in secondary use into the northern face of the Southern Wall and can be seen today inside Solomon's Stables. Several similar fragments were found by the B. Mazar expedition (Peleg-Barkat 2007: Nos. 1171–1177, 2017: Fig. II.75). These fragments, which are more complete, show that the laurel garlands begin in a crescent-shaped form and are arranged in groups of three or five leaves and two bay fruits.

Modillions decorated with various patterns (that are not acanthus leaves) appear in several instances in Augustan Rome. Thus, for example, a guilloche pattern decorates the modillions of the cornices in the Basilica Aemilia and the Temples of Mars Ultor and Concordia (Strong 1963: Pl. VIII: 3–4; Mattern 1997: Pl. 3: 2). Nevertheless, there are no examples of modillions decorated with a laurel garland or branch. Laurel branches and garlands appear regularly in Hellenistic art, especially on burial altars. However, the simplified and geometrical design of the garlands decorating the fragments from the Temple Mount area have parallels mainly in the East. Garlands comprised of laurel fruit and leaves that are almost identical to the ones that are seen on the Temple Mount area modillions appear on one of the sarcophagi covers found in the Tomb of Queen Helena of Adiabene dated to the mid-1st century CE (Foerster 1998: 297, Fig. 1, Pl. 125: 1). A similar design appears on the doorframe of the Temple of Bel in Palmyra, also dated to the 1st century CE (Seyrig *et al.* 1975: 207, Pls. 20: 1, 21: 3).[5] Earlier this pattern can be found on *simae* of 3rd–2nd centuries BCE terracotta cornices from Seleucia on the Tigris (Hopkins 1972: 133, Figs. 44–46). The design of the laurel garland in all of the above mentioned Eastern examples is a simplification of the classical garland. The leaves are not arranged freely, but rather in symmetrical groups. The ribbon twisted around the branches is reduced to a crescent-shaped leaf at the edge of each group of leaves. The resulting design is flat and does not give a sense of a three-dimensional garland.

Type C

One fragment (Fig. 8.2: 7) belongs to a cornice that originally crowned an entrance, niche or orthostat. One face of this fragment is molded with a *cyma recta* profile decorated by an alternating pattern of acanthus leaves and simple, narrow leaves with pointed edges. The *cyma* ends with a fillet and a slanting fascia above it carved with a pattern of a three-strand guilloche. Three similar fragments were found by the B. Mazar expedition south of the Temple Mount (Peleg-Barkat 2007: Nos. 1488–1492, 2017: Fig. II.99).[6] On two of the fragments the fascia was left plain, while on the third fragment, a similar guilloche pattern appears. An ornamentation with acanthus leaves and narrow, simple leaves alternately carved on a *cyma* profile is not widespread, but occasionally appears on the upper edge of various types of cornices, as can be seen, for example, at the Temple of Concordia in Rome, dated between 7 to 10 CE (Stamper 2005: 141–144, Fig. 105). The guilloche was a popular motif in the late Second Temple period on wall decorations, as evidenced in the frescoes found in the Upper City of Jerusalem and in Herod's Third Palace in Jericho (Broshi 1972: Pl. 7; Rozenberg 2003: 307–308, Figs. 22–23). It also appears often on mosaic floors, as can be seen at Masada (Foerster 1995: Pl. XIII: a), Herodium (Netzer 1999: Fig. 145), and in the Upper City of Jerusalem (Avigad 1983: Figs. 108–109; Avigad 1989: 51). Nevertheless, the specific combination as presented by the fragments from south of the Temple Mount is unprecedented.

Soffits/Decorated Ceilings

Seven fragments of decorated soffits were found (Figs. 9.3: 8–15). Most of them are too small to enable us to determine whether they came from a ceiling or a cornice soffit (of Type B).[7] Some

---

[5]   This design appears in several additional places in Palmyra, such as on the frame of a ritual niche from the 1st century BCE, found in the Agora (Colledge 1976: 33, Fig. 11).

[6]   Another similar fragment is found in the collection of the École Biblique et Archéologique Française de Jérusalem and originates, according to Jean-Baptiste Humbert, with French Christian pilgrims who collected the fragment in the 1970s from the dumps of B. Mazar exacavations south of the Temple Mount.

[7]   A soffit decorated with geometrical panels and floral designs is carved on the bottom of the lintel at the entrance to the Tomb of the Grapes in Jerusalem (Macalister 1900: Pl. 3; Peleg-Barkat 2007: Figs. 516–518).

fragments may have originated in architrave soffits, lintel soffits, or the unpreserved domes of the Double and Triple Gates' underground passageways. It should be noted that more than half of the architectural fragments found in the Temple Mount excavations headed by B. Mazar seem to belong to soffit decorations (Peleg-Barkat 2007: Nos. 1207–1471).

Five of the fragments (Fig. 8.3: 8–13) show remains of the frames that divided the ceilings into various decorated geometric fields or panels. These fields could be either square, rectangular, triangular, rhombus, hexagonal, octagonal or round. The frames have a profile of a simple, flat fillet with a plain *cyma reversa* molding on each side. This profile appears quite often in various media of stone carving in Jerusalem from the time of Herod until the destruction of the Temple. Thus, for example, several monumental inscriptions, such as the inscription of King Uzziah or the inscription of Theodotus (Weill 1920: 186–190, Pl. XXVA; Sukenik 1931: 217–221; *CII* 1.1: 9), bear similarly designed frames, and the same holds true for several contemporary sarcophagi with framed decorated panels (Foerster 1998: 303, Pls. 120, 121: 4, 122, 123: 3–4). Frames with identical profiles are also common around decorated panels of early Roman sarcophagi (Brandenburg 1978: 280, Figs. 1–35), as well as in Augustan architectural decoration; for example, around the decorated panels of the Ara Pacis (Mathea-Förtsch 1999: Pls. 57, 75: 1–3) or those of the stucco ceilings in the House of Augustus on the Palatine Hill (Carettoni 1983: Pl. Y1).

The other two fragments (Fig. 8.3: 14–15) are decorated with floral and geometrical motifs. One is decorated with a pattern of scales and buds (Fig. 8.3: 14) and the other is carved with a flat horizontal garland (Fig. 8.3: 15). The two fragments constitute two examples of the varied repertoire of motifs that were used to adorn the interior of the geometrical fields framed by the above-discussed frames.[8]

The decoration of ceilings with square panels originates in decorated ceilings of temples and auxiliary buildings, which were common from the Classical period onward and appear, for example, in the Propylea (437–432 BCE) on the Athenian Acropolis (Lawrence 1996: 117, Figs. 180–182). In order to alleviate the weight of these ceilings, equal-sized coffers were carved, uniformly covering the ceiling. This design imitates the wooden beams that generally support the ceilings of large buildings and cross over at right angles (Barbet 1993: 365). The coffers often remained without ornamentation, but sometimes rosettes were carved into the center of each. The stucco decorations of the concrete vaulted ceilings that developed in Italy during the 1st century BCE were much more complicated in their design; since in the stucco ceilings there was no need to decrease the weight of the mass of the ceiling, the panels lost their functional role and could be used more freely as decorations (Ling 1972: 20–43). Fragments of stucco moldings found in Herod's palaces in Herodium, Jericho, Masada, Kallirrhoe and Machaerus

---

[8] The fragment decorated with buds and scales is reminiscent of the modillion decorated with a design of scales and buds, carved on the cornice fragments found in Avigad's excavations in the Upper City of Jerusalem (Avigad 1983: Fig. 184). Several variants of horizontal garlands also appear on fragments found by the B. Mazar expedition (Peleg-Barkat 2007: Nos. 1427–1439; Peleg-Barkat 2017: Figs. II.93–94). One of the variants is similarly carved with garlands made of simple leaves arranged in four rows, organized in a mirror image on both sides of a central axis (Peleg-Barkat 2007: Nos. 1435–1439). Simple horizontal garlands also decorated the stucco ceilings in Herod's construction projects, such as that found in excavations on the southern Tell of Herod's Third Palace in Jericho (Netzer 1999: Fig. 70). A garland of various types of leaves and flowers decorates the doorframe on the façade of the Tomb of Queen Helena of Adiabene (Kon 1947: Pls. IX–XI).

8

9

10

11

12

13

14

15

0 5 10

Figure 8.3: Soffit Fragments

No.	Registration no.	Locus	Description H: height; D: diameter; L: length; W: width	Fig.
8	60402	6092	Soffit fragment, hard limestone (*mizzi hilu*). Two angles from two adjacent rectangular framed coffers have survived. Frame ca. 6 cm wide and made of central fillet and two undecorated *cyma reversa* moldings, one on each side. From patterns that decorated coffers that were bordered by these frames only faint signs have remained; apparently, they were carved off during phase of secondary use. Measurements: H. 23 cm; L. 20.1 cm; W. 17.5 cm	Fig. 8.3: 8

9	60401	6092	Fragment from soffit, hard limestone (*mizzi hilu*), slightly reddish with gray-purple surface (perhaps outcome of conflagration). Small part of frame, 7 cm wide, similar to no. 8, has survived. Measurements: H. 17 cm; L. 14 cm; W. 13.5 cm	Fig. 8.3: 9
10	60416	6093	Fragment from a soffit, hard limestone (*mizzi hilu*). Small part of frame, 7 cm wide, similar to no. 8, has survived. Measurements: H. 42 cm; L. 17.5 cm; W. 14.7 cm	Fig. 8.3: 10
11	60400	6092	Fragment from soffit, hard limestone (*mizzi hilu*), slightly reddish. Small parts from two parallel frames, ca. 7 cm wide each, similar to no. 8, have survived. Measurements: H. 27 cm; L. 12 cm; W. 24.3 cm	Fig. 8.3: 11
12	60580	6120	Fragment from soffit, hard limestone (*mizzi hilu*), slightly reddish. Small part of a frame, similar to no. 8, has survived. Measurements: H. 6.5 cm; L. 6 cm; W. 3 cm	Fig. 8.3: 12
13	60434/2	6097	Fragment from soffit, hard limestone (*mizzi hilu*), grayish surface. Small part of frame comprised of fillet band and only one undecorated *cyma reversa* profile. Measurements: H. 10.4 cm; L. 7.2 cm; W. 2.9 cm	Fig. 8.3: 13
14	60403	6092	Fragment from soffit, hard reddish limestone (*mizzi hilu*). Fragment decorated with scale and bud pattern. This pattern bordered on one side by simple fillet, 3.1 cm wide. Measurements: H. 11.5 cm; L. 14 cm; W. 10 cm	Fig. 8.3: 14
15	60404	6092	Fragment of acanthus leaf or garland, hard reddish limestone (*mizzi hilu*), gray surface. Measurements: H. 6.8 cm; L. 8.5 cm; W. 2.8 cm	Fig. 8.3: 15

(Rozenberg 2006: 339–349; Peleg-Barkat 2007: Figs. 299–308) show that ceilings in Herod's construction projects were decorated in a similar style. However, despite some similarities between their compositions and patterns, the stone ceilings display a much wider and richer variety than the local stucco ceilings, and they differ in many details both from these ceilings and from their Roman prototypes. It would appear, therefore, that the decorated soffits from the Temple Mount area should be attributed to a group of sophisticated stone ceilings created during the Early Roman period in the eastern provinces of the Roman Empire. These stone ceilings were perhaps inspired by contemporary Italian stucco ceilings, but they mostly represent local and Mesopotamian influences. The ceiling decoration of the portico and the thalamoi in the Temple of Bel at Palmyra, and those of the corridors and staircases in the large altar of the Temple of Jupiter in Baalbek, also belong to this group.[9]

---

[9]   Despite the fact that inscriptions date the two monuments, respectively, to 32 CE and the second half of the 1st century CE, some researchers suggest dating the planning of the structures and the carving of their architectural decoration to a slightly earlier period in the last third of the 1st century BCE and the first half of the 1st century CE, accordingly (Collart and Coupel 1951: 121–132; Seyrig *et al.* 1975; Freyberger 1998: 69, 75).

TEMPLE MOUNT WALLS PILASTER DECORATION

Three fragments of drafted margin ashlars[10] with complex profiles were found (Fig. 8.4: 16). They are similar in shape and style (but not in size) to the flat pilasters that originally adorned the exterior of the walls of the Temple Mount (see below). Two of the fragments originate from the projecting pilasters (one has the full width of the pilaster, 1.13 m), while the third originates in the base of the recessions between the pilasters that slanted outward.[11]

The three fragments join several other ashlars retrieved by the B. Mazar expedition at the collapse of the Temple Mount at the foot of its western and southern enclosure walls. The ashlars have a complex profile and testify to the fact that the exterior of the walls above the level of the inner plaza of the Temple Mount complex were decorated by flat pilasters, 1.45 m wide (Mazar 1971: 2, Fig. 1; Mazar 1972: 75; Ben-Dov 1982: 93; Ritmeyer and Ritmeyer 1989: 33). These pilasters are of the same width as the pilasters (with the recession between them being ca. 2.6 m wide) documented *in-situ* in 1873 by Conder (Warren and Conder 1884: 213–215) on a short section in the northern part of the Western Wall. Another such pilaster can still be seen on the Northern Wall of the Temple Mount in a tomb located in the center of the Madrasat al-Is'ardiyya (Burgoyne 1987: 373, Pl. 33.18). Similar pilasters decorate the walls of the Cave of the Patriarchs in Hebron and the ritual compound in Mamre (Vincent, Mackay and Abel 1923: 43; Magen 2003: 250–252, Figs. 9–10).[12] It has been suggested that the pilasters were intended to "diminish the sense of monotony and give the walls a monumental feeling" (Levine 1998: 111).

It should be noted that 1.13 m-wide-pilasters, similar in size to the ones discussed here, were also found in the destruction debris below the western enclosure wall of the Temple Mount (Reich and Billig 1999: 38). I have suggested that these pilasters that are about three quarters the width of the pilasters that adorned the Temple Mount's enclosure walls originated in the upper floor of the Royal Portico (Peleg-Barkat 2011: 47, 2017: 107–109).

---

[10] Ashlars with drafted margins were also used in the construction of the walls in the Cave of the Patriarchs in Hebron and in the ritual enclosure in Mamre (Magen 1991: 47). According to Jacobson, the drafted margins on the Temple Mount's retaining walls derive from the need to adapt the construction in the Herodian period to earlier construction from the Hellenistic period, which remained exposed in the Eastern Wall of the Temple Mount, north of Herod's expansion (between the "seam" and the "turning"). This section was also built from ashlars with drafted margins, but their boss is more prominent and coarsely chiseled (Jacobson 2000). Ashlars carved with drafted margins were common in Greek architecture from the Archaic period onward and can be seen, for example, in the foundations of the Parthenon, built by Pericles (Brouskari 1997: 106). This style of chiseling became common in Asia Minor and Mesopotamia in the 5th century BCE, mainly in funerary art and architecture (Nylander 1970: 81–88) and gained renewed popularity under Augustus, as can be seen in the Temple of Mars Ultor in the Forum of Augustus in Rome (Wilson-Jones 2003: Fig. 7.1) and the Temple of Augustus in Ankara (Krencker and Schede 1936: 21, Fig. 23, Pls. 13–18, 23, 38).

[11] The reason for the slanting base was perhaps to prevent accumulation of rainwater. It should be noted, though, that this design is unusual and does not appear at other sites decorated with pilasters. Stiebel suggests, based on a section of the Temple Scroll describing the Temple walls, that this design of recessed sections should be understood as sealed metaphorical windows, which expressed the centrality of the Temple and the eruption of the divine light from it to the outer world (Stiebel 2007: 219–234).

[12] The best-preserved pilaster decoration has survived on the enclosure walls of the Cave of the Patriarchs in Hebron, where 11 columns appear along the short walls, and 19 columns along the longer walls (including the wide corner columns). The width of the columns, excluding the corners, is ca. 1.14 m, while the recessions between the pilasters are approximately 2.07 m (Vincent, Mackay and Abel 1923: 43). A similar ornamentation was partially preserved on the northern and eastern walls of the ritual compound in Mamre. The pilasters in this monument are ca. 0.88–0.90 m wide and the recessions between the pilasters are 1.90–2.05 m in width (Magen 2003: 253).

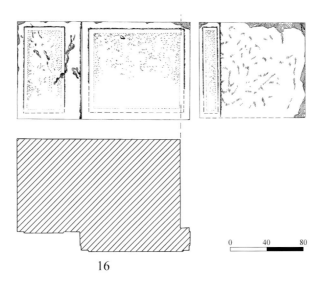

16

Figure 8.4: Ashlar Pilasters

No.	Registration no.	Locus	Description H: height; D: diameter; L: length; W: width	Fig.
16	60635	Topsoil	Ashlar building stone, hard limestone (*meleke*). The front is divided in two blocks, each with its own drafted margins, one that relates to recessed part of the wall and the other to a projecting pilaster. The pilaster projects 0.2 m and it is 1.13 m long. Measurements: H. 1.0 m; L. 1.78 m; W. 1.15 m	Fig. 8.4: 16
17	60631	Topsoil	Fragment of ashlar building stone, hard limestone (*meleke*). The front is divided in two blocks, each with its own drafted margins, one that relates to the recessed part of the wall and the other to a projecting pilaster. Pilaster projects 0.17 m and its preserved length is 0.33 m. Measurements: H. 1.19 m; L. 1.28 m; W. 0.99 m. On bottom face three rectangular sockets are preserved	-
18	60632	Topsoil	Fragment from obliquely fashioned lower portion of interstices between pilasters, hard limestone (*meleke*). Measurements: H. 0.96 m; L. 0.84 m; W. 0.79 m	-

The use of engaged columns or pilasters first appeared as an internal decoration in late Calssical temples (e.g., in the Temple of Athena Alea in Tegea; Norman 1984: 184–186). As an external type of ornamentation, pilasters exist mainly in Late Hellenistic and Roman funerary monuments, but also in temples and public buildings, such as the Bouleuterion of Termessos, dated to the 2nd century BCE. Among the temples decorated in this style are the temple on Mount Gerizim, dated to the 2nd century BCE (Magen 2000: 96–113), the Temple of Jupiter in Damascus (Creswell 1989: 50, Fig. 25), the external gate towers of the Temple of Jupiter Heliopolitanus in Baalbek (Segal 1999: 3–4), and the Temple of Bel in Palmyra (Seyrig *et al.* 1975: Pl. 1: 1–2), dated to the 1st century CE.

MOLDED DOORFRAMES

Four fragments of molded doorframes were found during the second season of excavations (Fig. 8.5: 19–22). The doorframes belong to Attic or Ionic style entrances and are carved with plain

19   20   21   22

0   5   10

Figure 8.5: Molded Doorframes

No.	Registration no.	Locus	Description H: height; D: diameter; L: length; W: width Measurements are given in meters	Fig.
19	60406	6092	Fragment of molded doorjamb or lintel, hard limestone (*meleke*), traces of rough comb chiseling. *Cyma reversa* followed by plain rectangular molding have been preserved. Measurements: H. 13.5 cm; L. 14 cm; W. 15.5 cm	Fig. 8.5: 19
20	60405	6092	Fragment of molded doorjamb or lintel, hard limestone (*meleke*). *Cyma reversa* followed by plain rectangular molding have been preserved. Measurements: H. 14.2 cm; L. 12 cm; W. 12.5 cm	Fig. 8.5: 20
21	60303/1	Topsoil	Fragment of molded doorjamb or lintel, hard limestone (*meleke*), traces of rough comb chiseling. *Cyma reversa* molding has been preserved. Measurements: H. 9.5 cm; L. 7.6 cm; W. 9.7 cm	Fig. 8.5: 21
22	60488	6093	Fragment of molded doorjamb, hard limestone, traces of rough chiseling. Rounded molding has been partially preserved. Measurements: H. 12.1 cm; L. 9.8 cm; W. 5.7 cm	Fig. 8.5: 22

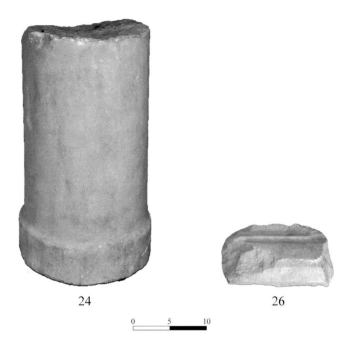

24   26

Figure 8.6: Byzantine/Umayyad Architectural Fragments

No.	Registration no.	Locus	Description H: height; D: diameter; L: length; W: width	Fig.
23	60536	6093	Fragment of column, brittle limestone, bad state of preservation, rough carving. Reconstructed diameter: 43 cm. Measurements: H. 30 cm; L. 8.5 cm; W. 16 cm	-
24	60293	6070	Simple column base and lower part of column shaft, gray marble. Column apparently stood against a wall or was attached to some other element. On the base there are traces of rough chiseling. Measurements: shaft: H. 28 cm; D. 17.5 cm; base: H. 5.9 cm; D. 20 cm	Fig. 8.6: 24
25	60303/2	Topsoil	Fragment from top part of a chancel screen post, hard gray limestone (*meleke*). At its center there is a small depression, 3.7 cm in diameter. Measurements: H. 16.9 cm; L. 11.7 cm; W. 8.7 cm	-
26	60311/3	6073	Small fragment from the frame of a chancel screen panel, gray marble. Measurements: H. 14.5 cm; L. 8.3 cm; W. 4 cm	Fig. 8.6: 26

undecorated moldings. Two main types of decorated doorframes are attested in this area; one is of a simpler style, characterized by few moldings, and the second is more sophisticated, with a more elaborate series of moldings. The doorframe of the gate that once stood above Robinson's Arch is of the Attic type[13] and is carved with a *cyma reversa* and an outer wide fillet; the same applies to fragments Nos. 19–22 (Fig. 8.5). This profile is common in the design of doorframes in the late Second Temple period, as can be seen in several contemporary tombs in Jerusalem, such as the Cave of Jehoshaphat, the Tombs of the Sanhedrin, the Tomb of the Grapes and several tombs in the Ben Hinnom Valley (Peleg-Barkat 2007: Figs. 535, 539–543, 547–549, 552–563). The decorated doorframe preserved on the western doorpost of the Triple Gate's western entrance is more elaborate; this doorframe is carved with five moldings, including an ovolo and *cyma reversa*, separated and flanked by fillets (Baruch and Reich 2016: 78, Fig. 46: 15; Fig. 47. For a general discussion and typology of chancel screen, see Habas 1994).[14]

BYZANTINE/UMAYYAD PERIOD ARCHITECTURAL FRAGMENTS

Four of the architectural fragments seem to date back to the Byzantine or Umayyad periods. One is a small fragment of a column with a reconstructed diameter of ca. 43 cm (No. 23; not illustrated). It is made of brittle stone and differs in material and chisel marks from the Second Temple period column drums revealed at the site, and probably dates to a later period. Also found was a small gray marble column, 17.5 cm in diameter (Fig. 8.6: 24). It is one of dozens of marble columns from the Byzantine and Umayyad periods scattered throughout the excavation site. Its minute dimensions suggest that its original function was as one of the feet for an altar table or ambo or perhaps as part of a railing of a window or a second-story exedra. A collar or a simple base is carved on one end.

Also found were a small fragment of a chancel screen post (No. 25, not illustrated) and a small fragment of a chancel screen panel (Fig. 8.5: 26). Dozens of similar fragments were found throughout the excavation area and date from the Byzantine period. The chancel screen panels retrieved during the B. Mazar excavations were decorated with various patterns, such as wreaths and conchs, harts, architectural structures, pomegranates and other floral and geometrical patterns (Peleg 2003: 135–152).

SUMMARY

The assemblage of architectural decoration found during the second season of the excavations near the Triple Gate and at the foot of the southeastern corner of the Temple Mount, led by Baruch and Reich, includes mainly Late Second Temple period pieces, with a few fragments that are of a later date, probably from the Byzantine or Umayyad periods. The 22 Herodian fragments join dozens of others found in this area in previous excavations and together they shed light on the decoration of the Herodian buildings on the southern flank of the Temple Mount and at its foot.

---

[13] The Attic entrance features a peripheral frame with the lintel protruding from both sides of the doorposts. The Attic frame originates in entrance and gate decorations in Classical and Hellenistic Greece. They appear, for example, in Macedonian tombs in Vergina and other sites (Miller 1982: Figs. 7–8, 12–13, 19, 24–25).

[14] This design has no parallel in local architecture, and it is possible that the intention was to distinguish the Triple Gate from the other gates with a special ornamentation, and to set it as the main entrance gate to the Temple Mount.

REFERENCES

Avigad, N. 1954. *Ancient Monuments in the Kidron Valley.* Jerusalem (Hebrew).

Avigad, N. 1983. *Discovering Jerusalem.* Nashville.

Avigad, N. 1989. *The Herodian Quarter in Jerusalem—Wohl Archaeological Museum.* Jerusalem (Hebrew).

Barbet, A. 1993. La peinture des plafonds et des voûtes à Rome, Herculanum, Stabies et Pompéi. In: dell'Orto, L.F., ed. *Ercolano 1738–1988*: 250 anni di ricerca archeologica, Atti del Convegno Internazionale Ravello-Ercolano-Napoli-Pompei, 30 ottobre–5 novembre, 1988. Ravello: 365–386.

Baruch, Y. and Reich, R. 2001. Second Temple Period Finds from New Excavations at the Ophel, South of the Temple Mount. *Qadmoniot* 122: 88–92 (Hebrew).

Baruch, Y. and Reich, R. 2016. Excavations near the Triple Gate of the Temple Mount, Jerusalem. ʿ*Atiqot* 85: 37–95.

Ben-Dov, M. 1982. *The Dig at the Temple Mount.* Jerusalem (Hebrew).

Brandenburg, H. 1978. Der Beginn der stadtrömischen Sarkophag-Produktion der Kaiserzeit. *JdI* 93: 277–327.

Broshi, M. 1972. Excavations in the House of Caiaphas, Mount Zion. *Qadmoniot* 19–20: 104–107 (Hebrew).

Brouskari, M. 1997. *The Monuments of the Acropolis.* Athens.

Burgoyne, M.H. 1987. *Mamluk Jerusalem—an Architectural Study.* London.

Carettoni, G. 1983. *Das Haus des Augustus auf dem Palatin.* Mainz.

Collart, P. and Coupel, P. 1951. *L'autel monumental de Baalbek.* Paris.

Colledge, A.R. 1976. *The Art of Palmyra.* London.

Corbo, V. 1989. *Herodion—gli edifici della reggia-fortezza.* Jerusalem.

Cotton, H.M., Di Segni, L., Eck, W., Isaac, B., Kushnir-Stein, A., Misgav, H., Price, J., Roll, I. and Yardeni, A. 2010. *Corpus Inscriptionum Iudaeae/Palaestinae,* Vol. 1: Jerusalem and Berlin.

Creswell, K.A.C. 1989. *A Short Account of Early Muslim Architecture,* revised and supplemented by J.W. Allan. Cairo.

Dentzer-Feydy, J. 2003. Le Décor sculpté et stuqué. In: Zayadine, F., Larché, F. and Dentzer-Feydy, J., eds. *Le Qasr Al-Bint de Pétra—L'architecture, le décor, la chronologie et les dieux.* Paris: 45–75.

Foerster, G. 1995. *Masada V: The Yigael Yadin Excavations 1963–1965, Final Reports: Art and Architecture.* Jerusalem.

Foerster, G. 1998. Sarcophagus Production in Jerusalem from the Beginning of the Common Era up to 70 CE. In: Koch, G., ed. *Akten des Symposiums "125 Jahre Sarkophag-Corpus," Marburg 4–7 Oktober 1995.* Mainz: 295–310.

Freyberger, K.S. 1998. *Die frühkaiserzeitlichen Heiligtümer der Karawanenstationen im hellenisierten Osten—Zeugnisse eines kulturellen Konflikts im Spannungsfeld zweier politischer Formationen* (Damaszener Forschüngen 6). Mainz.

Habas, L. 1994. The Relief Art of Chancel Screens in Churches and Synagogues in Palestine in the Byzantine Period: A Stylistic and Iconographic Study (M.A. thesis, Hebrew University of Jerusalem). Jerusalem (Hebrew).

Hizmi, H. 1992. Archelais: The Village of Archelaus. In: Erlich, Z.H. and Eshel, J., eds. *Judea and Samaria Research Studies: Proceedings of the 2nd Annual Meeting.* Ariel: 185–213.

Hopkins, C. 1972. *Topography and Architecture of Seleucia on the Tigris.* Ann Arbor.

Humbert, J.B. 1999. Qumrãn, esséniens et architecture. In: Kollmann, B., Reinbold, W. and Steudel, A., eds. *Antike Judentum und Frühes Christentum (Festschrift für Hartmut Stegemsnn zum 65 Geburtstag).* Berlin and New York: 183–196.

Jacobson, D.M. 2000. Decorative Drafted-Margin Masonry in Jerusalem and Hebron and Its Relations. *Levant* 32: 135–154.

Kähler, K. 1939. *Die römischen Kapitele des Rheinsgebietes.* Berlin.

Kon, M. 1947. *The Tombs of the Kings.* Tel Aviv (Hebrew).

Krencker, D. and Schede, M. 1936. *Der Tempel in Ankara* (Denkmäler Antiker Architecktur 3). Berlin.

Lawrence, A.W. 1996. *Greek Architecture,* revised by R.A. Tomlinson. New Haven and London.

Levine, L.I. 1998. *Jerusalem in Its Splendor: A History of the City in the Second Temple Period.* Tel Aviv (Hebrew).

Ling, R. 1972. Stucco Decoration in Pre-Augustan Italy. *Papers of the British School at Rome* 40: 11–57.

Ling, R. 1991. *Roman Painting.* Cambridge.

Macalister, R.A.S. 1900. On a Rock-Tomb North of Jerusalem. *Palestine Exploration Fund Quarterly Statement* 32(1): 54–61.

Macalister, R.A.S. 1902. The Newly Discovered Tomb North of Jerusalem. *Palestine Exploration Fund Quarterly Statement* 34: 118–120.

Magen, Y. 1991. Elonei Mamre—Herodian Cult Site. *Qadmoniot* 93–94: 46–55 (Hebrew).

Magen, Y. 2000. Mt. Gerizim: A Temple City. *Qadmoniot* 120: 74–118 (Hebrew).

Magen, Y. 2003. Mamre. A Cultic Site from the Reign of Herod. In: Bottoni, G.C., Di Segni, L. and Chrupcala, L.D., eds. *One Land—Many Cultures: Archaeological Studies in Honour of Stanislao Loffreda.* Jerusalem.

Mathea-Förtsch, M. 1999. *Römische Rankenpfeiler und Pilaster.* Mainz.

Mattern, T. 1997. Die Bauphasen der frühkaiserzeitlichen Basilica Aemilia. *Boreas* 20: 33–41.

Mazar, B. 1971. *The Excavations in the Old City of Jerusalem near the Temple Mount: Preliminary Report of the Second and Third Seasons, 1969–1970.* Jerusalem.

Mazar, B. 1972. Excavations near the Temple Mount. *Qadmoniot* 19–20: 74–90 (Hebrew).

Mazor, G. and Bar-Nathan, R. 1998. The Bet She'an Excavation Project 1992–1994. *Hadashot Arkheologiyot* 17: 7–36.

Miller, S.G. 1982. Macedonian Tombs: Their Architecture and Architectural Decoration. In: Barr-Sharrer, B. and Borza, E.N., eds. *Symposium Series I: Macedonia and Greece in Late Classical and Early Hellenistic Times* (Studies in the History of Art 10). Washington, D.C: 153–171.

Netzer, E. 1975. Cypros. *Qadmoniot* 30–31: 54–61.

Netzer, E. 1999. *The Palaces of the Hasmoneans and Herod the Great.* Jerusalem (Hebrew).

Netzer, E. 2001. *Hasmonean and Herodian Palaces at Jericho: Final Reports of the 1973–1987 Excavations,* Vol. 1: *Stratigraphy and Architecture.* Jerusalem.

Netzer, E. and Ben-Arieh, S. 1983. Remains of an Opus Reticulatum Building in Jerusalem. *Israel Exploration Journal* 33: 163–175.

Norman, N.J. 1984. The Temple of Athena Alea at Tegea. *American Jornal of Archaeology* 88(2): 169–194.

Nylander, C. 1970. *Ionians in Pasargadae: Studies in Old Persian Architecture* (Boreas: Uppsala Studies in Ancient Mediterranean and Near Eastern Civilizations 1). Uppsala.

Peleg, O. 2003. Decorated Byzantine Chancel Screen Panels and Posts Discovered in the Temple Mount Excavations. In: Mazar, E., ed. *The Temple Mount Excavations in Jerusalem 1968–1978 Directed by Benjamin Mazar, Final Reports,* Vol. 2: *The Byzantine and Early Islamic Periods* (Qedem 43). Jerusalem: 135–152.

Peleg, O. and Rozenberg, S. 2008. Stuccowork in the Herodian Palaces. In: Rozenberg, S., ed. *Hasmonean and Herodian Palaces at Jericho: Final Reports of the 1973–1987 Excavations,* Vol. 4: *The Decoration of Herod's Third Palace at Jericho.* Jerusalem: 475–522.

Peleg-Barkat, O. 2007. *The Herodian Architectural Decoration in Light of the Finds from the Temple Mount Excavation* (Ph.D. dissertation, Hebrew University of Jerusalem). Jerusalem (Hebrew).

Peleg-Barkat, O. 2011. The Royal Stoa of the Herodian Temple Mount: A Proposed Reconstruction. In: Amit, D., Stiebel, G.D. and Peleg-Barkat, O., eds. *New Studies in the Archaeology of Jerusalem and Its Region* 5. Jerusalem: 38–51 (Hebrew).

Peleg-Barkat, O. 2017. *The Temple Mount Excavations in Jerusalem 1968–1978 Directed by Benjamin Mazar, Final Reports,* Vol. 5: *Herodian Architectural Decoration and King Herod's Royal Portico* (Qedem 57). Jerusalem.

Peleg-Barkat, O. and Chachy, R. 2015. The Architectural Decoration of the Mausoleum. In: Porat, R., Chachy, R. and Kalman, Y., eds. *Herodium: Final Reports of the 1972–2010 Excavations Directed by Ehud Netzer,* Vol. 1: *Herod's Tomb Precinct.* Jerusalem: 314–348.

Reich, R. 2003. Stone Vessels and Architectural Fragments. In: Geva, H., ed. *Jewish Quarter Excavations in the Old City of Jerusalem, Final Report,* Vol. 2: *The Finds from Areas A, W and X-2.* Jerusalem: 263–291.

Reich, R. and Billig, Y. 1999. Excavations near the Temple Mount and Robinson's Arch, 1994–1996. *Qadmoniot* 117: 31–40 (Hebrew).

Ritmeyer, K. and Ritmeyer, L. 1989. Reconstructing Herod's Temple Mount in Jerusalem. *Biblical Archaeology Review* 15(6): 23–53.

Rozenberg, S. 2003. Wall Painting Fragments from Area A. In: Geva, H., ed. *Jewish Quarter Excavations in the Old City of Jerusalem, Final Report*, Vol. 2: *The Finds from Areas A, W and X-2*. Jerusalem: 302–327.

Rozenberg, S. 2006. Herodian Stuccowork Ceilings. In: Netzer, E., ed. *The Architecture of Herod, the Great Builder* (Texts and Studies in Ancient Judaism 117). Tübingen: 339–349.

Schick, C. 1879. Neue Funde im Norden von Jerusalem. *Zeitschrift des Deutschen Palästina-Vereins* 2: 102–104.

Schiller, E. 1967. *Cave of Machpela (Hebron)*. Jerusalem (Hebrew).

Segal, A. 1999. The Temples of Baalbek: An Architectural-Historical Survey. *Qadmoniot* 117: 2–16 (Hebrew).

Seyrig, H., Amy, R. and Will, E. 1975. *Le Temple de Bel á Palmyra*, 2 vols. (Bibliothèque Archéologique et Historique 83). Paris.

Stamper, J.W. 2005. *The Architecture of Roman Temples: The Republic to the Middle Empire.* Cambridge.

Stiebel, G.D. 2007. "A Light Unto the Nations": Symbolic Architecture of Ritual Buildings. *Eretz-Israel* 28: 219–234 (Hebrew).

Strong, D. 1963. Some Observations on Early Roman Corinthian. *The Journal of Roman Studies* 53: 73–84.

Sukenik, E.L. 1931. Funerary Tablet of Uzziah, King of Judah. *Palestine Exploration Fund Quarterly Statement* 63(4): 217–221.

Turnheim, Y. 1996. Formation and Transformation of the Entablature in Northern Israel and the Ğōlān in Roman and Byzantine Periods. *Zeitschrift des Deutschen Palästina-Vereins* 112(2): 122–138.

Vincent, L.H., Mackay, E.J.H. and Abel, F.M. 1923. *Hebron, Le Haram el-Khalil: Sepulture des Patriarches.* Paris.

Vincent, L.H. and Steve, P.M.A. 1954. *Archeologie de la Ville—Jérusalem de l'Ancien Testament. Recherches d'archéologie et d'histoire*, Vol. 1. Paris.

Warren, C. and Conder, C.R. 1884. *The Survey of Western Palestine: Jerusalem*. London.

Weill, R. 1920. *La Cité de David: Compte rendu des fouilles exécutée à Jérusalem sur le site de la ville primitive, Campagne de 1913–14*. Paris.

Wilson-Jones, M.W. 2003. *Principles of Roman Architecture*. New Haven and London.

CHAPTER 9

STAMP IMPRESSIONS OF THE *LEGIO X FRETENSIS* FOUND NEAR THE SOUTHEASTERN CORNER OF THE TEMPLE MOUNT

Benjamin J. Dolinka and Filip Vukosavović

The southeastern corner of the Temple Mount excavations yielded a corpus of 53 ceramic tiles that dated to the 2nd and 3rd centuries CE. Fifty were *tegulae* (flat roof tiles) and the remaining three were *imbrices* (semicircular roof tiles).[1]

The three *imbrices* and 36 of the *tegulae* bear stamp impressions of the *Legio X Fretensis* (Roman Tenth Legion). The tiles were recovered from loci attributed to the 2nd and 3rd centuries CE, a date range which is supported by the large quantities of pottery stamped with the *Legio X Fretensis* impression (see Chapter 7). The richest loci were Locus 6071 (ten tiles, as well as three *tubuli*), Locus 6073 (ten tiles), and Locus 6113 (15 tiles). Loci 6083 (three tiles), 6088 (two tiles), 6093 (four tiles) and 6120 (two tiles) contained fewer items. A selection of 15 tiles that bore stamp impressions of the *Legio X Fretensis* is presented below.

PREVIOUS RESEARCH

All *Legio X Fretensis* stamp impressions from the southeastern corner of the Temple Mount excavations conform to the typo-chronology developed by D. Barag (1967), who discerned two main types, Type I, the round stamp, and Type II, the rectangular stamp, with 10 variants. The inscriptions are formulaic; they are written in Latin and consist of three elements:

- The indication that the stamp belongs to a Roman legion (Lat. *Legio*) abbreviated as L, LE or LEG
- A Roman numeral X (Lat. *decem/decimus*) representing the Roman Tenth Legion, occasionally accompanied by a horizontal bar above the letter
- The moniker of the legion itself, *Fretensis* (Lat. for "of the sea straits"), abbreviated as F, FR, FRE or FRT
  The only exception is Type IIa, which contains only the first two elements, LX.

The Type I round stamps bear the inscription LEG•X•F in the central portion of the stamp, accompanied by two insignia of the legion: what has been interpreted as either a warship or a galley, located above the inscription, and a wild boar with its head facing to the right, located below the inscription. The round stamps have been dated to the period between the two Jewish revolts against the Roman Empire, i.e., 70–132 CE.[2] Significantly, no Type I stamp

---

[1] This article is based on the preliminary research, readings, parallels and a draft report on the stamped tiles of the *Legio X Fretensis* from the southeastern corner of the Temple Mount excavations.

[2] But see Beeri and Levi (2019) and Weksler-Bdolah (2020: 47–48) for a possibility that roof tiles were not stamped until the 2nd century CE.

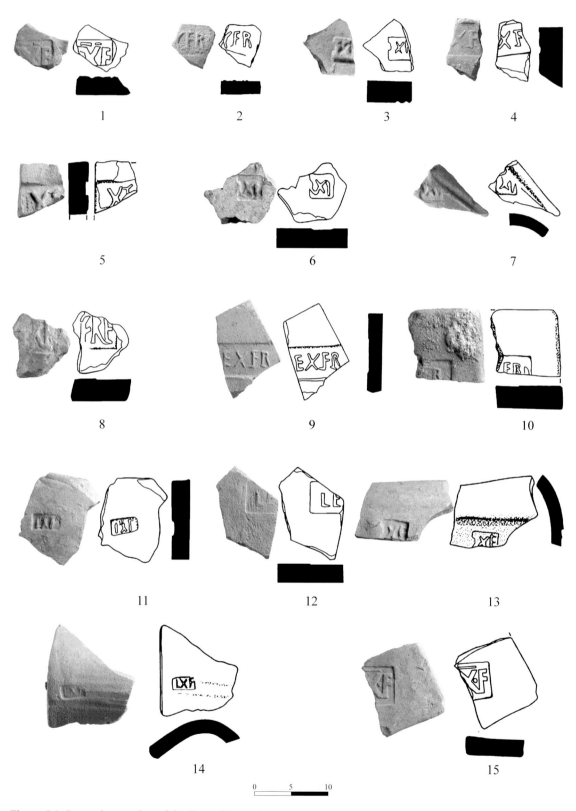

Figure 9.1: Stamp impression of the *Legio Fretensis*.

impressions were recovered from the Hulda Gate, which supports evidence for the limited number of finds for this type in Jerusalem.[3]

The Type II rectangular stamps are ubiquitous, date from the 2nd and 3rd centuries CE, and comprise all the examples of the stamped impressions recovered from the excavation (Fig. 9.1).

Several important excavation reports dealing with the tiles of the *Legio X Fretensis* from the Jewish Quarter (Geva 2003, 2006; Nenner-Soriano 2010, 2014, 2017; Gutfeld and Nenner-Soriano 2012; Weksler-Bdolah 2021), the Temple Mount (Mazar 1969, 1971; Adler 2011) and Gloria Hotel in the Christian Quarter (Dolinka 2021) in the Old City of Jerusalem shed light on the corpus presented here and provide both the comparative evidence and parallel examples. This information can be supplemented by other fieldwork conducted in and around Jerusalem, such as at Herod's Gate (Baruch and Zissu 2006), the Armenian Garden (Tushingham 1985), the City of David (Bliss and Dickie 1898; Behar 2013; Reich 2021), Damascus Gate (Hamilton 1944), Ramat Raḥel (Aharoni 1962; Tepper, Bocher and Koch 2016) and previous excavations on the Ophel (Macalister and Duncan 1926).

CATALOG

While 39 of the 53 tiles recovered from the southeastern corner of the Temple Mount excavation were stamped with impressions of the *Legio X Fretensis*, many were fragmentary, with only one or two letters preserved, thereby making positive identification of a type tenable at best. The following catalog consists of 15 of the best-preserved exemplars. The majority of the corpus was represented by Variants IIb (LXF) and IId (LEXFR), which came predominantly from Loci 6113 (five tiles), 6071 (three tiles) and 6093 (three tiles).

Variant IIb was represented by six exemplars (Catalog Numbers 3, 6–7, 11, 13–14). While one (Catalog Number 11) conforms to Barag Sub-Variant b5, the rest are of interest because they are not included in that typo-chronology. Four examples are of a new Sub-Variant b14 (Catalog Numbers 3, 6–7, 13) identified by Adler (2011: 325, Fig. 17.2: 12–13) from the Temple Mount excavations. The last exemplar is hitherto unidentified Sub-Variant b16 (Catalog Number 14). It differs from the others in its thick upturned letters and elliptical frame and is paralleled from excavations near the Damascus Gate (Hamilton 1944: 11–12, Fig. 23).

Variant IId was also commonplace in the corpus of stamp impressions from the Hulda Gate, five of which are illustrated here (Catalog Numbers 4–5, 9–10, 12). Completing the catalog are two exemplars of Sub-Variant IIe1 (Catalog Numbers 1, 15) and a single exemplar for each of Sub-Variants IIg5 (Catalog Number 2) and IIf6 (Catalog Number 8).

---

[3] Barag initially reported that the Type I round stamp impressions are not well attested. He characterized them as "rare" (Barag 1967: 245–247). None were found during the excavations in the Armenian Garden (Tushingham 1985: 61). Evidence from the Temple Mount indicates that only four out of 250 of the tiles were of Type I (Adler 2011: 323–324, Table 17.1). In the Jewish Quarter, a single exemplar was represented in the assemblages from the Cardo and the Nea Church (Gutfeld and Nenner-Soriano 2012: 122), another one in Areas J and N (Nenner-Soriano 2014), none in Areas H, Q, O-2 (Nenner-Soriano 2017) and a mere two out of 48 were recovered in Areas A and W (Geva 2003: 409). None was discovered at the Western Wall Plaza excavation (Weksler-Bdolah 2021), while two were found in the Gloria Hotel excavation (Dolinka 2021). Thus far, only one exemplar was uncovered in the City of David excavations (Bliss and Dickie 1898; Behar 2013; Reich 2021). Conversely, the Type I stamps are found in far greater numbers from or nearby the Roman legionary kilnworks on the Givat Ram ridge near Binyanei Haʾuma (Arubas and Goldfus 1995; Goldfus and Arubas 2019).

CONCLUSION

The assemblage of stamped tiles from the southeastern corner of the Temple Mount excavation is remarkable, especially given the rather limited size of the excavated area, and the presence of types not found within the Barag typo-chronology, including new Sub-Variant IIb16. The sheer number of tiles uncovered, together with the bricks, pipes, *tubuli* and marble slabs found at the site, seems to suggest the presence of a bathhouse nearby.

REFERENCES

Adler, N. 2011. Impressions of the Tenth Legion from the Temple Mount Excavations. In: Mazar, E., ed. *The Temple Mount Excavations in Jerusalem 1968–1978 Directed by Benjamin Mazar, Final Reports,* Vol. 4: *The Tenth Legion in Aelia Capitolina* (Qedem 52). Jerusalem: 319–332.

Aharoni, Y. 1962. *Excavations at Ramat Rahel, Seasons 1959–1960.* Rome.

Arubas, B. and Goldfus, H. 1995. The Kilnworks of the Tenth Legion Fretensis. In: Humphrey, J.H., ed. *The Roman and Byzantine Near East*, Vol. 1 (JRA Supplementary Series 14). Ann Arbor: 95–107.

Barag, D. 1967. Brick Stamp Impressions of the Legio X Fretensis. *Bonner Jahrbücher* 167: 244–267.

Baruch, Y. and Zissu, B. 2006. Jerusalem, the Old City, Herod's Gate, Final Report. *Hadashot Arkheologiyot* 118.

Be'eri, R. and Levi, D. 2019. Roman Period Workshops at the Crown Plaza Hotel at Giv'at Ram. In: Geva, H., ed., *Ancient Jerusalem Revealed, Archaeological Discoveries, 1998–2018.* Jerusalem: 195–205.

Behar, S. 2013. The Stamped Impressions of the Legio X Fretensis. In: Ben-Ami, D., ed. *Jerusalem: Excavations in the Tyropoeon Valley (Giv'ati Parking Lot),* Vol. 1 (IAA Reports 52). Jerusalem: 305–307.

Bliss, F.J. and Dickie, A.C. 1898. *Excavations at Jerusalem, 1894–1897.* London.

Dolinka, B.J. 2021. Stamped Tiles of *Legio Decimae Fretensis* from Gloria Hotel, Jerusalem. In: Zelinger, Y., Peleg-Barkat, O., Uziel, J. and Gadot, Y., eds. *New Studies in the Archaeology of Jerusalem and Its Region* 14. Jerusalem: 193–197 (Hebrew).

Geva, H. 2003. Stamp Impressions of the Legio X Fretensis. In: Geva, H., ed. *Jewish Quarter Excavations in the Old City of Jerusalem, Conducted by Nahman Avigad, 1969–1982,* Vol. 2: *The Finds from Areas A, W and X-2, Final Report.* Jerusalem: 405–422.

Geva, H. 2006. Stamp Impressions of the Legio X Fretensis. In: Geva, H., ed. *Jewish Quarter Excavations in the Old City of Jerusalem, Conducted by Nahman Avigad, 1969–1982,* Vol. 3: *Area E and Other Studies, Final Report.* Jerusalem: 307–309.

Goldfus, H. and Arubas, B. 2019. The Legio X Fretensis Kilnworks at the Jerusalem International Convention Center. In: Geva, H., ed. *Ancient Jerusalem Revealed, Archaeological Discoveries, 1998–2018.* Jerusalem: 184–194.

Gutfeld, O. and Nenner-Soriano, R. 2012. Stamp Impressions of the Legio X Fretensis from the Cardo and the Nea Church. In: Gutfeld, O., ed. *Jewish Quarter Excavations in the Old City of Jerusalem, Conducted by Nahman Avigad, 1969–1982,* Vol. 5: *The Cardo (Area X) and the Nea Church (Areas D and T), Final Report.* Jerusalem: 378–392.

Hamilton, R.W. 1944. Excavations Against the North Wall of Jerusalem, 1937–8. *QDAP* 10: 1–54.

Macalister, R.A.S. and Duncan, J.C. 1926. *Excavations on the Hill of the Ophel, Jerusalem 1923–1925* (PEFA 4). London.

Mazar, B. 1969. *The Excavations in the Old City of Jerusalem: Preliminary Report of the First Season, 1968.* Jerusalem.

Mazar, B. 1971. *The Excavation in the Old City of Jerusalem near the Temple Mount: Preliminary Report of the Second and Third Seasons, 1969–1970.* Jerusalem.

Nenner-Soriano, R. 2010. Stamp Impressions of the Legio X Fretensis. In: Geva, H., ed. *Jewish Quarter Excavations in the Old City of Jerusalem, Conducted by Nahman Avigad, 1969–1982,* Vol. 4: *The Burnt House of Area B and Other Studies, Final Report.* Jerusalem: 322–323.

Nenner-Soriano, R. 2014. Stamp Impressions of the *Legio X Fretensis* from Areas J and N. In: Geva, H., ed. *Jewish Quarter Excavations in the Old City of Jerusalem, Conducted by Nahman Avigad, 1969–1982*, Vol. 6: *Areas J, N, Z and Other Studies, Final Report*. Jerusalem: 318–327.

Nenner-Soriano, R. 2017. Stamp Impressions of the Legio X Fretensis from Areas Q, H and O-2. In: Geva, H., ed. *Jewish Quarter Excavations in the Old City of Jerusalem, Conducted by Nahman Avigad, 1969–1982*, Vol. 7: *Areas Q, H, O-2 and Other Studies, Final Report*. Jerusalem: 263–268.

Reich, R. 2021. Roof Tiles. In: Reich, R. and Shukron, E., eds. *Excavations in the City of David, Jerusalem (1995–2010): Areas A, J, F, H, D and L, Final Report* (Ancient Jerusalem Publications Series 1). University Park and Jerusalem: 576–577.

Tepper, Y., Bocher, E. and Koch, I. 2016. Roman Army Stamp Impressions and Related Objects. In: Lipschits, O., Gadot, Y. and Freud, L., eds. *Ramat Raḥel III: Final Publication of Yohanan Aharoni's Excavations (1954, 1959–1962)*, Vol. 1 (Monograph Series of the Institute of Archaeology of Tel Aviv University 35). Tel Aviv and Winona Lake: 461–472.

Tushingham, A.D. 1985. *Excavations in Jerusalem 1961–1967*, Vol. 1. Toronto.

Weksler-Bdolah S. 2020. *Aelia Capitolina—Jerusalem in the Roman Period in Light of Archaeological Research* (Mnemosyne Supplements 432). Leiden and Boston.

Weksler-Bdolah, S. 2021. A Military Stamp Impression of the Roman Tenth Legion from the 2017 Excavation Season. In: Weksler-Bdolah, S. and Onn, A., eds. *Jerusalem: Western Wall Plaza Excavations*, Vol. 3: *The Roman and Byzantine Periods: Small Finds from the Roman Refuse Dump and Other Contexts* (IAA Reports 67). Jerusalem: 141–142.

CHAPTER 10

LATE ROMAN DUCK HEAD FOUND NEAR THE SOUTHEASTERN CORNER OF THE TEMPLE MOUNT

Yuval Baruch and Dèbora Sandhaus

During the excavation of the southern corner of the Temple Mount, the fill layer below Floor 6110 yielded a fragment of a pottery duck head (Fig. 10.1). The fragment is made of well-burnished reddish-brown clay and is covered with a dark brown slip. It has puncture marks around the neck for decoration with feathers, and its eyes are marked with a sharp stylus in the form of two concentric circles. The beak is missing. Duck heads are known from the Jerusalem ceramic repertoire and are considered to be part of the local fine wares associated with Legionary activity. Several duck heads were found at the site of the Binyanei Ha'uma Tenth Roman Legionary workshop (Rosenthal-Heginbottom 2005: 277, Fig. 200, a–b; Magness 2005: 80–81, Fig. 13: 1), and in the Armenian Garden (Tushingham 1985: Fig. 25.21; Hershkovitz 1987: 322, Fig. 12.2.10). The duck head most likely was part of a *simpula*—a long handle with a duck's head at its end that was used for ladling wine in ritual services (after Rosenthal-Heginbottom 2005: 277), following metal prototypes. (For other possible uses, such as plastic adornments applied to deep bowls or tall oil lamps, see Magness 2005: 81.)

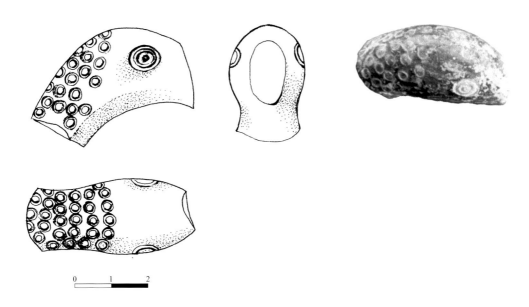

Figure 10.1 Fragment of Late Roman duck head.

REFERENCES

Hershkovitz, M. 1987. The Pottery of the First-Second Centuries CE from Giv'at Ram. *Eretz-Israel* 19 (M. Avi-Yonah Vol.): 314–325 (Hebrew).

Magness, J. 2005. The Roman Legionary Pottery. In: Arubas, B. and Goldfus, H., eds. *Excavations on the Site of the Jerusalem International Convention Center (Binyanei Ha'uma): A Settlement of the Late First to Second Temple Period, the Tenth Legion's Kilnworks, and a Byzantine Monastic Complex; The Pottery and Other Small Finds* (JRA Supplementary Series 60). Jerusalem: 69–194.

Rosenthal-Heginbottom, R. 2005. The 1968 Excavations. In: Arubas, B. and Goldfus, H., eds. *Excavations on the Site of the Jerusalem International Convention Center (Binyanei Ha'uma): A Settlement of the Late First to Second Temple Period, the Tenth Legion's Kilnworks, and a Byzantine Monastic Complex; The Pottery and Other Small Finds* (JRA Supplementary Series 60). Jerusalem: 229–282.

Tushingham, A.D. 1985. *Excavations by K.M. Kenyon in Jerusalem 1961–1967*, Vol. 1: *Excavations in the Armenian Garden of the Western Hill*. Toronto.

CHAPTER 11

COINS AND A FLAN MOLD FROM EXCAVATIONS NEAR THE SOUTHEASTERN CORNER OF THE TEMPLE MOUNT

Donald T. Ariel

COINS

Twenty-four coins were found in the excavations near the southeastern corner of the Temple Mount. Of these, six were unidentifiable.[1]

No coins were contextualized to the earliest Strata V–IV. Numerous coins derived from contexts from the end of the 1st century BCE to 70 CE (Stratum III). The best contextualized coin was No. 4, which dated to 24/25 CE; it was found in a crushed limestone floor (Locus 1114) associated with Wall 663. Nos. 2 and 11 were also from Stratum III—one from the 1st century BCE and the other from the 1st century CE (Locus 6115). In addition, Nos. 1, 6, 8 and 17 were found in the earth layer covering Walls 6090 and 6119. This includes the autonomous coin with a suggested date after 70 CE (90/91 CE?; No. 17). If the date is correct, however, the coin must be intrusive (Fig. 11.1).

Figure 11.1: Possibly autonomous coin.

Three coins (Nos. 3, 13, 15) were found in Late Roman contexts, including the latest coin in the main Second Temple period assemblage dating to year three of the first Jewish Revolt (68/69 CE; No. 15).

As has often been observed, the bronze coins in circulation in Judea at the end of the Second Temple period came almost exclusively from the Jerusalem mint. Confirmation of that observation in the numismatic profile of the present excavations also supports the reading of the uncertain date of No. 17 to 90/91 CE. That observation notwithstanding, the excavations are located near a focal point of activity in the century after the destruction of Jerusalem in 70 CE, based on archaeological finds (see, e.g., Weksler-Bdolah 2020: 23) as well as coins (Ariel 2013: 241). Specifically with regard

---

[1] The coins were cleaned in the laboratories of the Israel Antiquities Authority by Ella Altmark, and were photographed by Clara Amit of the IAA photography studio. The flan mold fragment was first noted in Ariel 2012: 63, but it does not appear on Table 3 there (pp. 65–66).

to No. 17, *minimas*—small imitative Roman provincial coins commonly ascribed to a Caesarean mint (Hamburger 1955)—although most are commonly found in Caesarea, some are also found in Jerusalem. They are found in significant numbers in Jerusalem excavations (close to a quarter of provenanced *minimas* in the Israel national coin collection). That quantity is primarily the result of the great number of excavations in the capital. In fact, only a half dozen *minimas* are dated from the period from 70 to the end of the 2nd century CE. One unpublished specimen that derives from B. Mazar's excavations is the same Tyrian type as No. 17. Another related type was excavated in the 2005–2010 excavations at the Western Wall Plaza (Bijovsky 2019: 181, No. 37).

A FLAN MOLD (FIG. 11.2)

A fragmentary block, part of a limestone mold (Reg. No. 60414) for casting flans, was found in an earthen fill in Stratum II (Locus 6088) that dated to the Late Roman period.

The fragment (referred to here as the Ophel fragment) is 12.9 cm high, 12.6 cm wide and 3.1 cm thick. Only one lateral edge is preserved. One side of the block is flat and smooth, with no chisel marks. The other side, ostensibly the face, has two indications that the block was involved in flan production.

The first indication is three columns of connected darkened circles of roughly 18 mm, evidence of the usage of the block as the flat side of the mold. The darkened circles give a sense of how the drilled side of the mold was organized, and what the strip of unstruck flans produced by the mold looked like when still connected. The longest such strip is preserved for roughly 10.8 cm and has remains of five or more "circles." The other two columns are preserved to smaller extents, one 7.5 cm (three or four "circles") and the other 3.7 cm (two "circles"). Most of these "circles" slightly overlap each other. However, in one case (in the smallest of the three columns), a channel of 4 mm is visible, indicating that although the darkened circles appear to be connected without a channel between them, channels did exist. They are not visible today because of the inexact alignment of the flat and drilled blocks with regard to each other. In other words, the "circles" as they appear are longer than the cavities drilled in the block's partner slab. This is also seen by the fact that the "circles" on this flan mold are not exactly circular. The phenomenon of the blackenings of the flat side being significantly larger than the drilled block has been noted for the three-part molds from Khirbet Rafi'a (Ariel 2012: 56 n. 21).

The second indication of the use of the block for flan production is a group of eight small "nipple drillings," no more than 2 mm in diameter, intended to guide the nipple of the drill bit into the limestone block and create the cavities. The eight small drillings are aligned in two parallel lines, one with five drillings preserved and the second with only three drillings. The "nipple drillings" are likely to have been made using the very top of the drill bit itself (below).

Two things can be learned from these nipple drillings. The first is that there was an intention to repurpose the flat block, with its darkened circles, to become the drilled side of a flan mold, the side with the connected cavities. From the details on the block, no apparent reason why such a change was desired can be suggested.

It may be noted that none of the eight nipple drillings are placed within the darkened circles on the block, perhaps because of fear that the heat that caused the darkening damaged the structure of the limestone at those points. This idea has some cogency. Unlike a darkened area in some unfinished drillings discussed on a possible flan mold from the Jewish Quarter (Ariel 2017: 261), there is no doubt that the darkened circles in this case are the result of use, judging from the irregular shapes of the circles. If the nipple drillings were purposefully distanced from the darkened circles on the block, this may support my opinion that the nipple drillings were prepared after the block functioned as the flat side of a mold.

The second lesson learned from the nipple drillings is that their presence indicates that the plan to convert the block to become the drilled side of a mold was abandoned, probably soon after the nipple drillings were prepared.

Many other Judean flan molds exhibit careless planning in their design (Ariel 2012: 62) and production. An example of a mold where the cavities were drilled but the channels connecting them were not made comes from the Jewish Quarter (Ariel 2014: 268, No. 6; Ariel 2012: 65, No. 3). This is a case where the project was abandoned a step earlier, before the full drillings were begun.

Another, still unpublished, case is known with this same feature. An unpublished fragmentary flan mold from Amaẓya (Permit 6125) attests to at least seven unfinished drillings on a block (Ariel forthcoming). On that fragment, four of the marks appear as on the Ophel fragment, with only the

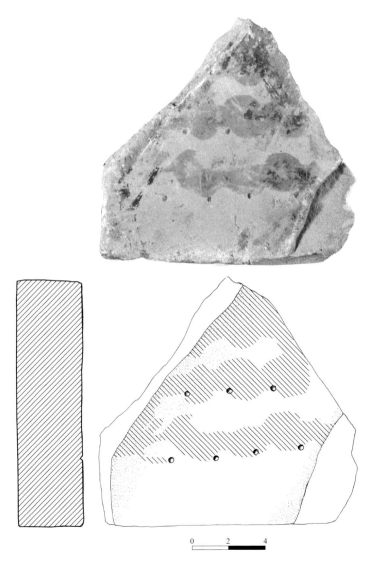

Figure 11.2: A flan mold.

176 DONALD T. ARIEL

nipple drillings visible. For the three others, there are signs of the unfinished beginnings of drilling, with part of the concentric circles of the rest of the drill bit visible. This suggests that all of the nipple drillings, those on the Amaẓya fragment and those on the Ophel fragment, were accomplished with the drill bits that later were intended for the preparation of the cavities themselves.

A difference between the Amaẓya fragment and the Ophel fragment is that in the Amaẓya fragment none of the nipple drillings are aligned in columns, and all are below the "height" of the correctly executed connected drillings located above them on the block. It is possible that the Amaẓya mold nipple drillings are the result of trials to see that the drill and bits work well. The nipple drillings on the Ophel fragment do not appear to be the result of testing the drill and its bits.

Fifty-six molds (or possible molds) are now known from Jerusalem, of which 18 are published. The most recent publications are from the excavations at the Western Wall Plaza, 400 m to the west of the Ophel fragment (Ariel 2021[2]) and from Area D3 at the City of David (Farhi 2022: 92–94).

---

[2] The number of 63 flan molds from Jerusalem, in Ariel 2021: 113, is an error. The total number of flan molds known from the southern Levant at that time was 63.

CATALOG

All the coins are bronze. The coins are arranged chronologically, according to coin types. The photograph of No. 17 is in Fig. 11.1

Cat. No.	Area/Locus (Baskets) (Weight [g], Diam. [mm], Axis)	Obverse	Reverse	Date	Mint	Reference	Notes	IAA No.
		Hasmoneans **Alexander Jannaeus (104–76 BCE)**						
1	B/6122 (60589/1) (0.52, 11)	Illegible	Six-pointed star	80/79 BCE and later	Jerusalem	*TJC*:210, Subgroup L9		96205
		Unclear Hasmonean ruler						
2	A/6115 (60525) (2.61, 15, ↑)	In wreath: [- - -]/ [- - -]	Double cornucopias with pomegranate between horns		Same			96201
3	B/6089 (60387) (1.59, 15)	Illegible	Same		Same			96192
		Roman Prefects in Judea **under Tiberius (14–37 CE)**						
4	A/6112 (60476) (2.12, 17)	In wreath: [- - -]	Palm branch; in fields: [- - -]-[- - -] [L]-IA	Year 11= 24/5 CE	Same	*TJC*:258, No. 329		96199
5	6111 (60466) (2.06, 18)	Same: [- - -]	Same: [- - -]-[- - -] [·]-[·]	17/8–24/5 CE	Same	Cf. *TJC*:257, No. 325		96198
6	B/6095 (60439) (2.04, 17, ↙)	[TIBEPIOY] KAICAP[OC] Lituus	In wreath: LIZ	Year 17= 30/1 CE	Same	*TJC*:258, No. 333		96195
7	B/6118 (60562) (1.53, 13×16, ↑)	[TIBEPIOY] ḳAICAPOÇ Same	In wreath: [LI]H	Year 18= 31/2 CE	Same	*TJC*:258, No. 334		96203

Cat. No.	Area/Locus (Baskets) (Weight [g], Diam. [mm], Axis)	Obverse	Reverse	Date	Mint	Reference	Notes	IAA No.
8	B/6095 (60451) (1.97, 16)	[- - -] Same	In wreath: [- - -]	30/1–31/2 CE	Same	Cf. *TJC*:258, No. 333		96196
Herod Agrippa I (37–44 CE)								
9–10	B/6120 (60569), A/6125 (60585)	BACIΛEWC– AΓPIΠA Canopy	Three ears of grain; in fields: L–ς	Year 6= 41/2 CE	Same	*TJC*:231, No. 120		96204, 96206
Roman Procurators in Judea Under Nero (54–68 CE)								
11	A/6112 (60447) (2.33, 17, ↑)	In wreath: [N] EP/[WNO/C]	[L]Ę KAI[C–APOC] Palm branch	Year 5= 58/9 CE	Same	*TJC*:260, No. 345		96200
12	A/6115 (60543) (1.67, 17)	In wreath: [- - -]	[- - -]A[- - -] Unclear	15/6–58/9 CE	Same	Cf. *TJC*:260, No. 345	Unclear Prefect/ Procurator	96202
First Jewish Revolt (66–70 CE)								
13–14	B/6089 (30375), 6096 (60546)	שנת–שתים Amphora	חרות ציון Vine leaf	Year 2= 67/8 CE	Same	*TJC*:241, No. 196		96191, 96197
15	B/6088 (60415) (2.63, 22, ↑)	שנת–שלוש Amphora with lid	חרות ציון Same	Year 3= 68/9 CE	Same	*TJC*:242, No. 204		96190
16	6091 (60417) (1.52, 15)	[- - -] Amphora?	[- - -] Vine leaf?	67/8–68/9	Same	Cf. *TJC*:241, No. 196		96193
Autonomous								

Cat. No.	Area/Locus (Baskets) (Weight [g], Diam. [mm], Axis)	Obverse	Reverse	Date	Mint	Reference	Notes	IAA No.
17*	B/6095 (60439) (1.31, 14, ↓)	Bust of Tyche r.	ΜΗΤΡΟΠΟΛ[ΕΩΣ] Palm tree; in fields: ϛΙ–Σ̣	Year 216?= 90/1? CE	Tyre?	Cf. *RPC* II:295, No. 2082; cf. *BMC Phoen.*:265, No. 338; cf. Hamburger 1955:123, No. 1	*minima?*	96194
18	- (60333) (1.36, 15, 0, ↑)	[- -] Draped bust r.	[- -] Victory advancing l., holding palm branch and wreath	364–375 CE		Cf. *LRBC* II:87, No. 2071		96207

REFERENCES

Ariel, D.T. 2012. Judean Perspectives of Ancient Mints and Minting Technology. *Israel Numismatic Research* 7: 43–80.

Ariel, D.T. 2013. The Coins. In: Ben-Ami, D., ed. *Jerusalem: Excavations in the Tyropoeon Valley (Givʿati Parking Lot)*, Vol. 1 (IAA Reports 52). Jerusalem: 237–264.

Ariel, D.T. 2014. A Group of Flan-Mold Fragments from Area N. In: Geva, H., ed. *Jewish Quarter Excavations in the Old City of Jerusalem, Conducted by Nahman Avigad, 1969–1982*, Vol. 6: *Architecture and Stratigraphy: Areas J, N, Z and Other Studies, Final Report.* Jerusalem: 266–271.

Ariel, D.T. 2017. A Possible Flan-Mold Fragment from Area H. In: Geva, H., ed. *Jewish Quarter Excavations in the Old City of Jerusalem, Conducted by Nahman Avigad, 1969–1982*, Vol. 7: *Areas Q, H, O-2 and Other Studies, Final Report.* Jerusalem: 260–262.

Ariel, D.T. 2021. A Flan Mold. In: Weksler-Bdolah, S. and Onn, A., eds. *Jerusalem: Western Wall Plaza Excavations*, Vol. 3: *The Roman and Byzantine Periods: Small Finds from the Roman Refuse Dump and Other Contexts* (IAA Reports 67). Jerusalem: 113–114.

Ariel, D.T. Forthcoming. A Possibly Unfinished Flan Mold. Appendix in G. Bijovsky. Coins from Amaẓya (Permits A-5973 and A-6125).

Bijovsky, G. 2019. Coins of the Hellenistic to Byzantine Periods. In: Weksler-Bdolah, S. and Onn, A., eds. *Jerusalem: Western Wall Plaza Excavations*, Vol. 1: *The Roman and Byzantine Remains: Architecture and Stratigraphy* (IAA Reports 63). Jerusalem: 165–193.

BMC Phoen.: Hill, G.F. 1910. *Catalogue of the Greek Coins of Phoenicia.* London.

Farhi, Y. 2022. The Numismatic Finds. In: Gadot, Y., ed. *The Landfill of Early Roman Jerusalem: The 2013–2014 Excavations in Area D3* (Ancient Jerusalem Publications Series 2). University Park and Jerusalem: 69–95.

Hamburger, H. 1955. Minute Coins from Caesarea. *ʿAtiqot* 1:115–138.

LRBC II: Carson, R.A.G. and Kent, J.P.C. 1965. Part II: Bronze Roman Imperial Coinage of the Later Empire, A.D. 346–498. In: *Late Roman Bronze Coinage, A.D. 324–498.* London: 41–114.

RPC II: Burnett, A.M., Amandry, M. and Carradice, I. 1999. *Roman Provincial Coinage II: From Vespasian to Domitian (AD 69–96).* London.

TJC: Meshorer, Y. 2001. *A Treasury of Jewish Coins: From the Persian Period to Bar Kokhba.* Jerusalem and Nyack, N.Y.

Weksler-Bdolah, S. 2020. *Aelia Capitolina—Jerusalem in the Roman Period in Light of Archaeological Research* (Mnemosyne Supplements 432). Leiden and Boston.

CHAPTER 12

EARLY ROMAN PERIOD STONE VESSELS AND OBJECTS FOUND NEAR THE SOUTHEASTERN CORNER OF THE TEMPLE MOUNT

Ronny Reich

Fragments of stone vessels and implements dating to the Early Roman period (late Second Temple period, 1st century BCE to 1st century CE) are ubiquitous in Jerusalem and were discovered near the southeastern corner of the Temple Mount as well. Most of the stone vessel fragments dealt with in this chapter originate from an Early Roman context. A few fragments of this period were found in strata of later periods.

The particular use and role of stone vessels in Jerusalem of the 1st century BCE and the 1st century CE are established facts and have been discussed extensively in the past (Gibson 1983; Cahill 1992; Deines 1993; Amit *et al.* 2000; Magen 2002; Reich 2003, and others).

The stone fragments in the following descriptions and figures are arranged by type of stone. The vessels made of chalk are divided by technique of manufacture, and further divided by morphological types.

MATERIAL

The majority of the fragments found are objects made of soft local chalk (i.e., limestone of biogenic origin), which was the softest and hence the easiest material to carve and manipulate for household objects (Figs. 12.1: 1–7; 12.2: 1–4; 12.3: 1, 9, 14).

Other types of stone that were in use in Jerusalem were local hard and medium-hard limestone (Figs. 12.3: 3–5), basalt (Figs. 12.3: 6–8, 10–13) and bituminous limestone (Fig. 12.3: 2). Although the present report presents its objects without any particular attention to precise statistical expressions, it is clear that vessels and objects made of chalk prevail (29 out of 44 objects; 66%), while only a few objects are of harder limestone and basalt.

Basalt was most likely imported from the Galilee and Golan Heights. The hardness, durability and rough texture of objects made of this type of stone made basalt a favored material for the production of mortars and millstones.

HAND-CARVED VESSELS AND OBJECTS

Although it seems that the mechanical method of carving objects on a lathe was very popular (as can be learned from the vast numbers of these, and the findings in the two known workshops, Amit, Seligman and Zilberbod 2000; Magen 2002: 5–17), it seems that the hand carving of certain types continued in large quantities. Were the hand-carved objects still in use parallel to those that were lathe-turned because they were cheaper? Probably not. It is interesting to note that the vast majority of hand-carved stone vessels were mugs. Religious tradition may stand behind the continuous use of the hand-carved objects. A definite proof is still called for. The modes of production have been listed by several scholars, as well as reconstruction suggestions to the production of these vessels (e.g., Cahil 1992: 218–225; Magen 2002: 118–131; Gibson 2016: 59–62).

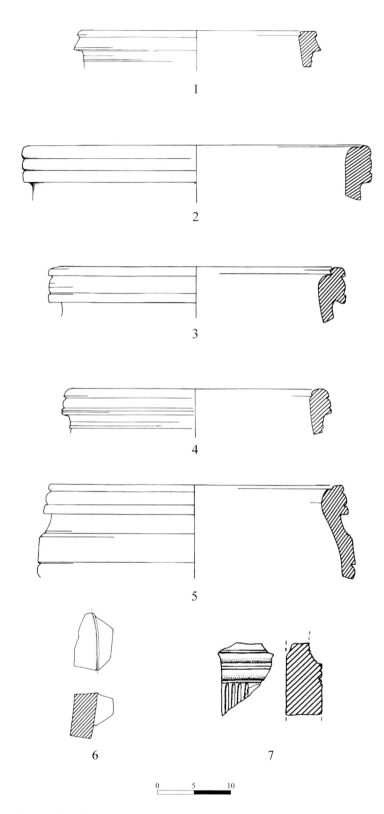

Figure 12.1: Stone objects.

Figure 12.1 Stone objects

No.	Reg. no.	Locus	Type	Description/Remarks	Fig.
1	60295/2	6070	*Qalal*	Lathe turned, rim, triangular profile, weathered inside	12.1: 1
2	60381	6086	*Qalal*	Lathe turned, rim, triple-band profile	12.1: 2
3	60410/1	6092	*Qalal*	Lathe turned, rim, triple-band profile, weathered inside	12.1: 3
4	60606/10	6128	*Qalal*	Lathe turned, rim, triple-band profile, weathered inside	12.1: 4
5	60502/1	6095	*Qalal*	Lathe turned, rim, triple-band profile, weathered inside	12.1: 5
6	60421/3	6091	*Qalal*	Lathe turned, body fragment with hand-carved trapezoidal ledge handle	12.1: 6
7	60392/1	6089	*Qalal*	Lathe turned, body fragment with vertical grooves	12.1: 7

Mugs

Although this type of vessel, among those carved by hand, is the most frequently discovered in excavations (Reich 2007), the present excavation produced a single item (Fig. 12.2: 13). They usually appear in three sizes: small, medium and large. The present fragment belongs to the medium-sized type.

According to the study carried out by Reich, these vessels were not used as measuring devices for volumes, therefore the term "measuring cup" attributed to them in the past should be replaced by the neutral term "mug." On the other hand, a new explanation for their use is still a desideratum (Reich 2007, 2016).

Basins

The second most frequent type of vessels carved by hand found in Jerusalem are basins with flat bottoms, straight but out-flaring sides, and plain rims. They generally have two flat, narrow ledge handles and come in two versions; one is circular and the other is elongated with two long straight sides and two semicircular short sides. It is not always possible to ascertain whether a circular fragment belongs to one of these two subtypes. Unfortunately, not many of them survived to an extent that permits measuring their exact volume. It is my belief that these vessels, or at least the circular ones, are the type of vessel called in the rabbinic literature מידה (*Middah*) (e.g., Mishnah *Terumoth* 1:7; *Shevi'it* 8:3) and was the actual vessel to measure volumes. Of the basins presented here (Fig. 12.2: 10–12), the latter seems to be of the circular type.

LATHE-TURNED VESSELS AND OBJECTS

The elaborate technique of producing stone vessels on a lathe has been described thoroughly as well as reconstruction suggestions to their production by several scholars (Magen 2002: 118–131; Gibson 2016: 59–62; Cahil 1992: 218–225).

The present finds cannot contribute any new insights to this matter, nor can they contribute much to the precise use of each type. It is hoped that the full study of the workshop discovered on Mount Scopus (Amit, Seligman and Zilberbod 2000) will take us further in the knowledge of this industry, which seems quite peculiar to this period (the 1st century CE, and perhaps slightly earlier).

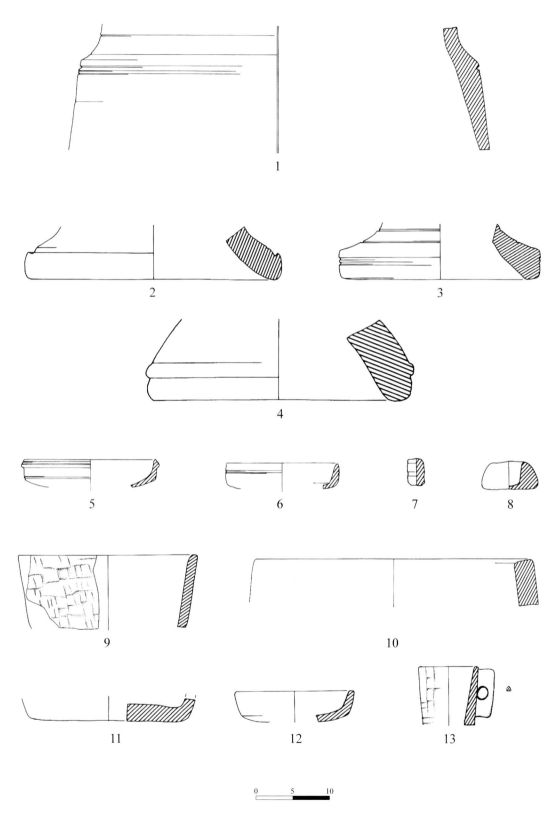

Figure 12.2: Stone objects.

Figure 12.2 Stone objects

No.	Reg. no.	Locus	Type	Description/Remarks	Fig.
1	60568/2	6120	*Qalal*	Lathe turned, body fragment	12.2: 1
2	60311/5	6073	*Qalal*	Lathe turned, conical base	12.2: 2
3	60573	6122	*Qalal*	Lathe turned, conical base	12.2: 3
4	60392/2	6089	*Qalal*	Lathe turned, conical base	12.2: 4
5	60394/8	6091	Bowl	Lathe turned, rim	12.2: 5
6	60394/9	6091	Bowl	Lathe turned, rim	12.2: 6
7	60475/10	6112	Miniature core		12.2: 7
8	60394/1	6091	Core	Core of large vessel, with depression on one side	12.2: 8
9	60591/1	6093	Basin	Hand carved, simple rim and thin body side	12.2: 9
10	60394/4	6091	Basin	Hand carved, simple rim and thick body side, weathered inside	12.2: 10
11	60384/1	6089	Basin	Hand carved, flat base of circular vessel, thin body side	12.2: 11
12	60561	6118	Bowl	Made of sandstone containing mica crystals, smoothed, severely charred inside	12.2: 12
13	60394/5	6091	Mug	Hand carved, base of medium size vessel ("measuring cup")	12.2: 13

KRATERS (*QALALS*)

The most frequent type of vessel presented here (Figs. 12.1: 1–7; 12.2: 1–4) are fragments of the largest type of known stone vessels, which might have been those named *Qalal* in the Second Temple period (Magen 1988: 53, 98, 156, n.14; 2002), as mentioned in the rabbinic literature (e.g., Mishnah *Parah* 3:3). It is the largest type of lathe-turned vessel known. Of these, quite a large number of complete, reconstructed items are already known from near the Temple Mount (Magen 2002: 30–82) and the Upper City (Avigad 1983: Figs. 125, 195, 196). It was used to hold sin-offering water (Mishnah *Parah* 3:3; 10:3; Tosefta *Parah* 9 (10), 5) or simply water (John 2:6).

These vessels differ particularly through the outer profile of their rims: Type 1 has a rim with a tripartite ridge on the outer side of the rim (Figs. 12.1: 2–5); and Type 2 is a rim with a triangular cross-section (Fig. 12.1: 1). Although these small numbers are statistically insignificant, they resemble other assemblages in which the triangular rim is less represented than the other. In the Jewish Quarter (Reich 2003: Pl. 8.2), there are seven items of Type 1 and three items of Type 2. In the City of David, Cahill (1992: Figs. 18–19) published nine items of Type 1 and five items of Type 2.

The difference in shape might point to the products of two different workshops, one more prolific than the other. On the other hand, this might be the outcome of the fact that Type 1 was produced sometime before Type 2 was introduced. In Area H of the Upper City of Jerusalem, which slightly predates the houses destroyed by the Romans, the breakdown is six items for Type 1 and one item for Type 2 (Geva 2006: Pl. 9.2). From the Burnt House (Area B), on the other hand, only the complete items were published (Geva 2010: Pl. 5.7). Here, one item of Type 1 and two items of Type 2 are present.

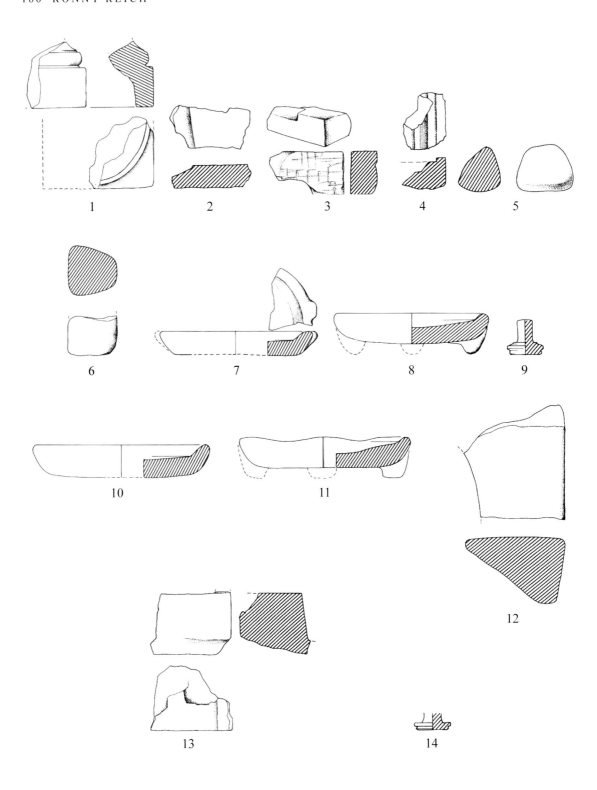

Figure 12.3: Stone objects.

Figure 12.3 Stone objects

No.	Reg. no.	Locus	Type	Description/Remarks	Fig.
1	60308/2	-	Table leg	Bottom of table leg resembling attic base. Square plinth worked with comb chisel. From *torus* upward lathe turned. Lower part hollowed with flat chisel	12.3: 1
2	60373	6089	Table top	Fragment of flat plate from black bituminous limestone	12.3: 2
3	60463/2	6109	Table top	Fragment of flat table top made of chalk, smoothed on top and side, flat chiseled below	12.3: 3
4	60533/1	6093	Table top	Fragment with raised edge (ca. 5 mm), made for inlay of stone veneer	12.3: 4
5	60538	6095	Table top	Heap of fragments of bituminous limestone, of a table top that disintegrated, some fragments have flat sides	12.3: 5
6	60513	6114	Pestle	Basalt, trapezoid cross-section	12.3: 6
7	60468/10	6113	Tripod mortar	Basalt, simple rim with small knob	12.3: 7
8	60518	6093	Tripod mortar	Basalt, one leg extant	12.3: 8
9	60509	6093	Stopper/lid	Chalk, lathe turned	12.3: 9
10	60508	6093	Tripod mortar	Basalt	12.3: 10
11	60474	6093	Tripod mortar	Basalt, one leg extant	12.3: 11
12	60408	6092	Hand millstone	Basalt, triangular fragment of upper stone	12.3: 12
13	60409	6093	Raw material	Gray/yellow mottled stone with traces of showing veneer sheets	12.3: 13
14	60514	6114	Stopper/lid	Lathe turned	12.3: 14

The rather large number of fragments of *qalal*s (11) against the lower number of other lathe-turned objects, or the mugs (a single object) might support the notion that these large kraters were related to storage of water mixed with the ashes of the red heifer, a possibility due to the proximity of the present excavation to the Temple Mount. This also coincides with the large number of these large objects retrieved in the B. Mazar and M. Ben-Dov excavations near the Temple Mount, published by Magen (2002: 80–90).

CHALICES AND BOWLS

Another type of lathe-turned vessel includes bowls and chalices (Figs. 12.2: 5, 6, 8). The waste of this lathe-turning industry is the stone cores extracted from the stone block to create a circular cavity (Fig. 12.2: 8). This is attested to by the considerably large quantities in the underground workshops discovered in Hizma (Magen 2002) and on Mount Scopus (Amit *et al.* 2000). However, they are occasionally found in areas of domestic architecture. Currently, no satisfactory explanation has been given for their presence outside of the stone vessel manufacturing workshop.

Two other lathe-turned objects which are found occasionally are objects which may be defined as lids or stoppers (Fig. 12.3: 9; 12.3: 14).

BITUMINOUS LIMESTONE

A black-colored chalk known as *Hajar Nabi Musa* is quarried in specific locations in the Judean Desert. Nabi Musa is one such area (Snyder, Hagbi and Szanton 2022: 106; Spiro *et al.* 1983). It is a limestone with a high concentration of organic substances which give it its black color and its distinct smell when wet (like kerosene or asphalt). The stone is soft and easy to cut, although too soft to be polished. Its softness occasionally causes it to flake.

Only a limited repertoire of objects has been made from it, especially table tops and trays. In construction work, it was used mainly to produce the black tiles in the *opus sectile* floors. This is the case of the fragment of table tops presented here (Fig. 12.3: 2).

BASALT

Basalt is the hardest type of stone in use in Jerusalem. Due to its specific virtues such as hardness, rough texture, black color (easy to spot a splinter in ground flour), and resistance to water, heat and mechanical wear, it was the ideal material for the production of mortars, mills and grinders of any kind through the ages. On the other hand, the durability of this type of stone means that while it is quite frequently found in private houses (e.g., Avigad 1983: Figs. 123, 209: 4), the objects did not break easily and therefore we rarely find them in city dumps. Several basalt objects (Figs. 12.3: 6–8, 10–12) are presented here.

HARD LIMESTONE

Occasionally grinding stones and millstones were produced from hard limestone rather than basalt, like the object shown here (Fig. 12.3: 5). This is a material considerably inferior to basalt for these purposes.

SUMMARY

What role or activity did the stone objects presented here play? As the assembly is similar in repertoire and in relative abundance between the various types (except perhaps the small number of mugs) to assemblages from the Upper City and the City of David areas, they seem to have belonged to private houses that existed here before their inhabitants were moved to other parts of the city (Reich 2014), before King Herod began his large construction operations to extend the perimeter of the Temple Mount.

REFERENCES

Amit, D., Seligman, J. and Zilberbod, I. 2000. Stone Vessel Workshops of the Second Temple Period East of Jerusalem. In: Geva, H., ed. *Ancient Jerusalem Revealed, Reprinted and Expanded Edition*. Jerusalem: 353–358.

Avigad, N. 1983. *Discovering Jerusalem*. Nashville.

Cahill, J.M. 1992. Chalk Vessel Assemblages of the Persian/Hellenistic and Early Roman Periods. In: De Groot, A. and Ariel, D.T., eds. *Excavations at the City of David 1978–1985, Directed by Yigal Shiloh*, Vol. 3: *Stratigraphical, Environmental, and Other Reports* (Qedem 33). Jerusalem: 190–274.

Deines, R. 1993. *Jüdische Steingefaesse und pharisaeische Froemmigkeit* (Wissenschaftliche Untersuchungen zum Neuen Testament 2, Reihe 52). Tübingen.

Geva, H. 2006. Stone Artifacts. In: Geva, H., ed. *Jewish Quarter Excavations in the Old City of Jerusalem, Conducted by Nahman Avigad, 1969–1982*, Vol. 3: *Area E and Other Studies, Final Report*. Jerusalem: 218–238.

Geva, H. 2010. Stone Artifacts. In: Geva, H., ed. *Jewish Quarter Excavations in the Old City of Jerusalem, Conducted by Nahman Avigad, 1969–1982*, Vol. 4: *The Burnt House of Area B and Other Studies, Final Report*. Jerusalem: 154–212.

Gibson, S. 1983 The Stone Vessel Industry at Hizma. *Israel Exploration Journal* 33: 176–188.

Gibson, S. 2016. Soft Limestone Vessels. In: Syon, D., ed. *Gamla III, The Shemarya Gutmann Excavations 1976–1989, Finds and Studies*. Jerusalem: 49–81.

Hovers, E. 1996. The Groundstone Industry. In: Ariel, D.T. and De Groot, A., eds. *Excavations at the City of David 1978–1985, Directed by Yigal Shiloh*, Vol. 4 (Qedem 35). Jerusalem: 171–203.

Magen, Y. 1988. *The Stone Vessel Industry in Jerusalem During the Second Temple Period*. Tel Aviv (Hebrew).

Magen, Y. 2002. *The Stone Vessel Industry in the Second Temple Period, Excavations at Hizma and the Jerusalem Temple Mount*. Jerusalem.

Reich, R. 2003. Stone Vessels, Weights and Architectural Fragments. In: Geva, H., ed. *Jewish Quarter Excavations in the Old City of Jerusalem*, Vol. 2: *The Finds from Areas A, W and X-2, Final Report*. Jerusalem: 263–291.

Reich, R. 2007. Stone Mugs from Masada. In: Stiebel, G.D. and Magness, J., eds. *Masada VIII: The Yigael Yadin Excavations 1963–1965, Final Reports*. Jerusalem: 195–206.

Reich, R. 2014. A Note on the Population Size of Jerusalem in the Second Temple Period. *Revue Biblique* 121(2): 298–305.

Reich, R. 2015. *Stone Scale-Weights of the Late Second Temple Period*. Jerusalem.

Reich, R. 2016. Stone Vessels and Implements of the Late Second Temple Period. In: Lipschitz, O., Gadot, Y. and Freund, L., eds. *Ramat Rahel III: Final Publication of Yohanan Aharoni's Excavations (1954, 1959–1962), Vol. 2*. (Monograph Series of the Institute of Archaeology of Tel Aviv University 35). Tel Aviv and Winona Lake: 624–631.

Shiloh, Y. 1984. *Excavations at the City of David*, Vol. 1: *1978–1982: Interim Report of the First Five Seasons* (Qedem 19). Jerusalem.

Snyder, F., Hagbi, M. and Szanton, N. 2022. Putting It All on the Table: From King Herod's Imitation of Roman Furnishings to the Bitumen Tables of the Elites of Jerusalem's Lower City. In: Gadot, Y., Zelinger, Y., Peleg-Barkat, O. and Shalev, Y., eds. *New Studies in the Archaeology of Jerusalem and Its Region* 15: 105*–125*.

Spiro, B., Welte, D.H., Rullokotter, J. and Schaefer, R.G. 1983. Asphalts, Oils and Bituminous Rocks from the Dead Sea Area: A Geochemical Correlation Study. *American Association of Petroleum Geologists Bulletin* 67: 1163–1175.

CHAPTER 13

FAUNAL REMAINS FOUND NEAR THE SOUTHEASTERN CORNER OF THE TEMPLE MOUNT

Abra Spiciarich and Lidar Sapir-Hen

A small assemblage of faunal remains was retrieved near the southeastern corner of the Temple Mount. A total of 132 faunal remains (NISP) were retrieved from eight loci dating to the Iron IIC, Early Roman, Late Roman and Byzantine periods (Table 13.1).

MATERIAL AND METHODS

The faunal remains were recovered by hand. The bones were washed in tap water in the laboratory to remove dust and adhering soil before analysis, and then dried indoors. Bone identification was done with reference to the comparative collection stored at the Steinhardt Museum of Natural History and at the Zooarchaeology Laboratory of the Institute of Archaeology, Tel Aviv University.

All epiphyses as well as diaphysis (shaft fragments) were studied and recorded. Completeness of identified fragments was coded according to five element's zones in the case of long bones (proximal epiphysis, proximal shaft, shaft, distal shaft and distal epiphysis). Other bones were recorded as the completeness percentages (e.g., 50% of a complete astragali).

Bone remains were identified to bone element and to the lowest possible taxonomic level. Separation of sheep (*Ovis aries*) from goats (*Capra hircus*) was based on morphological criteria of selected bones (following Zeder and Lapham 2010). Sheep and goat skeletal elements that could not be identified to species were combined in a sheep/goat (caprines) category. Bones that could only be identified to species were assigned to a body size group—either large mammal (cattle/donkey size) or medium mammal (caprines/pig size). All fully fused epiphyses were measured, following Von den Driesch (1976).

Recorded elements were inspected for various macroscopic bone surface modifications that are related to taphonomic processes, i.e., the processes that the remains went through from the time they were prepared for consumption to the time they were discarded. Recorded modifications include: butchery marks (based on Binford's [1984] cut marks typology); signs of animal activity (i.e., carnivore punctures, scoring, and digestion [Lyman 1994]); stage of weathering (Behrensmeyer 1978), which could indicate whether the bones were buried quickly or left exposed to the elements; and signs of burning, which were recorded based on a visible change in bone calcification. The percentage of element completeness (MNE/NISP) was assessed in order to understand the degree of bone fragmentation.

Abundance and demographic quantifications were conducted primarily on the Early Roman period assemblage, as it is the only one large enough to allow such analysis. The relative abundance of different taxa was quantified using NISP (number of identified specimens) and MNI (minimum number of individuals) (Grayson 1984; Lyman 2008). MNI's values are based on MNE (minimum number of elements) and calculated per locus. MAU (minimum animal units) was calculated in order to compare the frequency of skeletal elements within the assemblages. MAU was calculated

Table 13.1: Loci province information with Number of Identified Specimens (NISP) per loci

Loci	Period	Area	NISP
6074	Byzantine	A	6
6091	Early Roman	A	53
6096	Early Roman	A	31
6115	Early Roman	A	4
6122	Early Roman	B	1
6126	Early Roman	B	8
6130	Early Roman	B	9
6136	Iron IIC	A	20

on the basis of MNE, and calculation followed Lyman (1994: 104) and Klein and Cruz-Uribe (1983). Age at death of culled species was analyzed in order to study the exploitation aim of the main livestock, on the basis of epiphyseal fusion stages (Zeder 2006 for caprines). The sample size of measurable bones did not allow estimation of sex profiles.

RESULTS

We present below a detailed analysis of the assemblage modifying factors, followed by analysis of major animal economy trends for the Early Roman periods. The small sample size of the Iron IIC, Late Roman and Byzantine faunal assemblages did not allow for a full assessment. All measurements are provided in Appendix 1.

SPECIES REPRESENTED IN THE ASSEMBLAGE

A total of 183 bone fragments were examined and 132 (NISP) bones were identified to species. Of the identified specimens, 20 (NISP) derived from Iron IIC context, 105 (NISP) from Early Roman context, one (NISP) from Late Roman context and six (NISP) from Byzantine context.

Domestic livestock (i.e., sheep, goat, cattle, donkey, and pig) are the most dominant species in all assemblages and they represent 85% of the Iron IIC assemblage, 94% of the Early Roman assemblage, 100% of the Late Roman assemblage and 83% of the Byzantine assemblage (Table 13.2). Wild species, specifically mountain gazelle (*Gazella gazella*) are only present in the Early Roman assemblages.

The most dominant livestock animals in the Iron IIC assemblage are the caprines (sheep and goat) with 55% of the assemblage; no elements allowed identification to sheep or goat. The second most common species in the Iron IIC assemblage is cattle (*Bos taurus*, combined with large mammal body size group) with 30% of the assemblage. This assemblage also included a variety of avian species, such as goose (*Anser anser*, N: 1) and domestic chicken (*Gallus gallus*, N: 1).

The Early Roman assemblage is dominated by domestic livestock but also contains a wide variety of other species. The most prominent livestock animals in the Early Roman assemblage are caprines with 90% of the assemblage, with a sheep to goat ratio of 2:1. The second most common species in this assemblage is cattle with 4% of the assemblage. This assemblage also included other species, namely gazelle (N: 3) and avian species, such as duck (*Anas platyrhynchos*, N: 1) and domestic chicken (N: 3) (Table 13.2). The Late Roman assemblage comprised solely of a single tooth of

Table 13.2: Number of Identified Specimen (NISP), Frequency of Species (NISP%), and Minimum Number of Individuals by Period

Species	Scientific Name	Common Name	Iron IIC			Early Roman			Late Roman			Byzantine		
			NISP	MNI	NISP%	NISP	MNI	NISP%	NISP	MNI	NISP%	NISP	MNI	NISP%
Domesticated Ungulates	*Capra hircus*	Goat				4	2	4%						
	Ovis aries	Sheep				8	2	8%						
	Caprine size	Sheep or Goat	11	1	55%	82	2	78%				3	1	50%
	Bos taurus	Cow	4	1	20%									
	A Size	Large Mammal	2	1	10%	4	1	4%						
	Sus scrofa	Domestic Pig										2	1	33%
	Equus asinus	Donkey							1	1	100%			
Wild Mammals	*Gazella gazella*	Gazelle				3	1	3%						
Aves	*Anas platyrhynchos*	Mallard Duck				1	1	1%						
	Anser Anser	Domestic Goose	1	1	5%									
	Gallus gallus	Chicken	1	1	5%	3	1	3%				1	1	17%
	Medium Aves	Medium Bird	1	1	5%									
Total			20	6	100%	105	10	100%	1	1	100%	6	3	100%

donkey (*Equus asinus*). The Byzantine assemblage is the only assemblage with evidence of pig (*Sus scrofa*, N: 2), and it also included caprines (N: 3), and domestic chicken (N: 1) (Table 13.2).

TAPHONOMIC ANALYSIS

Weathering

Overall, weathering moderately affected the bones, with 69% of the total assemblage falling between Stages 0–2 of Brehensmeyer's scale (1978: 157) (69%; Table 13.3), suggesting that the majority of bones were covered soon after disposal (three years or less). However, little more than a quarter of the bones were exposed for longer than 3 years (Stages 3–6; Brehensmeyer 1978; see Table 13.3).

Burning

Only a single identifiable fragment showed evidence of charring: a left caprine radius from the Early Roman assemblage (#51; L.6115).

Butchery and Cut Marks

A small number of bones showed evidence of butchering. A total of 15 cut marks (11% of the total assemblage) were recorded (Table 13.4). The majority of cut marks (93%) were recorded on caprines and cattle bones. The frequency of both primary butchery (i.e., skinning and dismemberment; 80%) and secondary butchery (i.e., filleting; 20%) present in the Early Roman assemblages suggests full

Table 13.3: Total of Fragments Recorded in Each Weathering Stage (Stages According to Behrenmeyer 1978)

Weathering	Stage 0		Stage 1		Stage 2		Stage 3		Stage 4		Stage 5		Assemblage Total
	N	%	N	%	N	%	N	%	N	%	N	%	
Iron IIC			3	15%	5	25%	1	5%	4	20%	7	35%	20
Early Roman	21	20%	40	38%	19	18%	17	16%	7	7%	1	1%	105
Late Roman							1	100%					1
Byzantine	1	17%	3	50%	2	33%							6
Total	*22*	*17%*	*46*	*32%*	*26*	*20%*	*19*	*14%*	*11*	*8%*	*8*	*6%*	*132*

Table 13.4: Cut Marks (NISP) for Mammals and Birds Based on the Typology of Binford (1984) and Laroulandie (2001)

Period	Species	Dismembering	Filleting	Skinning	Total	Assemblage%
Byzantine	Caprine		1		1	17%
Early Roman	Cattle	1			1	11%
	Caprine	7	2	1	10	
	Ovis	1			1	
Iron IIC	Caprine	1			1	10%
	Goose		1		1	
Total		*10*	*4*	*1*	*15*	*11%*

processing of carcasses took place on-site. Butchery evidence was also present in the Iron IIC and Byzantine assemblages. In the Iron IIC assemblage, there is evidence of dismembering a caprine and filleting a goose and in the Byzantine assemblage there was only evidence of filleting (Table 13.4).

Fragmentation

Examination of the fragmentation of caprine elements (calculated as MNE/NISP) was only conducted on the Early Roman assemblage. The fragmentation suggests that the Early Roman assemblage was moderately fractured with the majority of elements 50–100% complete, leading to the assumption that the assemblage was in primary deposition (Fig. 13.1).

DOMESTIC LIVESTOCK EXPLOITATION

Age Profiles

The sample sizes of cattle and caprine bones in most of the assemblages were inadequate for quantitative demographic analysis. While the sample sizes of caprine bones are very small, a hypothetical model for herding strategy based on epiphyseal fusion was conducted for caprines in the Early Roman assemblage. Aging of caprines by epiphyseal fusion for the Early Roman period suggests that 79% of the ageable assemblage was young (Table 13.5), and that caprines were culled

Table 13.5: Aging Based on Epiphyseal Fusion of Elements for Early Roman Caprines (NISP based)

Element	Portion	Fused age range*	Total	Fused	Unfused	unfused%
Radius	Proximal	0–6 months	1	1	0	100%
Humerus	Distal	6–12 months	1	0	1	100%
Pelvis		6–12 months	1	0	1	100%
Scapula		6–12 months	0	0	0	0%
Phalanx II		12–18 months	4	2	2	50%
Phalanx I		12–18 months	2	2	0	0%
Tibia	Distal	18–30 months	1	0	1	100%
Metacarpal	Distal	18–30 months	3	0	3	100%
Metatarsal	Distal	18–30 months	0	0	0	0%
Calcaneus		30–48 Months	6	0	6	100%
Femur	Proximal	30-48 Months	0	0	0	0%
Femur	Distal	30-48 Months	1	0	1	100%
Ulna	Proximal	30-48 Months	0	0	0	0%
Radius	Distal	30-48 Months	1	0	1	100%
Tibia	Proximal	30-48 Months	3	0	3	100%
Humerus	Proximal	48+ months	0	0	0	0%
Total			*24*	*5*	*19*	*79%*

* Fusion aging based on Zeder (2006)

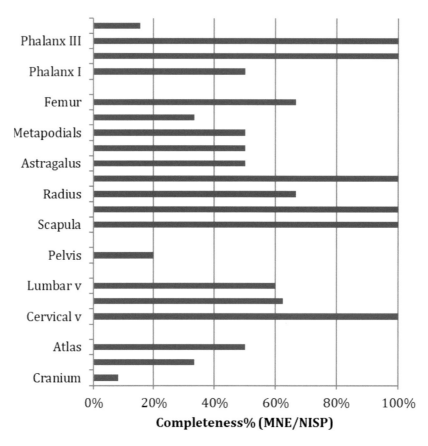

Figure 13.1. Early Roman completeness% (MNE/NISP) of caprine elements.

around 1–1.5 years of age, with none surviving passed 1–1.5 years of age. This pattern fits the model of herd exploitation geared toward meat consumption (Payne 1973).

Body Part Frequencies

Detailed analysis of anatomical frequencies was limited to caprines in the Early Roman assemblage. In this assemblage, elements from the entire body were present with an equal representation, based on MAU% of crania, mandibles, pelvis, humerus, radius, ulna, tibia, femur and tarsals, specifically astragalii and calcanei (Table 13.6). Anatomical elements of caprines represented in the Iron IIC assemblage included crania, mandibles, ribs and long bones, such as radius, ulna and femur. In the Byzantine assemblage, the only caprine elements present were ribs and scapulae.

Cattle elements present in the Iron IIC included a humerus and mandibular teeth, specifically the dP4, M1, M2 and M3. In the Early Roman assemblage, cattle elements included cervical vertebrae, ribs, a tibia and a femur (Table 13.6). Pig, which was only present in the Byzantine assemblage, was represented by a maxillary third molar tooth and a tibia. Overall, throughout every assemblage, the most common anatomical elements were cranial remains and long bones.

CONCLUSIONS

Our results suggest that the faunal remains from sections A.A, Area 1B and Area C/B of the sections along the southern Temple Mount wall were dominated by domestic livestock in the Iron IIC, Early

Table 13.6: Skeletal Elements Frequencies of Caprine and Cattle for the Early Roman Assemblage

Early Roman Body Part Frequencies	Caprines				Cattle			
Element	NISP	MNE	MAUi	MAU%	NISP	MNE	MAUi	MAU%
Cranium	12	1	1.00	100%	0	0	0.00	0%
Mandible	6	2	1.00	100%	0	0	0.00	0%
Atlas	2	1	1.00	100%	0	0	0.00	0%
Axis	0	0	0.00	0%	0	0	0.00	0%
Cervical v	2	2	0.40	40%	1	1	0.20	40%
Thoracic v	8	5	0.38	38%	0	0	0.00	0%
Lumbar v	5	3	0.43	43%	0	0	0.00	0%
Sacrum	0	0	0.00	0%	0	0	0.00	0%
Pelvis	5	1	1.00	100%	0	0	0.00	0%
Sternum	0	0	0.00	0%	0	0	0.00	0%
Scapula	1	1	0.50	50%	0	0	0.00	0%
Humerus	2	2	1.00	100%	0	0	0.00	0%
Radius	4	2	1.00	100%	0	0	0.00	0%
Ulna	2	2	1.00	100%	0	0	0.00	0%
Astragalus	4	2	1.00	100%	0	0	0.00	0%
Calcaneus	4	2	1.00	100%	0	0	0.00	0%
Metapodials	4	2	0.50	50%	0	0	0.00	0%
Tibia	6	2	1.00	100%	1	1	0.50	100%
Femur	3	2	1.00	100%	1	1	0.50	100%
Patella	0	0	0.00	0%	0	0	0.00	0%
Phalanx I	4	2	0.25	25%	0	0	0.00	0%
Phalanx II	1	1	0.13	13%	0	0	0.00	0%
Phalanx III	1	1	0.13	13%	0	0	0.00	0%
Rib	16	5	0.38	38%	1	1	0.08	15%

Roman, Late Roman and Byzantine periods, as is typical of south Levantine faunal assemblages of these periods (Horwitz and Dahan 1996). Dominance of domestic livestock is also characteristic of Jerusalem in these periods (Horwitz and Tchernov 1989; Lernau 1995; Horwitz 1996; Horwitz and Tchernov 1996; Bar-Oz *et al.* 2007; Bar-Oz and Raban-Gerstel 2013; Reich *et al.* 2015; Tamar and Bar-Oz 2015; Sapir-Hen *et al.* 2016; Spiciarich *et al.* 2017).

Demographic analysis of the Early Roman assemblage suggests that caprines, which were represented mainly by sheep, were nearly anatomically complete and were culled young for their meat or as sacrifices. Sheep were preferred over goats for cultic use, as they carried a symbolic connotation (Sapir-Hen 2019). In comparison to other Early Roman assemblages, this assemblage follows already-known patterns present in the Early Roman period of Jerusalem (Horwitz 1996; Bar-Oz et al. 2007; Reich 2015; and Spiciarich et al. 2017).

APPENDIX

MEASUREMENTS

Element	Period	Loci	Species	Measurements (in mm)			
Phalanx 1				Glpe	Bp	Sd	Bd
67	Early Roman	6091	Ovis/Sheep	39.71	12.16	9.75	11.97
Phalanx 2				Glpe	Bp	Sd	Bd
116	Early Roman	6096	*Ovis*/Sheep	23.73	11.33	8.9	9.16
Astralagus				GL1	GLm	D1	Bd
95	Early Roman	6091	*Capra*/ Goat	31.14	29.49	15.98	20.28
111	Early Roman	6096	*Capra*/Goat	33.4	31.8	18.19	21.22
Humerus				GL	Bp	SC	Bd
1	Iron IIC	6136	*Anser*/Goose			10.95	23.69
40	IAIIC/ER	6126	*Gallus*/Chicken	75.44	19.79	7.18	15.36
Ulna				Dip	Bp	SC	Did
107	Early Roman	6096	*Anas*/Duck	10.33	7.63	3.64	
108	Early Roman	6096	*Gallus*/Chicken			3.55	8.8

REFERENCES

Bar-Oz, G., Bouchnik, R., Weiss, E., Weissbrod, L., Bar-Yosef Mayer, D.E. and Reich, R. 2007. Holy Garbage: A Quantitative Study of the City-Dump of Early Roman Jerusalem. *Levant* 39(1): 1–12.

Bar-Oz, G. and Raban-Gerstel, N. 2013. The Faunal Remains. In: Ben-Ami, D., ed. *Jerusalem: Excavations in the Tyropoeon Valley (Givʿati Parking Lot),* Vol. 1 (IAA Reports 52). Jerusalem: 349–380.

Behrensmeyer, A.K. 1978. Taphonomic and Ecological Information from Bone-Weathering. *Paleobiology* 4: 150–162.

Binford, L.R. 1984. Butchering, Sharing, and the Archaeological Record. *Journal of Anthropological Archaeology* 3: 235–257.

von den Driesch, A. 1976. *A Guide to the Measurement of Animal Bones from Archaeological Sites* (Peabody Museum Bulletin 1). Cambridge, MA.

Grayson, D.K. 1984. *Quantitative Zooarchaeology: Topics in the Analysis of Archaeological Faunas.* New York.

Horwitz, L.K. 1996. Faunal Remains from Areas A, B, D, H, and K. In: Ariel, D. and De Groot, A., eds. *Excavations at the City of David 1978–1985, Directed by Yigal Shiloh*, Vol. 4 (Qedem 35). Jerusalem: 302–337.

Horwitz, L.K. and Dahan, E. 1996. Animal Husbandry Practices During the Historic Periods. In: Ben-Tor, A., Avissar, M. and Portugali, Y., eds. *Yoqneʿam I: The Late Periods* (Qedem 3). Jerusalem: 245–255.

Horwitz, L.K. and Tchernov, E. 1989. Subsistence Patterns in Ancient Jerusalem: A Study of Animal Remains. In: Mazar, E. and Mazar. B., eds. *Excavations in the South of the Temple Mount: The Ophel of Biblical Jerusalem* (Qedem 29). Jerusalem: 144–154.

Horwitz, L.K. and Tchernov, E. 1996. Bird Remains from Areas A, D, H, and K. In: Ariel, D. and De Groot, A., eds. *Excavations at the City of David 1978–1985, Directed by Yigal Shiloh*, Vol. 4 (Qedem 35). Jerusalem: 298–301.

Klein, R.G. and Cruz-Uribe, K. 1983. The Computation of Ungulate Age (Mortality) Profiles from Dental Crown Heights. *Paleobiology* 9(1): 70–78.

Lernau, H. 1995. The Faunal Remains of Cave I. In: Eshel, I. and Prag, K., eds. *Excavations in Jerusalem 1961–1967: The Iron Age Cave Deposits on the South-East Hill and Isolated Burials and Cemeteries Elsewhere.* Oxford: 201–208.

Lyman, R.L. 1994. *Vertebrate Taphonomy.* Cambridge.

Lyman, R.L. 2008. *Quantitative Paleozoology.* Cambridge.

Payne, S. 1973. Kill-off Patterns in Sheep and Goats: The Mandibles from Asvan Kale. *Anatolian Studies* 23: 281–304.

Reich, R., Billig, Y., Hakker-Orion, D. and Lernau, O. 2015. Faunal Remains from the 1994–1996 Excavation at the Temple Mount. *ʿAtiqot* 80: 19–34.

Sapir-Hen, L. 2019. Late Bronze and Iron Age Livestock of the Southern Levant: Their Economic and Symbolic Roles. *Tel Aviv* 46(2): 227–236.

Sapir-Hen, L., Gadot, Y. and Finkelstein, I. 2016. Animal Economy in a Temple City and Its Countryside: Iron Age Jerusalem as a Case Study. *BASOR* 375: 103–118.

Spiciarich, A., Gadot, Y. and Sapir-Hen, L. 2017. The Faunal Evidence from Early Roman Jerusalem: The People behind the Garbage. *Tel Aviv* 44(1): 98–117.

Tamar, K. and Bar-Oz, G. 2015. Zooarchaeological Analysis of the Faunal Remains. In: Mazar, E., ed. *The Summit of the City of David Excavations 2005–2008.* Jerusalem: 497–510.

Zeder, M.A. 2006. Reconciling Rates of Long Bone Fusion and Tooth Eruption Wear in Sheep (Ovis) and Goat (Capra). In: Ruscillo, D., ed. *Recent Advances in Aging and Sexing Animal Bones.* Oxford: 87–118.

Zeder, M.A. and Lapham, H. 2010. Assessing the Reliability of Criteria Used to Identify Post-Cranial Bones in Sheep, *Ovis*, and Goats, *Capra. Journal of Archaeological Science* 37: 2887–2905.

CHAPTER 14

BONE IMPLEMENTS FOUND NEAR THE SOUTHEASTERN CORNER OF THE TEMPLE MOUNT

Ronny Reich

TYPE

RODS

The four items presented below are small, circular and thin bone rods found in excavations near the southeastern corner of the Temple Mount (Table 14.1). As these items were only ca. 3–5 mm thick, they were probably too thin to serve as spoon handles and the like. It is more likely that they were used as cosmetic rods to apply pigments, as *styli* to write on waxed plates (*pinakes*), or as pins. Similar objects from the Early Roman period (late Second Temple period) were found in private houses in the Upper City of Jerusalem (Geva 2006: 268–269, Nos. B12–B18; Nenner-Soriano 2010: 286, Nos. B10–B14; 2014: 307, Nos. B5–B7).

RECTANGULAR PLAQUE

The bone plaque, which was perfectly worked into a small rectangle, was probably made for inlaying in furniture or in a platter. Currently, examples are thin stone inlays in the *opus sectile* technique (e.g., Avigad 1983: 116, Fig. 110), but bone plaques could be used as well.

Table 14.1: Bone Implements

Locus	Reg. no.	Type	Measurements (mm)	Material	Remarks
6093	60511	Circular elongated rod	Length: 64 Diam. 4–5	Bone	One edge rounded, the other broken
6089	30386	Circular elongated rod	Length: 57 Diam. 3.5–4	Bone	Broken on both edges
6093	60522	Circular elongated rod	Length: 23 Diam. 5	Bone	One side rounded, with three parallel grooves around; other side broken; black (charred)
6130	60621	Circular elongated rod	Length: 91 Diam. 2.5–3	Bone	Long thin round rod, broken on both edges
6071	60343	Rectangular plaque	47 × 13 × 4	Bone	One flat side smoothed. Seems to be complete item (not manufacturer's waste). Yellowish color

DATE

All bone items came from earthen fills containing Roman pottery. Three of them also contain impressed tiles of the Tenth Roman Legion.

Although the various bone items do not have clear stratigraphical contexts, it seems that by their morphological characteristics, they should all be attributed to the Early Roman period. Four of these items are cosmetic rods and are thus household objects; they must therefore be attributed to the residential locale that existed in this area before the start of Herod's megaproject to extend the boundaries of the Temple Mount (Reich and Baruch 2017).

REFERENCES

Avigad, N. 1983. *Discovering Jerusalem.* Nashville.

Geva, H. 2006. Bone Artifacts. In: Geva, H., ed. *Jewish Quarter Excavations in the Old City of Jerusalem, Conducted by Nahman Avigad, 1969–1982*, Vol. 3: *Area E and Other Studies, Final Report.* Jerusalem: 266–271.

Nenner-Soriano, R. 2010. Bone Artifacts. In: Geva, H., ed. *Jewish Quarter Excavations in the Old City of Jerusalem, Conducted by Nahman Avigad, 1969–1982*, Vol. 4: *The Burnt House of Area B and Other Studies, Final Report.* Jerusalem: 284–287.

Nenner-Soriano, R. 2014. Bone Artifacts from Areas J and N. In: Geva, H., ed. *Jewish Quarter Excavations in the Old City of Jerusalem, Conducted by Nahman Avigad, 1969–1982*, Vol. 6: *The Finds from Areas J, N, Z and Other Studies, Final Report.* Jerusalem: 306–310.

Reich, R. and Baruch, Y. 2017. On Expansion of the Temple Mount in the Late Second Temple Period. *Cathedra* 164: 7–24 (Hebrew).

CHAPTER 15

SUMMARY OF EXCAVATIONS NEAR THE SOUTHEASTERN CORNER OF THE TEMPLE MOUNT

Yuval Baruch and Ronny Reich

The excavations focused on two defined areas close to the southeastern corner of the Temple Mount complex and adjacent to the Southern Wall itself. In Area A, a south-to-north section was excavated. In this section, remains from the late Iron II to the end of the Byzantine period were discovered. Five squares were excavated in Area B; remains related to the Temple Mount structure and its destruction were documented. Above these squares, there were two archaeological strata that dated to the Late Roman and Byzantine periods. Some of the remains in this area were removed by the archaeologists who preceded us. Our excavations are a direct continuation of their work.

Iron Age: The earliest remains unearthed in this defined area are part of a system of three installations hewn and plastered in the lower part of the bedrock. A surface made of stones and limestone was constructed between the installations, with an assemblage of broken pottery vessels dating to the 7th–6th centuries BCE.

Pre-Herodian Period: The excavation revealed that the Iron Age installations were still used in the 2nd and 1st centuries BCE. The numerous sherds in the installations indicated that they may have been used as garbage pits. Moreover, additional rock-hewn installations were unearthed, including the lower part of a stepped installation, which was identified as a *miqweh*.

The Herodian Period: The main building component in the area was the Southern Wall of the Temple Mount, built at the end of the 1st century BCE. We uncovered remains of a construction system that, in conjunction with the Southern Wall, supported a sloping ramp. In Area A, three hewn compartments (Compartments 10–13) that supported the ramp were cleared of debris and documented, while in Area B, two additional compartments were unearthed. The excavation showed that at least three additional built-up compartments were constructed to the east of the rock-hewn compartment system. In contrast to the hewn compartments that were open to the south, the built compartments were sealed and filled to capacity with earth. The earth fill contained finds that date construction, or at least the earth fill, to the first half of the 1st century CE. This suggests that the foundations of the wall that abuts the southeastern corner of the Temple Mount complex (documented in Warren's excavations) are in fact part of the same engineering system that carried the ramp ascending toward the Triple Gate in the east.

In Area A additional remains, which we believe are a related hewn compartment system, were exposed, including the construction of an ashlar wall built parallel to the row of hewn compartments. It is possible that this wall was either a boundary fence, a built path or an alley that passed parallel to the compartments. Walls of crushed limestone approach the wall from the south and north.

Several dozen fallen Herodian stones were discovered in Area B, including some unique construction items and even decorated stone fragments. These stones are clear evidence of the destruction of the compound in 70 CE. In contrast to the situation at the foot of Robinson's Arch, or at the foot of the Triple Gate, no pile-up or rich stone complex was discovered. Some of the stones that avalanched here may have been taken later for construction; however, the reason may also be that the wall of the Herodian compound in this area was less damaged than elsewhere.

Late Roman Period: A large number of pottery sherds, square ceramic pipes and shingles with imprints of the Tenth Roman Legion were discovered within a thick fill of earth and gravel material in Area B and in earth fills documented in Section A of Area A. These findings indicate activity in the Late Roman period in this area. The square clay pipes, typically used in bathhouses, indicate that there was a drainage ditch nearby. Analysis of the earth fills in Area B indicates that these layers of dirt and gravel were poured here deliberately to level the surface. The fillings were piled on top of the Southern Wall and on the lower courses of the wall that abuts the southeastern corner of the Temple Mount complex (which integrates with the Byzantine Ophel Wall). It is therefore suggested that this ashlar wall, characteristic of fortifications, is from the Late Roman period.

The Late Byzantine Period: In Area A, a northern, outer wall was excavated. It was part of a multi-room architectural complex that was revealed in its entirety in the archaeological excavations that preceded ours. Our contribution to the investigation of this complex came in an excavation of the foundation trench of the wall. A wall that supported a passage that ran parallel to the entire complex was excavated north of the wall and parallel to it. The finds that emerged enabled us to date the wall, and possibly also the entire architectural complex, to the end of the Byzantine period (6th–7th centuries CE). In Area B, a leveled earth and gravel fill had been poured onto the fortification wall that abuts the southeastern corner of the compound. As we noted earlier in the context of the Late Roman period, this wall, which we assume was built as early as the Late Roman period, was incorporated into the construction of the Byzantine Ophel Wall. The leveled surface in Area B indicates that the area on the inner side of the wall, in the section that abuts the southeastern corner of the Temple Mount complex—that is, the one within the city—was a vacant, open lot.

INDEX OF LOCI AND WALLS

Wall	Area	Square	Upper level	Lower level	Period	Description	Fig.
651	B	A1			Late Roman (upper part of wall)	Abuts southeast corner of Temple Mount; integrated with Ophel Wall system	
652 a-b	A				Byzantine	Preserved to 7.8 m. Northern face plastered with rough grayish plaster. Comprised of lower part, Wall 652b and upper part, Wall 652a	4.5 4.6 4.7
653	A		713.92	713.53	Iron II B–C	Eastern wall of plastered installation	4.5 4.6
654	A				Iron II B–C	Northeast-southwest wall	4.5 4.6
656		1B	708.87	706.06	Early Roman	Western face of wall. Part of Compartment system C18/C19	4.16
657	A				Post-installation (Early Roman?)	Partition wall inside installation (1.1 m long)	4.5
659	A		717.71	715.78	Byzantine	Terrace wall built on top of earthen fills. Seems contemporary to Byzantine structure and may have served as wall at side of alley running to north of structure	4.7
660	A		717.85	715.90	Byzantine	Terrace wall built on top of earthen fills.	4.7
661	B	1B/1C	707.98	706.10	Early Roman	Common wall for C17 for C18	4.16 4.20 4.22
662	B/ C					Wall between C1/B1	4.16 4.19 4.20 4.21
663	A		714.80/97	714.12	Early Roman	Ashlar wall constructed parallel to wall south of Temple Mount	4.5 4.6 4.7 4.8 4.11

Wall	Area	Square	Upper level	Lower level	Period	Description	Fig.
664			714.60	714.27	Early Roman–Late Roman	Wall, only 4 stones of which are preserved (one course)	4.7
668	B	1C	708.89	707.97	Early Roman	Rock-cut Wall C16/C17. Upper part hewn as flat surface; circular cup-mark cut on top	4.16 4.20 4.22

Locus	Area	Square	Upper level	Lower level	Dating	Description	Fig
6027	A					Top soil	4.7
6070	B	Eastern area A1 A2 B1	Surface level	709.60	End of Byzantine	Surface level represents accumulated earth of Mazar and Ben-Dov's excavation (which preceded ours)	4.16 4.17
6071	B	2B	709.60	708.97	Late Roman (?)–Byzantine	Fills under Locus 6070. Gravelly material, many bricks	4.16 4.17
6072	B	Ophel Wall			Late Roman (?)–Byzantine	Upper layer of fills	4.16
6073	B	1A	Surface level	708.85	Up to Byzantine	Fills under surface level. Gravelly material. Leans diagonally to north, covering lower courses of Ophel Wall. Excavation halted	4.16
6074	A		714.18	Approx. 713.50	Late Byzantine	Stone foundation of Byzantine structure	4.6
6077	A		714.42–46	714.23	Early Roman	Water channel, plastered on east. Constructed of middle-sized, roughly hewn stones, glued together by grayish clay	4.5 4.6 4.14 4.15
6078	A		715.25	714.88	End of 1st and continues to 3rd century CE	West-east drainage channel built over earthen fills. Channel is unplastered, hence seems to be drainage channel. Same as Locus 6077	4.6 4.7 4.14 4.15
6079	A		713.67	713.53	Middle of 1st–beginning of 2nd century CE	Fills within the plastered installation, Unit A. Same as Locus 6086	4.5

Locus	Area	Square	Upper level	Lower level	Dating	Description	Fig
6080	A		714.80	714.77	Early Roman	Limestone floor underneath Locus 6112 on top of thick limestone foundation. Covers Wall 663	4.5 4.6 4.7
6081	A		713.55	713.25/23	Iron II B–C	Small-scale surface of stones leveled (floor?). Adjacent to wall of Installation 653	4.5 4.6
6082			714.45		Early Roman	C11, covered by thin layer of plaster. Pit 6137 and drainage channel cut into floor	
6083	B	1B	709.02	708.50	Late Roman	Earthen fills beneath 6070. Relatively tightly packed fill containing many stone grits—material has appearance of stone-cutting waste and earth	4.16 4.17
6084	A				Deleted		
6085			714.46	713.23/10	Late Roman	Earth from our predecessors' excavations	
6086	A		713.73	713.00	Middle of 1st–beginning of 2nd century CE	Fills within plastered installation, Unit A.	4.5 4.9 4.10
6087					Modern (?)	Modern terrace that seems to have been erected by previous excavators on top of Byzantine earthen fills	
6088	B	1C	708.92	708.20	Late Roman	Earthen fills beneath 6070. Includes many middle-sized ashlar stones, among them fragments of decorated Herodian building stones. Fill also includes many potsherds and bricks stamped by Roman Tenth Legion	4.16
6089	B	1B	708.50	708.10/ 79.00	Late Roman	Fills of dark brown earth underneath fill of rubble (6083), containing thin layers of limestone. Fill covers Wall 656 (C18/ C19) and contains Roman potsherds and bricks bearing Roman Tenth Legion stamps	4.16 4.17

Locus	Area	Square	Upper level	Lower level	Dating	Description	Fig
6091	A		713.07	712.26	Early Roman	Earthen fills in plastered installation, Unit A	4.5
6092	B	1B	708.56	708.02	Late Roman	Earthen fills and rubble underneath Locus 6089. Fill contains stones fallen from Western Wall as well as fragments of hewn stones, some of them decorated	4.17
6093	B	1C	709.00	708.89	Late Roman	Earthen fills and rubble underneath Locus 6088. Only upper part excavated	4.16
6095	B	1B	708.10/ 707.90	706.30	End of 1st century BCE–70 CE	Earthen fills under Locus 6089. Fill is yellowish-brown	4.16
6096	A		713.00	Never completed	Early Roman	Excavation of remaining side of Wall 658. Earthen fill on top of installation's floor; Fill includes large amount of restorable pottery, Unit A.	4.5
6097			717.90	717.20	Mixed	Accumulation of earth from previous excavations. While cleaning this earth, continuation of a wall belonging to Byzantine structure uncovered	
6100			717.20	715.90	Byzantine	Level of gravel beneath surface and above level of Byzantine structure's "alley" between that structure and Wall 660	
6101	A		715.90	715.40/35	Byzantine	Plaster layer (*rolka*) sealing foundation trench 6104	4.7
6102	A		717.75	716.55	Byzantine	A fill of earth and small stones between Walls 659 and 660	4.7 4.6
6103	A		717.70	716.70	Byzantine	Earthen fill adjacent to northern face of Wall 659 in its upper part	4.7
6104	Area		716.85	715.60	Byzantine	Foundation trench of northern wall of Byzantine structure/complex, filled with earth and small stones	4.7

Locus	Area	Square	Upper level	Lower level	Dating	Description	Fig
6105	A		715.60	714.20	Byzantine	Foundation trench continuation underneath Locus 6104. This part of trench filled with grayish dirt, almost devoid of gravel	4.7
6107	A		712.28	712.25	Late 1st–early 2nd century CE	Layer of dirt on bottom of plastered installation	4.6
6108	A		716.70	716.00	Middle of 1st–2nd century CE	Earthen fills north of Wall/ terrace 659, accumulated in lower part of wall's northern face and is later than its construction	4.7
6108a	A						4.6
6109	A		716.00	715.60/40	Late Roman	Hard-trodden floor	4.6 4.7
6110	A		715.40/60	715.40	End of 1st– beginning of 2nd century CE	Floor of crushed limestone on top of foundation floor 6111 of Early Roman period	4.6 4.7 4.8
6111	A		715.35	715.15	1st–2nd century CE	Foundation of Floor 6110, light gray colored with few stones	4.6 4.7 4.8
6112	A		715.15/45	714.80	Early Roman	Layer of earth on top of Floor 6080 and below Locus 6111 including potsherds and procurators' coin	4.7 4.6
6113	B	2B	708.97	Never completed	Late Roman	Fills of earth and gravel containing building stones and fragments of stones fallen from Southern Wall	4.16 4.17
6114	A		715.11	715.03	Early Roman	Floor (?)	4.6 4.7
6115			715.03	713.86	ER (unclean fill)	Thick soil level discerned in this accumulation	4.6
6117	B	1C	708.89	708.34	Late Roman	Earth and stone fills with brick and *tubuli* fragments	4.16
6118	B	1B	70630	705.65	End of 1st century BCE–70 CE	Earthen fills below Locus 6095	4.16 4.22
6120		B/C	707.60	709.05	Early Roman	Earthen fills	

Locus	Area	Square	Upper level	Lower level	Dating	Description	Fig
6121		1B/2B	Surface level	708.97	Mixed. Mainly Late Roman	Continuation of dismantling of balk's western half	
6122		C/B	Not recorded	Not recorded	Early Roman	Thin layer of crushed limestone	
6123	A		716.25	715.50	Byzantine	Earthen fills	4.7
6124	A		715.04	Unfinished	Mixed material from earlier excavation seasons up to Late Roman	Rock-cut space located under Compartment C10	4.5 4.6
6125	A		714.03	713.86	Late Hellenistic (Hasmonean)	Remains of plastered installation (*Miqweh*)	4.5 4.6 4.12
6126	B	1B	705.65	705.50	Late 1st century BCE–70 CE	Packed earthen fills	4.16 4.22
6127	B	1B/1C	706.50	Unfinished	Early Roman	Rock-cut foundation trench (very narrow--0.2 m), part of cutting of Southern Wall itself	4.16 4.23
6128	A		713.28	712.33	Early Roman–Late Hellenistic	Rock-cut installation plastered with gray hydraulic plaster	4.5 4.6 4.13
6130	B	1B	705.50	705.50	Late Iron Age	Packed earthen fills	4.16
6131	A		714.88	714.76	End of 1st–3rd century CE	Foundation of packed dirt (light brown) with few small stones. Drainage channel laid above it	4.5 4.7
6132	A		714.65/70	714.60	Early Roman–Late Roman	Layer of gray gravel under foundation floor (6131) of drainage channel (6078)	4.7
6133	A		714.60	714.27	Early Roman–Late Roman	Stones arranged in straight level (dry construction) under Layer 6132. In northern part, these stones are laid directly on floor of grayish plaster, and in part this serves as foundation for drainage channel (6077)	

Locus	Area	Square	Upper level	Lower level	Dating	Description	Fig
6134	A		713.23/10	Unexcavated	Iron Age	Rock-cutting in area between plastered installations, filled with small-to middle-sized field stones, serving as foundation to floor of crushed limestone (6136), fragmentarily preserved	4.6
6135	A		714.12	Unexcavated	Early Roman/ Late Hellenistic?	Floor of grayish plaster on top of rock's continuation to south of Installation (*Miqweh*) 6125. Wall 663 is built on top of this floor. Probably related to 6077	
6136	A	C	713.25/23	713.23/10	Iron II B–C	Floor of crushed beige-colored limestone, underneath layer of stones (6081). Laid down on top of foundation of small stones (6034). On top of floor, broken pottery and large amount of charcoal. Probably floor of a room	4.5 4.7 4.9
6137	A		714.63	714.49	Unclear	Flat surface of rock (C11) which contains water cistern (unexcavated)	4.5
6138						Deleted	
6139	A		712.20	Unexcavated	Late Hellenistic (?)	Installation covered with dark grayish plaster	4.5 4.6 4.7
6140	A		714.76	714.21	Early Roman	Fill of stones (probably foundation) below floor of crushed limestone (6080) and part of Wall 663	
6141	A	C			Iron II b–c?	Rock-cut	4.5 4.7
6143	A				Unclear	Rock-cut channel	

PART IIb:
THE WESTERN WALL FOUNDATIONS: STATIGRAPHY AND ARCHITECTURE

CHAPTER 16

THE WESTERN WALL FOUNDATIONS: STRATIGRAPHY AND ARCHITECTURE

Moran Hagbi and Joe Uziel

From December 2013 to March 2014, an excavation was conducted along the foundations of the Western Wall (OIG 172297/131452; NIG 222297/631452), as part of the tourist development of the City of David and Davidson Archaeological Park. The excavation covered an expanse of 2 × 10 m along the southern portion of the Western Wall Foundations, reaching the southwestern corner of the Temple Mount (Hagbi and Uziel 2015, 2016).[1] The area is located on the west bank of the Tyropoeon Valley, 6 m below the 1st century CE street that ran alongside the Temple Mount (Figs. 16.1, 16.2).

HISTORY OF RESEARCH

WILSON AND WARREN EXCAVATIONS (1864–1865, 1867)

The area of the southwestern corner of the Temple Mount was surveyed by Wilson and Warren (1871), who excavated a series of east-to-west shafts across the Tyropoeon Valley. One of the shafts, No. 22, was dug at the southwestern corner of the Temple Mount (Warren 1884: Pl. XXVIII).[2] Later, Warren renewed the excavations (1876), where he revealed the Early Roman Street and continued through an artificial breach in the pavement into the main drainage channel located beneath the street. Warren accessed the Western Wall foundations through two tunnels excavated from within the drainage channel, the first 10 m from the southwestern corner, and another 9 m to its north. Both Wilson and Warren dated the complex, Robinson's Arch, the street and the drainage channel to the Herodian period (Wilson and Warren 1871).

B. MAZAR AND BEN-DOV EXCAVATIONS (1968–1978)

B. Mazar and Ben-Dov conducted extensive excavations along the Southern and Western Walls of the Temple Mount (Mazar 1969, 1971, 1975; Ben-Dov 1985), where they revealed substantial remains dating to the Early Roman period, including the Herodian streets to the south and west of the

---

[1] The excavations (License A6971, A7016 and A7320) were carried out by the authors on behalf of the Israel Antiquities Authority, within the confines of the Davidson Archaeological Park. Funding and logistics were provided by the EL-AD Foundation. Assistance was provided by V. Essman and Y. Shmidov (surveying and plans), A. Peretz (photography), N. Nehama (foreman), G. Berkovitz and A. Ajami (foremen), T. Winter and Y. Gorin-Rosen (glass finds), D.T. Ariel (coins), A. Zilberstein (stone vessels), N. Agha and N. Marom (faunal analysis), H. Roth and D. Langgut (charcoal), D. Namdar (residue analysis), E. Ivanovski, A. Van Zuiden and S. Zach (preservation) and H. Atun (preservation plans). We would also like to thank Dr. Gabriel Mazor and Nahashon Szanton for their important comments on the report. Wet sifting was carried out in the Emek Tzurim National Park and was overseen by G. Zagdon and I. Novoselesky. We are grateful to all those people who assisted in the excavations, especially the workers.

[2] The base of this shaft was uncovered during our excavations, see Fig. 16.32.

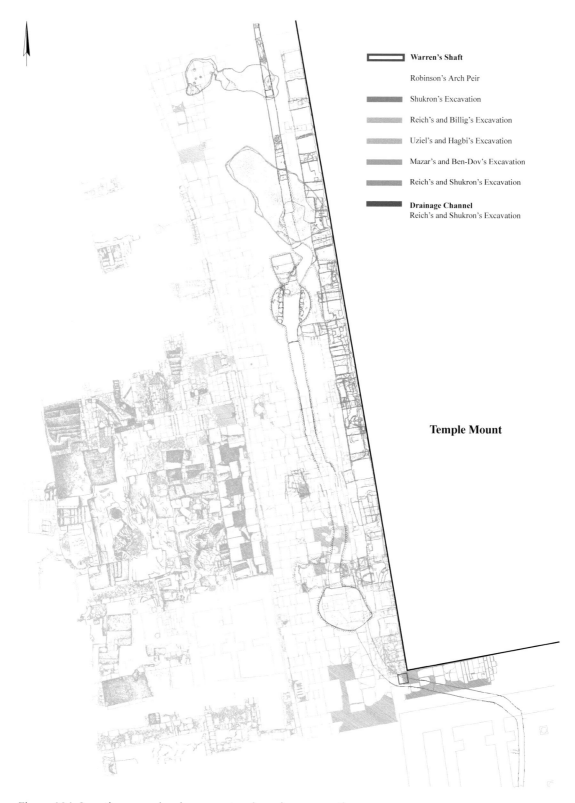

Figure 16.1: Location map, showing current and previous excavations.

Figure 16.2: View of the excavation area, looking south.

Temple Mount, the pier of Robinson's Arch and the monumental staircase along the Southern Wall, one of the main entrances to the Temple Mount in the Early Roman period. Beneath the pavement along the Southern Wall, Mazar and Ben-Dov exposed the infrastructure that was constructed to raise and support the street level of the city. Mazar and Ben-Dov also documented the drainage channel beneath the street, although they did not conduct any excavations in it.

REICH AND BILLIG EXCAVATIONS (1994–1996)

From 1994–1996, Reich and Billig excavated the Early Roman Street located at the foot of the Temple Mount, which ran beneath Robinson's Arch (1998, 1999, 2008). The street was uncovered under a pile of fallen stones that seem to have belonged to the walls of the Temple Mount and fell onto the street during the destruction of Jerusalem in 70 CE. Recently, Gibson (2014: 23–26) challenged this dating of the stone collapse, suggesting it should be attributed to the earthquake of 363 CE. This suggestion has been rebutted by Reich and Baruch (2020), who present evidence supporting the initial dating by the excavators. The excavations fully exposed the southwestern corner of the Temple Mount to the street level. Additionally, they excavated the area adjacent to Warren's Shaft, exposing a small part of the main drainage channel, where it cuts an earlier, round, rock-cut installation. Another section was excavated underneath the street pavement, between Warren's breach and the street's eastern curbstone. The latest coin that was found in this section dated to the era of Prefect Pontius Pilate (26–36 CE, Reich and Billig 2008: 1809; see Chapter 19). Reich and Billig (1998: 180) postdated the street to the 50s of the 1st century CE, due to historical considerations (Reich 2015).

Shukron Excavations (2011–2012)[3]

In 2011, Shukron and Reich accessed the foundations of the Western Wall through Warren's tunnels (Warren 1884: 175–176, Pl. XXVIII). They excavated between the foundations of the Western Wall and a parallel supporting wall (Wall 102) from south to north, between Warren's excavations (Reich and Shukron 2011a, 2011b, 2011c, 2012). Subsequently, Shukron continued the excavation to the north until the ascent to the Mughrabi (Moors) Gate (Shukron 2012). He revealed a series of structures and installations that preceded the Western Wall and the street above. These excavations, similar to our own, exposed a system of compartments and earth fills that had been built along the Western Wall in order to support the 1st century CE street and the structures to its east (see Reich and Billig 1999: 36–37). Shukron dated the compartments to the 1st century CE. Subsequently, excavations within the earlier installations led him to conclude that the construction of the Western Wall itself also occurred in the 1st century CE (Shukron 2012: 18–20; Reich and Shukron 2011b: 69; see discussion below). Reich later suggested that the supporting system was used for the erection of Robinson's Arch (Reich 2015).

EXCAVATION METHODOLOGY

The excavations presented here created numerous challenges and required extensive methodological adjustments in order to facilitate the gathering of scientific data and understanding within the confines of the nature of the project. The excavation was conducted below existing remains of the Jerusalem Archaeological Park—Davidson Center and therefore had to be dug horizontally, from the Shukron excavations (see above and Reich and Shukron 2012; Shukron 2012) southward. Furthermore, as an unexcavated 2.5-m-thick layer of fill lies above the current project, it was necessary to coordinate all progress and advancement with engineers in order to ensure the safety of workers. Previous excavations at the site (i.e., the Shukron expedition) dealt with the same issues, developing a system of horizontal excavations beneath and in between metal supports built to avoid the collapse of the fill above the excavations.

In order to ensure the proper gathering of finds and stratigraphic distinction of layers within the excavated area, each exposed section was carefully examined, and loci were assigned to each layer of sediment that was discerned. These layers were subsequently excavated from top to bottom within the 2 × 0.5 m area. If any additional features were discerned, they were also distinguished with different loci. Once the entire 2 × 0.5 m area was fully excavated to bedrock, the section that had been exposed was reevaluated in order to examine whether any features had been missed and whether the deposition of sediments had changed. Only walls running east–west, between the Western Wall and Wall 102 (Fig. 16.3, see full description below), were dismantled, after having been fully cleaned and documented (drawn and photographed).

Selected sediments from the excavation were wet-sifted at the Emek Tzurim National Park. Of the three compartments excavated (C1–C3, Fig. 16.3, see below), Compartment C1 was fully sifted, providing a complete sample of one compartment for analysis of finds. This compartment also served as the basis of the ceramic and faunal analysis, where the entire assemblage was considered, whereas the finds from Compartments C2 and C3 were used in order to complete the various finds assemblage, where types were missing from Compartment C1. In Compartments C2 and C3, wet

---

[3] The excavation permit was issued to E. Shukron alone, while most of the preliminary reports are by Reich and Shukron.

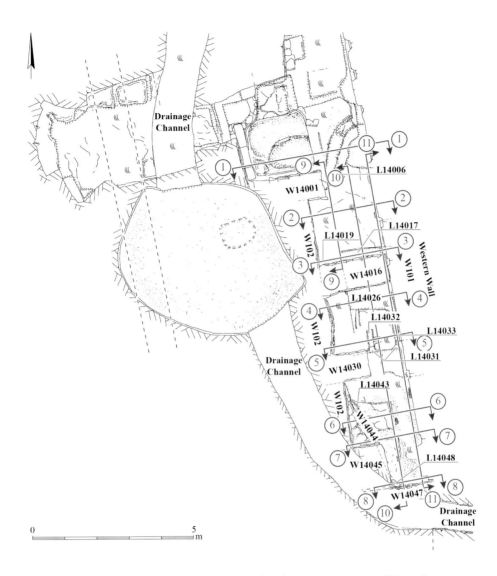

Figure 16.3: General plan of the excavations, showing compartments of Phase 3.

sifting was conducted on a small sample (10%) of the sediments, other than the accumulations on the bedrock, below the compartments, which were completely sifted.

ARCHITECTURE AND STRATIGRAPHY

Three distinct phases were discerned in the excavation: the quarrying of the bedrock (Phase 3); the construction of the Western Wall and particularly in the case of the current excavations, its foundations (Phase 2); and the building of a compartment system constructed in order to raise the level of the 1st century CE street and structures alongside it (Phase 1). As the three phases are interconnected and seen as stages within a single construction project, it was decided to divide them according to phases and not strata. Nevertheless, there is no doubt that each represents a distinct act that preceded the following stage. Within the 10 m area, three compartments of Phase

1 were excavated (labeled C1–C3 from north to south), with the remains of Phases 2 and 3 exposed alongside and underneath this system. As such, almost all of the finds from the excavation belong to Phase 1, and therefore a firm dating can be provided for this building activity (1st century CE, see below). While Phases 2 and 3 must predate this, no *terminus post quem* can be provided for either. Furthermore, despite being the last phase recognized, nothing precludes dating both of these phases to the same general time period as Phase 1—i.e., the 1st century CE, or essentially earlier (for further discussion on the debate of the dating of the Western Wall, see Shukron 2012; Weksler-Bdolah 2015; Reich and Baruch 2017 and further discussion below).

PHASE 3: THE BEDROCK AND ITS QUARRYING (FIG. 16.4)

The bedrock (Locus 14049–51, Figs. 16.4, 16.5, 16.6) exposed in the excavation area showed no signs of permanent structures or installations that predate the construction of the Western Wall. This is in

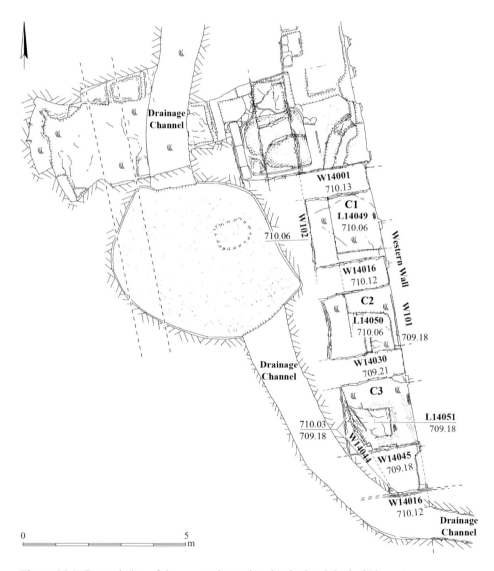

Figure 16.4: General plan of the excavations, showing bedrock loci of Phase 1.

contrast to the area excavated directly to the north by Reich and Shukron (2011a, 2011b, 2011c, 2012) and Shukron (2012), where the remains of structures and installations that preceded the Western Wall were discovered. The inhabitants of these houses were probably evacuated in order to build the Western Wall (Reich and Shukron 2012: 227). The bedrock in the current excavation showed signs of quarrying as well as smoothing, the latter of which almost certainly can be linked to the preparation of the area for the construction of the Western Wall and is therefore discussed in Phase 2.

Two clear signs of quarrying were noted in this area. The first is as a series of channels forming a "U" shape along the rock step separating Compartments C2 and C3. The channels were defined as three different loci—Locus 14032 to the west (length 0.6 m), Locus 14033 (length 1 m) to the east

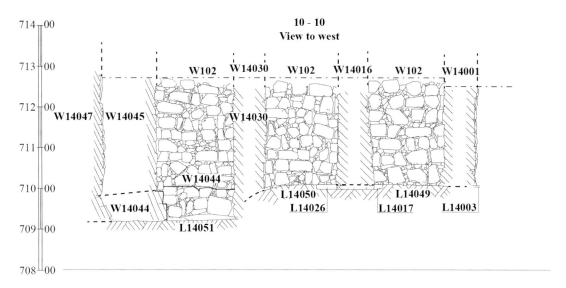

Figure 16.5: Section 10–10, Walls 102, 14044, 14045 and 14047, looking west.

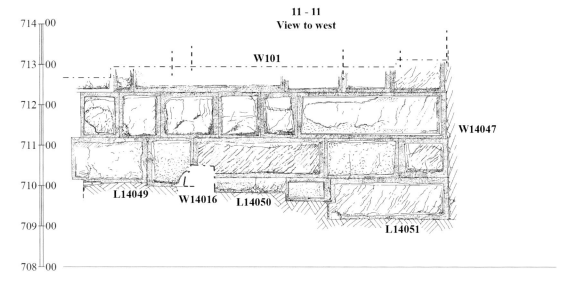

Figure 16.6: Section 11–11, the Western Wall (Wall 101), looking east.

and Locus 14031 (length 0.5 m) connecting between the two (see Fig. 16.7). The first two channels are approximately 0.35 m deep and 0.15 m wide, running north to south. Locus 14031 as well as the southern portion of the first two channels are sealed by Wall 14030 of Phase 1. It appears that these channels are quarry channels, connected with quarrying activities that predate the Phase 1 and likely the Phase 2 constructions.

In addition to these channels, a shallow depression was hewn into the bedrock (Loci 14017, 14026; see Figs. 16.5, 16.8), also likely related to the quarrying activities in this area. This feature spreads across Compartments C1 and C2 of Phase 1 (Fig. 16.3) and is sealed by both Wall 14016 and a chalk floor (Locus 14027, Section 4–4, see Phase 2) laid on a layer of beaten earth.

PHASE 2: THE WESTERN WALL FOUNDATIONS (FIGS. 16.4, 16.6)

Prior to the construction of the Western Wall, and in relation to the placement of its first course, the bedrock was smoothed and leveled (710.06 m asl in Compartments C1–2 and 709.18 in C3; Figs. 16.9, 16.10). The leveling was done with a comb-shaped chisel in the entire area (Fig. 16.11). The same type of chisel was used for the finishing of the typical "Herodian Masonry" around the ashlars of the Western Wall. In addition to the smoothing, several small niches noted on the bedrock were likely used in order to position the first course of the Western Wall (Figs. 16.9, 16.10, 16.11 and see 16.13). A thin, shallow chiseled line, incised in the rock from north to south, is seen along Loci 14049 and 14050 (Figs. 16.3, 16.12). The line is parallel to the Western Wall at a distance of 1.4 m. The function of this line is not clear, although a possible suggestion is that the line is related to the preliminary planning that was done at the site, before the onset of construction. In this sense, it is

Figure 16.7: Quarry (Loci 14031–14033), looking south.

Figure 16.8: Rock-hewn installation in C2 (Loci 14017, 14026), looking north.

Figure 16.9: The foundations of the south-western corner of the Temple Mount, looking east.

important to note that the line was not found along the entire length of the excavation, although this may be a result of later construction activities related to Phase 1.

During the excavations, a 10 m section of the Western Wall was uncovered, extending from the southern end of Shukron's excavation to the southwestern corner of the Temple Mount (Fig. 16.9). Four courses of the Western Wall, 3.5 m high, were exposed (710.06 m asl in C1–2, 709.18 m asl in C3; R, S, T and U in Warren's labeling; Warren 1884: Pl. XXVIII; Mazar 2011: Fig. 3.1.1 and see Fig. 16.6). The height exposed extended from bedrock to the highest point in the excavated area (712.81 m asl). It is important to note that the street level is 715.35 m asl, creating a gap of 2.5 m above that remained unexcavated. Previous probes beneath the street—such as those of Warren (1884: Pl. XXVIII)— indicate that the nature of the unexcavated section above is the same as the exposed section.

The ashlars of the Western Wall were not fully worked, with only the typical drafted margins of the "Herodian Masonry" notable, having left the bosses of the ashlars not fully flattened (Fig. 16.13). Warren and later Reich and Shukron assumed that the ashlars had not been fully worked due to the fact that they had been placed beneath street level and would not be seen (Warren 1884; Reich and Shukron 2012: 222). Remains of plaster patching can be seen between the ashlars, applied in places where the ashlars had been damaged or cracked during placement. In some instances, the plaster was finished with chisel marks or incised lines, mimicking the working of the original stone or the joint between the ashlars (Figs. 16.14, 16.15). This point questions the logic behind the unfinished stones; if the portion of the wall was not meant to be seen, why would the plaster repairs (likely meant to hermetically seal the foundations) be decorated?

Figure 16.10: The bedrock leveling work. Note niche used to place the ashlars, looking east.

Figure 16.11: Niche. Note bedrock comb-chisel work, looking east.

Figure 16.12: The chiseled planning line, looking west.

Figure 16.13: The Western Wall (Wall 101), looking east. Note the chiseled niche.

Figure 16.14: Plaster repair at the ashlar chiseled frame, looking east. Note the comb-chisel work on the plaster.

Figure 16.15: Plaster repair at the joint between the ashlars, looking east. Note the line mimicking the joint.

One possible answer is that changes were made in the planning of the street level during the building project, creating a situation where the actual exposed portion of the wall remained uncertain. This seems unlikely, as it appears that the planning of the project took into account the height of the street—and as a result, the courses that would be buried. This is notable most prominently in the positioning of the gates at a height that is coordinated with the street level. Furthermore, it is difficult to imagine that the plaster repairs were made at an early stage of construction.

Another option is that the courses below street level were used as a training area for new workers. The nature of the training exercises would probably have focused on aesthetic aspects of the walls, such as the final dressing of the ashlars, and would not have affected the stability of the foundations (Hagbi and Van Zuiden 2019, and see Chapter 37). Perhaps the plaster was used to cover flaws that could have caused instability to the stones (for example, through the growth of vegetation in the cracks, which could weaken the stone). The chiseling would then have been done subsequently during these practice exercises on the stones, also covering the plaster unintentionally.

Each course of the Western Wall (Fig. 16.6) in the excavated section is of uniform height—1.15 m in Course S; 0.99 m in Course T. The height of Course R could not be determined, as only its lower half was uncovered, although according to Warren's measurements, this course is also 0.99 m (Warren 1884: Pl. XXXVIII). Course U, placed directly on the bedrock, was used in order to create a leveled surface so that the course above it would be level and the ashlars could be manufactured following a uniform standard. Ashlars and portions of broken ashlars were laid on the surface after the course was in place in order to level the positioning of Course U. In the northern section, the bedrock was quarried in order to fit it to the blocks that were laid there. In the Shukron excavations to the north, Courses S and T were also used for leveling the subsequent courses. This can be noted in the slight changes in the height of the blocks along the northern portion of the Western Wall exposed by Shukron (Shukron 2012: Figs. 2, 11).

PHASE 1: THE COMPARTMENT SYSTEM

The main feature uncovered in the excavation is a system of walls (Walls 14001, 14016, 14030, 14045, 14047 and 102, Fig. 16.3), built as a compartment system for the 1st century street and the structures surrounding it (see Chapters 4 and 5). The system is comprised of a long wall (Wall 102, Fig. 16.5), parallel to the Western Wall, with perpendicular walls built between the two. Wall 102, also excavated to the north in Shukron's excavation, is parallel to the Western Wall at a distance of approximately 2 m and placed directly beneath the street's eastern curbstones (Reich and Shukron 2012: 221). Another wall, Wall 104 (*ibid.* 2012: Figs. 1–2, 7), excavated by Shukron, is parallel to Wall 102 and the drain from the west (2012: Fig. 1, Locus 16), situated approximately 4 m west of Wall 102, providing support at the center of the street (Reich and Shukron 2012: Fig. 7).

A set of walls was built between Wall 102 and the Western Wall (Fig. 16.3 and Figs. 16.16–16.24), from west to east. The walls are built at an average distance of 2.05 m from one another. Aside from Wall 14045, which is 1.3 m thick, the walls are all 0.80–0.90 m thick. These perpendicular walls created a system of compartments, three of which were excavated in the current project. Farther to the north, this substructure network was excavated by Reich and Shukron (2011b) and Shukron (2012). The compartments formed between the Western Wall and Wall 102 were labeled C1–C3 from north to south. Each compartment measures approximately 2 × 2.1 m. The walls are built from various types of stones, such as ashlars, refined stones, fieldstones and fragments of architectural elements in secondary use on both faces of the wall. The core of the walls is built of fieldstones, gravel and earth containing pottery sherds dating to the 1st century CE (see pottery analysis, Chapter 17).

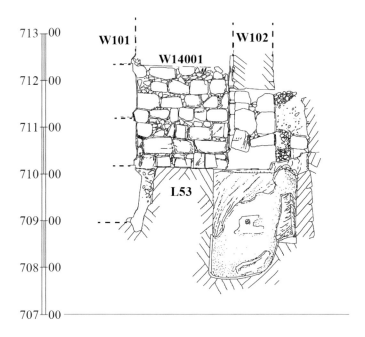

Figure 16.16: Section 1–1, Wall 14001, looking south.

Figure 16.17: Walls 14001, 101 and 102, looking south.

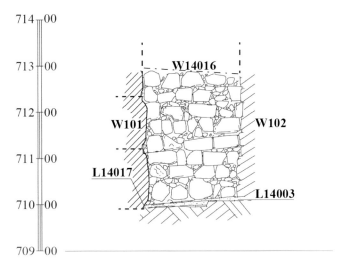

Figure 16.18: Section 3–3, Wall 14016, looking south.

Figure 16.19: Walls 14016 and 101 at C1, looking south. Note the earth fills and the inscribed planning line.

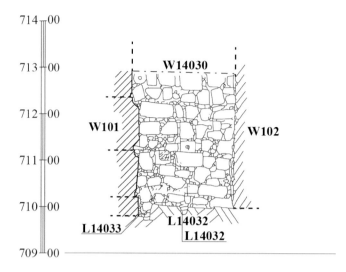

Figure 16.20: Section 5–5, Wall 14030, looking south.

Figure 16.21: Wall 14030 at C2, looking south. Note the quarry under Wall 14030.

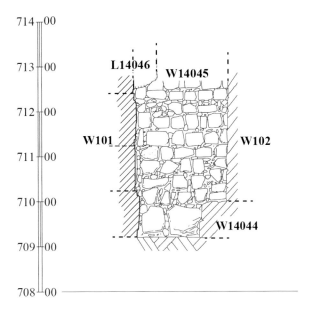

Figure 16.22: Section 7–7, Walls 14045, 14044 and Shaft
Locus 14046.

The compartments were built in warp and woof technique, where the lower courses of Wall 14001 abut Wall 102 and the lower courses of Wall 14016 adjoin Wall 102. The upper courses of Wall 14001 bond with Wall 102, and the courses of Wall 14016 abut Wall 102 and vice versa (Figs. 16.25–16.26). As seen in the first compartment, the layers of earth fill within the compartments correspond with the seams in the walls (Figs. 16.5, 16.27), indicating that the walls were built in stages, where the lower courses were built, the compartments were filled, and then the upper courses were added, after which additional layers of fill were placed in the upper portion of the compartment. Interestingly, the lower layers of fill were leveled, while the upper layers sloped down toward the Western Wall.

An additional wall (14047) was built against and parallel to Wall 14045 (Figs. 16.3, 16.5, 16.24). The wall is built close to the southern side of the southwest corner. It is likely that the wall is not part of the support system along the Western Wall and belongs to the system that was built along the Southern Wall of the Temple Mount, partially excavated by B. Mazar (1969, 1971).

In preservation work conducted on Wall 102 (License A7320; see Chapter 37), some earth was excavated from underneath it and replaced by refined stones. The earth was sifted and one coin, which was dated to Archelaus (4 BCE–6 CE, see Chapter 19), was extracted from it.

The compartments were packed with intentionally stratified earth fills (C1: Loci 14007, 14009–15, Figs. 16.28, 16.27, 16.19; C2: Loci 14020–22, 14024–25, 14028–29, Fig. 16.29; C3: Loci 14034–42, Fig. 16.30). The base of the compartments was filled with stone chips, with a few ashlars and refined stones found in the stone fill (C1: Loci 14007, 14015, Figs. 16.28, 16.27; C2: Locus 14025, Fig. 16.29; C3: Loci 14039–41, Fig. 16.30). The chips are probably the result of waste material from the finishing of the raised bosses of the Western Wall's ashlars. The stone chips formed a mound up to 1.2 m high at the base of the compartments, with broken vessels (a storage jar and cooking pots) at times overlying the stone chips (see Chapter 37, Fig. 16: 9).

Figure 16.23: Walls 101, 14045 and 14044 at C3, looking south.

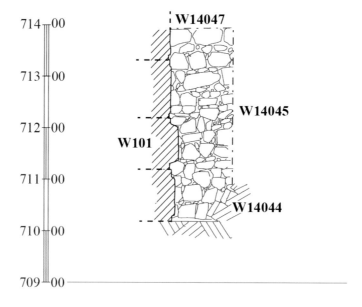

Figure 16.24: Section 8–8, Walls 14047 and 14044, looking south.

Sealing the stone chips were a series of stratified earth fill layers rich with finds, including pottery sherds and whole vessels (see Chapter 17), stone vessels (Chapter 21), animal bones and bone artifacts (Chapter 22 and below), glass sherds (Chapter 20), charcoal (Chapter 23) and metal artifacts (Chapter 18). As mentioned above, the first layers of earth were leveled, while

Figure 16.25: Walls 14016 and 102 at C1, looking southwest. Note course of walls.

Figure 16.26: Walls 14030 above courses of Wall 14044 and Wall 102.

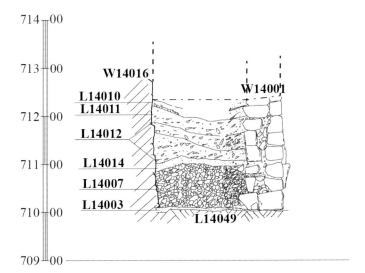

Figure 16.27: Section 9–9, the phases at the earth fills abutting Walls 14001 and 14016.

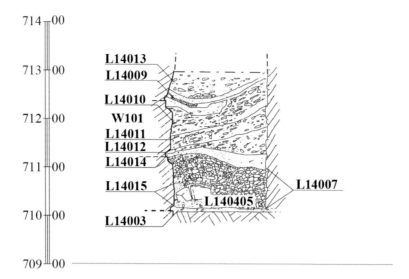

Figure 16.28: Section 2–2, the earth fills at C1.

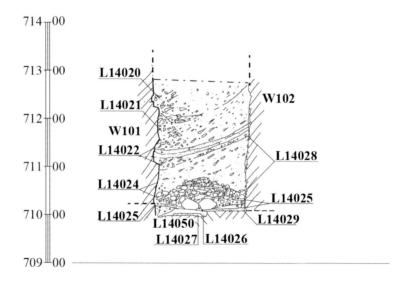

Figure 16.29: Section 4–4, the earth fills at C2.

the upper layers were dumped diagonally from west to east (from Wall 102 to the Western Wall). Unique to Compartment C3 was an additional layer, sealing the earth fills, composed of large, refined fieldstones and architectural elements (Locus 14034, Fig. 16.30). It is possible that this layer was only dumped into the southernmost compartment, or alternatively, that it was located above the roofing of the excavation in the other compartments in the unexcavated section above.

At the western end of C3, underneath Wall 102 (710.06 m asl), Wall 14044 was uncovered (Figs. 16.3, 16.22–24, 16.31). The wall follows the path of the drainage channel (Locus 12 following Reich and Shukron 2011b) from the north and curves southeast to east, passing adjacent to the southern face of the southwest corner. The height of Wall 14044 is ca. 0.85 cm (lower level 709.18 m asl). It

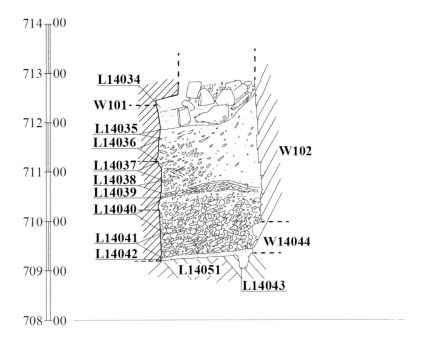

Figure 16.30: Section 6–6,the earth fills at C3.

seals the vault roofing of the drainage channel stones and may have served as an additional support between the vault and the walls of the compartments (Fig. 16.31). Three walls (Walls 102, 14045 and 14047) meet above Wall 14044, placing extreme pressure on this point, therefore creating a need for a vaulted system as opposed to the flat-roofed channel found to the north and south, in order to support the massive weight of the walls and the earth fills raised to a height of 6–7 m (Fig. 16.3, and see Ritmeyer 2006: 234).

Beneath Compartments C1–C3, a thin, light gray beaten earth layer that covered the bedrock and abutted the Western Wall (Locus 14003 in C1 Sections 2–2, 3–3 and 9–9; Locus 14029 in C2, Section 4–4; Locus 14042 in C3, Section 6–6) was discovered. The layer is 3–10 cm thick and consisted of very small amounts of pottery and several coins (17/18–24/25 CE; Ariel, Nos. 74–76, Chapter 19). In some cases, the small stone chips were pressed into the layer, as in Loci 14026 and 14041 (Fig. 16.30). The function of this layer is not completely clear. It is possible that it served as a surface at the time of the onset of the construction of the compartments, or that it predates the compartments and should be linked to the construction of the Western Wall, as suggested by Weksler-Bdolah (2015: 49). Nevertheless, as it clearly abuts the lowermost course of the Western Wall, it is clear that at least the lower courses of the Western Wall predate this layer. Therefore, it should be linked to the construction of the compartments and not to the construction of the Western Wall (see discussion below).

In the uppermost layer of fill in Compartment C3, north of Wall 14045, an intrusive pit was noticed (Locus 14046), which also partially dismantled the exposed upper portion of wall (Fig. 16.32). The pit was discernable through the loose earth and gravel fill that was observed in the missing part of the wall. It appears that this pit represents the base of Warren's Shaft XXII, excavated at the southwest corner of the Temple Mount (Warren 1884: Pls. XXXVIII, XXVII; Wilson and Warren 1871: 84). Mazar and Ben-Dov, who sealed it from the street level down (Fig. 16.32), had previously located the shaft.

Figure 16.31: Wall 14044 under Wall 102, looking west.

Figure 16.32: Warren's Shaft XXII (Locus 14046), looking east.

REFERENCES

Ben-Dov, M. 1985. *In the Shadow of the Temple: The Discovery of Ancient Jerusalem.* New York.

Gibson, S. 2014. The Pilaster Enclosure Wall of the Temple Mount in Jerusalem. In: Baruch, E. and Faust, A., eds. *New Studies on Jerusalem* 20. Ramat Gan: 17–39 (Hebrew).

Hagbi, M. and Uziel, J. 2015. Jerusalem, The Old City, The Western Wall Foundations. *Hadashot Arkheologiyot* 127. http://www.hadashot-esi.org.il/Report_Detail_Eng.aspx?id=15729&mag_id=122 (accessed December 31, 2015).

Hagbi, M. and Uziel, J. 2016. Jerusalem, The Old City, The Western Wall Foundations. *Hadashot Arkheologiyot* 128. http://www.hadashot-esi.org.il/report_detail.aspx?id=25029&mag_id=124 (accessed August 21, 2016).

Hagbi, M. and Van Zuiden, A. 2019. "Shaping the Stones"—Technical Aspects in the Endeavor to Lay the Foundation Stones of the Western Wall. In: Meiron, E., ed. *City of David: Studies of Ancient Jerusalem* 14. Jerusalem: 42–59 (Hebrew).

Mazar, B. 1969. The Excavations in the Old City of Jerusalem, *Eretz-Israel* 9: 161–174 (Hebrew).

Mazar, B. 1971. The Excavations in the Old City of Jerusalem near the Temple Mount—Second Preliminary Report, 1969–70 Seasons. *Eretz-Israel* 10: 1–34 (Hebrew).

Mazar, B. 1975. *Mountain of the Lord: Excavating in Jerusalem.* Jerusalem.

Mazar, E. 2011. *The Walls of the Temple Mount.* Jerusalem.

Reich, R. 2015. The Construction and Destruction of Robinson's Arch. *Eretz-Israel* 31: 398–407 (Hebrew).

Reich, R. and Baruch, Y. 2017. On Expansion of the Temple Mount in the Late Second Temple Period. *Cathedra* 164: 7–24 (Hebrew).

Reich, R. and Baruch, Y. 2020. A Note on the Date of the Stone Collapse at the Western Wall of the Temple Mount. *Israel Exploration Journal* 70(1): 99–105.

Reich, R. and Billig, Y. 1998. Jerusalem, Robinson's Arch. *Hadashot Arkheologiyot* 108: 180 (Hebrew; English summary: 135).

Reich, R. and Billig, Y. 1999. Excavations near the Temple Mount and Robinson's Arch. *Qadmoniot* 117: 33–40 (Hebrew).

Reich, R. and Billig, Y. 2008. Jerusalem: The Robinson's Arch Area. In: Stern, E., Geva, H., Paris, A. and Aviram, J., eds. *The New Encyclopedia of Archaeological Excavations in the Holy Land*, Vol. 5. *New York*: 1809–1811.

Reich, R. and Shukron, E. 2011a. Jerusalem, Robinson's Arch. *Hadashot Arkheologiyot* 123. http://www .hadashot-esi.org.il/report_detail_eng.aspx?id=1884&mag_id=118 (accessed May 21, 2015).

Reich, R. and Shukron, E. 2011b. Excavations in Jerusalem Beneath the Paved Street and in the Sewage Channel next to Robinson's Arch. *Qadmoniot* 142: 66–73 (Hebrew).

Reich, R. and Shukron, E. 2011c. The Second Temple Period Drainage Channel in Jerusalem—Upon the Completion of the Unearthing of its Southern Part in 2011. In: Meiron, E., ed. *City of David: Studies of Ancient Jerusalem* 6. Jerusalem: 67–94 (Hebrew).

Reich, R. and Shukron, E. 2012. Excavations next to Robinson's Arch 2011, from the Level of the Paved Street to Bedrock. In: Baruch, E., Levy-Reifer, A. and Faust, A., eds. *New Studies on Jerusalem* 17. Ramat Gan: 219–238 (Hebrew).

Ritmeyer, L. 2006. *The Quest: Revealing the Temple Mount in Jerusalem.* Jerusalem.

Shukron, E. 2012. Did Herod Build the Foundations of the Western Wall? In: Meiron, E., ed. *City of David: Studies of Ancient Jerusalem* 7. Jerusalem: 14–27.

Warren, C. 1876. *Underground Jerusalem: An Account of the Principal Difficulties Encountered in Its Exploration and the Results Obtained.* London

Warren, C. 1884. *Plans, Elevation, Sections, etc. Shewing the Results of the Excavations at Jerusalem, 1867–70, Executed for the Committee of the Palestine Exploration Fund.* London.

Weksler-Bdolah, S. 2015. The Enlargement of the Herodian Temple Mount: An Archaeological Perspective. In: Ben-Arieh, Y., Halamish, A., Limor, O., Rubin, R. and Reich, R., eds. *Study of Jerusalem Through the Ages.* Jerusalem: 19–72 (Hebrew).

Wilson, E. and Warren, C. 1871. *The Recovery of Jerusalem, Exploration and Discovery in the City and the Holy Land.* New York.

CHAPTER 17

POTTERY FROM THE WESTERN WALL FOUNDATIONS

Moran Hagbi and Joe Uziel

Finds from the Western Wall Foundations excavation can be attributed almost exclusively to the fills in the Phase 1 compartments (see Chapter 16). As no typological or chronological differentiation was notable in the varying layers of the fill, the pottery was treated as a single assemblage. The pottery from Compartment 1 served as the basis for the typological analysis, with finds from the other two compartments included for completing the ceramic profile of the excavation, or in cases where whole or complete profiles were only available from Compartments 2 and 3. The earth fills of the excavated compartments consisted of a large quantity of pottery, mostly sherds, with several whole vessels also found and partially restored. The whole vessels, along with some of the other finds, likely originated from discarding by the workers in the construction project (see Chapter 22), while the rest of the finds may have come from earth fills brought to the site and dumped into the compartments to serve as constructional fill (see discussion below). The source of the fills dumped into the compartments may have been a nearby refuse dump, or perhaps the immediate domestic areas that were evacuated due to the building activities (such as those found in the northern areas of excavation; see Shukron 2012). It is important to note that in the current excavations there were no finds that predated the Early Roman period, suggesting that the fill did not originate in the secondary deposition of a long-lived primary context, such as a building that would have been cleared for the construction of the Western Wall.

The pottery was defined according to rim morphology. The finds were compared to various excavations in the immediate vicinity, such as Areas B, E and J in the Jewish Quarter (Geva and Hershkovitz 2006, 2014; Geva 2010) and the Jerusalem International Convention Center (Binyanei Haʾuma) excavations (Berlin 2005). Parallels were also brought from HR3 and the Zealot occupation phases at Masada (Bar-Nathan 2002), the HR3 Phase at Jericho's palatial complex (Bar-Nathan 2006) and Herodium (Bar-Nathan 1981), as well as the refuse layers excavated along the eastern slopes of the City of David (Machline and Gadot 2017).

BOWLS

IN-CURVED RIM BOWLS (FIG. 17.1: 1–6)

Small, deep bowls with an in-curved rim can be divided into two types: one with a gently in-curved rim (Fig. 17.1: 1–2) and the other with a sharply in-curved rim, creating a clear carination (Fig. 17.1: 3–6). Parallels were found in the Jewish Quarter, Area E, Stratum 3 (Geva and Hershkovitz 2006: Pls. 4.8: 2; 4.9: 14–15; 4.10: 12), Area B, Stratum 2 (Geva 2010: Pl. 4.6: 2); Binyanei Haʾuma, Phases 3–4 (Berlin 2005: Pl. 17: 4–6). According to parallels found, these vessels usually have a flat base. This type was common in the 2nd–1st century BCE and continued to appear in the 1st century CE.

DOWN-TURNED RIM BOWLS (FIG. 17.1: 7–9)

Bowls with gentle carination in the upper part, a down-turned rim, ridges on the interior and exterior and a flat base were prevalent at Masada, Zealot occupation (Bar-Nathan 2006: Pl. 25: 20).

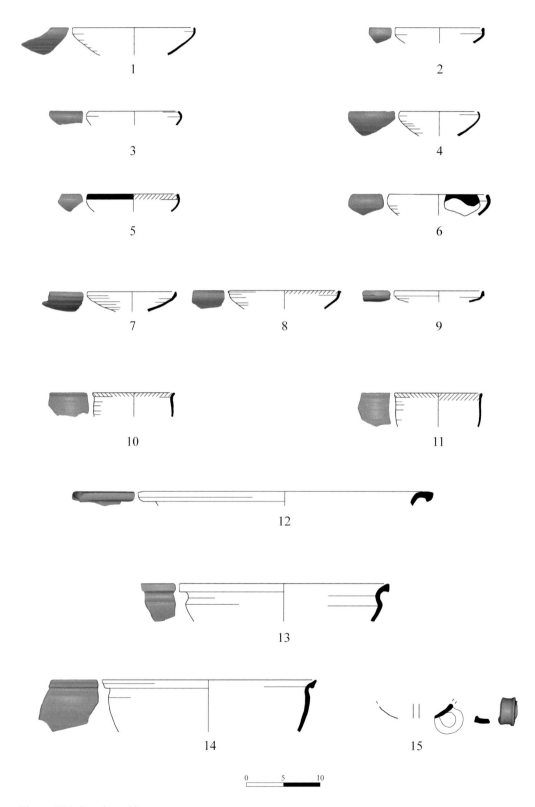

Figure 17.1: Bowls and kraters.

Figure 17.1: Bowls and Kraters

No.	Basket no.	Locus	Type	Description
1	140020	14009	Bowl	Orange clay with grits, inner red-brown decoration
2	140031.7	14014	Bowl	Orange clay with grits
3	140017.4	14012	Bowl	Orange clay with grits
4	140031.5	14014	Bowl	Orange clay with grits
5	140031.8	14014	Bowl	Orange clay with grits, lipstick decoration—red (inner) black (outer)
6	140113.2	14039	Bowl	Yellow clay with grits, inner black wave decoration
7	140028.1	14010	Bowl	Brown clay with grits
8	140057.2	14028	Bowl	Orange clay with grits, red lipstick decoration
9	140020.6	14009	Bowl	Orange clay with grits
10	140056	14022	Bowl	Orange clay, red lipstick decoration
11	140057.3	14028	Bowl	Orange clay with grits, red lipstick decoration
12	140041.7	14022	Krater	Orange clay with grits
13	140040.1	14022	Krater	Light brown clay with grits
14	140079.4	14039	Krater	Light brown clay with grits
15	140004.4	14004	Krater	Light brown clay

This type was also found in the Masada bowls (Bar-Nathan 2006: Pl. 25: 21). These bowls were also found at Binyanei Haʾuma, Phases 3–4 (Berlin 2005: Pl. 17: 7–9).

CUPS WITH AN OUT-CURVED RIM AND THIN FLARING WALLS (FIG. 17.1: 10–11)

Similar cups were found in the Zealot occupation context at Masada (Type M-CU3, Bar-Nathan 2006: Pl. 26: 66), in Jericho, HR2 15 BCE–6 CE (Bar-Nathan 2002: Pl. 16: 278).

KRATERS

OPEN HEMISPHERICAL KRATER (FIG. 17.1: 12–14)

Hemispherical kraters with triangular rim, no neck, and ring base are known from the Jewish Quarter excavations, although limited to Area E, Stratum 3 (Geva and Hershkovitz 2006: Pls. 4.10: 15–16; 4.12: 10). They were also found at Masada, Zealot occupation (Type M-KR2B1, Bar-Nathan 2006: Pl. 23: 7–10) and Jericho, HR3 (Type J-KR1B1, Bar-Nathan 2002: Pl. 27: 509–511). They were also found at Binyanei Haʾuma, Phase 4 (Berlin 2005: Pl. 18: 3–5).

KRATER WITH THREE RING BASES (FIG. 17.1: 15)

These kraters have a wide mouth, grooved ledge rim and rounded base with three ring feet. This vessel is a local imitation of the three astragal-shaped feet Cypriot Sigillata ware (Geva and Rosenthal-Heginbottom 2003: 179). The type does not appear in contexts later than the mid-1st century CE (Bar-Nathan 1981: 61). Parallels were found in the Jewish Quarter, Area N, Stratum 2

(Geva and Hershkovitz 2014: Pl. 3.13: 15) and Area E, Stratum 2 (Geva and Hershkovitz 2006: Pl. 4.13: 14). This type was not found in Area B (the Burnt House).

COOKING WARE

Cooking Jugs (Fig. 17.2: 1–3)

The cooking jugs have a triangular rim, a short, flaring neck with a ridge on its base, loop handles extending from the rim to the shoulder and a globular body with a pointed, convex base. They first appear at the end of the 2nd century BCE. The presented type developed in the second half of the 1st century BCE and is commonly found in 1st century CE contexts, e.g., Jewish Quarter excavations, Area E, Strata 2 and 3 (Geva and Hershkovitz 2006: Pls. 4.13: 18; 4.10: 23; 4.12: 17), although missing from Area B (the Burnt House). It was also found at Binyanei Haʾuma, Phases 2–4 (Berlin 2005: Pl. 6: 1–8), Masada, Zealot occupation (Type M-CJG1A, Bar-Nathan 2006: Pl. 31: 85) and Jericho, HR3, Triclinium B70 in Herod's Third Palace and Building No. 13 (Type JCJG1A, Bar-Nathan 2002: Pl. 27: 504).

Casserole (Fig. 17.2: 4–7)

Casseroles from the assemblage have a wide mouth, rounded to triangular rim, short neck, two loop handles from the rim to a carinated shoulder (sharp to round), semi-rounded body and convex base. The vessels are made from typical cooking ware fabric. This type is widespread in Masada's Zealot occupation phase (Type M-CS1A, Bar-Nathan 2006: Pl. 30: 51–55). The type is present in Jericho, HR1 to post-Herodian phases, dating from 31 BCE–115 CE (Type HR3 J-CS3, Bar-Nathan 2002: Pls. 27: 495–499), the Jewish Quarter, Area E, Strata 4–2 (Geva and Hershkovitz 2006: Pls. 4.5: 22; 4.12: 16; 4.10: 21; 4.13: 17), Area J, Stratum 3 (Geva and Hershkovitz 2014: Pls. 3.7: 3; 3.10: 6) and Binyanei Haʾuma, Phases 3–4 (Berlin 2005: Pl. 7: 1–11).

Cooking Pots (Fig. 17.2: 8–15; 17.3: 1)

The cooking pots are closed, globular to squat vessels with a triangular rim, short neck, convex base and two flattened loop handles from rim to shoulder. Dense exterior wheel ridging is notable on the shoulder, base, and occasionally on the body. Bar-Nathan (2006) divided these vessels into four subtypes on the basis of body shape and size (A–D, with the present type falling under her Type B). All the cooking pots are made of typical red cooking ware fabric. This is the most common closed cooking pot in Judea in the 1st century CE, with widespread distribution in Masada, Zealot occupation and Garrison 2 contexts (Type M-CP1B1–2, Bar-Nathan 2006: Pls. 27–28: 6–25) and Jericho, HR1–3 (Type J-CP2C2, Bar-Nathan 2002: Pl. 12: 150). They are also common in the Jewish Quarter, Area E, Stratum 3 (Geva and Hershkovitz 2006: Pls. 4.8: 9–10; 4.9: 18; 4.13: 16), Area B, Stratum 2 (Geva 2010: Pl. 4.5: 1–8) and Binyanei Haʾuma, Phase 2–4 (Berlin 2005: Pl. 4: 1–7).

Cooking Cup (Fig. 17.3: 2)

A thin-walled cup with oval, grooved strap handle on the shoulder was found, made from fine red-brown cooking fabric with soot marks on its wall, indicating its purpose. Two similar fragments were found in the Jewish Quarter excavations, Area J (Rosenthal-Heginbottom: 2014, Pl. 4.4: 17–18) and identified as cooking pots. Petrographic analysis there indicates these vessels were made in workshops in the Southern Coastal Plain of Israel or the Shephelah (Ben-Shlomo 2014).

STORAGE VESSELS

STORAGE JAR WITH RIDGED NECK (FIG. 17.3: 3–12)

Bag-shaped or cylindrical storage jars with everted, vertical or inward sloping necks, with a ridge at the base of the neck and a convex base were found. The jars have two loop handles from the shoulders to the body. This type first appears during the 1st century CE. The type was found in various contexts in the Jewish Quarter, such as the Burnt House, Area B, Stratum 2 (Geva 2010: Pl. 4.2: 1–4); Area E, Stratum 2 (Geva and Hershkovitz 2006: Pl. 4.13: 1–3). This is the main type of jar that was found in Masada's Herodian and Zealot occupation contexts, including all variants of this type (Type M-SJ7A-B, Bar-Nathan 2006: Pls. 4–7: 19–38), also found in Jericho, Area F (Type J-SJ7A-B, Bar-Nathan 2002: Pl. 6: 39–43).

STORAGE JAR WITH TRIANGULAR RIM (FIG. 17.4: 1–9)

These storage jars have an ovoid form with triangular rim, sometimes concave on the upper surface, a low neck with ridge around the lower end, convex base pointed in the center, two loop handles from shoulder to body and random exterior wheel ridging. The type first appeared at the beginning of the 1st century CE and by the end of the Second Temple period became more popular than the ridged-neck storage jar type. The type was found in the Burnt House in the Jewish Quarter, Area B, Stratum 2 (Geva 2010: Pl. 4.2: 8). The type is absent from Area E, Stratum 2. At Masada this type was found only in Zealot occupation context and was absent from contexts dated to Herod's reign (Type M-SJ8, Bar-Nathan 2006: Pl. 8: 39–42). Other parallels originate from Jericho, HR3 (6–48 CE), (Type J-SJ13, Bar-Nathan 2002: Pl. 24: 415–417).

JUGS

JUG WITH TRIANGULAR RIM (FIG. 17.5: 1–3)

Globular piriform jugs with a triangular rim with an inner groove, concave neck, ring base, usually with central knob, and a strap handle from rim to shoulder were discovered in the Phase 1 fill. Bar-Nathan subdivided the type according to the color of the jug's ware, suggesting that the types were made in two separate workshops (Type M-JG5B, Bar-Nathan 2006: Pls. 18–19: 6–18). Both types are present in the Phase 1 fills. The type is very common in the Jewish Quarter, e.g., Area B, Stratum 2 (Geva 2010: Pl. 4.3: 3–4), Area E, Stratum 3 (Geva and Hershkovitz 2006: Pls. 4.7: 8; 4.10: 6) and Area J, Stratum 3 (Geva and Hershkovitz 2014: Pl. 3.8: 6–7).

JUG WITH CUP-SHAPED RIM (FIG. 17.5: 4)

This globular jug has a ridged narrow neck, everted thickened rim, ring base, occasionally concave, and a flat handle from the rim to the upper body. The general type first appears at the end of 1st century BCE and develops into the discussed subtype in the 1st century CE, found mainly in Zealot occupation contexts at Masada (Type M-JG9C, Bar-Nathan 2006: Pl. 19: 27–31). It appears in the service building of Phase II at Herodium (Bar-Nathan 1981: Pl. 4: 17, 19) and in the Jewish Quarter, Area E, Stratum 4 (Geva and Hershkovitz 2006: Pl. 4.4: 7) and Area B, Stratum 2, the Burnt House (Geva 2010: Pl. 4.3: 1–2). This type is absent from contemporary Jericho contexts.

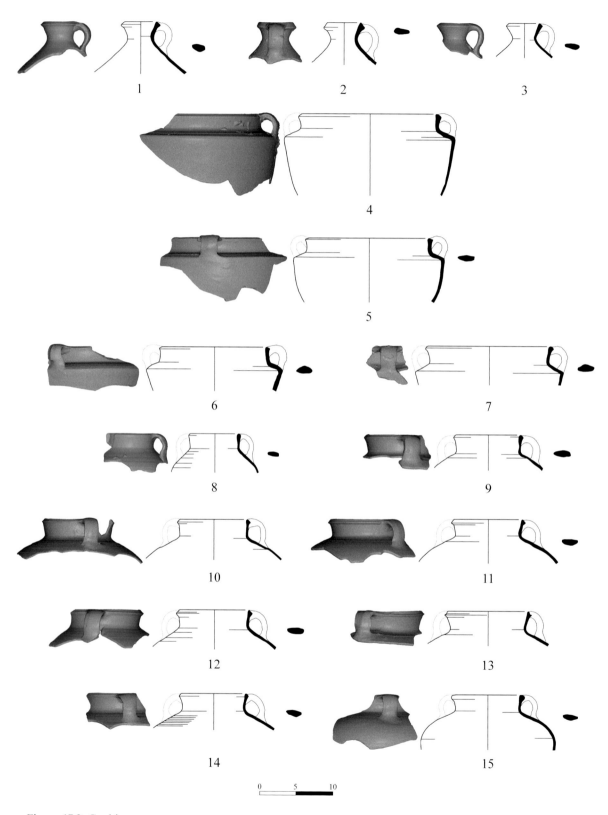

Figure 17.2: Cooking ware.

Figure 17.2: Cooking Ware

No.	Basket no.	Locus	Type	Description
1	140102.3	14039	Cooking jar	Red-brown clay with grits
2	140004.1	14007	Cooking jar	Red-brown clay with grits
3	140006.5	14004	Cooking jar	Red-brown clay with grits
4	140010	14004	Casserole	Red-orange clay with grits
5	140031.2	14014	Casserole	Red-brown clay with grits, thin gray core
6	140014.1	14009	Casserole	Red-brown clay with grits, thin gray core
7	140016.3	14011	Casserole	Red-brown clay with grits, thin gray core
8	140056.3	14022	Cooking pot	Red-brown clay with grits
9	140031.1	14014	Cooking pot	Red-brown clay with grits
10	140018.1	14012	Cooking pot	Red-orange clay with grits
11	140029.4	14011	Cooking pot	Red-brown clay with grits
12	140030	14012	Cooking pot	Red-brown clay with grits
13	140018.3	14012	Cooking pot	Red-brown clay with grits
14	140020.5	14009	Cooking pot	Red-brown clay with grits, gray core
15	140028	14010	Cooking pot	Red-brown clay with grits

FLASK (FIG. 17.5: 5–6)

Flasks with tall, narrow cylindrical necks, thickened rims, asymmetrical globular bodies with a pointed center at one side, a convex base, and two twisted loop handles from neck to body are very common in the assemblage. This is the most common flask at Judean sites in the 1st century BCE, where the flask continued to be used in the 1st century CE without any special changes. Such vessels were found in the Jewish Quarter, Area E, Stratum 3 (Geva and Hershkovitz 2006: Pls. 4.7: 20–21; 4.9: 1; 4.10: 13; 4.11: 11–12; Stratum 2, Pl. 4.13: 9), Area J, Stratum 3 (Geva and Hershkovitz 2014: Pls. 3.7: 12–13; 3.8: 21), Area N, Stratum 2 (Geva and Hershkovitz 2014: Pl. 3.13: 4) and Area B, Stratum 2 (Geva 2010: Pl. 4.3: 12–14). They are also common at Masada, Herod's reign and Zealot occupation contexts (Type M-FL1, Bar-Nathan 2006: Pl. 22: 70–73) and Jericho, HR3, the Industrial Area (Type J-FL1, Bar-Nathan 2002: Pl. 26: 468–475).

JUGLETS

CUP-SHAPED RIM JUGLET (FIG. 17.5: 7–8)

This type is a globular or elongated piriform juglet with a short narrow neck and flattened handle from rim to shoulder. Random exterior and occasionally interior wheel ridging is notable on the body. Bar-Nathan (2006) divided it into three subtypes according to the form of the base. In the present excavation, only the upper part of this type was found, therefore no division was made. It is the most common juglet in contemporary contexts, such as the Jewish Quarter, the Burnt House, Area B, Stratum 2 (Geva 2010: Pl. 4.3: 7–10), Area E, Strata 4–2 (Geva and Hershkovitz

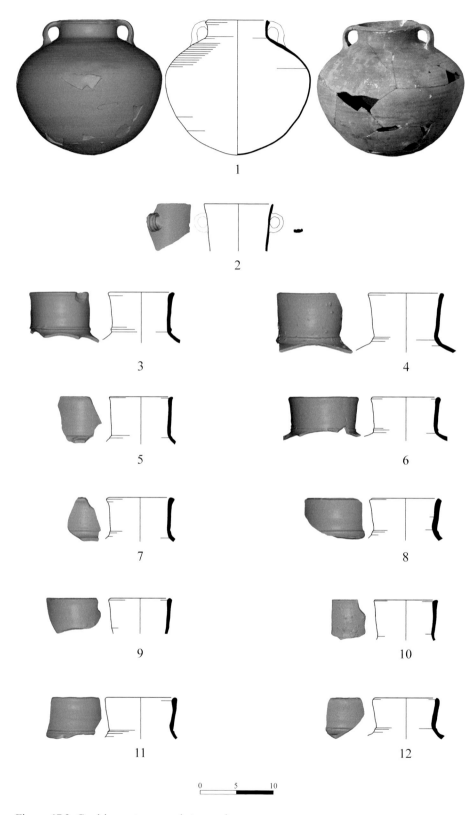

Figure 17.3: Cooking pot, cup and storage jars.

Figure 17.3: Cooking Pot, Cup and Storage Jars

No.	Basket no.	Locus	Type	Description
1	140018	14012	Cooking pot	Red-orange clay
2	140057	14028	Cooking cup	Fine red-brown clay
3	140079.3	14039	Storage jar	Light orange clay
4	140013.1	14007	Storage jar	Orange clay and core
5	140016.1	14011	Storage jar	Light brown clay, gray core
6	140020.9	14009	Storage jar	Orange clay, gray core
7	140020.3	14009	Storage jar	Light brown clay, gray core
8	140020.4	14009	Storage jar	Orange-brown clay with grits
9	140023.1	14012	Storage jar	Orange clay, gray core
10	140016.2	14011	Storage jar	Light brown clay, gray core
11	140041.3	14022	Storage jar	Orange clay, gray core
12	140020.7	14009	Storage jar	Light brown clay, gray core

2006: Pls. 4.4: 11–12; 4.7: 12; 4.9: 8; 4.10: 9; 4.11: 1–5; 4.13: 6), Area J, Stratum 3 (Geva and Hershkovitz 2014: Pls. 3.7: 6; 3.8: 11–14) and Area N, Stratum 2 (Geva and Hershkovitz 2014: Pl. 3.13: 5–6). At Masada, it was found in the Herodian and Zealot occupation context (Type M-JT1A1–3, Bar-Nathan 2006: Pl. 33: 1–14) and in Jericho, HR3 (Type J-JT1A1–2, Bar-Nathan 2002: Pl. 25: 443–447).

JUGLET WITH FLARING RIM (FIG. 17.5: 9)

An additional type of juglet found is represented by two fragments. The juglet is a small globular or piriform juglet with a rounded or out-curved rim, long narrow conical neck and strap handle from rim to shoulder. This type was found in the Jewish Quarter, Area B, Stratum 2 (Geva 2010: Pl. 4.3: 5) and Area E, Strata 3–2 (Geva and Hershkovitz 2006: Pls. 4.11: 6; 4.13: 7). It was also found at Masada in Zealot occupation context (Type M-JT3, Bar-Nathan 2006: Pl. 33: 16–19). This juglet appears to have a prototype in Jericho during the Hasmonean 2 Phase (85/75–31 BCE) and later developed during Herod's reign into Jericho Type J–JG3A2, also similar to J–JG3B (Bar-Nathan 2002: 41–42).

UNGUENTARIA

FUSIFORM UNGUENTARIUM (FIG. 17.5: 10)

Fusiform unguentaria with a triangular rim, tall cylindrical neck, small globular body, and well-made, tall, slim spindle foot were found in the assemblage. The examples here were not decorated and made from a gray clay. This form was found mostly in 1st century BCE contexts, such as Jericho, HR1–2 Phases (Type J-UN1, Bar-Nathan 2006: 58–59, Pl. 10: 93–95 and see discussion there). Only two fragments were found in the Masada Zealot occupation phase, both attributed by Bar-Nathan to Herod's reign (Type M-UN1, Bar-Nathan 2006: 201, Pl. 34: 1). The same type was

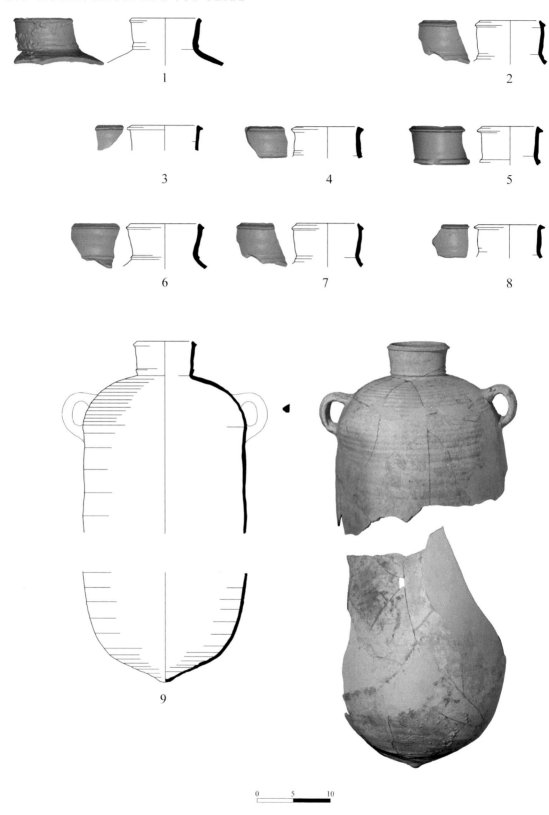

Figure 17.4: Storage jars.

Figure 17.4: Storage Jars

No.	Basket no.	Locus	Type	Description
1	140006.1	14004	Storage jar	Pale orange/yellow clay, gray core
2	140087.1	14039	Storage jar	Light orange clay
3	140014.11	14009	Storage jar	Light brown clay
4	140017	14012	Storage jar	Light brown clay
5	140087.3	14039	Storage jar	Pinkish-orange clay
6	140029	14011	Storage jar	Orange clay with grits, gray core
7	140102.2	14039	Storage jar	
8	140017.3	14012	Storage jar	Light brown clay, gray core
9	140113	14039	Storage jar	Light brown clay, yellow slip

found in Hasmonean to Herodian contexts in the Jewish Quarter, Area E, Strata 4 and 3 (Geva and Hershkovitz 2006: Pls. 4.4: 1–2; 4.7: 3), and was missing from the Burnt House, Area B, Stratum 2. The type disappeared around the beginning of the 1st century CE.

Piriform Unguentarium (Fig. 17.5: 11–13)

The small piriform unguentaria with long, everted neck, simple or triangular rim and flat base were also found. The type first appears in Judea at the end of the 1st century BCE and becomes more popular in the 1st century CE. Parallels are found in Masada's Zealot occupation context (Type M-UN3A, Bar-Nathan 2006: Pl. 34: 8–9), Jericho, HR1–3 (Type J-UN2A, Pl. 10: 103–105) and the Jewish Quarter, Area E, Stratum 3 (Geva and Hershkovitz 2006: Pl. 4.7: 13, 15) and Area B, Stratum 2 (Geva 2010: Pl. 4.4: 4–7).

Within the piriform unguentaria, an additional type was noted (Fig. 17.5: 13), which has a more elongated body, varied rim form, a tall, narrow cylindrical neck, concave or flat bottom. These vessels are particularly common in Zealot occupation contexts at Masada (Type M-UN2B, Bar-Nathan 2006: Pl. 34: 3–7) and Phases HR1–3 at Jericho (Type J-UN2A, Bar-Nathan 2002: Pl. 10: 103–105).

OIL LAMPS

Knife-Pared Oil Lamps (Fig. 17.6: 1–2)

The wheel-made "Herodian Lamp" is the most common lamp in the assemblage. The lamp has a round body with curving sides, a flat base and a short, arched speculate nozzle, which is knife pared on its bottom. A short rim around the filling hole surrounded by a sharp low ridge is typical on these lamps. The lamp lacks decoration. Three whole examples were found in the excavation. This type was produced in Jerusalem and was the typical oil lamp in Judea in the Early Roman period. Parallels were found in the Jewish Quarter, Area B, Stratum 2 (Geva 2010: Pl. 4.7: 3–6) and Area E, Stratum 2 (Geva and Hershkovitz 2006: Pl. 4.13: 19–20); Masada (Barag and Hershkovitz 1994: Fig. 6: 28–31).

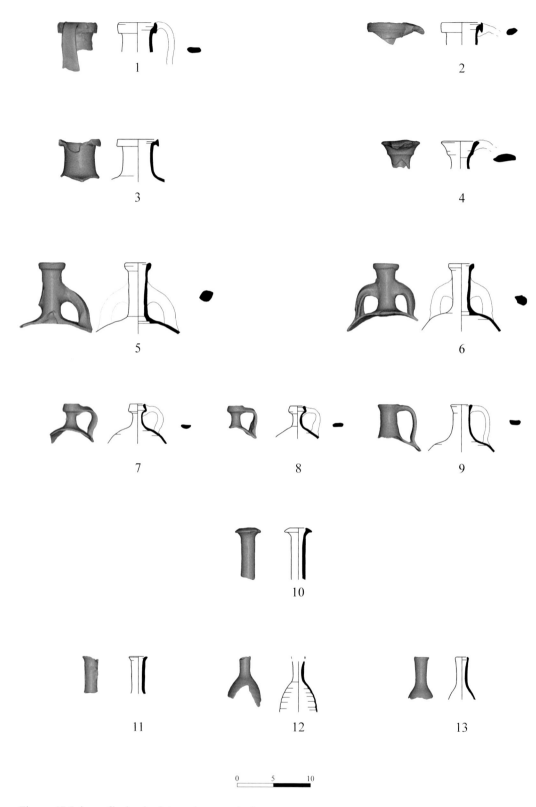

Figure 17.5: jugs, flasks, juglets and unguentaria.

Figure 17.5: Jugs, Flasks, Juglets and Unguentaria

No.	Basket no.	Locus	Type	Description
1	140041.4	14022	Jug	Light brown clay, orange core
2	140098	14036	Jug	Orange clay with grits
3	140027	14009	Jug	Orange clay with grits, gray core
4	140098.1	14036	Jug	Orange clay/light brown
5	140079	14039	Flask	Orange clay with grits
6	140079.1	14039	Flask	Light brown clay with grits, gray core, yellow slip
7	140006.4	14004	Juglet	Light brown clay
8	140102.6	14039	Juglet	Orange clay with grits
9	140004.2	14004	Juglet	Orange clay with grits
10	140107	14038	Unguentarium	Brown clay with grits
11	140004	14004	Unguentarium	Orange clay with grits
12	140070		Unguentarium	Orange clay with grits
13	140011	14007	Unguentarium	Orange clay with grits

JUDEAN RADIAL OIL LAMPS (FIG. 17.6: 3–4)

These are mold-made lamps of reddish-pink ware with brown or red slip on the exterior, thick walls, decorated with radial ridges or semi-concentric circles and other motifs. These oil lamps are very common during the 1st century BCE and were found in Area J, Stratum 3 (Geva and Hershkovitz 2014: Pl. 3.11: 5–9), Area E, Stratum 3 (Geva and Hershkovitz 2006: Pls. 4.6: 6–8; 4.8: 15–18) and Masada (Barag and Hershkovitz 1994: Fig. 2: 4–5, 13).

GRAY-SLIPPED OIL LAMPS (FIG. 17.6: 5)

Two nozzle fragments of such lamps were recovered from the earth fills. This type is mold made, with gray ware and a dark gray slip. According to parallels, these oil lamps are characterized by floral decorations. This type is a known group of locally made oil lamps, produced in Judea in the Early Roman period, and continuing after the 70 CE destruction (see Geva 2010: 129, Pl. 4.7: 7; for parallels from Masada, see Barag and Hershkovitz 1994: Fig. 14: 92).

STANDS

CYLINDRICAL STAND (FIG. 17.7: 1)

A tall, cylindrical to slightly convex stand (dimensions: 21 cm) with a flaring foot and rim was found in the excavation. The stand has a ridge under the rim. Black decoration is seen in the center of the stand. The vessel is made of light brown clay with grits. Air bubbles are notable on the body due to firing conditions. This type of stand is known from the Zealot occupation context at Masada (Type M-SD1, Bar-Nathan 2006: Pl. 38: 1), with other known parallels of this type in Jerusalem at the pottery workshop at Jerusalem's Convention Center

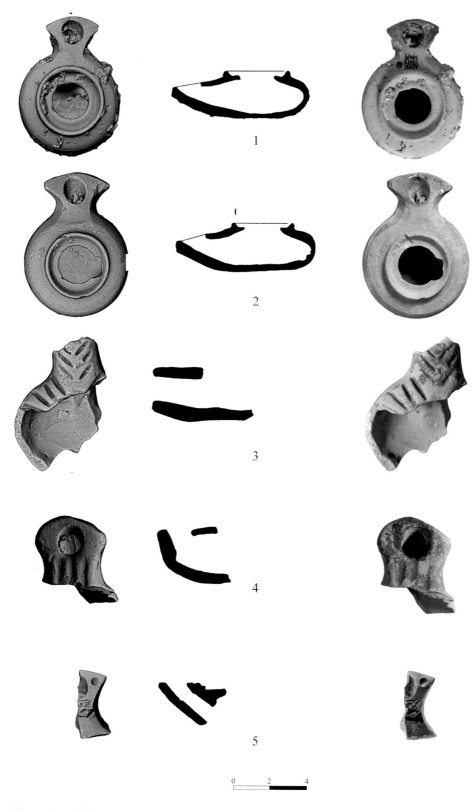

Figure 17.6: Oil lamps.

Figure 17.6: Oil Lamps

No.	Basket no.	Locus	Type	Description
1	140019	14013	Lamp	Light brown clay
2	140004.15	14004	Lamp	Brown-red clay with grits
3	140089.4	19035	Lamp	Light brown clay, dark brown slip
4	140044	14026	Lamp	Orange clay, red slip
5	140004	14004	Lamp	Gray clay, dark gray slip

(Be'eri and Levi forthcoming) and an additional stand from the City of David (Moni-Kedem Givon, personal comment). Bar-Nathan assumed that it was used as a stand for a hand-washing basin (Bar-Nathan 2006: 235–238, Fig. 74). The fact that this type was not found in context at the Jewish Quarter, Jericho or any other contemporary assemblages raises some questions as to the function, provenance and distribution of the vessel. It should be noted that the stand's rim is similar to some krater types, and it is possible that stand fragments were identified as such kraters erroneously.

SHORT STAND (FIG. 17.7: 2)

A short, ring-shaped stand with curved inner wall, the rims are rounded and have ridges between them. These stands, used for vessels with round bases, were made from an orange clay with white grits and have a gray core. The stand is widespread in Judea, found in the Jewish Quarter, Area E, Stratum 3 (Geva and Hershkovitz 2006: Pl. 4.12: 9), Area B, Stratum 2 (Geva 2010: Pl. 4.6: 12–14) and Binyanei Ha'uma, Phase 1–4 (Berlin 2005: Pl. 10; Be'eri and Levi forthcoming; Amit 2010).

VARIA

LADLE (FIG. 17.7: 3)

Only one handle fragment of a ladle was found. These vessels were cup-shaped, with a low disk base and simple rim and a long, rounded handle with a pointed tip rising from the upper body. The example here is made from light brown clay painted red. More complete parallels were found in the Jewish Quarter, Area B, Stratum 2 (Geva 2010: Pl. 4.6: 10–11).

NOTES ON THE POTTERY ASSEMBLAGE

The pottery assemblage exposed in the current excavation is typical of 1st century CE Jerusalem, well known from contemporary published assemblages predating the Roman destruction of Jerusalem, for example, from the Jewish Quarter, Area B, Stratum 2 (the Burnt House), dated to the first half of the 1st century CE to 70 CE (Geva 2010) and Areas E, N and J (Geva and Hershkovitz 2006; 2014). Functional vessels found in the earth fills of the Phase 1 support system, such as the cooking pot, cooking jugs, casseroles and stands, may have been produced in the Phase 3–4 kilns at Binyanei Ha'uma that yielded a similar repertoire (Berlin 2005). Outside of Jerusalem, similar assemblages were found in Masada's Zealot occupation and Garrison 2 contexts (Bar-Nathan 2006) and at Jericho, HR3 (Bar-Nathan 2002). Several of the types presented here give us a clear idea

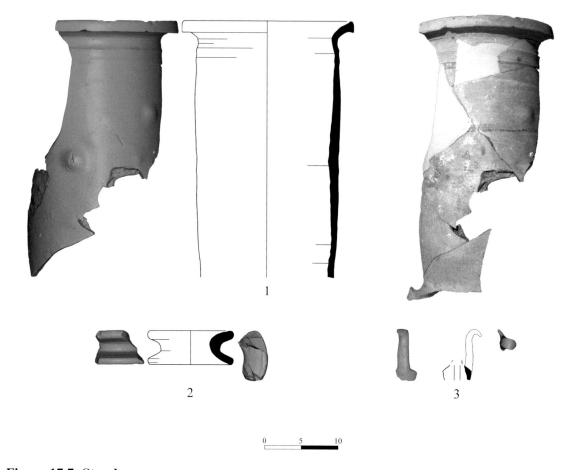

Figure 17.7: Stands

No.	Basket no.	Locus	Type	Description
1	140087	14039	Stand	Light brown clay with grits
2	140041.5	14022	Stand	Orange clay with grits, gray core
3	140013.2	14007	Ladle	Fine light brown clay, red slip

about the dating of the support system, also bolstered by the numismatic evidence (see Ariel, Nos. 74–76, this volume). Storage jars with ridged necks and those with triangular rims seem to date exclusively to the 1st century CE, while the cooking pots and piriform unguentaria are also more typical of 1st century CE assemblages. The cylindrical stand (Fig. 17.7: 1), found to date exclusively in Masada's Zealot occupation context (66 CE–73/74 CE, Bar-Nathan 2006: 225, 235–238), is of interest, as it is the earliest appearance of this type. Furthermore, to date the vessel is only known from Masada. As mentioned above, this may be a case of misidentified rim fragments. That said, the lack of such vessels in Jerusalem may be of significance. Regardless, the stands and storage jars provide a *terminus post quem* for the construction and fill of the compartments built along the Western Wall. This is in conjunction with the dates provided for the construction of the street above the support system, both beneath Robinson's Arch (Reich and Billig 1998) and lower downhill in Area S in the City of David (Szanton *et al.* 2019).

The fragmentary nature of much of the pottery may suggest secondary deposition of the finds, perhaps from a nearby refuse area as a source of constructional fill. That said, the homogenous nature of the assemblage, dating almost exclusively to the 1st century CE, seems to indicate that such a fill could not have been built up over years, but represents a single deposition episode in its primary context, and its almost immediate secondary deposition in the support compartments. Other findings, such as the residue analysis (Chapter 24) and faunal assemblage (Chapter 22), suggest a similar scenario of immediate burial, without a long period of exposure to the environment. It is possible that such refuse fills were available in Jerusalem, such as those found along the eastern slopes (Gadot 2014; Machline and Gadot 2017). The presence of several complete and whole vessels suggests that alongside the fills which included broken finds, the workers involved in the construction project likely threw in their own refuse as the construction fills were poured in (see Chapter 25).

REFERENCES

Amit, D. 2010. Incisions and Impressions on Ring Stands from the Binyanē Ha-ʾUma Workshop: A Preliminary Report. In: Amit, D., Peleg-Barkat, O. and Stiebel, G., eds. *New Studies in the Archaeology of Jerusalem and Its Region* 4. Jerusalem: 130–140.

Avigad, N. and Sass, B. 1997. *Corpus of West Semitic Stamp Seals*. Jerusalem.

Barag, D. and Hershkovitz, M. 1994. Lamps from Masada. In: Aviram, J., Foerster, G. and Netzer, E., eds. *Masada IV: The Yigael Yadin Excavations 1963–1965, Final Reports*. Jerusalem: 1–147.

Bar-Nathan, R. 1981. Pottery and Stone Vessels of the Herodian Period. In: Netzer, E., ed. *Greater Herodium* (Qedem 13). Jerusalem.

Bar-Nathan, R. 2002. *Hasmonean and Herodian Palaces at Jericho: Final Reports of the 1973–1987 Excavations*, Vol. 3: *The Pottery*. Jerusalem.

Bar-Nathan, R. 2006. *Masada VII: The Yigael Yadin Excavations 1963–1965, Final Reports: The Pottery of Masada*. Jerusalem.

Be'eri, R. and Levi, D., eds. Forthcoming. *Excavations at the Site of the Jerusalem International Convention Center (Binyanē Ha-ʾUma–Crowne Plaza Hotel) 2009–2010, Pottery Workshops from the Second Century BCE to the Second Century CE near Jerusalem*, Vol. 1 (IAA Reports).

Be'eri R., Levi, D. and Sandhaus, D., eds. Forthcoming. *Excavations at the Site of the Jerusalem International Convention Center (Binyanē Ha-ʾUma–Crowne Plaza Hotel) 2009–2010, Pottery Workshops from the Second Century BCE to the Second Century CE near Jerusalem*, Vol. 2 (IAA Reports).

Ben-Shlomo, D. 2014. Petrographic Analysis of Early Roman Periods from Areas J and N. In: Geva, H., ed. *Jewish Quarter Excavations in the Old City of Jerusalem, Conducted by Nahman Avigad, 1969–1982*, Vol. 6: *The Finds from Areas J and N, Final Report*. Jerusalem: 200–201.

Berlin, A. 2005. Pottery and Pottery Production in the Second Temple Period, In: Arubas, B. and Goldfus, H., eds. *Excavations on the Site of the Jerusalem International Convention Center (Binyanei Ha'Uma): A Settlement of the Late First to Second Temple Period, the Tenth Legion's Kilnworks, and a Byzantine Monastic Complex; The Pottery and Other Small Finds* (JRA Supplementary Series 60). Jerusalem: 29–60.

Gadot, Y. 2014. Preliminary Report on the Excavations at Jerusalem's Southeastern Hill, Area D. *Hebrew Bible and Ancient Israel* 3: 279–292.

Geva, H. 2006. Bone Artifacts. In: Geva, H., ed. *Jewish Quarter Excavations in the Old City of Jerusalem, Conducted by Nahman Avigad, 1969–1982*, Vol. 3: *Area E and Other Studies, Final Report*. Jerusalem: 266–271.

Geva, H. 2010. Early Roman Pottery. In: Geva, H., ed. *Jewish Quarter Excavations in the Old City of Jerusalem, Conducted by Nahman Avigad, 1969–1982*, Vol. 4: *The Burnt House of Area B and Other Studies, Final Report*. Jerusalem: 118–153.

Geva, H. and Hershkovitz, M. 2006. Local Pottery of the Hellenistic and Early Roman Periods. In: Geva, H., ed. *Jewish Quarter Excavations in the Old City of Jerusalem, Conducted by Nahman Avigad, 1969–1982*, Vol. 3: *Area E and Other Studies, Final Report*. Jerusalem: 94–143.

Geva, H. and Hershkovitz, M. 2014. Local Pottery of the Hellenistic and Early Roman Periods from Areas J and N. In: Geva, H., ed. *Jewish Quarter Excavations in the Old City of Jerusalem, Conducted by Nahman Avigad, 1969–1982*, Vol. 6: *The Finds from Areas J and N, Final Report*. Jerusalem: 134–175.

Geva, H. and Rosenthal-Heginbottom, R. 2003. Local Pottery from Area A. In: Geva, H., ed. *Jewish Quarter Excavations in the Old City of Jerusalem, Conducted by Nahman Avigad, 1969–1982*, Vol. 2: *The Finds from Areas A, W and X-2, Final Report*. Jerusalem: 176–191.

Gutfeld, O. and Nenner-Soriano, R. 2006. Metal Artifacts. In: Geva, H., ed. *Jewish Quarter Excavations in the Old City of Jerusalem, Conducted by Nahman Avigad, 1969–1982*, Vol. 3: *Area E and Other Studies, Final Report*. Jerusalem: 272–282.

Machline, H. and Gadot, Y. 2017. Wading Through Jerusalem's Garbage: Chronology, Function, and Formation Process of the Pottery Assemblage of the City's Early Roman Landfill. *Journal of Hellenistic Pottery and Material Culture* 2: 102–139.

Nenner-Soriano, R. 2010. Bone Artifacts. In: Geva, H., ed. *Jewish Quarter Excavations in the Old City of Jerusalem, Conducted by Nahman Avigad, 1969–1982*, Vol. 4: *The Burnt House of Area B and Other Studies, Final Report*. Jerusalem: 284–287.

Nenner-Soriano, R. 2014. Metal Artifacts from Areas J and N. In: Geva, H., ed. *Jewish Quarter Excavations in the Old City of Jerusalem, Conducted by Nahman Avigad, 1969–1982*, Vol. 6: *The Finds from Areas J, N, Z and Other Studies, Final Report*. Jerusalem: 311–317.

Reich, R. and Billig, Y. 1998. Jerusalem, Robinson's Arch. *Hadashot Arkheologiyot* 108: 180 (Hebrew; English summary: 135).

Rosenthal-Heginbottom, R. 2014. Lamps, Table and Kitchen Ware from Areas J and N. In: Geva, H., ed. *Jewish Quarter Excavations in the Old City of Jerusalem, Conducted by Nahman Avigad, 1969–1982*, Vol. 6: *The Finds from Areas J and N, Final Report*. Jerusalem: 134–211.

Shukron, E. 2012. Did Herod Build the Foundations of the Western Wall? In: Meiron, E., ed. *City of David: Studies of Ancient Jerusalem* 7. Jerusalem: 13–21 (Hebrew).

Szanton, N., Hagbi, M., Uziel, J. and Ariel, D.T. 2019. Monumental Building Projects in Jerusalem in the Days of Pontius Pilate: A View from the Stepped Street. *Tel Aviv* 46: 147–166.

CHAPTER 18

CATALOG OF SMALL FINDS FROM THE WESTERN WALL FOUNDATIONS EXCAVATIONS

Moran Hagbi and Joe Uziel

Below is a concise catalog of the complete spectrum of small finds unearthed in the fills of Phase 1 of the Western Wall Foundations excavations. The finds presented here may be useful in understanding the formation processes of the excavated compartments, i.e., where the fills in the chambers were brought from.

BULLA

A typical Iron IIB bulla was discovered, similar to many bullae found in Jerusalem in late Iron Age contexts (Fig. 18.1: 1. See, e.g., Avigad and Sass 1997). Two names appear on this bulla type, one above the other, in two registers divided by a single line separator. The fragment found here is the right end of the bulla, meaning that it is the first part of the name. The line separator is visible. Other than the base of the first letter, which may be a *lamed,* the upper name is almost completely illegible. A *lamed* often appears as the first letter on seals; it indicates "belonging to" (e.g., Avigad and Sass 1997: 49). The first letter of the lower name is a *nun,* the only complete letter to have survived. Following the *nun* is the leg of an additional letter that is not complete. It may be a *gimel,* although names beginning with a *nun* and then *gimel* are not common (see Avigad and Sass 1997: 43 for the use of the name Negbi). The most common name beginning with a *nun* would be Neriyahu or one of its variants (*ibid.*: 42), making the second letter a *resh*. This is the most likely scenario, although no secure identification can be made.

METAL ARTIFACTS

Complete copper alloy tack (Fig. 18.1: 2). Parallels found in the Jewish Quarter at Area B (Nenner-Soriano 2010: Pl. 8.2: M24) and Area E (Gutfeld and Nenner-Soriano 2006: Pl. 12.1: M5).

Copper alloy pin head, complete (Fig. 18.1: 3).

Copper alloy rod, fragment 4.5 cm long (Fig. 18.1: 4).

Bronze-made, square-shaped weight, length: 0.5 cm, width: 0.5 cm, weight: 0.68 g (Fig. 18.1: 5).

Bronze-made, square-shaped weight, length: 1.5 cm, width: 1.5 cm, weight: 12.9 g (Fig. 18.1: 6).

Bronze-made, square-shaped weight, length: 1.7 cm, width: 1.7 cm, weight: 13.62 g (Fig. 18.1: 7. Nenner-Soriano 2010: Pl. 8.3: M56; Gutfeld and Nenner-Soriano 2006: Pl. 12.1: M20).

Copper alloy arched-shaped bracket, complete, 3.5 cm. According to parallels, this artifact was likely the leg of a bronze bowl (Fig. 18.1: 8. Nenner-Soriano 2014: Fig. 14/1: M18).

BONE ARTIFACTS

BONE DICE

Solid bone dice, complete, rectangular (dimensions: $1 \times 1 \times 0.5$ cm). Full numeric setting, marked by concentric circles (Fig. 18.1: 9).

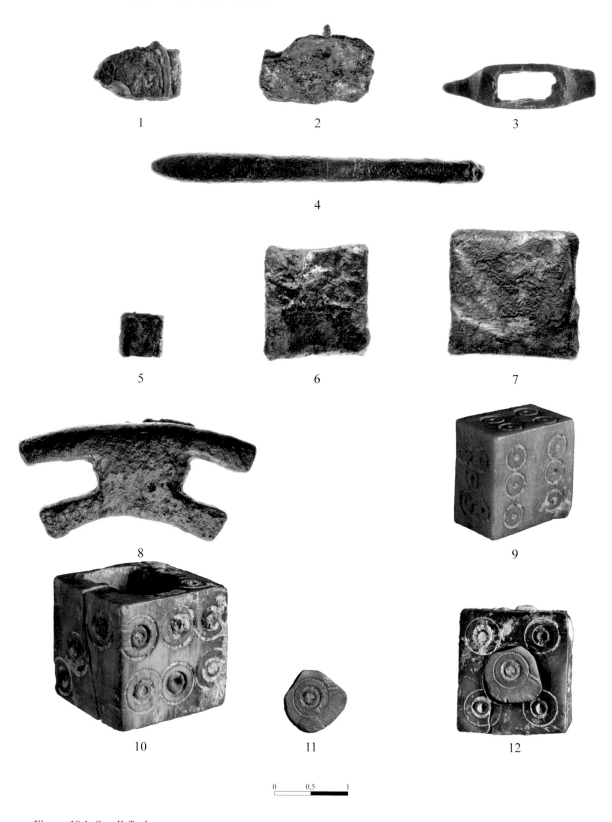

Figure 18.1: Small finds.

Bone-made dice, complete (dimensions: $1 \times 1 \times 1$ cm. Fig. 18.1: 10–12). Full numeric setting, marked by concentric circles. The dice is made from hollow, cut limb bone. The holes from both sides were covered by cut bone round plate. One piece was found in the same locus and probably was part of the dice (Fig. 18: 11). Parallels were found in the Jewish Quarter, Area E (Geva 2006: Pl. 11.1: B19).

Bone Inlays

Many small bone-made inlays of various shapes were found during the excavation. Most of the inlays were triangular, with a few others square or diamond-shaped. The inlays were used to decorate tables or other wood furnishings.

REFERENCES

Avigad, N. and Sass, B. 1997. *Corpus of West Semitic Stamp Seals*. Jerusalem.

Gutfeld, O. and Nenner-Soriano, R. 2006. Metal Artifacts. In: Geva, H., ed. *Jewish Quarter Excavations in the Old City of Jerusalem, Conducted by Nahman Avigad, 1969–1982*, Vol. 3: *Area E and Other Studies, Final Report*. Jerusalem: 272–282.

Nenner-Soriano, R. 2010. Bone Artifacts. In: Geva, H., ed. *Jewish Quarter Excavations in the Old City of Jerusalem, Conducted by Nahman Avigad, 1969–1982*, Vol. 4: *The Burnt House of Area B and Other Studies, Final Report*. Jerusalem: 284–287.

Nenner-Soriano, R. 2014. Metal Artifacts from Areas J and N. In: Geva, H., ed. *Jewish Quarter Excavations in the Old City of Jerusalem, Conducted by Nahman Avigad, 1969–1982*, Vol. 6: *The Finds from Areas J, N, Z and Other Studies, Final Report*. Jerusalem: 311–317.

CHAPTER 19

COINS FOUND ALONG THE WESTERN WALL FOUNDATIONS EXCAVATIONS

Donald T. Ariel

The excavations along the Western Wall Foundations yielded 217 coins. Of these, 138 could not be identified.[1]

STRATIGRAPHY, COIN CURRENCY AND CHRONOLOGY

The southern portion of the Western Wall of the Temple Mount has been subjected to excavations almost since the beginning of scientific exploration of Jerusalem. In recent years, coins have played a large role in understanding the chronology of the structures alongside the wall (e.g., Weksler-Bdolah 2015: 40, 46; Ariel forthcoming) and most recently, the date of the construction of the Western Wall itself.

The coin currency of Jerusalem in the 1st century CE, before the city came under siege and was subsequently conquered by the Romans, was almost exclusively composed of bronze coins from the municipal mint, and silver coins, more rarely in the archaeological record, of the mint of Tyre. Consequently, when a coin is identified in context, one can determine the date of the context with relative certainty by considering the date of the next known municipal issue and its relative rarity.

The first case in which I participated in providing the numismatic component of the chronology of the structures alongside the Western Wall was the dating of the street below Robinson's Arch. The latest coins to securely derive from below the street were of Pontius Pilate (Reich and Billig 1998: 180; 1999: 35). The coins were dated to 26–36 CE (*ibid.*: 180; 2008: 1809).[2]

Based on the coins, Reich and Billig first concluded the street's date to be around the time of the reign of Agrippa I (38–44 CE). This is perhaps because that king was a likely candidate to construct such a street.

In 2008, Reich and Billig adjusted their dating. Rather than the 40s CE as the date of the street, the revised date was the last generation of the Second Temple period (Reich and Billig 2008: 1809). Reich and Shukron (2012: 220) added a number date to this revision, i.e., the 50s of the 1st century CE. From the perspective of coin currency, both of these dates (the reign of Agrippa I and the 50s CE) are problematic. In Agrippa I's sixth regnal year (41/2 CE), the king produced a massive coin issue in Jerusalem (*TJC*: 231, No. 120). *TJC*: No. 120, in fact, was the largest coin issue struck in the capital in the 1st century CE.

---

[1] The coins were cleaned in the laboratories of the IAA by Victoria Nosikovsky, and were photographed by Clara Amit.

[2] Although I identified these coins, I cannot now reconstruct the exact details of the context with "Pontius Pilate" coins noted by Reich and Billig. Clarifications of the details must await the research for the final report of the excavations.

Had the street alongside the Western Wall been paved in the 50s of the 1st century CE, one certainly would have expected there to be some coins of the enormous issue of Agrippa I under the pavers.[3] In fact, had the street even been paved after 41–42 CE, one would have expected some of these common coins to be found in the foundations. I am not saying that Reich, Billig and Shukron were in error in their dating. After all, only 15 coins were found (Reich and Billig 1999: 35), and it is therefore possible that coins then associated with Pilate did appear, coins of Agrippa did not, and still the context would postdate Agrippa I's reign. Nevertheless, it would seem to me that Reich, Billig and Shukron had non-numismatic considerations which brought them to the later date, and that they found those considerations to be compelling.

In another part of the massive constructions alongside the Western Wall, Weksler-Bdolah dated Wilson's Arch to sometime after 29/30 CE, based upon a coin excavated in the foundations of the staircase that led to the causeway atop the arch (Weksler-Bdolah 2015: 40, 46). There was no assemblage of coins, just the one, a coin of a governor in Jerusalem in 29/30 CE (*TJC*: 258, No. 331). This *terminus post quem* date cannot be analyzed using coin currency tools, because the quantity of latest dated material in the context is too small (one coin). I cannot argue that for lack of coins of Agrippa I the causeway should date before 41/2 CE.

In 2011, Shukron excavated below Reich and Billig's street underneath Robinson's Arch. These excavations are located just north of the area of the 2013–2015 seasons of excavation in this report. Shukron's excavations relate very directly to the coins published here and therefore will be covered in detail. The general findings of those excavations, their Area P, have thus far been published only in a few summary articles. The details of their findings have been considered in the current excavations' final stratigraphic report, using those preliminary reports. In order to understand the numismatic profile reported here, I will relate to both what is published and what I know of those coins as the individual who identified them.

In general, the coin quantities and their profiles from Shukron's Area P and those from the current 2013–2015 excavations just to the south are the same. Among the registered coins in the Israel national collection are 57 identified coins from Area P, which is a similar scale to the 79 reported here. Both assemblages have earlier coins in appropriate proportions. By this I mean that the quantities are commensurate with the age of the coins and their presumed original output. In both groups, the earliest coin is a small issue of Antiochus III minted in 'Akko-Ptolemais material (cf. No. 1). There follow a small number of Hasmonean coins, dominated by the smallest issues of Alexander Jannaeus (*TJC*: 210, Subgroups L7–14; cf. Nos. 7–19). Early Herodian (Herod I, Archelaus) coins are in evidence (cf. Nos. 23–43), as well as a larger group of ear of barley/palm tree issues struck under a Roman governor under Augustus (cf. Nos. 44–68).[4]

All these coins were probably circulating at the time of the latest coins in the assemblages. In other words, there is no indication that the coins from either expedition accumulated slowly along the strip west of the Western Wall of the Temple Mount at its foundation level. Both excavation areas seem to be part of a one-period fill.

The latest coins of both assemblages date to the reign of Tiberius (14–37 BCE) and were struck by appointed governors to the province of Judea. The dates of the rule of these governors are unclear.

---

[3] One thousand forty-one coins of the type in the Israel national collection were documented from excavations in Jerusalem. This may be compared to 289 of types *TJC*: Nos. 327–329 (17/8–24/5 CE) discussed here. In other words, roughly speaking, for every coin of *TJC*: Nos. 327–329 found in archaeological assemblages dating after 41/42 CE in Jerusalem, more than three-and-a-half coins of Agrippa 1 would also be expected in those contexts.

[4] On Augustus's coins, see Kokkinos 2012 and comments on Kokkinos's arguments in Ariel 2014b: 387–388.

On the coins only the name of the reigning Roman emperor (Augustus, Tiberius, Claudius or Nero) and his regnal year appear. Nevertheless, until recently, numismatic literature tended to classify the coins in question according to the names of these various Roman governors, who seem to have been called *praefecti* up to 41 and *procuratores* after 44 CE. However, because there remains a sufficient amount of uncertainty regarding the chronology of the governors, it is best to abandon the conjectural dates formerly given for these governors' terms and prefer a heading composed of the emperor's name and year of rule.[5]

This is not simply a semantic change. The latest coins in Shukron's Area P are reported as dating to the governorship of Valerius Gratus. However, there is no longer a consensus regarding the end of Gratus's rule and the installation of his successor, Pontius Pilate. Hoffeditz (2006: 88, n. 4) discussed earlier suggestions to redate the beginning of Pilate's period of governorship (noting Eisler 1931; Schwartz 1992; Bond 1998; and Lønnqvist 2000). Hoffeditz ultimately rejected the attempts, in favor of the traditional dating. Mason, however, endorsed Schwartz's proposal.[6] The problematics of the chronology of those two governors have recently been reiterated by Schwartz (2013: 140–141).

Part of scholars' attempts to understand the import of Shukron's argument to redate the foundation of the Western Wall entails considering the feasibility that one provincial governor or another would have endorsed the project. As the governorship of Valerius Gratus and Pontius Pilate are perceived to have been quite different, the intersection of their chronologies with the coins found in *Miqweh* Locus 55 may be significant.

At this point, I must return to the numismatic analysis. Shukron wrote of the eight coins post-dating Herod in *Miqweh* Locus 55 in Area P, stating that the latest four coins were of Valerius Gratus and that they were struck in 17/8 CE (2012: 21). This is an error. The four latest coins are all of the same type. They bear Tiberius's name and title within a wreath on the obverse and a palm branch on the reverse. An inscription naming Tiberius's wife Julia flanks a palm branch, below which the date appears, as usual. Three regnal dates are known: years 4, 5 and 11, corresponding to years 17/8, 18/9 and 24/5 CE. On the four latest coins from *Miqweh* Locus 55, the date was clear on *none* of the coins. This means that the date of the latest coin might also have been year 11, or 24/5 CE, and that we must relate to them as dating from the range of 17/8–24/5 CE.

North of *Miqweh* Locus 55, still along the strip west of the Western Wall of the Temple Mount at its foundation level, part of another plastered installation was discerned and designated *Miqweh* Locus 91. There, too, I found an error in the 2012 reporting: Shukron wrote that the latest coin was minted by a governor under Augustus in 5/6 CE, and such a coin was found there (Shukron 2012: 23, Fig. 21 [IAA 138490]), but the actual latest coins were of the wreath/palm branch type of Tiberius. One coin bore the date of year 4 (17/8 CE; Shukron 2012: 21, Fig. 16 [IAA 141570]), and two others (one uncertain) bore year 5 dates, meaning that the latest coin in *Miqweh* Locus 91 was issued in 18/9 CE.

The two errors noted, discrepancies between the exact breakdown of the coins registered in the Israel national collection and Shukron's 2012 reporting of them[7] and others' re-reporting[8] of the

---

[5] See Editors' Note, *Israel Numismatic Research* 2 (2007): 3–4.

[6] "D.R. Schwartz (1992: 182–217), however, makes a compelling argument for the years *ca.* 19 to 37 as Pilate's term" in Mason's commentary [No. 1054] to Josephus, *War* 2.169 (Mason, n.d.).

[7] The discussion here is based on the coins' identifications in the Israel national collection.

[8] For example, Weksler-Bdolah 2015: 48 reports that 17 coins from *Miqweh* Locus 55 date to Valerius Gratus, and that four of them date to 15/6 CE. Unless some of the Area P coins have not yet been registered in the Israel national collection, no coins of 15/6 CE are found among Shukron's 2011 season coins. Moreover, the 15/6 CE (regnal year 2 of Tiberius) coin is a rare type.

dates and quantities of these coins, are not uncommon for preliminary reports. No doubt these will be ironed out with the publication of the final report of Shukron's 2011 excavations. It must be stressed that none of the coins examined by me from any of the 57 identified coins from Area P were datable beyond the profile described above. Hence, from a numismatic perspective, the picture is stable, as I presently will explain.

What is this picture of chronological stability? The quantities of coins issued in Jerusalem in the regnal years 4, 5 and 11 of Tiberius are similar. In both *Miqweh* Locus 55 and *Miqweh* Locus 91, there are no coins in which year 11 (*TJC*: 258, No. 329) has been read. One might wish, therefore, to date the filling of the *miqwaʾot* to between 18/9 and 24/5 CE. It may not be fortuitous that no wreath/palm branch coins of Tiberius bore an explicit year 11 date. However, as we cannot be sure that one of the coins with illegible date is *not* dated to 24/5 CE, we prefer a different formulation of the assemblage's chronological horizon. The coins were deposited "sometime in the 20s CE." This is because after the striking of the year 11, 24/5 CE, coin, the following issue of the Jerusalem mint occurred in 29/30 CE, in Tiberius's 16th regnal year. This coin, depicting a *simpulum* on the obverse and three ears of grain on the reverse (*TJC*: 258, No. 331), is plentiful in the archaeological record, and probably was a much larger production than *TJC*: 258, No. 329. Moreover, in the two years following that coin issue, in 30/31 and 31/2 CE, equally common mintings were made. In terms of the numismatic profile of Jerusalem, therefore, it would be difficult to imagine a coin assemblage the size of the fill of *Miqweh* Locus 55— and, *a fortiori*, that of the *Miqweh* Locus 55 fill together with the *Miqweh* Locus 91 fill—would date to the 30s of the 1st century CE, and not have had any of the coins of Tiberius's 16th through 18th years.

The finds from the 2013–2015 excavations along the Western Wall of the Temple Mount at the southernmost point serve to reinforce the chronological conclusions ("sometime in the 20s CE") above. From the reign of Tiberius, coins have been identified from year 2 (No. 69, the rare issue noted in note 6), year 4 (No. 70), year 5 (No. 71, and possibly Nos. 72–73). Four coins, coincidentally the same number as that found in Shukron's excavations, are of the same type without a legible date. My conclusions given to the first excavation team are therefore the same argued here.

Clearly, considerations other than numismatics are involved in dating the foundation of the Western Wall of the Temple Mount. Another numismatic consideration, however, supports the above. The street laid above the 2011 and 2013–2015 excavations contained coins in *its* foundation considered to be of Pontius Pilate and—according to their preliminary excavation report—dating to 26–36 CE (Reich and Billig 1998: 180; 1999: 35). Reich and Billig undoubtedly referred to the coins which Meshorer considered to have been struck by Pilate: *TJC*: 258, Nos. 329–333 (29/30 to 31/2 CE). The absence of those coins in the lower excavations and their presence in the upper ones are likely to somehow reflect the period of time from the beginning of the urban development of the street to its completion. A period of between a decade to two decades is reasonable for such a large construction project. Moreover, the coin excavated in the foundations of the staircase that led to the causeway atop Wilson's Arch (above), with its date in the early 30s CE, may have been part of the same urban development scheme.

This is not to say that there are no alternative explanations for Shukron's proposal that the Western Wall of the Temple Mount was constructed some 30 years after Herod's death in 4 or 3 BCE (Kushnir-Stein 1995: 83–86). Alternative explanations exist, as Weksler-Bdolah has noted (2015: 48). This discussion only lays out, in a careful fashion, the numismatic evidence for the dating of the filling alongside the Western Wall and up to the street above it.

In 2011, with 12 coins dating from Herod to Tiberius in *Miqweh* Locus 55—and with 30 coins dating from those dates in all of the elements excavated by Shukron—I considered the quantities of coins sufficient to suggest a numismatic *terminus post quem* date for the fill alongside the Temple Mount's western retaining wall: "sometime in the 20s CE." With the current addition of 55 more coins from that period from the 2013–2015 excavations, there is no doubt in my mind that enough numismatic material is available to provide a range of dates for the street project. It appears that, in the 20s, work began in that area, and in the 30s, or at the latest in the early 40s, it was completed. The absence of the massive Jerusalem issue of Agrippa I from any foundations of the undertaking, in my mind, is compelling.

It is another issue to draw conclusions from the coins found in these excavations on the question relating to the actual beginning of the Western Wall's construction. A consensus on the meaning of the stratigraphic relationship of the *Miqweh* Locus 55 and *Miqweh* Locus 91 fill to the Western Wall must be reached first.

NUMISMATICS

No. 78 is described as mint debitage. It is a bronze channel, part of a casting process. Although this could be any casting process because it is identical to the "negative" of many such channels chiseled on limestone flan molds known in the southern Levant, the shape of the fragment compellingly points to an identification of the fragment as coming from the production of flans.

The existence of bronze casting channels in the archaeological record in Israel was first seen in 1968 or 1969, when an assemblage of debitage from a minting operation in Jerusalem was excavated at the Jerusalem Citadel (Jaffa Gate). What is known about this find was reported by Schauer in 2010. Alongside other nondescript remains of the metallurgical processes involved in casting flans (Schauer 2010: 101, Fig. 1) were three separated casting channels similar to No. 78 (Schauer 2010: 103, Fig. 3b).

Another related category found in the Jerusalem Citadel assemblage were three pairs of unstruck flans attached by their common casting channels (Schauer 2010: 103, Fig. 3a). Pairs of unstruck flans have been identified in the past in sites (Ariel 2012: 49, N. 15). Two permutations of the category, both found in close proximity to the 2013–2015 excavations, are a pair of unstruck flans attached to each other but without a common casting channel (Ariel 1990: 105, C133) and an unstruck flan with casting channels protruding from two sides—and the remains of the leakage of the metal during casting still extant (Ariel 2012: 60, Fig. 3a).

The three full casting channels (Schauer 2010: 103, Fig. 3b), as separate objects, are the first such cases of which I am aware. Such casting channels are difficult to uncover in normal excavation conditions, owing to their minute dimensions. Because of the vagaries of their preservation, they are even more challenging to identify. Casting channels also have little or no value in the antiquities market. Therefore, they are not well known, although it is logical to find them in places where mints existed.

Separate casting channels are now known, but still unpublished, from a number of sites, besides No. 78 of the Western Wall Foundations. One was found in the excavations in Area S of the City of David (IAA 144655),[9] and five derive from the East Talpiyot site with evidence of flan production (and possibly also minting; see Ariel 2011a; IAA 144210–144211, 144218–144219, 144227).

Especially in mints, the manufacturing waste of bullion—be it of precious metal such as silver and gold, or less valuable metal such as the components of bronze (copper, tin) and lead—is saved and recycled back into the minting process. No doubt the precious metal waste is more carefully saved and reused. The debris of less valuable precious metal is perforce a bit less carefully collected.

---

[9] My thanks to Nahshon Szanton and Joe Uziel for permission to note this find.

The debitage of the Jerusalem Citadel mint seems to be a case of remains from a mint whose operation was closed or temporarily discontinued. The reason for the deposition of the other objects noted above may be different, as unstruck flans are known to have circulated alongside struck coins in the period of activity of the Jerusalem mint (Ariel 1990: 115; see also the unstruck flan from a hoard found in the Jewish Quarter of Jerusalem: Avigad 1983: 75; *TJC*: 219, No. 36l). Of the provenanced bronze unstruck flans in the Israel national collection, most have the characteristics of flans cast in molds of the likes of the Jerusalem mint. Over 20% of these derive from sites outside of Jerusalem—another indication that they behaved as coin currency. Might the separate casting channels, the pairs of unstruck flans and the like have entered circulation alongside the unstruck flans? Such an argument can be made.

However, the relevance of the separate casting channel from the excavations at the Western Wall foundations (No. 78) seems to go beyond the possibility that it functioned as currency. Sixty-four percent of the apparently Judean-related unstruck flans were found at sites where flan molds were also found (Ariel 2012: 65–66, Table 3): East Talpiot (×27 coins), Jerusalem Citadel (×17), City of David (×13), Temple Mount Western Wall (×10), Jewish Quarter (×4), Mount Zion (×4), Pisgat Ze'ev (×2) and even Zippori (×4). While many of the unstruck flans may have functioned like money and circulated alongside coins, considering the proximity of the unstruck flans to finds of flan molds, one can also say that the unstruck flans circulated close to the places where they were produced. The separate casting channels, so far found in three places—East Talpiot, Area S, and at the Western Wall—as well as the attached pair of unstruck flans from earlier excavations in the City of David and the unstruck flan with long casting channels, noted above, all also appear to have been deposited near their production areas. This suggests that the Western Wall foundations, where No. 78 was found, were very close to a flan production site, if not a full-fledged mint.

The clustering of No. 78 and the other related objects in the vicinity of the City of David, the oldest part of Jerusalem, raises the possibility that a mint existed there, before the city expanded to the west (Ariel 2012: 71).[10] These new finds, which hint at the existence of a nearby bronze mint, do not place in doubt the evidence for the other municipal mint, at the Jerusalem Citadel (Ariel 2011b: 392). There may be a diachronic relationship between the two.

A listing of the coins by locus is found in Table 19.1.

Table 19.1. List of Coins According to Loci. Coins Bearing an Asterisk Appear in Fig. 19.1

Locus	Qty.	Date (CE)	Cat. no.	Total per locus
1502	1	4 BCE–6 CE	34*	1
14001	1	4 BCE–6 CE	37*	3
	1	17/8–24/5	77	
	1	Unidentified		
14003	3	Unidentified		3

[10]   The presence of fragments of six flan molds in Area N in the Upper City would be another possibility for a nearby ("secondary"; cf. Ariel 2014a: 269) mint.

Locus	Qty.	Date (CE)	Cat. no.	Total per locus
14004	1	80/79 BCE or later	14	23
	1	129–37 BCE	20	
	2	104 BCE–6 CE	31	
	1	4 BCE–6 CE	35, 38	
	1	8/9	46	
	1	10/11	50*	
	2	5/6–10/11	59–60	
	14	Unidentified		
14005	1	Unidentified	1	1
14007	1	198–187 BCE	1	3
	1	80/79 BCE (or later)	6*	
	1	Unidentified		
14009	1	8/9	47	9
	7	Unidentified		
14010	1	10/11	51	13
	1	17/8	70*	
	1	18/9?	73	
	10	Unidentified		
14011	1	10/11	55	8
	1	5/6–10/11	61	
	6	Unidentified		
14012	1	129–37 BCE	22	8
	1	ca. 24 BCE–6 CE	27	
	1	104 BCE–6 CE	30	
	1	8/9	44	
	1	10/11	53*	
	2	5/6–10/11	58, 62	
	1	Unidentified		
14014	3	80/79 BCE or later	39, 13, 15	18
	1	ca. 27–24 BCE	23	
	1	8/9	45	
	2	10/11	52, 54	
	10	Unidentified		
	1	Unidentified		

Locus	Qty.	Date (CE)	Cat. no.	Total per locus
14016	1	ca. 24 BCE–6 CE	26	10
	1	4 BCE–6 CE	33	
	1	5/6–10/11	64	
	1	18/9? [BCE?]	72	
	6	Unidentified		
14020	2	4 BCE–6 CE	32, 39	7
	1	5/6–10/11	65	
	1	Unidentified		
14021	2	4 BCE–6 CE	36, 40	18
	2	5/6–10/11	66–67	
	1	1st c. BCE–1st c. CE	79	
	13	Unidentified		
14022	1	173/2–168 BCE	2	38
	1	104–76 BCE	3	
	1	104–80/79 BCE	5	
	2	80/79 BCE or later	16–17	
	1	ca. 24–12 BCE	25	
	1	ca. 24 BCE–6 CE	29	
	2	4 BCE–6 CE	41–42	
	1	9/10–10/11	56	
	1	5/6–10/11	68	
	1	15/6	69*	
	3	17/8–24/5	74–76	
	22	Unidentified		
14023	1	Unidentified		1
14024	3	Unidentified		3
14025	1	104–80/79 BCE	4	6
	1	9/10–10/11	57	
	4	Unidentified		
14028	1	ca. 24–12 BCE	24	5
	1	5/6–10/11	63	
	3	Unidentified		
14029	1	18/9	71*	1

Locus	Qty.	Date (CE)	Cat. no.	Total per locus
14030	5	80/79 BCE or later	7–8*, 10–11, 18	13
	1	129–37 [BCE?]	21	
	1	ca. 24 BCE–6 CE	28	
	1	129 BCE–69/70 CE	78*	
	5	Unidentified		
14037	1	4 BCE–6 CE	43	1
14038	2	Unidentified		2
14059	1	Unidentified		1
Unstratif.	2	80/79 BCE or later	12, 19	22
	1	9/10?	48	
	1	10/11	49	
	18	Unidentified		

Total: 217

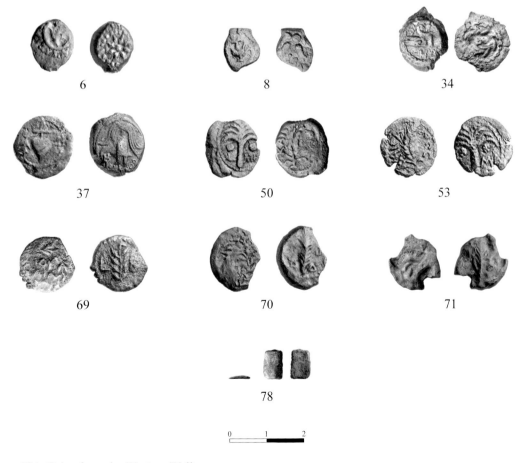

Figure 19.1: Coins from the Western Wall.

CATALOG

The coins are arranged chronologically, according to coin types. All of the coins are bronze. Coins bearing an asterisk have photographs in Fig. 19.1

Cat. no.	Locus reg. no.	Weight (g)	Diam. (mm)	Axis	Obverse	Reverse	Date (CE)	Mint	Reference	Notes	IAA no.
					Seleucids **Antiochus III (222–187 BCE)**						
1	14007 (140011/2)	1.42	11	↑	Head r.	[- -] Apollo stg. l., testing arrow and resting hand on grounded bow	198–187 BCE	'Akko-Ptolemais	SC I/1:416, No. 1096		149546
					Antiochus IV (175–164 BCE)						
2	14022 (140056/7)	2.58	13	↑	Laureate head of Apollo r.; behind head: [·]	[- - -] Veiled and draped female figure, stg. facing, holding long scepter or torch	173/2–168 BCE	Same	SC II/1:92, No. 1479	Serrated	149593
					Hasmoneans **Alexander Jannaeus (104–76 BCE)**						
3	14022 (140047)	1.39	14	→	In wreath: -]הכ[·]/[- -] ה/[- - -] [- - -]/[- - -]הכ/[-	Double cornucopias with pomegranate between horns		Jerusalem	Cf. TJC:212, Group P		149589
4	14025 (140043/14)	1.51	15		[BAΣ]ΙΛΕ[ΩΣ ΑΛΕΞΑΝΔΡΟΥ] Anchor	Star; between rays: Paleo-Hebrew inscription: [- - -]	104–80/79 BCE	Same	TJC:209, Group K		149575

Cat. no.	Locus reg. no.	Weight (g)	Diam. (mm)	Axis	Obverse	Reverse	Date (CE)	Mint	Reference	Notes	IAA no.
5	14022 (140056/1)	1.77	16		[- -] Same	[- -] Same	Same	Same	Same		149590
6*	14007 (140011/3)	1.62	12×14		ΒΑΣΙΛ[ΕΩΣ ΑΛΕΞΑΝΔΡ]ΟΥ Anchor in circle	Eight-pointed star in border of dots; around, unclear Aramaic inscription	Year 25= 80/79 BCE (or later)	Same	TJC:210, Subgroups L1–6	Possibly an imitation	149547
7	14030 (140068/1)	0.56	10×12		Anchor in circle	Six-pointed star in border of dots	80/79 BCE or later	Same	TJC:210, Subgroup L9		149598
8*	14030 (140068/2)	0.71	10×12		Same	Same	Same	Same	Same		149599
9	14014 (140031/1)	0.27	8×11		Illegible	Same	Same	Same	Same		149567
10	14030 (140068/5)	0.41	912		Same	Same	Same	Same	Same		149600
11	14030 (140066/3)	0.38	9×11		Same	Same	Same	Same	Same		149603
12	Unstratif. (140027/3)	0.30	10		Same	Same	Same	Same	Same		149608
13	14014 (140031/2)	0.34	9		Same	Same	Same	Same	TJC:210, Subgroups L7–14		149527
14	14004 (No Reg. No.)	0.78	13		Same	Same	Same	Same	Same		149538
15	14014 (140031/5)	0.47	10		Same	Same	Same	Same	Same		149569

Cat. no.	Locus reg. no.	Weight (g)	Diam. (mm)	Axis	Obverse	Reverse	Date (CE)	Mint	Reference	Notes	IAA no.
16	14022 (140056/4)	0.38	9×11		Same	Same	Same	Same	Same		149592
17	14022 (140056/8)	0.55	10		Same	Same	Same	Same	Same		149594
18	14030 (140069/2)	0.33	10		Same	Same	Same	Same	Same		149602
19	Unstratif. (140028/2)	0.35	8×10		Same	Same	Same	Same	Same		149609
Unclear Hasmonean ruler											
20	14004 (140004/15)	1.00	13	↘	In wreath: [- - -]/[- - -]/[- - -]	Double cornucopias with pomegranate between horns		Same			149540
21	14030 (140069/1)	2.21	16	↖	Same: [- - -]/[- - -]/[- - -]	Same		Same			149601
22	14012 (140087/1)	1.35	13		Illegible	Same		Same			149606
Herodians **Herod (37–4 BCE)**											
23	14014 (140031/4)	0.62	11	→	Inscription in lines: BACI[Λ]/EVC H/PWΔH/C	Anchor flanked by palm branches	*ca.* 27–24 BCE	Same	*TJC*:223, No. 60; Ariel and Fontanille 2012:62, Type 10 [Dies O2(-R1?) on Pl. 58]		149528

Cat. no.	Locus reg. no.	Weight (g)	Diam. (mm)	Axis	Obverse	Reverse	Date (CE)	Mint	Reference	Notes	IAA no.
24	14028 (140048/4)	1.58	14	↙	[- -] Anchor	Double cornucopias; between horns, caduceus; above, four dots	*ca.* 24–12 BCE	Same	*TJC*:222–223, No. 59; Ariel and Fontanille 2012:63, Type 15		149597
25	14022 (140040/16)	1.23	1315	6	[- -] Same	Same; above, three dots	Same	Same	Same		149587
26	14016 (140035/2)	0.99	13	↑	[- -] Same	Same	*ca.* 24 BCE–6 CE	Same	Cf. *TJC*:222–224, Nos. 59, 67–68	Ruler uncertain	149570
27	14012 (140030/3)	1.49	13×15	↑	[- -] Same	Same	Same	Same	Same	Same	149561
28	14030 (140069/4)	1.39	14	↙	[- -] Same	Same	Same	Same	Same	Same	149604
29	14022 (140040/15)	0.64	13		[- -] Same	Illegible	Same	Same	Same	Same	149586
30	14012 (140030/6)	1.37	13		[- -] Same	Same	104 BCE–6 CE	Same		Same	149565
31	14004 (140006/6)	0.95	12		[- -] Same	Same	Same	Same		Same	149542
Archelaus (4 BCE–6 CE)											
32	14020 (140045/1)	2.07	17	↑	Two parallel cornucopias; on r.: H[PW/Δ/HC]	[- -] Galley with ram, prow, aphlaston oars, and rudder, sailing l.; on stern, cabin of navigator		Same	*TJC*:224, No. 70		149576

Cat. no.	Locus reg. no.	Weight (g)	Diam. (mm)	Axis	Obverse	Reverse	Date (CE)	Mint	Reference	Notes	IAA no.
33	14016 (140036/1)	1.03	13×15	↑	[- - -] Two parallel cornucopias; on r.	EΘ[N]/[X]PA Galley with ram, prow, aphlaston oars, and rudder, sailing l.		Same	TJC:225, No. 71		149571
34*	1502 (15005)	1.64	15	↑	H-P-W Prow of galley l.	In wreath: EΘ		Same	TJC:225, No. 72g		149535
35	14004 (140004/4)	1.36	16	→	HPW[ΔOY Grape cluster	[EΘNAPX]OY Crested helmet with two cheek pieces; to bottom l., caduceus		Same	TJC:226, No. 73		149525
36	14021 (140046/2)	1.73	15×17	↗	[- - -] Same	[- -] Same; to bottom l., caduceus		Same	Same		149532
37*	14001 (140001/3)	2.43	16	↗	[HP]W[Δ]OY Same	EΘNA[PX]OY Same; to bottom l., caduceus		Same	Same		149536
38	14004 (140012/5)	1.74	16	↗	[HP]WΔOY Same	[- - -] Same; caduceus illegible		Same	Same		149544
39	14020 (140045/2)	1.26	15	→	[HPWΔ]OY Same	[- - -] Same; caduceus illegible		Same	Same		149577
40	14021 (140055/2)	1.54	16	→	[H]PW[ΔOY] Same	[- - -] Same; caduceus illegible		Same	Same		149582
41	14022 (140040/7)	1.24	16	→	[HPW]ΔO[Y] Same	[- - -] Same; caduceus illegible		Same	Same		149583

Cat. no.	Locus reg. no.	Weight (g)	Diam. (mm)	Axis	Obverse	Reverse	Date (CE)	Mint	Reference	Notes	IAA no.
42	14022 (140004/12)	2.28	16		[H]PWΔO[Y] Same	Illegible		Same	Same		149584
43	14037 (140111)	1.75	15	↙	[- - -] Same	EΘN[APXOY] Same; to bottom l, caduceus		Same	Same		149605
Roman Procurators in Judea under Augustus (27 BCE–14 CE)											
44	14012 (140030/1)	1.62	17	↑	KAICA–POC Ear of barley	Palm tree. In fields, date: L–ΛΘ	Year 39= 8/9	Same	TJC:256, No. 313		149562
45	14014 (140024/1)	1.87	16	↙	[K]AIC[A–POC] Same	Same; in fields: [L]–ΛΘ	Same	Same	Same		149526
46	14004 (140004/1)	0.94	15	↑	KAICA–[POC] Same	Same; in fields: L–ΛΘ	Same	Same	Same		149539
47	14009 (140020/7)	1.99	17	↑	KAICA–POC Same	Same; in fields: L–ΛΘ	Same	Same	Same		149549
48	Unstratif. (140027/2)	0.95	15	↑	[K]AICA–[POC] Same	Same; in fields: L–Ṃ	Year 40?= 9/10?	Same	Cf. TJC:256, No. 314		149607
49	14010 (140015/3)	0.86	16	↑	[KAI]CA–P[OC] Same	Same; in fields: [L]–MA	Year 41= 10/11	Same	Cf. TJC:256, No. 314		149534
50*	14004 (140012/1)	1.58	16	↑	KAIC[A]–POC Same	Same; in fields: L–MA	Same	Same	Cf. TJC:256, No. 315		149543
51	14010 (140028/1)	1.39	16	↙	KAICA–[P]OC Same	Same; in fields: L–MA	Same	Same	Same		149551

Cat. no.	Locus reg. no.	Weight (g)	Diam. (mm)	Axis	Obverse	Reverse	Date (CE)	Mint	Reference	Notes	IAA no.
52	14014 (140024/4)	1.34	15	↑	[K]AIC[A–P]OC Same	Same; in fields: L–MA	Same	Same	Same		149566
53*	14012 (140030/4)	1.29	16	↑	KAICA–POC Same	Same; in fields: [L]–MA	Same	Same	Same		149564
54	14014 (140031/3)	1.33	16	↑	[K]AICA–PO[C] Same	Same; in fields: L–MA	Same	Same	Same		149568
55	14011 (140022/5)	1.12	16	↑	KAIC[A–P]OC Same	Same; in fields: L–MA	Same	Same	Same		149553
56	14022 (140041/4)	1.35	15	↑	KAICA–POC Same	Same; in fields: L–M[·?]	9/10–10/11	Same	Same		149588
57	14025 (140049)	1.58	16	↑	[K]AICA–P[OC] Same	Same; in fields: L–M[·?]	Same	Same	Same		149595
58	14012 (140030/2)	1.61	16	↗	KAI[CA]–POC Same	Same; illegible date	5/6–10/11	Same	Same		149563
59	14004 (140006)	1.47	15	→	[- - -] Same	Same; illegible date	Same	Same	Same		149541
60	14004 (140004/18)	1.43	16	↙	KAI[CA]–POC Same	Same; illegible date	Same	Same	Same		149548
61	14011 (140022/4)	1.24	15	↙	[KAICA–P]OC Same	Same; in fields: L–[·]	Same	Same	Same		149552
62	14012 (140030/5)	0.94	15	↑	KAI[CA]–POC Same	Same; in fields: L–[·]	Same	Same	Same		149545
63	14028 (140048)	1.46	18	↑	[KAICA]–POC Same	Same; illegible date	Same	Same	Same		149596
64	14016 (140037/6)	1.78	17	↙	KA[ICA]–POC Same	Same; in fields: L–[·]	Same	Same	Same		149573

Cat. no.	Locus reg. no.	Weight (g)	Diam. (mm)	Axis	Obverse	Reverse	Date (CE)	Mint	Reference	Notes	IAA no.
65	14020 (No Reg. No.)	1.89	16	↙	[KAICA]–POC Same	Same; illegible date	Same	Same	Same		149574
66	14021 (140046/1)	1.31	17	↖	KAICA–POC Same	Same; illegible date	Same	Same	Same		149578
67	14021 (140046/3)	1.14	15	↙	[KAICA]–POC Same	Same; illegible date	Same	Same	Same		149580
68	14022 (140040/13)	0.96	14	↖	KAICA–[POC] Same	Same; illegible date	Same	Same	Same		149585

Roman Procurators in Judea under Tiberius (14–37 CE)

Cat. no.	Locus reg. no.	Weight (g)	Diam. (mm)	Axis	Obverse	Reverse	Date (CE)	Mint	Reference	Notes	IAA no.
69*	14022 (140056/6)	1.29	16	↙	In wreath: IOY/ΛIA	Palm branch; in fields: laurel branch; in fields: L–B	15/6	Same	TJC:257, No. 317		149591
70*	14010 (140015/7)	1.74	17	→	In wreath: [- - -]	Palm branch; in fields: [IOY]–ΛI[A] L–Δ	17/8	Same	TJC:257, No. 327		149533
71*	14029 (140046/2)	1.22	15		In wreath: [- - -]	Palm branch; in fields: [- - -]–[- - -] [L]–Є	18/9	Same	TJC:257, No. 328		149579
72	14016 (140037/1)	1.78	15		In wreath: [- - -]	Palm branch; in fields: IOY–Λ[IA] L–Є	18/9?	Same	Cf. TJC:257, No. 328	Date uncertain	149572

Cat. no.	Locus reg. no.	Weight (g)	Diam. (mm)	Axis	Obverse	Reverse	Date (CE)	Mint	Reference	Notes	IAA no.
73	14010 (140015/8)	1.777	15		In wreath: [- - -]	Palm branch; in fields: [IOY]-ΛIA L–Є	Same	Same	Same	Same	149550
74	14022 (140056/2)	1.44	15	↖	In wreath: TIB/KAI/CAP.	Palm branch; in fields: [IOY]-ΛIA [L]-[·]	17/8–24/5	Same	Cf. TJC:257, No. 327		149529
75	14022 (140056/5)	1.58	15		Illegible	Palm branch; in fields: [I]OY-[ΛIA] [L]-[·]	Same	Same	Same		149530
76	14022 (140056/2)	0.59	12		Same	Palm branch; in fields: [IOY]-Λ[IA] [L]-[·]	Same	Same	Same		149531
77	14001 (140005/4)	1.45	15		In wreath: [- -]	Palm branch; in fields: [IO]Y-ΛI[A] [L]-[·]	Same	Same	Same		149537
Mint Debitage											
78*	14030 (140068/6)	0.07	5×8		Remains of casting channel from flan casting			Same	Schauer 2010:103, Fig. 3b		149610
Autonomous											
79	14021 (14055/1)	2.22	15		Head of Tyche r.	Illegible	1st c. BCE– 1st c. CE				149581

REFERENCES

Ariel, D.T. 1990. *Excavations at the City of David 1978–1985, Directed by Yigal Shiloh*, Vol. 2: *Imported Stamped Amphora Handles, Coins, Worked Bone and Ivory, and Glass* (Qedem 30). Jerusalem.

Ariel, D.T. 2011a. A First Century CE Mint South of Jerusalem? Numismatic Evidence. In: Stiebel, G.D., Peleg-Barkat, O. and Amit, D., eds. *New Studies in the Archaeology of Jerusalem and Its Region 5*: 16–23 (Hebrew).

Ariel, D.T. 2011b. Identifying the Mints, Minters and Meanings of the First Jewish Revolt Coins. In: Popović, M., ed. *The Jewish Revolt Against Rome: Interdisciplinary Perspectives* (Supplements to the Journal for the Study of Judaism 154). Leiden: 373–397.

Ariel, D.T. 2012. Judean Perspectives of Ancient Mints and Minting Technology. *Israel Numismatic Research* 7: 43–80.

Ariel, D.T. 2014a. A Group of Flan-Mold Fragments from Area N. In: Geva, H., ed. *Jewish Quarter Excavations in the Old City of Jerusalem, Conducted by Nahman Avigad, 1969–1982*, Vol. 6: *Architecture and Stratigraphy: Areas J, N, Z and Other Studies, Final Report*. Jerusalem: 266–271.

Ariel, D.T. 2014b. Review of *Judaea and Rome in Coins, 65 BCE–135 CE: Papers Presented at the International Conference Hosted by Spink, 13th–14th September 2010*, by David M. Jacobson and Nikos Kokkinos, eds. *Numismatic Chronicle* 174: 385–391.

Ariel, D.T. Forthcoming. Coins from Excavations in Jerusalem Alongside the Western Wall of the Temple Mount, Appendix: Coins from Room 41. In: Onn, A. and Weksler-Bdolah, S., eds. *Jerusalem: Wilson's Arch and the Great Causeway* (IAA Reports). Jerusalem.

Ariel, D.T. and Fontanille, J.-P. 2012. *The Coins of Herod: A Modern Analysis and Die Classification* (Ancient Judaism and Early Christianity 79). Leiden and Boston.

Avigad, N. 1983. *Discovering Jerusalem*. Nashville.

Bond, H.K. 1998. *Pontius Pilate in History and Interpretation* (Society for New Testament Studies Monograph Series 100). Cambridge.

Eisler, R. 1931. *The Messiah Jesus and John the Baptist*. London.

Hoffeditz, D.M. 2006. Divus of Augustus: The Influence of the Trials of Maiestas upon Pontius Pilate's Coins. *Israel Numismatic Research* 1: 87–96.

Kokkinos, N. 2012. The Prefects of Judaea 6–48 CE and the Coins from the Misty Period 6–36 CE. In: Jacobson, D.M. and Kokkinos, N., eds. *Judaea and Rome in Coins, 65 BCE–135 CE: Papers Presented at the International Conference Hosted by Spink, 13th–14th September 2010*. London: 85–111.

Kushnir-Stein, A. 1995. Another Look at Josephus' Evidence for the Date of Herod's Death. *Scripta Classica Israelica* 14: 73–86.

Lønnqvist, K. 2000. Pontius Pilate—An Aqueduct Builder? Recent Findings and New Suggestions. *Klio* 82: 459–474.

Mason, S.N. n.d. Commentary on The Judean War. http://pace.hypervisions.it/york/york/showText?text=wars &version=whiston.

Reich, R. and Billig, Y. 1998. Jerusalem, Robinson's Arch. *Ḥadashot Arkheologiyot* 108: 180 (Hebrew).

Reich, R. and Billig, Y. 1999. Excavations near the Temple Mount and Robinson's Arch, 1994–1996. *Qadmoniot* 117: 33–40 (Hebrew).

Reich, R. and Billig, Y. 2008. Jerusalem: The Robinson's Arch Area. In: Stern, E., Geva, H., Paris, A. and Aviram, J., eds. *The New Encyclopedia of Archaeological Excavations in the Holy Land*, Vol. 5. New York: 1809–1811.

Reich, R. and Shukron, E. 2012. Excavations next to Robinson's Arch 2012, from the Level of the Paved Street to Bedrock. In: Baruch, E., Levy-Reifer, A. and Faust, A., eds. *Recent Innovations in the Study of Jerusalem* 17: 219–238 (Hebrew).

SC I/I: Houghton, A. and Lorber, C. 2002. *Seleucid Coins: A Comprehensive Catalogue*, Part 1: *Seleucus I through Antiochus III*, Vol. 1: *Introduction, Maps and Catalogue*. New York, Lancaster and London.

SC II/I: Houghton, A., Lorber, C. and Hoover, O. 2008. *Seleucid Coins: A Comprehensive Catalogue*, Part 2: *Seleucus IV Through Antiochus XIII*, Vol. 1: *Introduction, Maps and Catalogue*. New York, Lancaster and London.

Schauer, Y. 2010. Mint Remains from Excavations in the Citadel of Jerusalem. *Israel Numismatic Research* 5: 99–107.

Schwartz, D.R. 1992. *Studies in the Jewish Background of Christianity* (Wissenschaftliche Untersuchungen zum Neuen Testament 60). Tübingen: 182–201.

Schwartz, D.R. 2013. *Reading the First Century* (Wissenschaftliche Untersuchungen zum Neuen Testament 300). Tübingen.

Shukron, E. 2012. Did Herod Build the Foundations of the Western Wall? In: Meiron, E., ed. *City of David: Studies of Ancient Jerusalem* 7. Jerusalem: 15–30 (Hebrew).

TJC: Meshorer, Y. 2001. *A Treasury of Jewish Coins: From the Persian Period to Bar Kokhba*. Translated by Robert Amoils from Hebrew. Jerusalem and Nyack, N.Y.

Weksler-Bdolah, S. 2015. The Enlargement of the Herodian Temple Mount: An Archaeological Perspective. In: Ben-Arieh, Y., Halamish, A., Limor, O., Rubin, R. and Reich, R., eds. *Study of Jerusalem Through the Ages*. Jerusalem: 19–72 (Hebrew).

CHAPTER 20

GLASS FINDS FROM THE WESTERN WALL
FOUNDATIONS EXCAVATIONS

Tamar Winter

The excavations along the Western Wall Foundations yielded ca. 100 small and poorly preserved glass fragments; about 40% of these were diagnostic pieces.[1] All the glass finds, except one (Fig. 20.1: 10), were recovered in the fills of the compartment system, attributed by the excavators to Phase 1, dated to the first quarter of the 1st century CE (see Chapter 16).

The glass finds date to the Early Roman period; the assemblage cosists of a core-formed vessel (Fig. 20.1: 1), a small piece of opaque red glass (Locus 14022, not illustrated; see Gorin-Rosen 2003: 381–382; Israeli 2010: 228), numerous cast bowls of the ribbed and linear-cut types (Fig. 20.1: 2–10) including a tiny fragment of mosaic glass (Fig. 20.1: 5), as well as several blown vessels (Fig. 20.2: 1–4) and a glass cabochon (Fig. 20.2: 5).

Analogous examples are cited from published excavations in Jerusalem (e.g., the City of David [Ariel 1990; Winter 2021], the Jewish Quarter Excavations [Gorin 2003; Israeli 2010; Katsnelson 2011]).

THE FINDS

CORE-FORMED VESSEL

The fragment discussed here is quite small (Fig. 20.1: 1), yet probably belonged to an amphoriskos. Core-formed vessels, particularly amphoriskoi, were commonplace in the region from the mid- or late 2nd century BCE to the early 1st century CE. A small fragment of an amphoriskos was discovered in Area A in the Old City's Jewish Quarter, in a context dated to the early 1st century CE (Gorin-Rosen 2003: 375, Pl. 15.3: G20).

CAST BOWLS

Ribbed Bowls (Fig. 20.1: 2–4)

Cast ribbed bowls were the most widespread type of drinking vessel from the mid-1st century BCE to the mid-1st century CE. They all bear vertical ribs on the exterior wall and occasionally horizontal grooves on the interior, yet they differ chiefly in the shape of the bowl and its rim, and the shape, finishing and density of the ribs.

Several small fragments of ribbed bowls were discovered at the site, none bearing horizontal grooves on the interior. They are classified under Grose's Group C, dated from the mid-1st century BCE to the mid-1st century CE (Grose 1979: 61–63; 1981: 67, 69, Fig. 1: C). Numerous bowls of this type were unearthed in Jerusalem, for example, in Area A in the Old City's Jewish Quarter; where

---

[1] This paper was completed in 2015. The excavations along the Western Wall Foundations were carried out in 2013 and 2014 (IAA Permit Nos. A-6971/2013 and A-7016/2014). Thanks are due to Y. Gorin-Rosen for her advice. The glass finds were cleaned by A. Ganor, drawn by C. Hersch and photographed by C. Amit.

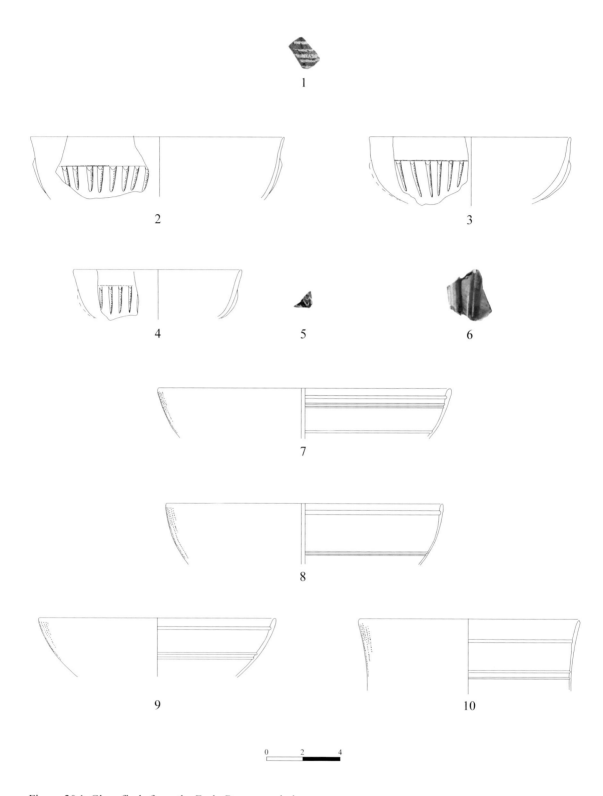

Figure 20.1. Glass finds from the Early Roman period.

Figure 20.1: Glass Finds from the Early Roman Period

No.	Permit	Locus	Basket	Description
1	7016	14020	140038.5	Tiny fragment of core-formed vessel, with opaque-white trail wound around body. Color undiscernible. Severe weathering
2	7016	14028	140048.3	Two fragments of cast bowl with rounded rim (D 140 mm) and convex walls, with vertical rounded ribs on exterior, ten of which are partly intact. Light greenish blue; spiral marks from production process on interior. Iridescence; slight pitting
3	7016	14028	140048.3	Cast bowl with pointed rim (D 110 mm) and thick convex walls, with vertical pointed ribs on exterior, seven of which are partly intact. Light greenish blue. Iridescence; slight pitting
4	7016	14036	140110.3	Cast bowl with rounded rim (D ca. 90 mm) and thick convex walls, with vertical, slightly pointed ribs on exterior, five of which are partly intact. Light greenish blue. Iridescence; crack on rim
5	7016	14010	140021.4	Tiny body fragment of mosaic-glass vessel, with opaque-white trail tooled in marble-like pattern. Light purple. Weathering; iridescence
6	7016	14010	140021.4	Body fragment of thick-walled cast bowl with vertical ribs on exterior, two of which are partly intact. Deep blue. Weathering; iridescence; slight pitting
7	7016	14010	140021	Cast bowl with rounded rim (D ca. 160 mm) and thick convex walls, with horizontal grooves on interior: one 4 mm below rim and two narrow grooves 24 mm below it. Light greenish blue. Iridescence; slight pitting
8	7016	14021	140039.14	Cast bowl with rounded rim (D ca. 150 mm) and thin convex walls, with horizontal grooves on interior: a wide one 4 mm below rim and two, two grooves 9 mm below it, and one, 26 mm below rim. Colorless with a greenish tinge; bubbles. Iridescence; slight pitting
9	6971	14001	140001.1	Cast bowl with rounded rim (D 130 mm) and convex walls, with horizontal grooves on interior: one 4 mm below rim and two 19 mm below it. Colorless with bluish-green tinge; bubbles. Iridescence; slight pitting
10	6971	14004	140004.3	Cast bowl with rounded rim (D 120 mm) and slightly outsplaying walls, with horizontal grooves on interior: one 11 mm below rim and two 27 mm below it. Blue. Iridescence; slight pitting

only one of these bowls had no interior grooves (Gorin-Rosen 2003: 379, Pl. 15.5: G52). Another bowl of this type was discovered in the City of David, in a context (Locus 1 in Area A1) dated no later than 70 CE (Ariel 1990: 161, Fig. 33: GL82).

Mosaic Glass (Fig. 20.1: 5)

The small fragment is made of light purple glass and adorned with an opaque-white trail tooled in a marble-like pattern. It probably belonged to a bowl, possibly a ribbed bowl (see above), made of mosaic glass. Bowls of this type were discovered along the Mediterranean and generally dated from the mid-2nd to the 1st century BCE; some are dated later, into the 1st century CE (see Gorin-Rosen 2003: 252).

Ribbed bowls displaying the same color combination as the presented example were excavated in the Old City's Jewish Quarter in a context (Stratum 2) dated from the 1st century CE (Gorin-Rosen

2006: 252, Pl. 10.5: G60), and in a construction fill, together with other glass vessels dated from the late 1st century BCE to the early 1st century CE (Katsnelson 2011: Fig. 14: 1). A similar ribbed bowl was recovered in the Burnt House in the Jewish Quarter; it was probably imported from Italy in the mid-1st century CE (Israeli 2010: 228, Pl. 6.3: G48).

Ribbed Bowl of the Pillar-Molded Type (Fig. 20.1: 6)

Several small fragments of ribbed bowls (Fig. 20.1: 6, and two additional pieces from Locus 14035, Basket 140089.3) belonged to a type of cast bowl known as pillar-molded, which is distinct from earlier types of ribbed bowls by the fine execution and the even distribution of the ribs that stretch down to the bottom. These bowls were generally well polished on and below the rim and on the rib tops.

Pillar-molded bowls are commonly found in Israel in excavated contexts from the 1st century CE. Pillar-molded bowls were unearthed in Jerusalem, for example, in Area A in the Jewish Quarter of the Old City (Gorin-Rosen 2003: 379–380, Pls. 15.5: G57; 15.6: G58–G59; 15.7: G76–G78; 15.8: G86–G87), and in the City of David (Winter 2021: 649, Fig. 46.2: 5–8).

Linear-Cut Bowls (Fig. 20.1: 7–10)

At least 14 linear-cut bowls were recovered at the site; they were found in nearly every basket that contained glass.[2] The bowls were made of glass in various hues, including light green, olive green, yellowish brown, blue, light blue and colorless glass.

The illustrated specimens include shallow bowls with curved walls (Fig. 20.1: 7–9) and a deep bowl with nearly vertical walls (Fig. 20.1: 10). Each is adorned with two sets of horizontal linear-cut grooves on the interior, a set below the rim and another farther down the wall. Bowl No. 7 has three grooves at the top and a single groove farther down the wall, while each of the other bowls, Nos. 8–10, has a single groove at the top and a set of two grooves farther down the wall.

Linear-cut bowls are classified under Grose's Group D and date from the mid-1st century BCE to the mid-1st century CE (Grose 1979: 63–65). Bowls of both the shallow and the deep subtypes, some with similar groove patterns, were excavated in Area A in the Jewish Quarter of the Old City (Gorin-Rosen 2003: 380–381, Pls. 15.3: G28–G29, G33; 15.5: G44–G45, G48), and in the City of David (Winter 2021: 649, Fig. 46.3).

BLOWN VESSELS

Several blown vessels were recovered at the site, including three beakers (Fig. 20.2: 1–3) and a jug handle (Fig. 20.2: 4), as well as a bottle neck and a small hollow ring base, both of yellowish-brown glass (from Locus 14009 and Locus 14039, respectively, not illustrated).

Thin-Walled Bowls or Beakers (Fig. 20.2: 1–3)

The thin-walled vessels presented are made of light greenish-blue or colorless glass, and their rims are worn and partly broken; those illustrated in Figs. 20.2: 1 and 20.2: 3 are adorned with horizontal incisions on the exterior wall, while the one in Fig. 20.2: 2 is undecorated.

---

[2]   Besides the bowls illustrated in Fig. 20.1: 7–10, ten additional pieces, not illustrated, were recorded: one from each of the following provenances: Locus 14010, B140015.6; Locus 14016, B140037.7; Locus 14020, B140038.5; Locus 14028, B140057.7; Locus 14036, B140098; Locus 14039, B140102; Locus 14047, B140122; drainage channel, B140012.3; as well as two from each of the following provenances: Locus 14022, B140056; Locus 14035, B140089.3.

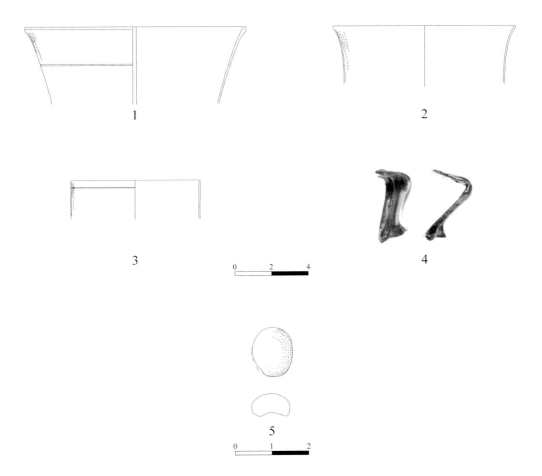

Figure 20.2: Glass Finds from the Early Roman Period

No.	Permit	Locus	Basket	Description
1	7016	14020	140038.5	Free-blown beaker with broken, probably rounded, thickened rim (D ca. 120 mm) and thin slanting walls, with horizontal groove on exterior 20 mm below the rim. Colorless with greenish tinge; bubbles. Iridescence; slight pitting
2	7016	14038	140101.4	Free-blown beaker with cut-off rim (D ca. 100 mm) and very thin, flaring walls. Light greenish blue. Iridescence; slight pitting
3	7016	14022	140040	Free-blown beaker with worn rounded rim (D ca. 70 mm) and very thin, vertical walls, with horizontal incision on exterior, 1–2 mm below the rim. Light greenish blue; bubbles. Iridescence; slight pitting
4	7016	14010	140021.4	Ribbed strap handle, broken on both sides, of a free-blown vessel. Colorless with light purple streaks. Weathering; iridescence
5	7016	14045	140121.1	Oval dome-shaped, un-pierced cabochon with slightly concave underside (L ca. 12 mm; max. W ca. 11 mm). Colorless. Iridescence; pitting

A thin-walled beaker with incisions on the exterior wall was discovered in Area A in the Jewish Quarter of Jerusalem's Old City (Gorin-Rosen 2003: 374, 382–383, Pl. 15.8: G88). Several beakers with no incisions, as in Fig. 20.2: 2, were unearthed in the City of David, in contexts dated up to 70 CE (Ariel 1990: 156, 163, Fig. 33: GL90–GL94).

Juglet (Fig. 20.2: 4)

This handle is typical of vessels of the Early Roman period, and it probably belonged to a juglet. A jug with a somewhat similar handle was recovered in the Burnt House, dated from the third quarter of the 1st century CE, excavated in Jerusalem's Jewish Quarter (Israeli 2010: 227, Pl. 6.3: G42).

MISCELLANEOUS

Cabochon (Fig. 20.2: 5)

Circular and oval dome-shaped glass cabochons probably imitated semi-precious stone jewelry; they were used as inlays or game pieces, and are generally associated with the Hellenistic and Early Roman periods.

Several cabochons were discovered in Jerusalem: in various fills dated from the Hellenistic period until 70 CE in the City of David (Ariel 1990: 157, Fig. 31: GL37–GL40, and see discussion therein); in the Burnt House in the Old City's Jewish Quarter, dated to the third quarter of the 1st century CE (Israeli 2010: 228, Pl. 6.3: G50); and in Area X-2 in the Jewish Quarter (Gorin-Rosen 2003: 388, Pl. 15.9: G106). One hundred and three glass cabochons are kept in the Israel Museum (Spaer 2001: 233, 236, Pl. 41: 548).

DISCUSSION AND SUMMARY

The glass finds recovered in the excavations along the Western Wall Foundations are noteworthy, as little material has thus far been published from this area of Jerusalem. The assemblage resembles contemporaneous glass corpora from the city (referred to above), as well as those from Jericho, Cypros and Herodium (Jackson-Tal 2013a; 2013b; 2015).

The glass assemblage includes household vessels, mostly bowls and beakers. It comprises a core-formed vessel, cast vessels and free-blown vessels, all from contexts of the same nature, some from the same locus and basket. Apparently, vessels made in these three techniques appeared contemporaneously in the late 1st century BCE and the 1st century CE.

Moreover, the cast vessels from the Western Wall Foundations significantly outnumber the blown vessels. This phenomenon was also observed regarding the glass corpus from Stratum 3 in Area E in the Jewish Quarter of Jerusalem's Old City, dated to the last quarter of the 1st century BCE; that corpus displays an 8:1 ratio of cast versus blown vessels (Gorin-Rosen 2006: 256–257). Similar circumstances were discerned in the excavations in Areas A and J in the City of David, where the glass assemblage comprised mostly cast bowls of various types, dating to the Late Hellenistic and Early Roman periods, particularly from the mid-1st century BCE to the mid-late 1st century CE (Winter 2021: 654). Conversely, in the glass assemblage of the Burnt House in the Jewish Quarter, dated to the third quarter of the 1st century CE, only a few fragments of cast vessels were recorded alongside blown vessels (Israeli 2010: 228–229).

It is therefore suggested that the date of the glass finds recovered in the excavations along the Western Wall Foundations may be narrowed down to the first half of the 1st century CE. This coincides with the date assigned by the excavators to the fills of the compartment system from which these glass finds were recovered.

REFERENCES

Ariel, D.T. 1990. Glass. In: Ariel, D.T., ed. *Excavations at the City of David 1978–1985, Directed by Yigal Shiloh*, Vol. 2: *Imported Stamped Amphora Handles, Coins, Worked Bone and Ivory, and Glass* (Qedem 30). Jerusalem: 149–166.

Gorin-Rosen, Y. 2003. Glass Vessels from Area A. In: Geva, H., ed. *The Jewish Quarter Excavations in the Old City of Jerusalem, Conducted by Nahman Avigad, 1969–1982*, Vol. 2: *The Finds from Areas A, W and X-2, Final Report*. Jerusalem: 364–386.

Gorin-Rosen, Y. 2006. Glass Vessels. In: Geva, H., ed. *The Jewish Quarter Excavations in the Old City of Jerusalem, Conducted by Nahman Avigad, 1969–1982*, Vol. 3: *Area E and Other Studies, Final Report*. Jerusalem: 239–265.

Grose, D.F. 1979. The Syro-Palestinian Glass Industry in the Later Hellenistic Period. *Muse* 13: 54–67.

Grose, D.F. 1981. The Hellenistic Glass Industry Reconsidered. *Annales du 8e Congrès Internationale d'Etude Historique du Verre*. (London and Liverpool, 18–25 Septembre 1979). Liège: 61–72.

Israeli, Y. 2010. Glass Vessels. In: Geva, H., ed. *Jewish Quarter Excavations in the Old City of Jerusalem, Conducted by Nahman Avigad, 1969–1982*, Vol. 4: *The Burnt House of Area B and Other Studies, Final Report*. Jerusalem: 221–235.

Jackson-Tal, R.E. 2013a. The Glass Finds from the Hasmonean and Herodian Palaces at Jericho. In: Bar-Nathan, R. and Gärtner, J., eds. *Hasmonean and Herodian Palaces at Jericho: Final Reports of the 1973–1987 Excavations*, Vol. 5: *The Finds from Jericho and Cypros*. Jerusalem: 100–119.

Jackson-Tal, R.E. 2013b. The Glass Finds from the Palatial Fortress at Cypros. In: Bar-Nathan, R. and Gärtner, J., eds. *Hasmonean and Herodian Palaces at Jericho: Final Reports of the 1973–1987 Excavations*, Vol. 5: *The Finds from Jericho and Cypros*. Jerusalem: 165–171.

Jackson-Tal, R.E. 2015. The Glass Finds from the Area of Herod's Tomb. In: Porat, R., Chachy, R. and Kalman, Y., eds. *Herodium: Final Reports of the 1972–2010 Excavations, Directed by Ehud Netzer*, Vol. 1: *Herod's Tomb Precinct*. Jerusalem: 396–408.

Katsnelson, N. 2011. Glass Vessels from the Early Roman Period. In: Billig, Y., ed. *Jerusalem, The Jewish Quarter: Final Report. Hadashot Arkheologiyot* 123 (December 29). http://www.hadashot-esi.org.il/report_detail_eng.aspx?id=1919&mag_id=118 (accessed February 29, 2012).

Spaer, M. 2001. *Ancient Glass in the Israel Museum, Beads and Other Small Objects* (Israel Museum Catalogue 447). Jerusalem.

Winter, T. 2021. The Glass Finds. In: Reich, R. and Shukron, E., eds. *Excavations in the City of David, Jerusalem (1995–2010): Areas A, J, F, H, D and L, Final Report* (Ancient Jerusalem Publications Series 1). University Park and Jerusalem: 647–655.

CHAPTER 21

STONE VESSELS FROM THE EXCAVATIONS ALONG THE WESTERN WALL FOUNDATIONS

Ayala Zilberstein

A large assemblage of stone vessels was exposed along the Western Wall Foundations (see Chapter 16) in the compartment fill that dates to the first quarter of the 1st century CE. The majority of the assemblage consists of chalk vessels.

The use of simple limestone, and especially chalk, as a raw material for large-scale production of tableware is a unique phenomenon that characterized the southern Levant settlements at the end of the Second Temple period. But in the Early Hellenistic period a relatively small number of bowls made of hard limestone is known; a phenomenon of mass production of tableware made of chalkstone developed only during the Early Roman period (e.g., Magen 2002). Some assemblages, published in recent decades, claim that this production process began to flourish as early as the second half of the 1st century BCE and increased considerably throughout the first part of the 1st century CE (Magen 2002: 162; Amit 2010: 63; Adler 2014: 76–80). However, new evidence brings to the fore additional cases that indicate that chalk-vessel production had already begun at the end of the Late Hellenistic (Hasmonean) period, albeit on a smaller scale (Geva 2014c: 350–351; 2014d: 369–370, Pl. 21.1: 6; Ben-Ami and Eshel 2016; Mizzi *et al.* in preparation). At the other edge of the chronological frame, it is possible that in most of the cases the popularity of this phenomenon declined radically after the failure of the Bar Kokhba Revolt (Cahill 1992: 233; Magen 2002: 162; Gibson 2003: 302; Adler 2017).

In spite of the fact that research on this phenomenon was expanded during recent decades, most of the reports published present assemblages with relatively large chronological ranges of the Early Roman period. Only a few assemblages would be attributed to a more specific time within this wide range. The early assemblages of the late 1st century BCE mentioned above include those from the Jewish Quarter excavation (Areas E and J, Strata 4–3; Geva 2006; Geva 2014b: 274–278, Pls. 10.1–3) and Jericho (Bar-Nathan and Gärtner 2013: 206–208, Pl. 9.1: 1–3). An additional assemblage that was suspected as relatively earlier than the other Early Roman vessels was discovered recently at Har Homa (Mizzi *et al.*, in preparation). The fact that the assemblage of the Western Wall Foundations came from a chronologically well-defined context of the early stages of the 1st century CE may contribute to the attempts at creating a more nuanced analysis of the chronological and typological development of these vessel types.

METHODOLOGY

The typology presented here is according to production method, i.e., vessels made by hand carving, small lathe turning, and large lathe turning.

Parallels are presented from the large assemblages from the immediate vicinity (Cahill 1992; Magen 2002). In order to examine and fine-tune the typological development of the chalk vessels, the types are examined by comparison with well-dated assemblages that have a short timeframe, i.e., the assemblages which were noted above. On the other hand, later assemblages that relate to the last decades of the Second Temple period are also used as an anchor for comparison. These include the Jewish Quarter excavations assemblages from Areas A, W and X–2 (Reich 2003, Stratum 3), and Area B (Geva 2010), as well as the Tyropoeon Valley (Givᶜati Parking Lot) excavation assemblage (Zilberstein and Nissim Ben Efraim 2013).

TYPOLOGY[1]

HAND-CARVED VESSELS

Mugs and Pitchers (Figs. 21.1: 1; 21.4)

These vessels have a cylindrical shape with high, straight, upright walls that are slightly angled outward near the flat base. Their rim is slightly tapered and has a flat top. The base diameter is smaller than the rim diameter, and the thin walls are straight with slight in-curving near the base. The exterior walls are designed with fine vertical chisel-faceting and the interior is almost smooth. Also worth noting is the presence of four body fragments of mugs that are rougher than the common fine mugs. These have short, deep horizontal knife marks along the vertical facets.

According to the common classification, this group is classified into two forms: mugs that are equipped with one or two large vertical pierced handles and often characterized by a relatively large volume; and pitchers that have relatively small measurements and are fitted with a single handle and spout fixed at a right angle to it (Cahill 1992: 209–211; Reich 2007: 196). In most cases, the fragmentary condition of vessels does not allow us to identify the exact form, although it can be assumed that the larger fragments belong to mugs.

Two almost complete mugs and 37 fragments of mugs were recovered, of which 12 are rims. Aside from one rim which is about 8 cm in diameter, the diameter of the rims ranges from 9–12.5 cm. The relatively large rims may rule out the possibility that they belong to pitchers and indicate the large presence of mugs in this group. Two fragments of spouts of pitchers are also included in this assemblage.

The almost complete preservation of the mug shown in Fig. 21.1: 1 enabled us to estimate its volume. According to the measurements based on the 3D scanning of three objects, the estimated volume of this vessel is 896 cc. This size fits the largest mugs (Type A1) from the corpus of complete mugs from Masada and other such vessels analyzed by Reich (2007: Table 9).

Parallels of cylindrical mugs are also known from the excavations near the Temple Mount (Magen 2002, Figs. 3.60: 1–2, 3.62), the City of David, Shiloh's excavations (Cahill 1992: Fig. 20: 3–4), the Jewish Quarter excavations (Area A, Reich 2003: Pl. 8.3: 11, 13, 15; Area B, Geva 2010: Pl. 5.4: 1–3) and the Tyropoeon Valley (Givᶜati Parking Lot) excavations (Zilberstein and Nissim Ben Efraim 2013: Fig. 9.2: 1–2, 4).

The absence of the early form of mugs in this assemblage is also noteworthy. The earlier form is characterized by concave rounded walls, which appear at sites dated to the second half of the 1st century BCE (Geva 2006: Fig. 9.1: 10–15; 2014b: Pl. 10.1: 13–14; Mizzi *et al.* in preparation). On the other hand, the mugs form with the in-curved walls, which is known in later assemblages (Geva 2010: Fig. 5.4: 5; Reich 2007: Fig. 1: B1, B2), was also not identified in the assemblage.

CUT-OFF MUG FRAGMENTS (FIG. 21.1: 2–9; FIG. 21.5)

An unusually large group of cut-off mug rim fragments was noted in the assemblage. The features of these items are identical to the rims of mugs. They have slightly tapered rims with a flat top and

---

[1] I would like to thank Y. Adler for advice regarding some important subjects in this assemblage, and A. Karasik for calculating the complete mug's volume.

relatively thin walls with a fine vertical chisel-faceted exterior and an almost smoothed interior face. However, the uniqueness of this group is reflected by their truncated bottom, characterized by rough cut marks. The height of these items is 1–3.3 cm. The range of the diameter of these rims is 9–12 cm, although two examples are very flat (Fig. 21.1: 2). Even though the rim and body of these items are usually characterized by a high-quality finish (Fig. 21.1: 3–8), in some cases the exteriors have a relatively rough face (Fig. 21.1: 9). Twenty-four fragments were securely assigned to this group, while three rims probably also belong to it. No parallels were found for this type.

The most conceivable suggestion is that these fragments represent production waste of mugs that were reworked to a smaller size. In such a case, the handle, which is usually located close to the rim, had to be removed. Perhaps this reworking turned the mugs into small bowls or cups without handles. In this context, it is worth noting the relatively narrow bowl/cup with a plain rim and vertical faceting design known from the Jewish Quarter excavation assemblage, Area W (Reich 2003: Pl. 8.3: 12). Nevertheless, the uniqueness of these items does not allow for the secure identification of their function. Perhaps further identification of this category, in other contexts, may help solve this issue.

Bowls (Fig. 21.1: 10–11; Fig. 21.6)

This group includes bowls carved by hand in various sizes and shapes. These bowls are characterized by fine horizontal or diagonal chisel marks on the exterior, almost smoothed interior walls and a flat base. A lug handle often appears adjacent to the rim. One almost complete bowl and 11 additional fragments were identified in the assemblage. The bowl in Fig. 21.1: 10 represents a wide and shallow medium-sized cylindrical bowl, with fine short horizontal chisel marks on the exterior. Only one example of this form exists in the assemblage. Three fragments of small, rounded, deep bowls, one of which has a small lug handle adjacent to the rim (Fig. 21.1: 11), were noted, as well as eight fragments of large oblong or rounded bowls (not illustrated).

The difference in the design of the hand-carved vessel types must be considered. Differences in the chisel marks between the mugs and pitchers compared with the bowls were noted in this chalk vessel assemblage. While all the mug fragments have an exterior typified by vertical chisel marks (Fig. 21.5), all the bowls include horizontal or diagonal chisel marks (Fig. 21.6).

In other assemblages mentioned above, this difference in design is also noticeable. Nevertheless, one exception can be made, of wide shallow bowls that appear in some cases with horizontal chisel marks or with an almost completely smoothed exterior, although in some other cases there are vertical marks (Cahill 1992: Fig. 20: 9; Magen 2002: Fig. 2.40: 5–6, Fig. 3.60: 10, Fig. 3.63: b; Bar-Nathan and Gärtner 2013: Fig. 9.1: 22). In light of this, it may be assumed that the direction of the chisel marks is dependent on the vessel form and on the positions of the raw material during the carving. It seems that vertical carving was more comfortable for cylindrical vessel production than in the case of the carving of rounded vessels.

Basin

One rim of a relatively rough medium-sized basin was identified in the assemblage (not illustrated). The diameter of this basin is ca. 30 cm. It has rough comb chisel marks on the exterior face and irregular chisel marks on the interior face.

SMALL LATHE-TURNED VESSELS

Small Lathe-Turned Bowls (Fig. 21.2: 1–2)

Thirteen indicative fragments of lathe-turned bowls were identified in the assemblage. They are characterized by a smoothed face and are sometimes decorated with simple horizontal lathe-turned incised lines or projecting ridges.

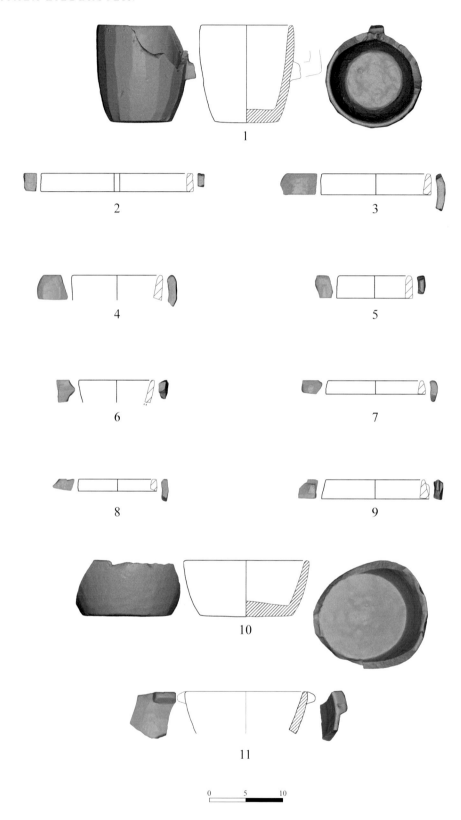

Figure 21.1. Hand-carved chalk vessels.

Figure 21.1: Hand-Carved Chalk Vessels

No.	Type	Locus	Basket	Description	Rim diameter (cm)	Height (cm)
1	Mug	14009	140014	Almost complete cylindrical mug	12.5	13
2	Cut-off mug	14020	140038.6-5	Cut-off mug fragment. Relatively flat wall	–	2.4
3	Cut-off mug	14004	140006.6-1	Cut-off mug rim. Cut marks on the bottom	11	2.7
4	Cut-off mug	14004	140006.6-4	Cut-off mug rim. Cut marks on the bottom	11	3.2
5	Cut-off mug	14020	140038.6-3	Cut-off mug rim. Cut marks on the bottom	10–11	3
6	Cut-off mug	14010	140021.1	Cut-off mug rim. Cut marks on the bottom only near the exterior	10–11	3.1
7	Cut-off mug	14001	140005.1-3	Short cut-off mug rim. Cut marks on the bottom	10–11	1.8
8	Cut-off mug	14001	14005.1-4	Cut-off mug fragment	10–11	1.6
9	Cut-off mug	14013	140502.1	Cut-off mug rim with rough horizontal protrusion on the exterior	12~	2.5
10	Bowl	14035	140083.1	Almost complete wide shallow bowl	17	7.2
11	Bowl	14036	140099.2	Rounded deep bowl with small lug handles	13	–

The dominant form in this group of bowls is the hemispherical bowls. These bowls are relatively deep and have a slightly spherical shape with a slightly in-curved tapered rim and disc base. Three rims, which measure 11–12 cm in diameter, four bases and one indicative body fragment of this form are included in the assemblage. The hemispherical bowl in Fig. 21.2: 1 represents a form with relatively straight walls. Parallels to this form are known in the excavations near the Temple Mount (Magen 2002: Fig. 3.13: 1), Shiloh's excavations in the City of David (Cahill 1992: Fig. 16: 3), the Jewish Quarter excavations (Areas A, W and X–2, Reich 2003: Pl. 8.3: 1; Area B, Geva 2010: Fig. 5.10: 7–8) and excavations in the Tyropoeon Valley (Givᶜati Parking Lot) (Zilberstein and Nissim Ben Efraim 2013: Fig. 9.2: 13–14).

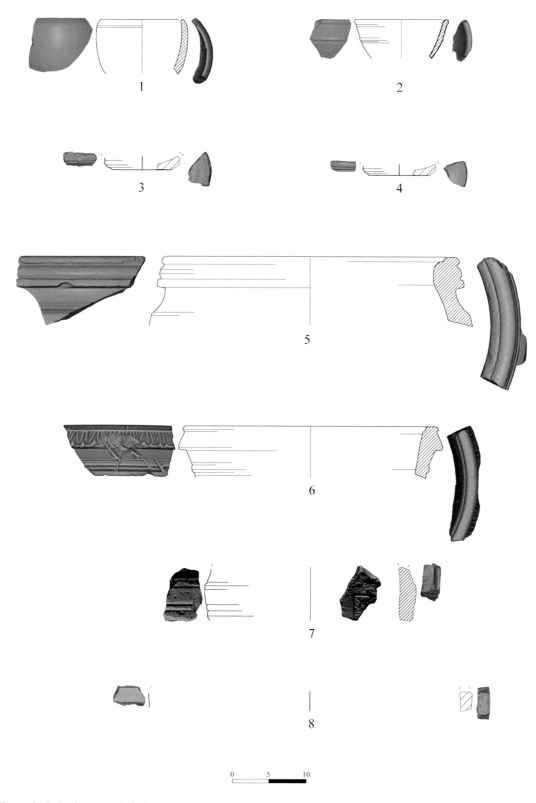

Figure 21.2: Lathe-turned chalk vessels.

Figure 21.2: Lathe-Turned Chalk Vessels

No.	Type	Locus	Basket	Description	Rim diameter (cm)
1	Bowl	14038	140075	Hemispherical bowl	12
2	Bowl	14010	140015-1	Flaring bowl	12
3	Core	14004	140500-1	Flat core	11 (near the top)
4	Core	14022	140056	Flat core	10 (near the top)
5	Krater	14010	140015-1	Triple-ridges profiled rim with shallow inner socket	40~
6	Krater	14022	140040-7	Triangular profiled flaring rim with leaf decoration	38~
7	Krater	14022	140040-29	Krater fragment with incision on the interior	–
8	Krater(?)	14009	140020-1	Greek incision on small krater fragment	–

One rim and two bases are identified as gentle bowls with flaring walls. The bowl in Fig. 21.2: 2 is a relatively narrow deep bowl with flaring rim and walls. The most similar parallels are to bowls known from Jericho (Bar-Nathan and Gärtner 2013: Pl. 9.4: 43–45). Other similar bowls are known in Shiloh's excavations in the City of David (Cahill 1992: Fig. 16: 17–18).

The lathe-turned bowls also include one wide, shallow bowl with straight walls (approximate diameter 23 cm) and one base of a narrow cup (approximate diameter 8 cm; not illustrated).

Flattened Cores (Fig. 21.2: 3–4)

Two fragments of rounded items with a flat, rough-finished top and base, and rough, deep lathe-turned grooves on the body, were noted in the chalk vessels assemblage. These items possibly represent cores of lathe-turned bowls that may have been in secondary use. Parallel cores were found in the excavations in the Tyropoeon Valley (Givʿati Parking Lot) assemblage (Zilberstein and Nissim Ben Efraim 2013: Fig. 9.6: 8).

In this regard, noteworthy is the absence of the regular high cylindrical lathe-turned cores in this assemblage compared to its high prevalence in other assemblages from the surrounding sites (Cahill 1992: Fig. 17: 26; Magen 2002: Fig. 3.29; Reich 2003: Fig. 8.3: 11; Geva 2010: Fig. 5.11: 8–11; Zilberstein and Nissim Ben Efraim 2013: Fig. 9.6: 11–15).

LARGE LATHE-TURNED KRATERS

Twenty-seven krater fragments, including four rims and three bases, were identified in the assemblage. Three fragments represent a form of krater with triple-ridged profiled rims. This form features an in-curved neck and a small shallow inner socket, a flat top and three horizontal ridges on the rim exterior (Fig. 21.2: 5). The second form (Fig. 21.2: 6), which is represented by a single example, is a krater with a triangular profiled rim and a flattened top and slightly outward-inclined neck. The example shown here is decorated with a leaf design on the exterior of the rim.

The dominance of the "triple-ridged rims" relative to the minor representation of the triangular profiled rim is also known in other early assemblages of the second half of the 1st century BCE from Areas A, E and J of the Jewish Quarter (Area A, Reich 2003: Pl. 8.3: 1–9; Area E, Geva 2006:

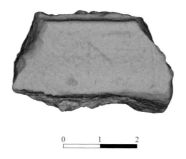

Figure 21.3: Krater fragment with Greek inscription.

Figure 21.4: Cut-off mugs.

Pl. 9.2: 1–7; Area J, Geva 2014b: Pl. 10.2: 2–3; see also Bar-Nathan and Gärtner 2013: Pl. 9.5: 66–69). These quantitative relationships are different from some later assemblages that include relatively more examples of the triangular profile rim than the triple-ridged profile rim (Geva 2010: Pls. 5.7: 1–3, 5.8: 1; Zilberstein and Nissim Ben Efraim 2013: 220, Fig. 9.3: 1–9). However, this situation is not consistent with all the late 1st century CE assemblages. In the huge assemblage from the eastern slopes of the City of David (Area D3. See Gadot and Adler 2016; Adler 2022), which are interpreted as the city dump, the triple-ridged rim type is much more dominant. Adler has pointed to the absence of the triangular profiled rim type from the Hizma and Mount Scopus workshops and suggests that the different types may represent different workshops that were developing different production methods or different designs, which may represent a trademark (Adler 2017). If so, that may raise a discussion about the meaning of the presence and/or absence of the different types together. Two body fragments with incisions also exist in the assemblage: One body fragment bears a relatively sloppy incision of a zigzag pattern encased by double frames (Fig. 21.2: 7). The incision, which is etched on the interior, was likely the secondary use of the krater fragment. This amateur decoration imitates a common, framed zigzag pattern that is well known on ossuaries (Rahmani 1994: 36–37).

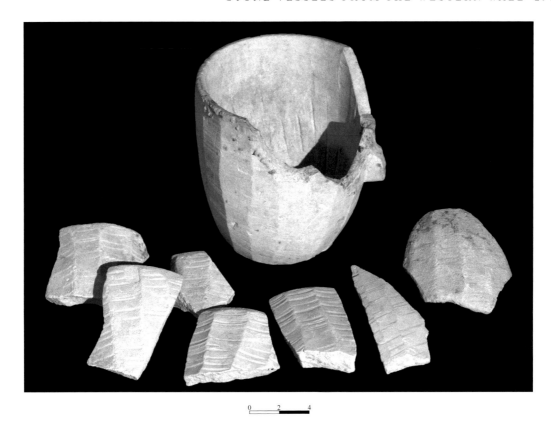

Figure 21.5: Hand-carved mugs.

Figure 21.6: Hand-carved bowls.

The presence of this pattern on a simple graffiti on chalk vessel fragments may indicate influence of popular artistic motifs on the decorative elements used by more common individuals.

Another fragment that probably belongs to a small krater bears an incision etched on the exterior. Two Greek letters were recognized on this fragment: Δ(?) and A (Figs. 21.2: 8; 21.3).

DISCUSSION

The large chalk vessel assemblage, which includes over 120 vessel fragments, was collected in the excavation along the southern part of the Western Wall Foundations. Items in the assemblage date from the first to the third decade of the 1st century CE (Table 21.1). The large number of chalk vessels and the variety of the types indicate the proliferation and development of the chalk vessel industry already at the beginning of the 1st century CE.

The main provenance of the chalk vessels was the earth fills of the Phase 1 compartments. Few other fragments were discovered in loci attributed to small stone chips found in the lowest layer of the constructional fills, which were the quarrying waste. With regard to spatial distribution of the various types, it is noteworthy that no concentration or absence of a specific type was observed in a particular location. The fragmentary preservation of most of the vessels indicates that these vessels were probably not used in the construction but brought with earth fills from the vicinity. Nonetheless, the fact that a few almost complete vessels were found in the second and third layers of the fills is significant.

Beyond providing a basic understanding of the formation of the constructional fills within the support chambers, the primary contribution of the assemblage is in the field of the chalk vessels research itself. The relatively short timeframe to which these vessels are dated enables us to nuance the typological development of these vessels through morphological and quantitative considerations.

The quantitative analysis discussed here is based only on the diagnostic fragments without counting body fragments. With regard to the techniques and methods used to form these vessels, the analysis shows that the prominent group is the hand-carved vessels, which constitute 74% (43 items) of the assemblage, while the vessels made by small lathe turning constitute 16% (9 items), and vessels (kraters) made by large lathe turning are 8% (6 items) of the assemblage. Among the group of bowls, the hemispherical bowl form is the most popular. This fact is also compatible with the situation at Jericho (Bar-Nathan and Gärtner 2013: 214). In contrast to the popularity of the lathe-turned bowls in this assemblage, there is a total absence of lids and stoppers. It is interesting to note the existence of a large quantity and a wide variety of bowls that were made by small lathe turn. The presence of this group in an assemblage from the beginning of the 1st century CE coincides with the chronological development that is reflected in other earlier sites. In the earliest assemblages, vessels made by small lathe turn are almost absent. Few examples related to Stratum 6 in Area A of the Jewish Quarter may represent the earliest evidence of such vessels (Reich 2003: Pl. 8.3: 2, 7).[2] In other assemblages of the 1st century BCE they are totally absent (Geva 2006; Mizzi et al. in preparation). Their first appearance known at Jericho is in contexts of the last two decades of Herod's region, 15 BCE–6 BCE (Bar-Nathan and Gärtner 2013: 213–216, Pl. 9.4). Some other lathe-turned vessels from Area A of the Jewish Quarter excavations are related to Strata 4–5 which are parallel in date to this assemblage (Reich 2003: Pl. 8.3: 3, 5). The vessels produced by the small lathes from the Western

---

[2] It must be considered that other than the mention of the stratum number in the plate descriptions, no additional details of the context were described.

Table 21.1: Chalk Vessels: Quantity and Analysis

Vessel type	Quantity	% of complete chalk vessel assemblage	Rim quantity	% of chalk vessel rims
Mugs and pitcher	41	33	18	31
Cut rims	27	22	16	28
Hand carved bowls and basin	13	11	9	16
Lathe-turned bowls	13	10	7	12
Kraters	27	22	6 (rims and bases)	10
Cores	2	2	2	3

Wall Foundation assemblage represent the next step in the chalk vessel development. The presence of the small lathe-turned vessels is more dominant in later assemblages, from the eve of the destruction of Jerusalem. The most prominent example is the assemblage from the Gadot excavations on the eastern slopes of the City of David (Area D), which contain 46% of the assemblage (Gadot and Adler 2016; Adler 2022). However, in the Tyropoeon Valley excavations assemblage (Givʿati Parking Lot—Area M1) the hand-carved vessels continue to be a dominant group (34%), and the large lathe-turned vessels comprise the most dominant group (49%) of the assemblage, while the small lathe-turned vessels make up the rest (Zilberstein and Nissim Ben-Efraim 2013: 225–228, Fig. 9.9). All this data together may point to a slowly growing popularity of the lathe-turned vessels over the course of the 1st century CE, beside continuation of the popularity of the mugs.

REFERENCES

Adler, Y. 2014. Tosefta Shabbat 1:14—"Come and See the Extent to Which Purity Had Spread": An Archaeological Perspective on the Historical Background to a Late Tannaitic Passage. In: Fine, S. and Koller, A., eds. *Talmuda de-Eretz Israel: Archaeology and the Rabbis in Late Antique Palestine* (Studia Judaica 73). Berlin: 63–82.

Adler, Y. 2017. The Decline of Jewish Ritual Purity Observance in Roman Palaestina: An Archaeological Perspective on Chronology and Historical Context. In: Weiss, Z. and Tal, O., eds. *Expressions of Cult in the Southern Levant in the Greco-Roman Period: Manifestations in Text and Material Culture* (Contextualizing the Sacred Series 6). Turnhout: 269–284.

Adler, Y. 2022. The Chalk Vessels. In: Gadot, Y., ed. *The Landfill of Early Roman Jerusalem: The 2013–2014 Excavations in Area D3* (Ancient Jerusalem Publications Series 2). University Park and Jerusalem: 97–122.

Amit, D. 2010. The Manufacture of Stone Vessels in Jerusalem and the Galilee: Technological, Chronological, and Typological Aspects. *Michmanim* 22: 49–66 (Hebrew).

Bar-Nathan, R. and Gärtner, J. 2013. The Stone Artifacts from the Hasmonean and Herodian Palaces at Jericho and Cypros. In: Bar-Nathan, R. and Gärtner, J., eds. *Hasmonean and Herodian Palaces at Jericho: Final Reports of the 1973–1987 Excavations,* Vol. 5: *The Finds from Jericho and Cypros.* Jerusalem: 205–227.

Ben-Ami, D. and Eshel, E. 2016. Stone Bowl Bearing the Name Hyrcanus from the Givati Excavations at the City of David. *Eretz Israel: Archaeological, Historical and Geographical Studies* 32: 16–20.

Cahill, J.M. 1992. The Chalk Vessel Assemblages of the Persian/Hellenistic and Early Roman Periods. In: De Groot, A. and Ariel, D.T., eds. *Excavations at the City of David 1978–1985, Directed by Yigal Shiloh,* Vol. 3: *Stratigraphical, Environmental, and Other Reports* (Qedem 33). Jerusalem: 190–274.

Gadot, Y. and Adler, Y. 2016. A Quantitative Analysis of Jewish Chalk Vessel Frequencies in Early Roman Jerusalem: A View from the City's Garbage Dump. *Israel Exploration Journal* 66(2): 202–219.

Geva, H. 2006. Stone Artifacts. In: Geva, H., ed. *Jewish Quarter Excavations in the Old City of Jerusalem, Conducted by Nahman Avigad, 1969–1982*, Vol. 3: *Area E and Other Studies, Final Report.* Jerusalem: 218–238.

Geva, H. 2010. Stone Artifacts. In: Geva, H., ed. *Jewish Quarter Excavations in the Old City of Jerusalem, Conducted by Nahman Avigad, 1969–1982*, Vol. 4: *The Burnt House of Area B and Other Studies, Final Report.* Jerusalem: 154–212.

Geva, H. 2014a. Hellenistic Stone Artifacts from Area Z. In: Geva, H., ed. *Jewish Quarter Excavations in the Old City of Jerusalem, Conducted by Nahman Avigad, 1969–1982*, Vol. 6: *Areas J, N and Z and Other Studies, Final Report.* Jerusalem: 369–372.

Geva, H. 2014b. Stone Artifacts from Areas J and N. In: Geva, H., ed. *Jewish Quarter Excavations in the Old City of Jerusalem, Conducted by Nahman Avigad, 1969–1982*, Vol. 6: *Areas J, N and Z and Other Studies, Final Report.* Jerusalem: 272–287.

Gibson, S. 2003. Stone Vessels of the Early Roman Period from Jerusalem and Palestine: A Reassessment. In: Botini, G.C., Di Segni, L. and Chrupcala, L.D., eds. *One Land—Many Cultures: Archaeological Studies in Honour of Stanislao Loffreda.* Jerusalem: 287–308.

Magen, Y. 2002. *The Stone Vessel Industry in the Second Temple Period: Excavations at Hizma and the Jerusalem Temple Mount.* Jerusalem.

Mizzi, D., Zilberstein, A., Sandhaus, D. and Kisilevitz, S. In preparation. *Chalk-Vessel Assemblage from Har Homa.* Jerusalem.

Rahmani, L.Y. 1994. *A Catalogue of Jewish Ossuaries in the Collections of the State of Israel.* Jerusalem.

Reich, R. 2003. Stone Vessels, Weights and Architectural Fragments. In: Geva, H., ed. *Jewish Quarter Excavations in the Old City of Jerusalem, Conducted by Nahman Avigad, 1969–1982*, Vol. 2: *The Finds from Areas A, W and X-2, Final Report.* Jerusalem: 263–291.

Reich, R. 2007. Stone Mugs from Masada. In: Stiebel, G.D. and Magness, J., eds. *Masada VIII: The Yigael Yadin Excavations 1963–1965, Final Reports.* Jerusalem: 195–206.

Zilberstein, A. and Nissim Ben Efraim, N. 2013. The Stone Vessels and Furniture of the Early Roman Period. In: Ben-Ami, D., ed. *Jerusalem: Excavations in the Tyropoeon Valley (Givᶜati Parking Lot)*, Vol. 1 (IAA Reports 52). Jerusalem: 213–228.

CHAPTER 22

ANIMAL BONE REMAINS FROM THE EXCAVATIONS ALONG THE WESTERN WALL FOUNDATIONS

Nimrod Marom

The construction fills exposed in the current excavations yielded a large 1st century CE faunal assemblage. The well-preserved remains probably accumulated during a short time slot and were then sealed by the street, providing an opportunity for excavators to examine animal consumption from a tightly framed spatiotemporal context in Roman Jerusalem. Moreover, a substantial part of the faunal assemblage was obtained by wet sieving, enabling relatively precise estimates of age at death, taxonomic and skeletal element frequencies.

Research on the bone assemblage focused especially on the consumption of meat during the massive construction works around the Temple Mount, particularly the construction of the Stepped Street and its infrastructure. Since the bones excavated originated in fills, they could have been an eclectic collection from diverse 1st-century CE consumption and discard episodes that were not related to the actual food eaten by the workers involved in the construction project. However, the analysis presented below demonstrates that the bones underwent a similar taphonomic trajectory with low rates of carnivore involvement and bone weathering, supporting the hypothesis of a uniform context of consumption (at least in terms of the faunal remains) related to the construction work. If the bones were discarded into the constructive fills immediately after consumption, as into huge garbage bins, we would expect to find neither signs of dog gnawing on bones nor bone surface degradation caused by prolonged exposure to the elements that are common marks of kitchen waste discarded in urban contexts (including Jerusalem city dumps; Bouchnick 2010).

If the assemblage was found to reflect direct discard of waste into the fills, we could proceed to investigate questions of provisioning: how the workforce was fed by the authorities employing them. Was a very restricted suite of animal species, age, sex, and body parts provided to the workers from a central kitchen (Zeder 1988)? Or was meat obtained haphazardly and intermittently from nearby suppliers, meaning that provisioning did not include an organized supply of meat?

The answer to the question of provisioning can provide a parallel line of evidence to the strength, wealth and logistical complexity of the period's administration. Although the huge scale of building does not need ancillary support from zooarchaeology to demonstrate Roman administrative potency, there does exist a nuanced difference between feeding a working force only with bread or with meat as well: The latter level of organization reflects an economic process that distinguishes imperial-scale monumental endeavors from conspicuous architectural feats that can be organized by rulers of polities on its proximate periphery.

METHODS

The faunal assemblage from the Western Wall excavations (A-6971, A-7016) is packed in six standard archive boxes, separated according to the method of recovery—by hand or by wet sieving. Wet-sieved (4 mm mesh) samples consisted of sediments from which bones were collected by hand before, and therefore the samples complement each other, with the wet sieving resulting in the recovery of specimens not collected in the field. The bone counts for the sieved and the hand-collected contexts were kept separate during analysis and were presented separately for some analyses (taxonomic and skeletal element representation), but not for others (metric analyses, age-at-death estimation based on mandibular tooth rows and epiphyseal fusion data).

The analysis of the large assemblage, which included many small fragments from wet sieving, was guided by a preference for extensive rather than intensive sampling. Ideally, each and every bone fragment would be identified to taxon (intensive sampling); this, however, would not be feasible within reasonable budget limitations and would have restricted the analysis and data recording to only certain loci. In order to collect a larger set of taxonomic, age-at-death and metric data, I employed a rapid method of bone recording (Davis 1992; see also Albarella and Davis 1996; Davis 2008; Albarella *et al.* 2009; for methodological discussion and validation, see Marom and Bar-Oz 2008; Trentacoste 2009). This, in addition to its efficiency, provides a more precise zooarchaeological dataset than "traditional," intensive protocols that create unwieldy and redundant datasets and introduce more room for inter-analyst identification bias.

Bone identification was carried out with reference to the comparative collection of the Laboratory of Archaeozoology at the University of Haifa, with morphologically similar sheep and goats distinguished by morphological and metric criteria (Zeder and Lapham 2010). Only POSACs (parts of the skeleton always counted; as in Davis 1992, with the addition of the ulnar articulation, the zygomatic bone and the second phalanx to the POSAC list) identifiable as to biological taxon were recorded in the database. The raw count of POSACs (henceforth also "the POSAC sample") form the basic unit for taxonomic and skeletal element frequency quantification (NISP, number of identified specimens), from which minimal number of animal units (MAU) were obtained by dividing the NISP value by the number of elements in a complete skeleton in order to present skeletal element abundance profiles. The highest MAU value calculated for any element was treated as a taxon's MNI (minimum number of individuals) statistic.

Age-at-death estimations relied on epiphyseal fusion data, calculated as the %Juvenile statistic ($100 * \frac{unfused}{(fused+unfused)}$) and on tooth eruption and wear (based on Payne 1973 for caprines and Grant 1982 for cattle). Caprine sex ratios were estimated by the shape of the iliopectineal eminence of the pubic bone (Edwards, Marchinton and Smith 1982) and by statistical analysis of measurements (taken following von den Driesch 1976; Davis 1992, 1996) obtained from sexually dimorphic elements (the metacarpus and humerus). Chicken bones were sexed by the presence or absence of a spur on the tarsometatarsus bone.

Bone surface modifications, including gnawing, burning and weathering (Behrensmeyer 1978), were recorded for all POSACs. Fractures with distinct morphology (Villa and Mahieu 1991) were coded as "spiral" (indicating breakage of fresh bone) or "dry" (indicating breakage of already dry bone). Butchery marks, which occurred on many specimens, were recorded on all bones (POSACs and others) from two boxes—labeled Box #1 (sieved) and Box #2 (hand collected)—and on POSACs only for the rest of the assemblage. Butchery mark typology consisted of (1) chopped specimens, which show a hacking mark inflicted by a heavy blade (a chopper); (2) sheared specimens, which showed damage from a chopper blow delivered in an oblique angle to the bone's longitudinal axis; (3) cleft specimens that were transversely chopped off by a heavy blade; (4) split bones, which were cleanly chopped along their longitudinal axis; (5) cut bones, nicked by a knife; and (6) sawn bones.

Statistical analyses were carried out on PAST 3.01 (Hammer, Harper and Ryan 2001).

RESULTS

TAXONOMIC COMPOSITION

The faunal assemblage consisted of 679 identified specimens (Tables 22.1 and 22.2), dominated by caprines (sheep, *Ovis aries*, and goats, *Capra hircus*; NISP=515, 74%; $NISP_{sieved}$=318, 88%; $NISP_{collected}$=197, 78%) followed by cattle (*Bos taurus*, NISP=98, 14%; $NISP_{sieved}$=44, 12%; $NISP_{collected}$=54, 22%). Chickens (*Gallus domesticus*, NISP=86, 12%) are not common in the assemblage, and are appreciably more numerous in the sieved sample ($NISP_{sieved}$=62) than in the hand-collected one ($NISP_{collected}$=24). Single bones of a crow (*Corvidae* sp.), gray goose (*Anser anser*; Fig. 22.1), an equid (*Equus* sp.) and a couple of pig bones (*Sus scrofa*; Fig. 22.2) complete the short taxonomic list of mammals and birds. In addition, the sieved sample contained 57 small fish vertebrae (not analyzed in the current report) and skull fragments, which were absent from the hand-collected sample and separated for future analysis.

TAPHONOMIC HISTORY

The bones in the sample are very well preserved. No weathered bones (weathering stage 2 and beyond, Behrensmeyer 1978) were noted in the POSAC sample, and only two specimens bore signs of carnivore gnawing. Three bones from the POSAC sample were burnt (cattle ulna and phalanx, goat astragalus). Fracture morphology analysis indicates similar frequency of spiral (N=50) and dry (N=42) types, suggesting a complex breakage process during food preparation and consequent mechanical breakage of buried and dry bone. The butchery process, which made extensive use of heavy choppers (N=89, 13% of the POSAC sample), is probably responsible for much of the fragmentation.

The bone surface modification data therefore suggest a very rapid burial of the faunal remains, in conditions that were protected from scavenging by urban commensals. Bone breakage was caused by butchery with a heavy blade and by consequent post-burial physical processes (for example, crushing by sediment weight). All in all, the data support the hypothesis that the animal remains accumulated rapidly, probably as the result of the immediate discard of consumption waste into the fills, which served as a midden. The competing hypothesis that the bones arrived with the fills from various urban contexts is not consistent with the homogeneous and excellent preservation of the sample. This is in contrast to the assemblages found in the refuse dumps of the same period where wearing patterns were clearly noted (Buchnik 2010).

SHEEP, GOATS, CATTLE AND CHICKENS

Sheep and Goats

Caprines, sheep and goats comprise by far the larger component in the assemblage (75%; Tables 22.1 and 22.2). The sheep-to-goat ratio is 3.4:1 (NISP values 109 sheep to 32 goats), based on morphological criteria. The dominance of sheep is confirmed by a metric analysis of metacarpus measurements, most of which show a high ratio (>62%, Zeder and Lapham 2010) between the depths of the lateral and medial distal condylar trochleae (sheep:goat ratio 2.5; Fig. 22.3). The breadth of the distal condylar articulation is notably larger than a reference population of unimproved Shetland female sheep (Davis 1996), which can be explained by either (1) the presence of a larger and improved sheep breed in Roman Jerusalem, or (2) a sample dominated by male animals, which are physically larger than females.

In order to address the different potential explanations, I employed a larger sample of (morphologically identified) sheep humerus measurements (Fig. 22.4). Again, the Jerusalem caprines

Figure 22.1: Ulna of a large anseriforme (Locus 14011, Basket 140029.2) probably a domestic goose (*Anser anser*).

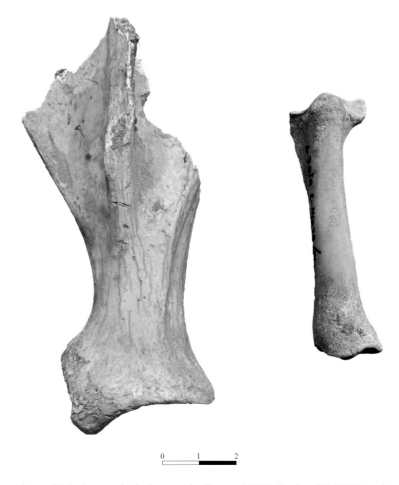

Figure 22.2: Cut-marked pig scapula (Locus 14011, Basket 140029.2) and an unfused pig metatarsus (Locus 14028, Basket 140048.1).

are found to have been larger than the Shetland female population. Significantly, however, the measurements from the assemblage at hand display a very large variance (Coefficient of Variation: BT=5.44; HTC=6.03) in comparison to Davis's female-only data (Coefficient of Variation: BT=3.2; HTC=3.7; only the mean is displayed in the figure). The probable explanation for this observation is that the Jerusalem sample comprises both male and female bones, *all of which are larger* than the Shetland sheep, thus supporting the hypothesis that a large, improved breed was present at the site. K-means clustering was employed to assign the Jerusalem humeri into two groups, reflecting the

Table 22.1: Taxonomic Frequencies in NISPs

Taxon	NISP	%
Sheep and Goat	515	73
Cattle	98	14
Chicken	86	12
Pig	2	0.2
Total	701	
Equid	*	
Goose	*	
Crow	*	

*=Present

Table 22.2: Bone Counts for Sheep and Goats (Sh/G) and Cattle, Presented Separately for the Sieved and Hand-Collected Samples

Portion	Bone/tooth	Fusion	Sieved		Hand-collected	
			Sh/G	Cattle	Sh/G	Cattle
Head	Zygomatic		6	2		1
	dP4		7		11	7
	P2				3	1
	P3				4	1
	P4		1		5	2
	M1/2		10	1	26	9
	M3		2		8	1
Forelimb	Scapula	U	5	1	5	2
	"	F	5	1	15	
	"	?	1	2		
	Humerus	UM	2	2	2	1
	"	UE	1			
	"	F	11		24	2
	Radius	UM	6	1	8	2
	"	UE	3			
	"	F		1	6	1
	Ulna	UM	7		1	
	"	UE				
	"	F	1			
	"	?		1		

Portion	Bone/tooth	Fusion	Sieved		Hand-collected	
			Sh/G	Cattle	Sh/G	Cattle
	Carpals 1+2		17	5		
Hindlimb	Ischium		5	1	12	1
	Femur	UM			10	
	"	UE	8		2	
	"	F			5	
	Tibia	UM	2		7	2
	"	UE	7		2	
	"	F	5		8	
	Calcaneum	U	13	2	1	3
	"	F	1			
	"	?	1			
	Astragalus		15	1	2	2
Feet	Metacarpal	UM	2	1	8	1
	"	UE	3			
	"	F	3		2	3
	Metatarsal	UM	1		8	4
	"	UE				
	"	F	3		6	1
	Metapodial	UM		1	1	
	"	UE	13			
	"	F	3	1		
	Phalanx I	UM	25	3	2	
	"	UE	22	2		
	"	F	17	2	3	6
	Phalanx II	UM	16	3		
		UE	8	3		1
		F	31	2		
	Phalanx III		29	5		
Totals	NISP		318	44	197	54
	%		88	12	78	22
	MNI		8	2	13	4
	%		80	20	76	24

UM=Unfused metaphysis; UE=Unfused epiphysis; F=fused; ?=epiphyseal fusion plain missing probable ratio of male (N=12) to female (N=11) animals in the assemblage. The similar frequencies of male-to-female sheep obtained by this analysis do not entirely agree with the male-biased ratio observed in the six sexed pubic bones, of which five were unmistakeably male. This disconformity may be the result of the small sample size of sexed pelves (Fisher's exact test P=0.54).

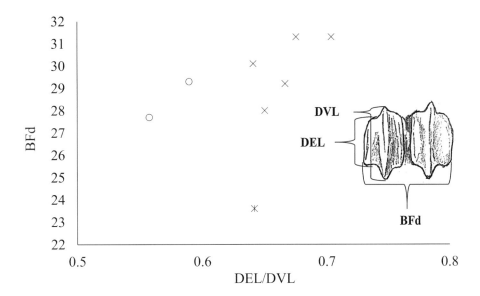

Figure 22.3: Caprine metacarpus measurements. BFd=Breadth of the distal articulatory facet; DEL=Depth of the lateral condylar trochlea; DVL=Depth of the medial condylar trochlea. X=Probable sheep; Open circle=Probable goat; Crossed X=Mean of a population of unimproved Shetland sheep female flock (Davis 1996).

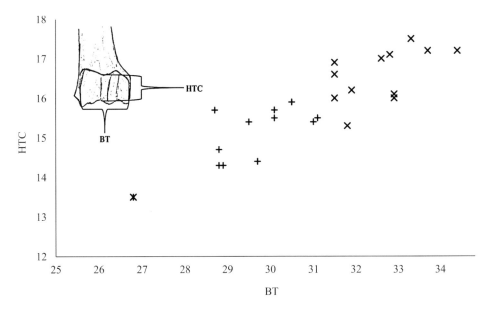

Figure 22.4: Sheep humerus measurements. BT=Breadth of the distal condylar trochlea; HTC=Height of the trochlear centre. X=Probable male; +=Probable female; Crossed X= Mean of a population of unimproved Shetland sheep female flock (Davis 1996).

The %Juveniles statistics calculated from the data in Table 22.2 indicate that many of the caprines were slaughtered as juveniles (57%). Mandibular tooth rows that could be assigned to a wear stage (Payne 1973; Fig. 22.5) support this observation, suggesting that 77% of the mandibles (N=17) belonged to animals younger than two years of age, with only five mandibles belonging to adult animals between four and six years of age at death. This culling profile indicates a herd maintenance strategy geared to specialized meat production, with most animals slaughtered upon reaching an optimal weight as young adults. Specialized milk or wool production is excluded because there are few (N=4) very young (less than six months old) or mature adult animals in the assemblage, respectively. Moreover, the concern for herd security (Redding 1981, Sasson 2010) as a major component of the production strategy is belied by the high percentage of sheep over goats, as demonstrated above.

Skeletal element frequencies calculated for the sieved and hand-collected samples (Fig. 22.6) complement each other, with smaller skeletal elements (carpals, tarsals, phalanges) found in the first and missing from the latter. Softer skeletal elements, such as the distal femur, are well represented in the combined sieved and hand-collected sample, supporting the evidence from the bone surface modifications to accumulation in an environment protected from carnivore gnawing and bone destruction. In summary, no selection for body part is observed, as opposed to models of provisioning in the zooarchaeological literature, which suggest that provisioning of meat would indicate patterns of selection according to specific body parts (Zeder 1988).

Cattle

Cattle are found in relatively low frequency in the assemblage (14%; Tables 22.1 and 22.2). At least some of the cattle were originally employed as draught animals, with two specimens bearing pathological bone alterations associated with stress on joins (exostoses on a third phalanx) and with foot infection that affected the periosteum (on a metacarpus; Fig. 22.7). Interestingly, one dorsal spine of a cattle thoracic vertebra was split, a morphological feature that distinguishes zebu cattle (*Bos indicus*; Fig. 22.8).

Although some of the cattle were retired draught animals, most were slaughtered as juveniles, based on epiphyseal fusion data (64%; Table 22.2). The dominance of juvenile cattle is also reflected in the high ratio of milk teeth (dp4; NISP=7) to posterior molars (M3; NISP=1) or adult premolars (P4; NISP=2). Therefore, there is strong support for the idea that veal, and not beef, was the prime cattle meat consumed. Veal is often the result of either an intensive cow milking industry (like in

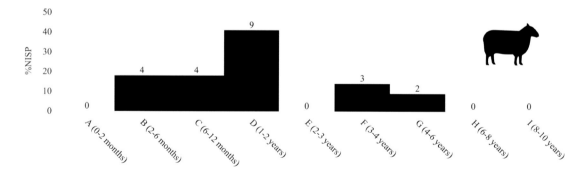

Figure 22.5: Caprine mandibular tooth row eruption and wear stages. X-axis=Wear stages and age in months or years (Payne 1973); Y-axis=Relative frequency in percentage of the number of aged mandibles. Numbers above columns are absolute NISP values.

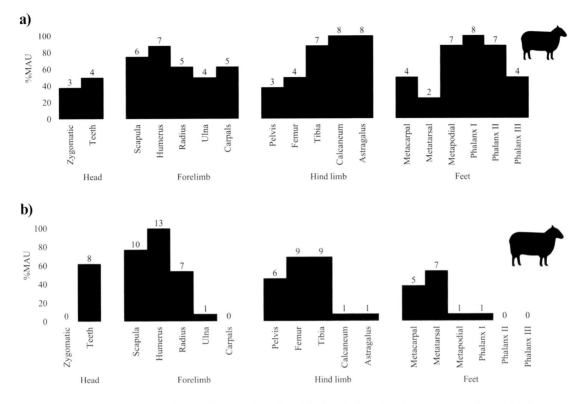

Figure 22.6: Caprine skeletal element frequencies, sieved loci only. Y-axis values are normalized MAU values; numbers above columns are absolute MAU values.

the modern era), which I do not think existed in Early Roman Jerusalem, or of the provisioning of large quantities of meat to feed many people (large carcass size).

The small number of cattle specimens was not sufficient for a meaningful reconstruction of skeletal element frequencies. General observations of the hand-collected assemblage (Fig. 22.9) indicate the presence of both slaughter (head, feet) and consumption (upper limb) waste in the assemblage. Skeletal element frequencies from the sieved assemblage are found in Table 22.2 but are too sparse to render graphically.

Chickens

Chickens comprise 12% of the identified bones in the assemblage, which makes them nearly as frequent as cattle; it should be remembered, however, that in terms of meat weights the contribution of these birds to the diet was negligible. Four out of five sufficiently complete tarsometatarsal bones did not bear a spur, indicating that most of the chickens were hens. Few (NISP=4; 10%) of the bones that were aged (N=37) had spongy epiphyses, typical of young birds. Both pelvic and shoulder girdle elements are present (Fig. 22.10). In summary, most of the chickens were adult hens, and are represented by all parts of the body. Chicken bone measurements appear in Appendix 22.2.

EVIDENCE FOR SPECIALIZED BUTCHERY

A detailed examination of butchery employed an inclusive sample of 161 butchered specimens (henceforth the "butchery sample"; see Methods section; data in Appendix 22.3). The variability in

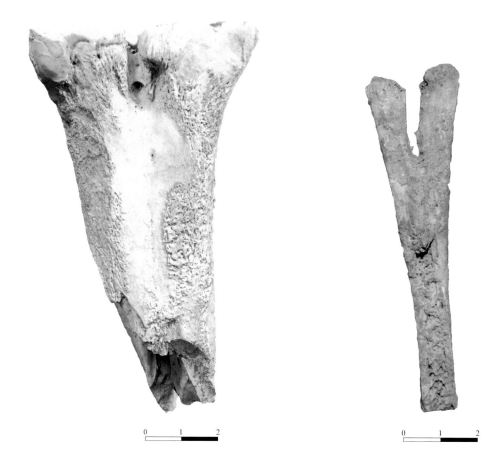

Figure 22.7: Caprine skeletal element frequencies, unsieved loci only. Y-axis values are normalized MAU values; numbers above columns are absolute MAU values.

Figure 22.8: Pathological cattle metapodial with lipping on the plantar aspect of the proximal shaft and osteoperiostitis (Baker and Brothwell 1980: 64—68). Locus 14022, Basket 140041.6.

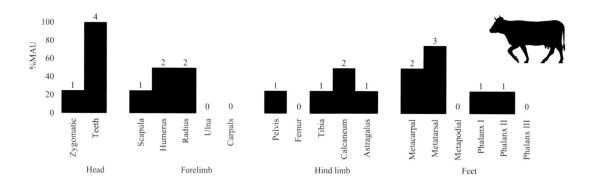

Figure 22.9: Split dorsal spine typical of zebu cattle (*Bos indicus*). Locus 14022, Basket 140041.6.

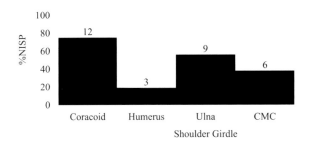
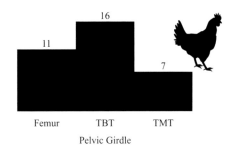

Figure 22.10: Cattle skeletal element frequencies, unsieved loci only. Y-axis values are normalized MAU values; numbers above columns are absolute MAU values.

the distribution of butchery marks with respect to location, taxon, butchery tool and type of damage to the bone does not easily lend itself to a robust statistical manipulation. Instead, I will concentrate on a qualitative analysis relating general features of the butchery sample to the characteristics distinguishing specialized Roman urban butchery. These include (Rixson 1989; Maltby 2007; Seetah 2006a, 2006b):

1. Extensive use of a chopper in carcass dismemberment and defleshing

2. Axial splitting of marrow-rich long bones

3. Transversely broken metapodials

4. Axially split vertebrae

These characteristics of Roman butchery are strongly evidenced from urban contexts in Roman Britain (Rixson 1989; Maltby 2007 and references therein) and were suggested (Seetah 2006b) to have originated in the catering practices of the Roman army born of the necessity to feed a large body of men, creating a "need for speed" in carcass processing. The specialized butchery process relied on traded livestock, mainly young, and on technological (special cleaver) and logistical infrastructure, which included a built space large enough to accommodate the skinning, evisceration and halving of hanged carcasses—with roof beams robust enough to carry the load of a ca. 450 kg carcass, plus the stress from chopper blows.

The fulfilment of the criteria for the practice of specialized butchery is seen in the very high frequency of chopper-inflicted damage to bones in the assemblage (Fig. 22.11); recorded marks of shearing, cleaving, chopping and splitting (N=89, 13% of the POSAC sample) outnumber thin knife slices in the same sample (N=58, 8%). This pattern is typical of Roman urban assemblages where specialized butchers were present (Maltby 2007). The axial splitting of upper limb bones using a chopper was observed on five humeri (two caprine, three cattle) and on a cattle radius in the butchery sample. Chopper blows or cleaving was recorded on four cattle and one caprine metapodial in the same sample; the chopper-assisted halving of hanged carcasses is amply demonstrated by the presence in the butchery sample of 14 axially split vertebrae (Fig. 22.12), three belonging to cattle and the remainder to caprines. Axial splitting of axial skeleton elements is also observed on a caprine skull (Fig. 22.13); sheep and goat skulls were further butchered by sawing/chopping off the horn cores (Fig. 22.14), probably in order to remove their sheaves for industrial use in glue or tool production.

A single worked bone (Fig. 22.15) is only remotely related to "butchery" but is nevertheless reported here in order to demonstrate the extensive use of animal carcasses for practical/aesthetic purposes, beyond their use as a food source.

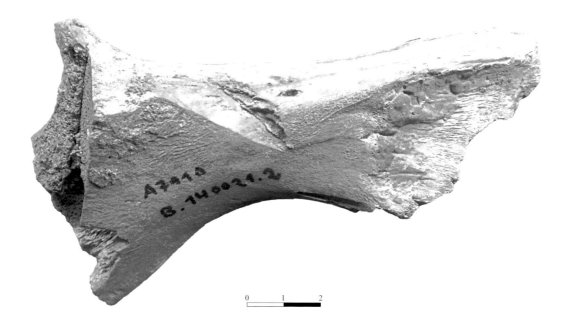

Figure 22.11: Chicken skeletal element frequencies, sieved loci only. Y-axis values are normalized NISP values; numbers above columns are absolute NISP values. CMC=Carpometacarpus; TBT=Tibiotarsus; TMT=Tarsometatarsus.

Figure 22.12: Chopped and cleft cattle pelvic fragment. Locus 14010, Basket 140021.2.

Figure 22.13: Longitudinally-split lumbar vertebra of a sheep or a goat. Locus 14010, Basket 140021.2

Figure 22.14: Sawn caprine horn cores from Loci 14021, 14028 and 14037.

Figure 22.15: Worked and decorated bone from
Locus 14020, Basket 140038.1.

SUMMARY AND CONCLUSIONS

The faunal assemblage from the constructive fills under the street running along the Western Wall probably reflects secondary deposition of animal remains consumed in a single activity episode, namely the construction of the supportive infrastructure to the street. This conclusion is supported by the complete lack of weathering and the near absence of carnivore gnawing, which are present in the slower accumulation of garbage on the slopes of the Kidron Valley, thought to represent the contemporary city dump (Bouchnick 2010: 122).

The workmen were supplied with a meat cuisine consisting mainly of younger sheep, from a larger (improved) breed, some goats and cattle meat. The cattle included some retired work animals but many younger animals (also known from other sites in 1st-century CE Jerusalem; Bar-Oz *et al.* 2007; Bouchnick 2010), reflecting the activity of cattle traders in an urban market. The presence of zebu cattle, which are well adapted to hot and dry climates, is remarkable; this breed made its first appearance in the Ancient Near East in the Late Bronze Age and appears sporadically at sites in east Israel during the Iron Age (Ziegler and Boessneck 1990; Wapnish and Hesse 1991; Marom 2012). To the best of my knowledge, no zebu finds were reported at sites from later periods. This may indicate a low percentage of redeposited fauna from other assemblages, although the bulk seems to have originated from the provision of meat for the workmen. Chicken and fish were recovered mainly from the wet-sieved sample, but probably contributed very little to the total meat consumption. Gray goose, probably domestic, was previously reported from Early Roman assemblages in Jerusalem (Horwitz and Tchernov 1996; Bouchnick 2010).

Caprine-dominated (~75%) assemblages in which sheep substantially outnumber goats are typical of the Roman period urban and military contexts (for example, Tel Anafa I and II: Redding 1994; Kidron Valley: Bouchnick 2010: 160, 164). This leads us straight to the question of provisioning, mentioned in the introduction: the taxonomic composition of the assemblage and the age at death of the livestock animals suggest that the workers were provisioned with meat. But is the urban/military taxonomic and demographic signature observed in the workers' midden substantially different from the urban garbage in other parts of Jerusalem? The taxonomic and demographic signature of the Early Roman garbage dump (Bouchnick 2010) is similar to this assemblage, suggesting that the two assemblages are similar in this manner.

Butchery patterns, however, bear a clear signature of Roman urban specialization not observed in the city dump. This signature comprises extensive use of the chopper, transverse breakage of metapodials and axial splitting of upper limb bones for marrow extraction, and the halving of hanged carcasses, including those of heavy cattle. While the provisioning of younger meat animals (cattle and caprines) was reported for the city at large (Bar-Oz et al. 2007; Bouchnick 2010), specialized Roman butchery, born in the legions' kitchens and spread across the empire along with the relevant technology and know-how, is unique to the present assemblage. Furthermore, the discard of slaughter waste (heads and feet) along with consumption remains (meaty limbs) into the workers' midden suggests the presence of the butchery facilities near the construction site: the garbage from the butcher's shop and the kitchen ended up in the same place.

In summary, I conclude that the massive construction works around the Temple Mount relied on a sophisticated provisioning chain consisting of herds geared toward meat production supplying the city at large (younger sheep and cattle), livestock traders plying their trade in the urban market (a phenomenon known from urban centers around the empire, including Jerusalem), and ending in a specialist employing Roman-style butchery technology and know-how in a dedicated facility located at the work site; this last link in the chain is unique to this context. The results of the zooarchaeological analysis supply a glimpse into the more ephemeral manifestation of imperial logistical organization—a specialized kitchen to an organized workforce—which hints at the (economic) infrastructure of lasting architectural achievements.

REFERENCES

Albarella, U., Beech, M., Curl, J., Locker, A., Moreno-García, M. and Mulville, J. 2009. *Norwich Castle: Excavations and Historical Survey, 1987–98,* Part 3: *A Zooarchaeological Study.* Dereham.

Albarella, U. and Davis, S.J.M. 1996. Mammals and Birds from Launceston Castle, Cornwall: Decline in Status and the Rise of Agriculture. *Circaea* 12: 1–156.

Bar-Oz, G., Bouchnick, R., Weiss, E., Weissbrod, L., Lernau, O., Bar-Yosef Mayer, D.E. and Reich, R. 2007. "Holy Garbage": A Quantitative Study of the City-Dump of Early Roman Jerusalem. *Levant* 39: 1–12.

Behrensmeyer, A.K. 1978. Taphonomic and Ecologic Information from Bone Weathering. *Paleobiology* 4: 150–162.

Bouchnick, R. 2010. *Meat Consumption in the Society of Judea* (Ph.D. dissertation, University of Haifa). Haifa.

Davis, S.J.M. 1992. *A Rapid Method for Recording Information About Mammal Bones from Archaeological Sites* (Ancient Monuments Laboratory Report 19/22). London.

Davis, S.J.M. 1996. Measurements of a Group of Adult Female Shetland Sheep Skeletons from a Single Flock: A Baseline for Zooarchaeologists. *Journal of Archaeological Science* 23: 593–612.

Davis, S.J.M. 2008. *Faunal Remains from Alcáçova de Santarém, Portugal.* Lisbon.

von den Driesch, A. 1976. *A Guide to the Measurement of Animal Bones from Archaeological Sites* (Peabody Museum Bulletin 1). Cambridge.

Edwards, J.K., Marchinton, R.L. and Smith, G.F. 1982. Pelvic Girdle Criteria for Sex Determination of White-Tailed Deer. *Journal of Wildlife Management* 46: 544–547.

Grant, A. 1982. The Use of Tooth Wear as a Guide to the Age of Domestic Ungulates. In: Wilson, B., Grigson, C. and Payne, S., eds. *Ageing and Sexing Animal Bones from Archaeological Sites.* Oxford: 91–108.

Hammer, Ø., Harper, D.A.T. and Ryan, P.D. 2001. PAST: Paleontological Statistics Software Package for Education and Data Analysis. *Palaeontologia Electronica* 4. http://palaeo-electronica.org/2001_1/past/issue1_01.htm.

Horwitz, L.K. and Tchernov, E. 1996. Bird Remains from Areas A, D, H and K. In: Ariel, D.T. and De Groot, A., eds. *Excavations at the City of David 1978–1985, Directed by Yigal Shiloh,* Vol. 4 (Qedem 35). Jerusalem: 298–301.

Maltby, M. 2007. Chop and Change: Specialist Cattle Carcass Processing in Roman Britain. In: Croxford, B., Ray, N. and Roth, R., eds. *TRAC 2006: Proceedings of the 16th Annual Theoretical Roman Archaeology Conference.* Oxford: 59–76.

Marom, N. 2012. Archaeozoological Analysis of Animal Bones from Selected Iron Age Contexts. In: Ben-Tor, A., Ben-Ami, D. and Sandhaus, D., eds. *Hazor VI.* Jerusalem: 604–623.

Marom, N. and Bar-Oz, G. 2008. Measure for Measure: Taphonomic Reconsideration of the Kebaran Site of Ein Gev I, Israel. *Journal of Archaeological Science* 35: 214–237.

Payne, S. 1973. Kill-Off Patterns in Sheep and Goats: The Mandibles from Aşvan Kale. *Anatolian Studies* 23: 281–303.

Redding, R.W. 1981. *Decision Making in Subsistence Herding of Sheep and Goats in the Middle East* (Ph.D. dissertation, University of Michigan). Ann Arbor.

Redding, R.W. 1994. The Vertebrate Fauna. In: Herbert, S.C., ed. *Tel Anafa II: Final Report of Ten Years of Excavation at a Hellenistic and Roman Settlement in Northern Israel.* Ann Arbor: 279–322.

Rixson, D. 1989. Butchery Evidence on Animal Bones. *Circaea* 6: 49–62.

Sasson, A. 2010. *Animal Husbandry in Ancient Israel: A Zooarchaeological Perspective on Livestock Exploitation, Herd Management and Economic Strategies.* London.

Seetah, K. 2006a. *Butchery as an Analytical Tool: A Comparative Study of the Romano-British and Medieval Periods* (Ph.D. dissertation, University of Cambridge). Cambridge.

Seetah, K. 2006b. Multi-Disciplinary Approach to Romano-British Cattle Butchery. In: Maltby, M., ed. *Integrating Zooarchaeology: 9th ICAZ Conference, Durham 2002.* Oxford: 111–118.

Trentacoste, A. 2009. Sometimes Less Is More: Comparison of Rapid and Traditional Recording Methods: Bantycock Mine, Balderton (M.Sc. thesis, University of Sheffield). Sheffield.

Villa, P. and Mahieu, E. 1991. Breakage Patterns of Human Long Bones. *Journal of Human Evolution* 21: 27–48.

Wapnish, P. and Hesse, B. 1991. Faunal Remains from Tel Dan: Perspectives on Animal Production at a Village, Urban and Ritual Center. *Archaeozoologia* 4: 9–86.

Zeder, M.A. 1988. Understanding Urban Process through the Studies of Specialized Subsistence Economy in the Near East. *Journal of Anthropological Archaeology* 7: 1–55.

Zeder, M.A. and Lapham, H. 2010. Assessing the Reliability of Criteria Used to Identify Postcranial Bones in Sheep, *Ovis,* and Goats, *Capra. Journal of Archaeological Science* 37: 2887–2905.

Ziegler, R. and Boessneck, J. 1990. Tierreste der Eisenzeit II. In: Fritz, V., ed. *Kinneret: Ergebnisse der ausgrabunden auf dem Tell el-Oreme am See Gennesaret 1982–1985.* Wiesbaden: 133–158.

APPENDIX 22.1

Mammal bone measurements in mm*

Bone/Taxon	Locus	Age	Measurements		
Astragalus			Bd	GLl	Dl
Sh/G	14001	F			
Goat	14007	F			
Goat	14021	U	17.6	29.7	15.4
Goat	14005		22.5	35.3	18.1
Goat	14016		19	31.1	16.4
Sheep	14001	F	20.9		
Sheep	14038	F	20.2	32.5	18.1
Sheep	14013	F	19.5	32	16.6
Sheep	14013	F	21.2		
Sheep	14005	F	22.9		
Sheep	14005	F			
Sheep	14021	F	21.2	32.4	17.1
Sheep	14016	F	20.9	32.7	18.2
Sheep		U	22.4		18.7
Sheep			22.3		
Cattle	14009	F			
Cattle	14011	F	43	71.1	38
Cattle	14011	U			
Calcaneus			GL		
Goat	14013	F	67.2		
Humerus			BT	HTC	
Sh/G		F	32.4	15.7	
Sh/G	14004	F	28.9	14.5	
Sheep	14038	F	33.3	17.5	
Sheep	14001	F	32.9	16.1	
Sheep	14004	F	29.5	15.4	
Sheep	14010	F	33.7	17.2	
Sheep	14022	F	32.8	17.1	
Sheep	14020	F	31.1	15.5	

* Abbreviations follow von den Driesch (1976) and Davis (1992, 1996). Sh/G=sheep or goat; UM=unfused metaphysis; UE=unfused epiphysis; F=fused

Bone/Taxon	Locus	Age	Measurements						
Sheep	14039	F	32.6	17					
Sheep	14039	F	31.8	15.3					
Sheep	14038	F	31.9	16.2					
Sheep	14037	F	30.5	15.9					
Sheep	14035-40	F	31.5	16					
Sheep	14037	F	30.1	15.7					
Sheep	14037	F	28.7	15.7					
Sheep	14004	F	28.9	14.3					
Sheep	14004	F	31	15.4					
Sheep	14036	F	28.8	14.7					
Sheep	14021	F	31.5	16.9					
Sheep	14014	F	32.9	16					
Sheep	14010	F	32.6						
Sheep	14028	F	34.4	17.2					
Sheep	14036	F	28.8	14.3					
Sheep	14028	F	30.1	15.5					
Sheep	14020	F	29.7	14.4					
Sheep	14020	F	31.5	16.6					
Cattle	14037	F	71.7	32.2					
M3			L	W					
Sh/G	14004	Payne F	23.8	9.3					
Sh/G	14022	Payne F	25	9.3					
Sh/G	14007	Payne G	25.5	9.5					
Cattle	14012	a,g,g,b	39.5	16.4					
Metacarpus			GL	SD	BFd	Dd	DEL	DVL	WC
Sh/G	14011	UM		15.7	31				
Sh/G	14012	UM							
Sh/G	14010	UM		14.8	30.6				
Sh/G	14010	UM		10.4	22.8				
Sh/G	14013	UM		16	32.9				
Sh/G	14039	UM		12.2	28.5				
Sh/G	14022	UM			31.7				
Sh/G	14036	UM			31.7				
Sh/G	14038	UM			31				

Bone/Taxon	Locus	Age	Measurements						
Sh/G	14037	UM		27.8					
Sh/G	14014	UM		30.5					
Sh/G	14004	UM		32.3					
Sh/G	14004	UM		30.1					
Sh/G	14028	UM		26.8					
Goat	14021	F	17.9	29.3	19	11.2	19	14.2	
Sheep	14011	F		31.3	19.9	12.9	19.1	14.2	
Sheep	14020	F	139.7	17.4	31.3	19	13.3	18.9	14.8
Sheep	14039	F	118.8	17.2	27.7	17.6	9.7	17.4	12.9
Sheep	14004	UE		28	17.4	10.6	16.3	12.2	
Sheep	14020	UE		29.2	19	12.4	18.6	13.8	
Sheep	14020	UE		30.1	20.2	12.5	19.5	14.4	
Cattle	14038	F	27.2	55.1	30.7				
Cattle	14035-40	F		54.7	31.8				
Cattle	14028	F		56.1	30.8				
Metatarsus			GL	SD	Bd	Dd	WLT	WMT	WC
Sh/G	14022	UM		11.7	27				
Sh/G	14022	UM		9.3	25				
Sh/G	14022	UM			28				
Sh/G	14021	UM			29.6				
Sh/G	14036	UM			26.7				
Sh/G	14036	UM			26.2				
Sh/G	14013	UM		12	26.1				
Sh/G	14012	UM			25.8				
Sh/G	14004	UM			27.4				
Sh/G	14028	UM			30.1				
Cattle	14038	UM			47.8				
Cattle	14036	UM			49.5				
Cattle	14004	UM			51.7				
Cattle	14028	UM			61.9				
Cattle	14022	UM			57.7				
Sheep	14005	F					12.7	18.7	12.8
Cattle	14037	F			63.5				
Goat	14037	F	125.1	12.6	25.3	16.6	10.2	16.8	11.7

Bone/Taxon	Locus	Age	Measurements						
Goat	14016	F			26.7	17.4	10.7	17.4	13.1
Sheep		F		14.1	28.1	18.6	12.8	18.6	13
Sheep	14037	F			29.8	19.5	12.5	19.6	13.7
Sheep	14004	F			25.1	18.2	11.7	18.2	12.7
Sheep	14028	F	163.4	14.3	28.7	19.6	13.1	19.6	13.8
Sheep	14028	F			28.5	18.9	11.7	18.4	12.8
Sheep	14020	F			29.3	20.5	13.3	20.3	14.3

Phalanx 1			SD	Bp	Bd	GLpe
Sh/G		F		11.7		
Sh/G		F				
Sh/G	14020	F		12.9		
Sh/G	14004	F				
Sh/G	14009	F	11.4	14.2	12.7	
Sh/G	14022	F	10.1	13.1	10.9	37.9
Sh/G		UE				
Sh/G		UE		13.2		
Sh/G	14001	UE		13		
Sh/G	14004	UE		12.6		
Sh/G	14001	UE		14.1		
Sh/G	14020	UE		13.9		
Sh/G	14020	UE		13.3		
Sh/G	14004	UE		13.4		
Sh/G	14004	UE	7.6	10	10.7	
Sh/G	14013	UE		11.5		
Sh/G	14011	UE		13		
Sh/G	14013	UE		12.1		
Sh/G	14013	UE		14.1		
Sh/G	14013	UE		13.5		
Sh/G	14005	UE		12.8		
Sh/G	14005	UE		12.3		
Sh/G	14005	UE		13.4		
Sh/G	14005	UE		13.8		
Sh/G	14014	UE		12.5		
Sh/G	14008	UE		15		

Bone/Taxon	Locus	Age	Measurements			
Sh/G	14021	UE		12.2		
Sh/G	14021	UE		11.1		
Sh/G		UM	10	12.3	12.2	
Sh/G	14001	UM	10.7	12.9	12.6	
Sh/G	14010	UM	19.3		11.4	
Sh/G	14004	UM	11.6	13.3	13.3	
Sh/G	14001.3	UM	12.8		13.9	
Sh/G	14011	UM	9.1	10.7	11.2	
Sh/G	14004	UM		12.6		
Sh/G	14005	UM	11.5	14.2	12.9	
Sh/G	14021	UM	10.6	12.8	12.7	
Sh/G	14021	UM	9.8	12.8	11.6	
Sh/G	14021	UM	9.7	11.7	11.4	
Goat	14039	F	9.4	13.3	12.2	40
Goat	14020	F	9.9	12.7	11.8	38
Goat	14004	F	11.5	15.1	14.1	45.1
Goat	14004	F			13.8	41.4
Goat	14016	F	10.7	13.7	13.1	38.9
Goat	14016	F	10.5	13.5		
Goat	14020	UM	12.1		13.5	
Goat	14011	UM	9.4	10.1	11.7	
Goat	14005	UM	12.3	13.3	13.9	
Goat	14005	UM	10.2	12.4	11.3	
Goat	14014	UM	9.9	12	12	
Sheep	14001	F	10.7	13.6	13.4	37.6
Sheep	14001	F	12		14	
Sheep	14010	F	10.6	13.1	12.7	39.5
Sheep	14011	F	10.4	14.3	13.6	42.2
Sheep	14013	F	10.6	13.6	12.9	41.5
Sheep	14013	F	11.8	14.2	13.5	
Sheep	14011	F	10.6	13.3	12.3	39.8
Sheep		UM			13.2	
Sheep		UM	11.6		13.8	
Sheep		UM	12.4	14.9	14.9	

Bone/Taxon	Locus	Age	Measurements			
Sheep	14004	UM	10.8	13	12.4	
Sheep	14035	UM	10.5		13.7	
Sheep	14004	UM	10.1	11.4	11.7	
Sheep	14013	UM	9.7	11	10.7	
Sheep	14013	UM			12.1	
Sheep	14005	UM	10.6	12.7	11.1	
Sheep	14021	UM	13.1	15.1	14	
Cattle	14004	F	21.9	27.4	28.7	62.8
Cattle	14022	F	21.8	26	25	56
Cattle	14038	F	24.2	28.7	27.4	64.9
Cattle	14021	F	225	27.5	27.1	62.2
Cattle	14035-40	F	20.2	25.6	24.9	54.5
Cattle	14020	F	21.9	25	23.2	59.2
Cattle	14009	F	21.1	24.9	24.4	61.8
Cattle		UE		22.4		
Cattle	14004	UE		23.8		
Cattle	14011	UM		25		

Radius			Bd			
Sh/G	14039	F	32.3			
Sh/G	14035	F	34.7			
Sh/G	14037	F	32.7			
Sh/G	14020	F	31			
Sh/G	14020	F	30.9			
Sh/G	14020	UE	30.7			
Sh/G	14039	UM	30			
Sh/G	14011	UM	33.7			
Sh/G	14028	UM	27.5			

Scapula			GLP			
Sh/G	14004	F	34.6			
Sh/G	14012	F	37.2			
Sh/G	14012	F	37.4			
Sh/G	14020	F	40.4			
Sh/G	14038	F	39.3			
Sh/G	14036	F	40.7			

Bone/Taxon	Locus	Age	Measurements	
Sh/G	14020	F	39.1	
Sh/G	14028	F	37.6	
Sh/G	14020	F	38.9	
Sh/G	14022	F	35.1	
Sh/G	14016	F	34.8	
Tibia			Bd	Dd
Sh/G	14001	F	30.4	22.3
Sh/G	14004	F	27.8	21.1
Sh/G	14020	F	32.2	25.4
Sh/G	14035-40	F	30.2	24.1
Sh/G	14013	F	28.9	22
Sh/G	14005	F	31.7	24.9
Sh/G	14005	F	29.4	23.2
Sh/G	14020	F	30.9	24.1
Sh/G	14004	F	26.3	19.1
Sh/G	14011	F	28.2	21.8
Sh/G	14020	F	32.2	25
Sh/G	14039	F	30.6	23.9
Sh/G	14001	UE	32.2	23.6
Sh/G	14011	UE	29	22
Sh/G	14009	UE	31.1	24.4
Sh/G	14021	UE	28.4	21.5
Sh/G	14021	UE	27.8	17.9
Sh/G	14011		34.9	26.2

APPENDIX 22.2

Chicken Bone Measurements in mm*

Bone/Locus	Age	Measurements		
Coracoid		GL		
14010		51.2		
14004		53.4		
14013		50.6		
14013		51.4		
Carpometacarpus		GL		
14020	F	38.8		
14028	F	41.8		
14022		40.5		
14004		38		
Femur		GL	Bp	Bd
	F	82		17.7
14010	F			14.3
14012	F	73.7	15.4	14
14020	F			16.4
14013	F			17
14005	F	76.5		14.3
14036	F	74.5		13.8
14022	F	82.4		
14011	F			15.1
14028	F	78.3		14.7
14028	F	89.8		17.5
				12.7
				12.7
Humerus		Bp	Bd	GL
14004	F		13.5	
14012	F	20.7	16.5	76.4
14037	F	22.5	16.5	84.3
14009	F		14.9	70.4

*F=Adult Bone; U=Young Bone (Porous Epiphyses)

Bone/Locus	Age	Measurements		
14037	F		15.8	78.5
Tarsometatarsus		GL	Bd	
14010	F		12.3	
14036	F	112.5	12.9	
14020	F		13.4	
14022	F	126.8	13.1	
14020	F	136.7	13	
14007	F		12.6	
14010	U		14.1	
			13	
14004			11.5	
14010			12.1	
14010			11.2	
14013		84.9		
14020			10.3	
14020			10.5	
14005		82	14.3	
Tibiotarsus		GL	Bd	
14013	F		15.8	
14016	F		15.4	
14010	F	69.3	11.5	
14009	F	88.9	14.2	
14038	F		14.7	
14020	F	87		
14013			13.5	
14005			12.3	

APPENDIX 22.3

Butchery marks recorded on a sample consisting of two crates of bones from the excavation*

Basket	Taxon	Bone	Butchery
14004.1	Sh/G	Astragalus	Sheared, lateral
140111	Sh/G	Atlas	Cut
140081	Sh/G	Atlas	Sheared
140005.3	Sh/G	Femur	Sheared, distal
140012.4	Sh/G	Femur	Cleft, distal
140038.1	Sh/G	Femur	Cut, shaft
140038.1	Sh/G	Femur	Cut, shaft
140039.1	Sh/G	Femur	Cut, proximal
140046.1	Sh/G	Femur	Cut, distal shaft
140109	Sh/G	Femur	Sheared, distal
140075	Sh/G	Femur	Cut, shaft
140075	Sh/G	Femur	Cut, shaft
140087	Sh/G	Femur	Cut, shaft
140102	Sh/G	Femur	Sheared, distal
140089.1	Sh/G	Femur	Cleft, distal
140021.2	Sh/G	Femur	Cut, caput
140005.3	Sh/G	Frontal	Split
140041.6	Sh/G	Horn	Chopped
140074	Sh/G	Horn	Sawn
140112	Sh/G	Horn	Chopped
140089.1	Sh/G	Horn	Chopped
140006.5	Sh/G	Humerus	Cleft, distal shaft
140006.5	Sh/G	Humerus	Sheared, proximal; chopped, distal
140012.4	Sh/G	Humerus	Split, proximal
140015	Sh/G	Humerus	Split, proximal
140109	Sh/G	Humerus	Cut, distal shaft
140073	Sh/G	Humerus	Chopped, proximal; cut, shaft
140021.2	Sh/G	Humerus	Cut, distal
140039.1	Sh/G	Metacarpus	Cut, proximal

* Sh/G=Sheep or goat; Cut=Cut-marks inflicted by a thin blade; Chopped=Chopper blow; Sheared=Oblique chopper blow that sheared off some bone tissue; Cleft=Chopper blow that cut through the bone in a right angle to its longitudinal axis; Split=Chopper blow that split the bone along its longitudinal axis

Basket	Taxon	Bone	Butchery
140029.2	Sh/G	Metacarpus	Cut, distal shaft
140030.2	Sh/G	Metacarpus	Sheared, distal
140084	Sh/G	Metacarpus	Cut, shaft
140006.5	Sh/G	Metapodial	Cleft, distal
140012.4	Sh/G	Metapodial	Chopped, distal
140012.4	Sh/G	Metapodial	Chopped, distal
140015	Sh/G	Metapodial	Cleft, distal
140006.5	Sh/G	Metapodial	Cleft, shaft
140041.6	Sh/G	Metapodial	Cut, proximal shaft
140102	Sh/G	Metapodial	Cut, proximal shaft
140006.5	Sh/G	Pelvis	Cleft, acetabulum
140028.2	Sh/G	Pelvis	Cut, ischium
140039.1	Sh/G	Pelvis	Cleft, ilium
140083	Sh/G	Pelvis	Sheared, ischium
140084	Sh/G	Pelvis	Cut, ilium
140074	Sh/G	Pelvis	Cut, ilium
140111	Sh/G	Pelvis	Cleft, ilium and ischium
140089.1	Sh/G	Pelvis	Chopped, cut, ilium
140046.1	Sh/G	Radius	Cleft, shaft
140072	Sh/G	Radius	Cut, distal shaft; sheared, distal
140078	Sh/G	Radius	Sheared, distal
140012.4	Sh/G	Rib	Cut
140039.1	Sh/G	Rib	Cut
140077	Sh/G	Rib	Cut
140075	Sh/G	Rib	Cut
140075	Sh/G	Rib	Cut
140102	Sh/G	Rib	Chopped
140021.2	Sh/G	Rib	Cut
14004.1	Sh/G	Scapula	Split; Cut, neck
140005.3	Sh/G	Scapula	Cut, glenoid; chopped, coracoid
140012.4	Sh/G	Scapula	Sheared, distal; cut, neck
140030.2	Sh/G	Scapula	Sheared, coracoid
140041.6	Sh/G	Scapula	Chopped, blade
140041.6	Sh/G	Scapula	Chopped, neck

Basket	Taxon	Bone	Butchery
140084	Sh/G	Scapula	Chopped, blade; sheared, coracoid
140075	Sh/G	Scapula	Cut, blade
140079	Sh/G	Scapula	Sheared, coracoid
140012.4	Sh/G	Tibia	Chopped, distal
140015	Sh/G	Tibia	Sheared, distal
140038.1	Sh/G	Tibia	Cut, shaft
140039.1	Sh/G	Tibia	Cut, shaft; sheared, shaft
140098	Sh/G	Tibia	Cut, shaft
140098	Sh/G	Tibia	Cut, shaft
140075	Sh/G	Tibia	Sheared, distal
140089.1	Sh/G	Tibia	Cut, shaft
140021.2	Sh/G	Tibia	Sheared, proximal
140012.4	Sh/G	Ulna	Sheared, proximal
14004.1	Sh/G	Vertebra	Split
140006.5	Sh/G	Vertebra	Split
140012.4	Sh/G	Vertebra	Cleft
140012.4	Sh/G	Vertebra	Split
140015	Sh/G	Vertebra	Cleft
140015	Sh/G	Vertebra	Split
140029.2	Sh/G	Vertebra	Chopped
140029.2	Sh/G	Vertebra	Sheared
140030.2	Sh/G	Vertebra	Split
140026.1	Sh/G	Vertebra	Cut
140041.6	Sh/G	Vertebra	Sheared
140041.6	Sh/G	Vertebra	Sheared
140109	Sh/G	Vertebra	Split
140085	Sh/G	Vertebra	Split
140111	Sh/G	Vertebra	Split
140021.2	Sh/G	Vertebra	Cleft
140021.2	Sh/G	Vertebra	Cleft
140021.2	Sh/G	Vertebra	Sheared
140021.2	Sh/G	Vertebra	Split
140021.2	Sh/G	Vertebra	Split
140021.2	Sh/G	Vertebra	Split

Basket	Taxon	Bone	Butchery
140029.2	Cattle	Astragalus	Cleft
140005.3	Cattle	Atlas	Cleft and split
140029.2	Cattle	Axis	Split
140109	Cattle	Calcaneus	Chopped, tuber calcis
140074	Cattle	Humerus	Sheared, distal; cut, distal
140074	Cattle	Humerus	Split; Sheared, distal
140079	Cattle	Humerus	Split, proximal
140021.2	Cattle	Humerus	Split, distal
140047.1	Cattle	Metacarpus	Cut, shaft
140100	Cattle	Metacarpus	Cut, shaft
140012.4	Cattle	Metacarpus	Cleft, distal
140089.1	Cattle	Metacarpus	Cut, shaft
140101	Cattle	Metacarpus	Cut, distal shaft
140089.1	Cattle	Metacarpus	Cut, distal
140027.1	Cattle	Metatarsus	Chopped
140038.1	Cattle	Metatarsus	Cut, shaft
140047.1	Cattle	Metatarsus	Cut, proximal shaft
140047.1	Cattle	Metatarsus	Cut, shaft
140075	Cattle	Metatarsus	Chopped, shaft
140101	Cattle	Metatarsus	Chopped, shaft
140102	Cattle	Metatarsus	Cut, shaft
140100	Cattle	Metatarsus	Chopped, shaft
140075	Cattle	Metatarsus	Cut, distal shaft
140111	Cattle	Metatarsus	Cleft, distal; cut, shaft
140047	Cattle	Pelvis	Cut, ilium
140021.2	Cattle	Pelvis	Chopped
140006.5	Cattle	Radius	Cleft, shaft; cut, distal shaft
140038.1	Cattle	Radius	Sheared, distal
140101	Cattle	Radius	Split; Sheared, distal
140079	Cattle	Radius	Cleft, proximal shaft
140012.4	Cattle	Rib	Cut
140033.1	Cattle	Rib	Cut
140038.1	Cattle	Rib	Chopped
140047.1	Cattle	Rib	Cut

Basket	Taxon	Bone	Butchery
140078	Cattle	Rib	Chopped
140112	Cattle	Rib	Cut
140079	Cattle	Rib	Cut
140089.1	Cattle	Rib	Cut
140087	Cattle	Sacrum	Split
140005.3	Cattle	Scapula	Cut, blade
140012.4	Cattle	Scapula	Split
140081	Cattle	Scapula	Sheared, spine
140021.2	Cattle	Scapula	Split
140101	Cattle	Tibia	Cleft, distal shaft; cut, distal shaft
140005.3	Cattle	Ulna	Cleft, proximal
140075	Cattle	Ulna	Chopped
140030.2	Cattle	Vertebra	Split
140077	Chicken	Tibiotarsus	Cut, distal
14004.1	Sheep	Astragalus	Chopped; cut, medial
140112	Sheep	Astragalus	Cut
140021.2	Sheep	Astragalus	Cleft
140005.3	Sheep	Calcaneus	Cut, sustenculum and lateral
140006.5	Sheep	Calcaneus	Cut
140039.1	Sheep	Horn	Sawn
140021.2	Sheep	Horn	Chopped
140005.3	Sheep	Humerus	Cut, distal shaft
140006.5	Sheep	Humerus	Chopped, distal shaft
140041.6	Sheep	Humerus	Sheared, distal
140111	Sheep	Humerus	Sheared, distal
140075	Sheep	Humerus	Cut, distal
140102	Sheep	Humerus	Cleft, shaft
140102	Sheep	Humerus	Sheared, distal; chopped, distal
140021.2	Sheep	Metatarsus	Sheared

DENDROARCHAEOLOGICAL ANALYSIS OF REMAINS FOUND AT THE EXCAVATIONS OF THE WESTERN WALL FOUNDATIONS

Helena Roth and Dafna Langgut

The excavations of the constructional fill exposed in the excavations presented here yielded 115 pieces of charcoal. The charred material was transferred for wood identification to the Laboratory of Archaeobotany and Ancient Environments at Tel Aviv University.

PHYSICAL SETTINGS

Jerusalem is located in the Judean Mountains, east of the watershed border, and enjoys a typical Mediterranean climate (precipitation >350 mm/year). The current natural vegetation of the Judean Mountains is characterized by Mediterranean forest-maquis, garrigue and batha formations. In the forest-maquis, *Quercus calliprinos-Pistacia palaestina* is the most common association, with the occasional *Pinus halepensis* and an open maqius of *Ceratonia siliqua-Pistacia lentiscus* mixed with *Quercus calliprinos*. The eastern slopes of the Judean Mountains are characterized by a narrow strip of semi-arid Irano-Turanian steppe vegetation, dominated by *Zizyphus lotus*, *Pistacia atlantica* and dwarf shrubs, e.g., *Artemisia herba-alba* and grasses. However, the natural landscape of the region was subjected to extensive changes over the period of human occupation of the area (Zohary 1962: 39, 98, 208–212). Because of the man-made changes to the landscape, the thinning of the Mediterranean maquis due to grazing, forest clearing for agriculture, cutting trees for timber, production of charcoal and other uses of wild plants, as well as the proximity of the city to the steppe Irano-Turanian phytogeographical zone (resulting in the replacement of the natural Mediterranean vegetation by semi-arid steppe vegetation elements), the current vegetation surrounding Jerusalem is highly anthropogenic, covered by low batha shrubs, predominantly *Sarcopoterium spinosum* (e.g., Lev-Yadun 1997).[1]

MATERIALS AND METHODS

The samples were systematically collected *in-situ* from the constructional fill in the three support chambers uncovered in the current excavation. The 115 specimens collected were from different loci in the same context of the constructional fill (Loci 14001, 14004, 14009, 14011, 14012, 14013, 14014, 14020 and 14021).

Since the three-dimensional structure of wood (transverse, radial and tangential) is well preserved even as charred material, it is possible to identify the wood remnants based on their anatomical structure when the state of preservation is satisfactory. The charcoal assemblage was examined under a Zeiss SteREO Discovery V20 epi-illuminated microscope at magnifications of up to ×360 with bright/dark field objective. A Scanning Electron Microscope (SEM: JOEL JSM-6300) was

---

[1] The Study refers to the Samaria Highlands, but applied to the Judean Mountains as well.

used when a higher magnification was required. Charcoal pieces larger than 0.5 cm were cut using razor blades and examined along the three wood axes. The abundance, arrangement and size of the wood's anatomical structures (e.g., annual growth rings, vessels, rays and fibers), along with a number of other diagnostic characteristics, were noted and compared with wood and charcoal reference collections of the southern Levant (provided by the Steinhardt Museum of Natural History, Tel Aviv University). Regional wood anatomy atlases were also used in order to make a determination (e.g., Fahn, Werker and Baas 1986; Wheeler, Baas and Gason 1989; Schweingruber 1990; Richter *et al.* 2004; Akkemik and Yaman 2012).

RESULTS AND DISCUSSION

The charred wood assemblage is characterized by a medium to poor state of preservation. Most of the charred pieces examined were between approximately 0.5–2.5 sq cm. The assemblage is also characterized by a low diversity of tree species and high occurrences of roots and tubers (Table 23.1 and Fig. 23.1). Twenty-nine percent (=33 samples) were identified as one of four species in declining frequency: *Olea europaea, Pinus halepensis, Cupressus sempervirens* and *Ficus carica.* Fifty-one percent of the assemblage was recognized as roots or tubers, which are characterized by a different set of diagnostic features and thus cannot be identified with a specific species. Twenty percent were determined undetectable due to poor states of preservation. One sample was identified as an unspecified coniferous tree. The sample was too small and poorly preserved to make a more accurate determination. The discussion below follows the data presented in Table 23.2 and Fig. 23.2.

Olea europaea (olive; 48.5%, Table 23.2, Fig. 23.2) is an evergreen tree of the Mediterranean forest-maquis in Israel and occurs both as a cultivated (more common than the wild since the Early Bronze Age) and natural element (Zohary 1973: 135, 372, 628). Economically it was the most important fruit cultivation of the Mediterranean basin (Zohary, Hopf and Weiss 2012: 116). Although olive orchards are currently a major component of the south Levantine landscape, the wild olive has always been a minor component in the natural Levantine environment, as is reflected in Late Pleistocene palynological diagrams (Horowitz 1979; Weinstein-Evron 1983; Langgut *et al.* 2011). A sudden and profound rise in olive pollen percentage was observed in the region's pollen diagrams

Table 23.1: Identification of Charred Wood Remains from Western Wall Foundations

Taxa / tree species	Absolute no.	Percentage
Root/tuber	59	51.3
Olea europaea (olive)	16	13.9
Pinus halepensis (Aleppo pine)	9	20.0
Cupressus sempervirens (Italian cypress)	5	7.8
Other conifers	1	4.3
Ficus carica (common fig)	2	1.7
Undetectable	23	0.9
Total	*115*	*100*

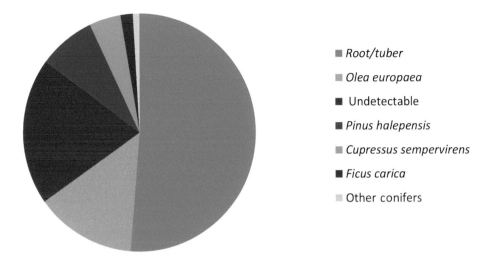

Figure 23.1: Relative frequencies of the identified taxa in the charred assemblage from the Western Wall Foundations.

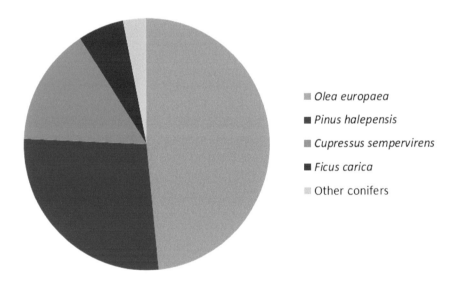

Figure 23.2: Distribution of taxa in the charred wood remains assemblage of the Western Wall Foundations (root/tuber and undetectable were excluded).

during the Chalcolithic period, which is considered to reflect the intensification of domesticated olive cultivation (Neumann *et al.* 2007; Litt *et al.* 2012; Langgut *et al.* 2019).[2]

Olive wood can be identified anatomically by the diffused porosity and the arrangement of the vessels in radial multiples of 2–4. Its rays are heterogeneous, mostly 2–3 seriate up to 12 cells high (and in some cases up to 20 cells), with mostly 1–3 (and in some cases up to 6) square and upright marginal cells (Fahn, Werker and Baas 1986: 136–137). This species has a large structural variability because of irregular growth forms (Schweingruber 1990: 573). The hard wood of the

---

[2] Evident also by archaeobotanical remains (Zohary and Spiegel-Roy 1975).

Table 23.2: Identification of Charred Wood Remains from the Western Wall Foundations (Root/Tuber and Undetectable Were Excluded)

Taxa/tree species	Absolute no.	Percentage
Olea europaea	16	48.5
Pinus halepensis	9	27.3
Cupressus sempervirens	5	15.2
Ficus carica	2	6.0
Other conifers	1	3.0
Total	*33*	*100.0*

olive tree makes it suitable for fuel as well as crafting small objects (Fahn and Werker 1992). *O. europaea* was identified in large quantities in the City of David excavations directed by Y. Shiloh in 1978–1985. The assemblages were dated to the Middle Bronze through the Iron Ages (Liphschitz and Waisel 1992; Fahn and Werker 1992; Werker and Baruch 1992). It was also identified within the Iron Age strata of the Ophel excavations (Liphschitz 1989) and in the late Iron Age to Persian period strata of the Scottish Church excavation (Liphschitz and Waisel 1980). The existence of the timber of fruit trees probably indicates that they were grown in the vicinity of the site (Liphschitz 2007: 104, 108).

Theophrastus (late 4th–early 3rd century BCE) mentioned the use of olive wood for kindling (*EiP* 5.9). Though Theophrastus predates the Early Roman period in Judea by approximately 300 years, he may have described conceptions that passed on through the ages. Vitruvius (1st century BCE) proposed using charred olive wood beams to strengthen unstable foundations (*TBoA* 3.4). In the 1st century CE, Pliny described this tree as one that was considered sacred (*NH* 13.2), and its use for fuel was forbidden even in cultic contexts (*NH* 15.40).

Pinus halepensis (Aleppo pine; 27.3%, Table 23.2, Fig. 23.2) is a native coniferous softwood tree naturally occurring in Israel as a characteristic arboreal species of the Mediterranean maquis, with an altitude range between sea level and 1000 m (Zohary 1973: 135, 341, 397, 502). *P. halepensis* is a relatively short-lived tree (Zohary 1973: 341), which usually lives up to 150 years (Zohary 1978: 218), but may attain an age of 200 years, mainly resulting from arboricultural care (Liphschitz, Lev-Yadun and Waisel 1981). It is a fast-growing tree species with moderate ecological requirements (Zohary 1978: 213). It can reach a height of 30 m in plantations with deep soil. However, in a mountainous environment with shallow soil, its height does not exceed 15 m (Bolotin 1963). It is the only naturally occurring pine species in the southern Levant (Weinstein-Evron and Lev-Yadun 2000). It is restricted to the Mediterranean climate with precipitation above 450 mm annually but is highly drought resistant (Bolotin 1963).

P. halepensis is one of the few species of softwoods growing in Israel and is anatomically distinguished from the others by the presence of longitudinal and horizontal resin ducts that appear regularly in every annual growth ring and within the infrequent multiseriate rays. Most of its rays are uniseriate up to 16 cells high (in some cases up to 22 cells) and the rays are characterized by bordered pits and tori (Fahn, Werker and Baas 1986: 57–58; Schweingruber 1990: 121).

P. halepensis was identified within the Iron Age and the Persian period strata in Shiloh's aforementioned excavations in the City of David (Liphschitz and Waisel 1992; Werker and Baruch

1992), the Scottish Church excavation (Liphschitz and Waisel 1980), as well as in the Ophel excavations south of the Temple Mount (Liphschitz 1989). One sample was unearthed in Area X-2 in the Jewish Quarter and was dated to the Hasmonean period (1st century BCE) (Liphschitz 2003). In total, nine pieces of various sizes of charred *P. halepensis* wood were identified within the Early Roman period layers in Jerusalem. Six of the samples were found in the Burnt House of the Jewish Quarter (Liphschitz 2010) and three samples were identified in a fill of a Herodian pool in the Ophel (Liphschitz 1989).

A relatively high percentage of *P. halepensis* wood was found in the Shephelah and Coastal Plain in Hellenistic and Roman–Byzantine period sites, which was interpreted by Liphschitz and Biger (2001) as indication of trade of pine logs with other regions. *P. halepensis* timber was widely used in the Greco-Roman culture in construction work, ship building, as well as other building and construction projects such as carpentry and furniture manufacture (Theophrastus *EiP* 5.7). Pine was also described by Pliny as resistant to rot and wood worms (*HN* 16.81).

Cupressus sempervirens (Italian cypress; 15.2%, Table 23.2, Fig. 23.2) is an evergreen species of a conifer tree that occurs naturally in the Mediterranean forest-maquis (Zohary 1973: 501). It can live for over 450 years and is able to grow up to 50 m high with a trunk diameter of up to 2 m (Lev-Yadun 1987). Its natural habitat is mountainous at altitudes of 500–1200 m asl and it is able to tolerate less rainfall and higher temperatures than many other conifers (Gale and Cutler 2000: 380). Although rare in this region, it is accepted that the species is native to Israel and surrounding areas since it is encountered in prehistoric sites (e.g., Lev-Yadun 1987; Lev-Yadun and Weinstein-Evron 1993). It is an important participant in several plant communities in the Middle East (Zohary 1973: 514, 529–532); however, it does not typically form large forests (Lev-Yadun and Weinstein-Evron 1993).

C. sempervirens is one of the few species of softwoods that grows in Israel and Transjordan and is anatomically distinguished from the others by its lack of resin canals in the wood, its uniseriate rays 3–20 cells high (and in rare cases up to 40 cells), and the occurrence of simple pits and smooth tori (Fahn, Werker and Baas 1986: 55; Schweingruber 1990: 137).

C. sempervirens was identified in the Iron Age strata in Shiloh's excavations in the City of David (Liphschitz and Waisel 1992). Nineteen samples of *C. sempervirens* were identified in Jerusalem within the Early Roman period strata: one was discovered in the Lower City of Jerusalem, 15 (mostly logs) in the Burnt House of the Jewish Quarter (Liphschitz 2010) and four in the palatial mansion (Liphschitz 2001). The straight, long trunks of the trees were used for a variety of purposes, including the construction of monumental buildings and boats, as roof timber, supporting beams, boxes, coffins, furniture and tools (e.g., Meiggs 1982).

Even though there is some evidence for the use of *C. sempervirens* in earlier periods, during the Roman period, a dramatic increase in the amount of cypress remnants was documented in south Levantine sites. The increase in cypress remains may derive from the common use in Roman monumental construction projects and/or, as was suggested by Langgut, Gleason and Burrell (2015), cypress was used as an ornamental tree in royal gardens dated to the Roman period in the southern Levant and beyond. Large numbers of logs and wood remnants were recorded in Herodium (Liphschitz and Waisel 1975), Tel Beer-Sheba (Liphschitz and Waisel 1973), Masada (Liphschitz, Lev-Yadun and Waisel 1981; Liphschitz and Lev-Yadun 1989; Lev-Yadun, Lucas and Weinstein-Evron 2010), Cypros (Liphschitz 2004), ʿEn Boqeq (Liphschitz 2000) and Jericho (Liphschitz and Waisel 1999). Moreover, large concentrations of cypress wood at sites in the arid regions of the Negev and the Jordan Valley were unearthed and dated to the Early Roman period (see Liphschitz 2007). Cypress wood, like pine, was described by Pliny as resistant to rot and wood worms (*HN* 16:81).

Ficus carica L. (common fig; 6.0%, Table 23.2, Fig. 23.2) is a deciduous fruit tree native to the Mediterranean region. The oldest known fig pips came from the ca. 780,000 YBP Acheulian Gesher Benot Ya'aqov site in Israel (Melamed *et al.* 2011). It was one of the first fruit trees to be cultivated in the Mediterranean basin (Zohary and Spiegel-Roy 1975) and can reach heights of up to 4 m in cultivated plantations. *F. carica* has been part of regular food production in the Levant since the Early Bronze Age, providing fresh fruit in summer and storable, sugar-rich, dry fruit all year round (Zohary, Hopf and Weiss 2012: 126). Wild common fig trees grow mainly in the low altitudes of the Mediterranean phytogeographical region, occupying stream sides, but are also found in habitats including rock crevices and gorges. Feral types of *F. carica* are widely distributed in secondary man-made habitats, such as edges of plantations and cultivated terraces, collapsed cisterns and cave entrances (Zohary, Hopf and Weiss 2012: 128). Pruning and training the cultivated trees is common at *F. carica* plantations. It allows for a sufficient amount of sunlight to reach all of the tree's branches and facilitates harvesting the fruit (Flaishman, Rodov and Stover 2008).

F. carica is distinguished by distinct annual growth rings, diffuse porosity, vessels arranged in radial multiples and clusters of 2–4 vessels (and in some cases up to 7), and up to 20% of solitary vessels. The parenchyma is comprised of 2–6 seriate tangential bands in vasicentric, marginal and fusiform performance. The rays are 1–4 cells wide and up to 45 cells high, heterocellular, with procumbent central cells, and upright and square marginal cells (Fahn, Werker and Baas 1986: 131; Schweingruber 1990: 551).

Only one uncertain identification of *F. carica* was made with two wooden bowls discovered in the En Gedi cemetery dating to the late Hellenistic period (Werker 1994). *F. carica* is not represented in the Early Roman period wood charcoal assemblages of Jerusalem.

Theophrastus described the fig wood as just as good for kindling as the olive wood because it ignites quickly and does not burn out quickly, but also as one that gives pungent smoke (*EiP* 5.9).

SIGNIFICANCE OF THE DATA FROM AN ARCHAEOLOGICAL PERSPECTIVE

According to the results of the identification of the charred wood remains, as well as the poor state of preservation of the samples unearthed, the assemblage may represent the contents of a garbage dump. The relatively large number of roots discovered may originate from the refuse created by agricultural activities in the fields outside the city. The botanic refuse that was cleared away from the field may have been used for fuel in domestic contexts, after which it was discarded into a dump. This form of recycling of agricultural refuse can still, to a certain extent, be seen in current rural populations of the Levant[3] and is also ethnographically recorded in other regions (e.g., in central Africa; Gelabert, Asouti and Martí 2011).

The large volume of olive wood identified in the assemblage may also represent refuse of agricultural activities, such as pruning, that took place in olive orchards in the vicinity of the city, and which was later also used as fuel. Pruning of olive tree branches is common and important since it helps moderate the alternate year bearing, keeps the trees at a height that allows easy harvest, helps remove branches infected with pests and fungi and therefore increases the fruit yield. Increasing yield following branch pruning that induces new branch formation occurs

---

[3]   Collection of tree roots and any flammable material is still performed by Bedouins and Palestinian farmers.

also because olive trees never bear fruit on the same branch twice (Zinger 1985). The removed branches would have been cleared from the plantation area to prevent the spreading of pests and fungi on the healthy trees. Thus, it seems that the large quantities of olive wood represent the large scale of olive cultivation practiced in the vicinity of the city, as was previously suggested by Liphschitz (1987; 2007: 104, 108), Liphschitz and Waisel (1992), and Fahn and Werker (1992). The high presence of charred olive wood found in ancient settlements (see Liphschitz 2007) may suggest that the *O. europaea* was indeed used as a common fuel source (Liphschitz 2007: 108), as was described by Theophrastus (*EiP* 5.9). However, due to the economic value of olives and possible sacred status of the tree, it is reasonable to suggest that its use as fuel was restricted to the products of pruning.

It seems that this "agricultural garbage" that accumulated in a dump in the area of the city was later reused as a fill during the construction of the foundation of the Stepped Street and adjacent drainage channel. The recycling of dump material as constructional fills is common and a well-known phenomenon throughout the ages (e.g., Sapir-Hen *et al*. 2012).

An alternative explanation to the relatively high percentage of olive wood in the assemblage comes from Vitruvius (*TBoA* 3.4), who proposed using charred olive wood beams to strengthen unstable foundations. It is possible that the constructors used charred olive wood as a frame for the constructional fill in order to stabilize the foundation of the Stepped Street and the drainage channel. Tamarisk beams used for stabilizing the construction of the Roman siege rampart were documented at Masada (Liphschitz, Lev-Yadun and Waisel 1981).

Two samples of the assemblage were identified as *Ficus carica* (common fig), the only other non-coniferous species within the assemblage apart from the olive that represents the Mediterranean maquis. Being a cultivated fruit tree, it could be argued that these samples originate from a domestic fuel context occurring as a result of agricultural activity, rather than a representation of the natural arboreal environment of the city's hinterland. The lack of other evergreen taxa of the Mediterranean maquis (such as *Pistacia spp.* and *Quercus calliprinos*) exemplifies the scarcity of these taxa from the vicinity of the city and their possible replacement by fruit tree plantations.

Palynological records from the Dead Sea (which mainly reflect pollen originating from the Judean Mountains) show increasing olive pollen percentages since the early Hellenistic period (Neumann *et al.* 2010; Litt *et al.* 2012; Langgut and Lipschits 2017). These data align with these dendroarchaeological investigations and demonstrate that the olive plantations around Jerusalem to a great extent replaced the Mediterranean forest-maquis.

It is possible that the conifer wood (of *P. halepensis* and *C. sempervirens*) that was favored in construction originated from the debris of a building destroyed by fire that was moved to a local garbage dump. The conifer wood was also retrieved from adjacent loci in Square C1 (Loci 14012, 14020 and 14021), which could represent the material resulting from the event of clearing debris into a garbage dump. Despite the scarcity of *C. sempervirens* in the local wild vegetation, charred wood assemblages of Early Roman period sites have yielded a high percentage of this wood (Langgut, Gleason and Burrell 2015 and references therein).

The low species diversity, high occurrence of presumed agricultural refuse and possible architectural debris all support the possibility that the assemblage originates within a local garbage dump. The poor state of preservation of the charred pieces may indicate a period of time when this assemblage accumulated above ground and was therefore subjected to erosion. Later, the material in this garbage dump was moved and reused as a constructional fill under the Stepped Street and adjacent drainage channel.

REFERENCES

Akkemik, U. and Yaman, B. 2012. *Wood Anatomy of Eastern Mediterranean Species.* Kessel.

Bolotin, M. 1963. Contributions to the Arboreal Flora of Israel: *Pinus halepensis Mill. La-Yaaran* 13: 120–127.

EiP: Theophrastus. 1961. *Enquiry into Plants.* Translated by Sir Arthur Hurt (Loeb Classical Library). London and Cambridge, Mass.

Fahn, A. and Werker, E. 1992. Macrobotanical Remains, Section B. In: De Groot, A. and Ariel, D.T., eds. *Excavations at the City of David 1978–1985, Directed by Yigal Shiloh*, Vol. 3: *Stratigraphical, Environmental, and Other Reports* (Qedem 33). Jerusalem: 106–114.

Fahn, A., Werker, E. and Baas, P. 1986. *Wood Anatomy and Identification of Trees and Shrubs from Israel and Adjacent Regions.* Jerusalem.

Flaishman, M.A., Rodov, V. and Stover, E. 2008. The Fig: Botany, Horticulture and Breeding. *Horticulture Reviews* 34: 96–132.

Gale, R. and Cutler, D. 2000. *Plants in Archaeology.* West Yorkshire.

Gelabert, L.P., Asouti, E. and Martí, E.A. 2011. The Ethnoarchaeology of Firewood Management in the Fang Villages of Equatorial Guinea, Central Africa: Implications for the Interpretation of Wood Fuel Remains from Archaeological Sites. *Journal of Anthropological Archaeology* 30: 375–384.

Horowitz, A. 1979. Palynology. In: Horowitz, A., ed. *The Quaternary of Israel.* New York: 180–259.

Langgut, D., Almogi-Labin, A., Bar-Matthews, M. and Weinstein-Evron, M. 2011. Vegetation and Climate Changes in the South-Eastern Mediterranean During the Last Glacial-Interglacial Cycle (86 ka): New Marine Pollen Record. *Quaternary Science Reviews* 30: 3960–3972.

Langgut, D., Cheddadi, R., Carrión, J.S., Cavanagh, M., Colombaroli, D., Eastwood, W.J., Greenberg, R., Litt, T., Mercuri, A.M., Miebach, A., Roberts, N., Woldring, H. and Woodbridge, J. 2019. The Origin and Spread of Olive Cultivation in the Mediterranean Basin. *The Holocene* 29: 902–922.

Langgut, D., Gleason, K. and Burrell, B. 2015. Pollen Analysis as Evidence for Herod's Royal Garden at the Promontory Palace, Caesarea. *Israel Journal of Plant Sciences* 62: 111–121.

Langgut, D. and Lipschits, O. 2017. Dry Climate During the Babylonian and the Early Persian Period and its Impact on the Creation of Idumea. *Transeuphraténe* 49: 141–172.

Lev-Yadun, S. 1987. Cupressus sempervirens L. A Native and Cultivated Tree in the East Mediterranean Region. *Rotem* 23–24: 33–40 (Hebrew; English summary: 162).

Lev-Yadun, S. 1997. Flora and Climate in Southern Samaria: Past and Present. In: Finkelstein, I., Ledermen, Z. and Bunimovitz, S., eds. *Highlands of Many Cultures, the Southern Samaria Survey: The Sites* (Monograph Series of the Institute of Archaeology of Tel Aviv University 14). Tel Aviv: 85–102.

Lev-Yadun, S., Liphschitz, N. and Waisel, Y. 1981. Dendrochronological Investigations in Israel: *Pinus halepensis*–the Oldest Living Pine in Israel. *La-Yaaran* 31: 1–8 (Hebrew; English summary: 49–52).

Lev-Yadun, S., Lucas, D.S. and Weinstein-Evron, M. 2010. Modeling the Demands for Wood by the Inhabitants of Masada and for the Roman Siege. *Journal of Arid Environments* 74: 777–785.

Lev-Yadun, S. and Weinstein-Evron, M. 1993. Prehistoric Wood Remains of *Cupressus sempervirens* L. from the Natufian Layers of El-Wad Cave, Mount Carmel, Israel. *Tel Aviv* 1: 125–131.

Liphschitz, N. 1987. The Landscape of Vegetation and Weather Conditions in Judah and Samaria in Ancient Times. *Rotem* 22: 21–26 (Hebrew; English summary: 114).

Liphschitz, N. 1989. Dendroarchaeological Studies 150: The Ophel (Jerusalem) 1986. (Appendix C). In: Mazar, E. and Mazar, B., eds. *Excavations in the South of the Temple Mount: The Ophel of Biblical Jerusalem* (Qedem 29). Jerusalem: 142–143.

Liphschitz, N. 2000. Dendroarchaeological Remains. In: Fischer, M., Gichon, M. and Tal, O., eds. *ᶜEn Boqeq: Excavations in an Oasis on the Dead Sea*, Vol. 2. Mainz: 127–130.

Liphschitz, N. 2003. Archaeobotanical Remains. In: Geva, H., ed. *Jewish Quarter Excavations in the Old City of Jerusalem, Conducted by Nahman Avigad, 1969–1982*, Vol. 2: *The Finds from Areas A, W and X–2, Final Report.* Jerusalem: 496–500.

Liphschitz, N. 2004. Dendroarchaeological Analysis of Wood Remains from Cypros. In: Netzer, E., Laureys-Chachy, R. and Meshorer, Y., eds. *Hasmonean and Herodian Palaces at Jericho: Final Reports of the 1973–1987 Excavations*, Vol. 2: *Stratigraphy and Architecture*. Jerusalem: 281–285.

Liphschitz, N. 2007. *Timber in Ancient Israel: Dendroarchaeology and Dendrochronology* (Monograph Series of the Institute of Archaeology of Tel Aviv University 26). Tel Aviv.

Liphschitz, N. 2010. Archaeobotanical Remains. In: Geva, H., ed. *Jewish Quarter Excavations in the Old City of Jerusalem, Conducted by Nahman Avigad, 1969–1982*, Vol. 4: *The Burnt House of Area B and Other Studies, Final Report*. Jerusalem: 300–304.

Liphschitz, N. and Biger, G. 2001. Past Distribution of Aleppo Pine (*Pinus halepensis*) in the Mountains of Israel (Palestine). *The Holocene* 11: 427–436.

Liphschitz, N. and Lev-Yadun, S. 1989. The Botanical Remains from Masada: Identification of the Plant Species and the Possible Origin of the Remnants. *BASOR* 274: 27–32.

Liphschitz, N., Lev-Yadun, S. and Waisel, Y. 1981. Dendroarchaeological Investigations in Israel (Masada). *Israel Exploration Journal* 31: 230–234.

Liphschitz, N. and Waisel, Y. 1973. Analysis of the Botanical Material of the 1969–1970 Seasons and the Climatic History of the Beer-Sheba Region. In: Aharoni, Y., ed. *Beer-Sheba I: Excavations at Tel Beer-Sheba, 1969–1971 Seasons* (Publications of the Institute of Archaeology 2). Tel Aviv: 97–105.

Liphschitz, N. and Waisel, Y. 1975. *Dendroarchaeological Investigations: Herodium* (Mimeographed Report No. 35). (Hebrew).

Liphschitz, N. and Waisel, Y. 1980. *Dendroarchaeological Investigations: The Scottish Church* (Mimeographed Report No. 83). (Hebrew).

Liphschitz, N. and Waisel, Y. 1992. Macrobotanical Remains, Section A. In: De Groot, A. and Ariel, D.T., eds. *Excavations at the City of David 1978–1985, Directed by Yigal Shiloh*, Vol. 3: *Stratigraphical, Environmental, and Other Reports* (Qedem 33). Jerusalem: 105–106.

Liphschitz, N. and Waisel, Y. 1999. Timber Analysis. In: Hachlili, R. and Killebrew, A.E., eds. *Jericho: The Jewish Cemetery of the Second Temple Period* (IAA Reports 7). Jerusalem: 88–92.

Litt, T., Ohlwein, C., Neumann, F.H., Hence, A. and Stein, M. 2012. Holocene Climate Variability in the Levant from the Dead Sea Pollen Record. *Quaternary Science Reviews* 49: 95–105.

Meiggs, R. 1982. *Trees and Timber in the Ancient Mediterranean World*. Oxford.

Melamed, Y., Kislev, M., Weiss, E. and Simchoni, O. 2011. Extinction of Water Plants in the Hula Valley: Evidence for Climate Change. *Journal of Human Evolution* 60: 320–327.

Neumann, F., Kagan, E., Leroy, S. and Baruch, U. 2010. Vegetation History and Climate Fluctuations on a Transect Along the Dead Sea West Shore and Their Impact on Past Societies Over the Last 3500 Years. *Journal of Arid Environments* 74: 756–764.

Neumann, F., Schölzel, C., Litt, T., Hense, A. and Stein, M. 2007. Holocene Vegetation and Climate History of the Northern Golan Heights (Near East). *Vegetation History and Archaeobotany* 16: 329–346.

NH: Pliny. 1952. *Natural History*. Translated by H. Rackham (Loeb Classical Library). Cambridge.

Richter, H.G., Grosser, D., Heinz, I. and Gasson, P.E. 2004. IAWA List of Microscopic Features for Softwood Identification. *IAWA Journal* 25: 1–70.

Sapir-Hen, L., Bar-Oz, G., Sharon, I., Gilboa, A. and Dayan, T. 2012. Understanding Faunal Contexts of a Complex Tell: Tel Dor, Israel, as a Case Study. *Journal of Archaeological Science* 39: 590–601.

Schweingruber, F.H. 1990. *Anatomy of European Woods*. Kessel.

TBoA: Vitruvius. 1999. *Ten Books on Architecture*. Translated by I.D. Rowland and T.N. Howe. Cambridge.

Weinstein-Evron, M. 1983. The Paleoecology of the Early Wurm in the Hula Basin, Israel. *Paléorient* 9: 5–19.

Weinstein-Evron, M. and Lev-Yadun, S. 2000. Palaeoecology of *Pinus halepensis* in Israel in the Light of Archaeobotanical Data. In: Ne'eman, G. and Trabaud, L., eds. *Ecology, Biogeography and Management of Pinus halepensis and Pinus brutia Forest Ecosystems in the Mediterranean Basin*. Leiden: 119–130.

Werker, E. 1994. Botanical Identification of Wood Remains from the 'En Gedi Excavation. *'Atiqot* 24: 69–72 (Hebrew; English summary: 10*).

Werker, E. and Baruch, U. 1992. Macrobotanical Remains, Section C. In: De Groot, A. and Ariel, D.T., eds. *Excavations at the City of David 1978–1985, Directed by Yigal Shiloh*, Vol. 3: *Stratigraphical, Environmental, and Other Reports* (Qedem 33). Jerusalem: 115–121.

Wheeler, E., Baas, P. and Gasson, P. 1989. IAWA List of Microscopic Features for Hardwood Identification. *IAWA Journal* 10: 219–332.

Zinger, A. 1985. *Olive Cultivation*. Tel Aviv (Hebrew).

Zohary, D., Hopf, M. and Weiss, E. 2012. *Domestication of Plants in the Old World* (4th ed.). Oxford.

Zohary, D. and Spiegel-Roy, P. 1975. Beginnings of Fruit Growing in the Old World. *Science* 187: 319–327.

Zohary, M. 1962. *Plant Life of Palestine: Israel and Jordan.* New York.

Zohary, M. 1973. *Geobotanical Foundations of the Middle East.* Stuttgart.

Zohary, M. 1978. *The Plant World: Morphology, Taxonomy, Evolution, Biology.* Tel Aviv.

APPENDIX

Table 23.A1: Classification of All Charred Wood Samples from the Western Wall Excavation (Area L)

Tree species/taxa	Area	Locus	Basket	Object number
Cupressus sempervirens	L	14021	140046.3	2
	L	14021	140046.3	5
	L	14021	140046.3	9
	L	14021	140046.3	11
	L	14021	140046.3	12
Ficus carica	L	14004	140004.14	7
	L	14004	140004.14	15
Olea europaea	L	14001	140005	1
	L	14004	140004.14	1
	L	14004	140004.14	4
	L	14004	140004.14	5
	L	14004	140004.14	8
	L	14004	140004.14	9
	L	14004	140004.14	11
	L	14004	140004.14	14
	L	14009	140014.3	6
	L	14009	140014.3	7
	L	14009	140014.3	10
	L	14009	140014.3	12
	L	14009	140014.3	13
	L	14011	140016.2	1
	L	14013	140026	2
	L	14020	140054	7
Pinus halepensis	L	14012	140030	1
	L	14020	140045.3	8
	L	14020	140045.3	18
	L	14021	140046.3	1
	L	14021	140046.3	3
	L	14021	140046.3	6

Tree species/taxa	Area	Locus	Basket	Object number
	L	14021	140046.3	7
	L	14021	140046.3	8
	L	14021	140046.3	10
Other conifer	L	14021	140046.3	4
Root/tuber	L	14004	140004.14	2
	L	14004	140004.14	3
	L	14004	140004.14	6
	L	14004	140004.14	10
	L	14004	140004.14	13
	L	14004	140004.14	16
	L	14009	140014.3	1
	L	14009	140014.3	2
	L	14009	140014.3	3
	L	14009	140014.3	4
	L	14009	140014.3	5
	L	14009	140014.3	8
	L	14013	140019.3	1
	L	14013	140019.3	2
	L	14013	140019.3	3
	L	14013	140019.3	4
	L	14013	140019.3	5
	L	14013	140019.3	6
	L	14013	140019.3	7
	L	14013	140026	1
	L	14013	140026.3	1
	L	14013	140026.3	2
	L	14014	1400316.6	1
	L	14020	140038.3	1
	L	14020	140038.3	1
	L	14020	140038.3	2
	L	14020	140038.3	2
	L	14020	140038.3	3
	L	14020	140038.3	3

Tree species/taxa	Area	Locus	Basket	Object number
	L	14020	140038.3	4
	L	14020	140038.3	4
	L	14020	140038.3	5
	L	14020	140038.3	6
	L	14020	140045.3	1
	L	14020	140045.3	2
	L	14020	140045.3	3
	L	14020	140045.3	4
	L	14020	140045.3	5
	L	14020	140045.3	6
	L	14020	140045.3	7
	L	14020	140045.3	9
	L	14020	140045.3	10
	L	14020	140045.3	11
	L	14020	140045.3	12
	L	14020	140045.3	13
	L	14020	140045.3	14
	L	14020	140045.3	15
	L	14020	140045.3	16
	L	14020	140045.3	17
	L	14020	140054	1
	L	14020	140054	2
	L	14020	140054	3
	L	14020	140054	4
	L	14020	140054	5
	L	14020	140054	6
	L	14021	140039.2	1
	L	14021	140039.2	2
	L	14021	140039.2	3
	L	14021	140039.2	4
Undetectable	L	14004	140004.14	12
	L	14009	140014.3	9
	L	14009	140014.3	11

Tree species/taxa	Area	Locus	Basket	Object number
	L	14013	140019.3	8
	L	14013	140019.3	9
	L	14013	140019.3	10
	L	14013	140019.3	11
	L	14013	140019.3	12
	L	14013	140019.3	13
	L	14013	140019.3	14
	L	14013	140019.3	15
	L	14013	140019.3	16
	L	14013	140019.3	17
	L	14013	140019.3	18
	L	14013	140019.3	19
	L	14013	140019.3	20
	L	14020	140038.3	5
	L	14020	140038.3	6
	L	14020	140038.3	7
	L	14020	140038.3	8
	L	14020	140038.3	9
	L	14020	140038.3	10
	L	14020	140038.3	11

CHAPTER 24

RESIDUE ANALYSIS OF FILLS EXCAVATED ALONG THE WESTERN WALL FOUNDATIONS

Dvory Namdar

This report discusses the results of residue analysis of 18 vessels discovered in the constructional fills excavated along the Western Wall Foundations (see Chapter 16) located 6 m below the 1st century CE street that ran alongside the Temple Mount. The main feature uncovered in the excavation is a system of walls built as a compartment system for the 1st century CE street and structures surrounding it. The system is comprised of a long wall, parallel to the Western Wall, with perpendicular walls built between the two. This created a system of compartments, three of which were excavated in the current project. Within the fills of the compartments, significant amounts of pottery as well as other finds were uncovered. Although three distinct phases were discerned by the excavators, the finds all originated from the Phase 1 fills within the compartments, dating to the 1st century CE.

MATERIALS AND METHODS

MATERIALS

Samples were gathered for analysis from all compartments. The compartments were filled with intentionally stratified earth fills. These fills were rich with finds and included many pottery sherds, complete vessels, stone vessels, animal bones, bone artifacts, metal artifacts, glass sherds and charcoal. As only Compartment C1 was fully sifted, this compartment served as the basis of the ceramic analysis, where the entire assemblage was considered. In Compartments C2 and C3 only a relatively small portion of the sample (10%) was gathered.

The vessel fragments sampled included the following types: one bowl, eight knife-paired oil lamps and nine juglets of two distinct types: small flat-based unguentaria and cupped-rim juglets, some with flat bases and others with rounded bases. Two of the latter juglets are a bit larger than the others. These were all analyzed using the described method. All items came from the constructional fill within compartment systems beneath Early Roman habitation levels and can be dated according to their form and context to the 1st century CE (see Chapter 16).

METHODS

Extraction of Organic Residues

All glassware was soaked overnight in fuming nitric acid, washed carefully with distilled water, and then washed with acetone, followed by dichloromethane, and dried in a fume hood. Method blanks were routinely run with each batch of extraction, for both archaeological and modern samples, as well as for plant extraction. This routine was employed in order to monitor and detect any introduction of contaminants during lab work.

Table 24.1: Inventory List of the Sampled Vessels Excavated from the Western Wall Foundations

Reg. no.	Locus	Locus description	Vessel type
140029/RAS-1	14011	Compartment 1, Layer 4 of constructional fill	Flat base juglet
140030/RAS-1	14012	Compartment 1, Layer 5 of constructional fill	Lamp
140030/RAS-2	14012	Compartment 1, Layer 5 of constructional fill	Jug
140031/RAS-3	14041	Earth fill under quarrying waste (Locus 14040)	Bowl
140032/RAS-1	14016	Compartments C1 and C2 separating wall	Rounded base juglet
140033/RAS-2	14013	Compartment 1, uppermost layer of constructional fill	Rounded base juglet
140038/RAS-2	14020	Compartment 2, uppermost layer of constructional fill	Lamp
140040/RAS-3	14022	Compartment 2, Layer 3 of constructional fill	Rounded base juglet
140041/RAS-0	14022	Compartment 2, Layer 3 of constructional fill	Lamp
140041/RAS-1	14022	Compartment 2, Layer 3 of constructional fill	Lamp
140041/RAS-2	14022	Compartment 2, Layer 3 of constructional fill	Lamp
140041/RAS-3	14022	Compartment 2, Layer 3 of constructional fill	Lamp
140041/RAS-4	14022	Compartment 2, Layer 3 of constructional fill	Lamp
140048/RAS-5	14028	Compartment 2, Layer 4 of constructional fill	Lamp
140048/RAS-6	14028	Compartment 2, Layer 4 of constructional fill	Flat omphalos base juglet
140054/RAS-3	14020	Compartment 2, uppermost layer of constructional fill	Unguentarium
140056/RAS-4	14022	Compartment 3, quarrying waste & earth fill Layer 7 of constructional fill	Rounded base juglet
140057/RAS-2	14028	Compartment 2, Layer 4 of constructional fill	Rounded base/flat base juglet

A 1 cubic cm fragment was broken off each ceramic vessel with pliers. Its surface was carefully cleaned with a sterile scalpel and then manually ground to powder in an agate mortar and pestle. A weighed 1 g sample of the homogenized powder was used for the extraction. Each sample was placed in a 20 mL centrifuge glass tube (HS, Kimble). The following steps were repeated twice: 10 mL of a dichloromethane: methanol mixture (2:1, v/v) was added to each sample, followed by sonication for 10 min.; the tubes were then centrifuged for 10 min. at 3500 rpm. The supernatant was removed to a clean glass vial and 10 μL of 1-nonadecanol (c_{19}ol) diluted in DCM:MeOH was added to serve as an internal standard. The accumulated solvents were evaporated under a gentle stream of nitrogen. Prior to analysis 100 μl of *N,O*-bis(trimethylsilyl)trifluoroacetamide (BSTFA) containing 1% trimethylchlorosilane (TMCS) was added to the dry extracts followed by heating at 65 °C for 20 min. One μL of each sample was injected into the gas chromatograph (GC) with mass selective detector (MS). All the samples were extracted twice, in totally separate extraction batches, to evaluate reproducibility.

Identification of Organic Residue Using Gas Chromatography/Mass Spectrometry (GC/MS)

GC/MS analyses were carried out using a HP7890 gas chromatograph coupled to a HP5973 mass spectrometer (electron multiplier potential 2 KV, filament current 0.35 mA, electron energy 70 eV, and the spectra were recorded over the range m/z 40 to 800) using a splitless injection mode. An Agilent 7683 autosampler was used for sample introduction. Helium was used as a carrier gas at a constant flow of 1.1 mL s^{-1}. An isothermal hold at 50 °C was kept for 2 min., followed by a heating gradient of 10 °C min.$^{-1}$ to 320 °C, with the final temperature held for 10 min. A 30 m, 0.25 mm ID 5% cross-linked phenylmethyl siloxane capillary column (HP-5MS) with a 0.25 μm film thickness was used for separation and the injection port temperature was 280 °C. The MS interface temperature was 300 °C. Peak assignments were carried out with the aid of library spectra (NIST 1.6) and compared with published data.

RESULTS AND DISCUSSION

The extraction of lipids from the sampled vessels showed an overall very good preservation of the absorbed commodities. The complete molecular assemblage of the lipids extracted, their calibrated total amounts and their suggested interpretations are presented in Table 24.2.

LAMPS

Eight lamps from the excavation were studied. They came mainly from one area (Compartment 2) and from most of its excavated layers. All the lamps date to the 1st century CE. Four of the lamps were found to have palm oil and four contained olive oil. As these lamps were part of the coherent study of the lamps of the City of David, this reflects a broader pattern noted in ancient Jerusalem at the time (Namdar *et al.* 2018). This shows that these deposits did not come from the richer population of the Upper City, which would have strictly used olive oil, due to its superior characteristics (lighting time, scent), despite its proximity, but reflects other classes (and/or possibly the workers located on site during the construction of the street) of the city. The oils used in the lamps were constrained to either the traditionally used olive oil or to the newly introduced substance of palm oil, and to them only. No mixtures of the two, or any other plant oils (or animal fat) were detected. This is also in accordance with the overall picture gained for other lamps from all over the City of David (*ibid.*).

JUGLETS

Nine juglets were analyzed and their content is much more varied than what was demonstrated for the oil lamps. The sampled juglets came from different loci and from all compartments and layers exposed during the excavation. GC/MS investigation of organic residues of plant oils and animal fats in archaeological lamps from Egypt (Copley *et al.* 2005; Evershed 2008) has made major contributions to our understanding of the chemical composition of plant oils and animal fats, in order to identify and distinguish them in archaeological samples.

Olive oil was detected in two juglets. The research conducted by Condamin *et al.* (1976) on oil lamps has contributed to identifying olive oil in archaeological ceramics. The identification of olive oil was based on the relative abundance of palmitic, stearic, oleic and linoleic acids, apparent in the relative abundance of $c_{16:0} > c_{18:0}$ and $c_{18:1} > c_{18:0} \gg c_{18:2}$ formulas. Linoleic acid is present in the extracts, but its amount exceedss 0.2% of the total lipid extract. This composition matches the one typical of ancient olive oil (Namdar *et al.* 2018).

Table 24.2: Total Lipid Extracts of All the Studied Items from the Western Wall Foundations Excavation*

Reg. no.	Type of vessel	Lipid analysis Fatty acids and Acylglycerols	Others	TOC (μg/g)	ID	Notes
140030. RAS-1	Lamp	$c_{16:0}$, $c_{18:2}$, $c_{18:1}$, $c_{18:0}$	β-sitosterol	120	Olive oil	
140048. RAS-5	Lamp	$c_{16:0}$, $mag_{16:0}$	Glycerol	70	Palm oil	
140038. RAS-2	Lamp	$c_{16:0}$	Glycerol	100	Palm oil	
140041. RAS-0	Lamp	$c_{16:0}$	Glycerol	120	Palm oil	
140041. RAS-1	Lamp	$c_{16:0}$, $c_{18:2}$, $c_{18:1}$, $c_{18:0}$	β-sitosterol	290	Olive oil	
140041. RAS-2	Lamp	$c_{16:0}$, $c_{18:2}$, $c_{18:1}$, $c_{18:0}$, $mag_{18:1}$, tag_{18}	β-sitosterol	90	Olive oil	
140041. RAS-3	Lamp	$c_{16:0}$	Glycerol	125	Palm oil	
140041. RAS-4	Lamp	$c_{16:0}$, $c_{18:2}$, $c_{18:1}$, $c_{18:0}$, $mag_{18:1}$		300	Olive oil	
140040. RAS-3	Rounded base juglet	$c_{16:0}$, $c_{18:0}$		---	n/a	No burning signs
140029. RAS-1	Flat base juglet	$c_{16:0}$, $c_{18:2}$, $c_{18:1}$, $c_{18:0}$		230	Olive oil	
140057. RAS-2	Rounded base juglet	$c_{16:0}$, $mag_{16:0}$	Glycerol	70	Palm oil	
140054. RAS-3	Unguentarium	$c_{16:0}$, $c_{18:1}$, $c_{18:0}$	Very high $c_{18:2}$	210	Plant oil (nigella?)	
140048. RAS-2	Flat omphalos base juglet	$c_{16:0}$, $c_{18:1}$, $c_{18:0}$, $c_{20:0}$	Glycerol, cholestanone, amines	130	Animal fat	
140056. RAS-4	Rounded base juglet	$c_{6:0}$, $c_{8:0}$, $c_{9:0}$, $c_{16:0}$, $c_{18:1}$, $c_{18:0}$, $c_{24:0}$, $c_{26:0}$	Benzaldehyde, n-c_{21} -n-c_{31}, c_{30}ol	200	Beeswax	(Coating?)
140032. RAS-1	Flat base juglet	$c_{16:0}$, $c_{18:2}$, $c_{18:1}$, $c_{18:0}$		160	Olive oil	
140033. RAS-2	Rounded base juglet	---		---	n/a	No burning signs
140030. RAS-1	Jug	$c_{16:0}$, $c_{18:2}$, $c_{18:1}$, $c_{18:0}$	Glycerol	200	Olive oil	
140031. RAS-3	Bowl	$c_{16:0}$, $c_{18:2}$, $c_{18:1}$, $c_{18:0}$	β-sitosterol	180	Olive oil	

* $C_{x:y}$, a fatty acid with x carbons chain and y degree of unsaturation, all in their trimethylsilylated form; $mag_{x:y}$, $tag_{x:y}$, mono/tri-acylglycerol bounded with fatty acid with x carbons chain and y degree of unsaturation; $c_x$ol, alcohol with x carbons chain; n-c_x, normal alkane with x carbons chain.

One juglet contained palm oil, which is less commonly found in juglets in the ancient city of Jerusalem. The fatty acid composition of pure date palm oil consists exclusively of palmitic acid ($c_{16:0}$). The extracts of Juglet 14028.RAS-1 demonstrated a similar composition, with only palmitic acid as its FFA component (Table 24.2).

One juglet contained animal fat. Animal fat can be identified in archaeological material by fatty acid ratios of stearic acid ($c_{18:0}$) showing more abundance over palmitic acid ($c_{16:0}$), along with traces of cholesterols (Dudd and Evershed 1998; Copley *et al.* 2005) or cholesterol degradation byproducts, like the cholestanone and amines detected in this particular juglet. Animal fat can be stored for its own use but is also a suitable basis for medical ointments (Evershed *et al.* 2002). In our case, no other plant materials of lipids were detected to indicate the presence of medicinal use. The animal fat was not heated as no ketones were observed (Evershed *et al.* 1995).

One juglet contained beeswax. Natural beeswax is dominated by the presence of palmitic and stearic acids along with a series of homologous, odd and even, long chain *n*-alkanes with 21–31 carbon atoms. C_{30}-alcohol and long chain fatty acids ($c_{24:0}$ and $c_{26:0}$) are also very typical of beeswax (Namdar *et al.* 2007). The presence of this particular assemblage of lipid extracts is consistent with the identification of heated beeswax in antiquity (Namdar *et al.* 2009). According to various publications and extensive research of beeswax in archaeological context (Evershed *et al.* 2002; Mazar *et al.* 2008; Namdar *et al.* 2009; Namdar *et al.* 2018), the results of the lipid extract of Juglet 14022.RAS-2 follow the compound assemblage classification and ratios characteristic of non-heated beeswax. As for the reason for the presence of beeswax in this juglet, it can be suggested that the juglet was used to store beeswax for its own merit or maybe the beeswax detected remained as a byproduct of storing bees' honey. It might also indicate the use of beeswax as a sealing agent or coating. In this second case, the content stored in the juglet would remain unknown. Beeswax might also have been used in the preparation of cosmetics (Namdar *et al.* 2007). At this stage, we cannot favor any one suggestion based on the analytical data, and all these suggestions are possible.

One juglet (14020) contained oil that had never before been reported or detected by us in an archaeological sample. Based on matching to modern degraded local oils, we carefully suggest that this juglet contained nigella seed oil, mainly based on the very high relative abundance of linoleic acid ($c_{18:2}$). As this is our first identification of this type of plant oil, the suggestion merits further separate study.

Two rounded base juglets (14022.RAS-1 and 140033.RAS-2) contained no signs of absorbed organic residues (Table 24.2). This may suggest that this context was fired and the absorbed lipids evaporated. That said, no such evidence was noted in the excavation. As the contexts excavated in these compartments are densely accumulated, it is unlikely that only one juglet was affected by a fire, whereas the others were not. Therefore, it is more likely to suggest that this juglet never contained any absorbable lipids. It is possible that this juglet held a commodity that is not traceable, like water or grains. Another possibility is that it was never used, either because it broke prior to use or simply because it was never used deliberately and served (in its original use) as a symbolic tribute or offering deposit. Bunimovitz and Zimhoni (1993) suggested that ceramic items buried as symbolic offerings were never used before their burial.

Jug and Bowl

One jug and one bowl were chosen from the same contexts as the lamps and juglets. Both the jug and bowl presented very well-preserved plant oil, probably olive oil. The olive oil was preserved in its best condition in the bowl.

CONCLUSIONS

Based on the "biomarker approach" (Evershed 2008) discussed in depth in the previous section, different plant oils were identified in the extracts of the different types of vessels analyzed. The lamps and their role in understanding socioeconomic choices are discussed in detailed manner elsewhere (Namdar *et al.* 2018).

Among the juglets analyzed, a very high diversity of materials was detected. Olive oil, palm oil, beeswax and animal fat were found in the juglet, along with the first report for nigella oil in the antiquity of the Levant, as far as we know. When the commodity is matched with the specific subtype of the juglet in which it was found, an interesting story starts to reveal itself. It is important to note that the very small number of juglets analyzed, even more drastic when coming to discuss each subtype (represented by 13 for each subtype), limits the extent of understanding the unique and particular use of a certain form. The broader study of similar vessels and in a similarly detailed manner will help in understanding the usage patterns of each type. That said, it seems that the focused study of the subtypes of juglets in relation to the commodities detected in them reveals very interesting initial insights. Our results will be used, therefore, to lay out the way we suggest addressing these aspects in pottery-commodity-preservation relations.

From our very small assemblage of vessels, it seems that we can carefully suggest a simple correlation between the base of the vessel and the commodity which it held. Juglets with flat bases contain olive oil-based materials and rounded base juglets contain other plant oil, such as date palm oil. Perhaps rounded base juglets were used as dipper juglets for measuring out a given amount of liquid from a larger sized jar, while flat base juglets were merchandized as their own article of trade. Thus, the rounded base juglets contained different commodities, as their function relates to their shape; each rounded base juglet was affixed to one jar/commodity type, in order not to mix the pure products held in the different jars.

One rounded base juglet preserved residues of beeswax. The beeswax in this juglet was most possibly used for coating the inner walls of the vessel in order to preserve other materials (such as wine or some medicinal ointment). This assumption cannot be further researched as the beeswax effectively sealed it from absorbing other compounds.

Two special juglet subtypes were identified in the sampled assemblage and their extracts demonstrate once again the simple commodity–subtype correlation suggested. The first one, the piriform unguentarium, contained plant oil identified as nigella oil. This unguentarium has a short flat base, no handles, piriform-shaped body and is made of pale yellowish clay. The term "unguentarium" is functional rather than descriptive. The common term used reflects modern usage based on assumptions about their use, although the organic content of unguentaria was never studied systematically. Small vessels of two shapes, usually without handles, are referred to as unguentaria. *Fusiform*, characteristic of Hellenistic unguentaria, is defined by a heavy ovoid body resting usually on a small distinct stem base, with a long tubular neck and cylindrical stem. The shape is comparable to a spindle (Latin *fusus*, "spindle," see Thompson 1934; Robinson 1959; Khairy 1980; Anderson-Stojanovic 1987). These ovoid unguentaria first appear in Cyprus around the turn of the 4th and the 3rd centuries BCE and may have been Near Eastern in origin or influence (Anderson-Stojanovic 1987). Early examples are similar in shape to the amphoriskos. They are believed to develop functionally from the *lekythos*, which they replace by the end of the 4th century BCE (Rotroff 2006). The second shape is the *piriform* with a footless body that is rounded or pear-shaped (Latin *pirus*, "pear"). Piriforms began to appear in the second half of the 1st century BCE and are characteristic of the Roman era, particularly the early Principate (Khairy 1980; Anderson-

Stojanovic 1987; Bikai and Perry 2001). These are regularly associated with graves (Robinson 1959). The piriform unguentaria were in use for a limited period of about a hundred years and replace the *fusiform* in late Second Temple Jerusalem (Geva and Rosenthal-Heginbottom 2003: 185). This special type of vessel indeed contained special plant oil extracted from the nigella seeds, native to our region.

A unique vessel sampled was a juglet with a flat omphalos base, which contained animal fat. This was probably used as a base for a medicinal ointment, but as other additives were not detected this suggestion cannot be further investigated.

As the juglets were all found in constructional fills, their original contextual source(s) is not clear and thus any further understanding regarding their original use cannot be deduced. The excavators believe that the fills originated from two sources. The first is fills that were brought to the area from other places in the city, containing ceramic discarded vessels, in other words, relocated garbage deposits. These deposits were not left exposed for long and were immediately covered. In addition, there are signs that the workers at the site were throwing their used ceramic vessels into the accumulated pile. Both scenarios do not contribute to deciphering the original use and source of the juglets analyzed. For example, two juglets presented no organic compounds in their extracts. As their immediate find location showed no signs of burning, it is impossible to know whether their original commodity was such that left no lipids (such as water or grains) or that its initial source of use was fired or affected by any other not-preserving environment for organic compounds.

Our results present an intriguing array of commodities, preserved particularly in the juglets, especially in specific subtypes of juglets. This initial, rather limited research is only an "appetizer," demonstrating the potential of systematic study of juglets with a close relation to their subtype. In any further focused study, careful attention should be devoted to contextual and typological considerations. Thus, social issues such as imported commodities, medicine and socioeconomic choices will be available for revision.

REFERENCES

Anderson-Stojanovic, V.R. 1987. The Chronology and Function of Ceramic Unguentaria. *American Journal of Archaeology* 91: 106–114.

Bikai, P.M. and Perry, M.A. 2001. Petra North Ridge Tombs 1 and 2: Preliminary Report. *Bulletin of the American Schools of Oriental Research* 324: 66–78.

Bunimovitz, S. and Zimhoni, O. 1993. Lamp-and-Bowl Foundation Deposits in Canaan. *Israel Exploration Journal* 43: 99–125.

Condamin, J., Formenti, F., Metais, M.O., Michel, M. and Blond, P. 1976. The Application of Gas Chromatography to the Tracing of Oil in Ancient Amphorae. *Archaeometry* 18: 195–201.

Copley, M.S., Bland, M.A., Rose, P., Horton, M. and Evershed, R.P. 2005. Gas Chromatographic, Mass Spectrometric and Stable Carbon Isotopic Investigations of Organic Residues of Plant Oils and Animal Fats Employed as Illuminants in Archaeological Lamps from Egypt. *Analyst* 130: 860–871.

Dudd, S.N. and Evershed, R.P. 1998. Direct Demonstration of Milk as an Element of Archaeological Economies. *Science* 282: 1478–1481.

Evershed, R.P. 2008. Organic Residue Analysis in Archaeology: The Archaeological Biomarker Revolution. *Archaeometry* 50: 895–924.

Evershed, R.P., Dudd, S.N., Copley, M.S., Berstan, R., Stott, A.W., Mottram, H., Buckley, S.A. and Crossman, Z. 2002. Chemistry of Archaeological Animal Fats. *Accounts of Chemical Research* 35: 660–668.

Evershed, R.P., Stott, A.W., Dudd, S.N., Charters, S. and Leyden, A. 1995. Formation of Long-Chain Ketones in Ancient Pottery Vessels by Pyrolysis of Acyl Lipids. *Tetrahedron Letters* 36: 8875–8878.

Geva, H. and Rosenthal-Heginbottom, R. 2003. Local Pottery from Area A. In: Geva, H., ed. *Jewish Quarter Excavations in the Old City of Jerusalem, Conducted by Nahman Avigad, 1969–1982*, Vol. 2: *The Finds from Areas A, W and X-2, Final Report*. Jerusalem: 176–191.

Khairy, N.I. 1980. Nabataean Piriform Unguentaria. *Bulletin of the American Schools of Oriental Research* 240: 85–97.

Mazar, A., Namdar, D., Panitz-Cohen, N., Neumann, R. and Weiner, S. 2008. Iron Age Beehives at Tel Rehov in the Jordan Valley. *Antiquity* 82: 629–639.

Namdar, D., Amrani, A., Ben-Ami, D., Hagbi, M., Szanton, N., Tchekhanovets, Y., Uziel, J., Dag, A., Rosen, B. and Gadot, Y. 2018. The Social and Economic Complexity of Ancient Jerusalem as Seen Through Choices in Lighting Oils. *Archaeometry* 60: 571–593.

Namdar, D., Neumann, R., Goren, Y. and Weiner, S. 2009. The Contents of Unusual Cone-Shaped Vessels (Cornets) from the Chalcolithic of the Southern Levant. *Journal of Archaeological Science* 36: 629–636.

Namdar, D., Neumann, R., Sladezki, Y., Haddad, N. and Weiner, S. 2007. Alkane Composition Variations Between Dark and Lighter Colored Comb Beeswax. *Apidologie* 38: 453–461.

Robinson, H.S. 1959. Pottery of the Roman Period: Chronology. *The Athenian Agora* 5: 15–29.

Rotroff, S.I. 2006. Fusiform Unguentaria, in Hellenistic Pottery: The Plain Wares. *The Athenian Agora* 33: 138–149.

Thompson, H.A. 1934. Two Centuries of Hellenistic Pottery. *Hesperia* 4: 472–493.

CHAPTER 25

THE EXCAVATION ALONG THE SOUTHWESTERN CORNER OF THE TEMPLE MOUNT: DISCUSSION AND ANALYSIS

Moran Hagbi and Joe Uziel

Our excavation along the southwestern corner of the Temple Mount, and the exposure of the lower courses of the Western Wall Foundation along its southern end, adds to the growing number of excavations in this area since the earliest explorations in the 19th century. It attempted to complement existing information, gather data regarding open questions and controversies, and provide new data and analyses not collected in previous excavations. Through analyses of similar contemporary contexts from Jerusalem and beyond, presentation of the finds from the current excavation will almost certainly further the study and add to the scholarship and debate on these various issues.

Our excavations identified three phases of human activity along the foundations of the Temple Mount. Although their relative chronological order is clear, the dating of the first two stages can only be given in broad terms, as no datable features or evidence was attributed to these phases. The earliest features discovered (Phase 3) include quarrying channels and marks on the bedrock. These were covered over by the massive construction of the Western Wall (Phase 2). The quarrying of the rock obviously predated the construction, although it is not clear when this occurred. As opposed to the areas to the north (Shukron 2012), where various rock-cut installations, such as ritual baths or basement floors, were excavated, in this area no such features were found, making it difficult to determine this first stage of human activity. It is possible that this area was settled in earlier periods as well (e.g., the Iron IIB, Hellenistic and Hasmonean periods) and cleared away during the preparation of the area for quarrying, although we found no evidence of this in our excavations. The singular finds (such as the bulla, see Chapter 18) dating from earlier periods cannot be interpreted as evidence of such activity as they clearly arrived with the massive earth fills of Phase 1.

THE DATING OF THE WESTERN WALL FOUNDATIONS

The dating of the remains of Phase 2, i.e., the remains of the Western Wall, is very important in order to understand the urban development of 1st-century CE Jerusalem. Elements and finds excavated alongside the Western Wall are of no help in arriving at a precise date for its construction. Rather, the finds from the current excavations only provide a *terminus ante quem* for the building of the Western Wall. As the finds date to the 1st century CE, it is clear that the expansion of the Temple Mount occurred either in the first half of the 1st century CE or earlier. In this sense, the finds from the excavations provide no new clear information for determining the date of the expansion. Traditionally, the construction of the entire Temple Mount was attributed to the 1st century BCE, in the days of Herod's rule (e.g., Warzawski and Peretz 1992). Recently, however, Shukron (2012) has proposed a date in the early 1st century CE, according to the numismatic evidence found in *Miqweh* Locus 55, which, according to Shukron, is sealed by the Western Wall. The coins found in the *miqweh* were attributed to the days of Valerius Gratus (15–17 CE). As Shukron suggested, the *miqweh* was sealed by the Western Wall, and the intentional blockage of the installation was assumed to have been undertaken prior to the construction of the Western Wall. In addition, Shukron suggested that two other rock-cut installations—Locus 71 and *Miqweh* Locus 91 (2012: Figs. 17–20) were canceled by the construction of the Western Wall and were used as a "foundation trench" for the ashlars of the Western Wall. The coins extracted from the earth fills from these installations led Shukron to propose a new date for the completion of the Temple Mount, in the first quarter of the 1st century CE.

Several important points must be made regarding the sealing of *Miqweh* Locus 55. The first is the so-called stone slabs that sealed *Miqweh* Locus 55. A closer look at the photographs and sections published by Shukron (2012: Figs. 5–12) suggests that the stone slabs were obviously not sealed by the construction of the Western Wall. If the slabs had been sealed by the Western Wall, Shukron would not have been able to extract them. The published photographs appear to indicate that the stones remaining abut the Western Wall and are therefore later. Moreover, the pottery types (see above) and the coins presented in Shukron's article are contemporary or even later than those found in the upper earth fills of the presently excavated cells and therefore belong to the same phase (Chapter 19).

Regarding the "foundation trench" presented by Shukron (2012: 21, Fig. 18), it seems that earlier rock-cut installations belong to the phase preceded by the construction of the Western Wall (Shukron 2012: Loci 71, 91; and Figs. 17–20). Locus 91 is a rock-cut basement floor or water installation which was filled with large boulders seen under the first course of the Western Wall. The narrow gap between Locus 91 and the foundation of the Western Wall was interpreted as a "foundation trench" by Shukron. Locus 71 was a rock-cut installation that was filled in the same way as Locus 91. The finds excavated from these elements and presented by Shukron are equivalent to the earth fills from the supporting system and therefore belong to the same event/phase.

Unfortunately, as mentioned above, the current excavation did not reveal any direct evidence for the dating of the construction of the southwestern corner. As a result, the numismatic evidence from *Miqweh* Locus 55 is no longer convincing (see Chapter 19 for a complete discussion of the numismatic evidence and its effect on the dating of both the wall and the street above), as these coins are in actuality one and the same as the other coins from the upper fills of the support cells (Phase 3), which had to have postdated the construction of the Western Wall, as they abut it. Therefore, it appears that the intentional blockage of the *miqweh* does not provide a date for the construction of the Western Wall but should be seen as part of the support systems built alongside it in the construction of the street and structures. These latter features can no longer be dated to the time of Herod, and must be placed within the 1st century CE, as clearly noted by the evidence of both the Reich-Billig excavations (2008), as well as excavations farther downslope in the City of David, where evidence for the 1st century construction of the road has also been published (Szanton and Uziel 2015; Szanton *et al.* 2016, 2019), and in the current report of the numismatic finds from the current excavation by Ariel (Chapter 19).

Another relevant feature is the layer of gray packed earth located some 20 cm above the bedrock. This layer has been termed "the Wall Builder's Floor" (Weksler-Bdolah 2015). If this surface is in fact related to the construction of the Western Wall, then its dating may be a key to dating the wall itself. This surface was also discovered in our excavations (Locus 14003, Sections 2–2, 3–3; Locus 14029, Section 4–4; Locus 14042, Section 6-6); however, save for one coin (Chapter 19: Nos. 74–76), no datable material was found beneath it. The coin has been dated to 18/19 CE. This would seem to support the 1st century CE date for the construction of the Western Wall. Furthermore, if this surface sealed the fill within *Miqweh* Locus 55, this would mean the surface must have postdated the coins in the *miqweh* and therefore place the construction of the Western Wall in the 1st century CE. There is, however, an alternate, more plausible explanation. First, there is no reason to assume that this surface should be linked to the building of the Western Wall. While it is reasonable to assume that the first course and the cornerstone of the Western Wall were moved into place directly from above the bedrock (and see further below), the massive construction of the wall's upper courses most likely occurred from the inner part of the Temple Mount, where backfill was laid regardless in order to create the artificial platform for the Temple. This would have made the construction much simpler without the need to raise large boulders to tremendous heights. It is more likely that this surface served as the floor level of those building the cells, prior to the interment of the first layers of constructional fill. The constructional fill must have been put in place only after the first few courses were laid, and the masons practiced their carving methods on the bosses of the stones that would be covered over later (Hagbi and Van Zuiden 2019). Support for this can be found in the fact that this floor actually abuts the first course of the Western Wall, making it later (although this may have been a very short time later). Furthermore, the floor seals the niches used to move the first course into place. These niches were carved into the bedrock and likely were used to precisely position the first course of the wall. The second point regarding the sealing of the *miqweh* is notable in a photo published of the *miqweh*, where it is clear that one of the support walls running between Wall 102 and the Western Wall was built into the *miqweh* (Shukron 2012: Figs. 8, 12). Therefore, the coins found within the *miqweh* were found in the fills abutting this small support wall and belong to the same horizon of the entire construction project of the raising of the street level, and not that of the Western Wall.

This is not to suggest that the Western Wall could not date to the 1st century CE, but rather that just as our excavations alongside the foundations of the Temple Mount offered no evidence in the dating of the foundation of the Western Wall and the southwestern corner, so too the excavations to the north including *Miqweh* Locus 55 and Locus Installations 91 and Locus 71. The dating of the Western Wall and the completion of the Temple Mount project must be sought by other means.

It is interesting to note that the data from the earth fills does coincide well with certain historical sources regarding the completion of the reconstruction of the Temple Mount. The work of reconstructing the compound, which began with the Temple itself, and followed with its enclosures, began in 20/18 BCE (*Ant.* 15.380–425). When considering that the latest coins found in the earth fills abutting the Western Wall date to 17/18–24/25 CE (Chapter 19: Nos. 74–77), including the coins extracted from *Miqweh* Locus 55 (Shukron 2012: Fig. 17), the likely *terminus ante quem* for the Western Wall foundations should be placed roughly under half a century after the commencement of the project in 20/18 BCE. If this is the case, the excerpt from John (2:20) in the New Testament may in fact be quite accurate in stating that the project lasted for 46 years: "Then said the Jews, 'Forty and six years was this temple in building, and wilt thou raise it up in three days?'" If we accept the traditional dating brought by Josephus (18/20 BCE), combined with the *terminus ante quem* of the foundations given by the latest date of the coins found in the earth fills (18/19–24/25 CE), the passage from John 2:20 fits with the latest date given by the coins. That notwithstanding, the historicity and dating of this narrative must be dealt with carefully.

Of no less interest are the methods of construction of the wall. The report by Van Zuiden (Chapter 37) shows that the massive building projects undertaken in Early Roman Jerusalem created a need for a large group of masons to be highly trained in the carving and dressing of the boulders used for the monumental structures (and see the *Tosefta Kelim, Baba Batra* 2:1). The foundations of the Western Wall provided ample opportunity for such on-site training, as noted by the different styles of tooling and chiseling of the bosses on these stones. As these courses were meant to be buried, they provided an on-site workshop for practice (Hagbi and Van Zuiden 2019).

While possibly speculative, this, however, may be of importance in the debate regarding the date of construction of the Western Wall. The clear distinction between the finely cut ashlars above ground and the roughly cut ashlars with varying degrees of finishing indicates that the architectural plan had intended for the lower 6–7 courses to be buried from the outset. This is further supported by the account in Josephus's *War* (5.188–189), stating that the foundations, although containing stones 40 cubits long, were buried in order to level the streets along the Temple Mount. In this sense, the street, the buildings surrounding it and the constructional cells and fill all belong to part of the master plan related to the construction of the Temple Mount. If this is the case, and the dating of the street and the constructional cells must be placed in the 20s and early 30s of the 1st century CE (for the difficulty in delaying the construction of the street to the days of Agrippa as suggested by Reich and Billig 1999; Szanton *et al.* 2019; see Chapter 19), then it is difficult to imagine that the lower 6 m of the monument would have been exposed and unfinished, whereas the superstructure was finely carved and dressed. This may suggest support for a 1st century CE dating, although alone it is not enough and must be considered with further evidence, such as historical sources (*War* 5.185–189) and archaeological evidence of other portions of the Temple Mount and its surroundings (for further such evidence and discussion of the dating of the Temple Mount, see Weksler-Bdolah 2015; Reich and Baruch 2017; Lieberman *et al.* 2021).

THE COMPARTMENTS SYSTEM AND THE STEPPED STREET

As mentioned above, the primary feature discovered in the current excavation is the cells and fill layers attributed to the raising and support of the street level and buildings alongside it in the 1st century CE. The support system was a planned part of the construction projects, in order to fill the Tyropoeon Valley and create a raised street level. As opposed to the support systems further downhill in the City of David (Szanton and Uziel 2015) and further uphill (Bahat 2013), the fills here were quite thick, reaching 6 m. The source of these fill layers seems to be mixed. The lowest of the layers is a thick layer of stone chips, probably related to the carving of the ashlars of the Western Wall. It is important to note that the stone chips were probably brought from a deposit close by, where the quarrying waste had piled up during the final dressing of the ashlars, whether it was done *in-situ* or at a nearby site. This layer may also relate to the training exercises noted above (Chapter 37). The stone chips could be used as fine filling material for the supporting system. An alternative explanation was recently suggested by Reich, who posited that the wall system is actually a scaffolding system used for the erection of Robinson's Arch (Reich 2015). This option could be reinforced by the *Tosefta* mentioned previously. Above it, the series of layers of fill yielded finds that on the one hand were quite uniform chronologically, yet on the other hand provided evidence for varying primary contexts of the finds. The evidence from the glass sherds (Chapter 20), charcoal (Chapter 23) and stone vessels (Chapter 21) seems to suggest that these fills were brought from a nearby refuse area, similar to that found along the eastern slopes of the City of David (e.g., Gadot 2014 and 2022). Evidence for such deposits is given by Josephus (*War* 5.185). The pottery found for the most part also fits with this, due to its fragmentary nature. However, the faunal analysis (Chapter 22) as well as numerous restorable pottery vessels seem to suggest otherwise, indicating that the fills contained the immediately discarded refuse of the workers located at the construction site. It seems that both of these assumptions are correct, and the constructional fill brought to the site was likely from a nearby refuse area; however, the workers likely discarded their garbage—including bones from the meat they consumed—into the fill.

The results of the excavations presented here shed additional light on the extensive construction projects undertaken in Jerusalem during the first half of the 1st century CE. While there is no doubt that Herod influenced the city's landscape and advanced many building projects, the archaeological data now confirms that these projects continued well into the 1st century CE, also seen in the historical sources of the period (*War* 5.38; John 2:20). The majority of the data presented here, related to the raising and construction of the street level, suggests that this project would have been primarily undertaken in the days of the Roman prefect Pontius Pilate (Szanton *et al.* 2016, 2019). This project included the construction of a support system that flanked the main drainage channel from both sides, adjusting the habitation level of the Early Roman city, supporting the street, while continuing above the street level in the area between the Western Wall and the eastern curbstone of the street, forming a series of small cells (Reich and Billig 1999: 36–37).

REFERENCES

Bahat, D. 2013. *The Jerusalem Western Wall Tunnel.* Jerusalem.

Gadot, Y. 2014. Preliminary Report on the Excavations at Jerusalem's Southeastern Hill, Area D. *Hebrew Bible and Ancient Israel* 3: 279–292.

Gadot, Y. 2022. *The Landfill of Early Roman Jerusalem: The 2013–2014 Excavations in Area D3* (Ancient Jerusalem Publications Series 2). University Park and Jerusalem.

Hagbi, M. and Van Zuiden, A. 2019. "Shaping the Stones"—Technical Aspects in the Endeavor to Lay the Foundation Stones of the Western Wall. In: Meiron, E., ed. *City of David: Studies of Ancient Jerusalem* 14. Jerusalem: 42–59 (Hebrew).

Lieberman, T., Regev, J., Boaretto, E. and Uziel, J. 2021. Under Construction: On the Access to the Temple Mount During Its Expansion. In: Zelinger, Y., Peleg-Barkat, O., Uziel, J. and Gadot, Y., eds. *New Studies in the Archaeology of Jerusalem and Its Region* 14. Jerusalem: 1–16 (Hebrew).

Reich, R. 2015. The Construction and Destruction of Robinson's Arch. *Eretz-Israel* 31: 398–407 (Hebrew).

Reich, R. and Baruch, Y. 2017. On Expansion of the Temple Mount in the Late Second Temple Period. *Cathedra* 164: 7–24 (Hebrew).

Reich, R. and Billig, Y. 1999. Excavations near the Temple Mount and Robinson's Arch. *Qadmoniot* 117: 33–40 (Hebrew).

Reich, R. and Billig, Y. 2008. Jerusalem: The Robinson's Arch Area. In: Stern, E., Geva, H., Paris, A. and Aviram, J., eds. *The New Encyclopedia of Archaeological Excavations in the Holy Land*, Vol. 5. New York: 1809–1811.

Shukron, E. 2012. Did Herod Build the Foundations of the Western Wall? In: Meiron, E., ed. *City of David: Studies of Ancient Jerusalem* 7. Jerusalem: 14–27.

Szanton, N., Hagbi, M., Haber, M., Uziel, J. and Tzvi-Ariel, D. 2016. Monumental Building Projects in Jerusalem in the Days of Pontius Pilate: A Numismatic View from the Stepped Street in the Tyropoeon Valley. In: Stiebel, G.D., Uziel, J., Cytryn-Silverman, K., Re'em, A. and Gadot, Y., eds. *New Studies in the Archaeology of Jerusalem and Its Region* 10. Jerusalem: 99–114 (Hebrew).

Szanton, N., Hagbi, M., Uziel, J. and Ariel, D.T. 2019. Monumental Building Projects in Jerusalem at the Days of Pontius Pilate: A View from the Stepped Street. *Tel Aviv* 46: 147–166.

Szanton, N. and Uziel, J. 2015. On the Question of the Stepped Stone Monument from the Second Temple Period in the City of David. *City of David: Studies of Ancient Jerusalem* 10. Jerusalem: 19–40 (Hebrew).

Warzawski, A. and Peretz, A. 1992. Building the Temple Mount: Organization and Execution. *Cathedra* 66: 3–46.

Weksler-Bdolah, S. 2015. The Enlargement of the Herodian Temple Mount: An Archaeological Perspective. In: Ben-Arieh, Y., Halamish, A., Limor, O., Rubin, R. and Reich, R., eds. *Study of Jerusalem Through the Ages.* Jerusalem: 19–72 (Hebrew).

INDEX OF LOCI AND WALLS

Locus/ Wall	L/W	Upper level	Lower level	Phase	Description	Dominant pottery dating
101	W	712.81	709.18	2	The Western Wall Foundation	Early Roman
102	W	712.81	710.06	3	Support Wall parallel to the Western Wall	Early Roman
14001	W	712.81	710.08	3	Support Wall between Western Wall and Wall 102, northern wall of Chamber C1	Early Roman
14003	L	710.11	709.95	2	Gray beaten earth surface on bedrock under C1	Early Roman
14004	L	712.68	711.48	1	Section cleaning	Early Roman
14005	L	709.97	710.06	na	Merged with Wall 14003	Early Roman
14006	L	710.05	709.95	2	Quarrying mark in the bedrock	Early Roman
14007	L	711.48	710.11	3	Quarrying waste, 7th layer of constructional fill in Chamber 1	Early Roman
14008	L	712.85	712.5	3	Earth fill above and north on Wall 14001	Early Roman
14009	L	712.81	712.3	3	2nd layer of constructional fill in Chamber 1	Early Roman
14010	L	712.41	712.16	3	3rd layer of constructional fill in Chamber 1	Early Roman
14011	L	712.16	711.91	3	4th layer of constructional fill in Chamber 1	Early Roman
14012	L	711.91	711.3	3	5th layer of constructional fill in Chamber 1	Early Roman
14013	L	712.9	712.43	3	Uppermost constructional fill in Chamber 1	Early Roman
14014	L	711.74	711	3	6th layer of constructional fill in Chamber 1, adjoins Locus 14014	Early Roman
14015	L	710.45	710.13	3	6th layer of constructional fill in Chamber 1, adjoins Locus 14014	Early Roman
14016	W	712.81	710.06	3	Wall separating Chambers C1 and C2	Early Roman
14017	L	710.06	709.95	1	Rock hewn under Wall 14016	Early Roman
14018	L	709.95	709.9	2	Niche	Early Roman
14019	L	710.08	710.06	1	Chalk floor on bedrock in C1	Early Roman
14020	L	713.26	712.33	3	Uppermost constructional fill in Chamber 2	Early Roman
14021	L	712.97	711.68	3	2nd layer of constructional fill in Chamber 2	Early Roman
14022	L	712.11	711.18	3	3rd layer of constructional fill in Chamber 2	Early Roman
14023	W	712.81	710.06	na	Wall - Cancelled	Early Roman
14024	L	711.18	710.32	3	Quarrying waste under Locus 14022, 5th layer of constructional fill in C2	Early Roman

Locus/Wall	L/W	Upper level	Lower level	Phase	Description	Dominant pottery dating
14025	L	710.32	709.94	3	Quarrying waste mixed with earth under Locus 14022, adjoins Locus 14024	Early Roman
14026	L	710.04	709.89	3	Rock hewn at C2 adjoins Locus14017	Early Roman
14027	L	710	709.96	3	Chalk floor at Chamber 2	Early Roman
14028	L	711.18	710.66	3	4th layer constructional fill in Chamber 2	Early Roman
14029	L	710.12	710.06	2	Gray beaten earth surface on bedrock under C2	Early Roman
14030	L	712.81	709.24	3	Wall separating Chambers C2 and C3	Early Roman
14031	L	710.06	710	1	Rock hewn under W14030	Early Roman
14032	L	710.06	709.76	1	Rock hewn under W14030	Early Roman
14033	L	710.06	709.91	1	Rock hewn under W14030	Early Roman
14034	L	713.06	711.78	3	Collapsed rocks upper constructional fill in Chamber 3	Early Roman
14035	L	712.98	711.7	3	2nd layer of constructional fill in Chamber 3	Early Roman
14036	L	711.7	711.37	3	3rd layer of constructional fill in Chamber 3	Early Roman
14037	L	711.38	710.96	3	4th layer of constructional fill in Chamber 3	Early Roman
14038	L	710.96	710.07	3	5th layer of constructional fill in Chamber 3	Early Roman
14039	L	710.96	710.18	3	6th layer of constructional fill in Chamber 3	Early Roman
14040	L	710.55	709.41	3	Quarrying waste and earth fill, 7th constructional fill in Chamber 3	Early Roman
14041	L	710.38	709.3	3	Earth fill under quarrying waste (Locus 14040)	Early Roman
14042	L	709.48	709.17	2	Gray beaten earth surface on bedrock under C3	Early Roman
14043	L	709.23	709.03	2	Drain at Chamber 3	Early Roman
14044	L	710.03	709.24	3	Wall above the main drainage channel's barrel vault	Early Roman
14045	W	712.68	709.18	3	Southern wall of Chamber 3	Early Roman
14046	L	712.81	712.58	NA	Warren's shaft No. 22	Early Roman
14047	W	712.81	710.06	3	Wall south of Wall 14045	Early Roman
14048	L	712.81	709.18	3	Earth fill between Wall 14045 and W14047	Early Roman
14049	L	710.06	710.06		Bedrock in C1	Early Roman
14050	L	710.06	710.06		Bedrock in C2	Early Roman
14051	L	709.18	709.18		Bedrock in C3	Early Roman

PART IIc:
EXCAVATION AT AN ISLAMIC CEMETERY

CHAPTER 26

AN EARLY ISLAMIC CEMETERY AT THE EDGE OF THE TEMPLE MOUNT

Ronny Reich, Yaakov Billig and Yossi Nagar

B. Mazar and M. Ben-Dov excavated along the southern edge of the Western Wall of the Temple Mount between 1968–1975 (Mazar 1969, 1971). The excavations were halted at a level that approximately represented the Early Islamic period (721.00 m asl on the average), where the excavators encountered remains of several burials. The path abutting the gigantic Herodian wall was paved with gravel as part of a local park, and the Hebrew inscription with a verse from Isaiah, one of Mazar's prize finds, could now be viewed by visitors to the park at eye level (see Chapter 29).

Excavations at this spot, which was directly below Robinson's Arch, were resumed in 1994.[1] A burial ground located just after the gravel on the tourist path (Locus 20) was removed (Fig. 26.1).

Mazar (1971: 21) and Ben-Dov (1982: 335–338) had already partially excavated burials to the south of our excavation, that is, in the area stretching from the southwest corner of the Temple Mount to our Burial No. 50. A short time prior to our dig, before the old tourist path was eliminated, R. Abu Raya (1997: 107) discovered some burials to the north of our Burial No. 30. The burial ground, or cemetery, that our expedition could excavate, therefore, was bounded by Burials Nos. 30 and 50—a strip pf earth ca. 19.5 m long and ca. 4 m wide. Between the Western Wall of the Temple Mount (Fig. 26.1, Wall 501) and Wall 502 (the Eastern Wall of B. Mazar's Umayyad Edifice IV), about 30 burials were unearthed (see list below). This chapter is the excavation report of our work (Figs. 26.2–3).[2]

All the tombs were simple inhumations without any traces of stone lining or cover stones. The level of the burials was relatively thin, mostly located ca. between 720.35–720.97 m asl. At these levels, 2–3 layers of burials were found.

It seems that the burials had been dug during a period that was lengthy enough so that any markings or traces of the burials, as simple as they may have been, had already vanished, and new burials were then dug into the older burials, disturbing the older ones to a lesser or a greater extent.

---

[1] Excavation Permit No. 2205, carried out by the authors on behalf of the Israel Antiquities Authority. Preliminary reports were prepared by Reich and Billig 1997, 1998, 2000. The excavation lasted for a considerable time, between the fall of 1994 and summer of 1996; the excavation of the cemetery presented here was the first act of the excavation.

[2] Our work at this cemetery proceeded as follows: In order to locate a burial, we excavated only in areas and levels where a burial was suspected. Only one burial or bone concentration was excavated at a time, cleaned and photographed. The excavated debris was sifted in its entirety. When remains were found, an anthropologist was summoned from the IAA premises at the Rockefeller Museum (Y. Nagar or J. Verdene in most cases; J. Zias for Burial 31). Only then were the bones, mostly broken into small splinters, lifted. On a daily basis, the late Rabbi Y.M. Getz (the Rabbi of the Wailing Wall) was notified. For this procedure, Rabbi Getz received an official *ad hoc* nomination from the Ministry of Religious Affairs/Department of Burials. The rabbi's assistant would then come to the dig to retrieve the bones and bone splinters for reburial, and provide us with a receipt.

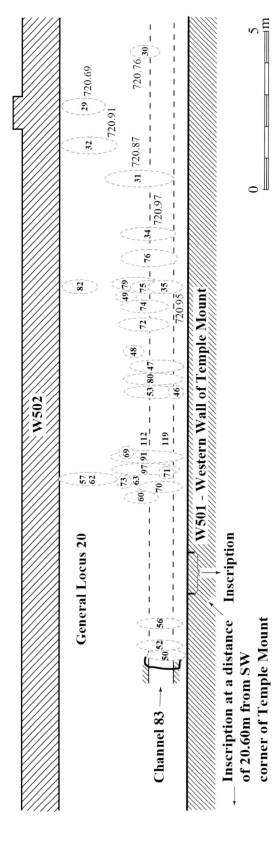

Figure 26.1: Plan of the cemetery near the Western Wall.

Thus, as the gravediggers buried new corpses, they piled the dug-up debris—which contained bones from the older graves—alongside the new graves. This is the cause of concentrations of bones without any articulation alongside graves, or parts of graves, with bones in correct anatomical articulation.

Several cases of skeletons buried in very close proximity (one next to the other; one just above the other) might point also to the burial of several bodies at the same time.

All the burials in which a complete skeleton was exposed (or a partial skeleton but of which enough was extant to establish the direction of burial) point to a burial of the dead in an east–west direction. In most cases, it could be established that the corpse was laid on its right side, with its front facing south. In Burial No. 31 the skeleton was found on its back; in Burial No. 75 it was laid on its foreside. In one burial (No. 31), remains of several iron nails and iron fittings were found

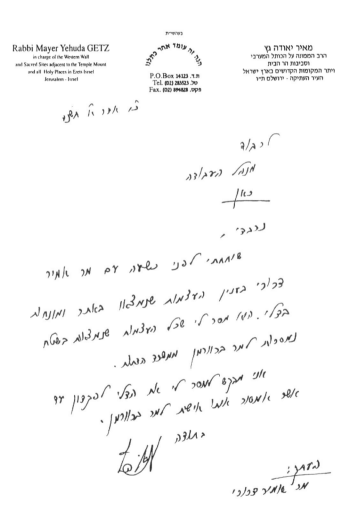

Figure 26.2: Letter by Rabbi M.Y. Getz to the director of the excavations requesting that the bucket of human bones discovered at the excavation be given to him for safekeeping and that it later be handed over to Mr. Braverman at the Ministry of Religious Affairs.

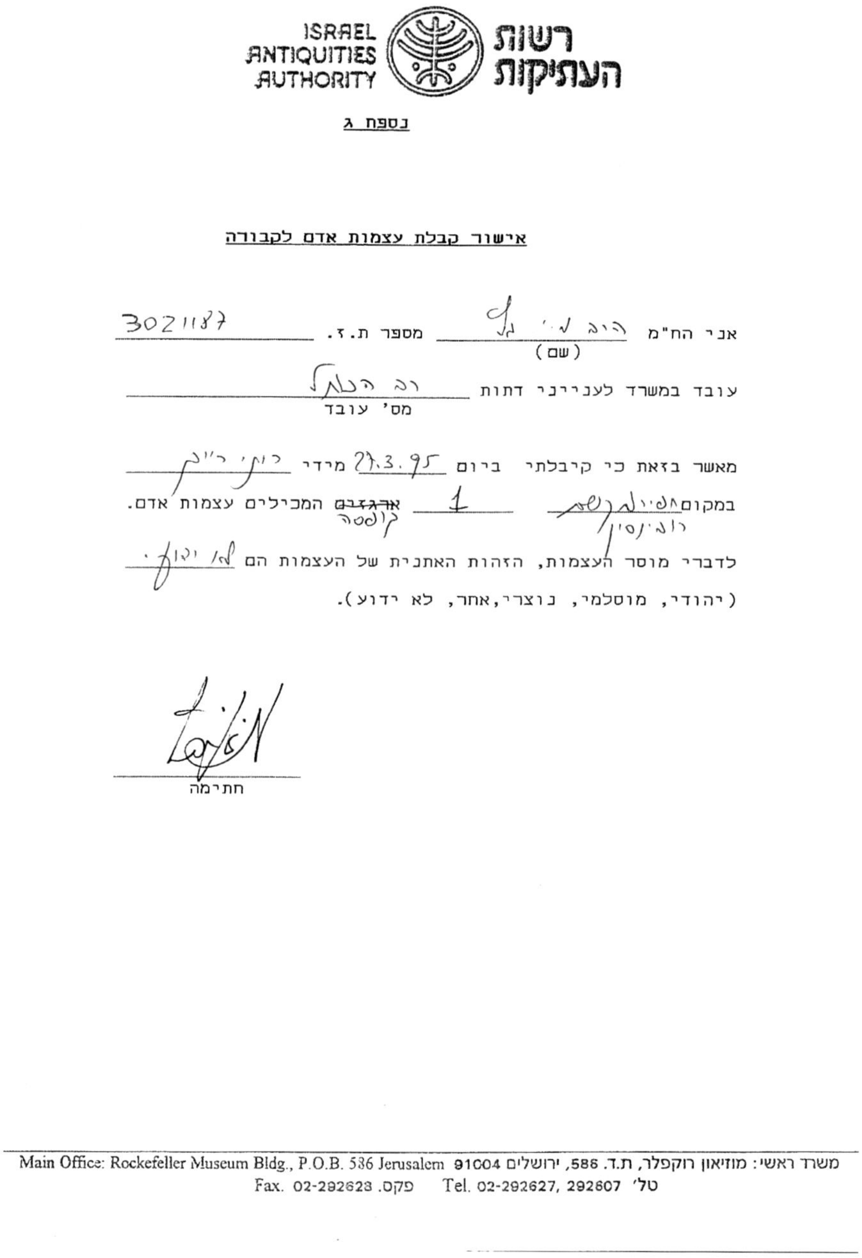

נספח ג

אישור קבלת עצמות אדם לקבורה

אני הח"מ _____ מספר ת.ז. 302ו187
(שם)

עובד במשרד לעניירני דתות _____
מס' עובד

מאשר בזאת כי קיבלתי ביום 27.3.95 מידי _____
במקום _____ ארגזים המכילים עצמות אדם.
(מספר)
לדברי מוסר העצמות, הזהות האתנית של העצמות הם _____ .
(יהודי, מוסלמי, נוצרי, אחר, לא ידוע).

_____
חתימה

Main Office: Rockefeller Museum Bldg., P.O.B. 536 Jerusalem 91004 משרד ראשי: מוזיאון רוקפלר, ת.ד. 586, ירושלים
Fax. 02-292623 פקס.   Tel. 02-292627, 292607 טל'

Figure 26.3: One of the receipts signed by Rabbi M.Y. Getz, confirming that a box containing human bones, excavated under Robinson's Arch, was consigned to him.

around the skeleton, pointing to the possible use of a wooden coffin. In other burials (e.g., Nos. 35, 47, 53, 97), nails were found scattered in association with the burials.

The fact that no burials were found in the area excavated to the west of Wall 502 points to the fact that the narrow alley or space, ca. 4 m wide, between Wall 502 and the Western Wall of the Temple Mount (Wall 501), was used for burial, while the Umayyad Building IV was still partially erect and functioning, or at least in ruins still piled up to a considerable height, which prevented the crossing of Wall 502 westward. In addition, there was probably also a strong tendency to choose for burial particularly the strip of land adjacent to or abutting the Holy Precinct of the Temple Mount.

It is impossible to know how far north the cemetery reached. It certainly extended northward as long as the span of Wall 502. However, it could well have extended all along the Western Wall of the Temple Mount or to a greater part of it, seemingly for religious reasons. In that case, it should be stressed that directly below the pavement of today's Wailing Wall prayer area, one should expect the extension of this cemetery!

Scattered bones, in a disturbed status, were found in two loci:

1. Locus 20, which is the general locus just below the gravel of the modern path and above the undisturbed burials.

2. Channel 83, which is part of the Umayyad building of the earlier stratum, passes below the cemetery. In some cases, burials were placed directly above cover stones of the channel, which later collapsed into the channel, dragging the bones with them.

Ben-Dov says (1982: 335) that the 30 burials he excavated contained only bones of young males, as identified by Haas. This observation is obviously different from the results of Nagar, Verdene and Zias as given here, who examined, on site, each of the burials we exposed and identified a variety of ages (adults and infants) of both genders (see Table 26.1).

Table 26.1: Burials Excavated Along Southern Edge of Western Wall of Temple Mount*

Burial (Locus) No.	Level	Minimal number of individuals buried	Age	Sex	Position of head	Direction of face	Remarks	Fig.
29	720.69	1	14–17		W		Disturbed by Locus 20	
30	720.76	2	20–30 4–5				Disturbed by Locus 20	
31	720.87				W	S	Iron nails and fittings around skeleton, skeleton on back	26.4
32	720.91	10	6 adult 4 child <7		W		Disturbed by Locus 20	
34	720.97	2	25–35 >35				Disturbed by Locus 20	
35	720.95	2	20–30 child				Disturbed by Locus 20 Inscribed gem**	
46		2	<40 6	M				
47		2	20–30 >35					26.5

Burial (Locus) No.	Level	Minimal number of individuals buried	Age	Sex	Position of head	Direction of face	Remarks	Fig.
48		2	20–25	F?			Ring	
			25–35	M				
49		2	20–30				Mainly remains of skull	26.6
			30–40					
50		1	?					
52		3	20–30					26.7
			adult?					
			child					
53		2	>40		W	S		26.8
			>35					
54, 55		1	20				Remains of burial, not indicated on plan	
56	720.14	1	20–30	M				26.9
57		1	25–35	F	W		Burial directly above Burial 62	26.10
60		2	30–40	F?			Iron nails around bones	26.11
			7					
62	720.20				W	S	Burial directly below Burial 57	26.12
63		2	20		W			
			adult?					
70		1	adult	M?				26.13
71		1	adult	M				
72							Traces of burial in an E–W orientation	26.14
73							Remains of skull under Burial No. 63	
74					W	S	Burial which cuts through Burial 49. A piece of bronze (coin?) found inside skull	

Burial (Locus) No.	Level	Minimal number of individuals buried	Age	Sex	Position of head	Direction of face	Remarks	Fig.
75	720.29 720.39				W	S	Skeleton lying on front side. Burial under Burial 75	26.15
76		1	25–40	F	W	S		26.16 26.17
79	720.29	1	20	F	W	S		26.18
80	720.29				W		Very fragmentary	
82	720.70						Fragmentary, probably disturbed by B. Mazar excavations	26.19
91		2	30–40 7–8		W			26.20
97		2	adult 3–5.5	M	W		Burial above cover stone of Channel 83	
112		1	30–50	F?	W		In baulk between Squares 2 and 3	
119							In baulk, below Burial 112	

*Essentials on age and sex concluded by Anthropologists Y. Nagar and J. Verdene.

**Whereabouts of object unknown.

DISCUSSION

No sepulchral finds or private objects of the deceased were found in association with the burials. All that was found in close connection with the bones were a few pottery sherds. These, of course, were present in the debris into which the graves had been dug, and were returned with the earth that had been used to cover the dead. They certainly are not part of any goods added to any burial. Examination by the authors of the few pottery sherds shows that they date from the late Iron Age to medieval times. Obviously, only the latest pieces might be the closest to the date of burial.

Mazar and Ben-Dov reported the discovery of a small *musalla* (praying ground with a *mihrab*) or small mosque, and a plastered water basin (Mazar 1971: 21). Mazar and Ben-Dov dated the cemetery to the 11th century, i.e., to the Fatimid period, which predated the Crusader conquest (Mazar 1971: 21). It seems that their main argument was based on the dated Arabic-inscribed tombstone they found (see below), and the fact that the cemetery was built over by a thick wall dated to the Crusader

Figure 26.4: Burial No. 31(IAA Archives).

Figure 26.5: Burial No. 47 (IAA Archives).

Figure 26.6: Burial No. 49 (IAA Archives).

Figure 26.7: Burial No. 52 (IAA Archives).

Figure 26.8: Burial No. 53 (IAA Archives).

period (Mazar 1970: Pl. 11 right; 16 upper right). Unfortunately, no archaeological data are extant on this wall.

A picture of the small mosque was published recently (Sharon 2018: Fig. 1). A comparison of this picture with Fig. 26.20 shows (as attested by the horizontal groove on the Western Wall of the Temple Mount) that the floor of that mosque is at the same level as, or a few centimeters higher than, the layer of burials. It seems that burials were carried out in the narrow space along the Temple Mount up to the mosque and in relation to it. In this case, this inscription gives us a *terminus post quem* for the cemetery (see Chapter 31).

Two Arabic inscriptions were discovered in this area by Mazar and Ben-Dov, published by M. Sharon 45 years apart (1973; 2018). Of extreme importance is the Arabic inscription found incorporated in the small mosque mentioned (Sharon 2018: Fig. 2), as it is dated to 32 AH (=652 CE).

The second Arabic inscription is on a tombstone (Sharon 1973: 217–220), which dates to 392 AH (=1002 CE). The excavation details of this stone have not been given. If it had been a tombstone of

Figure 26.9: Burial No. 56 (IAA Archives).

Figure 26.10: Burial No. 57 (IAA Archives).

Figure 26.11: Burial No. 60 (IAA Archives).

Figure 26.12: Burial No. 62 (IAA Archives).

Figure 26.13: Burial No. 70 (IAA Archives).

a particular burial in this cemetery, then it was the only tombstone used within the several scores of burials excavated by Mazar and Ben-Dov and by ourselves. Sharon pointed to the extraordinary formula, which convincingly points to the burial of a Christian. The deliberately erased name might support this supposition (see Chapter 31).

Referring back to the Arabic inscription of the Christian person, we would like to underscore the words of curse against "whoever does harm to the burial in this house" expressed on it. Sharon drew attention to the ambiguity of the phrase "in this house," and has suggested that it refers to Jerusalem in general, which is called in Arabic *Bayt al-Maqdis.*

We suggest that the narrow (4 m wide) and long space between Wall 502 (the Eastern Wall of Umayyad Building IV) and the Western Wall of the Temple Mount was roofed over in medieval times, and two or even three floors were constructed (Chapter 27). In this case, the cemetery under discussion was located inside a closed and dark space, between two mighty walls and a roof. This situation can be the "house" to which the Arabic inscription refers.

Figure 26.14; Burial No. 72 (IAA Archives).

Figure 26.15: Burial No. 75 (IAA Archives).

Figure 26.16: Burial No. 76 (IAA Archives).

Figure 26.17: Burial No. 76 (IAA Archives).

Figure 26.18 Burial No. 79 (IAA Archives).

Sharon has suggested, correctly, that the burial of many (several scores) humans in a limited space might point to some disaster predating the Crusader conquest of Jerusalem in 1099, which caused this. He suggested the Seljuk conquest of Jerusalem (1070–1098 CE) to be a possible cause. To this, we may add as a cause the severe earthquake of 1033 CE, particularly because earthquakes do not discriminate between people, followed by the fact that in this location Muslims, Christians and even Jews were buried.

At this point we should refer the reader to the Hebrew inscription which bears a biblical verse (Isaiah 66:14), which was published by B. Mazar (1971: 20-21). It should be noted that it is incised a short distance (ca. 1–1.1 m) above the layer of burials discussed here. Mazar and other scholars who referred to it did not relate it to the burials under discussion, but one can see in it a sort of epitaph. On some of our observations relating to this inscription see Chapter 30.

Figure 26.19: Burial No. 82 (IAA Archives).

Figure 26.20: Burial No. 91 (IAA Archives).

REFERENCES

Abu Raya, R. 1997. Jerusalem, Hama'araviyim Gate. *Excavations and Surveys in Israel* 16: 106–108.

Ben-Dov, M. 1982. *In the Shadow of the Temple: The Discovery of Ancient Jerusalem.* Jerusalem.

CIIP: Cotton, H.M., Di Segni, L., Eck, W., Isaac, B., Kushnir-Stein, A., Misgav, H., Price, J., Roll, I. and Yardeni, A. 2010. *Corpus Inscriptionum Iudaeae/Palaestinae*, Vol. 1: *Jerusalem* Part 1: 1–704. Berlin and New York.

Könen, K. 1990. Zur Inschrift unter dem Robinsonbogen. *Zeitschrift des Deutschen Palästina-Vereins* 106: 180–182.

Mazar, B. 1969. *The Excavations in the Old City of Jerusalem: Preliminary Report of the First Season, 1968.* Jerusalem.

Mazar, B. 1971. *The Excavations in the Old City of Jerusalem near the Temple Mount: Preliminary Report of the Second and Third Seasons, 1969–1970.* Jerusalem.

Mazar, B. 1975. *The Mountain of the Lord: Excavating in Jerusalem.* New York.

Reich, R. and Billig, Y. 1997. Jerusalem, Robinson's Arch. *Excavations and Surveys in Israel* 16: 108–109.

Reich, R. and Billig, Y. 1998. Jerusalem, Robinson's Arch. The Archaeological Park of the Second Temple Period. *Excavations and Surveys in Israel* 18: 88–90.

Reich, R. and Billig, Y. 2000. Excavations near the Temple Mount and Robinson's Arch, 1994–1996; Appendix: A Group of Theater Seats from Jerusalem. In: Geva, H., ed. *Ancient Jerusalem Revealed, Reprinted and Expanded Edition.* Jerusalem: 340–352.

Sharon, M. 1973. Arabic Inscriptions from the Excavations at the Western Wall. *Israel Exploration Journal* 23: 214–220.

Sharon, M. 2018. Witnessed by Three Disciples of the Prophet: The Jerusalem 32 Inscription from 32 AH/652 CE. *Israel Exploration Journal* 68: 100–111.

Warren, C. 1884. *Plans, Elevations, Sections, etc. Shewing the Results of the Excavations at Jerusalem, 1867–70, Executed for the Committee of the Palestine Exploration Fund.* London.

PART III:
STUDIES
IN THE
VICINITY
OF THE
WALLS

CHAPTER 27

OBSERVATIONS ON THE ARCHITECTURE OF THE SOUTHERN WALL

Yuval Baruch and Ronny Reich

INTRODUCTION

Herod the Great's project to expand the Temple Mount is doubtless one of the peak architectural feats and achievements the Land of Israel has ever known. Merged in this project were issues of planning, complicated land surveys, engineering and work management on a cultic site frequented by vast waves of worshippers constantly on the move. Added to these issues were technical matters that pertained to construction with extremely large ashlars that required particular expertise in quarrying, transporting, lifting and precision laying. Each of these architectural aspects called for the work of qualified and experienced professionals. While examining the architectural results, on still erect walls or on scattered stones, the success of these professionals is evident. The identities of almost all of them—surveyors, architects, engineers, masons, stone cutters, work managers, technicians and others—did not survive, and they remain buried in anonymity. Their work, however, speaks for them across the millennia. Only an allusion to one such master mason was found in a Hebrew/Aramaic inscription incised upon an ossuary found in Jerusalem, mentioning "Simon, the Temple Builder" (CIIP I/1 2010, No. 54).

Our Study

As scientists present for a considerable time at the Temple Mount, we had the rare opportunity to set up an outdoor "laboratory" to examine firsthand not only the walls left standing, but the collapsed stones piled up around them. This chapter presents our observations of various aspects of the Temple Mount walls. Some of these observations have already been hinted at by those who came before us, but we believe that every observation has the potential to reveal new data not seen by others, and new insights that might add to our understanding of Herod's spectacular ancient undertaking.

Today, several hundred ashlars from the original construction of the Temple Mount retaining walls have been exposed. At the site near Robinson's Arch, we studied several dozen ashlars that were pushed and dropped from the top of the Western Wall following the Roman conquest of Jerusalem.

Wilson (1865) and Warren (1884) provided early detailed descriptions of the walls, and Mazar (2011, 2020) later improved on their observations. We found there was still a great deal to be learned from the extant remains, both quantitatively and especially from Herodian construction methods—particularly the minute details. Such research requires comprehensive and thorough investigation, which we will hopefully be able to carry out in the future.

When scaffoldings were attached to the Western Wall, we used the opportunity to carry out conservation work (2019–2020) and return a collapsed ashlar to the Wall. We were also able to learn a great deal about the thickness of the walls by setting up on-site Ground Penetrating Radar inspection (Chapter 32).

What follows are some of our thoughts and observations as we worked along these ancient, holy and after 2000 years still magnificent and awe-inspiring walls:

Carved Bedrock in Preparation for the Southern Wall Construction

As part of the construction of the Southern Wall, in the section extending from the Triple Gate to the southeastern corner of the Temple Mount, the early builders invested significant effort in carving the bedrock (Fig. 3.14). The natural hill had been quarried in order to lower its elevation so that it could be designed appropriately for the placement of the foundation courses of the Southern Wall. This process attests to the architectural planning of the Herodian complex prior to its construction, including the sloping street on the southern side, which was built adjacent to the Temple Mount.

The bedrock's surface was carved in a stepped manner, descending from west to east, only between the Triple Gate and Compartment 14 (Chapter 5). The pace of the descent, also from west to east, precisely matches the plan of the street. It, therefore, appears that the cutting of the foundations was undertaken from the Triple Gate eastward, as opposed to the building of the wall itself, which was constructed in the opposite direction (Reich and Baruch 2019: 158–164).

Furthermore, the quarrying not only served as the basis for the foundation of the Southern Wall but as part of the design of the compartments that were constructed beneath the sloped street level. The lower part of the walls of the compartments was also carved from the bedrock, save for the southern wall of the compartments, which is completely missing. This wall was most probably constructed of stones, like the excavated shops facing the streets running along the Western Wall of the Temple Mount. The roof of the compartments, in the form of a vault, was also stone-built.

As opposed to the carefully stepped carving of the bedrock in the section described above, the bedrock in Compartment 15 eastward was treated differently. In this small stretch, the Southern Wall foundation stones of the Temple Mount were placed in quarried trenches.

Interestingly, a comparison of the architectural system described above to other entrance complexes to the Temple Mount (such as Robinson's Arch and Wilson's Arch on the west) emphasizes one major difference: the street here was built as an integral part of the Temple Mount complex and must have been constructed prior to the placement of the upper courses of the Southern Wall. In contrast, it is possible that the other entrances to the Temple Mount were added at later stages of the construction of the holy compound. This fact may be considered the primary evidence for the integral importance of this architectural system within the function of the Temple Mount, as is discussed below. This goes hand in hand with the dating of the system, in the early years of the construction of the Temple Mount during Herod's reign.

The Size of the Herodian Stones of the Southern Wall

The exposure of an additional part of the mighty wall's southern face at the southeastern corner of the Temple Mount contributed further details relevant to the construction of the walls. Noteworthy are the long ashlars incorporated here. In the southeastern corner itself, the long stones were incorporated in alternating courses. This can be seen in the lower stone layers exposed by Warren (1884: Pls. 10, 12, 18–20) as well as in much higher levels exposed by us and the upper courses that have always been exposed (Fig. 27.1).

Warren exposed three long stones here:

- *Layer d*, which extended from the corner northward (Warren 1884: Pl. 18), is 14'6" (= 4.42 m) long.

- *Layer c*, above *Layer d*, is a stone that extended westward. It is 14'4"3/4 (= 4.38 m) long.

- *Layer b*, above *Layer c*, which also extended westward. It is 20' (= 6.1 m) long.

Figure 27.1: The eastern part of the Southern Wall. Oversized Herodian stones indicated in color.

We recorded the following long stones in much higher levels (Fig. 27.2): In Courses I, K, M, O, Q and S, the long stones are laid along the southern face, while in the alternating courses between (i.e., J, L, N, P, R and T), they are laid along the eastern face. This is the method also employed in the southwestern corner of the Temple Mount. However, the stones at the southeastern corner, which are between 4.5 m (Layer Q) and 6.8 m (Layers M, O) long, are far shorter than those at the southwestern corner. There, the stones are ca. 10 m long. Here, at the southeastern corner, two long stones are incorporated in Layers M and Q, and three long stones in Layer O. They serve as stretchers, with one or two small stones in between serving as headers. This type of phenomenon is not present in the southwestern corner. The difference in construction between the southeastern corner and the southwestern corner might be the result of the long history of construction of the Temple Mount walls. Since the construction of the Temple Mount walls extended over several decades, the methods employed in the earlier phases of construction differed from those employed in the later stages, due to the experience gained. This topic deserves further study.

The Grand Course

Our attention was drawn to a particularly noticeable course of stones on the Southern Wall near the Triple Gate that is much taller than the other courses of the Herodian masonry. While the average height of the courses is 1.1 m, this so-called Grand Course is ca. 1.80 m high.

Figure 27.2: Southeastern corner of Southern Wall. Note the oversized stones. The grand course is indicted by arrow.

This course is known as the נדבך רבא (Grand Course; Bahat 2013: 242). We were looking for answers to three specific questions:

1.   Where would we find stones of the Grand Course on the Temple Mount walls?

2.   To what other elements (rock levels of the Temple Mount, level of the inner esplanade, etc.) did the stones relate?

3.   What was the function of this course of tall stones?

Apparently, a course of tall stones might circumscribe the entire Temple Mount at a specific level, but a careful examination showed that this was not the case. We had at our disposal Warren's (1884), E. Mazar's (2011) and Bahat's (2013) documentation as well as the possibility of examining a greater number of the stones firsthand. The level of the course's base near the Triple Gate is, according to Warren, 2380 feet which equals 725.42 m asl. The Grand Course is listed as E and F according to Warren's numbering.

The tall course of stones was identified in the Eastern Wall, the Southern Wall and the Western Wall.

The Eastern Wall
According to Warren (1884: Pl. 19, Layers E and F), only the cornerstone belongs to the Grand Course. At this elevation, Warren marked the level of its base to be 2379 feet which equals 725.11 m asl. This figure is somewhat lower (by ca. 19 cm) from the figure given above. On the latter elevation, Warren states that this is the "Level of floor of vaults (Solomon's Stables)."

The Southern Wall
Eastern Part: From the Triple Gate to the southeastern corner of the Temple Mount (Warren 1884: Pl. 20), the Grand Course is extant from the corner of the mount to near the Single Gate. Eight stones survived along some 21 m. Another tall stone survived a few meters east of the Triple Gate (Fig. 27.3).

It seems that all other stones here are from a late masonry (Umayyad?), and originally the Grand Course extended along the entire stretch, from the gate to the corner.

Central Part: Between the Triple Gate and the Double Gate. In this part, the tall course is fully preserved for ca. 64 m. It seems that along the entire length of this part, or its greatest part, the Grand Course is founded upon bedrock (Warren 1884: Pls. 25–26), which is quite high at this point (Figs. 27.4–6).

Western Part: From the Double Gate to the southwestern corner of the Temple Mount. The part next to the Double Gate is obstructed by a large medieval building that abuts the outer face of the Southern Wall (*Madrasat al-Hatuniya*). From this medieval building up to the southwestern corner, there is no Grand Course (Warren 1884: Pl. 27). On the other hand, there is a seam or an inconsistency between the stone layers at a distance of ca. 19 m east of the corner. Warren adds a remark on the plate: "Junction of beveled and stones." This inconsistency between the stone courses might be the outcome of the need to adjust the Grand Course from the east and its continuation westward with average or common stone courses. The inconsistency of two types of stone masonry precisely at the "seam" reinforces the notion we presented elsewhere (Reich and Baruch 2017) that the extension of the Temple Mount by Herod was performed in large segments. The present "seam" and the "seams" near Robinson's Arch support this suggestion.

The Western Wall

Southern Part: The tall course is absent from the southwestern corner through Robinson's Arch, Barclay's Gate and the prayer area (Wailing Wall).

Central Part: (Wilson's Arch area). The Grand Course does not exist in this area (Warren 1884: Pls. 33–34).

Northern Part: (from Wilson's Arch and northward to the northwestern corner of the Temple Mount). Here, instead of the Grand Course there is a course of super large stones. These are three stones set one next to the other (Bahat 2013: Loci 1000–1001), as follows:

- Southern stone (Bahat 2013: Figs. 7.03, 8.01, 1.01p; Photos 7.15, 7.16, 8.01, 8.02): this is the largest stone in the group, 3.30 m high, 13.55 m long (Bahat 2013: 242).

- Northern stone (Bahat 2013: Fig. 1.01o): 11.65 m long; height not given.

- Central stone (Bahat 2013; Fig. 1.01o): set between the two large stones mentioned above, 2.0 m long; height not given.

- Stone incorporated as the doorjamb of Warren's Gate (Locus 1003, Bahat 2013: 10, Fig. 1.01n): 8.2 m long (Bahat 2013: 242); height not given.

Bahat states (2013: 243, n. 3) that these stones are 4.5 m thick. This assertion is incorrect according to the data that Bahat himself gathered. In an appendix to his report, he published the results of a Ground Penetrating Radar (GPR) examination (Jol, Bauman and Bahat 2013), according to which the measured thickness of the Grand Course is between 1.8–2.5 m (about half of the figure of 4.5 m given by Bahat himself, above). The figure that Bahat gave is probably based on an unpublished report written by Amos Levanon (1968) of an examination made in September 1968 on behalf of the Geophysical Institute of Israel. The experiment was carried out in the B. Mazar excavation area. Mazar was at this time just beginning work (started in February 1968) next to the southwestern corner of the Temple Mount. From this report, it is not clear if the GPR examination was on the western side of the corner or on the eastern side.

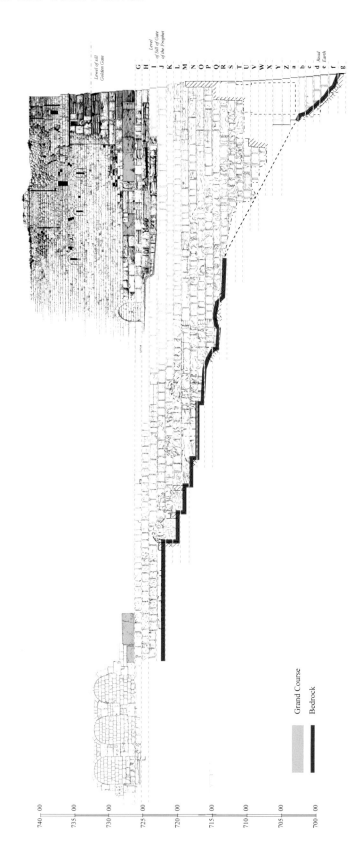

Figure 27.3: The eastern part of the Southern Wall.

Figure 27.4: The central part of the Southern Wall. The Double Gate is on the right and the Triple Gate on the left. The Grand Course is indicated in green.

Figure 27.5: The central part of the Southern Wall. The Double Gate is on the right and the Triple Gate on the left. The Grand Course, looking northwest. Note original doorjamb of the Triple Gate.

According to the measurements given above (thickness between 1.8–2.5 m), and assuming a specific weight of 2.2 tons for this stone, the large stone weighed between 177 and 246 tons. The super large stones do not resemble those of the Grand Course of the Southern Wall, neither by height nor by length. The super large stones create a category of their own and should be evaluated separately from the Grand Course of the Southern Wall.

What is clear is that two different uses of large or thick stones can be distinguished in the Herodian masonry of the Temple Mount walls: (1) extremely large stones on the Western Wall, north of Wilson's Arch, and (2) a tall layer of stones (the so-called Grand Course) on the eastern part of the Southern Wall.

Figure 27.6: The central part of the Southern Wall. The Double Gate is on the right and the Triple Gate on the left. Grand Course, looking northeast.

Other Contemporary Mega-Construction in the Region

A building project with super large stones took place precisely between the middle of the 1st century BCE and 1st century CE in Heliopolis (Baalbek) in the Beqaa Valley in Lebanon. There, use was made of even larger stones (the largest ever cut by man, detached from the quarry, transported and incorporated in a building). Kropp and Lohmann (2011) have pointed to possible relations between these two holy precincts, in Baalbek and in Jerusalem, especially because Herod financed show-off public building projects in various cities in Lebanon (*War* 1.422). In Baalbek, the super-sized masonry has a flaunting effect. There, the temple rests on three large stones (the Trilithon), each of which weighs 900 tons. One stone was abandoned on the way from the quarry (the stone dubbed Hajar al-Hibla), and two additional stones were recently discovered there (Abdul Massih 2014: Figs. 62–63) that were transported to the construction site (Adam 1977).

No less impressive is the fact that the engineers were able to construct a crane that could raise architraves weighing up to 108 tons (Gilad 2014). It seems that in Jerusalem, too, the construction crew was set for the show-off effect, since the super large stones face the Jerusalem main street and the luxurious residential quarters of the Upper City. Also, the fact that they are taller than they are wide speaks for this.

The tall course of stones on the Southern Wall is a different matter.

The fact is that this Grand Course has been found to be on the level of the sills of the Double Gate, the Triple Gate and the Warren Gate at the Western Wall, and the Golden Gate in the Eastern Wall of the complex, although the last-mentioned monument is not a Herodian structure. The cornerstone of the Grand Course in the southeast angle is a large block. It is on the floor level of the vaults of Solomon's Stables and consequently more than 30 m above the foundation stone at this corner.

We assume that the masons tried to create a sort of bonding and stabilizing belt for the entire masonry located under it, particularly for the part between the Triple Gate and the southeastern corner, which descends to a significant depth.

Elsewhere (Reich and Baruch 2017), we argued that this part was the first to be constructed in the project of extending the Temple Mount. It is possible that at the outset of the project the masons were of the opinion that such a belt was necessary. Later, as their experience grew, they abandoned this idea, hence it does not appear in the parts mentioned above. And indeed, heavier stones do not have any advantage over stones lighter in weight but greater in quantity. On the other hand, there is an advantage, statically, of long stones, as they bind the stones in a wall lengthwise. In the Southern Wall, many stones with an average length of 6 m were used (see above), while later when the southwestern corner was constructed, the masons made use of stones 10 m long.

It is possible that originally the masons planned to create a tall course all around the Temple Mount (ca. 1200 m, after deducting the Eastern Wall, which already existed). However, obtaining stones of this height (1.80 m) in large numbers was not easy (against stones that are particularly long), since locating quarries where there are no bedding planes in the rock for such a height is very rare. It seems they started their project with the tall course but soon found that obtaining such stones was not feasible and abandoned it.

Margin Drafting

Many stones of the collapsed Temple Mount walls remained on-site following the destruction of the complex in 70 CE, particularly next to the southwestern corner. All of the stones were worked in a similar fashion, i.e., they had drafted margins around the stone, leaving a central, slightly raised and flat boss. The width of the worked margins of the stones in the Southern Wall varies—ca. 10 cm on average for the upper margin and ca. 5 cm on average for the lower and lateral margins. The margins are set back from the central boss, ca. 1–1.5 cm on average. While not all of the stones follow this rule, most show these 1:2 proportions scrupulously.

The result is a neat appearance of straight, horizontal lines. Jacobson (2000: 145) pointed out that these proportions of drafted margins are also found in the Cave of the Patriarchs (Me'arat ha-Makhpelah) in Hebron, which is another holy compound built by Herod, but missing in other contemporary monumental edifices.

Drafted-margin masonry is a well-known component of Roman architecture. However, its roots are far more ancient, going back as early as the Late Bronze Age (Jacobson 2000: 139–141). Still, it seems to us that there is no functional difference between the Bronze Age margin drafting and the one that reached the peak of sophistication in the Roman period and particularly in the days of Emperor Augustus.

Warszawski and Peretz suggested that margin drafting was performed in the quarry as part of the processing of the stones. They went as far as calculating and found that the task of stonecutting called for the investment of ca. two hours per meter (Warszawski and Peretz 1992: 33). In our opinion, this suggestion should be reconsidered; we believe that since margin drafting is a delicate handicraft that is to be meticulously and carefully performed, it must have been carried out at the building site and not in the quarry. We believe that margin drafting was a functional device designed to enable the precise laying down of the stones.

We base our suggestion on three principal considerations: first, there is an absence of flaws and defects which would have been caused to the margins during the transportation of the stones from the quarry to the building site. Additional support for this suggestion lies in the fact that many of the margin-drafted stones were laid in the foundation of the walls in such a way that they were hidden from sight. The requirement for margin drafting and the willingness to invest in its implementation derived from an engineering or practical need rather than from an aesthetic desire.

Further support for our suggestion comes from the examination of stone quarries documented north of Jerusalem, in the Shuafat and Ramat Shlomo neighborhoods (ca. 5 km northwest of the Old City), where remains of Second Temple/Early Roman gigantic stones were found, still resting in the quarry prior to being transported to the construction site. Not one of these stones has drafted margins (Sion *et al.* 2011). In addition, excavations west of the Western Wall of the Temple Mount revealed a stonemason's chisel, 15 cm in length, which testifies, according to the excavator (Weksler-Bdolah 2017: 6), that the finishing touches were given by chiseling conducted on-site.

Use of the Anathyrosis Method

Today, several hundred ashlars from the original construction of the Temple Mount walls are exposed. In the excavation site near Robinson's Arch, several dozen ashlars are scattered on the paved street along the wall. These stones were pushed and dropped from the top of the Western Wall following the Roman conquest of Jerusalem.

Already at the outset of the exploration of the Temple Mount's walls, researchers noted the high degree of adjustment between the ashlars, creating straight joints with barely any gaps in between. A survey of the wall in the area of Robinson's Arch revealed that this was indeed true in most cases, except for gaps of a few millimeters here and there.

In regard to this question of compatibility between adjacent ashlars, we inspected several ashlars in the collapse on the paved street west of the Temple Mount. Evidence of two types of masonry methods were revealed:

The method of anathyrosis is attested to in the collapsed Herodian ashlars. One of the main tools used by masons and woodworkers/carpenters was the try-square (Latin *norma*; Reich 2000: 64). It was designed to make sure that certain details in a structure are at right angles; this is particularly crucial in creating openings with matching doors. In chiseling stones for masonry, this tool also aids in forming angles smaller than a right angle. The Temple Mount's ashlars are extremely large and heavy, and manipulating them in order to lay them down with precision in their courses was not an easy task. An average-sized ashlar could be laid down and manipulated by a worker or two trying to move it into place next to the ashlar laid down before it. In the case where the compatibility between both ashlars was not the best, because their sides had not been hewn in a straight manner and at a right angle in relation to the ashlar's front side, the stone would be taken back, the hewing corrected, and another attempt to lay the ashlar in place carried out. With extremely heavy ashlars, the supervisor had only a single opportunity to lay the ashlar in place. In that case, it had to be confirmed in advance that the sides of both ashlars—the one already in place and the one being driven toward it—were connected with a perfectly straight joint perpendicular to the course and without a space. Since the smallest protrusion on the ashlar's lateral faces, including protrusions invisible to the naked eye, could prevent a perfect interface, in many cases one lateral face of an ashlar was lightly chiseled to be slightly less-than-perpendicular to the ashlar's front side. As a result, ashlars were actually touching only in the joint, while in the depth of the wall their faces were not in effect perpendicular to the ashlar's front. This fact is easily discernible when a square is placed close to an ashlar's corner (Fig. 27.7).

Another phenomenon observed on the ashlars is that of beveling—the creation of a moderate incline on a 4–5 cm wide strip along the ashlar's edge. An ashlar with this kind of incline will create a few millimeters of open joint. We find it hard to trace the reason for creating this kind of incline (Figs. 27.8–9).

Engaged Pilasters

Three ashlars that fell from the Southern Wall were discovered in the excavation area and are discussed in the report by Peleg-Barkat (Chapter 8). The three stones came from the Southern Wall's engaged pilasters, that is, from the upper part that was designed with pilasters slightly protruding from the wall. One pilaster was preserved to its full width (1.13 m). Peleg-Barkat notes that excavations by B. Mazar and Ben-Dov and later by Reich and Billig unearthed pilasters whose full width was 1.45 m and this is the width of the "regular" pilasters, while the narrower pilasters probably adorned the

Figure 27.7: Anathyrosis on stone ashlar in the collapse of stones next to Temple Mount. Note the Anathyrosis space (photo by Y. Baruch).

Figure 27.8: The beveling of anathyrosis on stone ashlar in the collapse of stones next to Temple Mount. Note the beveled space (photo by Y. Baruch).

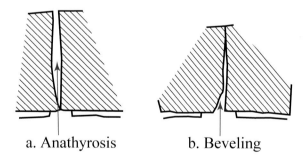

Figure 27.9: Schematic rendering of anathyrosis (a), beveling (b).

exterior of the upper part of the Royal Portico. We agree with this view. In addition, Peleg-Barkat points out that a complete recession between pilasters, 2.66 m wide, was documented in 1873 by Conder on a short section in the northern part of the Western Wall (Fig. 27.10).

It is well known that in the holy enclosures attributed to Herod, in Jerusalem, Hebron and Mamre, the exterior faces of the walls were adorned in their upper parts by engaged pilasters (Table 27.1).

The Temple Mount complex employed the Greek measurement of *orgyia* (ὄργυια) in its construction (Reidinger 2004: 9–10). One *orgyia* (known in English as fathom) is equivalent to six Greek feet or 1.86 m. The Southern Wall, which measures 279 m, equals 150 ὀργυιαί, and so the pier of Robinson's Arch is built with four compartments open to the street, with 1.86 m high walls in between. In light of this, it is noteworthy that the width of the pilasters, be it the narrower or the wider variant, as well as the recessions between the pilasters, were not designed according to this measurement. That said, the width of a narrow pilaster together with the width of a recession equals two ὀργυιαί (1.13 + 2.66 = 3.79, approximately 3.72 m).

FROM A SKETCH BY LIEUT. C. CONDER, R.E.

Figure 27.10: Engaged Pilasters *in-situ*, close to the northwestern corner of the Western Mount (Warren and Conder 1884: 213; Vincent and Steve 1956: 544).

Table 27.1: Select Measurements of the Walls and Pilasters in the Holy Enclosures at Jerusalem, Hebron and Mamre (after Jacobson 2000: 139)

Enclosure	Reference	Pilaster width, m	Distance between pilaster, m	Pilaster protrusion, m	Course height, m
Jerusalem	Vincent, Mackay and Abel 1923: 108	1.48	2.68	0.3	1.11 (average)*
Hebron	Vincent, Mackay and Abel 1923: 43, 108, Pl. IV	1.14	2.07	0.3	1.13 (average)*
Mamre	Mader 1957: 68–70, Z23, Z27; Magen 1993: 941	0.90 0.88	2.07 1.9	0.27	0.88, 1.13 (two lowest courses)

*For the finely dressed masonry only; see the analysis in the appendix of Jacobson 2000.

Gibson (2014) described in detail the pilaster enclosure wall of the Temple Mount with many parallels to this architectural phenomenon, in particular from Roman *temenoi* in the Middle East that exhibited wide popularity of engaged pilasters in ritual architecture, especially under Emperor Augustus. Gibson uses this detailed description to support his thesis that the upper part of the Temple Mount's walls was not dismantled by the Roman Tenth Legion following the destruction in 70 CE, but rather during the earthquake of 363 CE (the *Ra'ash Shevi'it*, "Sabbatical Year Earthquake"). Recently, Reich and Baruch (2020) presented arguments rebutting this view.

It should be mentioned that the inventory of ashlars found fallen in the excavation along the Southern Wall was scanty compared to the collapse of these stones found heaped upon the stone-paved street along the Western Temple Mount Wall. We suggest only a partial answer to this difference, namely, that this scarcity is due to the fact that, in this area along the Southern Wall, the outer surface is very close to the underground level of the Temple Mount, and therefore it was easier to carry fallen ashlars from this spot in order to reuse them for building inside the complex (for example, in the part known as Solomon's Stables). Note that an examination of the stones integrated in secondary use in the walls of buildings following the destruction of the Temple Mount, including in Solomon's Stables, has not revealed stones that may be identified as belonging to the engaged pilasters.

Rectangular Holes in Robinson's Arch

The scaffolding erected on Robinson's Arch for the conservation work enabled us to take a close look at the arch (Fig. 27.11). Examining Robinson's Arch from up close revealed three, perhaps four rectangular holes (the southernmost is decimated) cut exactly into the joint between Course B and Course C that underlies it so that the upper half of each hole is in the upper course and the lower half of each hole is in the lower course. This means that they were cut after the courses of the arch were already constructed. The holes are uniform in shape and size, some 15 × 35 cm, and ca. 30 cm in depth (Figs. 27.12–16).

The holes are perfect rectangles, well cut, with straight sides with right angles, most probably meant to receive wooden struts, likely with metal shoes or fittings. Particularly remarkable is the fact that the inner (eastern) part of the hole is cut flat and smooth. It can be assumed that if these holes were cut at any later period, say in medieval times, the holes, and especially their inner part, would not have been cut in so meticulous a fashion. This brings us to assume that these holes were cut in conjunction with the construction of the arch, namely as part of the scaffolding system used for its construction.

Course B is composed of two extremely large stones. The construction of these did not require any scaffolding or support during construction since part of each stone is incorporated into the Temple Mount Western Wall. This part was most probably larger than the western part of the stones, which already hovered in the air. This can perhaps be said about the stones of Course A as well. The stones of Course A were also stuck in the wall (although it seems to a lesser depth than those of Course B, which underlie and carry them). The stones of Course A could have been supported during construction also transversely with long wooden beams held on the other, western side of the arch (at Course A the distance along the opening of the arch was ca. 10.1 m).

We suggest that the beams that were placed in these holes were part of the hovering scaffolding that was supported mainly on the protruding stones of Course D. The construction of the arch using this Roman technique of hovering scaffolding (also called: centring) terminated in an accident: two large voussoirs survived and became stuck in the main drainage channel below, under the paved street, and the arch was eventually constructed by a different method (see below).

Figure 27.11: Scaffoldings mounted on Robinson's Arch 2020
(photo by Y. Baruch).

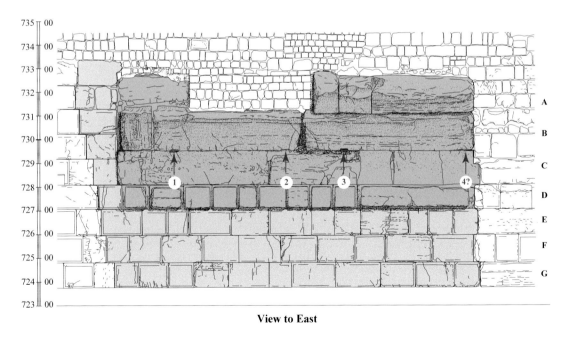

View to East

Figure 27.12: Robinson's Arch. Elevation. Indicated are the location of the four rectangular holes (model and sketch by Or Roz).

Figure 27.13: Robinson's Arch, hole number 1 (photo by Y. Baruch).

Figure 27.14: Robinson's Arch, hole number 1 (photo by Y. Baruch).

Figure 27.15: Robinson's Arch, hole number 2 (left), hole number 3 (right) (photo by Y. Baruch).

Figure 27.16: Robinson's Arch, hole number 2 (left), hole number 3 (right) (photo by Y. Baruch).

The "Seams" on the Sides of Robinson's Arch

Elsewhere, we have discussed a constructional "seam" visible south of Robinson's Arch, between it and the southern part of the Western Wall (Reich and Baruch 2019: Fig. 4, indicated with an arrow) The mounting of modern scaffolding on Robinson's Arch for conservation work enabled us to observe the seam closely (Fig. 27.17). The joints to its left (north) are barely visible when standing on the Paved Street below; however, they are easily discernible on closer inspection. The "seams" descend to Course G (inclusive). On the right side (south) of the arch is a single "seam," almost straight and vertical. On the left side of the arch (north) in fact two "seams" are extant. The one on the left is slanted and stepped. When Robinson's Arch was inserted, the gap between the vertical side of the arch and the graded edge of the vertical wall was filled in with masonry, thus leaving behind two "seams."

This observation reinforces the suggestion (see below) that the construction of Robinson's Arch was begun twice. The first attempt terminated in a construction accident, traces of which survived under the Paved Street. It took time to clear the collapsed stones. In the interim, the construction of the vertical wall continued north of the planned arch, leaving behind the required gap in which the arch, in the second attempt at construction, was inserted (Fig. 27.18).

Horizontal Grooves on the Ashlars of the Western Wall Near Robinson's Arch

In the southern part of the Temple Mount's Western Wall, from the ramp of the Bab al-Maghariba gate down to the compound's southwestern corner, one can easily observe three long horizontal grooves carved in the wall, one above the other (Figs. 27.19–20). These grooves are found solely in the Herodian ashlars of the wall. They were exposed when the larger part of this section of the Herodian wall was unearthed in the 1969–1978 Mazar and Ben-Dov excavations (Mazar 1971). Prior to that, the surface elevation reached the base of Robinson's Arch, hence the grooves were invisible. These grooves do not appear in Warren's documentation (Warren 1884: Pls. 28–29).

The need to discuss the Western Wall's ashlar grooves became pressing following the collapse of a piece of one of the wall's ashlars and the realization that one of the main reasons for the stone's collapse was the existence of the groove cut in that ashlar (Chapter 35).

The details of the three grooves are as follows (Fig. 27.21):

1. The lower groove. Cut on the lower part of Course H (according to Warren's numbering). Its base is the top of Course I and runs for 67.5 m along the wall from the area of the ramp leading up the Bab al-Maghariba, down to the Temple Mount's southwestern corner. The groove also continues beyond the southwestern corner on the Southern Wall of the Temple Mount, along the same course of the Herodian ashlars, for an additional distance of ca. 22.5 m from the corner eastward (Fig. 27.22).

    The elevation of its floor is 722.18 m asl.

2. The middle groove. Cut on the lower part of Course D, which is the course that protrudes directly under Robinson's Arch. Its bottom is not the top of Course E, as is the case with the lower groove and the upper groove, but it is cut some 5–6 cm into the top of Course E, thus eliminating the upper drafted margin of this course (Figs. 27.23, 27.26).

    The groove runs for ca. 45 m from the Bab al-Maghariba ramp to the stump of Robinson's Arch. The level of the bottom is 726.55 m asl. This groove ends in a square cut in the wall, ca. 4.5 m, north of Robinson's Arch (see below).

    The faces of the cuttings of this groove were found devoid of any cement or plaster, meaning that it did not, at any time, carry a water channel or water pipe. On the other hand, the ^{14}C experts experimented with a patch of cement containing carbonized seeds at the inner part of the groove but not on the level bottom of it (see Chapter 33, Figs. 27.23, 27.26) Two samples were taken for [14]C

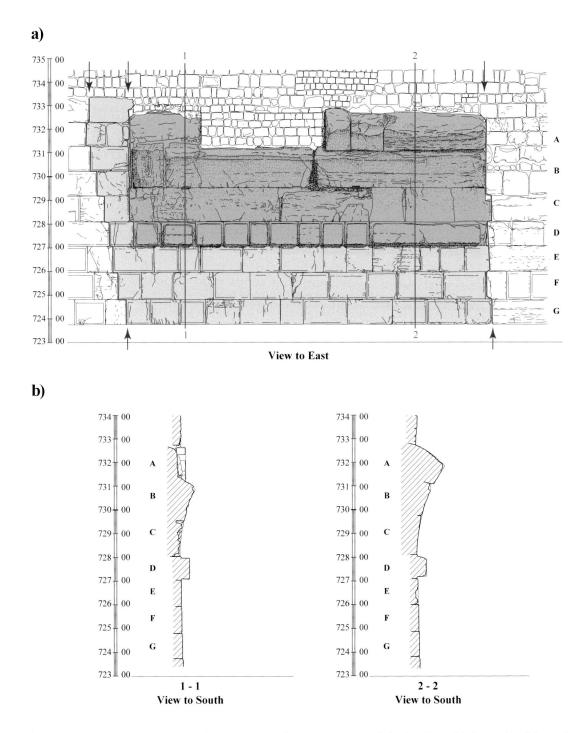

Figure 27.17: (a) Robinson's Arch. Elevation. Note the "seams" to the right (south) and left (north) of the arch. (b) Robinson's Arch, cross section (model and sketch by Or Roz).

dating. This observation is problematic. One may easily claim that these are the remains of a water channel, similar to the remains of the one observed on the lower groove. However, the middle groove leads nowhere. It terminates at the northern edge of Robinson's Arch, which is not a destination, clearly different from the lower groove, which is related to the Umayyad Palace II. The existence of the patch of plaster within the groove cannot be explained, while its ^{14}C date is certainly valid.

Figure 27.18: Robinson's Arch. "Seam" indicated by arrows (photo by Y. Baruch).

Figure 27.19: The southwestern corner of the Temple Mount. Note the stump of Robinson's Arch with the three grooves cut to the north of it, looking northeast (photo by Y. Baruch).

A similar groove was documented in excavations conducted beneath Wilson's Arch (Uziel, Lieberman and Solomon 2017: 244).

One may think that the groove documented in Wilson's Arch, at about a similar elevation and ca. 140 m apart from the present middle groove to the north, is in effect a continuation of the said middle groove. However, the substantial distance between the grooves (the one near Robinson's Arch and the one in Wilson's Arch) cannot be interconnected, since Barclay's Gate is located between them (Warren 1884: Pl. 32) and this prevents such a continuity (Fig. 27.24).

Figure 27.20: The southwestern corner of the Temple Mount. Note the stump of Robinson's Arch with the three grooves cut to the north of it, looking southeast.

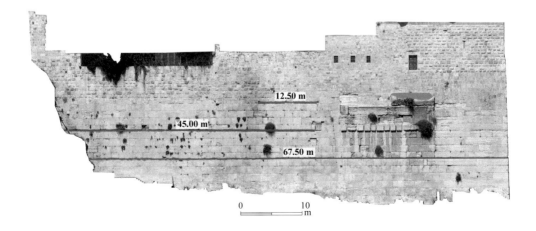

Figure 27.21: Southern part of the Western Wall of the Temple Mount, indicating elevation.

Figure 27.22: The lower groove at the point where the Wall turns around the southwestern corner of the Temple Mount, looking northeast (photo by S. Halevi).

Figure 27.23: The middle groove, looking southeast. Note that there are no extant traces of cement or plaster (photo by Y. Baruch).

3. The upper groove. Cut in the lower part of Course 1 according to Warren's numbering (Warren and Conder 1884: 120), which is the course right above Course A. Its bottom elevation is 732.14 m asl. It runs along some 12.5 m, ending on its southern edge in a square cut similar to the one documented in the middle groove. It is impossible to tell whether the groove originally continued northward, since beyond its northern end the ashlars are not of Herodian masonry.

Cutting of the Grooves

A close examination shows that the cutting of all the grooves, to all their lengths, in the area of Robinson's Arch, is relatively uniform in shape: their height is 30 cm on average, as is their depth. The cross-sections of all three grooves slant, forming a cut in the shape of right-angled triangles, sometimes with a curved profile (Fig. 27.25).

Dating the Cutting of the Grooves

The three grooves were exposed by the Mazar and Ben-Dov expedition. The southern part of the lower groove, in the area underneath Robison's Arch down to the southwestern corner, was exposed first. The middle and upper grooves are missing on this part of the wall. The expedition reported finding the lower groove (Mazar 1969: 163, Fig. 2, Course 12; Fig. 4, Course 12; Pl. 84: 2). They identified it as a water carrier, leading water from the north southward and further around

Figure 27.24: The middle groove, in the center, with holes at its southern edge, looking north. Note that the bottom of the groove is at a level several cm lower than the Herodian ashlar to the south (right) of it, indicated by an arrow (photo by Y. Baruch).

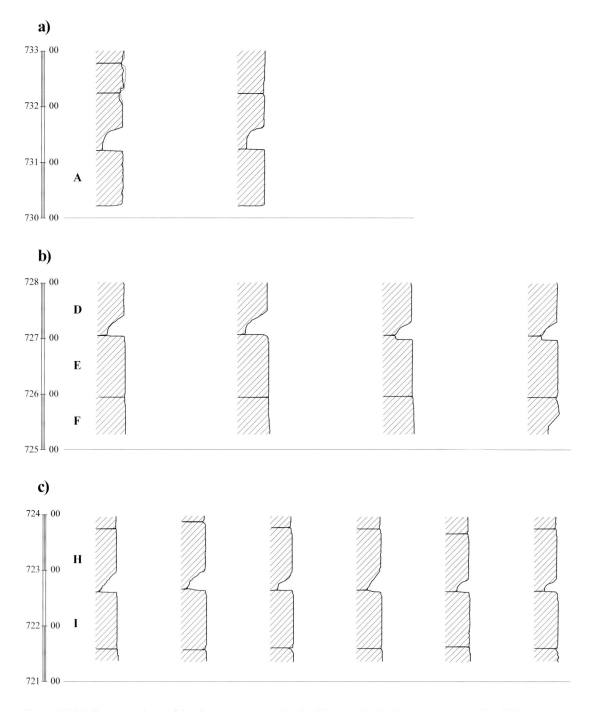

Figure 27.25: Cross-sections of the three grooves cut in the Western Wall: (a) upper groove; (b) middle groove; (c) lower groove.

Figure 27.26: The lower groove on the Southern Wall of the Temple Mount at the point where it terminates and turns downward. Note that the last stone in which it is cut is also the last stone of Herodian masonry with marginal drafting.

the corner eastward toward the Double Gate.[1] Mazar and Ben-Dov suggested that it was probably constructed in the Byzantine period, but that it continued to serve through the Umayyad period. At that point a diversion was created down to the Umayyad main gutter, and through the northern wall of Umayyad Palace II (Fig. 27.7; Ben-Dov 1973: 76–78).

The Mazar and Ben-Dov expedition exposed the middle and upper grooves by (Mazar 1971: Pl. 11) but the excavators did not comment on them.

Regarding the date of the grooves, the following observations and facts should be considered:

1. All the grooves are carved only in the Herodian courses of the complex.

2. All three grooves are similar in size in their cross-section. It is reasonable to believe that they are the product of a single operation. It is possible that the three grooves were originally cut only on the Western Wall of the Temple Mount, adjacent to the stump of Robinson's Arch on the north. At a later stage, the lower groove was continued southward and around the corner eastward for the sake of the water channel it carried.

3. The lower groove terminates on the Southern Wall exactly where the Herodian masonry terminates. At this point, the groove continues downward, while the course of masonry continues eastward in a different style (that of the Umayyad period). This makes it possible that the carving of the lower groove was done only on what was left of the Herodian ashlar-built walls and prior to the restoration of the breaches (see above).

---

[1]   This assertion cannot be accepted since the level of the Double Gate is some 4 m higher than the level of the lower groove.

4. Two samples were taken for ^{14}C dating from the cement found in the inner part of the middle groove. The absolute dates obtained (Chapter 33) were Sample RTD-11140: 674–702 CE; Sample RTD-11141: 741–772 CE. This datum, at most, may provide a *terminus ante quem* for the cutting of the groove. It might date the water channel that might have been inserted into the groove.

5. Traces of a water channel or water pipe are clearly seen in the lower groove. It is inconceivable that such a device was also present at the time in the middle groove; even if it was later hacked out, a trace would have been left as in the lower groove. These devices were almost totally absent when the excavation revealed the face of the wall.

The Use of the Grooves

Several possibilities should be considered:

1. Water carrier. This suggestion was first put forward by Ben-Dov, who based it on a possible connection between the channel in the lower groove and a water channel running beneath the Northern Wall of Umayyad Structure II (Ben-Dov 1973: 76, 78–79, Fig. 4). Contrary to Ben-Dov's reconstruction, although remains of binding material or plaster were found along the lower groove, no remains of a clay pipe or its imprint were documented in the recent conservation project (1973, Fig. 4: left side). In addition, the binding material documented by the conservators was not hydraulic (Chapter 34). In the middle and upper grooves, almost no traces of a binding material are extant.

2. Grooves supporting wooden beams of floors, for a structure leaning onto the Western Wall. The excavation conducted close to Robinson's Arch by Reich and Billig (1994–1996) unearthed a long wall of considerably good masonry. The wall was constructed exactly parallel to the Western Wall, at a distance of 4 m from it (Wall 502, Fig. 27.27, see Chapter 26).[2] This wall was built directly on the collapse of Herodian ashlars caused by the Roman army following the city's destruction in 70 CE. This wall is in fact the eastern boundary wall of Umayyad Structure IV opposite the Western Wall. The 4-m wide space between Structure IV and the Western Wall of the Temple Mount was planned as an alley, as was the custom with the other contemporary structures in this area.

We suggest that the narrow (4-m) and long (at least 70-m) space between Wall 502 and the Western Wall was used for a housing project. This narrow and long space was divided into two or three stories. The grooves in the wall were designed to receive the eastern ends of the wooden beams of the floors. We assume that Wall 502 had similar grooves on the same levels. Unfortunately, the said wall was not preserved to its full height, but it was strongly built with ashlars and may have risen to a significant height, carrying the suggested floors on the western side. All in all, this created two long and narrow stories with a roof above them, possibly even three stories. Each story was equal in height to four Herodian courses (ca. 4.5 m).

Here, another architectural element comes to support this suggestion: on the ashlars of the Herodian wall, close to Robinson's Arch and north of it, near the southern edges of the middle and upper grooves, between the lower and middle grooves and between the middle and upper groove, pairs of square cuts are visible in the stone. Between these pairs of cuts, the face of the Herodian ashlars is partly missing. These pairs of cuts are located almost one above the other, the upper pair slightly closer to Robinson's Arch (Fig. 27.27).

---

[2] In order to expose the collapse of Herodian ashlars at the foot of Robinson's Arch, the wall was dismantled in its entirety by the Reich and Billig expedition.

Figure 27.27: Wall 502 (on the right). Constructed parallel
to the Western Wall of the Temple Mount (on the left).

We suggest that in the space between the middle and upper grooves and Robinson's Arch, and in the two pairs of cuts mentioned above, parts of a stairway were inserted. The square cuts accommodated pairs of square-sectioned horizontal wooden beams; between them were fixed ladders or stairs, as suggested in the following reconstruction (Figs. 27.28–27.29).

No direct data exists that enables us to date the suggested building with the wooden floors which left the grooves on the wall. Wall 502, which is part of Umayyad Building IV, does, however, provide a *terminus post quem*.

If this reconstruction is accurate, then under the lower floor which was inserted along the lower long groove, a space remained between the wooden floor and the cover-tones of the Umayyad main gutter, some 1.50–1.80 m high. The cemetery described by Reich and Billig (Chapter 26) is situated directly upon the gutter cover stones. This cemetery might be contemporary with the building with the wooden floors, meaning that those who created the multifloored construction took advantage and concealed a cemetery under the building.

Alternatively, it is more likely that this cemetery was created at a later period—taking advantage of the narrow, dark and difficult to access long space under the building. A cemetery would not usually be located inside the boundaries of an urban area, but it seems that some unusual conditions demanded it in this case. A Hebrew inscription was also inscribed upon the wall of this dark and unapproachable space. This was not a display inscription. While it cites Isaiah 66:14, "You shall see, and your heart shall rejoice; your bones shall [flourish] like the gra[ss]," its beginning, "You shall see," stands in contrast to the totally dark conditions that prevented its view (see Chapter 29). The cemetery was not easily dated as it lacks indicative finds for this. A possible date, based on historic considerations, places it in the early 11th century CE. This seem to be the lower date for the building with the wooden floors.

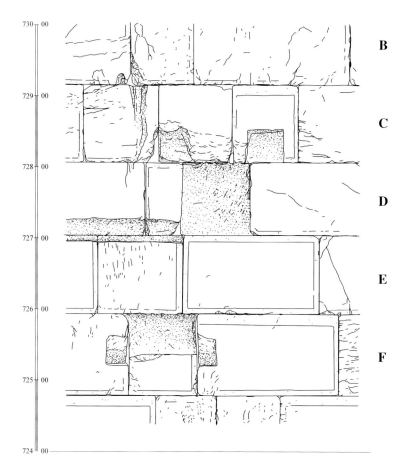

Figure 27.28: The Western Wall of the Temple Mount. Rectangular holes cut above and below the middle groove.

CONSTRUCTION OF ROBINSON'S ARCH[3]

The expansion of the Temple Mount in Jerusalem, initiated by King Herod, was undoubtedly the largest building project carried out in the Land of Israel in ancient times. A short time after its completion, its mighty retaining walls were described by Flavius Josephus: "both (porticoes) were (supported) by a great wall, and the wall itself was the greatest ever heard of by man" (*Ant.* 15.396). Later, the Jewish sages exclaimed: "He who has not seen the Temple of Herod has never seen a beautiful building" (Babylonian Talmud, *Bava Batra* 4[a]), and "He who has not seen the Temple in its full construction has never seen a glorious building in his life" (Babylonian Talmud, *Sukkah* 51[b]).

In 1838, a monumental arch in the southwestern corner of the Temple Mount was found and named for the American Bible scholar Edward Robinson.[4] Scholars at the time claimed that this arch, Robinson's Arch, was the largest and easternmost of a series of arches that supported a bridge

---

[3]   The following section was originally published in Hebrew by Reich (2015).

[4]   On this subject, see H. Goren (2020).

Figure 27.29: Reconstruction of the three-story building, making use of the three grooves cut in the Western Wall (reconstruction by R. Reich; art: Or Zakaim).

leading from the Upper City of Jerusalem to the Temple Mount. B. Mazar years later convincingly proved that it was a part of a monumental staircase that provided access to the holy precinct.

The arch was destroyed by the Roman army shortly after the sack of Jerusalem in 70 CE. Several elements withstood the carnage. The stump of the eastern springer built into the Western Wall survived, as did the western pilaster, built in the same masonry style as the Western Wall.

The pilaster was first discovered by Wilson (1865: 75, Pl. XXVI: 4, Area VIII, Photos 13b, 14a) and Warren (1884: Pls. VII, XXVIII–XXX; Warren and Conder 1884: 178–186). The greater part of the arch and its stones, including steps and handrails, were found scattered in a massive collapse on the paved street that ran under it. Part of it was exposed by B. Mazar and Ben-Dov and part by Reich and Billig.

On the Construction of Robinson's Arch

Robinson's Arch (Fig. 27.30) was a vast stone arch constructed to carry a monumental staircase that led toward one of the western gates of the Temple Mount. It is situated 12 m north of the southwestern corner of the Temple Mount. The arch was in effect a vault that was ca. 15.35 m wide with a 12.68 m wide span.[5] Its eastern side is incorporated in the Western Wall of the Temple Mount itself, while the western side is supported on a pilaster constructed of the same masonry as the Temple Mount walls. The lowest three courses of this pilaster survived almost completely, as well as two stones of the fourth layer. The western pilaster measures 3.60 × 15.35 m.[6] Four cubicles, which open onto the street and were used as shops, were located within it. The lintels above these cubicles survived, as well as parts of the relieving arch over the northernmost shop.[7]

The volume of the suspended part of the arch can be calculated to be ca. 750 cu m. This is based on the measurements of the arch, as well as on the level of the Temple Mount's esplanade into which it led. At a density of 2.2 tons per cu m for the stone, this part of the arch weighed ca. 1600 tons (Fig. 27.31).

The size of the stones in the arch was of the same magnitude as the other stones of the Temple Mount walls, as can still be seen from the stump, three courses of which survived. The second course includes a stone as long as approximately a third of the width of the arch, with an estimated weight of 20 tons.

Apart from the square fallen stones of the pilaster and the fallen voussoirs of the arch, several other types of stones were discovered in the collapse of the arch (Fig. 27.32):

- A large number of stairs (Fig. 27.33). These are small stones, relative to the fallen stones of the pilaster and voussoirs. They have a step-like lower profile with which they were fitted to one another. Their upper faces are smooth due to erosion by the feet of the users.

- Several flat blocks of stone that were rounded on one side. In one of these stones, two opposing sides were at an oblique angle to the other two sides (Fig. 27.34). The angles were similar to the angle of the staircase. This implies that these stones were in fact handrails on the sides of the monumental staircase. The rounded side supports this assumption.

- A large-profiled stone and several large fragments indicate that these were fragments of the frame of the gate that opened into the Temple Mount at the point where the arch reached it (Reich and Billig 2000: 347).

On the Western Wall of the Temple Mount, under the springer course of the arch, is a stone course that protrudes from the face of the wall. This is a common architectural feature on Roman arches and vaults; these were used in supporting the centring scaffolds for the construction of the arch (Fig. 27.30). Part of this course is designed as a continuous course while the other part is cut into protruding cubic stones. The western pilaster of the arch survived to a level lower than this course. However, in the pile of collapsed stones, several were found with a cubic protrusion, which was part of a similar course on the western side of the arch.[8]

The collapse of Robinson's Arch brought down in an instant some 1600 tons of stones on a relatively small area of ca. 200 sq m. This area was not affected uniformly by the impact. In the southeast, excavated by Reich and Billig (2000: 344), the paving of the street sank ca. 2 m. This was due to the fact that there were cellars and *miqwaʾot* (Fig. 27.35) under this street, and their vaults gave

---

[5] For the distance between the pilaster of the arch and the Western Wall of the Temple Mount one cannot give a definitive figure because the Temple Mount's wall is not vertical. Each stone course is set back 2–3 cm in relation to the course upon which it rests.

[6] The figure provided by Ritmeyer (2006: 47, in the box) for its width (6.5 m) is incorrect.

[7] The final excavation reports of these cubicles were published by E. Mazar (2020: 71–90).

[8] Several of these stones can be seen scattered in the adjoining park.

Figure 27.30: Robinson's Arch, looking northeast.

Figure 27.31: Robinson's Arch, reconstruction (Urban Simulation Team UCLA. Architecture: L. Snyder).

Figure 27.32: Stone collapse of Robinson's Arch leaning onto the western pilaster (Reich and Billig excavations).

Figure 27.33: Stone stairs extracted from the stone collapse of Robinson's Arch (Reich and Billig excavations).

Figure 27.34: Stones that were part of the handrail of the staircase on Robinson's Arch (Reich and Billig excavations).

way (Shukron and Reich 2011). On the northeastern part of this area of the street, the cave-in was moderate due to the large drain that crossed under the street in a north–south line.[9] On the western half of the street, which received the impact of the collapsing arch, the paving is still at its original level, due to the layers of packed earth that underlie it.

While the cave-in process is obvious, the stability of the pavement on the western side of the street requires examination. The stone-paved road was found to be laid upon a ca. 5 m thick layer of bedded and hard-trodden debris, which reaches down to bedrock (Reich and Shukron 2011: 222, Fig. 2). Moreover, these layers are supported by a network of subterranean walls that also reach down to the bedrock between which these debris layers were laid (Fig. 27.36). The question here is whether the street's paving required such a thick and stable subterranean construction. If the underground support described was not the aim of the road paver, what was the purpose of this subterranean construction?

I suggest that this construction is the lower part of a much higher construction that was prepared in relation to the construction of Robinson's Arch a long time before the street was paved. As mentioned above, the arch is in fact a vault, some 15.35 m wide with a 12.7 m span, all built as one solid construction. At Nîmes in southern France, for example, each of the arches in the two low tiers of the Pont du Gard Aqueduct has an average span of ca. 24.4 m (see Gockel 1986: 158–161; Adam 1994: 174–177) (almost

---

9   This cave-in did not necessarily occur at the moment of the collapse's impact. The earthen fills under the street could have been washed into these spaces from rain runoff that occurred in the following decades, and as the main drain under the street removed part of the wash, this could have created hollows under the street. The impact on the street accelerated this process.

Figure 27.35: Foundation course of the Western Wall, under Robinson's Arch, constructed over an ancient *miqweh* (Shukron excavation).

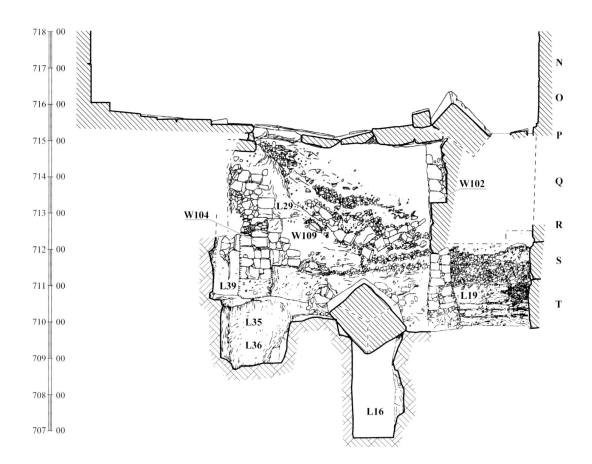

Figure 27.36: Cross-section, perpendicular to the Western Wall under the street paving at Robinson's Arch. Note earthen fills abutting the Western Wall (Locus 19, Shukron excavation).

twice the size of the span of Robinson's Arch). However, each one of the arches in the low tier is made of four narrow arches abutting each other (and three arches in the second tier; Adam 1994: Fig. 420), each only 1.55 m wide on average. This method enabled the constructors to prepare a narrow centring scaffold, construct one arch and move the centring sideways to construct the neighboring arch and so forth. The centring method is the most efficient scaffolding method and is also the most economical in terms of material—long and thick wooden logs. In addition, the arches of Pont du Gard are constructed of stones only some 5 tons in weight. The fact that Robinson's Arch was constructed as a single arch, using extremely large blocks of stone, implies that its construction presented the builders with a formidable task. The type of scaffold and the material required for its construction were of utmost importance.

Mention should be made here of the protruding course on the arch's springer course. In Roman architecture, these protruding stones were anchoring points sufficient for constructing the centring scaffold and the arch, without using a "forest" of vertical long and thick wooden logs for this purpose. Did the local builders in Jerusalem master this technique? Did they have the proper know-how at their disposal? Did they have a sufficient supply of adequate long trunks, especially for an arch that springs at a level of ca. 12 m above the street under it?

At this point, we should turn to examine the space beneath the paved street. Here, cut in bedrock, there is a large drain (some 1.20 m wide and 3.5 m deep) that is roofed over with an elongated vault. At the spot right under Robinson's Arch, in 1867, Charles Warren discovered two large voussoirs stuck in the upper edges of the drain (Fig. 27.37). The drain was open and the road above it had not

Figure 27.37: The main sewer under Robinson's Arch, with the collapsed stone voussoir stuck in its upper part, as seen before the excavations.

yet been paved when these stones fell, most probably as a result of an accident, during construction. The constructors had decided not to extract these two stones, and they were left as-is. The vault over the drain, the network of subterranean walls and the compact layers of debris were all constructed and laid after this incident, as the remains imply.

I suggest that the builders of Robinson's Arch, probably by centring (Fig. 27.38), which required specific know-how, had an accident during construction. They switched from the Roman method of arch building to the method of building with vertical supports, with which Jerusalem constructors were better acquainted. This required preparing the area involved by packing and treading the earth upon which the vertical supports were about to be constructed. For this purpose, they constructed a wall network and packed layers of earth found under the street's paving, taking no chances, and lowering it down to bedrock. To what level did they raise this construction of packed earth? If it would have been constructed only to the level of the planned paved street (as is the case now), it would have required preparing thick wooden trunks some 12 m long at the springers of the arch to 18.5 m at the arch's apex (Fig. 27.39), and this over the entire space covered by the arch (some 200 sq m). Although the Judean Hills were covered with forest (*War* 5.264, 496, 522–523; 6.5–7, 9–11, 375), these trees did not have long and thick trunks, as was the case in Europe. We have no clue, historical or archaeological, that timber was imported from Europe. On the other hand, the builders could have raised the construction of the network of supporting walls and layers of packed earth in between, up to the level of the arch's springer, or somewhat lower than this, that is, some 12 m more (Fig. 27.40). This would have resulted

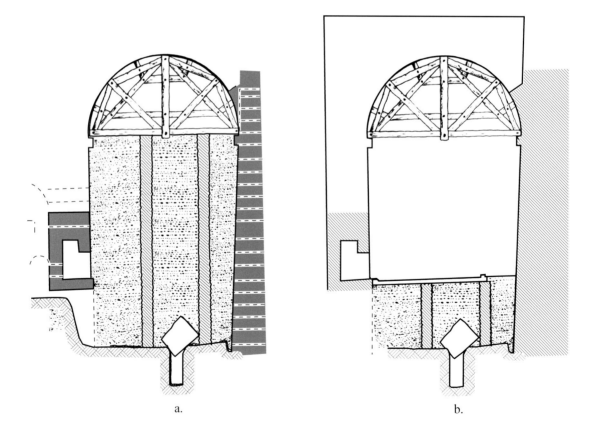

a.   b.

Figure 27.38: Possible scaffolding system for the construction of Robinson's Arch: centring.

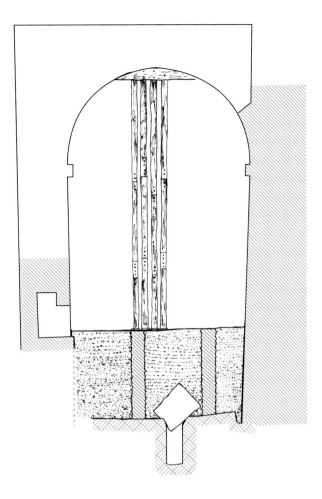

Figure 27.39: Possible scaffolding system for the construction of Robinson's Arch: high, upright scaffolding (only four polls are illustrated).

in the need for only 28% of the timber for the full project, and of a small number of trunks, 6.5 m long at most, to be used at the arch's apex. After the completion of the arch, the auxiliary construction would have been cut down slightly to the level desired for the planned street under the arch and removed. The lower parts of this construction were left useless *in-situ*.

Date of Construction

The eastern springer of Robinson's Arch is incorporated in the Western Wall of the Temple Mount; hence, its date of construction seems easy to determine. It is common knowledge that the Temple Mount was constructed by King Herod the Great (37–4 BCE). Flavius Josephus has it that the construction started in his 18th regnal year (22 BCE; *Ant.* 15.380) and that it lasted for eight years, that is, until 15 BCE (15.420).

At face value, this span of time—eight years—seems considerably too short for the completion of these four mighty retaining walls that create the Temple Mount, and all other related constructions. However, a study made by two civil engineers concluded that this figure is feasible (Warszawski and Peretz 1992: 3–46). It seems that this time span relates to the construction of the stoa and secondary

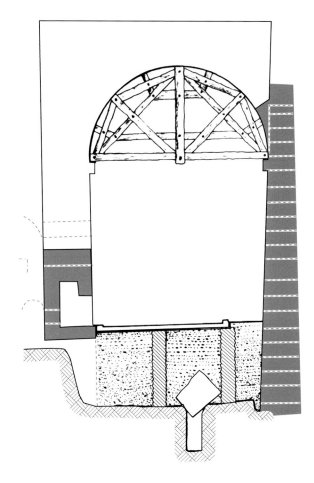

Figure 27.40: Possible scaffolding system for the construction of Robinson's Arch: short, upright scaffolding, constructed over a high podium made of trodden earth, between vertical walls.

building operations on top of the completed Temple Mount rather than the main extension project of the Temple Mount.

Toward the end of *Antiquities*, Josephus presents another assessment that has a bearing on the time required for the extension project of the Temple Mount: "Just now, too, the Temple has been completed. The people therefore saw that the workmen, numbering over eighteen thousand, were out of work and would be deprived of pay ... but he did not veto the paving of the city with white stone" (*Ant.* 20.219, 222). The time described is the reign of Agrippa II and Albinus's procuratorship in Jerusalem, i.e., 62–64 CE. This implies that the construction works at the Temple Mount lasted some 80 years. This certainly is a reasonable time span for the completion of such a project.

Another statement concerning the long time required for the construction of the holy precinct finds support in the sayings related to Jesus of Nazareth while visiting Jerusalem: "Forty and six years was this Temple in building and wilt thou raise it up in three days?" (John 2:20). The number of years quoted—46 years—seems to indicate that during his visit to Jerusalem, the Temple Mount was under construction for the considerable time mentioned, much longer than the figure of eight years given by Flavius Josephus.

In the excavation of a segment of the street along the Western Wall of the Temple Mount, a probe was carried out under the paving stones (Reich and Billig 2000). The probe retrieved 15 coins. The latest coin retrieved from under the paving was struck under Pontius Pilate (26–36 CE), thus giving a *terminus post quem* for the paving. Later excavations carried out on the same paved road in a location more to the south of the Temple Mount have demonstrated that during the procuratorship of Pilate the street was paved (Szanton *et al.* 2019).

In the excavation carried out by Shukron at the base of Robinson's Arch (Shukron 2012), a small segment of the foundation layers of the Western Wall were exposed and the debris next to it excavated. The greater parts of this segment's first layer of stones were found based upon bedrock.

It should be borne in mind that the Western Wall of the Herodian Temple Mount (in addition to the Southern and Northern Walls) belongs to the enlargement project envisaged by King Herod and carried out accordingly. To this end, large built-up areas with domestic dwellings were cleared away. In these areas, the upper structure of houses was demolished and discarded, while rock-cut installations like cisterns, cellars and *miqwa'ot* were filled in with debris. Remains of these were exposed south of the Temple Mount (Chapter 4). The excavation abutting the Western Wall under Robinson's Arch exposed under the street several such installations.

One installation—a *miqweh*—is of special importance. It is cut in bedrock and plastered with the gray plaster typical of the late Second Temple period (Reich and Shukron 2011: 69). Its plastered steps descend from east to west. In relation to the Western Wall of the Temple Mount, it survived in part under it and in part west of it. For the construction of the first layer of the wall, the *miqweh* was filled in with debris and medium-sized stones. The stones of the Western Wall were not fit into the space of the *miqweh* but upon the debris filled in it. This is currently the first and the only known installation that runs right under one of the Temple Mount walls; hence, the debris and artifacts it contained are of utmost importance in dating the construction of this particular segment of the Temple Mount wall and Robinson's Arch. It is clear that the *miqweh* predates the Western Wall of the Temple Mount, and the date of the artifacts found in it provide a *terminus post quem* to the date of construction of this wall.

Seventeen bronze coins were retrieved from sifting the earthen fill from within the *miqweh*. All are small bronze *perutot*. For the present discussion, only the latest coins are important. These are four coins minted by the Roman procurator Valerius Gratus under Tiberius. The latest coins date to the year 17/18 CE (Shukron 2012: 19).

Three complete oil lamps found inside the *miqweh* provide supporting evidence for the dating of the construction of the segment of wall under Robinson's Arch. They are of the most common type of oil lamps at the later part of the Second Temple period (mid–1st century CE).

These belong to the type made of light brown-orange ware, fine-grained clay, well fired, wheel-made body, with a handmade nozzle attached to it, an arched outer outline and the typical signs of knife paring on its lower side. The nozzle carries clear traces of soot (Shukron 2012: Fig. 15).

This type of lamp was found in large quantities in strata in which traces of the Roman destruction were exposed, such as in the Burnt House in the Upper City of Jerusalem (Geva 2010: 128–129), in the Sicarii quarters at Masada during the Roman siege on the fort (Barag and Hershkovitz 1994: 24–53) and at Gamla (Adan-Bayewitz *et al.* 2008: 37–85), to name only the most significant locations.

From these stratigraphic and chronological considerations, one concludes that the wall under Robinson's Arch was constructed sometime during the 20s or 30s of the 1st century CE. It must have been one of the last constructed segments on the perimeter of the Temple Mount. The question is whether this is also the date of construction of the arch proper.

Architectural Considerations

The construction of the Temple Mount walls in the extension project required large numbers of skilled and unskilled workers, large-scale auxiliary works and equipment, such as roads, ramps, machinery, carts, cranes and the like, and a large supply of stone. One could have worked simultaneously on the entire circumference of the holy precinct—ca. 1600 m long—laying a single stone layer at a time all around, or alternatively, work could have been carried out simultaneously at a few spots, and a smaller segment could have been constructed in each from foundation to coping course, moving after its completion to construct a new segment. This seems to be a more economical way to work as it concentrates the auxiliary constructions and machinery at a few points, and does not spread them along a long line, or moving them constantly around the long perimeter. While the moving of workers is a relatively simple task, this is not the case with the auxiliary constructions and machinery. The authors have opted elsewhere for construction in segments (Reich and Baruch 2019: 158–164).

Herod extended the old *temenos* of the Temple Mount to the south, west and north. The old pre-Herodian eastern original wall is still visible, as well as the joint or "seam" with the new Herodian wall that extended it to the south. It is reasonable to suggest that at these two points, that is, the northeastern and the southeastern corners of the old *temenos* walls, the Herodian construction started, working from here to the Southern and the Northern Walls, and concluding the project by constructing the Western Wall, or at least the southern part of this Western Wall, in which Robinson's Arch is incorporated.

Above we presented the two "seams" that are visible on the sides of the arch. They are present in the wall down to Course G (inclusive). This implies that the Western Wall was constructed here in the following manner: first six stone courses of foundations, based upon bedrock (Courses U–P; Warren 1884: Pl. 29), were constructed, followed by eight courses of upper structure (Courses O–H). At this point in the construction, the accident occurred, and the first attempt at constructing Robinson's Arch failed. Construction of the wall continued, leaving a gap for a second attempt to construct the arch using a different method of scaffolding. Further on, the arch was constructed. Its southern side was adapted to a wall on its south and the vertical "seam" was created. On the northern side, a wider gap was left between the arch and the wall to the north, which had to be filled in with masonry, hence the double "seams."

Summing up the archaeological and historical data given above, we may conclude that Robinson's Arch was one of the latest elements constructed on the vast perimeter of the Temple Mount, in the second quarter of the 1st century CE, that is, half a century after Herod's death. The paving of the street which runs under it followed.

Destruction of the Arch

The destruction of this gigantic stone arch was an achievement in itself. Certainly, the keystones could not be extracted from it to cause the destruction, as the force required would have been extremely great, and no ancient machinery had the ability to do so. We actually do not know how the arch was destroyed. One possibility was to quarry out the keystones while supporting the gap with wooden logs, as it was created, and finally burning down the wood. The few seconds in which some 1600 tons of stone collapsed upon the paved street must have been a spectacular and traumatic sight (Fig. 27.32).

While there are currently no archaeological clues for a date more precise than 70 CE for the destruction of the Temple Mount walls, it seems that such clues do exist for the date of the destruction of Robinson's Arch. This topic has been discussed in the past, and a short note will do here (Reich and Billig 2003: 243–247; Reich 2009: 117–132).

It was observed that one of the handrail stones of the arch was found reshaped (Fig. 27.41), inscribed and reused as a Roman milestone. The inscription on the milestone bears the names of Vespasian and of Titus, the conqueror of Jerusalem. As the stone carries Titus's title as imperator, it points to the fact that the milestone was inscribed during Titus's principate (79–81 CE). Thus, at this time the arch was already in ruins, and worked stones were obtained from the pile of collapsed stones for secondary use.

It seems that the Roman army carried out some demolishing operations at the Temple Mount immediately following the capture of Jerusalem in 70 CE. We can only guess about the reason. It should be borne in mind that this large arch was extremely prominent in the urban landscape. It protruded from the high and long Western Wall of the Temple Mount, and it faced the Upper City, to be seen by many. Since single monumental arches were used by the Romans in Rome to commemorate their triumphs, it is not unlikely that the arch was destroyed only for its shape and size.[10]

In summary, Robinson's Arch, together with Wilson's Arch, were the largest arches, created from the largest stones, ever erected in Jerusalem and the Land of Israel. The erection of Robinson's Arch was a great engineering achievement. The remains that survived on-site point to difficulties in its construction, as well as to a solution to overcome these.

It seems that Robinson's Arch was erect and in use for a relatively short time. It was constructed toward the middle of the 1st century CE and ceased to be in use with the sack of Jerusalem in 70 CE, and was destroyed around the year 80 CE, making its time of use, altogether, a generation long.

Postscript

E. Mazar suggested that Robinson's Arch was approached by monumental staircases from three different directions. In addition to the accepted reconstruction of the staircase leading up to the arch from the south, she reconstructed an approach by means of a monumental staircase from the north, similar and symmetrical to the southern staircase. This idea was already suggested by Brian Lalor, who served as the B. Mazar expedition architect (Mazar 2020: 387). In addition, E. Mazar suggested that a third monumental staircase approached the arch from the west, descending from the Upper City toward the arch (Mazar 2020: 20, 48).

This, indeed, is a novel and daring idea, and Eilat Mazar should be thanked for presenting it. This major urban monument was almost certainly planned as she suggested. I doubt, however, if the plan was ever carried out and completed. I base my reservation on the fact that west of Robinson's Arch no large stone ashlars were found. These would certainly have been left behind if such a monumental edifice had been destroyed, like the stones exposed on the Herodian stone-paved street and south of the arch. These could have been taken away after the sack of Jerusalem by Rome and reused elsewhere, but alternatively, it is possible that they were never there, since the northern part of this approach was never constructed.

Unfortunately, E. Mazar did not present the remains of the suggested vaults to the north and to the west of Robinson's Arch in the common stone-by-stone detailed plan. There are several general photos for the northern vaults and staircase (Mazar 2020: 163–164, 166, 170–171, 174) and the same for the western vaults and staircase. A schematic plan of the entire monument was published (Mazar 2020: 51: red, and its derivatives in the following pages), which presents her reconstruction rather than the walls and stones as found. I find it difficult to navigate through the photographs and to detect the bases of the suggested northern and western vaults. It is expected that they would have left traces similar in magnitude to the bases of the southern walls of the vault (Mazar 2020:

---

[10] A fragmentary monumental inscription was discovered that points to a triumphal arch constructed in the vicinity of the Temple Mount (Grüll 2006: 183–200).

Figure 27.41: Lower part of a milestone bearing a Latin inscription, made of a handrail stone of the staircase leading up to Robinson's Arch.

131–150), and yet they do not meet this expectation. A proof of this is the fact that such a possibility did not spark the idea during the B. Mazar excavations.

As we said, it is not impossible that such a monumental approach was planned. It remains to be proved that it was carried out. As a small parallel, one can bring forward the so-called "eastern Robinson's Arch." There are traces of an arch, smaller than Robinson's Arch, on the eastern wall of the Herodian extension of the Temple Mount, close to the southeastern corner. Elsewhere it was demonstrated (Reich and Baruch 2014: 176–189) that this arch was never constructed. Charles Warren was seeking the foundations of its pier and came to negative results (Warren 1884: Pl. 18). This and other arguments clearly show that plans were changed. We believe that the ramp along the Southern Wall of the Temple Mount replaced the function of this arch and gate (see above). In the same sense, it is possible that the monumental staircase at the southwestern corner of the Temple Mount, which approaches and mounts Robinson's Arch, was carried out only in part.

Restoration of Ruined Southern Wall of Temple Mount After Destruction

The walls of the Temple Mount were destroyed by the Tenth Roman Legion *Fretensis* sometime after 70 CE.

The excavations along the Southern Wall of the Temple Mount demonstrated that most of the accumulated debris and architectural remains at the foot of the Southern Wall was the result of various construction and destruction operations that lasted until the Early Islamic period (7th–8th century CE). This accumulation, which reached the height of ca. 12 m, covered the lower courses of the Southern Wall, especially near its corners. On the other hand, between the Double Gate and the Triple Gate, the accumulation was only about 1 m in height.

Only a few building remains dating from the Umayyad period and onward have been unearthed in the excavations conducted in this area. Most of these remains have been exposed in the western part of the area and the amount diminishes gradually as one goes east along the wall. Some have attributed the reasons for this to modern excavations which may have used mechanical tools during the Jordanian rule over Jerusalem (Ritmeyer 2006: 101). However, comparing photographs from the 19th century with photographs from the days of the first excavations in the area, probably in the 1970s, indicates that only debris was removed and not built-up remains (see Chapter 2). This lack of building remains along the Southern Wall and particularly near the eastern part of the wall reinforces the idea that part of the city was not included in the built-up area of the city, probably as early as medieval times. This probably also had a bearing on the construction and restoration processes of the Southern Wall and its gates.[11]

In our review of the Southern Wall to its full length, we noted many differences in the nature of the construction of the ruined walls. This topic is discussed in detail in the work of E. Mazar, Shalev and Reuven (2011: Chapter 7). We have chosen to describe and discuss here mainly the stages of construction relating to the first restoration of the destroyed wall, in an attempt to establish the architectural context of these restorations and to estimate their date.

For the sake of the present discussion, we have chosen to describe the restoration of the Southern Wall in three sections:[12]

1. The wall between the Double Gate and the Triple Gate.

2. From the southwestern corner to the Double Gate.

3. From the Triple Gate to the southeastern corner.

It is difficult to make the stones speak and determine just when they were used. And yet, in relation to the dating of the walls of the Temple Mount, several attempts have been made that began with the pioneering work of Warren (1880: 161–166), especially with regard to the Temple Mount's Southern and Western Walls. With respect to the southwest corner of the compound, five types of building blocks were described (Warren and Conder 1884: 174–175). In our case, the two ancient types, Type 1 and Type 2,[13] are important: Type 1 refers to the original building blocks identified as Herodian ashlars with drafted margins. The stones of Type 2, as defined by Warren and Conder, date to the Roman-Byzantine period—between Hadrian and Justinian, that is, between the 2nd and 6th centuries CE—and are always laid on top of the Herodian courses and complement them. These stones clearly date after 70 CE and represent the restoration of the ruined walls of the Temple Mount. B. Mazar and M. Ben-Dov proposed to date the restoration of the breaches, that is, the use of Type 2 stones, to the Umayyad period (Mazar 1971: 4–5; Ben-Dov 1973: 78–79) and to relate it to the Umayyad building projects on the Temple Mount and the structures at the foot of it. E. Mazar, Shalev and Reuven (2011) also maintained this date, although their division into types of building blocks is much more detailed—and was associated with 23 different construction periods.

---

[11] For the history of the area south of the Temple Mount in light of the archaeological finds unearthed in the excavations of the Givᶜati Parking Lot, south of the Temple Mount, see Ben-Ami and Tchekhanovets 2020: 703–707.

[12] Similar to Mazar, Shalev and Reuven's (2011: 199–253) division of the wall. The gates in the Southern Wall—the Double Gate, the Triple Gate and the Single Gate—will be described separately.

[13] This typology is based on Warren and Conder's work in the Southern and Western Walls and therefore ignores the stones of the Eastern Wall, which represent, as is commonly accepted, the pre-Herodian phase of the Temple Mount complex (north of the so-called "seam").

Weksler-Bdolah, often contrary to other proposals, suggested that the restoration of the Temple Mount after its destruction in 70 CE was done in the Roman period—that is, the period of Aelia Capitolina—and as part of its construction as a Roman compound with a temple of Jupiter at its center (Weksler-Bdolah 2020: 119–123). The study by Burgoyne concentrated on the thorough and detailed documentation of the Eastern Wall, using pioneering methods of advanced documentation and photography. Six types of building blocks were classified in this study, ranging from the pre-Herodian structure to the Ottoman construction associated with the construction works of Sultan Suleiman the Magnificent (Burgoyne 2000: 483–486).

As far as we know, this section of the Southern Wall is the most ravaged among the sections along the wall as well as in comparison to the Western and Eastern Walls of the Temple Mount (Fig. 27.42). The destruction of the wall in this section was thorough, and it was dismantled to its full height down to the Grand Course, which is here the foundation course of the Southern Wall. In this strip of the wall, we identified two main sections, as follows:

1a. From the Double Gate eastward to a distance of 15.4 m.
1b. Continuing eastward to the Triple Gate to a distance of 49 m to the south lintel of the gate.

The first section (1a) is similar in its general character to the section from the southwest corner eastward to the Double Gate (see below), and therefore it can be suggested that, despite certain differences in the construction details, it was a single construction operation. This reconstruction can also be associated with the restoration or reconstruction of the Double Gate. On the other hand, the second section (1b) in this strip is built in a completely different manner which, in our opinion, indicates a different construction period. This also has implications for the very determination that the Temple Mount was restored from its ruins in one fell swoop.

Figure 27.42: Southern Wall of the Temple Mount between the Double Gate and the Triple Gate. Note the courses constructed above the Herodian Grand Course.

From the Double Gate Eastward

This section is 15.4 m long. Above it is the eastern part of the Al-Aqsa Mosque and the Mosque of Omar, which is adjacent to it from the east (Fig. 27.43). The stones that were used to restore the ruined wall were placed directly above the Grand Course. These are rectangular blocks of stone, of varying lengths, with an average height of ca. 1.05 m. This height is similar to the average height of the Herodian courses of the wall. The joints were plastered with a thin layer of binding material. This section of the Southern Wall bears the southern façade of the Al-Aqsa Mosque. Thus, it is possible to speculate and point to a possible chronological connection between the construction of the mosque in its first phase (as a stone building) and this construction of the ruined wall.

Continuing Eastward to the Triple Gate

As far as is known, the other northern face of the wall, inside the Temple Mount compound, has never been explored. The restoration of this section, and for a distance of ca. 17 m west of the Triple Gate, was carried out with ashlars with drafted margins and a prominent protrusion that were placed directly on top of the Grand Course of the wall. According to the style of the stones, it can be suggested, without the ability to be more precise about the dating, that this is a medieval

Figure 27.43: Southern Wall of the Temple Mount and the southern façade of the Al-Aqsa Mosque built on top of it, looking north (photo by S. Halevi).

construction, and that in the Middle Ages this section was rebuilt or, alternatively, that it remained ruptured and was never completed at least until then (Figs. 27.44–45).

From the Southwestern Corner to the Double Gate

This section of the Southern Wall now supports the western part of the Al-Aqsa Mosque and other buildings built along it to the west, mainly in the Middle Ages and the Ottoman period. This section is the clearest representation of the restoration of the walls after their destruction at the end of the Second Temple period. Our description is given from west to east: First, two rows of stones were laid upon the extant Herodian masonry, equal in height to the Herodian course (ca. 1.05 m on average) and later to Courses C–E according to Warren's numbering. Course B and above were shorter courses, which retreated a bit internally from the wall face (Fig. 27.46).

The stones used to rehabilitate this section are *meleke* or *mizzi hilu*-type stones; a thick yellowish-brown patina covers their faces, and they are usually well and finely chiseled (Fig. 27.47). No stones with drafted margins were found among the stones used for the restoration of the walls. Similar

Figure 27.44: The Double Gate. Shown are the stone blocks of the reconstruction on top of the Grand Course (photo by S. Halevi).

Figure 27.45: Southern Wall, looking northwest.

to the manner in which the Herodian stones were laid, here too the stones were laid in a constant retreat inward—ca. 2 cm for each course. Small stones were inserted in the joints between the stones, and the joints were then lightly pointed.

From the Triple Gate Eastward to the Temple Mount's Southeastern Corner

On the northern face of the wall in this section and in the inner part of the complex, there is an underground architectural space known as Solomon's Stables. The floor level here is more or less the same as the level of the Triple Gate's threshold.

We suggest that the restoration of the breaches in the Southern Wall in this section was carried out simultaneously with the complete construction of Solomon's Stables, and probably in place of an earlier Herodian underground space (Gibson and Jacobson 1996: 179–259).

The physical condition of the restored section of the walls of the Temple Mount is very poor; patches of repair are visible (Chapter 34). Above the Herodian building block, one can see courses of building stones that are similar in size to those of the Herodian stones, lacking drafted margins and central flat bosses; however, their construction is less meticulous than the Herodian construction (Fig. 27.42). The joints between the stones were gently pointed, and the lines of pointing are visible. Similar to the Herodian construction, these stones were also given a constant inward retreat of about 2 cm for each course. Above these courses—which in our opinion represent the first restoration of the complex from its ruins—the walls were built of smaller stones, following the principle of three courses equaling in height the height of one Herodian course.

Another point of reference for the restoration of the ruined walls is the southeastern corner of the Temple Mount (Figs. 27.48–49). In this area, the original Herodian wall was preserved to the maximal height, or, as put by Warren and Conder: "This is probably the so-called 'pinnacle of the Temple,' spoken of by the Bordeaux Pilgrim and others" (Warren and Conder 1984: 159).

A stone cornice is placed at the top of the Herodian stones (Figs. 27.50–51). This cornice was also documented and visible in the Eastern Wall of the Temple Mount compound (Burgoyne 2000: 491). Since the cornice also runs over a construction that is not Herodian but later, it certainly cannot be Herodian.

As detailed below, it turns out that the level of the cornice in the southeast corner of the Temple Mount compound is similar to the level of the cornice above the Double Gate. We therefore propose that both cornices, i.e., that of the southeastern corner and that of the Double Gate, are part of a single ornamental system built on one occasion, as part of an operation aimed at restoring the breaches (as mentioned above, the Double Gate is discussed separately).

Figure 27.46: Slight grading between the stone layers at the point of contact between the Herodian ashlars where the breach was restored.

Figure 27.47: The western part of the Southern Wall, looking north (photo by S. Halevi).

Figure 27.48: Southeastern corner of the Temple Mount, looking northwest. Note the height to which the Herodian masonry survived, with a cornice on top (photo by S. Halevi).

Figure 27.49: Southeastern corner of the Temple Mount, looking northwest. Note the arrow indicating height to which the Herodian masonry survived, with a cornice on top. Note, also, the cubicle and window above the cornice. Both are no longer extant.

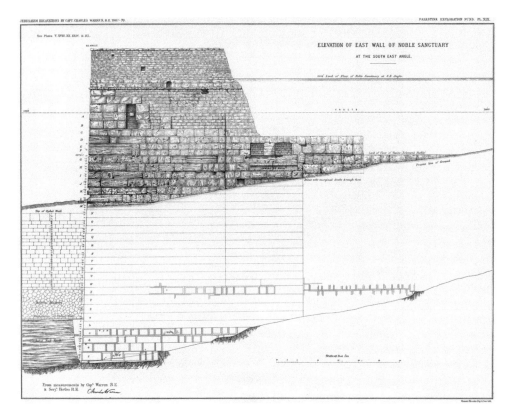

Figure 27.50: Southeastern corner of the Temple Mount, looking west. Note stone cornice on top of the Herodian courses (Warren 1884: Pl. XIX).

CONCLUSIONS

Our excavations in the area near the southeastern corner of the Temple Mount compound revealed remains, the latest of which are dated to the end of the Byzantine period. An analysis of the finds and the condition of the surface shows that the accumulation of remains in this area and at least up to the Byzantine period refers only to the Herodian courses of the wall and that they do not cover or abut the later stages of restoration.

As regards the excavations conducted near the southwestern corner, the picture is more complex. A retrospective examination of Mazar and Ben-Dov's excavations and especially the descriptions of the section made by them south of the Temple Mount (Mazar 1971: 4, Fig. 5; Ben-Dov 1971) shows that the head of this section was sealed by a narrow street separating the Southern Wall and Umayyad Building II (Fig. 27.52). The pavement is made of smoothed flagstones of various sizes, bound together by a chalky material. The southern edge of the street undoubtedly relates to a wide threshold installed at the top of the Umayyad building, which opens directly onto the street. It is conceivable that this street functioned in the context of Umayyad Building II and therefore also dates to the period of its construction. On the other hand, the northern edge of the street abuts the stones of the Southern Wall: on the western side/edge of the street, it abuts the upper part of the Herodian course of the Temple Mount (Courses K and J, Fig. 27.53).

However, in its route sloping up to the east—toward the Double Gate—the pavement stones abut the Type 2 courses of the wall defined by Warren and Conder, or Course 11 as defined by B. Mazar (1971: 4, Fig. 5) and cover parts of them. This situation, where the Umayyad Street covers the Type 2 courses of the wall, indicates that the street postdates them, at least technically, and on the other hand, the street undoubtedly connects and refers to the monumental structure south of it. Hence, the restoration of the wall was done prior to the construction of the street and the monumental structure that was opened to it, at least technically, as mentioned above.

The above refers to the level of the street that seals the section, but what about the accumulation below the street's pavement? The remains of the Herodian Street built at the foot of the Southern Wall were exposed at the bottom of the section. Between these two, that is, between the street that seals the section and the components of the Herodian Street below, fills and layers were documented that indicate an activity later than the system associated with the Herodian street and preceding the Umayyad street. For the most part, and at least according to the archaeological sections excavated by Mazar and Ben-Dov and earlier by Warren, it appears that this accumulation was made entirely adjacent to Type 1 stones (the Herodian stones). Therefore, since the levels of soils and floors documented by Mazar and Ben-Dov and which covered parts of the Herodian Wall included only pre-Umayyad finds and, according to their reports, at least until the end of the Byzantine period, the excavators' conclusions can be adopted that in the area near Robinson's Arch, intensive activity also took place after the destruction of the walls in 70 CE and at least until the Byzantine period.

From this state of affairs, it can be concluded that the accumulation of remains—between the time of the destruction of the walls and at least until the end of the Byzantine period—indicates that after the destruction of the Temple no special importance was given to leaving the walls clean and exposed, and we believe that the results of our excavations near this part of the Temple's walls reflect this notion. On the other hand, only with the restoration of the breaches in the wall and its gates was the symbolic importance restored to the complex, including the idea of leaving the walls exposed at least during the first restoration period.

Back to the question of the date of the restoration of the breaches: Earlier we pointed out that parts of the Southern Wall, especially in the area between the two gates, were completely destroyed by the Roman army, and in our opinion this was done deliberately, as a symbolic act of destroying the systems of entrance to the Temple for the Jewish pilgrims.

Hence, the restoration work carried out in the southern part of the Temple Mount, at least on the technical side, preceded the construction work on the Temple Mount itself. In other words, if indeed it was a construction project of the Umayyad rulers, as proposed in the past, then at least from the engineering and technical aspects this restoration operation of the walls preceded the construction of the buildings in the inner part of the complex, i.e., the Al-Aqsa Mosque (the construction of which is customarily dated to the years 701–705 CE), the Double Gate, the Triple Gate, as well as Solomon's Stables—and as proposed, also preceded the construction of the monumental building south of the Temple Mount (Building II).

In conclusion, there is reason to believe that the restoration of the breaches in the walls of the Temple Mount was carried out by the Umayyad Caliphate. We accept the proposal that this was in fact the first construction operation that the rulers of this caliphate undertook in Jerusalem under their rule. However, in our opinion, this operation of restoring the breaches actually began and was even completed before the construction of the buildings within the Temple Mount proper, as well as those rulers' construction operations outside the compound.

Figure 27.51: Southeastern corner of the Temple Mount, cornice on top of the Herodian masonry (photo by Y. Baruch).

Figure 27.52: The street at the foot of the Southern Wall, covering the Type 2 courses of the Wall (photo by Y. Baruch).

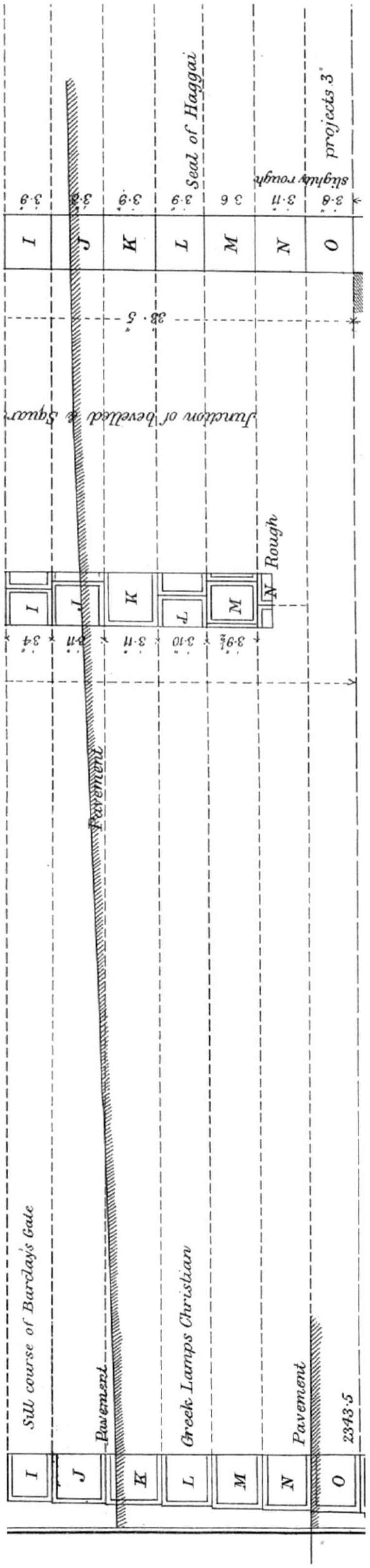

Figure 27.53: Cross-section of the street covering Courses K and J (Warren 1884: Pl XXVII, part).

REFERENCES

Abdul Massih, J. 2014. Von den Steinbrüchen zu den Tempeln. In: Van Ess, M. and Rheidt, K., eds. *Baalbek— Heliopolis, 10000 Jahre Stadtgeschichte.* Darmstadt: 52–57.

Adam, J.P. 1977. A propos du trilithon de Baalbek. Le transport et la mise en œuvre megaliths. *Syria* 54(1/2): 31–63.

Adam, J.P. 1994. *Roman Building: Materials and Techniques.* London.

Adan-Bayewitz, D., Asaro, F., Wieder, M. and Giauque, R.D. 2008. Preferential Distribution of Lamps from the Jerusalem Area in the Late Second Temple Period (Late First Century B.C.E.–70 C.E.). *BASOR* 350: 37–85.

Bahat, D. 2013. *The Jerusalem Western Wall Tunnel.* Jerusalem.

Barag, D. and Hershkovitz, M. 1994. Lamps from Masada. In: Aviram, J., Foerster, G. and Netzer, E., eds. *Masada IV: The Yigael Yadin Excavations 1963–1965, Final Reports.* Jerusalem: 1–147.

Ben-Ami, D. and Tchekhanovets, Y. 2020. *Jerusalem: Excavations in the Tyropoeon Valley (Giv'ati Parking Lot),* Vol. 2: *The Byzantine and Early Islamic Periods.* Part 2: *Strata IV–I: The Early Islamic Period* (IAA Reports 66/2). Jerusalem.

Ben-Dov, M. 1971. The Omayyad Structure near the Temple Mount. In: Mazar, B. *The Excavations in the Old City of Jerusalem near the Temple Mount: Preliminary Report of the Second and Third Seasons, 1969–1970.* Jerusalem.

Ben-Dov, M. 1973. Building Techniques in the Omayyad Palace near the Temple Mount, Jerusalem. *Eretz-Israel* 11 (Immanuel Dunayevsky Volume): 75–91 (Hebrew, English abstract: 24–25).

Burgoyne, M.H. 2000. The East Wall of the Haram Al-Sharif: A Note on Its Archaeological Potential. In: Auld, S. and Hillenbrand, R., eds. *Ottoman Jerusalem: The Living City, 1517–1917.* Jerusalem: 479–491.

CIIP: Cotton, H.M., Di Segni, L., Eck, W., Isaac, B., Kushnir-Stein, A., Misgav, H., Price, J., Roll, I. and Yardeni, A. 2010. *Corpus Inscriptionum Iudaeae/Palaestinae,* Vol. 1: *Jerusalem,* Part 1: *1–704.* Berlin and New York.

Geva, H. 2010. Early Roman Pottery. In: Geva, H., ed. *Jewish Quarter Excavations in the Old City of Jerusalem, Conducted by Nahman Avigad, 1969–1982,* Vol. 4: *The Burnt House of Area B and Other Studies, Final Report.* Jerusalem: 118–153.

Gibson, S. 2014. The Pilaster Enclosure Wall of the Temple Mount in Jerusalem. In: Baruch, E. and Faust, A., eds. *New Studies on Jerusalem* 20. Ramat Gan: 17–39.

Gibson, S. and Jacobson, D.M. 1996. *Below the Temple Mount in Jerusalem: A Sourcebook on the Cistern, Subterranean Compartments and Conduits of the Haram al-Sharif* (BAR International Series 637). Oxford.

Gilad, J. 2014. Roman First Century CE Technology, The Tower Crane, Engineering Analysis and Proposed Reconstruction (M.A. thesis, University of Haifa). Haifa (Hebrew).

Gockel, B. 1986. Bilddokumente. In: *Wasserversorgung im Antiken Rom, Herausgeber Frontinus Geselschaft.* Munich: 158–161.

Goren, H. 2020. *"The Loss of a Minute Is Just So Much Loss of Life": Edward Robinson and Eli Smith in the Holy Land* (Studia Traditionis Theologiae 39). Turnhout.

Grüll, T. 2006. A Fragment of a Monumental Roman Inscription at the Islamic Museum of the Haram ash-Sharif, Jerusalem. *Israel Exploration Journal* 56: 183–200.

Jacobson, D.M. 2000. Decorative Drafted-Margin Masonry in Jerusalem and Hebron and Its Relations. *Levant* 32: 135–154.

Jol, H.M., Bauman, P. and Bahat, D. 2013. Looking into the Western Wall, Jerusalem, Israel. In: Bahat, D., ed. *The Jerusalem Western Wall Tunnel.* Jerusalem: 395–400.

Kropp, A. and Lohmann, D. 2011. "Master, Look at the Size of Those Stones! Look at the Size of Those Buildings!" Analogies in Construction Techniques Between the Temples at Heliopolis (Baalbek) and Jerusalem. *Levant* 43: 38–50.

Levanon, A. 1968. *Report on Electrical Resistivity Carried out on the Southern Wall of the Temple Mount, Jerusalem,* Job 68/635גה/, File No. 484, The Geophysical Institute of Israel, Ministry of Labour, Public Works Department. Azor (Hebrew).

Mader, A.E. 1957. *Mambre: Die Ergebnisse der Ausgrabungen im heiligen Bezirk, Ramet el-Halil in Südpalästina 1926–1928.* Freiburg im Breisgau.

Magen, I. 1993. Mamre. In: Stern, E., ed. *The New Encyclopedia of Archaeological Excavations in the Holy Land.* Jerusalem: 939–942.

Mazar, B. 1969. The Excavations in the Old City of Jerusalem. *Eretz-Israel* 9 (William Foxwell Albright Memorial Volume): 161–174 (Hebrew).

Mazar, B. 1971. The Excavations in the Old City of Jerusalem near the Temple Mount—Second Preliminary Report, 1969–70 Seasons. *Eretz-Israel* 10: 1–34 (Hebrew).

Mazar, E. 2011. *The Walls of the Temple Mount.* Jerusalem.

Mazar, E. 2020. *Over the Crossroads of Time: Jerusalem's Temple Mount Monumental Staircase as Revealed in Benjamin Mazar's Excavations (1968–1978).* Jerusalem.

Mazar, E., Shalev, Y. and Reuven, P. 2011. *The Southern Wall and the Western Wall, Chronological Maps.* In: Mazar, E., ed. *The Walls of the Temple Mount.* Jerusalem: 257–283.

Reich, R. 2000. Measuring Tools in the Service of Architects and Masons in Antiquity. In: Rimon, O., ed. *Measuring and Weighing in Ancient Times* (Hecht Museum Catalogue). Haifa: 61*–67* (English, Hebrew version: 93–100).

Reich, R. 2009. The Roman Destruction of Jerusalem in 70 CE, Flavius Josephus' Account and the Archaeological Record. In: Thiessen, G., Steymans, H.U., Ostermann, S., Schmidt, K.M. and Moresino-Zipper, A., eds. *Jerusalem und die Länder, Max Kuechler Festschrift.* Göttingen: 117–132.

Reich, R. 2015. The Construction and Destruction of Robinson's Arch. *Eretz-Israel* 31: 398–407 (Hebrew).

Reich, R. and Baruch, Y. 2017. On Expansion of the Temple Mount in the Late Second Temple Period. *Cathedra* 164: 7–24 (Hebrew).

Reich, R. and Baruch, Y. 2019. The Herodian Temple Mount in Jerusalem: A Few Remarks on its Construction and Appearance. In: Eisenberg, M. and Ovadiah, A., eds. *Cornucopia: Studies in Honor of Arthur Segal* (Archaeologica 180). Rome: 157–169.

Reich, R. and Baruch, Y. 2020. A Note on the Date of the Stone Collapse at the Western Wall of the Temple Mount. *Israel Exploration Journal* 70: 99–105.

Reich, R. and Billig, Y. 2000. Excavations near the Temple Mount and Robinson's Arch, 1994–1996; Appendix: A Group of Theater Seats from Jerusalem. In: Geva, H., ed. *Ancient Jerusalem Revealed, Reprinted and Expanded Edition.* Jerusalem: 340–352.

Reich, R. and Billig, Y. 2003. Another Flavian Latin Inscription from the Excavations near the Temple Mount, Jerusalem, ʿAtiqot 44: 243–247.

Reich, R. and Shukron, E. 2011. Excavations at Robinson's Arch 2011: From the Paved Street to Natural Rock. In: Baruch, E., Levi-Reifer, A. and Faust, A., eds. *New Studies on Jerusalem* 17. Ramat Gan: 219–238 (Hebrew; English abstract: 56*–57*).

Reidinger, E.F. 2004. The Temple Mount Platform in Jerusalem from Solomon to Herod: An Archaeological Re-Examination. *Assaph* 9: 1–64.

Ritmeyer, L. 2006. *The Quest: Revealing the Temple Mount in Jerusalem.* Jerusalem.

Shukron, E. 2012. Did Herod Build the Foundations of the Western Wall? In: Meiron, E., ed. *City of David: Studies of Ancient Jerusalem* 7. Jerusalem: 15–30 (Hebrew).

Shukron, E. and Reich, R. 2011. The Second Temple Period Central Drainage Channel in Jerusalem—Upon the Completion of the Unearthing of its Southern Part in 2011. In: Meiron, E., ed. *City of David: Studies of Ancient Jerusalem* 6. Jerusalem: 67–95.

Sion, O., Sasson, A., Zilberbod, I. and Rapuano, Y. 2011. Quarries and Quarrying Methods in the Second Temple Period in the North of Jerusalem. *Judea and Samaria Studies* 20: 39–48 (Hebrew).

Szanton, N., Hagbi, M., Uziel, J. and Ariel, D.T. 2019. Pontius Pilate in Jerusalem: The Monumental Street from the Siloam Pool to the Temple Mount. *Tel Aviv* 46: 147–166.

Uziel, J., Lieberman, T. and Solomon, A. 2017. Two Years of Excavations Beneath Wilson's Arch: New Discoveries and Ponderings. In: Gadot, Y., Zelinger, Y., Cytryn-Silverman, K. and Uziel, J., eds. *New Studies in the Archaeology of Jerusalem and Its Region* 11. Jerusalem: 239–261 (Hebrew).

Vincent, L.H., Mackay, E.J.H. and Abel, F.M. 1923. *Hébron, le Haram el-Khalil, sepulture des Patriarches.* Paris.

Warren, C. 1880. Notes on Colonel Wilson's Paper on the Masonry of the Haram Wall. *Palestine Exploration Fund Quarterly Statement* 12(2): 159–166.

Warren, C. 1884. *Plans, Elevations, Sections, etc. Shewing the Results of the Excavations at Jerusalem, 1867–70, Executed for the Committee of the Palestine Exploration Fund*. London.

Warren, C. and Conder, C.R. 1884. *The Survey of Western Palestine: Jerusalem*. London.

Warszawski, A. and Peretz, A. 1992. Building the Temple Mount: Organization and Execution. *Cathedra* 66: 3–46 (Hebrew).

Weksler-Bdolah, S. 2017. A Cache of Iron Quarrying Tools from Excavations near Jerusalem's Third Wall. ʿ*Atiqot* 88: 1–8 (Hebrew; English abstract: 153–154).

Weksler-Bdolah, S. 2020. *Aelia Capitolina—Jerusalem in the Roman Period in Light of Archaeological Research* (Mnemosyne Supplements 432). Leiden and Boston.

Wilson, C.W. 1865. *Ordnance Survey of Jerusalem*. London.

CHAPTER 28

SCULPTURAL DECORATION OF THE FAÇADE OF THE DOUBLE GATE: A NEW STYLISTIC APPROACH

Svetlana Tarkhanova

The historical, religious, architectural and artistic aspects of the Double Gate, located in the Southern Wall of the Temple Mount, have attracted the attention of scholars since the late 19th century, and a considerable number of publications have been devoted to its dating and detail (Fig. 28.1).[1] Scholars are in general agreement that the architectural-constructional framework of the façade of the gate, its monumental threshold, jambs and lintels with the two relieving arches over them built of large and delicately carved ashlars with drafted margins and voussoirs, are in a recognizable architectural style known from other Herodian monuments and are therefore in a Herodian/Early Roman style. In its initial phase, the gate was not decorated sculpturally; if it had been, there would have been lining on the sides of the doorways (Gibson and Jacobson 1996: 258).

The dating of the sculptural decoration of the façade, which includes the spring course (cornice) over the relieving arches and two archivolts over the doorways, is not so obvious and needs greater discussion. Two main theories have been proposed. According to the first, the Double Gate was restored during the Byzantine period. Most of the early architectural and decorative renovation of the gate was related to the activity of Empress Eudocia during her presence in Jerusalem (mid-second half of the 5th century CE; Vincent and Abel 1914–1926: 910–911). A more widely accepted opinion connected the decoration of the gate to the erection of the Nea Church during the reign of Emperor Justinian (530s CE; Lewis 1888: 96; Vogüé 1864: 12, 64–68, Figs. 10, 36–38, Pls. V–XII) (Fig. 28.2).[2] Dating of the renovation of the gate to the 6th century CE was supported by the initial proposal that the Nea Church was built on the Temple Mount (at the spot now occupied by the Al-Aqsa Mosque), and the entrance to it was through the Double Gate. Thus, when the location of the Nea Church was revealed to be elsewhere, in close vicinity to the Temple Mount (Avigad 1970), the theory of 6th-century phasing of the Double Gate was rejected as untenable; there was no need for the gate to lead to the allegedly deserted Temple Mount (Avi-Yonah 1954: 53). As a compromise between the stylistic impressions and historical testimonies, the restoration of the Double Gate was ascribed to the time of Emperor Heraclius, to the days subsequent to the return of the True Cross to

---

[1]   The most extensive publications are those of Gibson (Gibson and Jacobson 1996: 235–282) and E. Mazar (Mazar *et al.* 2011: 226–238). All known historical sources, references and scientific research work ever applied to the Double Gate, as well as their plans, drawings and photos, have now been assembled. The Mazar publication presents meticulous surveys and measurements conducted at the site and contains the complete plan and drawing of the façade (Mazar *et al.* 2011: 227, Fig. 6.4.1; 233; Fig. 6.4.12). The primary difficulty with the material is the inability to correlate the observations of several parts of the Double Gate, which are blocked and separated by later architectural additions (Khunthaniya Tower) from their outer side. Some important and rare archive photos of the exterior of the Double gate belong to the Library of Congress in Washington and are applicable online (URL: https://jcpa.org/secrets-under-the-al-aqsa-mosque-a-photographic-essay/).

[2]   The drawings of the Double Gate and the anticipated restoration of their archivolts presented in the early publications contain many discrepancies; for the analysis, therefore, only photographic materials were used.

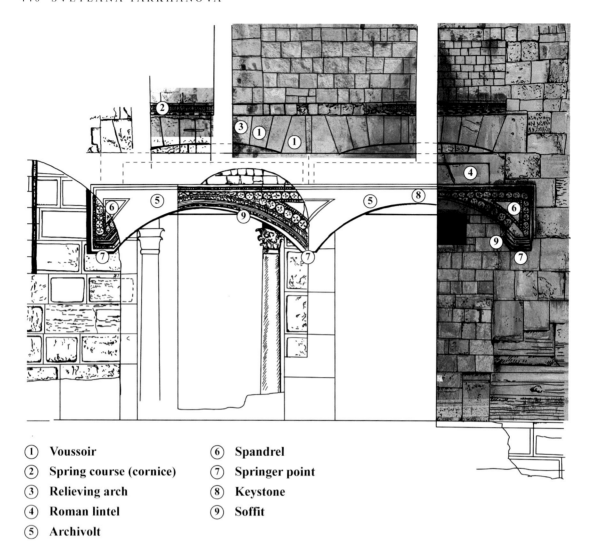

① **Voussoir**   ⑥ **Spandrel**

② **Spring course (cornice)**   ⑦ **Springer point**

③ **Relieving arch**   ⑧ **Keystone**

④ **Roman lintel**   ⑨ **Soffit**

⑤ **Archivolt**

Figure 28.1: Drawing of the Southern Wall of the Temple Mount with the Double Gate behind the Khatiniyya Tower. Plan (drawing by A. Yoffe-Pikovsky after Mazar 2011: 233, Figure 28. 6.4.12).

Jerusalem (after 629/630 CE; Creswell 1969: 381–389, 465). Wilkinson characterized the decoration of the Double Gate as Coptic and explained its appearance in Jerusalem by the presence of workmen from Egypt at the time of Patriarch Modestus (after 638 CE; Wilkinson 1987: 10). Talgam shortly referred to the reliefs of the Double Gate as the expression of the "Byzantine-Classical tradition in Syria and Palestine during the 7th–8th centuries" (Talgam 2004: 36).

Another group of scholars proposed that the sculptural decoration appeared during the reign of Caliph Abd al-Malik (685–705 CE). This theory was first proposed by Watzinger (1935: 115) and then Hamilton (1947: 68). The dating was supported by Rosen-Ayalon (1989: 42–45), Ben-Dov (Ben-Dov and Friedman 1982: 286–288), Burgoyne (1992: 110) and Gibson (Gibson and Jacobson 1996: 256, 258). As a result of a detailed article by Shani and Chen devoted to the stylistic analysis of the sculptural decoration of the Double Gate, mainly of its inner part (Shani and Chen 2001), there has been almost complete scholarly acceptance regarding the Umayyad phasing of the restoration (see Mazar *et al.* 2011: 226–238; Bahat 2020: 82–86).

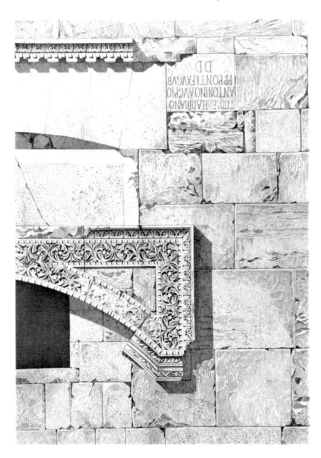

Figure 28.2: General drawing of the eastern section of the Double Gate. Note the discrepancies and inaccuracies in the details: the egg-and-dart pattern on the spandrel is replaced by a lotus-palmette motif; the sequence of the decorated astragali on the intrados and the impost are also confused (Vogüé 1864: Plate V).

It might be concluded from the short overview above that while discrepancies between stylistic observations and historical testimonies often invalidated one date or another, the actual point in time for the construction of the Double Gate has gradually shifted forward from the 5th to the 8th century CE. It should also be emphasized that the dating of the façade decoration to any period was always based only on partial stylistic analysis (mainly on the frieze with the "inhabited scrolls" pattern) without the overall research of all the peculiarities. The aim of this article is to provide consistent analysis of the order and stylistic peculiarities of the sculptural decoration of the façade together with the consequent dating.

THE DOUBLE GATE IN COMPARISON TO THE GOLDEN GATE: A BRIEF ARCHITECTURAL ANALYSIS

There are several aspects of the architecture of the Double Gate that should be treated individually. First, there are several mismatches between the Herodian/Roman architectural-constructional framework and its later sculptural decoration (Figs. 28.1, 28.3–28.4). The cornice as well as the archivolts with the spandrels are not connected to the masonry of the gateways structurally, so their role is not constructive but purely decorative. The cornice was incorporated over the relieving arches rather accurately (Figs. 28.5–28.7), while the archivolts were fixed over the surface of the jambs and lintels more carelessly and fixed by means of clamps. Though a major part of the gate is blocked by later walls, it seems that two archivolts attached to the Herodian lintels were symmetrical.

Figure 28.3: General view of the eastern section of the eastern archivolt and the cornice above it (photo by H. Shkolnik).

Figure 28.4: Eastern archivolt attached to the Herodian/Early Roman lintel. Note that it is not connected to the masonry structurally, but was attached to it (photo by H. Shkolnik).

Figure 28.5: An uninterrupted line of the cornice over the large, well-carved voussoirs of the Roman relieving arches. The cornice over the western doorway is severely eroded. Its stones were replaced by plain masonry of the same scale. The photo was taken from the roof of Khatiniyya Tower (photo by D. Czitron and Y. Baruch. Courtesy of the Israel Antiquities Authority).

Figure 28.6: The cornice over the eastern doorway (photo by D. Czitron and Y. Baruch. Courtesy of the Israel Antiquities Authority).

Figure 28.7: Cornice over the eastern section of the eastern doorway (photo courtesy of the Israel Antiquities Authority Archive, British Mandate Scientific Record Files [SRF_79(172/172)]).

The eastern spandrel of the eastern archivolt was not well attached to the wall and juts slightly forward. The soffits and some of the other decorative elements of the eastern archivolt were considerably chiseled so that the span of the arch was widened and raised. Some of the ashlars and voussoirs of the archivolt and spandrel are not in their original places: their upper parts were chiseled so the stones could be raised. I assume these changes were connected to the phase when the passageway was blocked with the later wall built of small ashlars. A window was inserted in the upper part of this wall, just below the archivolt, so that the complete archivolt blocks it. This explains the odd proportions of the eastern end of the eastern archivolt, which I suppose was originally symmetrical with its western end and symmetrical with the entire western archivolt and its spandrels. The western archivolt is much better preserved since the doorway was not blocked, though it went out of its original use because of the abutting Khatiniyya Tower (Mazar *et al.* 2011: 228, Fig. 6.4.2).

From these observations, it may be concluded that the archivolts and the cornice were not manufactured especially for the doorways of the gate but were reused for its decoration as *spolia* (secondary used details). Thus, the execution of these elements and their affixing to the façade belonged to two different phases, while their genesis is from another monumental edifice. Is it possible to highlight these phases and the initial architectural origin of the sculptural elements?

It has been observed (see publications mentioned above) that the sculptural decoration of the Double and Golden Gates is similar. Some of the decorative patterns of the moldings are identical (Wilkinson 1987: 11, Fig. 7; 12, Fig. 9), but the general architectural forms and the sequence in which the moldings are combined are different in many ways (Table 28.1). In the Double Gate, the upper parts of the semicircular archivolts are joined by a straight molded line and flanked by lateral triangular spandrels. The junction of the archivolts is inapplicable because of the later abutting walls of the tower so it is impossible to conclude whether they were originally integral or artificially attached to each other. The soffits of the archivolts in parts that were not chiseled preserved the decorative floral elements (Mazar *et al.* 2011: 232, Fig. 6.4.10), so the pilasters with the caps were not implied under them. The thickness of the archivolts is inconsiderable, the rear facets seem to be undecorated, and the archivolts were therefore initially manufactured as a decorative application over the walls.

In the Golden Gate, the frontal and rear façades are adorned with double semicircular arches joined in the center and flanked by the lateral horizontal shoulders on both sides instead of spandrels (Mazar *et al.* 2011: 162–170). In the interior, the wall is decorated with the straight entablature with protrusions/imposts for pilaster caps below (Fig. 28.8). The spans and the rises of the semicircular arches in the Golden Gate (4 m wide, ca. 1.8 m high)[3] and segmental archivolts of the Double one (ca. 6.4 m wide, 1.2 m high) are not equal, so from the architectural point of view, they are structurally different. The pilaster caps used below the entablature and shoulders of the arches in the Golden Gate do not fit each other in scale and style.

Due to the stylistic similarity, the entablature and arches from both gates were manufactured at the same time in one workshop. My assumption is that in both gates the details were in secondary use, deriving from one workshop or even one common building with lavishly decorated arcades and pilastered walls. By the architectural forms of these elements, it might be another monumental gate with several arcuated passages, a civil basilica, a church in the shape of a basilica with several apses, hexa- or octagon with an inner circumference of arches, a multi-apsidal building (tetra-, hexa- or octaconch), etc. The shape of the monolithic archivolts with the spandrels is rarely used in Classical architectural edifices. For parallel, the Triumphal Arch of Constantine the Great in Rome can be mentioned (Wilson Jones 2000: 51, Fig. 1). The shape of monolithic arches with spandrels is attested in liturgical furnishings such as ciboria/canopies of the Byzantine period (Niewöhner 2021: 102, Fig. 266 [from Lycia, Museum Antalya]; 138, Fig. 366 [Museum Burdur in Pisidia]). A decorated spandrel of a small arch was revealed in the Alacahisar Church in Lycia (Harrison 1963: 147–148, Pl. XLIIIf). The reconstruction of this hypothetical architectural edifice is a challenge for further investigations.

---

[3]   Measurements taken by the author from IAA Archive photos, British Mandate Scientific Record Files (SRF_79(172 172) and drawings of Balogh (Mazar *et al.* 2011: 162, Fig. 5.2.1; 227, Fig. 6.4.1).

Table 28.1: Comparative Table of the Similar Architectural Elements of Double and Golden Gates

	Double Gate	Golden Gate
Architectural elements	Double segmental archivolts with spandrels (exterior)	Double semicircular arches with lateral shoulders (exterior);
		Straight entablature with imposts (interior)
Span of archivolt/arch	6.4 m wide	4 m wide
Rise of archivolt/arch	1.2 m high	1.8 m high

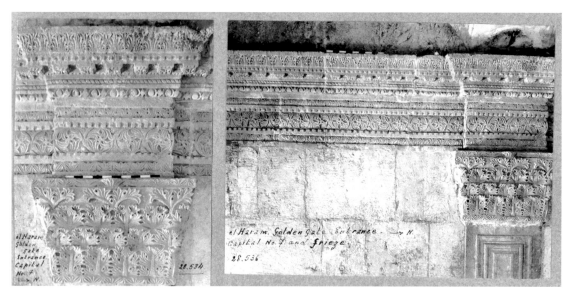

Figure 28.8: Fragment of the interior decoration of the Golden Gate (photo courtesy of the Israel Antiquities Authority Archive, British Mandate Scientific Record Files (SRF_89[151/150])).

DECORATION OF THE FAÇADE OF THE DOUBLE GATE

The consistent analysis of the cornice and archivolts of the Double Gate will include three main features: (1) order morphology; (2) decorative patterns; (3) style of sculpting. However, before proceeding with this three-stepped approach, there is a need for a short excurse into the Classical Roman tradition, and its further development is necessary in order to evaluate the features from a proper perspective.

The sculptural decoration of the façade is deeply rooted in the Roman tradition. The Roman entablatures manufactured from marble or limestone showed stable conformity throughout the territories of the Empire and its provenances. There are many samples of Roman entablatures in the Land of Israel, including Beth She'an, Kedesh, Omrit, Hippos-Sussita and Jerusalem[4] (Ovadiah and Turnheim 1994; Turnheim 1996: 122–127), which are comprised of canonical moldings with minor variability. The entablatures consisted of two blocks: cornice with bed molding and architrave. The

---

[4] A Classical Roman cornice (Hadrianic?) (Coüasnon 1974: Pl. 22) was reused in the façade of the Holy Sepulchre.

cornice with bed molding usually included[5] cyma with anthemion adorned by palmetto/acanthus leaves, astragalus with a bead-and-reel pattern, corona with tongues (short flutes), s-shaped modillions and coffers framed by a narrow band of egg-and-darts, Lesbian cyma, astragalus with twisted rope pattern, a row of dentils, and egg-and-dart pattern (Fig. 28.9). The architrave was decorated by convex frieze, crowning and three receding fasciae with astragali between them (adorned with bead-and-reel or egg-and-dart patterns, depending on the local traditions) (Fig. 28.10). During the Early Byzantine period, this abundant collection of moldings was considerably altered, simplified and reduced (Turnheim 1996: 122–124; Niewöhner 2017). The process of simplification and deviation from Classical conventions progressed during the Late Byzantine and Early Islamic periods, especially during and after the 8th century CE (Talgam 2004: 73–78), so that the order morphology was severely blurred. Though the Umayyad art was heterogeneous even in the geographically and chronologically close monuments (for example, the palaces of Khirbet al-Mafjar, Mshatta, Qasr al-Hayr), they followed some common stylistic tendencies, which implied the disturbance of the proportions between the order elements in favor of a purely ornamental approach, geometrization and overall lattice-like covering of the surface (Talgam 2004: 73–97). What place did the decorative features of the Double Gate take in this process?

ORDER

Cornice

The integral line of the cornice leans on the upper horizontal edge of two relieving arches (Figs. 28.1, 28.5–28.6, 28.11–28.12). The cornice is comprised of medium stones of equal height (ca. 0.38 m) and various widths (ca. 0.35 m, 0.50 m, 0.68 m, etc.), regularly arranged into one even course. The length of the cornice slightly overlaps the edges of the relieving arches, but due to the poor state of preservation of the lateral edges (as well as the middle part), its exact length cannot be determined (ca. 15.4 m long). Many other stones of the cornice are severely eroded or completely lost, so the decoration, which seems to be regular all over the length of the cornice, is restorable based only on the well-preserved elements. The cornice was comprised of plain flat molding (0.07 m high), cyma (0.163 m high) adorned with a lotus-palmette pattern, corona with dentils (ca. 0.7 m high), and modillions (0.094 m high) framed with zigzag/chevron/dogtooth pattern, all carved from one piece of stone (Fig. 28.12).[6] The state of preservation of the modillions is very poor, but on several of them the remnants of the densely twisted rope are discernable (Fig. 28.11). The modillions were adorned with acanthus leaves and the coffers between them seem to be decorated with rosettes (almost not preserved).

In relation to the Roman canon, the sequence of the moldings of the cornice of the Double Gate has an arbitrary interpretation: 1) the corona is decorated with a row of dentils instead of tongues; 2) the row of dentils should not be above the modillions but below them; 3) the astragali and egg-and-dart patterns are absent.

Archivolts and Spandrels

The archivolts and the spandrels of the Double Gate were constructed of separate ashlars and voussoirs of irregular sizes and shapes (Fig. 28.14). On the eastern corner, these elements were

---

[5]   The descriptions of the moldings of the details are given here and below from top to bottom.

[6]   This pattern is better preserved on similar cornices in the interior of the Golden Gate (Wilkinson 1987: 11, Fig. 7; 12, Fig. 9).

① **Cornice**   ⑥ **Modillions and coffers**
② **Bed molding**   ⑦ **Lesbian cyma**
③ **Cyma with anthemion**   ⑧ **Astragalus with twisted rope pattern**
④ **Bead-and-reel**   ⑨ **Dentils**
⑤ **Corona**   ⑩ **Egg-and-dart**

Figure 28.9: Fragment of the cornice part of the Roman entablature reused in the southern façade of the Holy Sepulchre in Jerusalem (photo by H. Shkolnik).

① **Architrave**
② **Frieze with "peopled scroll"**
③ **Architrave crowning**
④ **Fasciae with astragali**

Figure 28.10: Fragment of the architrave part of the Roman entablature from Beth Sheʾan theater (photo by S. Tarkhanova).

① **Cyma with lotus-palmette frieze**   ④ **Coffer**
② **Corona with dentils**   ⑤ **Zigzag/chevron/dog-tooth pattern**
③ **Modillion**   ⑥ **Twisted rope**

Figure 28.11. Fragment of the cornice (photo by D. Czitron and Y. Baruch,
courtesy of the Israel Antiquities Authority; drawing by A. Yoffe-Pikovsky).

severely eroded, partially chiseled and probably in secondary use, so the integrity of the decoration
is considerably shattered. The decorative program is theoretically but rather firmly restored based
on the preserved fragments and symmetrical decoration of the eastern archivolt (Mazar *et al.* 2011:
227, Fig. 6.4.1; 233, Fig. 6.4.12).

The main decorative element of each archivolt is the uninterrupted slightly convex frieze with a
"peopled scroll" pattern, framed by various moldings from outer and inner edges. The rectangular
part of the archivolts is framed with the plain ledge and ovolo molding embellished with a large-
scaled egg-and-tongue pattern between two fillets (Fig. 28.15). These moldings consistently recede

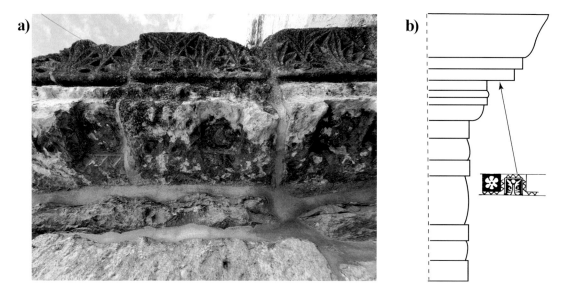

Figure 28.12: (a) Fragment of the cornice; view from below. Modillions and coffers of the cornice (photo by D. Czitron and Y. Baruch, courtesy of the Israel Antiquities Authority). (b) Section of the entablature from the interior of the Golden Gate. Modillions, coffers, and their adornment are similar to those in the Double Gate (Wilkinson 1987: 12, Figure 28. 7).

toward the sunken frieze and flat surface inside the spandrels. The "peopled scroll" frieze follows the perimeter of the rectangular part and the span of the arch. The medallions of the "peopled scroll" pattern are presented by complete circumferences over the length of the frieze. They diminish only toward the keystone and sharply bend at the springer points. The frieze, with "inhabited scroll", is framed with rows of dentils placed in a mirror-like manner and their tips turned toward the frieze. On the horizontal segments, the dentils of the lower range are inverted; on the vertical segments, they lie on their sides. Such locations of the dentils, which usually hang down, contradict the logic of their original order in the canon. Interestingly, on the lower horizontal segment of the spandrel over the impost, the dentils are oriented downward, complying with the proper logic of their original canonic order.

At the springer point of the eastern spandrel of the eastern archivolt, an impost is partially preserved (apparently, the other imposts were adorned in the same manner; Fig. 28.16). It is comprised of the aforementioned dentils, the concave molding (torus?) with wavy acanthus branch,[7] the twisted rope and the row of turned-up slanted trefoils. All the decorative moldings of the impost are separated from each other by fillets. The directions of the grooves of the twisted rope and the axes of the trefoils coincide, inclining to the right. The soffit of the impost is decorated with a row of palmettoes directed by their tops toward the center of the archivolts ("Milesian" type) (Fig. 28.17); the pattern is flanked by two rows of dentils turned by their points inside. These moldings on the impost together with the decorative soffit also continue over the intrados of the arch.[8] In addition, they stretch to the lateral side of the impost, joining with the egg-and-tongue row and fillets of the vertical part of the frame into one integral collection of moldings that consistently recede (Fig.

---

[7] At the corner, wavy tendril with slanted leaves delicately transformed into vertical five-lobed leaf (palmetto?).

[8] As mentioned above, the intrados of the eastern archivolt is chiseled, but the intrados of the western archivolt is preserved (Mazar *et al.* 2011: 228, Fig. 6.4.2; 232, Fig. 6.4.10).

28.18). This three-dimensional feature that joins several surfaces into one complicated composition is virtuously executed.

In Roman tradition, the cornice with bed molding might be used separately from the architrave part when it was necessary for architectural and aesthetic purposes, for example, on the façade of the Triumphal Arch in Gerasa (Kraeling 1938: Pl. IV; date: 130 CE), on the Triumphal Arches of the Great Colonnade Street in Palmyra (Browning 1979: 141–143, Fig. 83; date: 2nd century CE), on the propylon of the processional way to Sebasteion in Aphrodisias (McKenzie 2007: 113–114, Fig. 186) and elsewhere. From this perspective, the decoration of the archivolts and spandrels of the Double Gate should be based on the order vocabulary of the architrave block. However, there are many discrepancies in relation to the Roman tradition: 1) ovolo with egg-and-tongue pattern and the row of dentils are actually bed molding elements; they should be carved from the same block as the cornice[9] and arranged inversely (dentils should be above the egg-and-dart); 2) architrave crowning under the frieze is absent; the second row of inverted dentils appears in its stead; 3) fasciae are omitted, while the repertoire of astragali moldings and their sequence became entirely free,[10] though not opulent.

The sequence of the moldings both on the cornice and on the archivolts with the spandrels contradicts the Roman canon, but still, the order regulations are firmly preserved and well-recognized; the experimentation with the molded elements—their relocation and distortion—are not as free and spontaneous as they appear in Late Byzantine and Early Islamic art. The critical point when the rules of the Greco-Roman order were no longer obligatory had not yet been reached. In its adherence to the Classical roots, the sculptural decoration of the Double Gate might be compared to some 5th-century monuments in Constantinople, such as the Palace of Antiochus/St. Euphemia (Niewöhner 2017: 264–265, Figs. 53–55) or the Church of St. John Stoudios (Niewöhner 2017: 269–270, Figs. 67–69). In a certain sense, it is even more traditional than the other entablatures of the late 4th or 5th centuries from the Forum of Theodosius (Niewöhner 2017: 252–254, Figs. 26–31), Theodosian St. Sophia (Niewöhner 2017: 257–258, Figs. 36–37) and some others revealed in Constantinople without exact provenances (Niewöhner 2017: 259–264), which are more abstract in relation to the Classical vocabulary. The crowded sculptural decoration of the Double Gate resembles the adornment of the Early Byzantine churches in Tur Abdin in Mesopotamia (Bell 1982: 58–60, 70–72, Pl. 49 [Mayafarqin], Pls. 74–79 [Nisibin], 81, Pls. 190–198 [Deir Za'faran]), Red and White Coptic monasteries in Sohag (Bolman 2016: 86–90, Figs. 7.10–7.15; Akermann 1976), South Church in Bawit (McKenzie 2007: 295–304, Figs. 49–508), the monastery of Apa Jeremiah at Saqqara in Egypt (McKenzie 2007: 306, Figs. 518–521), churches in Qal'at Si'man (Krautheimer 1986: 145–150, Figs. 103–107; Peña 2000: 110–111), Qalb Loze in Syria (Krautheimer 1986: 151–152, Figs. 109–110; Lassus 1947: 193, Pl. XXXIII; Strube 1977: 181–191), edifices in Rusafa (Schulz and Strzygowski 1904: Fig. 58), etc. These monuments stand out with prevailing arcuated forms and articulation of rich sculptural elements. No complete parallels for the decoration of the Double Gate have as yet been found among the regional architectural schools, which are deeply rooted in the

---

[9]   When the blocks of the cornice and architrave were split, the bed molding might be repeated on them both. Thus, the cornice block and the archivolts of the Double Gate might initially have comprised common construction separated from each other lately due to the architectural peculiarities of the gate (early lintels and relieving arches).

[10]   The entablature and arches of the Golden Gate are carved in the same manner but with additional decorative bands and patterns arranged in a different sequence and with some additional moldings bearing tendrils and geometric motifs not used in the Double Gate.

antique tradition. And even remote similarities cannot be found in the local Byzantine architecture of the Holy Land.

There is a minimal sense in the systematic comparison of the entablature of the Double Gate with the Byzantine entablatures in general because the sequence and the collection of the moldings were unregulated, free and rarely repeated each other. Only for the separate patterns the parallels from the general artistic vocabulary of the period might be highlighted. Niewöhner noticed that:

> Whilst fifth-century entablatures were still recognizably Roman and their deviations from the ancient canon may be described in terms of decline, the tradition seems to have lapsed sometime around the turn of the sixth century. All later carvings were eclectic hybrids and may thus be termed the afterlife of the Roman entablature. (Niewöhner 2017: 239)

Based on these partial observations, I suppose that the sculptural elements of the Double Gate were manufactured during the 5th or early 6th century at the latest.

DECORATIVE PATTERNS

Some of the decorative patterns used on the molded elements and their arrangement deserve special attention and analysis as they may serve as chronological indicators and criteria. All of them are rooted in antique art and interruptedly developed from the Greco-Roman until the Early Islamic or even Medieval period.

Cyma with Lotus-Palmette Frieze

The cyma of the cornice is adorned with the lotus-palmette frieze (Figs. 28.6, 28.11–28.12). It is comprised of alternating, five-lobed fan-like leaves (palmettoes) and three-lobed trefoils (lotuses), all arranged vertically. The floral motifs are at the base, with the lower tips of the palmettoes forming eyes, and the lateral lobes of neighboring lotuses touching each other at the tips and forming arches over the palmettoes. All the lobes are deeply grooved with the angularity at the bottom; the lateral lobes of the lotuses overlap the central one, creating a light three-dimensional effect.

The lotus-palmette pattern is known from the Middle Roman period at the latest. For example, it was applied for the decoration of the cyma on the gable of Hadrian's Gate in Gerasa (Browning 1982: 104–108, Figs. 43–45 [before reconstruction]; Wikimedia commons [after reconstruction]) and on the member of the Roman cornice revealed in secondary use in Ramat al-Khalil church in Mamre/Mambre (Mader 1957: Fig. 94). Its artistic interpretation and morphology in these Classical monuments are creative and detailed. The pattern was rarely applied for the decoration of the cornices during the Byzantine period. The only examples are the cornice of the pier that derived from the Church of St. Polyeuktos in Constantinople (currently in Venice; Krautheimer 1986: 220–221, Fig. 177; date: 524–527 CE) and the intrados of the monolithic arch of the ciborium from the Burdur Museum in Pisidia (Niewöhner 2021: 138, Fig. 366). However, the lotus-palmette pattern was sometimes used on the abaci of the Early Byzantine capitals: one example is known from the Edirne Museum in Thrace and the other one was reused in the Pammakaristos Monastery (Niewöhner 2021: 101, Fig. 264; 109, Fig. 289; both capitals are dated to the 6th century).[11] The most geographically close artifact where the lotus-palmette pattern was applied is a basket capital from the monastery of St. Martyrius in Ma'ale Adumim (Magen 2015: 224–225, Fig. 257b) (Fig. 28.19). The same pattern, albeit stylistically completely altered toward stronger ornamentation and

---

[11] The morphology and style of the lotus-palmette frieze on these capitals is mostly similar to that of the Double Gate.

abstraction, was applied in the decoration of the Khirbet al-Mafjar Palace (Hamilton 1959: Pl. LV). It is noteworthy that this pattern survived even during the Late Byzantine art of the 11th–12th centuries (cornices in the Crusader chapels) of the Holy Sepulchre (Corbo 1981–1982: Photo 191), unprovenanced cornice from Constantinople (Niewöhner 2017: 318, Fig. 175), Proskynetarion icon frame, Hosios Loukas Monastery, Greece (Bogdanovic 2017: 97–97, Fig. 2.42). According to the stylistic and morphological similarities, I would relate the lotus-palmette motif of the cornice under consideration to the Early Byzantine period (5th–6th centuries CE) rather than the Early Islamic.

Zigzag/Chevron/Dogtooth[12] Pattern on the Modillions

The modillions of the cornice are framed with the zigzag/chevron/dogtooth pattern (Fig. 28.12). The modillions in the Classical tradition were usually decorated with the egg-and-dart pattern, sometimes supplied by an ancillary row of the bead-and-reel motif. In the Early Byzantine period, the framing of the modillions was frequently omitted (cornice from the church in Khirbet el-Beiyudat, Hizmi 1990: 260, Fig. 21). Sometimes the pattern was replaced by beads, for example, on the cornice from St. Thecla/Meriamlik Church in Asia Minor (Niewöhner 2017: 279–280, Fig. 93). The only parallel for the decoration of the modillions with chevrons is known from the Mausoleum of Diocletian at Split (Nikšić 2011: 193, Fig. 4; dated to the late 3rd century CE) (Fig. 28.13). The zigzag/chevron/dogtooth pattern was very popular in Early Byzantine art and particularly in the Negev churches. The cornices, voussoirs and pilaster caps from the South Church in Shivta (Segal 1988: 98–99; Golan 2020: 47–49, 51, 338, Pls. 89–97), from the North Church in Oboda/Avdat (Woolley and Lawrence 1914–1915: 101, Fig. 32; Golan 2020: 70, 470, Pls. 175–176), from Nessana (Golan 2020: 94–96, 547–548, Pls. 250–254), and from some unknown sites in the Negev (Golan 2020: 128, 616, Pl. 321) are adorned with the zigzag/chevron/dogtooth pattern.[13] The recently found marble relief voussoir associated with a church in Ascalon also bears a molding with the finely carved chevrons.[14] The zigzag/chevron/dogtooth motif was also applied in the decoration of Qasr Kharana and the Umayyad palace in Amman (Creswell 1989: 101–103, Fig. 64; 169–171, Fig. 97), but in the other Umayyad monuments, for example, in Khirbet al-Mafjar or Mshatta, it was completely excluded from the repertoire.

Dentils

This pattern was a compulsory element of the Greco-Roman and Byzantine entablatures, but it was frequently omitted in the Umayyad sculptural decoration. This molding was repeated five times on the cornice and archivolts of the Double Gate, including positions that contradict their order sense. This repetition resembles the popularity of the pattern in Early Byzantine Negev art (though not so frequently used as the zigzag/chevron/dogtooth pattern). It was applied on the pilaster caps, lintels and cornices in Oboda, Shivta, etc. (Golan 2020: 20–21, 28, 35, 39, 44, 70–71, 107, 152, 163). Thus, I suppose the frequency of the moldings with the dentils on the façade of the Double Gate is connected to Byzantine stylistic trends rather than to Early Islamic ones.

---

[12] In various sources, different terms are used for the same pattern.

[13] Statistically, there were 102 examples on which the zigzag/chevron pattern was applied: "8 different doorjamb bases, 30 different doorjamb capitals, 12 different cornices and 8 different arches" (Golan 2020: 152). Voussoirs from Oboda (Golan 2020: 470, Pl. 175) by the collection of their moldings resemble the decoration of the intrados and imposts of the archivolts of the Double Gate.

[14] The site was excavated by Erickson-Gini in 2019. Some preliminary results were published (Erickson-Gini 2021).The voussoir was published only in the short interview available online (URL: https://www.friendsofiaa .org/news/2019/12/16/roman-fish-sauce-made-in-ashkelon).

Figure 28.13: Cornice with the zigzag/chevron/dog-tooth pattern framing the modillions. Mausoleum of Diocletian in Split, 3rd century CE (photo by M. Atayants).

"Peopled Scroll" Pattern on the Frieze

This pattern is the most important one for dating, as it bears some distinctive features. It originated in Hellenistic times, and its morphology and style modified and developed distinctively during the Roman, Byzantine and Early Islamic periods, in accordance with the general artistic streams of each epoch (Toynbee and Ward-Perkins 1950; Dauphin 1987; Ovadiah and Turnheim 1994; Tarkhanova 2020).

The scroll of the frieze of the Double Gate is comprised of complete medallions, interconnected to each other by one general stem (Figs. 28.2–28.3, 28.14–28.15). Cauliculi are placed at the junctions of the neighboring circumferences. Their bodies are corrugated and three tunnelings diminish toward the bottom. Lotus-like vegetal patterns (trefoils) stretch from them, covering the triangular segments left between the medallions. In style, these trefoils strongly resemble the lotuses of the cornice. On the opposite segments, heart-shaped leaflets grow from the medallions. Each medallion is comprised of a single thin stem that curls inward. Inside the medallions, there are four stiff-acanthus bundles, each comprised of three-pointed grooves. The medallions curl alternately in clockwise and counterclockwise directions. There are diamond-like patterns in the centers.

The "peopled scroll" pattern was very popular during Byzantine architecture of the 5th–6th centuries. It was frequently used on the friezes and lintels in Coptic (Drioton 1942: 32–55), Syrian (Peña 1997: 85f; Deir Seta, 88f; Qalb Loze, 89f; Baqirha, 140f; Qalat Siman, 144; Ruweiha, 188; Ba'ude), Lycian (Harrison 1963: 131–136, Pls. XLI–XLIII [Karabel, Alacahisar], Gough 1985: 80–120, Fig. 27–34, Pls. 10–14, 40 [Alahan monastery]), and Constantinopolitan Early Byzantine edifices (Niewöhner 2017). By its morphological features, albeit with some differences in the interpretation and ancillary details, the "peopled scroll" pattern of the Double Gate resembles the lintel of the Red Monastery in Egypt (Bolman 2016: 88, Figs. 7.12–7.13; dated to the 4th–5th centuries CE) (Fig. 28.20), the lintels in the Moudjeleia (Vogüé 1865–77: 82, Pls. 32, 45; dated to the 5th century CE) and el-Barah in Syria (Vogüé 1864: 68, Fig. 40; dated to the 6th century CE) (Fig. 28.21), the lintel of the church in Karabel in Lycia (Harrison 1963: 131–134, Pl. XLIIe; dated to the 5th–6th centuries CE) (Fig. 28.22), the frieze in the Capernaum synagogue in the Galilee

① **Ledge**

② **Ovolo molding with egg-and-tongue pattern**

③ **Fillet**

④ **Frieze with "peopled scroll"**

Figure 28.14: General view of the eastern spandrel of the eastern archivolt (photo by H. Shkolnik; drawing by A. Yoffe-Pikovsky).

Figure 28.15: Fragment of the eastern spandrel of the eastern archivolt (photo by H. Shkolnik).

Figure 28.16: Impost and intrados of the eastern spandrel of the eastern archivolt
(photo by H. Shkolnik; drawing by A. Yoffe-Pikovsky).

(Tarkhanova 2020: 201–202, Fig. 1 [First group]; dated by me to the 5th–6th centuries) (Fig. 28.23), and the lintel recently found in the chapel on the slope of the Mount of Olives (dated to the 6th century).[15] But strikingly similar, both stylistically and morphologically, is the "peopled scroll" pattern of the "bowl" capital located in the Islamic Museum on the Temple Mount (Wilkinson 1987: 203, no. 145; Rosen-Ayalon 1989: 143, Fig. 25; dated to the 5th century). Recently a similar capital, transformed into a small baptismal font, was discovered in the large octagonal baptismal font in the Basilica of the Nativity in Bethlehem (Bacci 2019) (Fig. 28.24). Both capitals are marble and thus imported.[16] In contrast to the non-religious nature of the "peopled scroll" frieze of the Double Gate (no crosses were noted), the medallions of the capitals are "inhabited" and "baptized" with the small

---

[15] Gethsemane Chapel was excavated in 2020 on behalf of the Israel Antiquities Authority in collaboration with Studium Biblicum Franciscanum (the excavation was directed by A. Reem and D. Eger). A brief interview with some illustrations was published online (URL: https://www.jpost.com/israel-news/ritual-bath-from-time-of-jesus-found-at-gethsemane-in-jerusalem-652826).

[16] The other known "bowl capitals" adorned with the "peopled scroll" pattern are different (Kautzsch 1936: Pl. 46, Capitals 799–800; Wilkinson 1987: 196, Fig. 31). Interestingly, this type of capital was popular mainly in the Holy Land churches.

Figure 28.17: Decoration of the soffit of the eastern spandrel of the eastern archivolt
(photo by H. Shkolnik; drawing by A. Yoffe-Pikovsky).

crosses, and their Early/Middle Byzantine dating is unquestionable. The medallions are formed by stiff-pointed acanthus[17] that seem to have been discontinued after the 5th century CE (Niewöhner 2021: 21). The similarities and parallels between the friezes of the Double Gate (and also of the Golden Gate) and the *kalathi* of these capitals are no less than astounding; it is therefore possible to propose that they are contemporaneous and apparently belonged to one architectural complex.

The "peopled scroll" pattern was still popular in Early Islamic art, but it was so much altered that almost nothing, save the general idea, remained in common, either in morphology or style, with the frieze of the Double Gate. For example, the "peopled scroll" friezes of Mshatta or entablatures

---

[17] Stiff-pointed (German: starrzackig) leaves are characterized by stiffly fanned out leaf tips or "points." The tips do not abut as in the case of soft-pointed leaves, nor do they enclose "eyes" as do broad- and narrow-pointed leaves. Outer tips typically touch (Niewöhner 2021: 21).

Figure 28.18: The lateral side of the eastern spandrel of the eastern archivolt (photo by H. Shkolnik).

Figure 28.19: Basket-capital with the ledge decorated with lotus-palmette pattern (photo by S Tarkhanova).

of the Dome of the Rock (when there are no Byzantine *spolia*) are deeply ornamental with almost no connection to any realistic features; the vegetal details became small, symbolic and covered the surface in a lattice-like manner (Wilkinson 1987: 14–16, Figs. 10–11; Creswell 1989: 24–25, Fig. 8, 27, 31, Figs. 10–11; Talgam 2004: 3–30, Figs. 43–58).

Wavy Stem with Alternating Tendrils

One of the astragali of the intrados and springer point is decorated with a single wavy stem from which soft acanthus leaves alternately grow (Fig. 28.25). This pattern was used comparatively often on Byzantine artifacts, for example, on the lintel from Gethsemane Chapel on the Mount of Olives

Figure 28.20: Door lintel of the Red Monastery with the "peopled scroll" pattern (photo by S. Tarkhanova).

40. — Porte à El-Barah. vɪᵉ siècle après J.-C.

Figure 28.21: Door lintel of the church in el-Barah, Syria, with the "peopled scroll" pattern (Vogüé 1864: 68, Figure 28.40).

(see Footnote 13), on the Byzantine ciborium from the Burdur Museum in Pisidia (Niewöhner 2021: 138, Fig. 366), on the capital of the Mayafarqin Church, el ʿAdhra (Bell 1982: Pl. 64), on the arch of the South Church in Bawit (McKenzie 2007: 299, Fig. 493), on the pediment from Oxyrhynchus (McKenzie 2007: 269, Fig. 447) and elsewhere.

Scales with Floral Patterns (Scale-and-Bud)

The lateral side of the eastern spandrel of the eastern archivolt is adorned with an original pattern of scales with vegetal motifs inscribed into them. There are four complete semicircular scales arranged vertically (Fig. 28.26). Their contours are formed by plain fillet molding. Segmental scales are located on the upper, lower and lateral sides of the field. The floral motifs of the complete scales consist of

Figure 28.22: Door lintel of the church in Karabel, Lycia (photo by A: Vinogradov).

Figure 28.23: Frieze with "peopled scroll" from the synagogue in Capernaum (photo by S. Tarkhanova).

two trefoils, with one overlapping the other. The trefoil in the background is larger in scale and flatter. The lobes of the trefoils are nicely grooved with angularity at the bottom. Their deepened surface combines nicely with the flat moldings of the scales and of the rectangular frame. Trefoils, slanted toward the central axis, are inscribed into the segmental parts of the scales. The feature of overlapping grooved motifs creates a delicate, voluminous effect that resonates with the lotus-palmette pattern of the cornice, wavy tendrils of the astragalus and rows of palmettos on the soffits of the archivolts.

a)

b)

Figure 28.24: (a) Bowl-capital with the "peopled scroll" pattern in the collection of the Islamic Museum; frontal side (Rosen-Ayalon 1989: 143, Figure 28. 25). (b) Bowl-like capital recently discovered in the Church of the Nativity in Bethlehem. Rear side (Photo credit: https://www.earlychristians.org/bethlehem-a-new-baptismal-font-found/ [open internet resource]).

Figure 28.25: Astragal of the impost (and intrados) decorated with the wavy floral pattern (photo by H. Shkolnik).

The pattern of scale-and-bud is rooted in Early Roman art at the earliest. The baltei of two monumental Ionic capitals found in the Jewish Quarter near the Temple Mount and dated to the Early Roman period are adorned with similar motifs though smaller in scale and less detailed (Ben Haim and Peleg-Barkat 2017: 75–76, 89, Pl. 3.3: 5). The excavators mention some other samples of capitals with the scale-and-bud pattern found in Jerusalem and in Asia Minor (Ben Haim and Peleg-Barkat 2017: 76). The scales were often used in Byzantine art in various kinds of art, including mosaics (Fig. 28.27), but an almost exact parallel with only minimal deviations is known from the Umayyad Palace Khirbet al-Mafjar in Jericho (Hamilton 1959: 271, Fig. 226c) (Fig. 28.28). Therefore, I suppose that this very pattern might be dated to the Umayyad period. By its proportions, style and pointless (from the perspective of order) location on the lateral side of the spandrel, the pattern breaks the integrality of the whole artistic complex, which is rather systematic and consistent in all of its other order and decorative elements. I assume it was added to the ready-made archivolts.

STYLE

The ornaments of the cornice and archivolts are arranged in a very regular manner, with the repetition of motifs. The patterns and moldings are interconnected structurally, stylistically and by small ancillary details. All elements are of conservatively Classical derivation, transposed into harsh forms. The proportions of the moldings and the scales of the patterns are well-balanced and not distorted; the only exception is the scale-and-bud motif on the lateral side of the eastern spandrel. The reliefs are mainly flat, stiff and two-dimensional, with chiseled contours, without undercutting or drilling. The style is already not as realistic as in Roman art, but also not yet so ornamental and symbolical as it turned out to be in Late Byzantine or Early Islamic periods. Apparently, the reliefs were initially implied for the external decoration of a monument with an abundant source of light.

Figure 28.26: Lateral side of the eastern spandrel decorated with a scale-and-bud pattern (photo by H. Shkolnik).

CONCLUSIONS

Based on the detailed analysis of the order, decorative and stylistic features of the cornice and archivolts of the Double Gate, I am of the opinion that they were manufactured not later than the 5th–early 6th century CE and not during the Umayyad period, as it was generally agreed according to the latest publications (Gibson and Jacobson 1996: 235–282; Shani, Chen 2001; Talgam 2004: 36; Mazar *et al.* 2011: 226–238). This conclusion strengthens the earliest theories that relied mainly on historical reasoning and not on stylistic analysis (Vogüé 1864: 12, 64–68; Lewis 1888: 96; Vincent and Abel 1914–1926: 910–911, etc.). There are no other such complete and opulent entablatures known from any other local buildings of the Byzantine period. In view of the extraordinary number of similarities between the "peopled scroll" frieze of the Double Gate and the two imported marble

Figure 28.27: Byzantine mosaic with a scale-and-bud pattern under the Al-Aqsa Mosque (below 9th pier) (photo courtesy of the Israel Antiquities Authority Archive, British Mandate Scientific Record Files [SRF_92 (102/102)]).

Figure 28.28: Scale-and-bud pattern on the stucco decoration of balustrade from Khirbet el-Mafjar (Hamilton 1959: 271, Figure 28. 226c).

capitals, it can be assumed, with due caution, that the decoration of the façade was carved under strong regional influences and possibly by visiting carvers who imitated and reproduced the style of the marble capitals. It is impossible to determine when exactly these elements were incorporated into the façade of the Double Gate, but in view of the discrepancies in sizes between the archivolts and the elements of the original doorways, they clearly were not originally manufactured for the Gate. The decoration of the lateral side of the spandrel during the Umayyad period (and apparently also of the soffits of the archivolts) could have been part of the general renovation of the elements, executed immediately prior to their attachment to the façade of the Double Gate. The practice of using Byzantine *spolia* and their re-elaboration during the Early Islamic period is well-known from numerous other examples (Lic 2013). Above all, the Dome of the Rock and the Al-Aqsa mosque, built on the Temple Mount during the Umayyad period, should be mentioned: most of their marble capitals, column sets, revetments, and some of the wooden entablatures are Byzantine *spolia* (Wilkinson 1987: 18–19; Reuven 2014; Guidetti 2017: 97–132; Talgam 2004: Fig. 124). Several capitals used in the interior of the Double Gate are also Byzantine *spolia* (Shani and Chen 2001: 23–28). Apparently, the renovation of the Double Gate with the reuse of the earlier details was part of the general architectural program of Abd al-Malik in Jerusalem in the late 7th century CE. These conclusions bring to life the old theory of the Byzantine genesis of the sculptural decoration of the façade of the Double Gate, though without omitting previous research works, where the Umayyad phase of the gate was confidently highlighted.

REFERENCES

Akermann, P. 1976. *Le Décor Sculpté du Couvent Blanc: Niches et Frises.* Cairo.

Avigad, N. 1970. New Church of the Theotokos: NEA. Excavations in the Jewish Quarter of the Old City of Jerusalem 1970: Second Preliminary Report. *Israel Exploration Journal* 20: 129–140.

Avi-Yonah, M. 1954. *The Madaba Mosaic Map.* Jerusalem.

Bacci, M. 2019. The Rediscovery of a Byzantine Capital, Reused as a Baptismal Font, in the Nativity Church, Bethlehem. *Convivium* 6(2): 122–127. https://doi.org/10.1484/J.CONVI.4.2019042.

Bahat, D. 2020. *Temple Mount: Holy Compound in Jerusalem.* Jerusalem (Hebrew).

Bell, G. 1982. *Churches and Monasteries of the Tûr 'Abdîn.* London.

Ben-Dov, M. and Friedman, I. 1982. *In the Shadow of the Temple: The Discovery of Ancient Jerusalem.* Jerusalem and New York.

Ben Haim, A. and Peleg-Barkat, O. 2017. Monumental Ionic Columns from Areas Q and H. In: Geva, H., ed. *Jewish Quarter Excavations in the Old City of Jerusalem, Conducted by Nahman Avigad, 1969–1982*, Vol. 7: *Areas Q, H, O-2 and Other Studies, Final Report.* Jerusalem: 68–95.

Bogdanovic, J. 2017. *The Framing of Sacred Space: The Canopy and the Byzantine Church.* Oxford and New York.

Bolman, E.S. 2016. *The Red Monastery Church: Beauty and Asceticism in Upper Egypt.* New Haven and London.

Browning, I. 1979. *Palmyra.* London.

Browning, I. 1982. *Jerash and the Decapolis.* London.

Burgoyne, M.H. 1992. The Gates of the Haram al-Sharif. In: Raby, J. and Johns, J., eds. *Bayt al-Maqdis, 'Abd al-Malik's Jerusalem*, Part 1. Oxford: 105–140.

Corbo, V.C. 1981–1982. *Il Santo Sepolcro di Gerusalemme: Aspetti archeologici dalle origini al periodo crociato.* Jerusalem.

Coüasnon, C. 1974. *The Church of the Holy Sepulchre in Jerusalem.* London.

Creswell, K.A.C. 1969. *Early Muslim Architecture*, Vol. 1, Part 2. Oxford.

Creswell, K.A.C. 1989. *A Short Account of Early Muslim Architecture.* Cairo.

Dauphin, C. 1987. The Development of the "Inhabited Scroll" in Architectural Sculpture and Mosaic Art from Late Imperial Times to the Seventh Century A.D. *Levant* 19: 183–212.

Drioton, E. 1942. *Les Sculptures Coptes du Nilomètre de Rodah.* Cairo.

Erickson-Gini, T. 2021. The Good Life: Evidence for the Production of Wine and Garum in an Early Roman Estate and Byzantine Monastery South of Ashkelon. In: Golani, A., Varga, D., Lehmann, G. and Tchekhanovets, Y., eds. *Archaeological Excavations and Research Studies in Southern Israel: Collected Papers (17th Annual Southern Conference).* Jerusalem: 7–24 (English section).

Gibson, S. and Jacobson, D.M. 1996. The Subterranean Areas at the Southern End of the Ḥaram al-Sharîf. In: Gibson, S. and Jacobson, D.M., eds. *Below the Temple Mount in Jerusalem: A Sourcebook on the Cisterns, Subterranean Chambers and Conduits of the Ḥaram al-Sharîf* (BAR International Series 637). Oxford: 235–282.

Golan, K. 2020. *Architectural Sculpture in the Byzantine Negev: Characterization and Meaning.* Berlin and Boston.

Gough, M. 1985. *Alahan: An Early Christian Monastery in Southern Turkey.* Toronto.

Guidetti, M. 2017. Material Transfers in the Early Medieval Mediterranean: Marble Columns from Churches to Mosques. In: Guidetti, M., ed. *In the Shadow of the Church: The Building of Mosques in Early Medieval Syria.* Leiden and Boston: 97–132

Hamilton, R.W. 1947. *The Structural History of the Aqsa Mosque.* Oxford.

Hamilton, R.W. 1959. *Khirbat al Mafjar: An Arabian Mansion in the Jordan Valley.* Oxford.

Harrison, R.M. 1963. Churches and Chapels of Central Lycia. *Anatolian Studies* 13: 117–151.

Hizmi, H. 1990. The Byzantine Church at Khirbet el-Beiyudat: Preliminary Report. In: Bottini, G.C., Di Segni, L. and Alliata, E., eds. *Christian Archaeology in the Holy Land: New Discoveries. Essays in Honour of Virgilio C. Corbo, OFM.* Jerusalem: 245–264.

Kautzsch, R. 1936. *Kapitellstudien.* Berlin and Leipzig.

Kraeling, C.H., ed. 1938. *Gerasa, City of the Decapolis.* New Haven.

Krautheimer, R. 1986. *Early Christian and Byzantine Architecture.* New Haven and London.

Lassus, J. 1947. *Sanctuaires Chrétiens de Syrie: Essai sur la Genèse, la Forme et l'Usage Liturgique des Édifices du Culte Chrétien, en Syrie, du IIIe Siècle à la Conquête Musulmane* (Bibliothèque Archéologique et Historique de l'Institut Français d'Archéologie de Beyrouth 42). Paris.

Lewis, T.H. 1888. *The Holy Places of Jerusalem.* London.

Lic, A. 2013. Functions of Spolia in Umayyad Architecture. *Art of the Orient* 2: 7–17.

Mader, A.E. 1957. *Mambre: Die Ergebnisse der Ausgrabungen in heiligen Bezirk, Ramat el-Halil in Sud-Palästina, 1926–1928.* Freiburg im Breisgau.

Magen, Y. 2015. *Christians and Christianity,* Vol. 5: *Monastery of Martyrius.* Jerusalem.

Mazar, E., Shalev, Y., Reuven, P., Steinberg, J. and Balogh, B. 2011. *The Walls of the Temple Mount.* Jerusalem.

McKenzie, J. 2007. *The Architecture of Alexandria and Egypt, c. 300 BC to AD 700.* New Haven and London.

Niewöhner, P. 2017. The Decline and Afterlife of the Roman Entablature: The Collection of the Archaeological Museum Istanbul and Other Byzantine Epistyles and Cornices from Constantinople. *Istanbuler Mitteilungen* 67: 237–328.

Niewöhner, P. 2021. *Byzantine Ornaments in Stone: Architectural Sculpture and Liturgical Furnishings.* Berlin and Boston.

Nikšić, G. 2011. Diocletian's Palace—Design and Construction. In: Bülow, G. von and Zabehlicky, H., eds. *Bruckneudorf und Gamzigrad: Spätantike Paläste und Großvillen im Donau-Balkan-Raum. Akten des Internationalen Kolloquiums in Bruckneudorf, 15–18 Oktober 2008.* Bonn: 187–202.

Ovadiah, A. and Turnheim, T. 1994. *"Peopled" Scrolls in Roman Architectural Decoration in Israel: The Roman Theatre at Beth Shean, Scythopolis.* Rome.

Peña, I. 1997. *The Christian Art of Byzantine Syria.* Reading.

Peña, I. 2000. *Lieux de pèlerinage en Syrie* (Collectio Minor 38). Jerusalem.

Reuven, P. 2014. Gilded Capitals on the Temple Mount. In: Meiron, E., ed. *City of David: Studies of Ancient Jerusalem* 9. Jerusalem: 31–63 (Hebrew).

Rosen-Ayalon, M. 1989. *The Early Islamic Monuments of Al-Ḥaram al-Sharīf: An Iconographic Study* (Qedem 28). Jerusalem.

Schultz, B. and Strzygowski, J. 1904. Mschatta. In: *Jahrbuch der Königlich Preussischen Kunstsammlungen* 25. Berlin: 205–373.

Segal, A. 1988. *Architectural Decoration in Byzantine Shivta, Negev Desert, Israel* (BAR International Series 420). Oxford.

Shani, R. and Chen, D. 2001. On the Umayyad Dating of the Double Gate in Jerusalem. *Muqarnas* 18: 1–40.

Strube, C. 1977. Die Formgebung der Apsis-dekoration in Qalbloze und Qalat Siman. *Jahrbuch für Antike und Christentum* 20: 181–191.

Talgam, R. 2004. *The Stylistic Origins of Umayyad Sculpture and Architectural Decoration.* Wiesbaden.

Tarkhanova, S. 2020. Dating Capernaum Synagogue by Stylistic Method: Some Aspects of Its Reconstruction. In: Bonnie, R., Hakola, R. and Tervahauta, U., eds. *The Synagogue in Ancient Palestine: Current Issues and Emerging Trends* (Forschungen zur Religion und Literatur im Alten und Neuen Testaments 279). Tübingen: 195–220.

Toynbee, J.M.C. and Ward-Perkins, J.B. 1950. Peopled Scrolls: A Hellenistic Motif in Imperial Art. *Papers of the British School at Rome* 18: 1–43.

Turnheim, Y. 1996. Formation and Transformation of the Entablature in Northern Eretz Israel and the Golan in the Roman and Byzantine Periods. *Zeitschrift des Deutschen Palästina-Vereins* 112(2): 122–138.

Vincent, L.H. and Abel, F.M. 1914–1926. *Jérusalem: Recherches de Topographie, d'Archéologie et d'Histoire II: Jérusalem Nouvelle.* Paris.

de Vogüé, M. 1864. *Le Temple de Jérusalem.* Paris.

de Vogüé, M. 1865–1877. *Syrie Centrale: Architecture Civile et Religieuse du Ier au VIIe siècle,* 2 vols. Paris.

Watzinger, C. 1935. *Denkmiiler Paliistinas*, Vol. 2. Leipzig.

Wilkinson, J. 1987. *Column Capitals in Al-Haram Al-Sharif (From 138 A.D. to 1118 A.D.) (with Over 200 Photos and 36 Illustrations And 94 Diagrams).* Jerusalem.

Wilson Jones, M. 2000. Genesis and Mimesis: The Design of the Arch of Constantine in Rome. *Journal of the Society of Architectural Historians* 59(1): 50–77.

Woolley, C.L. and Lawrence, T.E. 1914–1915. *The Wilderness of Zin: Archaeological Report.* London.

CHAPTER 29

HEBREW INSCRIPTIONS

Ronny Reich, Yuval Baruch, Dror Czitron and Hélène Machline

Several short Hebrew inscriptions and markings were observed at various locations on Herodian masonry of the Temple Mount's Southern Wall.

INSCRIPTION EAST OF THE TRIPLE GATE

On the Southern Wall of the Temple Mount, on the lower drafted margins of a Herodian ashlar located to the east of the Triple Gate, is an array of incised signs that looks like the Jewish script of the Early Roman (=late Second Temple) period (Figs. 29.1–2).[1] When first reviewed, it was difficult to differentiate the incised strokes from chisel marks.

Like many other incisions of the period, these strokes had been inscribed while the ashlar was still in the quarry, before it had been set in its course, or while it was being prepared for the construction site. As it turned out, when the ashlar was set in the wall, the inscription was set upside down. After a picture of the ashlar was taken and was turned right side up, the strokes that were previously difficult to differentiate immediately became a legible inscription (see reading below). This phenomenon was observed in the past on Herodian ashlars incorporated in the lower courses of the southeastern and northeastern corners of the Temple Mount (Reich and Baruch 2016a, 2016b).

The inscription reads: גלם.

The word גלם (*glm*) denotes an object or vessel that is still in its raw, unfinished state. We find in Mishnah *Eduyot* (3:9) גלמי כלי מתכות (*unfinished metal vessels*) and in Mishnah *Kelim* (12:8) גלמי כלי עץ (*unfinished wooden vessels*). In this sense, one can understand that the present inscription refers to the ashlar upon which it is inscribed, namely that something in its workmanship requires completion, such as the dressing or beveling on its sides.

INSCRIPTION AT JESUS'S CRADLE

An inscription in square Jewish script is incised on the inner face of the southern window of the room dubbed Jesus's Cradle, located at the pinnacle of the southeastern corner of the Temple Mount (Figs. 29.3–4). The window is constructed of well-dressed ashlars, and is in fact part of the Herodian construction of the Temple Mount. The inscription is incised in the center of the stone, at about 1.5 m from the windowsill. The letters are ca. 3 cm high, and the inscription is 18–20 cm long.[2]

---

[1]   Unfortunately, the provenance was not recorded.

[2]   The inscription was photographed without a scale.

Figure 29.1: Inscription, with text upsidedown, on the Herodian masonry, east of the Triple Gate (photo by Y. Baruch).

Figure 29.2: Facsimile of inscription of Fig. 29.1 with text turned right side up.

The inscription reads:

משרי יהו

Or

ה
משת יהו
ח

Comments on the letters:

Mem—The letter is very clear. It is totally open on the left side; the type is frequently found on ossuaries.[3]

---

[3]   For example: Corpus CIIP, Nos. 54, 69, 75 and more.

Figure 29.3: Inscription at Jesus's Cradle (photo by D. Czitron and Y. Baruch).

Figure 29.4: Facsimile of Fig. 29.3.

Shin—The letter is very clear. Note the vertical stroke, which is slightly longer downward from the point where the right stroke connects to it, as is customary on ossuary inscriptions.[4]

Taw/Heh or Het—the two vertical strokes of the letter are very clear. It is not certain whether there is a short horizontal bar on the lower part of the left vertical stroke, which might render the letter as a *taw*, or if these are just a line of shallow dots left by the chisel of a stonecutter or mason.

The upper horizontal bar of the letter is clearly connected to the top of the right vertical stroke. However, due to the lighting of the picture, it is not clear whether it is connected to the top of the left vertical stroke. If there is no connection, there are two possibilities: *dalet/resh* and *waw/yod*.

---

4   For example: Corpus CIIP, Nos. 16, 19 and more.

It seems that the case of a single letter is more likely. It is difficult to know whether the upper horizontal bar is cut as a very thick line so that the right vertical stroke does not protrude above the top of the horizontal bar. Hence, it is difficult to know whether this is a *het* (if the right vertical line rises above the horizontal bar) or a *he*. To the left of this letter, the space is slightly wider than the spaces between the other letters, and these are probably two words separated by a space, as is suggested below.

Waw/yod or *zayin*—It is difficult to say if there is a thickening to the right at the top of the vertical stroke, as in a *zayin*, or to the left, as in a *waw* or *yod*. As the letter *zayin* is somewhat rare in use in the Jewish script, one has to choose *waw/yod*, which are the most frequently used letters. On the other hand, it is not possible to choose between the *waw* and the *yod* as they are similar and even identical in the Jewish script in this period.

He—The fifth letter is very clear, whether the left vertical stroke is connected or unconnected to the upper horizontal bar.

Waw—Although the upper part of the letter is damaged by a fracture in the stone, the letter is quite long and can easily be identified.

In addition, it should be noted that on each side of this inscription a vertical short stroke is incised. The distance of these strokes from the inscription indicates that they are not part of the inscription and are not letters (*waw* or *yod*).

The shape of the letters points to a date in the Early Roman (late Second Temple) period, namely to the 1st century BCE and 1st century CE, down to the sack of the city in 70 CE.

DISCUSSION

If it were an inscription from the Iron II, one could point without hesitation to a private name with a theophoric suffix—*Yahu*. In the late Second Temple period, this is no longer possible, although the left part of the inscription can be identified as holding the name of the God of Israel (the defective form of the tetragrammaton, lacking its last letter). This is supported by the fact that the inscription is located within the boundaries of the Temple Mount.

The first suggested reading, משת יהו, introduces the Aramaic word *MšRI*, which denotes a place to stay, rest or camp. The root שר"ה refers among others to a spirit that rests in a place, or even the Divine Presence (the *Shekhinah*) that rests in this place, which serves as its holy abode.

From other, alternative readings one can find some sense only in משת יהו.

There are two possible derivations of the root שת"ה: the word (משת(ה, which is a banquet where wine is consumed, and so the inscription could have been incised by one of the frequenters to the Temple Mount during one of the festivals. Another derivation is from the root שת"ת, foundation. Since this inscription is not an official one, it could have been incised by one of the masons who, during the construction of the Temple Mount in the 1st century BCE or CE, was providing instructions for the location of the stone in the construction. Alternatively, one of the persons who celebrated the inauguration of the newly constructed Temple Mount walls could have incised his name. In any case, the location of the stone at the southeastern corner of the Herodian Temple Mount excludes it from the boundaries of the *halakhic* Temple Mount.

There is no doubt that this is an unofficial inscription, incised by a private, literate person. As we have at our disposal only a few non-funerary Hebrew/Aramaic inscriptions in the Jewish script from the late Second Temple period, this seems to be an important, welcome addition. It is not possible to determine whether the inscription was incised after the stone had already been set in its place on the Temple Mount Wall or when it was still in the quarry and was marked as destined to be taken to the Temple Mount Wall, as can be inferred from the first reading alternative (above).

INSCRIPTION AT THE SOUTHWESTERN CORNER

The excavations conducted in July 2021 by Yuval Baruch and Hélène Machline in the lower courses of the southwestern corner of the Temple Mount revealed the lowest courses of the corner, numerated S, T, U and V by Charles Warren (Warren 1884: Pls. 28, 29), with Course V based upon bedrock. In several places, incised letters were revealed:

1. Three letters incised in one level line were found on the face of Course S pointing west, at a distance of 1 m from the corner (Fig. 29.5). The letters, whose average height was ca. 7 cm, were deeply incised into the flat face of the ashlar, which bore rough chisel markings.

     The letters read: קר ח *(qof, resh* and *het).*

At first, another letter was suspected in the space between the *resh* and *het*, but a careful on-site examination with lighting from various directions ruled out this possibility.

The letters are written in the so-called Jewish Script in its lapidary form, which prevailed in the 1st century BCE and 1st century CE.

The *qof* has a precise parallel in the "Place of Trumpeting" inscription that was installed on the same corner of the Temple Mount, more than 30 m higher up (CIIP, No. 5).

There are several parallels for the *resh* and *het* on the "Tomb of the Sons of Hezir" inscription (CIIP, No. 137). The single occurrence of the letter *qof* is unfortunately damaged.

Figure 29.5: Inscription that reads qof, resh and het, at the southwestern corner of the Temple Mount (photo by S. Halevi).

A considerably large number of the original Herodian stones that construct the Temple Mount's vast retaining walls are extant, exposed and known to science. Yet on the majority, there are no markings from their period of construction. Until recently, only single letters and signs were known from stones incorporated in their southeastern (Warren 1884: Pls. 19, 20, 21: F, G; 22, 23) and northeastern corners (Warren 1884: Pl. 21: C, D, E). It should be noted that the said signs are marked on foundation stones, and when construction works on the Temple Mount concluded, these were not seen by anyone.

An interpretation of the meaning of these markings was published recently (Reich and Baruch 2016a, 2016b). The newly found markings published here augment and support the former interpretation (see Chapter 27).

The letters discovered by Warren were read as initials: *qof* for *QRBN* (*qorban,* sacrifice), *het* for *HRM* (*herem,* consecration) and *taw* for *TRMH* (*terumah,* heave offering).

The three letters published here should be read in the same way:

קר[בן] ח[ר]ם]

QRBN HRM

The sign *QR* supports the former reading, since here the letter *resh* is added to the *qof,* and the reading QRBN becomes definitive.

It should be added that in the present case the letters can be read right away, different from letters marked on the eastern corners, where some of them are in an upside-down stance. That disposition was explained by saying that those letters were marked when the stones were still in the quarry and destined for the Temple Mount works. The present stone does not add any information on this issue.

The letters marked on the stones at the three corners of the Temple Mount were interpreted as dedications when the construction of each one of the corners was initiated. This marks the corners not only as locations where construction started but also as "cornerstones" in the ceremonial meaning of the idiom. These letters stand in contrast to the fact that there are absolutely no contemporary markings or graffiti on any other stone of the seen parts of the Temple Mount Walls, pointing to the fact that the local population, as well as that of the many pilgrims who frequented the site and were in close proximity to the walls, avoided any undesired contact or damage to the walls of the sacred precinct.

2. On the face of Course T pointing south at a distance of 2.53 m from the corner, one letter and a vertical stroke, incised in one level line, were observed (Fig. 29.6). The average height of the letters was ca.10 cm. The markings were deeply incised into the flat face of the ashlar which bore rough chiseling marks.

The letters read: | ח

That is: *het* and a vertical stroke.

The *het* should be interpreted as all other occurrences of this letter on the Temple Mount's corners, that is, an abbreviation of *herem* (religious dedication), as stated above. The vertical line seems not to be a *waw,* as it lacks the upper short turn to the left. It might be the beginning of a second letter, the execution of which was not completed, but also a dividing line between separate letters.

3. On the face of Course T that points westward at a distance of 0.34 m from the corner, several signs incised in one level line were observed (Fig. 29.7). The average height of the letters was ca. 10 cm. The letters were deeply incised into the flat face of the ashlar which bore rough chiseling marks. There were traces of four or five letters. It is almost impossible to decipher the signs, since the letters were severely damaged, either deliberately, or by later chiseling of the face of the stone, or both.

Figure 29.6: Inscription 2 at the southwestern corner of the Temple Mount (photo by S. Halevi).

Figure 29.7: Inscription 3 at the southwestern corner of the Temple Mount (photo by S. Halevi).

REFERENCES

CIIP: Cotton, H.M., Di Segni, L., Eck, W., Isaac, B., Kushnir-Stein, A., Misgav, H., Price, J., Roll, I. and Yardeni, A. 2010. *Corpus Inscriptionum Iudaeae/Palaestinae*, Vol. 1: *Jerusalem*. Berlin and New York.

Reich, R. and Baruch, Y. 2016a. The Meaning of the Inscribed Stones at the Corners of the Herodian Temple Mount. *Revue Biblique* 123(1): 118–124.

Reich, R. and Baruch, Y. 2016b. The Meaning of the Inscribed Stones at the Corners of the Herodian Temple Mount (Y. Naveh Volume). *Eretz-Israel* 32: 187–190 (Hebrew).

Warren, C. 1884. *Plans, Elevations, Sections, etc. Shewing the Results of the Excavations at Jerusalem, 1867–70, Executed for the Committee of the Palestine Exploration Fund.* London.

CHAPTER 30

THE ISAIAH 66:14 INSCRIPTION RECONSIDERED

Ronny Reich and Yaakov Billig

During the B. Mazar excavations (1971: 20–21, Pl. 32; 1975: 94), the now famous incomplete and defective Hebrew inscription of the verse from Isaiah 66:14 (Figs. 30.1–3) was noticed on the Western Wall of the Temple Mount by Y. Margovsky.. The inscription is carved on the Western Wall, 21.90 m north of the southwest corner, above and close to burials Nos. 52 and 56 in the Early Islamic cemetery. It is our opinion that the inscription relates to that cemetery (see Chapter 26).[1]

The inscription reads:

וראיתם ושש לבכם ועצמותם כדש]א

And when ye see this, your heart shall rejoice, and your bones shall flourish like an herb.

The inscription is carved on the Herodian masonry (Stone Course I, according to Warren's numbering; Warren 1884: Pl. 29), just below the long lower horizontal groove cut in the wall. Although this fact seems irrelevant to the inscription, there might be a relation (see Chapters 26 and 27). We attribute relevance to the thus far unnoticed fact that the inscription is located on the wall ca. 1.1 m above the level of the burials and abuts the bottom of Course J and the upper part of Course K, just above the drain (Warren 1884: Pl. 29).

Unfortunately, this inscription has never been dealt with paleographically in order to scientifically fix its dating, and we do not venture to do this here either. The only dating of the inscription and quest for its significance done thus far has sought historical events favorable to Jews in order to justify the incising of a Hebrew inscription which expresses a messianic or optimistic sentiment or feeling. B. Mazar first suggested the mid-4th century CE incident during the reign of Emperor Julian the Apostate (360–363 CE). Ben-Dov (1986: 16–19) offered several suggestions, including the reign of Theodosius II (408–450 CE), the Persian-Sassanid raid (614 CE), the Muslim conquest of Jerusalem (638 CE) or the Umayyad period, when 70 Jewish families were moved from Tiberias and settled near the Temple Mount (Ben-Dov 1985: 219, 222; 1986: 16–19; CIIP, No. 790).

K. Könen (1990) discussed the meaning and nature of the inscription, dwelling mainly on the facts that it is defective and deviates from the Masoretic Text in two points. These differences were already mentioned in the past, but no explanation was suggested, and Könen's seems to be the first to suggest a meaning. Könen indicates that the defective form of the inscription might lead to understanding it in two different ways:

1. In which דשא *DŠ'* (grass) is understood positively, and its third person plural ending refers to the dead. As this is not the case of a theological text but of a short inscription, Könen is of the opinion that specific persons are referred to in the inscription, i.e., martyrs.

---

[1] The facsimile of the inscription published by Mazar (1971: 20, Fig. 14) gives the full version of the word דשא although on the clear picture published (Mazar 1971: Pl. 32), the *alef* is not extant. This was already observed by Ben-Dov (1986: 17). We present a new drawing of the inscription (Fig. 30.3).

2. In which *DŠ'* is seen in a negative light. Unlike the spirit expressed in the Masoretic Text, it is not the regeneration of bones that is meant but rather their temporary existence. The bones mentioned here are not the bones of specific dead persons but represent a group of people. The third person plural (as opposed to the second person plural in the Masoretic Text) might refer to enemies, whose bones the writer of the inscription wishes might perish like grass. According to Könen, the lack of data for the precise dating prevents us from identifying the persons referred to in the inscription, whether they be martyrs or enemies.

On the other hand, one can argue that the inscription was incised not necessarily in conjunction with a particular historical event of the magnitude mentioned above, which created an atmosphere that favored the Jews, and that it was carved by a Jew in times hard to bear, which brought about the choice of this particular verse that expresses a hope in future relief based on deep religious faith.

There was also a suggestion to see the defective writing in *W'SMWTM* (their bones) as a ligature between the *taw* and a *kaf* that is embedded in the long upper bar of the *taw* on its left-hand side (Giesser and Erlich 2013: 326). This suggestion should be rejected as it inserts another deviation, a third one, from the Masoretic Text, as it omits the *yod*.

If the inscription is indeed related to the cemetery, the following facts should be borne in mind (Figs 30.4–5):

1. The cemetery is located *intra muros*, a fact outstanding for a cemetery of any denomination. There are no such cemeteries (different from single burials) known in Jerusalem.

Figure 30.1: The Isaiah 66:14 inscription.

Figure 30.2: Close-up of the Isaiah 66:14 inscription.

Figure 30.3: Facsimile of the Isaiah 66:14 inscription.

Figure 30.4: Burial 91 at the Western Wall. The worker is pointing to the Isaiah 66:14 inscription.

Figure 30.5: Excavating burial at the Western Wall. The Isaiah
66:14 inscription is ca. 1 m above the man's head.

2. The cemetery included burials mostly of Muslims. An inscribed stone slab mentioning a
    Christian name might be related to it. And the Hebrew inscription might refer to Jews as well.

3. The location of the cemetery is outstanding. It occupies a narrow (4 m wide) and very long (at
    least 50–60 m) strip of land, between an external wall of a main building (Umayyad Building
    IV) and the Western Wall of the Temple Mount. In addition, it is possible that the long, incised
    groove on the wall, which might have served as a water channel in earlier times, supported a
    wooden floor that ran all along this strip and above it (Chapter 27).

We would like to suggest that the inscription was incised by a Jewish passerby, but not someone
who accidentally found himself here at the Western Wall of the Temple Mount and expressed
his feelings, which were aroused by a general religious or political situation. We believe that the
inscription was incised by a Jewish passerby in direct relation to the cemetery that was situated right
below it. However, it can still be understood in either a positive or a negative sense.

If understood positively, the inscription should be considered almost as a tombstone, or perhaps
an epitaph, which foresees or wishes a resurrection for the persons buried below it. In this case it

must refer to a Jewish identity of at least some of the persons buried, as the archaeological finds point to burial customs of different types. Most seem to be Muslim, but some might be Christian, as alluded by the Arabic inscription found by Mazar (Mazar 1971: 21; Sharon 1973: 217–220) and corroborated by the fact that several burials were carried out in wooden coffins from which some iron nails survived, as the archaeological record shows. We are aware of the fact that followers of different faiths were, and still are, buried in separate cemeteries, usually outside the city's limits. However, one should not exclude the extreme situation (siege, plague, the earthquake of 1033 CE?), in which the dead of various denominations could not be brought to traditional burial and were buried, rather hastily, inside the city's boundaries.

A possible negative attitude of the inscription cannot be ruled out either. Again, it would have been incised by a Jew, who during a period of religious and political tolerance would have dared to approach the cemetery along the Western Wall of the Temple Mount and wrote his verse above a cemetery of his religious opponents (mostly Muslim, perhaps some also Christian), gaining by this act personal revenge. The second person plural in *WR'YTM* (you will see, you will observe)[2] refers to his fellow Jews whom he calls upon to rejoice, and the third person plural of *W'ṢMWTM* (their bones) and the deliberate omission of the last word of the original verse, in contradiction to the Masoretic Text, refers to his opponents' bones, which will turn into grass.

REFERENCES

CIIP: Cotton, H.M., Di Segni, L., Eck, W., Isaac, B., Kushnir-Stein, A., Misgav, H., Price, J., Roll, I. and Yardeni, A. 2010. *Corpus Inscriptionum Iudaeae/Palaestinae*, Vol. 1: *Jerusalem*. Berlin and New York.

Ben-Dov, M. 1985. *In the Shadow of the Temple: The Discovery of Ancient Jerusalem*. New York.

Ben-Dov, M. 1986. Hebrew Inscriptions Carved on Stone from the Temple Mount. *Cathedra* 40: 3–30 (Hebrew).

Giesser, A. and Erlich, Z.H. 2013. "*Ve'azmotechem*" and also "*Ve'azmotam*"! The Graffiti Artist Who Turned to Be a Torah Scholar: On the Meaning of the "*Ure'item*" Inscription on the Western Wall. In: Baruch, E. and Faust, A., eds. *New Studies on Jerusalem* 19. Ramat Gan: 323–329.

Könen, K. 1990. Zur Inschrift unter dem Robinsonbogen. *Zeitschrift des Deutschen Palästina-Vereins* 106: 180–182.

Mazar, B. 1971. The Excavations in the Old City of Jerusalem near the Temple Mount—Second Preliminary Report, 1969–70 Seasons. *Eretz-Israel* 10: 1–34 (Hebrew).

Mazar, B. 1975. *Mountain of the Lord: Excavating in Jerusalem*. Jerusalem.

Sharon, M. 1973. Arabic Inscriptions from the Excavations at the Western Wall. *Israel Exploration Journal* 23: 214–220.

Warren, C. 1884. *Plans, Elevations, Sections, etc. Shewing the Results of the Excavations at Jerusalem, 1867–70, Executed for the Committee of the Palestine Exploration Fund*. London.

---

[2]   One could argue that in *W'ṢMWTM*, the *taw*, which has an extremely long upper bar, is in fact a ligature of the *taw* and the *kaf* of the original Masoretic test. Such a suggestion, however, leaves out the *yod* of the original text.

CHAPTER 31

ARABIC INSCRIPTIONS

Moshe Sharon

In 1969, Arabic inscriptions dating to the 11th century CE were found during the excavations directed by Benjamin Mazar outside the Southern and Western Walls of the Temple Mount. Subsequently, Israel Antiquities Authority archaeologists discovered Arabic inscriptions from the 1st century until about the end of the 5th century after the Hijrah (AH; 11th century CE).

In 1973, I published a few of the inscriptions in the *Israel Exploration Journal (*1973: 214–222): two fragments of epitaphs and one fragment of a monumental inscription (one word), apparently of a construction text (Fig. 31.1–3). In Vol. 7 of the *CIAP*, I published an additional inscription from the 1st Hijrah century (7th century CE), although I was still unable to read part of it (*CIAP* 32–41). I also added another inscription to those already published in the *IEJ*, which I ascribed to the year 105 AH (723 CE). This inscription embodied a special feature. It was, in fact, an elaborate graffiti. I did not define it as such, however, because of the fine script that revealed the inscription's date (more or less), which led to my ability to determine the reason for engraving it. It had been engraved on the shallow-dressed margin of a typical Herodian ashlar. When the inscription was engraved at the Western Wall near Robinson's Arch, the area was already covered with earth and rubble so an individual standing upright could easily reach the margin of the ashlar in order to engrave on it.

Engraving inscriptions on the margins of Herodian building stones was taken up by others in the vicinity of Robinson's Arch. One or two inscriptions were discovered by later archaeologists, but they were of bad quality and only one of them, which seems to be the last part of an epitaph, can be read. In every case, the remaining letters seem to belong to the beginning of the 2nd century AH (8th century CE). The complete inscription that I published in *CIAP* 7: 113, No. 11, is about 1 m long, and although one tends to think that it is similar in style and content to the inscriptions more recently discovered, that is not necessarily so. These inscriptions were engraved on a different level and, although graffiti in style, they seem to belong to another period, which could not be much later than the end of the 2nd/8th century. The letters of most of these inscriptions were on the whole destroyed except for a few, which might indicate their age (Fig. 31.4).

The three fragments and the one complete epitaph that I published in 1973 in the *IEJ* belong to different periods. Two fragments (Sharon 1973: Pls. 55B and C, Figs. 31.1–2) are the beginnings of epitaphs readings *hādhā qabr m…* (this is the grave of M…). They continue with the names of the deceased, both of which begin with an *m*. The two fragments are from the same period, even the same year, and were found *in-situ* in a small cemetery of about 15 graves situated to the north of the southwestern corner of the Temple Mount (Sharon 1973: 214). The cemetery was used for a short period; the graves seem to have been dug for a group of victims buried at the same time. Since a Crusader structure was built over it, the cemetery antedates the Crusader period (Sharon 1973: 216).

This cemetery, therefore, could have been dug at the very latest at the beginning of 1099 CE, just before the Crusader conquest of Jerusalem. However, this is merely a theoretical attempt to establish a chronological sequence of events. Since the small cemetery seems to have been used at one time for a small number of victims, we must look for a tragic event in which a group of

Figure 31.1: An epitaph from the 8th century CE.

Figure 31.2: An epitaph from the 8th century CE.

Figure 31.3: Fragment of a building inscription. 11th–12th century CE.

Figure 31.4: Declaration of faith from the time of Caliph ʿAbd al-Malik.

people all died at the same time and had to be buried in a makeshift cemetery. Only one such tragic event fits; it occurred during the Seljūq conquest of Jerusalem, probably in 1076. In that year, the Seljūq commander of Atsiz had to deal with an uprising of the Jerusalemites against him. He unleashed a terrible slaughter on the rebellious Jerusalemites, sparing not even those who took refuge in the Al-Aqṣa Mosque. Some of the victims of this tragedy were most probably buried in this cemetery. When the Crusaders built the structure over the cemetery, they must have used stones with inscriptions from the graves. The letters of the inscriptions in Figs. 31.1 and 31.2 belong to the 5th century AH (11th century CE) and agree with the above discussion. In the same area of the cemetery, another small fragment of a monumental inscription was found in secondary use. It is not part of an epitaph but seems to belong to a building inscription (Fig. 31.3). The monumental style of this fragment takes us to the time of the Fatimid Caliph aẓ-Ẓahir (1021–1036) or even Muṣtanṣir (1036–1094). These were the dates of extensive building activity on the Temple Mount.

COMPLETE EPITAPH

In the same area of the cemetery, although not part of it, a complete inscription was found—an epitaph dated to 1002 (Fig. 31.5). It is not *in-situ* and was brought from somewhere else to the cemetery. It was broken in two; one section was used to cover the grave and the other was used as part of its side. In spite of its broken state, the inscription was not affected. The complete slab of marble measures 0.85 × 0.625 m, nine lines of beautiful, monumental angular script ornamented with barbs; incised. In line two, the name of the deceased was dug out intentionally and a different

Figure 31.5: A complete epitaph, 392 AH (1002 CE).

name (illegible) was engraved. The epitaph seems to belong to a Christian and has parallels (Sharon 1973: Pl. 56: B). It reads as follows:

١)بسم الحي الذي لايموت ٢)هذا قبر ... ٣)...ايا توفي يوم الثلثا ٤)لخمس بقين من شعبان٥)شنة اثنين وتسعين وثلثما ٦)ية رحمه الله ورحم والد ٧)يه محروم من ٨)تعرض للدفن٩) في هذا البيت

In the name of the living one who will not die. This is the grave of … ayā. He died on Tuesday 24 of Shaʻbān in the year 392 (8 July 1002). May Allah forgive him and his two parents, excommunicated will be whoever objects to the burial in this house.

The inscription was engraved some 60–70 years before the cemetery became operative and was brought from elsewhere to be used as building material for a grave in the cemetery, and as mentioned above, for this purpose it was broken in two.

THE EARLIEST INSCRIPTION FROM THE SAME AREA

The most exciting find from this area is an inscription from the 1st century AH/7th century CE. The inscription itself is a block of limestone in secondary usage, serving as a building stone in the right wall of a miḥrāb of a small mosque, next to the southwestern corner of the Temple Mount, not far from Robinson's Arch (Fig. 31.6). I mentioned it in my *IEJ* article (1973: 24), observing, "Undoubtedly it dates from the first century." At the time, in spite of investing great effort, I could

Figure 31.6: The earliest Arabic inscription found in the Holy Land, probably from the year 32 AH (652–653 CE).

not decipher more than the last five lines. Now, more than half a century later, I can only add one more line (Line 4), which enables me to define the nature of the inscription, which I published in *CIAP* 7 (J2: No. 01: 33–41). I believe that it is a rare document that commemorates the agreement between the Muslim conquerors of Jerusalem and its citizens and specifies the Muslim leaders who witnessed (*shahidū*) the agreement (See also Sharon 2018).

SPECIAL CATEGORY: GRAFFITI ON THE MARGINS OF THE WESTERN WALL ASHLARS

This is an interesting category. I describe it as graffiti although, in fact, it is properly engraved in what can be described as a very early, simple, Umayyad, nonprofessional script, which may be allocated from the late 7th to the very early 8th century CE. The inscriptions, or what remains of them, were incised on the finely dressed margins of the typical, huge Herodian ashlars of the southern part of the outer Western Wall. The earliest inscription of this category was found in the same area in 1969, during the B. Mazar excavations; more were found almost completely defaced in recent excavations near Robinson's Arch. The inscription found in 1969 seemed to me complete at the time. However, recent photographs revealed the *basmalah* with which it opens (Fig. 31.7). It is published here, complete, for the first time. In the original publication of this inscription in the *CIAP*, I attributed it to the year 723 CE to keep the inscriptions in chronological order.

The inscription uncovered by Mazar in 1969 was found near the southwestern outside corner of the Temple Mount on the shallow dressed margin of a typical Herodian ashlar, 1 m long. One line was discovered in the third or fourth course of the wall facing north. At the time, it was the height of an average person, which should also have been its height above the ground when it was incised, which means that the excavators reached the original height of the inscription above the ground when it was engraved, with no points and no vowels (*CIAP* 7 (2) no. 11: 113–116). The style of the script enables the dating of the inscription to the time of ʿAbd al-Malik, about the beginning of the 2nd century AH/8th century CE (Fig. 31.7).

TEXT AND TRANSLATION

بسم الله الرحمن الرحيم اسمعيل بن الحسين يشهد الا اله الا الله وحده لا شريك له

Basmalah. Ismaʿil b. al-Ḥusayn testifies that there is no god but Allah alone He has no companion.

This is a simple declaration of faith representing the mood of the time and the policy of the Caliph, ʿAbd al-Malik, after he succeeded in unifying the empire and putting an end to the rebellion of ʿAbd Allah b. al-Zubayr in Arabia and the eastern provinces of the empire. He then declared Mecca, once again, as Islam's major shrine and as the House of Allah, the only God (*ibid.*: 114). It does not affect the message of the inscription, which was circulated throughout the empire with the message of Allah's unity and singularity. It became fashionable for people to declare this message, which appeared on every official document and on every silver and gold coin (see *CIAP, ibid.* 114 and figure there). For instance, we read on the coins: *lā ilāh illa allah waḥdahu la sharīka lahu*—There is no god but Allah alone He has no companion. The coins were a very effective means of disseminating the wishes of the caliph.

Another inscription, 2 m long, is located not far from the inscription above, on the shallow dressed margin of a Herodian ashlar on the Western Wall of the Temple Mount, to the south of Robinson's Arch (Fig. 31.8). It seems to be a copy of the last inscription (Fig. 31.7), with some unreadable additions at its beginning and/or its end. When engraved, it was no higher than the height of an average man who could easily reach the lower margin of the ashlar with his tools. Umayyad script, simple, well-defined, angular letters, no points, no vowels and no signs; incised. Most of the inscription is defaced, but the end of it, about 1 m, is preserved (Fig. 31.9). It reads: *raḥima allah man taraḥḥama ʿalayhi*—May Allah forgive whoever asks forgiveness for him [the deceased].

Figure 31.7: Declaration of faith from the time of Caliph ʿAbd al-Malik (photo by Y. Vaknin).

Figure 31.8: Declaration of faith from the time of caliph 'Abd al-Malik (photo by Y. Vaknin).

Figure 31.9: Invocation from the 8th century CE (photo by Y. Vaknin).

The inscription seems to refer to a deceased person in the Islamic cemetery. The Umayyad script dated this inscription to the 7th/early 8th century CE. However, since the cemetery itself was dated, as explained above, to the 11th century CE, the inscription indicates the burial of people already in the 7th/early 8th century CE. This inscription was then reused in the 11th century CE. This is a wild guess, but without which, we cannot find any relation between the cemetery and the WW1 and WW2 inscriptions, which should be treated independently. There was no doubt that the defaced and lost part in the beginning of the inscription bore the name of the deceased before the last part of the inscription, that contains the invocation, although it is difficult to know how it could be attached to a specific grave. Before the last readable part of the inscription there is one letter that is very clear. It is either *dāl* (D) or *kāf* (K), followed by an invocation. This letter was the end of the name of the deceased or the name of his father. A creative reconstruction of the text might read something like the following:

Basmalah. This is the grave of 'Abdallah b Dāwud may Allah forgive him and whosoever asks mercy for him.

REFERENCES

CIAP: Sharon, M. 1997–2021. *Corpus Inscriptionum Arabcarum Palaestinae*, Vols. 1-7. Leiden. Vols. 1–7. Leiden.

Sharon, M. 1973. Arabic Inscriptions from the Excavations at the Western Wall. *Israel Exploration Journal* 23: 214–220.

Sharon, M. 2018. "Witnessed by Three Disciples of the Prophet." *Israel Exploration Journal* 68(1): 100–111.

CHAPTER 32

THE THICKNESS OF THE WESTERN WALL: GROUND PENETRATING RADAR IMAGING

Uri Basson

King Herod's plans for and execution of the expansion of the Temple Mount enclosure was undoubtedly the most massive building project ever undertaken in the Land of Israel in antiquity, and indeed until modern times. Of this vast project, the Eastern, Southern and Western Walls have been preserved until today—evidence of the high quality of execution by architects and masons who lived 2000 years ago.

For religious and political reasons, archaeological excavations have not been carried out inside the enclosure, and excavations will undoubtedly not be carried out in the foreseeable future. The walls, however, have been explored for over 16 decades now, and we must content ourselves with excavating and understanding their outer faces.

Three times prior to the research described in this paper, scientists attempted to inspect the internal structure of several of the walls' stones by geophysical means. The first attempt was undertaken by Amos Levanon in 1968 on behalf of the Geophysical Institute of Israel during Hebrew University archaeological excavations near the Southern Wall. The wall's stability had become an issue and experts were called in. Measurements were taken using Electrical Resistivity (ER) (Schlumberger method with four electrodes) in two locations on the Southern Wall (Levanon 1968). The exact location where the measurements were taken is not marked in their report, but it was probably done at the excavation level of September 25, 1968. The measured ER values of the two locations showed the following: (1) from the outer face of the wall to a depth of 4.2–4.9 m, the ER values were relatively high—a good fit for hard, dense limestone; (2) beyond this depth, a drop was noted in the ER values—a good fit for loose fill materials behind the wall. Therefore, the conclusion of the ER measurements was that the thickness of the stones can be estimated at 4.2–4.9 m. A second attempt was carried out during the Israel Ministry of Religious Services' clearing of the Western Wall tunnels, where a monumental ashlar, extending over three courses of the Western Wall (13.60 m long and 3.50 m tall), was found. GPR imaging was undertaken using a frequency of 225 MHz (Jol *et al.* 2006). The resolution of the 2006 imaging was poor; nevertheless, the thickness of the stone was estimated to be 1.8–2.5 m. The next attempt was made by me on May 16, 2017, on behalf of the City of David Foundation, during the excavation of the Herodian Street and its substructure (Basson 2017). During this attempt, sharp results of Ground Penetrating Radar (GPR) images conducted on the foundation course of the southwestern corner of the Temple Mount, founded directly on bedrock, presented a thickness of ca. 2.2 m for the cornerstone, and penetrating the next stone as well. This stone and others nearby, which were also imaged and measured, revealed thicknesses ranging from about 2.2 m to ca. 3.2 m and established a scientific basis for the extensive research described in this paper.

In 2020, I had the unique opportunity to research and image the structure of the Western Wall in complete large segments (Fig. 32.1) using state-of-the-art GPR (see part of the findings: Baruch

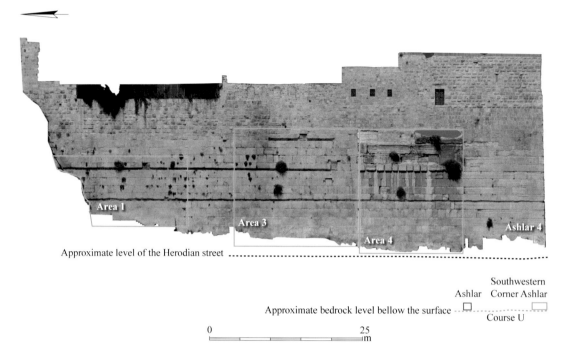

Figure 32.1: Location of the GPR imaging areas on the Western Wall: Area 1) south of the Mughrabi Gate; Area 4) Robinson's Arch. Locations of the specific GPR imaging profile conducted in each area are presented in Fig. 32.2a and Fig. 32.2b (model by Alex Wigmann).

et al. 2021; Basson 2021). The imaging was conducted together with measurements of the physical properties of the propagating electromagnetic waves (EMW) and calibration of typical ashlars. High Dynamic Range (HDR) GPR imaging measurements were conducted to explore the structure of the wall and its stones and to measure their thicknesses. It should be stressed that, in comparison to the past local, specific analyses, this investigation scanned and imaged the Herodian ashlars to the full height of the wall and along considerable stretches.

The opportunity to conduct this unique imaging of complete sections of the Western Wall and explore the structure and measure the thicknesses of its stones was carried out in cooperation with the preservation activities of the Israel Antiquities Authority (IAA). The research included the southern part of the Western Wall, from the ramp of the Mughrabi Gate to the southwestern corner of the Temple Mount. This section was divided into five segments, according to the scaffolding that was built for the conservation activities and moved respectively. During the days of the imaging, many GPR profiles with different frequencies (Table 32.1) were conducted above and below the surface level of the Western Wall and Course U (founded on top of the bedrock of the southwestern corner of the Temple Mount; Warren 1884: Pl. XXVIII), together with calibration measurements of electromagnetic properties of various ashlars (see Baruch *et al.* 2021; Basson 2021).

The thickness of the ashlars revealed in the GPR imaging and described in my previous papers may not explain the structural stability of the Temple Mount. In this paper, I present indications and results for the talus-like fill behind the wall supporting the structure of the Temple Mount enclosure.

Table 32.1: Compilation of the GPR Imaging Setting and Average EMW Velocities of the Various Measurements

GPR Imaging	GX–160	GX–450	GX–750
Dates of measurements	11–12.03.2020	11–12.03.2020; 23,25.08.2020	11–12.03.2020; 23,25.08.2021
Center frequency	160 MHz	450 MHz	750 MHz
Sampling frequency	2.240 GHz	5.120 GHz	9.600 GHz
Step interval	0.05 m	0.05 m	0.02 m
Time window	216 ns	146 ns	75 ns
Stack	Automatic, typically ≥ 64	Automatic, typically ≥ 64	Automatic, typically ≥ 64
Average penetration depth range	7–10 m	4–5.5 m	2–2.5m
EMW velocity (avg. ashlars 1–4)	–	0.100 m/ns ($\pm$ 0.005 m/ns)	0.100 m/ns ($\pm$ 0.005 m/ns)
EMW velocity range into the fill	0.100–0.110 m/ns ($\pm$ 0.005 m/ns)	–	–

METHODS

GROUND PENETRATING RADAR IMAGING

GPR is a non–invasive (non–destructive) geophysical method for high-resolution imaging, characterization and mapping of shallow subsurface properties, targets and structures based on differences in the electromagnetic (EM) properties of the materials (Ulriksen 1982; Davis and Annan 1989; Basson *et al.* 1994; Basson 2000; Basson *et al.* 2002). GPR generates and uses high–frequency EMW to detect changes in EMW properties (dielectric permittivity, electric conductivity and magnetic permeability), that in a geologic setting are a function of bulk density and water content. GPR has been recognized as an ASTM D6432–19—*Active Standard for Using the Surface Ground Penetrating Radar Method for Subsurface Investigation.* Data is normally acquired using antennas placed on the ground surface or on the face of the structure (such as a wall). The transmitting antenna radiates EMW that propagates the subsurface or inside the structure and reflects from boundaries at which there are property contrasts for the EMW. The receiving GPR antenna records the reflected waves over a selectable time window. The EMW propagation velocity inside the structure can be measured or estimated so that the depths (and thicknesses) of the reflecting interfaces are measured or calculated respectively through the arrival times in the GPR imaging data.

GPR is currently applied in many different fields of research, such as geology, sedimentology, hydrology, environment, archaeology, civil engineering and tectonics. Vaughan (1986), Goodman (1994), Marco *et al.* (1997), Basson and Ginzburg (2009) and others describe GPR studies and simulations used in archaeological investigations. The research described in the paper was aimed mainly to image a variety of ashlars along courses of the Western Wall, measuring their thickness and evaluating their structural integrity.

DESCRIPTION OF THE GPR SYSTEM

The GPR system used for the imaging and mapping of the Western Wall was a MALÅ GeoScience AB Ground Explorer (GX). The GX system is based on innovative, patent-pending MALÅ High Dynamic Range (HDR) technology that allows near real time sampling that permits hyper stacking, which dramatically reduces random noise. The result is a significant increase in penetration when using 32-bit high-resolution data.

MEASUREMENT SETTING

The antennas used for the research were mainly 450 MHz and 750 MHz. During the general walkover, measurements at the beginning of the imaging, GX–160MHz profiles were conducted as well, but the results did not justify the use of this frequency for this research. Since the thicknesses of the ashlars were of greater importance, the main imaging was carried out using the GX–450 MHz.

The GPR imaging measurements of the Western Wall were conducted in 2020 during two periods and in two locations: March 11–12 (beginning of spring), south of the Mughrabi Gate (Area 1); August 23 and 25 (end of summer) at Robinson's Arch (Area 4), (Fig. 32.1). The imaging was done by GeoSense Ltd. using Ground Explorer HDR GPR GX–450 MHz, GX–750 MHz and transceivers (Figs. 32.2–32.3), according to the setting of parameters presented in Table 32.1.

IMAGING AND MEASUREMENTS OF THE EMW VELOCITIES OF FOUR REPRESENTATIVE ASHLARS

GPR systems measure time gaps between transmitted waves and reflected waves (as well as other returned waves; see Basson 2000). In order to compute depths and thicknesses at the radargrams, EM wave velocities of the substance should be measured as well. There are several ways to measure the EM velocities of stone, the most straightforward being a direct method that can also be used for assessing the visibility and resolution (quality) of the imaging together with a calibration. The places chosen to demonstrate the visibility of the GPR imaging and to measure the EM velocities (calibration) of typical wall ashlars that are exposed were described in Baruch *et al.* 2021 and Basson 2021. Since the EM velocities of limestone/dolomite (and any type of stone/rock) depend also on their moisture content (Davis and Annan 1989; Basson 1992), the qualitative and quantitative results of the imaging of the exposed stones are also a function of the seasons of the year. Therefore, the calibration imaging measurements were done twice, in early spring (March 11–12), when the moisture content was close to the maximum, and in mid-summer (August 23, 25), when the moisture content was close to the minimum.

The results of the HDR GPR calibration measurements that were conducted for several known ashlars were done at the beginning of the imaging, both in the wet and in the dry seasons, as described in Baruch *et al.* 2022, and in Basson 2021, using GX–450 MHz and GX–750 MHz settings. The calibration profiles were also used to verify the possible penetration thicknesses/depths for each frequency and the possibility to present of the internal reflections from ashlar layering and defects/flows (such as fractures, weathering and small voids), as well as the interface between the back of the ashlar and returns from the fill behind it. The penetrations in measuring ashlar thicknesses for the GX–750 MHz setting proved to be not more than ca. 1.9–2 m, while for the GX–450 MHz the decaying reflections of the higher frequency were shown clearly. The measured EMW velocity at the calibration was: 0.100 m/ns (±0.005). The measured EMW velocity for deeper returns from the inner fill using the GX–160 MHz varied from 0.100 m/ns to 0.110 m/ns (±0.005).

a)

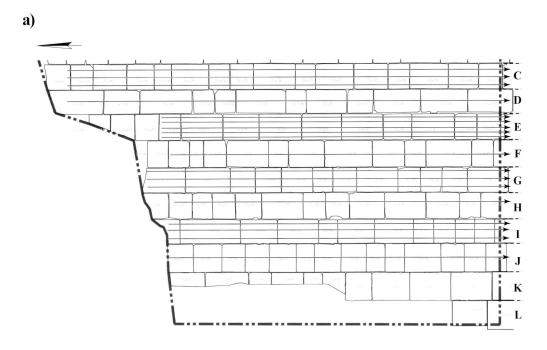

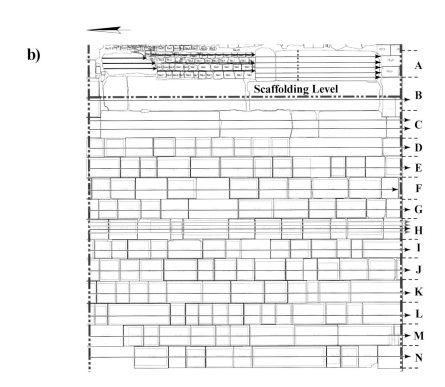

Figure 32.2: (a) The location of the GPR GX–450 MHz imaging profiles conducted at the area south of the Mughrabi Gate (Fig. 32.1, Area 1). (b) The GPR imaging profiles' location at the Robinson's Arch area (Fig. 32.1, Area 4; model and sketch by Or Roz).

Figure 32.3: Operation of the GPR GX–450 MHz system on the face of the Western Wall (operators: U. Basson and O. Nachum, GeoSense Ltd.). Left – from the operations at Area 1. Center and right – from the operations at Area 4.

ACCURACY OF THICKNESS MEASUREMENTS

The accuracy of the thickness measurements of the ashlars is mainly a function of the physical parameters of the imaging and the values of the calibrated EMW velocities. The physical parameters are the interaction of the EMW (at 450 MHz or at 750 MHz) with bulk physical properties of the rock/stone/ashlar, resulting in the quality of the visibility of the image. Since the GPR system is an HDR 32-bit data, the visibility of the images generally varied from medium to high, therefore allowing a fairly sharp interpretation and measurement of the thicknesses. The average accuracy, which takes into account the abovementioned aspects of the GPR imaging, is as follows: location/ position along the profile/courses ~ 0.10 m; thickness/depth of an ashlar ~ 5%.

THE IMAGING OF THE WESTERN WALL

THE SEGMENT ABOVE THE EARLY ROMAN STREET LEVEL

The GPR imaging of the Western Wall in Area 1 began after the field processing, interpretation and evaluation of the profiles conducted during the walkover and visibility demonstrations and measurements of the EMW velocities of the typical wall ashlars. The same procedure was carried out for the measurements of Area 4, including new measurements for calibration of the EMW velocities. As a result of the these explorations, the central frequency chosen for the complete measurements of the area was 450 MHz, although several courses were also imaged using the central frequency of 750 MHz (Table 32.1).

The location of each of the GPR profiles is presented in Fig. 32.2a (Area 1) and in Fig. 32.2b (Area 4). The GX–450 MHz and the GX–750 MHz imaging profiles are marked on each course in black. Photographs of the imaging operation using GX–750 MHz in both areas are presented in Fig. 32.3.

Typical results of the HDR GPR imaging in 450 MHz and 750 MHz of the Western Wall are presented and analyzed in several representative images (Figs. 32.4–32.6 and Figs. 32.9–32.10). The GX–450 MHz imaging along Course E, Area 1, indicates an average depth of about 5.2 m (Fig. 32.4). This GPR image was processed to enhance the back of the ashlars, but meaningful returns from the fill behind the ashlars have also been detected. These reflections/diffractions at 3–4 m deep may indicate the existence of boulders inside the fill. Prominent reflections from the interfaces of the ashlars are detected and shown clearly and sharply. Those reflections are marked on the GPR image with black lines. The dashed lines mark places where possible cracks and fractures in the ashlars were detected. The thickness of the ashlars in this course varies from about 1.0 m to 2.25 m. The results show that the thicknesses of the ashlars differ substantially along the course; moreover, the back sides of several stones have not been processed and straightened in the same manner as the outer faces. Behind the course, reflections from the internal discontinuities such as boulders inside the fill are detected as well. The GX–450 MHz imaging along Course H, Area 4, presented in Figure 32.5 also shows an average depth of about 5.2 m. This GPR image was processed the same as the one presented in Fig. 32.4. Here, too, prominent reflections from the interfaces of the ashlars are detected and shown clearly and sharply, marked on the GPR image with black lines. Like the course in Area 1, the thicknesses of the ashlars here also differ substantially along the course, and the back sides of the stones are not necessarily processed and straightened. Note that the thickness of the ashlars in this course varies from about 0.95 m to about 3.00 m, but in several locations, the enlarged thickness is due to deeper ashlars that were detected. Behind it, reflections from the internal discontinuities such as boulders inside the fill are detected as well.

Several high-resolution imaging profiles of the same course were mapped using the GX–450 MHz imaging, as presented in Fig. 32.6. The imaging of Course H, Area 4, was produced at the request of the IAA's Conservation Department, in order to enhance the visibility inside the ashlars for the ability to detect internal flaws, such as cracks and voids. This part of the course is built from rather porous and layered *mizzi hilu* and *meleke* limestones. The imaging conducted at the center of the course shows that the depth is ca. 2.6 m. Part of the near-surface flaws were fixed by the IAA conservation team: drillholes filled with glued fiberglass poles were inserted in order to reinforce fractured fragments in the massive parts of the ashlars. These reinforced poles are detected in the GPR imaging as well. It is interesting to note that between Ashlar IV.H.12 and Ashlar IV.H.11, there is a segment/ashlar (marked as 12b in Figs. 32.5–32.6) that on the surface looks like part of Ashlar IV.H.12, but according to the GPR imaging is thicker and different. It therefore may be a broken part of Ashlar 12 that was repaired in the past or an entirely different ashlar.

Vertical cross-sections of the courses at two locations in Area 1 (1.1–1.1'; 1.2–1.2') and at two locations in Area 4 (4.1–4.1'; 4.2–4.2') were compiled from the results of the imaging conducted along the courses, to present the measured thicknesses and the variations of the ashlars vertically (to the height of the Western Wall). It should be noted that the thickness of the ashlars at the cross-sections is on average about 0.9–1.6 m wide. Therefore, in places, where the cross-section passes between two ashlars it was repositioned to be on one of the ashlars. Even so, the thickness can be affected partly by the adjacent ashlar. The comparison between the areas is presented in Fig. 32.7: In Area 1, the cross-sections describe the ashlars from Course J to Course C; in Area 4, the cross-section describes the ashlars from Course N to Course A of Robinson's Arch. The one-piece ashlars

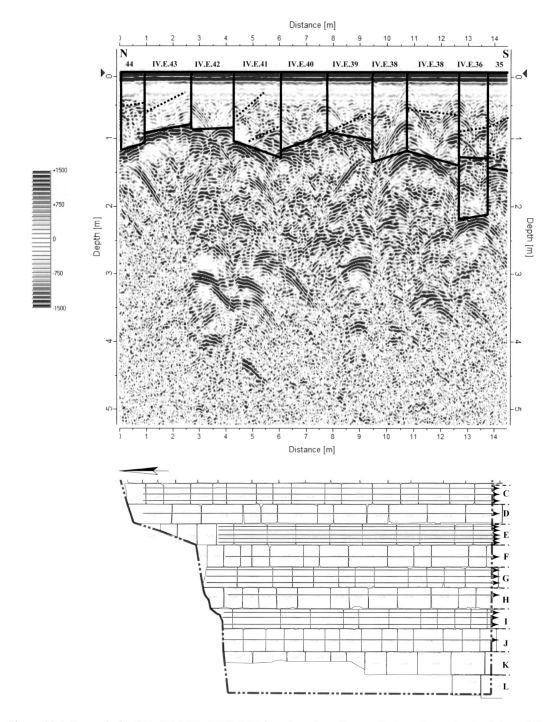

Figure 32.4: Example for GX–450 MHz HDR GPR imaging along Course E, Area 1 to a depth of about 5.2 m. The horizontal scale presents the location of the measurement along the profile (along the surface of the ashlars' course); the vertical scales present the thickness of the first ashlar and the depth/thicknesses of the "deeper" ashlars/events. The phase and the amplitude of the returned waves are displayed on the color palette. The back interface of each ashlar is marked on the GPR image with black lines. The dashed lines marked cracks and fractures inside the ashlars. Note the returns detected behind the ashlars: these reflections/diffractions at 3–4 m deep may indicate the existence of boulders inside the fill of Temple Mount (model and sketch by Or Roz).

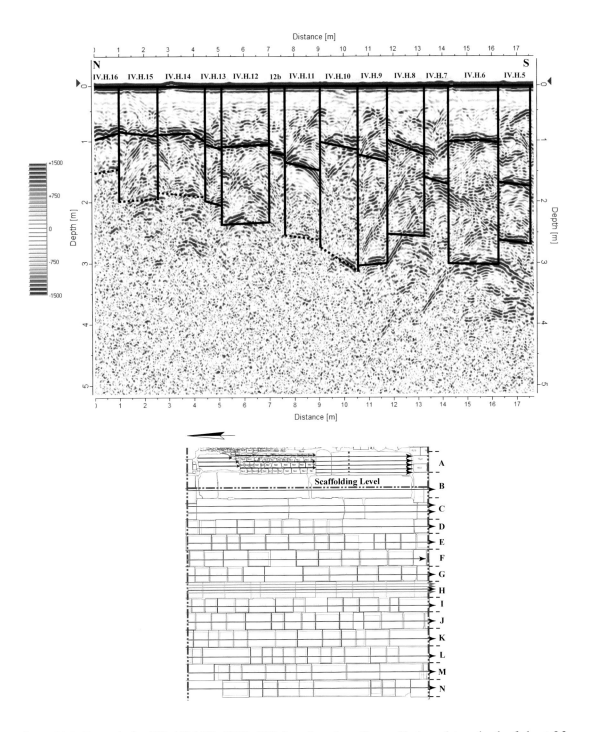

Figure 32.5: Example for GX–450 MHz HDR GPR imaging along Course H, Area 4 to a depth of about 5.2 m (for scales and palette description—see Fig. 32.6). The back interface of each ashlar is marked on the GPR image with black lines (model and sketch by Or Roz).

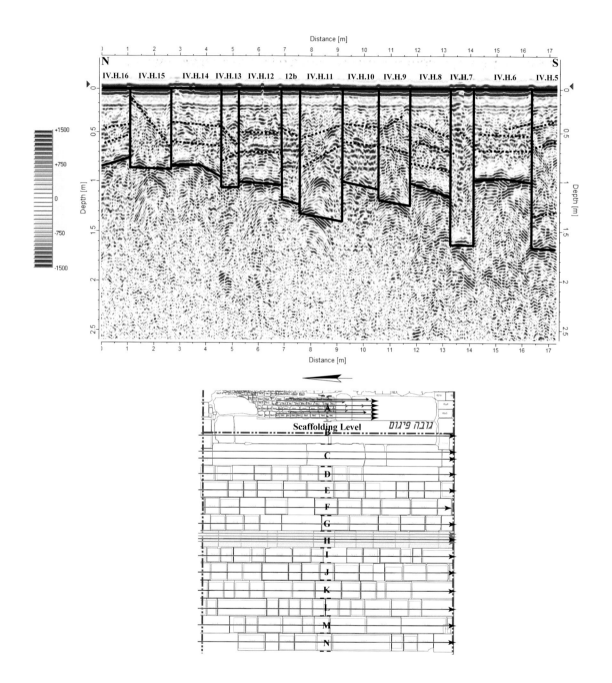

Figure 32.6: Example for GX–750 MHz HDR GPR high–resolution imaging along Course H, Area 4 to a depth of about 2.6 m (for scales and palette description, see Fig. 32.4). The back interface of each ashlar is marked on the GPR image with black lines. The dashed lines marked cracks and fractures inside the ashlars. Cracks and fractures inside the ashlars are not marked on this image since they are marked on the deeper penetration image presented in Fig. 32.5. Also, diffractions from drills done by the preservation of IAA, filled with glued fiberglass poles that were inserted for reinforcing fractured fragments, are detected as well (for example: in positions: 2.8 m, 3.4 m, 6.1 m, 7.0 m and 13.6 m; model and sketch by Or Roz).

are marked in thick black lines. In places where the ashlar looks broken or as if it may be built of two close ashlars (as Ashlar 2 and Ashlar 3 at the calibration, see Baruch *et al.* 2022; Basson 2022), the second part of the continuation is marked in a dashed black line.

The results of the GPR imaging show that adjacent ashlars in the same course may differ in thickness and in rock type and orientation. In order to demonstrate the difference in average thicknesses of the Western Wall between Area 1 and Area 4, a statistical analysis of the complete set of imaging/measurements was compiled (Fig. 32.8). The comparison was made for the courses of the same levels, along their lengths, that were imaged and mapped. The average thickness of the courses based on the complete one-piece ashlar (see Fig. 32.7, marked in thick black) were calculated and plotted in light orange (Area 1) and light blue (Area 4). The matched thickness of courses based on the ashlar pair (Fig. 32.7, marked in thin dashed black) were calculated and plotted in dark orange (Area 1) and in dark blue (Area 4). In both segments (Figs. 32.7–32.8), it is clear that the Western Wall is thicker in Area 4, which is, according to the engineering rationale of the architects and masons who constructed the wall, providing additional support needed for the foundations of Robinson's Arch.

BELOW THE SURFACE—THE WESTERN AND SOUTHERN WALLS

Several HDR GPR GX–450 MHz profiles were also conducted to measure the thicknesses of two representative ashlars below the surface: the southwestern cornerstone of Course U, founded on the bedrock (the same corner of Ashlar 4); an ashlar about 12 m north of the southwestern corner of the Temple Mount, below Robinson's Arch (Fig. 32.9). Six GPR profiles were conducted to map this corner ashlar. The corner ashlar was detected as being ca. 2.20 m thick. In addition, the ashlar behind it, which is actually part of the Southern Wall, was detected as well: it is about 1.40 m wide and (clearer in Profile 2) about 2.20 m thick. The other profiles are presented without marks to show the raw data.

Three more HDR GPR GX–450 MHz profiles were conducted along the ashlar located some 12 m north of the corner (Fig. 32.10), indicating a thickness of about 3.35 m (on Profile 1). The other profiles are shown without interpretation of the back of the ashlar. This is the thickest complete ashlar that was detected thus far.

DEEP BEHIND THE WESTERN WALL

Although the purpose of the research was to measure the thicknesses of the ashlars in large areas and assist the preservation operations, I was curious about what was behind the wall. Therefore, I decided to make a deeper imaging profile as an example and for future investigation. The results of this profile, presented in Fig. 32.11, reveal a mixture of reflections and diffraction up to depth range of 4.5–6.2 m from the surface of the wall, which scatters the GPR energy and may indicate a boulder/talus-like fill behind the wall. The boulder-like fill behind the wall together with the wall itself may explain the ability to support the tremendous structure of the Temple Mount enclosure.

DISCUSSION AND CONCLUSIONS

Our HDR GPR imaging of the Western Wall is the first comprehensive geophysical research to study and reveal the hidden nature and structure of the wall, the variety of rock types, and the thicknesses of many dozens of its ashlars. An important result of our research is the discovery that the Western Wall is not built uniformly. On the contrary, it was constructed of different types of rocks that

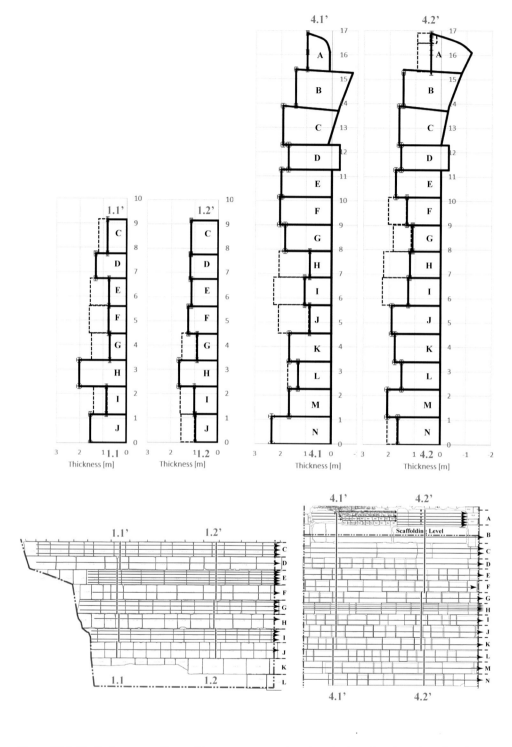

Figure 32.7: Vertical cross-sections of the courses at two locations in Area 1 and two locations in Area 4 (1.1–1.1'; 1.2–1.2' and 4.1–4.1'; 4.2–4.2' respectively). The cross-sections were compiled from the results of the imaging conducted along the courses, to present the thicknesses and the variations of the ashlars vertically. It should be noted the thicknesses of the ashlars in the cross-sections is an average of about 0.9–1.6 m wide (modified from Baruch *et al.*, 2022; model and sketch by Or Roz).

Courses Thicknesses (m) per (1/m²)

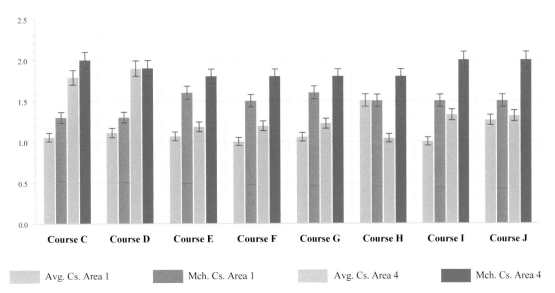

Figure 32.8: Statistical analysis of the complete set of imaging, compiled for the courses of the same levels, along with their total lengths. The average thickness of the courses based on the complete/one-piece ashlar (see Fig. 32.7, marked in thick black) have been calculated and plotted in light orange (Area 1) and light blue (Area 4). The matched thickness of courses based on the ashlar pair (see Fig. 32.14, marked in thin dashed black) have been calculated and plotted in dark orange (Area 1) and in dark blue (Area 4).

were processed into ashlars in a variety of sizes and layer orientations. The results of our imaging show that adjacent ashlars in the same course not only differ in rock type and orientation but may also differ in thickness. Moreover, the results show that as opposed to the invested appearance of the faces of the ashlars, the internal interfaces—especially the back sides of the ashlars—were not necessarily processed.

The results of the GPR imaging of the Western Wall show ashlar thickness distribution varies from ca. 0.70 m to 3.35 m. Averages along courses built only from the complete (one-piece) ashlars (non-broken ones or non-pair of ashlars) show a distribution of thicknesses of about 1.00–1.35 m for Area 1 (of four areas) and about 1.05–1.70 m in Area 4. When taking into account fractured or two close ashlars (broken or a close pair), the matched thicknesses are about 1.30–1.60 m for Area 1 and about 1.80–2.00 m for Area 4. The accuracy of the results is roughly ±5% of the thickness value.

The statistical analysis of the data clearly shows the difference in thicknesses between the two areas. According to the GPR imaging, Area 4, which is below Robinson's Arch, was built from ashlars that are about 25%–38% thicker and more massive than those in Area 1. We believe this was according to the engineering rationale of the architects and masons who worked here 2000 years ago; they did this to provide the extra support needed for the foundations of Robinson's Arch and the entrance road to the Temple Mount.

The thickest complete ashlar (as one stone) that was detected so far in this research was in Course U at the excavations below Robinson's Arch. The thickness of the ashlar which is located about 12 m north of the southwestern corner of the Temple Mount is about 3.35 m. This is not surprising, given the other dimensions of the ashlars that have been detected, together with the fact that it is the lowest course that is founded directly on the bedrock of Mount Moriah.

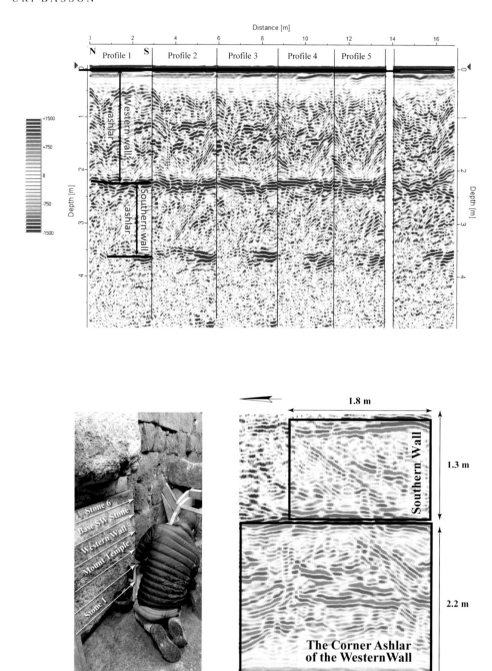

Figure 32.9: Six GX–450 MHz imaging profiles at the southwestern corner ashlar of the Temple Mount at the subsurface excavations below the level of the street (for a description of scales and palette—see Fig. 32.4; for the location map—see Fig. 32.1). The profile photo on the left is of the corner ashlar, detecting a thickness of about 2.20 m. The interpretation of the back interface between this ashlar and the second one behind it is marked on Profile 1, while the other profiles are presented as is. Also, the ashlar behind it, which is actually on the Southern Wall, is detected as well: its width is about 1.40 m and its thickness is detected more clearly in Profile 2 and is about 2.20 m. The other profiles are presented without marks to show the raw data. Another presentation of the cornerstone from the Western and the Southern Walls is presented in a 45° rotated mirror image, compiled from Profile 2.

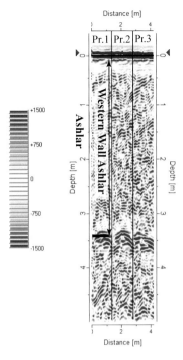

Figure 32.10: Three GX–450 MHz imaging profiles at an ashlar about 12 m north of the southwestern corner of the Temple Mount (for a description of scales and palette—see Fig. 32.4; for location map—see Fig. 32.1, Course U, bellow the southern edge of Robinson's Arch). A mark at the back of the ashlar, a reflection interface mapping a thickness of about 3.35 m is shown on Profile 1. The other profiles are shown without interpretation on the back of the ashlars. This ashlar is the thickest complete/one–piece stone that has been detected in this research. Note the reflections from the boulders' fill behind the ashlars.

We are aware of the fact that according to the current engineering design criterion of retaining walls the thickness of the wall should be at least a third of its height in order to support its structure. According to this criterion, the thickness of the ashlars of the walls cannot support the structure of the Temple Mount. The imaging of the Western Wall reveals the ashlars' thicknesses, which can support the structure of Robinsons' Arch, but apparently are not thick enough to fulfill this engineering criterion. However, although the HDR GPR imaging was focused on the ashlars' thicknesses, images such as Fig. 32.11 that reveal reflections/diffractions at 3–4 m deep may indicate the existence of boulders inside the fill. This deeper imaging profile combined with evidence from other profiles that were not conducted for deep penetration, the imaging indicates that behind the wall there is a fill that may be composed of talus-like piles of boulders and rocks that could assist in supporting the wall. Using the 450 MHz systems' setting was the appropriate choice for mapping thick ashlars but not for a substantial penetration behind them; therefore, it is now our plan to perform deeper imaging using lower HDR GPR frequencies to penetrate 10–15 m deeper, to investigate the structural fill of the Temple Mount enclosure.

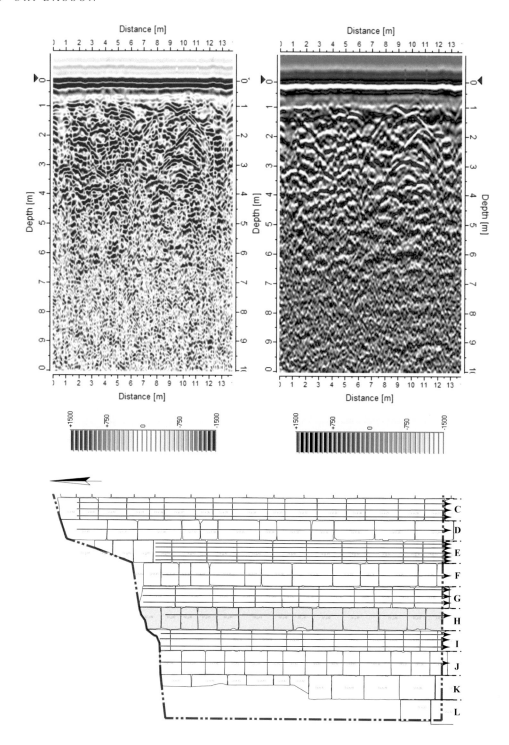

Figure 32.11: GX–160 MHz imaging profiles conducted at Area 1 along course H about 12 m north of the southwestern corner of the Temple Mount (for the location map – see Fig. 32.1). The profile that was made to penetrate deeper to detect inner ashlars or the fill behind the wall is presented in two processing algorithms and palettes: The color one on the left present reflections and diffractions from the inner wall and the fill. The one on the left present a proprietary algorithm for the automatic detection of the stronger reflections and diffractions (blue) on the black and white images (model and sketch by Or Roz).

ACKNOWLEDGMENTS

I would like to thank the EL-AD Foundation for financing the GPR imaging of the southwestern subsurface corner of Temple Mount. My thanks also go to GeoSense Ltd. for financing the imaging of Area 1 and to the Israel Antiquities Authority for financing the GPR imaging of Area 4.

Special thanks to Mr. Omry Nachum of GeoSense Ltd. for his helpful assistance in the field measurements and documentation of the GPR data.

REFERENCES

ASTM D6432–19. *Standard Guide for Using the Surface Ground Penetrating Radar Method for Subsurface Investigation.* ASTM International, West Conshohocken, PA, 2019, www.astm.org. DOI: 10.1520 /D6432-19.

Baruch, Y., Basson., U., Nachum, O. and Reich, R. 2021. Robinson's Arch: Results of a Geophysical Study. In: Meiron, E., ed. *City of David: Studies of Ancient Jerusalem* 16. Jerusalem: 99–116.

Basson, U. 1992. Mapping of Moisture Content and Structure of Unsaturated Sand Layers with Ground Penetrating Radar (M.A. thesis, Tel Aviv University). Tel Aviv (Hebrew with English abstract).

Basson, U. 2000. *Imaging of Active Fault Zone in the Dead Sea Rift: Evrona Fault Zone as a Case Study* (Ph.D. dissertation, Tel Aviv University). Tel Aviv.

Basson, U. 2017. *Detection of the Continuation of the Herodian Street Through the Underground Sewage Tunnel Using Ground Penetration Radar Imaging.* GeoSense report 0125052017.

Basson, U. 2021. Ground Penetrating Radar Imaging of the Western Wall. In: Zelinger, Y., Peleg–Barkat, O., Uziel, J. and Gadot, Y., eds. *New Studies in the Archaeology of Jerusalem and Its Region 14*. Jerusalem: 65*–88*.

Basson, U., Ben-Avraham, Z., Garfunkel, Z. and Lyakhovsky, V. 2002. Development of Recent Faulting in the Southern Dead Sea Rift According to GPR Imaging. Tectonophysics. European Geophysical Society (EGS) Stephan Mueller Special Publication Series 2. European Geosciences Union: 35–48. http://dx.doi .org/10.5194/smsps-2-35-2002

Basson, U., Enzel, Y., Amit, R. and Ben-Avraham, Z. 1994. Detecting and Mapping Recent Faults with Ground Penetrating Radar in the Alluvial Fans of the Arava Valley, Israel. *Fifth International Conference on Ground Penetrating Radar, June 12–16, 1994, Kitchener, Ontario, Canada*, Vol. 2: 777–788. https://doi .org/10.3997/2214-4609-pdb.300.57

Basson, U. and Ginzburg, A. 2009. Mapping Archaeological Remains at the Banias Using Ground Penetrating Radar. In: Tzaferis, V. and Israeli, S., eds. *Paneas*, Vol. 2: *Small Finds and Other Studies* (IAA Reports 38). Jerusalem: 189–194.

Davis, J.L. and Annan, A.P. 1989. Ground Penetrating Radar for High Resolution Mapping of Soil and Rock Stratigraphy. *Geophysical Prospecting* 37: 531–551.

Goodman, D. 1994. Ground–Penetrating Radar Simulation in Engineering and Archaeology. *Geophysics* 59(2): 224–232.

Jol, H.M., Bauman, P. and Bahat, D. 2006. Looking into the Western Wall, Jerusalem, Israel. In: *Proceedings of the 11th International Conference on Ground Penetrating Radar, Columbus, OH, June 19–22*. Columbus.

Levanon, A. 1968. *Report on Electrical Resistivity Measurements Conducted at the Southern Wall—Jerusalem, for Ministry of Work, Department of Public Works.* The Institute for Petroleum and Geophysics. Work No. GE/635/68 (Hebrew).

Marco, S., Agnon, A., Ellenblum, R., Eidelman, A., Basson, U. and Boas, A. 1997. 817-Year-Old Walls Offset Sinistrally 2.1 m by the Dead Sea Transform, Israel. *Journal of Geodynamics* 24(1–4): 11–20.

Reich, R. and Billig, Y. 2000. Excavations near the Temple Mount and Robinson's Arch, 1994–1996; Appendix: A Group of Theater Seats from Jerusalem. In: Geva, H., ed. *Ancient Jerusalem Revealed, Reprinted and Expanded Edition*. Jerusalem: 340–352.

Ulriksen, C.P.F. 1982. *Application of Impulse Radar to Civil Engineering* (Ph.D. dissertation, Lund University). Lund.

Vaughan, C.J. 1986. Ground-Penetrating Radar Surveys Used in Archaeological Investigations. *Geophysics* 51(3): 595–604.

Warren, C. 1884. *Plans, Elevations, Sections, etc. Shewing the Results of the Excavations at Jerusalem, 1867–70, Executed for the Committee of the Palestine Exploration Fund.* London.

CHAPTER 33

RADIOCARBON ABSOLUTE CHRONOLOGY OF THE SOUTHWEST CORNER OF THE TEMPLE MOUNT

Johanna Regev and Elisabetta Boaretto

While we were involved in a major ongoing radiocarbon chronology project on ancient Jerusalem, the area surrounding the southwestern corner of the Temple Mount became available to us for research. The samples that pertain to this area of excavation are presented in this paper.

In 2020–2021, contexts were studied and sampled from features uncovered during earlier excavation seasons (Mazar 1971; Reich and Shukron 2011: 68; Shukron 2012: 29–30). Among the contexts available for sampling, four major features were considered: a large cistern; a later wall within the cistern that leaned against the Western Wall; material between the lowest course of stones of the Western Wall and the bedrock upon which it was founded; and a long channel (the middle of three channels) chiseled into the Western Wall. Material with short lifespans was collected from building materials and sediments that could be securely associated with the features intended for dating. In the following report, some first results are discussed.

CONTEXT DESCRIPTION

CISTERN

The stratigraphically earliest context dated in this study was a large cistern (Shukron 2012; Fig. 33.1). The walls of the cistern were coated with 10-cm-thick plaster, made from four layers, one on top of the other. Each layer was about 2 cm thick. Analyzing the plaster layers in an FTIR (Fourier Transform Infrared) spectrometer shows that all the layers have similar mineralogy, composed mainly of calcite, but with extraordinarily high peaks in 606 and 566 cm^{-1} (Fig. 33.2), suggesting that a significant amount of organic compound had been added to the plaster. A more detailed future study of this plaster composition will be of interest, as this composition seems unique and should be compared with other contemporaneous cisterns. A chunk of plaster was taken from an area with unbroken plaster to eliminate the possibility of intrusive material and contamination. In the second layer of plaster (from the bedrock), several grape seeds were extracted and identified, and one of them was dated as sample RTD-10670.

WALL WITHIN CISTERN

With building projects related to the Temple Mount enclosure, a wall was built in the middle of the cistern, probably to close a gap created in the cistern wall when the Western Wall was constructed. Gray mortar with some charred material had been applied between the large stones in antiquity. The binder material consisted almost entirely of calcite, with a clear presence of phosphates and very little clay. The calcite atomic order is higher than expected for mortar, which is usually relatively disordered. It can be explained by recrystallization of the calcite crystals, a suggestion supported by the larger-than-average crystal size in the mortar sample (Fig. 33.3). Several small seeds, within

Figure 33.1: The cistern. Note the supporting wall left of the ladder.

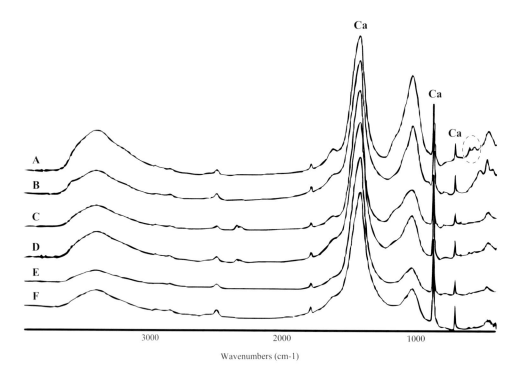

Wavenumbers (cm-1)

Figure 33.2: FTIR spectra of the materials dated in this study. (A) Cistern wall; notice the unusually high peaks associated with phosphates marked within the dashed circle. (B) Fill material as control sediment. (C) Middle channel, pink plaster. (D) Middle channel, gray mortar. (E) Wall within cistern, gray mortar. F) Under the lowest course of the Western Wall, gray mortar.

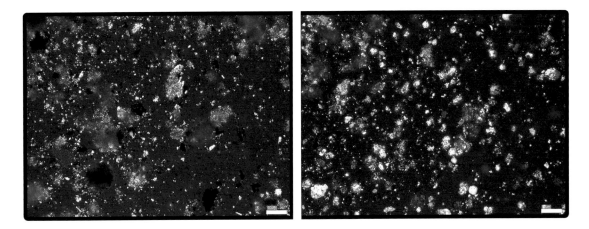

Figure 33.3: Grain mount slides under cross-polarized light. Left: the large, recrystallized calcite crystals in the mortar between the stones of the supporting wall of the cistern. Right: The mortar with smaller-sized crystals that had been covered by hard plaster in the middle channel, chiseled into the Western Wall. The scale bar in both images is 50 μm.

what might have been a fraction of a charred fruit, were extracted from the mortar. The seeds were too distorted for further botanical identification. One of them was dated as sample RTD-10673.

Western Wall—Under Lowest Stone Course

Another area where construction materials related to the Western Wall could be sampled was directly underneath the first course of Western Wall stones, where the leveled bedrock had some cavities that needed to be filled prior to placing the stones above them (Fig. 33.4; see Chapter 16). These holes were filled with gray-brown mortar that had been mixed with some fine charred material. The FTIR spectra of the binder material is similar to that of the supporting wall within the cistern, but the calcite order is that of between ash and plaster, probably indicating in this case that both were used. First, the outer surface was cleaned by removing 2 cm of material, and then the mortar was collected in two parts: Sediment A, closer to the outside surface, and Sediment B, deeper within the mortar. Later, in the laboratory under a binocular, charred material was recovered from Sediment B. Two small twigs were dated as samples RTD-11170.1 and RTD-11170.2.

Western Wall—Middle Channel

The fourth context dated was sampled during conservation works on the Western Wall (Mazar 1971; see Chapter 4). At some point in the past, three small channels had been chiseled into the wall at the base of the large ashlar rows at different elevations (Fig. 33.5). Out of these channels, the middle channel was sampled for radiocarbon dating. The channel was made non-permeable to water by a hard 1–2-cm-thick pink plaster, spread above gray mortar, filling the cracks and smoothing the surface for the plaster. This underlying gray mortar included many small pieces of charred remains, mainly chaff, fragile seeds and some charcoal, from which samples RTD-11140 (barley seed) and RTD-11141 (olive pit) were measured.

METHODS

All samples were collected in the field by the authors, aimed specifically for chronology building by radiocarbon dating. Therefore, the strategy was to find contexts securely linked to the feature

Figure 33.4: Gray mortar above bedrock and underneath the lowest course of the Western Wall Foundations. Tag width is 4.5 cm.

Figure 33.5: The chiseled channel in the Western Wall with gray mortar covered with pink plaster.

dated. The screening for preservation and quality of the material for radiocarbon dating, as well as the pre-treatment process toward dating, was tailored according to the type of material and sample size as presented in previous studies (Regev *et al.* 2014, 2020; Boaretto *et al.* 2009; Boaretto 2015). After careful separation of the contaminants from the original material, the samples were graphitized and measured at the Dangoor Research Accelerator Mass Spectrometry Laboratory (D-REAMS) at the Weizmann Institute of Science (Regev *et al.* 2017). Radiocarbon ages (Libby Age) are reported in conventional radiocarbon years (before present=1950) in accordance with international convention (Stuiver and Polach 1977). All calculated ^{14}C ages have been corrected for fractionation so the results are equivalent to the standard δ^{13}C value of -25‰ (wood). Calibrated ages in calendar years have been obtained from the calibration tables of IntCal20 (Reimer *et al.* 2020) by means of OxCal v. 4.4.4 (Bronk Ramsey 2009). The charred botanical remains were identified using binocular microscope SMZ-800N (Nikon) and metallurgical microscope Eclipse LV150N (Nikon) prior to ^{14}C analysis. The sediments were characterized using FTIR analysis using Nicolet iS5 (Thermo) FTIR instrument at 4 cm^{-1} resolution. The spectra could be used to identify the presence of anthropogenic substances, such as burnt clay (Berna *et al.* 2007), phosphate (Weiner 2010), and disordered calcite (Regev *et al.* 2010, displayed in Fig. 33.3). Grain mount slides were used for search of ash pseudomorphs, dung spherulites and size of calcite crystals in the sediment.

RESULTS

THE CISTERN

The calibrated range of sample RTD-10670 covers the 300-year-long, wiggly-shaped "Hallstatt plateau" of the calibration curve (around 700–400 BCE), making a single measurement with no stratigraphically associated material merely to point to the First Temple period, between 750–540 BCE (Fig. 33.6; Table 33.1). As it is not expected that building projects immediately after the Babylonian destruction (587 BCE) were undertaken in Jerusalem, the range can be narrowed to between 750–587 BCE. However, the highest statistical probability is between 750–685 BCE (Fig. 33.6; Table 33.1), coinciding with the early part of the lengthy reign of King Uzziah. Interestingly, 2 Chronicles 26:10 mentions various building projects in Jerusalem undertaken by this king, as well

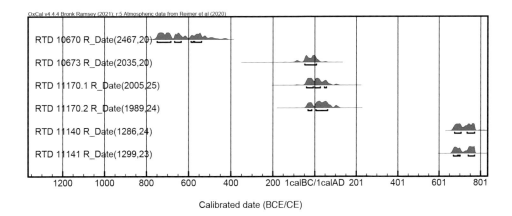

Figure 33.6: Multiplot of the calibrated ranges of single radiocarbon measurements. The lines underneath the probability distributions of each date mark the 68.3% range (meaning there is 68.3% chance that the correct date is within this range).

as him cutting many cisterns in the surrounding areas. The second relevant, smaller-probability distribution of the calibrated range falls between 670–640 BCE, during the long rule of the highly capable Judean monarch King Manasseh. In the future, with more measurements and samples from additional contexts, the range might be narrowed down further.

Wall Within the Cistern

The calibrated age ranges of RTD-10673 are between 49 BCE and 8 CE, suggesting a Herodian or slightly later date for the construction of this wall. This date fits well with the interpretation that the cistern was damaged by the construction of the Western Temple Mount Wall, and that the wall under discussion was constructed in that period to repair this damage (Fig. 33.6; Table 33.1).

Table 33.1: Radiocarbon dating results*

Lab number	Feature	Eff. %	C %	δ¹³C [‰]	Libby Age ±1σ [BP]	Calibrated range 68.3%	Calibrated range 95.4%
RTD 10670	The cistern	20.2	62.0	-23.5	2467±20	750BCE (34.8%) 685BCE 667BCE (14.3%) 636BCE 588BCE (3.8%) 578BCE 572BCE (15.4%) 539BCE	758BCE (37.1%) 678BCE 672BCE (57.9%) 476BCE 430BCE (0.5%) 426BCE
RTD 10673	Wall within the cistern	27.0	40.6	-22.8	2035±20	49BCE (68.3%) 8CE	96BCE (7.6%) 72BCE 56BCE (87.0%) 26CE 49CE (0.8%) 55CE
RTD 11170.1	Western Wall— lowest stone course		61.8	-27.1	2005±25	R_Combine 36BCE (26.2%) 14BCE	R_Combine 44BCE (95.4%) 70CE
RTD 11170.2			65.1	-27.9	1989±24	4CE (29.5%) 28CE 45CE (12.6%) 58CE	
RTD 11140	Western Wall— middle channel	32.0	61.0	-20.8	1286±24	R_Combine 674CE (27.2%) 702CE	R_Combine 665CE (42.6%) 710CE
RTD 11141		69.5	65.4	-22.0	1299±23	741CE (41.1%) 772CE	720CE (52.8%) 774CE

*Efficiency percentage (Eff %) is the percentage of material left through the chemical cleaning, and carbon percentage (C %) is the carbon content within the pre-treated sample. Libby Age is the date before calibration in years BP. The calibrated ranges are according to 68.3% or 95.4% probability that the true age is included in each range. The calibration was done by IntCal20 calibration curve (Reimer *et al.* 2020)

Western Wall—Under Lowest Stone Course

As the two dated twigs (Samples RTD-11170.1 and 11170.2) are from the same mortar sample, it is possible to combine the two results (using the R_Combine function in the OxCal software, Bronk Ramsey 2009). The similar $\delta^{13}C$ values of the two twigs (Fig. 33.6; Table 33.1), which are somewhat lower than the typical -25‰ of wood, suggest that the two twigs might be from the same plant. The calibrated date has three possible ranges: 26% probability between 36–14 BCE (Herod's time), 29% probability between 4–28 CE (during the time of the Roman prefects), and 13% probability between 45–58 CE. In this case, the precise building date remains open until more samples, that can be stratigraphically related, will be measured.

Western Wall—Middle Channel

The two measurements (RTD-11140, RTD-11141) gave almost identical uncalibrated ages and were combined using the R_Combine function (Fig. 33.7). As the date falls on a wiggle in the calibration curve, the probability distribution has two distinct calibrated ranges. Both ranges postdate the Muslim conquest of the city in 638 CE. The earlier part of the range has 27% probability and falls between 674–702 CE, and it coincides with the starting time of the construction of Al-Aqsa Mosque by Abd al-Malik. The later range has 41% probability and dates between 741–772 CE, the time of the earthquake of 749 CE and reign of Abbasid Caliph al-Mansur. If this part of the calibrated range is the correct historical time of the events, it would point to reconstruction works undertaken

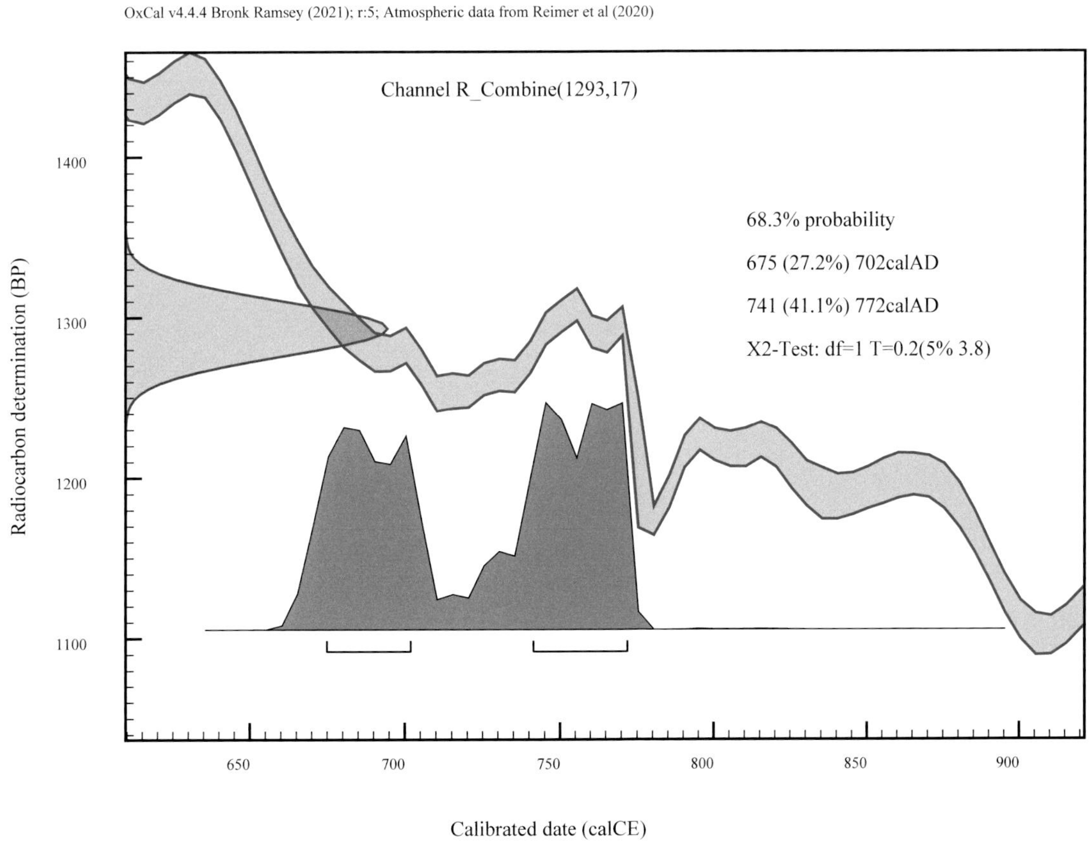

Figure 33.7: R_Combine results of the two dates from the chiseled middle channel in the Western Wall.

following the earthquake. However, based on the large-scale building projects undertaken in and around the Temple Mount, we consider the late 7th century part of the calibrated range more likely to be the real building date of the channel.

REFERENCES

Berna, F., Behar, A., Shahack-Gross, R., Berg, J., Boaretto, E., Gilboa, A., *et al.* 2007. Sediments Exposed to High Temperatures: Reconstructing Pyrotechnological Processes in Late Bronze and Iron Age Strata at Tel Dor (Israel). *Journal of Archaeological Science* 34: 358–373. https://doi.org/10.1016/J.JAS.2006.05.011.

Boaretto, E. 2015. Radiocarbon and the Archaeological Record: An Integrative Approach for Building an Absolute Chronology for the Late Bronze and Iron Ages of Israel. *Radiocarbon* 57(2): 207–216.

Boaretto, E., Wu, X., Yuan, J., Bar-Yosef, O., Chu, V., Pan, Y., Liu, K., Cohen, D., Jiao, T., Li, S., Gu, H., Goldberg, P. and Weiner, S. 2009. Radiocarbon Dating of Charcoal and Bone Collagen Associated with the Early Pottery at Yuchanyan Cave, Hunan Province, China. *Proceedings of National Academy of Science* 106(24): 9595–9600.

Bronk Ramsey, C. 2009. Bayesian Analysis of Radiocarbon Dates. *Radiocarbon* 51(1): 337–360.

Mazar, B. 1971. *The Excavations in the Old City of Jerusalem near the Temple Mount: Preliminary Report of the Second and Third Seasons, 1969–1970*. Jerusalem.

Regev, J., Finkelstein, I., Adams, M.J. and Boaretto, E. 2014. Wiggle-Matched ^{14}C Chronology of Early Bronze Megiddo and the Synchronization of Egyptian and Levantine Chronologies. *Ägypten und Levante* 24: 243–266.

Regev, J., Uziel, J., Lieberman, T., Solomon, A., Gadot, Y., Ben-Ami, D., Regev, L. and Boaretto, E. 2020. Radiocarbon Dating and Microarchaeology Untangle the History of Jerusalem's Temple Mount: A View from Wilson's Arch. *Plos One* 15(6): e0233307.

Regev, L., Poduska, K.M., Addadi, L., Weiner, S. and Boaretto, E. 2010. Distinguishing between Calcites Formed by Different Mechanisms Using Infrared Spectrometry: Archaeological Applications. *Journal of Archaeological Science* 37: 3022–3029. https://doi.org/10.1016/J.JAS.2010.06.027.

Regev, L., Steier, P., Shachar, Y., Mintz, E., Wild, E.M., Kutschera, W. and Boaretto, E. 2017. D-REAMS: A New Compact AMS for Radiocarbon Measurements at the Weizmann Institute of Science, Rehovot, Israel. *Radiocarbon* 59(3): 775–784.

Reich, R. and Shukron, E. 2011. Excavations in Jerusalem Beneath the Paved Street and in the Sewage Channel next to Robinson's Arch. *Qadmoniot* 142: 66–73 (Hebrew).

Reimer, P., Austin, W., Bard, E., Bayliss, A., Blackwell, P., Bronk Ramsey, C., Butzin, M., Cheng, H., Edwards, R., Friedrich, M., Grootes, P., Guilderson, T., Hajdas, I., Heaton, T., Hogg, A., Hughen, K., Kromer, B., Manning, S., Muscheler, R., Palmer, J., Pearson, C., van der Plicht, J., Reimer, R., Richards, D., Scott, E., Southon, J., Turney, C., Wacker, L., Adolphi, F., Büntgen, U., Capano, M., Fahrni, S., Fogtmann-Schulz, A., Friedrich, R., Köhler, P., Kudsk, S., Miyake, F., Olsen, J., Reinig, F., Sakamoto, M., Sookdeo, A. and Talamo, S. 2020. The IntCal20 Northern Hemisphere Radiocarbon Age Calibration Curve (0–55 cal kBP). *Radiocarbon* 62(4): 725–757.

Shukron, E. 2012. A Public Reservoir from the First Temple Period near the Western Wall. In: Baruch, E., Levin, Y. and Levy-Reifer, A., eds. *New Studies on Jerusalem* 18. Ramat Gan: 29–30 (Hebrew).

Stuiver, M. and Polach, H.A. 1977. Discussion: Reporting C-14 Data. *Radiocarbon* 19(3): 355–363.

Weiner, S. 2010. *Microarchaeology: Beyond the Visible Archaeological Record*. New York.

PART IV:
CONSERVATION
OF THE
SOUTHERN WALL
AND THE AREA OF
ROBINSON'S ARCH

CHAPTER 34

CONSERVATION OF THE SOUTHERN WALL
Ofer Cohen

Over the past few years, a bulge was noted on the Southern Wall near the upper southeastern corner of the Temple Mount. It is unknown when this bulging first began and how it developed over time (Fig. 34.1).

As the walls of the Temple Mount are a primary concern for those dealing with Jerusalem, it has been of major concern to determine the nature of the bulge, how it evolved and whether it constitutes a source of danger to the monument itself and for those visiting, praying and working in its vicinity. The Conservation Department of the Israel Antiquities Authority took upon itself the execution of a physical-conservation survey of the bulge to locate, identify and define the affected area close to the southeastern corner of the Temple Mount and to provide initial solutions to the problems it created. This report is a summary of that research.

The survey was conducted in consideration of the limitations of the site and of those beyond the control of the Conservation Department. As a consequence, the work utilized three-dimensional documentation through laser scanning technology, photographic documentation, binocular scanning and archival research.

FINDINGS

Within the limitations of the survey and following analysis of the data, it was established that the bulge originated near the southeastern corner of the Temple Mount, where there is evidence of stone erosion. The bulge covers an extensive area (over 190 sq m, and a protrusion of 10 cm beyond the line of the wall) and reaches an apex of 70 cm from the line of the wall. The center of the bulge is located 30 m from the southeast corner, 9.5 m from the top of the wall, close to the blocked Single Gate. The erosion of the stone is severe and in places reaches a depth of 20 cm from the original stone face.

There are many possible causes for such lacunae but at this stage of the research, it is not possible to assess with certainty the degree of influence of each causal factor. We detail the possible causes in the concluding section at the end of this report.

DOCUMENTATION OF THE SOUTHEASTERN CORNER

Laser scanning was used for the survey of the Southern Wall of the Temple Mount from the Triple Gate steps to the southeastern corner, and 25 m of the Eastern Wall from the corner. The documentation was conducted by "Mabat—Three-Dimensional Technology" (Fig 34.2).

OBJECTIVE

The data collected by the survey had several objectives. Foremost was the mapping of the bulge, which included the vertical and horizontal sections of required density, to quantify the phenomena and produce isobars of the bulge parallel to the theoretical face of the wall. The data is necessary to

Figure 34.1: General location of the bulge in the eastern corner of the Southern Wall of the Temple Mount (see arrow).

Figure 34.2: 3D laser scanning of the Southern Wall of the Temple Mount.

plan consequent research and treatment of the eroded area and enable comparison of deformations or any changes in the bulge in the future.

IMPLEMENTATION

The survey conducted included general mapping: 10 scans from seven angles at three positions at an average resolution of 20 × 20 mm. Mapping of eroded areas included seven scans from five angles at two positions at an average resolution of 5 × 5 mm.

The scans were collated to cross-register the points in a geodesic system, cross-referenced with artificial targets and connected to actual building elements.

The points were connected with a localized coordinate system. A localized coordinate system was set in place at the site for future comparison and reference.

CAD elements that statistically characterize the wall in its different areas were constructed to receive a dimensional indication of the behavior of the contoured surface. It was thus possible to receive the contour of the actual section (the surface of the bulge) together with a theoretical surface of the wall without the influence of the bulge to provide a reference surface (Figs. 34.3–34.5).

DOCUMENTATION PRODUCTS

The primary information resulting from scans is a collection of points in space that represent the scanned section. The cloud of points can be processed to provide various products and can be used directly to display the scanned element. The Cloud of Points is an essential tool for comparison and follow-up analysis of the development of the wall lacunae by using additional scans with which to compare the original scan.

Horizontal and vertical sections were interspaced at 4 m across the scanned area and spaced at 25 cm in the area of the bulge and erosion. Each section has a line representing the actual face of the wall and a line showing the theoretical face of the wall as it should be (reference surface).

The collation of the information in the area of the bulge employs the model of a topographical plan with contours (isobars) every 5 cm relative to the theoretical surface of the wall (reference surface).

OUTPUT

Cross 11% file (DXF and CGP) including:

- Vertical sections (contour) spaced at every 4 m (20 sections)
- Horizontal sections (contour) spaced at every 4 m (8 sections)
- Vertical sections (contour) spaced at every 25 cm in bulge area (approx. 100 sections)
- Horizontal sections (contour) spaced at every 25 cm in bulge area (approx. 50 sections)
- Surfaces—CAD elements representing the wall
- A full cloud of points 11%—general (only CGP)
- Help line layer of coordinates for sections
- *Blita* (Bulge) file (DXF and CGP) including isobars (topography) perpendicular to wall
- Erosion.cgp file: cloud of points 100% for analysis of the erosion (Fig. 34.6)

ARCHIVAL RESEARCH

The archival research concentrated on two elements—analyzing the structural changes of the eastern part of the Southern Wall over time and pursuing information concerning the interior side

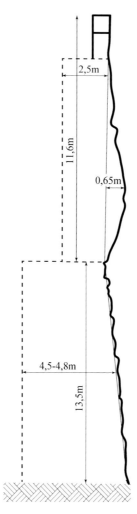

Figure 34.3: Section of the Southern Wall of the
Temple Mount, showing the bulge.

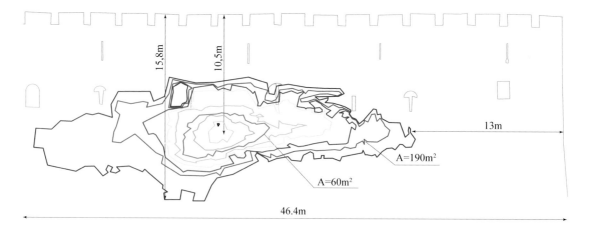

Figure 34.4: Elevation lines, demonstrating the extent of the bulge.

Figure 34.5: The extent of the bulge on the Southern Wall of the Temple Mount.

of the wall to which access was impossible. The research utilized plans, sections, drawings and historical photographs of the southeastern corner of the Temple Mount.

Photographs from 1864–1865 of the southeastern corner of the Southern Wall (Wilson 1865) show that the ruined state of the upper portion of the wall, in the vicinity of the present problematic area, is in good condition and shows no clear erosion or movement.

COMPARISON BETWEEN THE 1864 PHOTOGRAPH AND THE PRESENT SITUATION

Comparison between the pictures and the present situation shows primarily that in the former period, the upper part of the wall was ruined and completely different from its present state. The thickness of the wall, where discernable, is relatively wide (at least 1.5 m), and the wall is built with debris and mortar (*debesh*). The erosion around the openings (windows) is not severe and is mainly concentrated in the sections above the openings where the entire wall is damaged. Erosion is evident in the wall portion above the large Herodian stones, though again much less than today. There are no signs of swelling of the bulge at the time of the early photograph, though it is difficult from this type of image to assess if the phenomena had already commenced.

SURVEY CONCLUSIONS

Within the limitations imposed on the execution of the survey and after assessing the situation on the basis of the data available, the present state of the Southern Wall of the Temple Mount is as follows:

The eastern section of the Southern Wall suffers from two paramount lacunae.

Figure 34.6: Close-up image demonstrating the extent of the erosion of the Southern Wall.

- A bulge covering a large area close to the southeast corner. If not treated, the problem is a source of danger in the medium term (in the range of a number of years), and its collapse may cause irreversible damage to the structure.
- Extensive erosion of the stones of the Southern Wall, causing major damage to the structure. If not treated, it may also cause structural instability.

DETAILS OF THE LACUNAE

There is deformation by extensive swelling over a large area. The area of the deformation is larger or equal to 10 cm above the reference surface is ca. 190 sq m. The area of the deformation is larger or equal to 35 cm above the reference surface is ca. 60 sq m. The dimensions of the greatest extrusion from the reference surface are 60–70 cm from that plane in specific places. The center of the deformation is 30 m west of the southeast corner and 9.5 m from the top of the wall, close to the blocked Single Gate.

There is severe extensive erosion of the stone above the large Herodian stones. The erosion appears primarily around the openings (windows) in the eastern section and in the vicinity of the deformation and the swelling. The erosion is deep and in certain places reaches a depth of 20 cm.

CAUSES OF THE DEFORMATION AND SWELLING

The deformation of the Southern Wall is probably relatively recent and cannot be identified in historical photographs. The deformation may be caused by a number of factors:

1. Separation of the external face of the wall from the core.
2. Excessive vertical load on the wall.
3. Excessive vertical load on the external face of the wall following incomplete integration of the building of the upper section of the wall with the previously existing structure.
4. Excessive horizontal load on the wall. The pressure may be the result of fill behind the wall or the result of horizontal forces swelling within the vaults.
5. Destabilization of the wall following the loss of binding material due to faulty drainage of the upper surface or of the subterranean spaces (Solomon's Stables).
6. Damage to the walls resulting from recent building/reconstruction or other structural changes.

CAUSES OF THE EROSION OF THE STONE

The erosion of the stonework of the upper part of the wall is already clear in the historical images. There are a number of possible reasons for the erosion:

1. Use of inappropriate stone, or stone with many veins.
2. Incorrect laying of the stones or faulty dressing.
3. Excessive load on the stones.
4. Faulty drainage of upper surface water, or incorrect drainage causing flow on the façade of the wall.
5. Faulty drainage of the subterranean vaults behind the wall and seepage through the wall.
6. Drainage on the face of the wall and damage to the stones.

RECOMMENDATIONS AND CONSERVATION ENGINEERING

It is essential that the survey be continued, and that collection of the following data be completed:

1. Detailed measurements and mapping of the spaces behind the Southern Wall.
2. A survey of the erosion of the stonework.
3. Inspection of the surface plane of the internal face of the wall.
4. Comprehensive investigation of the building technology of the eroded area and of the bulge deformation.
5. Comprehensive investigation of the structural results of the new building in the area of Solomon's Stables.

If continuation of the survey becomes impossible, or if access to the area is denied, then it will become essential to continue the monitoring of the development of the erosion and of the bulge deformation using laser scanning by "Mabat" and photographic image analysis.

REFERENCES

Wilson, C.W. 1865. *Ordnance Survey of Jerusalem*. London.

CHAPTER 35

CONSERVATION SURVEY OF THE ASHLARS OF THE WESTERN WALL

Yonathan Tzahor, Yosef Vaknin, Yael Kalman and Dorit Tsipshtein

Following the collapse of one of the Western Wall ashlars in the summer of 2018, the Jerusalem municipality pronounced its southern section a danger zone. The urgent need for meticulous inspection of the physical condition of the Wall's ashlars led to a detailed conservation survey carried out by a team of conservators, engineers and planners (Tzahor 2019).

Aside from historical-archaeological research, the survey's objectives were to locate immediate hazards that might compromise visitors and to establish a plan for conservation and stabilization works. Due to the sensitivity associated with the Temple Mount complex and especially the Western Wall, both the survey and conservation work were carried out under the auspices of the Prime Minister's Office and directed by the Israel Antiquities Authority's Jerusalem district and Conservation Department.

The survey and conservation work that followed was carried out in the southern section of the Western Wall, from the Mughrabi Gate ramp to the complex's southwestern corner. The southern section is ca. 63 m long and its height varies from 17.30 m to 28.90 m (Tzahor 2019). This section, located in the Davidson Archaeological Center, was divided into five sub-sections. The northern sub-section, closest to the Mughrabi Gate ramp, was surveyed in 2019, after which conservation work was carried out (Tzahor 2020b). Two additional sub-sections, including the section from Robinson's Arch to the Temple Mount's southwest corner, were surveyed in 2020, after which conservation work was conducted (Tzahor 2020a, 2020c).

The first part of this report presents the conservation survey as a whole, its methodologies, features and scope, and results and conclusions regarding the Wall's physical condition. The second part presents conservation plans and work carried out to remove hazards and to stabilize and preserve the Wall's ashlars. In addition, professional dilemmas are discussed and various limitations introduced, as well as unconventional conservation solutions.

SURVEY OF THE WESTERN WALL ASHLARS

The conservation survey comprised innovative measuring techniques, historical documentation, detailed cataloging of the ashlars, and the collection of a variety of data and their presentation in a clear, accessible manner for online viewing. This unique survey, conducted on three different sections of the Wall, inspected some 590 different ashlars. The first sub-section surveyed 248 ashlars and served as a test case for the other sub-sections. It measured, identified, mapped and characterized the main conservation problems and dilemmas regarding the individual stones (Tzahor 2020b). These conservation surveys exposed preservation problems and engineering malfunctions, and led to dramatic conclusions regarding the severity of the Wall's physical condition and to the establishment of the fact that a large number of its original ashlars are prone to destabilization and eventual collapse (Tzahor 2020a, 2020b, 2020c).

DOCUMENTATION AND MAPPING

A precursory demand for the conservation survey was the creation of a detailed dataset of the Wall's ashlars. Precise dimensions, including laser measuring, were taken in December 2018, using two different techniques that produced color and black-and-white maps. These maps displayed the Wall's ashlars in detail, highlighting cracks, fissures, holes, evidence of stone-working, and well-rooted vegetation (Figs. 35.1–35.2). To these were added photogrammetrical measurements of the entire southern part of the Western Wall (Fig. 35.3). The Wall was also photographed that same month, with a detailed, stone-by-stone image of each ashlar recorded as a preliminary stage for each of the surveys.

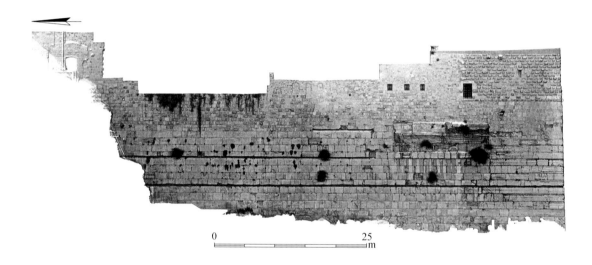

Figure 35.1: Using a color laser scan to measure the façade of the southern section of the Western Wall (by "Mabat" for the Israel Antiquities Authority).

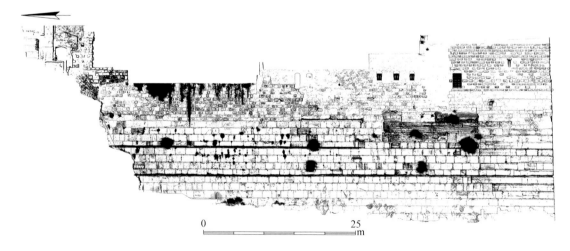

Figure 35.2: Measuring the façade of the southern section of the Western Wall, using a black and white laser scan (by "Mabat" for the Israel Antiquities Authority).

The measurements and photographic documentation were used to create a precise, detailed map of the entire southern sector of the Western Wall. In this map, every ashlar of the Wall was drawn in high resolution and included the designation of margin drafting, rooted vegetation, crack locations and more. Each ashlar was thus thoroughly documented and numbered (Fig. 35.4). This map was meant to serve as a basis for managing the dataset of the conservation surveys on a Geographic Information System (GIS) (Tzahor 2019, 2020b).

The numbering method of the ashlars was designed to assign each ashlar to the period of its quarrying, to its proper course and location in the wall, and to prevent a case of overlap or duplication. Numbering was based on historical numbering as put forward in the British map of the survey conducted by Warren in 1867–1870 (Warren 1884). Our map and the historical map both numbered the courses from top to bottom, since both maps referred to the possible presence of underground courses, invisible at the time (Fig. 35.5). In addition, this numbering method was meant to enable possible unification of data of a future survey in the other walls of the Temple Mount complex with the existing dataset from the Western Wall's conservation survey (Tzahor 2019, 2020b; Fig. 35.6).

COLLECTION OF DATA IN SURVEY CARDS

The set of data collected and measured from the maps and on-site was summarized in detailed conservation cards prepared for each ashlar. This information in the conservation cards was based on data and variables that had been checked in previous surveys made at the central Western Wall Plaza in 2003 and 2008. The gathering of data on-site was performed by an expanded survey team that included conservation engineers, senior conservators and conservation planners. The work method included the documentation and filling out of the conservation cards prepared for each ashlar, pinpointing of problems and structural shortcomings, and the suggestion of solutions and the treatment of the problems encountered. The array of solutions that we offered referred both to individual ashlars and to the assemblage of adjacent ashlars on a course, and occasionally in a whole section, according to the global information gathered following the collection of data on-site. A typical ashlar's survey card included some 120 paragraphs divided into five categories (Tzahor 2020b):

Figure 35.3: Photogrammetrical measurement of the façade of the southern section of the Western Wall (by A. Wiegmann, Israel Antiquities Authority).

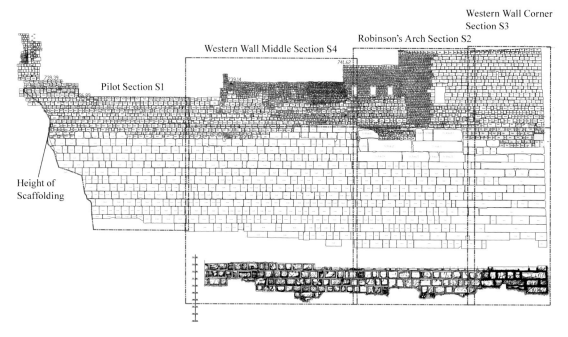

Figure 35.4: Diagram of the southern section of the Western Wall's ashlars (interim report for the engineering conservation survey, Israel Antiquities Authority).

1. General description: location, construction of wall, date, type of stone, etc.

2. Cracks in the stone: characterization of the cracks—continuing cracks, local cracks, micro-cracks.

3. Stone erosion: erosion of the ashlar's surface, gaps in the stone, peeling and detachment of stone parts, vegetation, evidence of past human activity, and more.

4. Ashlar joints: state of preservation of binding materials, effects of cement binding, etc.

5. Summary: grading of the stone's state of preservation, urgency of intervention and treatment needed, specification of guidelines and recommendations for treatment and specification of required conservation actions.

The data gathered were processed and presented using GIS, enabling the presentation of information in a clear, precise manner and the production of an up-to-date status view, which assists in decision-making. Conservation tools included the following:

1. A GIS online system: the mapping of the Wall, analysis of risk and state of ashlars on a geographic spread displaying the Wall as a map.

2. A GIS-Collector system: an application used for the gathering of data on-site.

3. A Dash-Board system: a tool for presenting data in a simple, clear manner.

THE PERFORMANCE OF RADAR INSPECTIONS

The size of the stone that fell from the Western Wall and the investigation of the physical factors that led to its collapse proved that the ashlar's collapse was caused by a deep, internal and invisible crack that developed over many years. This crack, which remained unseen on the ashlar's façade, was located parallel to the façade deep inside the stone and therefore was invisible until the day the ashlar fell. In order to pinpoint other internal, parallel cracks, different radar scans of the Wall's ashlars were conducted with the aim of receiving a precise and true status of the ashlar's composition without performing intrusive or destructive procedures to the sacred stones. These ultrasonic radar scans were carried out in an array of frequencies, literally shedding new light on the state of internal cracking and cavities located behind the stone face of the Wall (Tzahor 2020b).

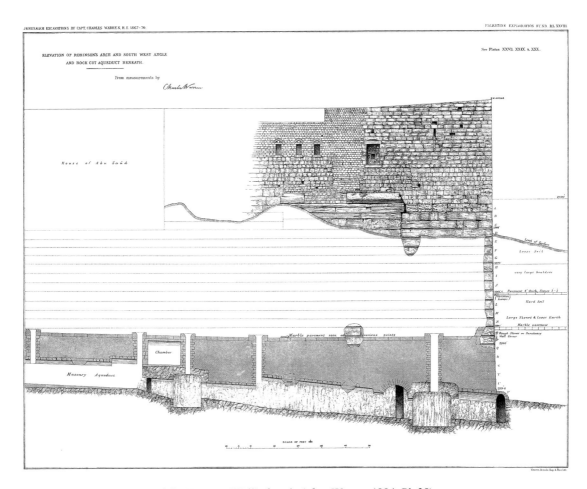

Figure 35.5: Measurement of the Western Wall's façade (after Warren 1884: Pl. 28).

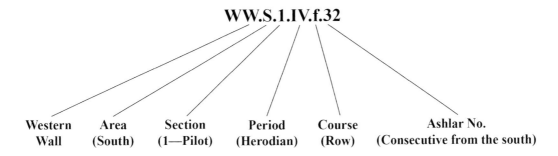

Figure 35.6: Example of ashlar numbering (after Tzahor 2019).

SURVEY FINDINGS AND QUANTITATIVE DATA

The mapping and documentation of the Wall's ashlars in our methodological conservation survey permitted us, for the first time, to inspect and retrieve quantitative data regarding them and their state of preservation (Tzahor 2020a).

- There are 4,577 ashlars in the Wall. Of them, 594 date to the Herodian period. While the chiseled colossal ashlars, which date to the first original construction of the Wall, are the most conspicuous stones due to their size and surface area, they are only 13% of the total number of ashlars in the Wall (Fig. 35.7).

- The number of ashlars surveyed in the three documented sub-sections is 2,879 or 63% of the total of the Wall's ashlars. Due to limited access and the height of the scaffolding authorized, it was possible to survey and treat only 589 ashlars in the three sub-sections. Three hundred and forty-six of them date to the original Herodian period, which is 57% of the total of Herodian ashlars. The other 244 ashlars date to later phases in the construction of the Wall, and they are generally located above the Herodian phase (Fig. 35.8).

The Herodian ashlars in the Western Wall were the stones that attracted most of our attention regarding the state of preservation and physical engineering deficiencies. All the Herodian ashlars in the three sections were treated.

EROSION FACTORS AND TYPICAL PROBLEMS IN PRESERVATION

- Cracking: Although the Western Wall exhibits a relatively small number of continuing cracks running along several ashlars and courses, the outer surface of many ashlars is cracked. This cracking cannot be uniformly defined due to the variety of different cracking formations—both in the number of cracks in each ashlar and in the depth of the cracks and the directions of their development. Sometimes the number of cracks in each ashlar is large, sometimes it is small, and

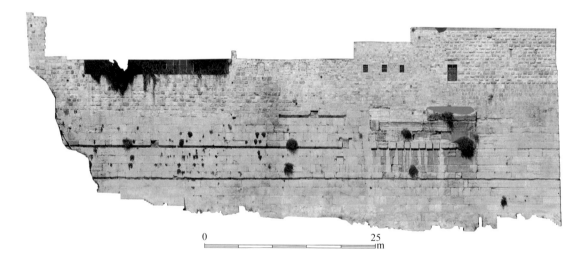

0   25
━━━━━━━━━━━━━━━━━━━━━━━m

Total ashlars in the southern part of the Western Wall: 4,577

The yellow part represents 594 Herodian ashlars.

Figure 35.7: Summation of ashlar numbers in the Western Wall's southern part (after Tzahor 2019).

sometimes it is nonexistent. The depth of the cracks is sometimes superficial and sometimes very deep. The directions of the cracks on the surface of the stone may be vertical, horizontal or diagonal, and in many ashlars, there is a combination of different types of cracks. The need to treat the cracks is obvious, as deep cracks can lead to loosening and detachment of stone parts.

The influence of young cracks (micro-cracks) was also studied, but similar to the examination of the cracks themselves, here, too, due to the variety of micro-cracking conditions, they cannot be characterized in a general manner.

One of the main objectives of the conservation survey was to identify the presence of cracks and internal cavities developing within the stone mass, deeply and parallel to the surface. These internal, invisible cracks could create an immediate danger and therefore called for urgent treatment. Since it was impossible to detect these cracks in the sacred stones by using intrusive methods, the cracks and cavities were examined and identified by non-invasive radar and sound tests. In the three sections of the survey, more than 200 internal cracks were identified in the ashlars of the Western Wall. It is evident that internal cracking is one of the main and most hazardous erosion factors, and one that may cause the detachment and collapse of additional stones.

• Erosion on the face of the ashlars: The examination of the ashlars' surface taught us a great deal about their physical conditions and permitted us to diagnose erosion patterns, such as the peeling of stone layers and their disintegration, occasionally into powder, its perforation, the development of micro-biology such as patina stains, natural patina and lichen. Due to the internal cracks and cavities within the stone mass, the assessment of the stone core's physical condition was precluded, leaving us with a conundrum.

• Stone deficiencies and cavities, loosening and detachment of stone parts: The loosening of stone parts and their detachment cause deficiencies in the Wall. An examination of the appearance of the stone surface reveals a variety of causes: mechanical damage, natural weathering and

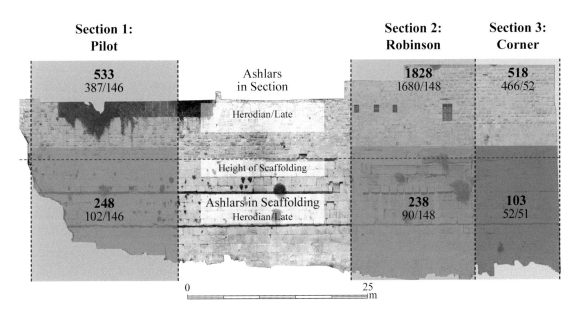

Figure 35.8: Total number of ashlars on three sub-sections of the survey executed on the Western Wall's southern section (after Tzahor 2019).

deep cracking. The mechanical damage, caused by ancient quarrying for secondary use of the Western Wall's ashlars, also included the removal of parts of the original stones. Natural weathering caused the wear of the Wall's face, mainly in those ashlars exposed to the elements for long periods of time or in those less resistant to the effects of time and climate.

- Human intervention: Damage to the Wall's ashlars caused by humans were also surveyed. They are discernible in two main ways: the first is modern intervention carried out with the aim of preserving and stabilizing the stones. This activity was mainly detected in the upper courses, which were exposed for a relatively long period. Although there is no documentation or dating for these actions, they clearly occurred during the 20th century as evidenced by the extensive use of cement-based binding material and iron pins. Most of the use of cement-based binding materials is found in joints and sometimes even as a supplement to deficiencies in the stones themselves. The use of cement is destructive to stone and serves as a factor that accelerates its weathering processes. The cement is stronger, harder and less porous than the stone and therefore causes water and salts to seep through the stone itself, which damages and weakens it further, to the point of detaching lumps of stone. That said, it is important to note that in most cases in which a cement-based binding material was identified between the ashlars of the Western Wall, it has not yet damaged the ashlars and joints to which it was applied. Thus, there is an extensive need for its immediate, overall replacement with lime-based binding materials that are more suitable for use in stone construction, which has yet to be undertaken. Another prominent human intervention at the Western Wall is related to the prevailing custom of inserting notes in the stone cracks and open interfaces, especially in the lower courses adjacent to the places of prayer and human hand contact. Although the effect of these paper notes on the Western Wall's ashlars is small, it has important historical and social research value.

- Fauna and flora in the Western Wall: As a complementary step to the conservation survey, a survey of fauna and flora was also conducted at the Western Wall. This survey traced the plants, the nests of the various birds and the rest of the animals present at the Western Wall. This mapping is important not only as documentation of a valuable and important stratum in the historical and cultural monument of the Western Wall, but it also enabled the establishment of precise guidelines of treatment required in sensitive places, in order to reduce, as much as possible, the negative impact the conservation work might have on the ecological fabric of the flora and fauna of the Western Wall. The vegetation at the Western Wall is typical wall vegetation, rooted mostly in the ashlar joints. The main plant species identified are Golden Henbane (*Hyoscyamus aureus*), Golden Drop (*Podonosma orientalis*), Pellitory of the Wall (*Parietaria judaica*) and the Caper (*Capparis spinosa*), which has become part of the Wall's symbols. Vegetation rooted in the joints can cause severe cracks and detachment of stone parts. To avoid future damage to the stones and possible danger, it was recommended to remove some of the plants.

ASSESSMENT OF THE PHYSICAL CONDITION OF THE WESTERN WALL ASHLARS

The detailed review of the Western Wall ashlars in the first sub-section revealed troubling findings about their state of preservation and the need for conservational care (Tzahor 2020b).

1. The state of preservation of most of the Western Wall ashlars in the three sub-sections surveyed and treated is poor and problematic. Only a minority of the ashlars have been found to be in a good state of preservation and require no treatment at present (Tzahor 2020a).

2. Examining the state of preservation of the ashlars from the Herodian period presents an even greater challenge. Of the 589 ashlars surveyed, the physical-engineering condition of 371 ashlars required preservative treatment, as their state of preservation was deemed moderate or poor. This is about two-thirds (63%) of the stones surveyed. Out of the 371 ashlars, 220 stones (37% of the stones surveyed) required immediate treatment and removal of the danger due to their poor state of preservation.

The physical condition of the Herodian ashlars, which are the essence of the Western Wall, is serious. Of the 346 ashlars from the Herodian period, no fewer than 267 ashlars (77%) were found to be in moderate to poor condition. One hundred sixty of the Herodian ashlars (46%) required immediate preservative treatment to remove the danger they present.

Only 218 ashlars, about one-third (37%) of the total ashlars examined, are in good condition and do not currently require treatment (Tzahor 2020a).

In addition to the severely problematic state of preservation of most of the Western Wall's ashlars, as revealed in the conservation surveys, other areas and parts of the Wall were also identified as having preservation problems and factors of danger and damage due to stone collapse: three long horizontal grooves, one above the other to a total length of ca. 125 m, were cut along the entire southern part of the Western Wall (Chapter 27). The quarrying of the horizontal grooves created deficiency in the support of the course above them and undermined the stability of its ashlars to the point of collapse, as happened with the stone that fell in the summer of 2018. All the ashlars in the hewn course were therefore defined as hazardous with immediate stabilization required.

Other areas in the Western Wall that were found to be problematic are in the lower part, such as the ancient shaft (Warren's Shaft) near the bottom of the Mughrabi ramp or the Western Wall courses near the current ground surface to which various built elements are adhered. In these areas, which are currently inaccessible, a large and significant internal cracking has been identified, and this, too, could lead to a serious engineering hazard (Tzahor 2019).

CONCLUSIONS AND RECOMMENDATIONS OF THE WESTERN WALL CONSERVATION SURVEYS

A summary of the physical condition of the Western Wall's ashlars, together with an assessment of their state of preservation and the urgency of treatment required, led to conclusions and recommendations for their preservation. These led to formulating work plans to carry out the required operations and conservation work.

1. Disengagement of stones at the Western Wall and their fall-off constitutes a genuine danger to worshipers and visitors, and therefore requires immediate treatment.

2. To the immediate and urgent hazards are added various defects and shortcomings which, although not urgent and currently non-hazardous, require conservation treatment to prevent exacerbation of existing problems. As stated above, about two-thirds of the ashlars surveyed require treatment and conservation, but of the Herodian stones, no less than 77% (!) are in danger (Tzahor 2020a; Fig. 35.9, Table 35.1).

WESTERN WALL ASHLAR CONSERVATION OPERATIONS AND HAZARD REPAIR— CONCERNS AND RESTRICTIONS

The significance of the conservation intervention required at the Western Wall is considerable and complex, especially due to the sensitivity of a place that is unique, sacred and of major import to the

Table 35.1: The State of Preservation and Urgency of Treatment of the Western Wall's Stones in the Three Sections of the Survey Conducted

		Section 1 Survey: Pilot				Section 2 Survey: Robinson's Arch				Section 3 Survey: Western Wall Corner				Summary (Intermediate)			
		Quantity	Herodian	Late	Total	Quantity	Herodian	Late	Total	Quantity	Herodian	Late	Total	Quantity	Herodian	Late	Total
State of Preservation	Good/Fair	Ashlars	59	82	141	Ashlars	42	54	96	Ashlars	9	0	9	Ashlars	110	136	246
		%	24%	33%	57%	%	18%	22%	40%	%	9%	0%	9%	%	19%	23%	42%
	Moderate	Ashlars	33	7	40	Ashlars	27	5	32	Ashlars	25	34	59	Ashlars	85	46	131
		%	13%	3%	16%	%	11%	3%	14%	%	24%	33%	57%	%	14%	8%	22%
	Poor/Problematic	Ashlars	54	13	67	Ashlars	79	31	110	Ashlars	17	18	35	Ashlars	150	62	212
		%	22%	5%	27%	%	33%	13%	46%	%	16.5%	17.5%	34%	%	25.5%	10.5%	36%
	Total	Ashlars	146	102	248	Ashlars	148	90	238	Ashlars	51	52	103	Ashlars	345	244	589
		%	59%	41%	100%	%	62%	38%	100%	%	49.5%	50.5%	100%	%	59%	41%	100%
Urgency of Intervention Needed	Immediate Treatment and Removal of Danger	Ashlars	72	17	89	Ashlars	71	25	96	Ashlars	17	18	35	Ashlars	160	60	220
		%	29%	7%	36%	%	30%	10%	40%	%	16.5%	17.5%	34%	%	27%	10%	37%
	Treatment of Defects	Ashlars	34	10	44	Ashlars	48	0	48	Ashlars	25	34	59	Ashlars	107	44	151
		%	14%	4%	18%	%	20%	0%	20%	%	24%	33%	57%	%	18%	8%	26%
	No Current Treatment Needed	Ashlars	40	75	115	Ashlars	29	65	94	Ashlars	9	0	9	Ashlars	78	140	218
		%	16%	30%	46%	%	12%	28%	40%	%	9%	0%	9%	%	13%	24%	37%
	Total	Ashlars	146	102	248	Ashlars	148	90	238	Ashlars	51	52	103	Ashlars	345	244	589
		%	59%	41%	100%	%	59%	41%	100%	%	49.5%	50.5%	100%	%	59%	41%	100%

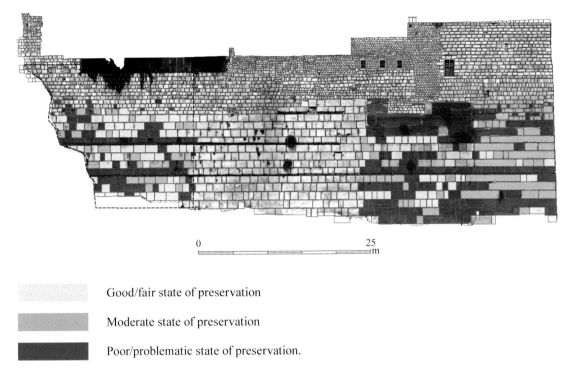

0 _____ 25
                                    m

Good/fair state of preservation

Moderate state of preservation

Poor/problematic state of preservation.

Figure 35.9: State of preservation of the Western Wall's ashlars in the three sections of the survey (after Tzahor 2020a).

three great monotheistic religions of the world. Therefore, conservation plans detailing the works required are bound by numerous special considerations and restrictions. Many of these restrictions have arisen in comprehensive discussions between the authorities of the Western Wall on the issue of sovereignty as well as on statutory aspects, research and scientific aspects, and cultural and religious aspects.

The main issue is the approval of the expected works by the Western Wall's rabbi, who is the religious authority of the Wall. The *halakhic* prohibition against smashing stones of the Temple and the Wall has created great difficulty vis-à-vis the required engineering stabilization technique of the stones in danger of undermining and disengaging. This technique, which requires drilling and inserting pins to anchor loose stone parts, by its very nature causes mechanical damage to the stones and removal of dust and sacred rock materials. The opposition by the rabbi, especially during the survey of the first sub-section, contradicted the fact that in other walls of the Temple Mount there was no delay and *halakhic* discussion about drilling during conservation work in previous years. This included even deeper, more drastic intervention such as stone replacement and deeply intrusive probes that entailed the removal of stone parts. The rabbi's objections also caused significant delay in the conservation work in the first sub-section (Tzahor 2020b).

The solution and compromise that were eventually reached included a substantial perceptual shift in the objectives of the conservation survey and planning of the conservation work. The initial premise was that the purpose of the intervention and conservation work was to stabilize and remove danger from the Wall's ashlars for the long term. The compromise agreement resolved that a mechanism of strict monitoring would be created, followed up by periodic treatment every two years. Through this monitoring system, it would be possible to significantly reduce the number of stones defined as hazardous, thus greatly reducing the amount of drilling required to stabilize the pins. This was acceptable to the Western Wall Rabbinate.

Although this solution of a constant, fixed and agreed-upon control and monitoring mechanism applied only to the area of the first sub-section of the survey which coincided with the area of "Ezrat Yisrael," defined as a sacred place of prayer, and was not required in other sections of the Western Wall—such dilemmas, having arisen more than once during our conservation work, have forced us to come up with flexible solutions, alternate thinking and unconventional execution methods when preserving the Wall's stones.

The designation of this area of the Western Wall, within the area of "Ezrat Yisrael" and for the use of all streams of Judaism, as initially determined in the Israeli government's "Western Wall Compromise," was the impetus to quickly proceed with the stabilization and conservation work, since following the collapse of the stone in the summer of 2018 access to that part of the Western Wall was denied and the prayer plaza and site remained closed to the public.

PLANS TO CARRY OUT CONSERVATION WORK

Due to the preservation problems found in the conservation surveys of the Western Wall's sub-sections, plans were formulated to carry out the conservation work. The conservation was divided into two categories: intrusive and non-intrusive operations. Intrusive operations included drilling, perforation and penetration of the ashlars. These are *halakhically* sensitive actions due to the prohibition of "smashing" sacred stones. The engineering necessary for the intrusive operations was considerable, and its purpose was to stabilize and anchor loose stone parts and severe cracks, which had been defined as prone to disengagement and collapse, through drilling, pin insertion and the use of epoxy glue. In contrast, non-intrusive operations mainly involved the use of lime-based binding materials. Binding materials were injected into parallel cavities and cracks within the stone and wall mass ("micro-grouting"), to stabilize and fill gaps, to stabilize small stone parts, and to fill and close cracks and deep joints ("grouting"). The non-intrusive operations also included the removal of previous destructive cement-based adhesives from stones and joints, replacing them with lime-based binding, removing vegetation rooted in the stones and joints, and reducing animal damage as part of preventive conservation (Tzahor 2020a; Fig. 35.10, Table 35.2).

EXECUTION OF CONSERVATION WORK AND THE DILEMMAS ASSOCIATED WITH IT

The discussions regarding the disagreements that arose during the conservation work in the first survey section were held intermittently for about a year, from March 2019 to March 2020. In contrast, the work in the next two survey sections—the Robinson's Arch section and the Western Wall corner section—was conducted without delays. The conservation survey in the second section was conducted from March to May 2020. Work began immediately after and was completed by September 2020 (Tzahor 2020c). The conservation survey in the third section was conducted in October of that year, and the work was done in the two months that followed (Tzahor 2020a).

The main discussions on the various conservation questions that arose during the execution of the work on the first section, which was a pilot, dealt with, among other things, the issues discussed below.

REDUCTION OF DRILLING IN THE WESTERN WALL'S ASHLARS

Dealing with the *halakhic* prohibition of drilling pins into the stones included a discussion of various alternatives, such as substitute preservation technologies and non-metallic materials, like basalt and fiberglass pins. In the first section of the survey, a very limited alternative to intrusive operations and internal drilling was agreed upon. This followed another thorough engineering review and the assurance of a regular and comprehensive follow-up and monitoring of the development of hazards in the stones (Tzahor 2020b).

Table 35.2: Conservation Work Required on the Western Wall Stones in the Three Sections of the Survey

No.	Conservation work	Herodian ashlars	Late ashlars	Total ashlars
1	Stabilizing detachments with pins	159	60	**219**
2	Stabilizing detachments with anchors	1	0	**1**
3	Treatment with binding materials only ("micro-grouting," for filling gaps and closing cracks and deep joints)	106	40	**146**
4	Chemical stabilization of stone surface (arch ashlars)	1	0	**1**
5	Detached ashlars for dismantling and rebuilding	0	4	**4**
8	Ashlars which require no current intervention	78	140	**218**
Total		*345*	*244*	*589*

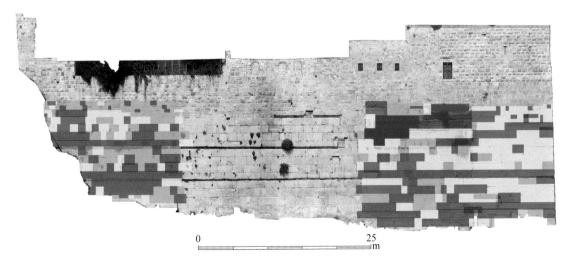

Figure 35.10: Urgency of treatment required in the three sections surveyed. See Table 35.1 for color analysis (after Tzahor 2020a).

TREATMENT OF ASHLARS ABOVE THE ANCIENT HORIZONTAL GROOVES ALONG THE WESTERN WALL

The cutting of these grooves undermined the stone courses above them, which resulted in the plummeting of the ashlar in 2018 (Chapter 27). The committee organized to resolve these issues included representatives from the Israel Antiquities Authority, the Nature and Parks Authority, the city engineer and conservation experts. Four alternatives were suggested, and a solution was chosen that included the filling of the grooves with plastered fieldstones and binding. This solution was chosen due to its reversibility and minimal damage to the stone (Figs. 35.11a–35.11d). In order to minimize the significant visual impact on the appearance of the Western Wall, it was executed in the least invasive manner possible and with a clear visual distinction between the new filling and the original stone. A number of casting samples were made for the filling and the best sample, concave in shape, was selected. Similarly, the final plaster shade, which has a great effect on the final appearance, was chosen from several samples mixed on-site. We chose a shade similar to the color of the stone but not too close in texture (Tzahor 2020b; Fig. 35.12).

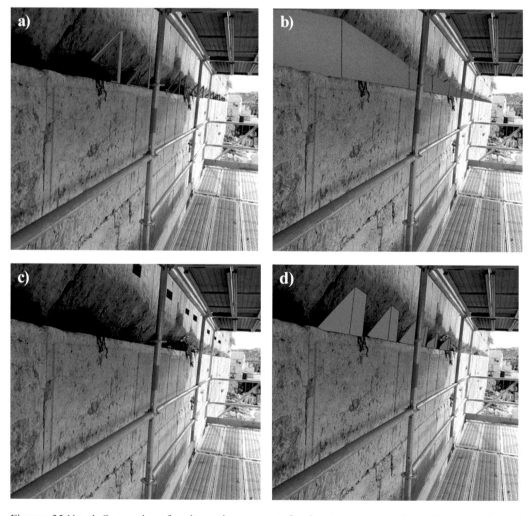

Figures 35.11a–d: Suggestions for alternative supports for the stone courses above the cut horizontal grooves along the Western Wall.

Treatment of the Collapsed Stone

The discussion of what is required and can be done with a stone that fell from the Western Wall, as well as the space left in the wall, the existence of which undermines the ashlars above it, led to a number of possible alternative engineering solutions. Among the alternatives were reinstating the original stone in place, the installation of a constructive frame using stainless steel profiles to support the stones above or filling the space with a casting similar to the solution used for the cut horizontal grooves. Several considerations were taken into account:

- Engineering—faults in the original stone makeup.
- *Halakhic*—fear of damage to the ashlars from the drilling of pins and anchors.
- Conservation—finding a solution where the visual appearance would not be overly conspicuous and would blend in with the texture of the Wall.

The solution eventually chosen was the same used for the rock-cut tunnel—filling the space by casting binding material and fieldstones. This solution addressed the engineering necessity to support the ashlars above the void, as well as the *halakhic* need to prevent damage by drilling in the stones. It also addressed the visual and conservational need for the Wall's appearance. The stone cavity was cast in two parts. The lower part, which is also part of the rock-cut tunnel, was cast as part of the tunnel; the upper part was cast with a binding material, matching the stone texture and the appearance around it (Tzahor 2020b; Fig. 35.13).

The religious and historical importance intensified the need for accurate and meticulous work. Executives of the Israel Antiquities Authority and its Conservation Administration attended many stages of the work, paying close attention to the finer details and decision-making, such as the color of the finishing plaster in the various filling layers, the color of the binding material at the joints, the number of centimeters left open at the grooves, etc. (Chapter 36).

Figure 35.12: Cut horizontal grooves after filling (photo by Y. Tzahor, March 2020).

Figure 35.13: Casting to fill the cavity caused by the ashlar's collapse (photo by Y. Tzahor, March 2020).

Figure 35.14: Condition of the first section following the conservation work (photo by Y. Tzahor, March 2020).

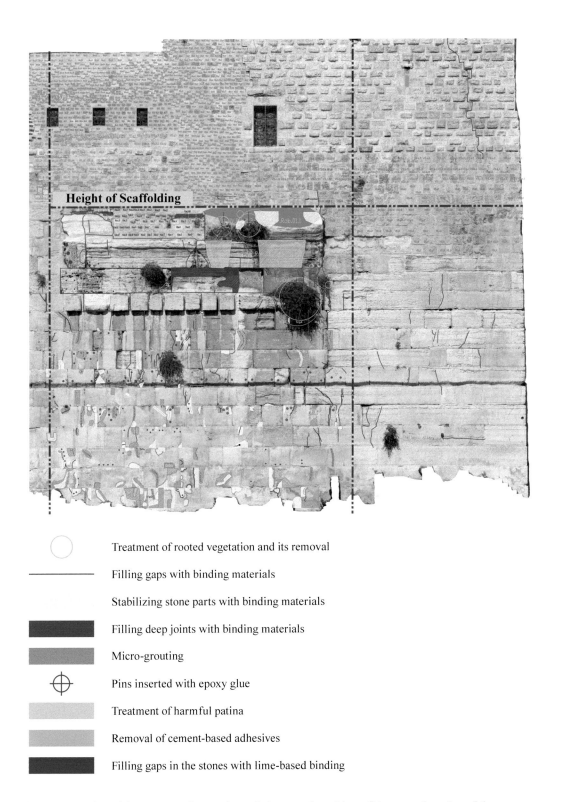

Treatment of rooted vegetation and its removal

Filling gaps with binding materials

Stabilizing stone parts with binding materials

Filling deep joints with binding materials

Micro-grouting

Pins inserted with epoxy glue

Treatment of harmful patina

Removal of cement-based adhesives

Filling gaps in the stones with lime-based binding

Figure 35.15: Plan of the conservation work carried out on the ashlars of the second section of the survey, at the end of the conservation work (after Tzahor 2020c).

SUMMARY

Only unforeseen circumstances, such as a large fragment of a Western Wall's ashlar breaking off, led to an examination of the Wall's engineering condition and the physical state of preservation. This large, complex and sensitive project, which was not planned in advance, was carried out by a team of conservators, engineers and planners who had already surveyed ca. 600 ashlars in the southern part of the Western Wall. The various stages of the survey, which included innovative measurements, historical documentation and the collection of copious data, led to the exposure of problems, failures and an assessment of the severity of the physical and engineering condition of the stones. The treatment and work to eliminate the dangers and repair faults that were discovered were coupled with the complexity of the site and its sensitivity due to its significance as a sacred World Heritage monument. Ultimately, the project was completed successfully, and we were able to stabilize, preserve and prevent additional stones from falling and endangering visitors to the site.

The Israel Antiquities Authority immediately mobilized to recruit a large team of professionals and experts to take part in this project—preserving, rescuing and investigating the Wall's stones. Together they created a comprehensive, meticulous and advanced survey. The extensive conservation work, which was carried out according to the survey's conclusions and with the greatest sensitivity, brought the Western Wall to an optimum state of preservation (Figs. 35.14–15).

The large surface area of the Western Wall's façade, the quality and great size of its ancient ashlars, and its cultural centrality place the extensive information that emerged from the conservation survey and the detailed data collected as a unique and valuable resource. This important database will aid future research and will serve as a basis for monitoring, controlling and managing the site. Aware of the great value of the information collected, the surveyors and researchers ensured that the information was presented online.

REFERENCES

Tzahor, Y. 2019. *Interim Report for Engineering Conservation Survey—Southern Section, First Sub-Section (WW. South.1)*. Submitted to the Israel Antiquities Authority's Conservation Department. Jerusalem.

Tzahor, Y. 2020a. *Interim Report for Engineering Conservation Survey—Southern Section, Third Sub-Section: Temple Mount's Corner*. Submitted to the Israel Antiquities Authority's Conservation Department. Jerusalem.

Tzahor, Y. 2020b. *Conservation of the Western Wall's Ashlars, Southern Section, First Sub-Section—Final Execution Report*. Submitted to the Israel Antiquities Authority's Conservation Department. Jerusalem.

Tzahor, Y. 2020c. *Conservation of the Western Wall's Ashlars, Southern Section, Second Sub-Section (Robinson's Arch)—Final Execution Report*. Submitted to the Israel Antiquities Authority's Conservation Department. Jerusalem.

Warren, C. 1884. *Plans, Elevations, Sections, etc. Shewing the Results of the Excavations at Jerusalem, 1867–70, Executed for the Committee of the Palestine Exploration Fund*. London.

CHAPTER 36

DEGRADATION OF THE STONES IN THE WESTERN WALL: SALT DISTRIBUTION OVER THREE DECADES

Yotam Asscher, Aliza Van Zuiden and Meidad Shor

INTRODUCTION

In this chapter, we present a new approach to studying degradation of stone. We consider past conservation efforts and new analytical examinations that focus on salt distribution in stone that may explain the current state of its preservation.

The Western Wall as seen today combines Early Roman monumental construction of both large stone ashlars (Ritmeyer 2006; Mazar 2011; Bahat 2013) with much smaller ashlars on its upper courses that date from later periods (Hillenbrand 2000). The state of preservation of the stones is directly related to their history, including destruction in Roman times by wars, by poor maintenance in later periods when walls were excavated, and by modern accelerators such as soluble salts, which promoted deterioration. An example of this is the southern part of the Western Wall, which includes the Prayer Area and Robinson's Arch area. It is currently only about half the height it was when it was partially destroyed by the Roman army in 70 CE (Fig. 36.1). According to an 1856 photo from the New York Public Library, this area was covered by soil and debris until the mid-19th century. The walls were exposed by a sequence of archaeological excavations performed in the 20th century, mainly by B. Mazar in 1968–1978 (Mazar 1971, 1976) and by Reich and Billig in 1994–1996 (Reich and Billig 2000) (Fig. 36.2).[1]

Different types of deterioration can be observed on the stones at the Ezrat Yisrael Prayer Area and Robinson's Arch. During the Roman destruction, the big bridge collapsed and battering rams were used to push stones from the level of the Temple platform to the Early Roman Street level, piling them to a height of 2–3 m. During their fall, it is likely that the stones bumped on the protruding edges of the ashlars in the wall. The stones suffered internal cracks, some visible, but mostly invisible to the naked eye (Figs. 36.3a, 36.3b). Large stone scales became either detached from the wall (Fig. 36.3c, 36.3e) or somehow remained in-situ (Figs. 36.3a, 36.3d), but in all cases presented serious safety issues for visitors and caused complicated conservation problems.

Fire missiles (or other flammable material) launched into shops at the base of the wall, causing fires and damage, as the ashlars burst and cracked. High temperatures (possibly 700–900 °C) caused heavy scaling (Fig. 36.3d) and may have converted part of the limestone scales into quicklime (Ashurst and Ashurst 1989), increasing porosity and further decay.

---

[1] Our thanks to R. Reich for providing much background information during many conversations at the site; Y. Baruch, Director of the Jerusalem District of the IAA, for helpful discussions during the planning of the project; Conservator R. Elberger who visited the site every 2–4 weeks and helped with mapping; Surveyor M. Kunin for measurements and base-drawing of the lower 6–7 courses of the Robinson's Arch area. We also wish to thank R. Kislev, Director of the Conservation Division in the IAA; Y. Schaffer, Director of the Conservation Department; A. Mashiah, Head of the Projects Department; and Y. Saad, Head of the Implementation Unit. Our special thanks go to the Conservator Y. Vaknin for his help in pushing the project forward in 2019–2020.

Figure 36.1: Reconstruction by Balage Balogh and Eilat Mazar of the Temple Mount before its destruction in 70 CE. The Western Wall faces left (photo courtesy of the IAA).

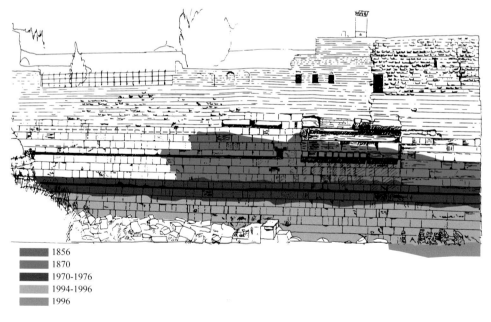

Figure 36.2: Excavation levels at different periods: Base drawing, from photos by A. Van Zuiden, IAA. Brown: 1856 (according to a picture from the archives of the New York Public Library). Blue: 1870 (Robinson excavation). Black lines: buildings in front of the Wall (the Mughrabi neighborhood). Red: 1970–1976 (Mazar excavation). Light brown: 1994–1996 (Reich, Billig excavation). Dark green: 1996, excavation to the original level of the Early Roman period.

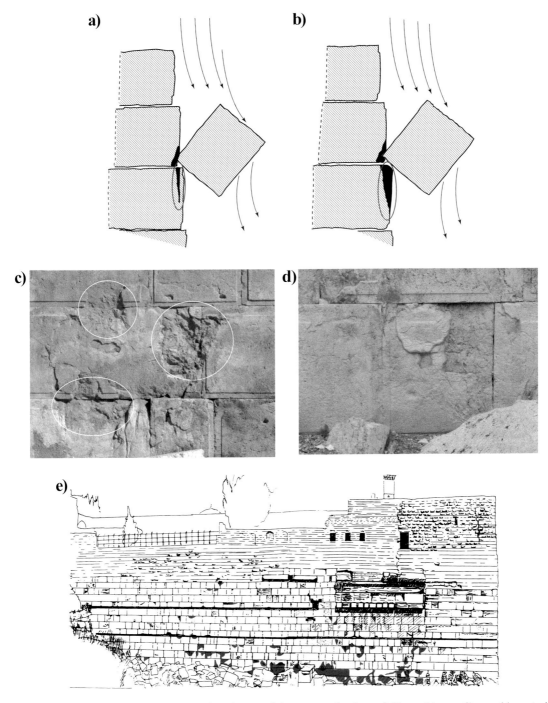

Figure 36.3: Internal cracks and complete detachment of the stone scales due to falling ashlars or flammable material. *Situation 4.1996:* (a) Stones fell on protruding edges of the ashlars of the wall and caused internal cracks (partial detachment). (b) Stones fell on protruding edges of the ashlars of the wall and caused complete detachment of stone scales. (c) Complete detachment of stone scales, presumably due to fallen stones on the protruding edges of the ashlars of the wall. *Situation 2.2015:* (d) Partial detachment of stone scales, presumably due to fire bombs thrown into the shops. *Situation 7.2014:* (e) Areas marked in red show a complete detachment of stone scales, presumably due to fallen stones on the protruding edges of the ashlars in the wall (see also Fig. 36.3c).

The retaining walls around the Temple Mount were built with huge ashlars (1.10 m high, 0.80–10 m wide, and 0.70–1.00 m, or even more, deep). The stone types are local *meleke* and *mizzi hilu*, a medium-hard and hard limestone, respectively; the latter shows stylolithes or dissolution planes (Gill 1996, 2019). During conservation work between 1996 and 1998, no mortar remnants were found in the joints between the ashlars at the lower 3–4 courses of the Western Wall, and no remnants of mortar was found on the pile of collapsed ashlars still remaining on the Herodian/Early Roman Street. These observations agree with finds from the underground base excavations of the Western Wall, showing dry building technique, i.e., no mortar was used between the ashlars (Hagbi and Van Zuiden 2019). The fill material behind the ashlars of the Western Wall is inaccessible, hence unknown, and has yet to be studied.

In addition to mechanical deterioration of Roman times, there is continuous deformation of the stone structure due to soluble salts. The presence of soluble salts can be extremely harmful to ancient building materials. While stones do not contain high levels of salt because their porosity is low, we find salts in the cracks between and in the middle of the stones, as well as in adhered materials such as mortars and soil which are porous materials. Hygroscopic salts such as chlorides transport easily in monuments or buildings, showing they can reach a height of 15 m in sandstone columns and up to 12 m in ancient brick walls. The salts transport by means of dissolution in the pore water of the material, which allows mobility to locations with higher temperatures, lower humidity and ventilation, allowing for evaporation and recrystallization of the salts ("wetting and drying cycle"). Different types of salts, such as gypsum, have different mineral forms depending on the structural water within their crystals, changing their volume during dissolution and crystallization. In dry areas, salts usually stay in their original volumes; however, in high relative humidity of the air or rain, the crystal absorbs water and their volume expands. These processes of salt expansion in pores and cracks can cause dramatic deterioration in stones and mortars, producing thick scales that detach from the stone mainly due to sulfates (hydration damage), which are less soluble than chlorides and nitrates, which produce thin scaling (crystallization damage). Price (1996) gives an interesting point of view on salts' role in the wetting and drying cycle. He writes:

> Salt damage is largely attributable to two mechanisms: the crystallization of salts from solution; and the hydration of salts. Any salt, in principle, is capable of causing crystallization damage, whereas hydration damage can be caused only by salts that can exist in more than one hydration state. Sodium chloride, for example, is only capable of crystallization damage, while sodium sulfate, which can exist as either the anhydrous salt thenardite (Na_2SO_4) or the decahydrate mirabilite (Na_2SO_4 10H2O), can cause both crystallization damage and hydration damage.

In this research, we use analytical tools to study the presence of salts in the Western Wall quantitatively, mapping their distribution and their influence on the stone deterioration, overviewing decades of salt monitoring from the late 1990s to 2020.

MAPPING VISUAL INDICATORS RELATED TO SALTS

Between 1996 and 1998 visual observations were used to map indicators that relate to the presence of salt. Leakage of water and salt crusts show degradation was mainly between the Ezrat Yisrael Prayer Area and Robinson's Arch. Leakage was noticed on a daily basis in 1996 between 13:00 and 15:00 p.m., north of Robinson's Arch, from the top of the Wall to the bottom (original street level). Due to the timing of the repeated leaks, the leakage was probably associated with the irrigation system in the garden next to the Islamic Museum (former Moors' Mosque), or from broken sewage pipes. These leakages caused the Early Roman ashlars to show stone scaling and thin salt crusts in the spring of 1996 (Figs. 36.4a, 36.4b). In addition, deformation ("belly forming") of the top part of the Wall was observed in the Umayyad and Ottoman additions. As a result, in 1997, the Waqf (Muslim religious authority) repointed the upper part of the Wall, using a non-porous white cement which was impermeable to water (Fig. 36.4c and inset).

Visual signs of moisture, water accumulation and salt crust on the stone surface were observed and mapped in 1997 (Fig. 36.5a), 1998 (Fig. 36.5b), and 2020 (Fig. 36.5c). The moisture, salts and degradation were prominent between the Ezrat Yisrael Prayer Area and Robinson's Arch area due to the repointing of the cement on the upper levels. In addition, accumulation of salts and salt damage were observed on the lower courses of the Wall and the original floor surface, due to the heavy percolation of the water toward the base. The moisture content on the stone surface at the bottom of the Wall and in the joints was tested with the Protimeter instrument (model 1989) in 1997, just before the rainy season, up to a height of 3–5 courses of ashlars. Maximum measurements of >60% moisture content were frequently tested (Fig. 36.6a). The same results were tested on the stone surface (with the pin electrodes) as in the joints, to a depth of 23 cm (with deep wall probes) (Fig. 36.6b).

Stone scaling (0.5–1.5 cm) was observed and mapped, showing overlap with moisture content at the bottom 3–5 courses of ashlars. "Acoustic" tests were performed in September 1997 with the aid of a small plastic hammer up to a height of the 3–4 lower courses to detect the location of internal cracks and partial detachment of stone scales. The detached areas were mapped by Van Zuiden on the base-drawings of the ashlars made by surveyor Mark Kunin of the IAA (Fig. 36.7). The biggest concentration of the internal cracks is right under the arch, which collapsed during the 70 CE destruction.

Plant growth and bird nesting was registered and compared with pictures from 1970 (Fig. 36.8). An enormous difference was noticed, probably due to water leakage and storage behind the walls, which changed over time. The main type of plants were the Caper bush and the Golden Henbane; the Caper showed roots reaching about 8–10 m, increasing the destructive potential in crack formation. Open joints gave birds the ability to nest, showing the Common Kestrel or Lesser Kestrel nesting in the upper Ottoman part of the Southern Wall. Bird nests were observed in 2020 as well, this time in the Western Wall. Birds and animals can hollow out the core of the wall.

SEMI-QUANTITATIVE INDICATORS OF DETERIORATION

During the 1990s, an empirical system was set up to evaluate semi-quantitatively the presence of salts in mortars and soils that were directly related to the stones. The semi-quantitative methods were adapted from exact sciences and conservation treatments, including test strips, titric methods, electrodes of electrical conductivity and colorimetric methods, that estimate the levels of salts in solution which includes distilled water and the sample. This would be used to recommend the necessity of desalinization or other preventive conservation measurements. Literature indicates the acceptable salt levels for each method, showing the precision and accuracy of various methods (Table 36.1).

The Electrical Conductivity test was used to assess the presence of the total amount of soluble salt, and test strips were used to estimate the concentration of major components in soluble salts. Electrical Conductivity allows estimating the amount of salts in a sample since it is directly related to the soluble salts which are emitted from the sample into the solution. Hence, by measuring the

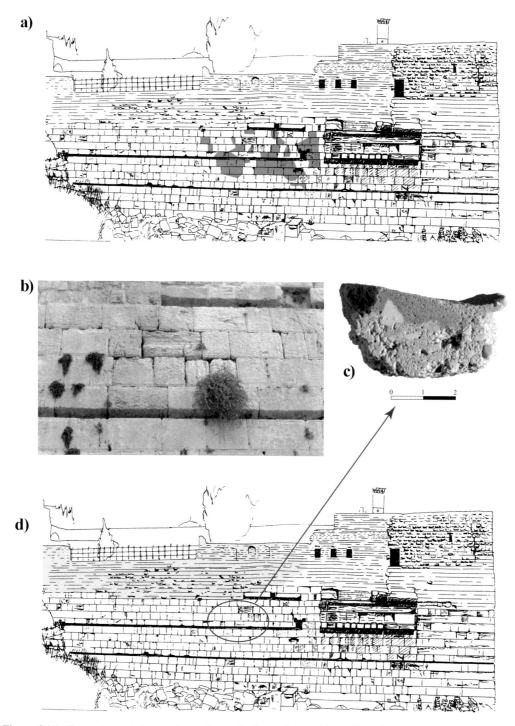

Figure 36.4: Cement repointing and deteriorated edges of the ashlars. Situation on Oct. 1997. Due to leakages, wide open joints with deteriorated edges of the ashlars. (a) Areas with thin stone scaling and thin salt crusts. Situation spring 1996, before conservation efforts. (b) The area below the repointed area with an impermeable white cement (marked with red circle), showing wide-open joints and heavy deteriorated edges of the ashlars Situation 2020. (c) Area repointed with an impermeable, non-porous white cement mortar that was applied on Oct. 1997 by the Waqf (marked in yellow). Cement repointing shows 2 layers (see c), which might have pushed leakages downward, below the cement.

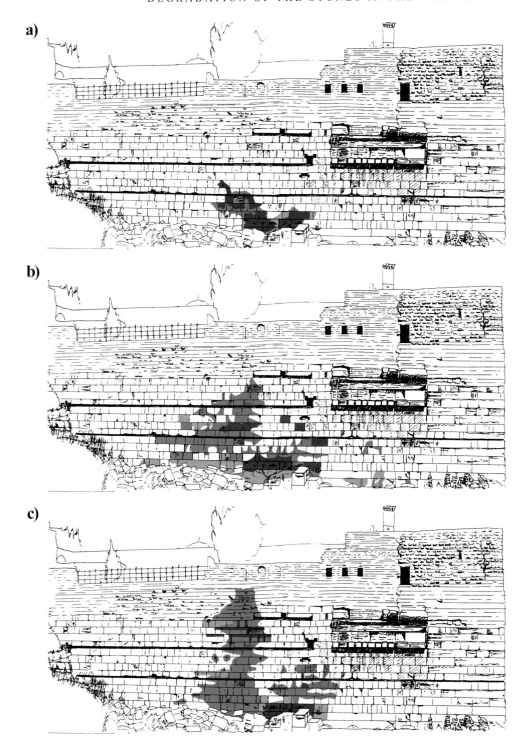

Figure 36.5: Areas with visible moisture (wet areas), showing increased salt efflorescence and salt encrustation with time. (a) Situation Nov. 1997. (b) Situation July 1998. (c) Situation 16 July 2020. Legend: Blue area with visible moisture (wet areas, no running water on the stone surface), Pink–salt efflorescence, Red–salt crust, red lines–wide open joints with heavily deteriorated edges and birds' nests.

Table 36.1: Acceptable Standard Salt Levels*

Electrical conductivity or type of salt	Coarse indication	Salt amounts— mS/cm–mgr p/l–D
Electrical Conductivity–EC (Hanna HI–8733 meter)	Low Medium High	0.00–1.00 mS/cm 1.00–1.50 mS/cm >1.50 mS/cm
Sodium–Na (Meter)	Low Medium High	0.00–200 mgr p/l 200–1000 mgr p/l >1000 mgr p/l
Chlorides–Cl (Merck test strips and titric method)	Low Medium High	0.00–100 mgr p/l 100–250 mgr p/l > 250 mgr p/l
Sulfates–SO_4 (Merck test strips)	Low Medium High	0.00–600 mgr p/l 600–1200 mgr p/l >1200 mgr p/l
Nitrates–NO_3 (Merck test strips)	Low Medium High	0.00–250 mgr p/l 250–500 mgr p/l >500 mgr p/l
Carbonates–$CaCO_3$ (Merck test strips)	Low Medium High	0–12° D 12–18° D > 18° D
Bi-Carbonates–$CaHCO_3$ (Merck test strips)	Low Medium High	0–8° D 8–16° D >16° D
Potassium–K (Merck test strips)	Low Medium High	–250 mgr p/l 250–750 mgr p/l >750 mgr p/l
Magnesium–Mg (Merck colorimetric method)	Low Medium High	–250 mgr p/l 250–750 mgr p/l >750 mgr p/l

*Empirical observation, according to the method of placing samples in a watery solution (ratio material: water as 1:4) before being tested.
1° D = 10 mgr CaO = 17.8 mgr p/l $CaCO_3$

conductivity of a solution in which a sample was mixed the amount of salts could be indirectly assessed. The method involves: samples of ca. 25 grams of material were placed in 100 cc distilled water for 24 hours. The salt content of the water was tested via a Hanna HI 8733 Electrical Conductivity meter, Merck test strips or via Merck colorimetric or titric test methods; chlorides, nitrates, sulfates, carbonates, sodium and potassium were the main salts to be tested (Arnold 1986) (Fig. 36.9). Most test strips do not have as wide a test range as the EC tests (0.00–199.99 mS/cm). The Electrical Conductivity showed extreme results (1.00–110 mS/cm, where values of normally 0.20 mS/cm are advised), as well as high values of chlorides and nitrates.

Thirty samples from different building materials were taken, including stone, mortars and soil from various locations (Fig. 36.10). These samples were aimed at correlating between the soil as a possible source of salts, and the salts in the stones and mortars. Soils were collected from the

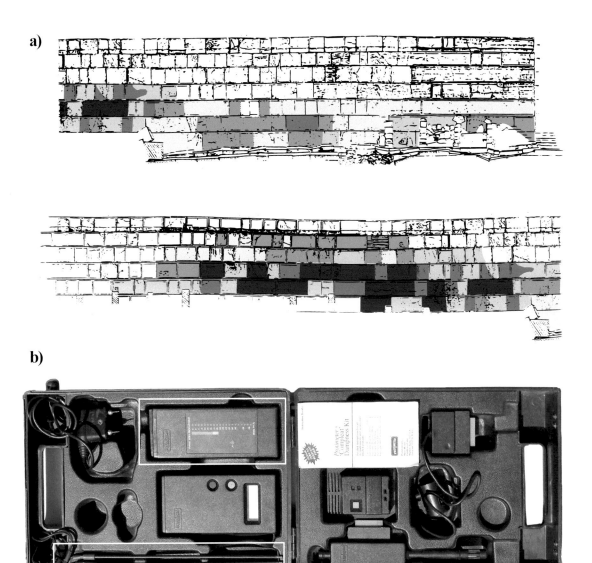

Figure 36.6: Moisture content measurements on the stone surface. *Situation 4-15.10.1997.* (a) Moisture Content measurements at the lower 3-4 courses of Robinson's Arch area: Yellow: 0−15% MC; Dark blue: 35−55% MC; Pink: 15–20 % MC; Purple: 55− 60% MC; Light blue: 20–35 % MC. The area with a high Moisture Content is situated behind the southern part of the heap of the collapsed ashlars.

(b) The "Protimeter 'Compleat' Dampness Kit," model 1989.

White squares:

Lower = the MC Moisture Content instrument with two pin electrodes for surface detection

Upper = deep wall probes for detection within the joint.

Green—0−15% moisture content—"air-dry" condition.

Yellow—15−20% moisture content—slightly in excess of normal.

Red—20−60% moisture content—excess moisture.

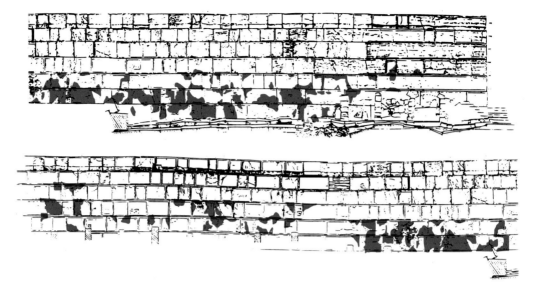

Figure 36.7: Internal, partial detachment of stone scales (not visible to the naked eye, observed only via acoustic tests with a plastic hammer). Top drawing is from the southwest corner of the Temple Mount to the collapsed ashlars. Bottom drawing is from the collapsed ashlars northward, to the area under the Mugrabi gate. Situation 9 Sept. 1997.

ground, between the joints of the ashlars, from stone chips of the pier of Robinson's Arch, the shops parallel to the Western Wall and from the Western Wall itself.

A high EC (between 50–100 mS/cm, marked in blue in Table 36.2) occurs very frequently in the Western Wall and Southern Wall, while the recommended values of EC are 0.2–1.00 mS/cm.

To understand if soils might have influenced the salt composition of the building materials, soil samples were measured by the same method (Table 36.3). The results show that soils EC vary greatly, depending on the context, ranging between 0.6 and 83.6 mS/cm. The EC of the stones from the Western Wall and the Southern Wall vary between 3.5 and 18.3 mS/cm (Table 36.3). The soil in the joints between the ashlars of the Western Wall and the Southern Wall is, however, extremely contaminated with salts, ranging between 58.6 and 83.6 mS/cm. A single sample of suspected lime/ mortar from the Southern Wall shows similar values (70.2 mS/cm), which is most likely to have arrived from inside the wall (the core) and migrated through cycles of dissolution and precipitation toward the surface. This shows that the proximity to a sewage or any water pipe will dictate if the soils contain salts or not. In general, EC values are higher in soils than in stone, which shows maximum of 18.3 mS/cm. Interestingly, the soil in the joints between the ashlars (83.6 mS/cm) in the Southern Wall (southwest corner) has extremely high salt content, including high chloride (Cl) and sodium (Na) ions, showing values higher than 6000 and 2000 parts per million (ppm), respectively. Although these ions show as halide salts (very soluble), visually, less stone deterioration is observed. The soil in the joints between the ashlars of the Western Wall and the Southern Wall is, however, extremely contaminated with salts, ranging between 58.6–83.6 mS/cm. A single sample of suspected lime/mortar from the Southern Wall shows similar values (70.2 mS/cm), which is most likely to have arrived from inside the wall (the core) and migrated through cycles of dissolution and precipitation toward the surface. This shows that the proximity to a sewage or any water pipe will dictate if the soils contain salts or not. In general, EC values are higher in soils than in stone, which shows maximum of 18.3 mS/cm. Interestingly, the soil in the joints between the ashlars (83.6 mS/ cm) in the Southern Wall (southwest corner) has extremely high salt content, including high chloride

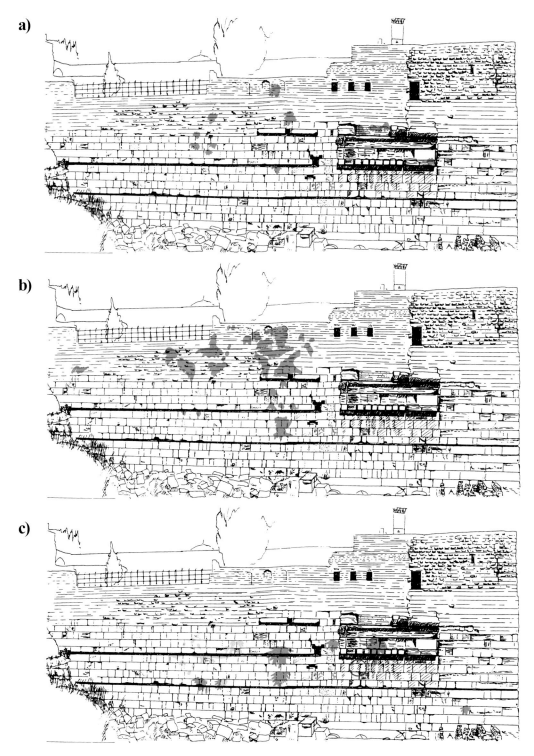

Figure 36.8: Plant growth in 1970 and in spring 1996, showing overlap with moisture distribution. (a) Situation of 1970 (according to old pictures), shows only a few Caper bushes. (b) Situation spring 1996, shows much plant growth (dark green is Caper bush, light green is Golden Henbane). (c) Situation summer 2020, shows plants with short roots like the Golden Henbane (light green) can only grow if water is present in the wall. A bird's nest is marked in red in an open joint.

Table 36.2: Electrical Conductivity (EC) in Different Building Materials in the Western Wall and Southern Wall

Place and date of sampling	Soil from floor level	Soil from inside joints	Stone	Mortar	Desalination— poultice material
Pier of Robinson's Arch 29.4.1996	1		4 3 1		
Herodian or Early Roman Street 29.4.1996 4.7.1997	3 1			2	
Shops along Western Wall 29.4.1996 4.7.1997	2 1		2	1	
Western Wall Behind the collapsed ashlars	1		4 2 3 1 2		1 2 19
Southern Wall, southwestern area 22.1.1998		5	5		1 1 4

Legend:

⬜ 0–1 mS/cm–EC   ⬜ 1–2 mS/cm–EC   ⬜ 2–5 mS/cm–EC

⬛ 5–10 mS/cm–EC   ⬛ >10.00–110.00, mS/cm–EC

Numbers in colored squares are number of samples taken from that area and from that material.

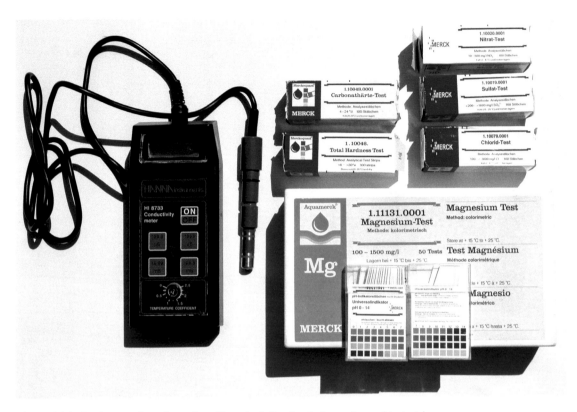

Figure 36.9: Equipment for salt testing: Electrical Conductivity meter and test strips.

(Cl) and sodium (Na) ions, showing values higher than 6000 and 2000 parts per million (ppm), respectively. Although these ions show as halide salts much sun exposure and the Wall showed visually a continuous high moisture content. The soils from the shops along the Western Wall show relatively low EC value (0.6 mS/cm), implying that the salts in the Western Wall and Southern Wall did not arrive from the environment, but most likely from inside or behind the wall.

The Western Wall has a much lower salt level than the Southern Wall. Most hygroscopic salt crystals expand with water from the environment and the salt crystal diminishes in size when drying out. This process of wetting and drying caused much more damage than the extreme high salt content in the Southern Wall with its stable high moisture content.

General salts tests, as conducted between 1996 and 1998, using the same protocol based on EC and test strips, were repeated in 2020 (Table 36.4). Six samples for additional salt analysis were collected (locations of samples in Fig. 36.11). The high EC in the white cement sample (Sample 1–109.70 mS/cm) is presumably not connected to the cement mixture itself, since Sample 4 has a much lower EC value (5.7 mS/cm). Sample 1 was taken from the top of Robinson's Arch, on the border between the destroyed Early Roman arch and the 19th century Ottoman addition. Eighteen hundred years of leakages are apparently responsible for this extreme EC value. The high chloride and nitrate levels point in this direction as well. Another extreme EC value was tested in the plaster of the channel (149.80 mS/cm, Sample 6). The channel is associated with a later period, and chiseled to a depth of some 50 cm, that is, into half to two-thirds of the depth of the ashlar. Probably leakages behind the ashlars (visible already in Fig. 36.5), from the core of the Wall toward the stone surface, are responsible for this extreme EC value. The high chloride and nitrate levels are a good indicator of leakages.

Table 36.3: Salt Test Card and Salt Analysis of Some Typical Samples

Site: Robinson's Arch—Western Wall and Southern Wall
Sub-site: – Shops 13.7.1998

— Western Wall behind collapsed ashlars: 30.7.1997

— Southern Wall, southwest corner: 2.2.1998: 11.3.98

Date: 13.7.1997/ 30.7.1997/ 2.2.1998/ 11.3.98
Sampled by: A. Van Zuiden

nr	Dilution	pH	EC—Electrical Conductivity mS/cm	pNa ppm	Cl ppm	SO₄ ppm	NO₃ ppm	CaCO₃ °D	CaHCO₃ °D	Ca ppm	Mg ppm	K ppm	Place/remarks
6	25/100	7.6	0.6	600				20	16				Shops—soil from floor
9	25/100	7.4	1.1	900	400			20	8–12				Shops—soil from floor
7	25/100		13.9		700	> 1600	>> 500	>>25	8–12			1000	Western Wall—Stone
8	25/100		3.5		1500	400–800	>500	>>25	4–8				Western Wall—Stone
10	25/100		7.4		500	>1600	>500	>>25	4–8		450		Western Wall—Stone
10	25/100		18.3	1900	0–500		500	>>25			250		Southern Wall—Stone
11	25/100		58.6	4700	1000	200	>> 500	>>25			450		Southern Wall—soil from joint
12	25/100		70.2	6000	1500	200	>> 500	>>25			700		Southern Wall—lime/mortar?
A	25/100	6.0	83.6	6000	2000-3000	400	>> 500	>>25	12–16		1500	500	Southern Wall—soil from joint

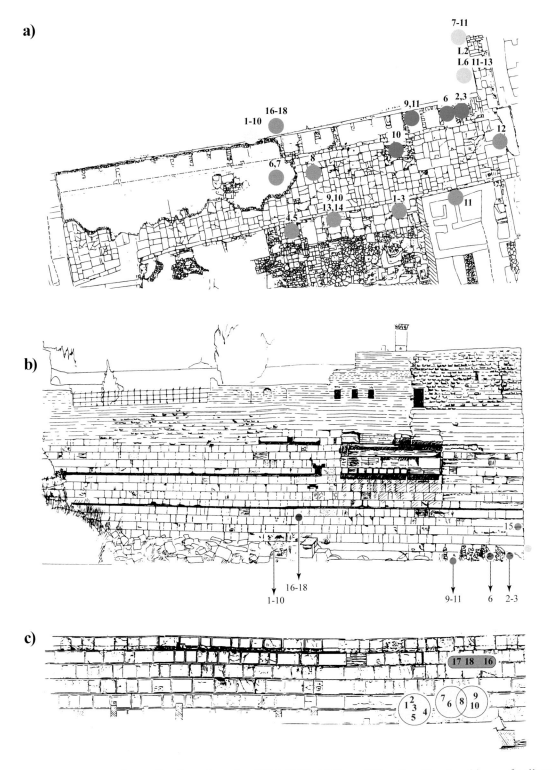

Figure 36.10: Place of sampling for salt testing 1996–1998. (a) Plan of Herodian Street and heap of collapsed stones in front of the Western Wall. (b) Western Wall, Robinson's Arch area. (c) Western Wall, behind the area with the collapsed stones. Orange: 29 Apr. 1996 (18 samples); Blue: 4 July 1997 (5 samples); Yellow: 31 July 1997 (10 samples); Green: 1 Feb. 1998 (12 samples). (d) Southern Wall—southwest corner.

a)

b)

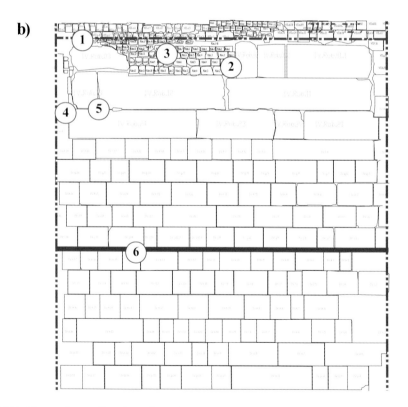

Figure 36.11: Place of sampling for salt testing 2020. (a) The seven-storey scaffolding at Robinson's Arch in June 2020. (b) Samples for salt analysis were taken from cement, soil encrustations, and lime-based mortar and plaster (scaffolding floors 3, 6, 7).

Table 36.4: Salt Test Card and Salt Analysis in 2020

Site: Robinson's Arch area—Western Wall

Sub-site: scaffolding level 3, 6, 7

Date: 17.6.2020

Sampled by A. Van Zuiden

No.	Dilution	pH	EC— Electrical Conductivity mS/cm	pNa	Cl ppm	SO₄ ppm	NO₃ ppm	CaCO₃ °D	CaHCO₃ °D	Ca ppm	K ppm	Mg ppm	Place/remarks
1	25:100	6–7	109.70		2000	200	>500	>>21	4–8		700		White cement—2 layers Floor 7
2	25:100	8	2.20		0–500	200	25	7	8–12				In joint—soil/encrustation Floor 7
3	10:100	6–7	1.60		0–500	200	25		4		0		In joint—lime mortar Floor 7
4	25:100	7	5.70		500	200	250	4–7	0–4		0		In joint—white cement Floor 6
5	25:100	8	5.30		500	200	250	7–14	8–12		0		In joint—soil and lime mortar Floor 6
6	25:100	7	149.80		>> 3000	1200	500	>>21	4–8		1000		In channel—pinkish plaster Floor 3

DISCUSSION

The analysis of the different types of indicators that could be mapped and semi-quantified to describe the salts and other parameters that influence the state of preservation in the Western Wall show different deterioration processes that could be treated by conservators. Many types of stone deterioration were observed, ranging from geological defects to human destruction in 70 CE. The geological defects do not provide any explanation about the narrative of the site, so the missing part of the ashlar was filled, using slaked lime with hydraulic aggregates, up to 1–2 mm under the stone surface (Fig. 36.12). Cracks and scales, affiliated with the 70 CE destruction of the Temple Mount and its retaining walls, were filled to a minimum, in order to show the destruction of the Temple Mount and its surroundings. A major aspect in conservation is the documentation of the visual changes that occur. Table 36.5 summarizes the events between 1996 and 1998, noting the 70 CE damages.

STONE DESALINATION AND CONSOLIDATION

These treatments might prevent future deterioration of the stones (Wihr 1980; Hanna 1984; Price 1984, 1996; Doehne and Price 2010). Desalination via electrolysis or rinsing baths is impossible because of the wall structure and size (Wihr 1980; van Bommel, Ex and Scholten 2001). Only poultice techniques came into consideration (Wihr 1980; Bradley and Hanna 1986; Price 1996; van Bommel, Ex and Scholten 2001; Doehne and Price 2010), and some results are shown in Table 36.6. Six to eight desalinization poultices, based on Kaolin or Attapulgite, were applied as a trial method on three limited areas behind the remaining collapsed area of the ashlars; the size of

Figure 36.12: Geological defects in the stone are not important for the narrative of the site; they are only visually disturbing. They were filled with 1–2 mm lime mortar under the stone surface.

Table 36.5: Events and Observations of Stone Damage

70 CE	Falling stones caused internal cracks or detachment of stone scales
	Fire caused internal cracks or detachment of stone scales
Spring 1996	Registration of 3 large areas with existing stone scaling and thin salt crust
Spring 1996	Registration of plant growth and comparison with pictures from 1970
Apr. 1996	Salt tests on soil and stone—20 samples (pier of Robinson's Arch, Herodian Street, Western Wall)
Early summer 1996	Flooding from the top of the Wall to the bottom between 13.00 and 15.00 p.m
July 1997	Salt tests on soil and stone—14 samples (shops and Western Wall)
Sept. 1997	Acoustic tests to locate internal cracks and hollow areas
Oct. 1997	Cement repointing by the Waqf of the upper part of the Wall
Oct. 1997	Moisture Content (MC) measurements on stone surface and in joints
Aug.–Nov. 1997	Trial out desalination poultices and salt tests—22 samples (Western Wall)
Nov. 1997	Visual observation 1—wet areas, salt efflorescence and salt crusts
Jan.–Feb. 1998	Salt tests on soil and stone—14 samples (Southern Wall)
	Desalination poultices and salt tests—5 samples (Southern Wall)
July 1998	Visual observation 2—wet areas, salt efflorescence and salt crusts

each poultice was 1 × 1 m. Reduction of the salt content inside the poultices began only after the fourth poultice (Table 36.6). Desalinization via poultices is an extremely labor-intensive method and rather useless if the source of salt contamination is not eliminated. Stone consolidation in a limited area of the lower three stone courses behind the collapsed ashlars could be possible with lime water. It would give some strength to the outer 5–8 cm, but the preparation of lime water is a labor-intensive procedure as well. As the Western Wall is exposed to the sun from 10:00 a.m. till 16:00 p.m., consolidants based on organic solvents are not advisable, as the solvent (together with the consolidant) returns quickly to the stone surface (in those years, water-based micro-lime and nano-lime consolidants did not yet exist). An attempted trial consolidation with the classic lime-water treatment (Price 1984) was performed on a part of a stone fence, which collapsed from the top of the Temple Mount into one of the shops. Eight to ten applications with lime water were performed with rather good success. The lime consolidant penetrated some 5–10 cm and strengthened the porous stone.

Fillings: stone scales and loose edges were fixed in place with a few points of epoxy glue before complete detachment would occur. Holes, cracks and empty places behind the stone scales were filled using a lime-based mortar or grout (liquid mortar), to prevent detachment and future plant-growing substrates (Table 36.7). The grout was injected via syringes and plastic tubes into the hollow areas and cracks. Open joints had to be filled as well to prevent plant growth (application at a deep level is advisable in order not to lose the visual impact of the "dry-building" technique). The lime mortar and grout were based on slaked lime and hydraulic aggregates (in the 1990s, hydraulic lime was not yet available in Israel). A drawback of this slaked lime mortar is its sensitivity to high salt contents. In salt-laden areas, many stone repairs crumbled after a few years and disappeared. In non-salt-laden areas, the mortar survived well to the present (2020).

Table 36.6: Electrical Conductivity Values (EC 10–200 mS/cm) Measured in the Different Desalination Poultices (Numbers I–VIII)

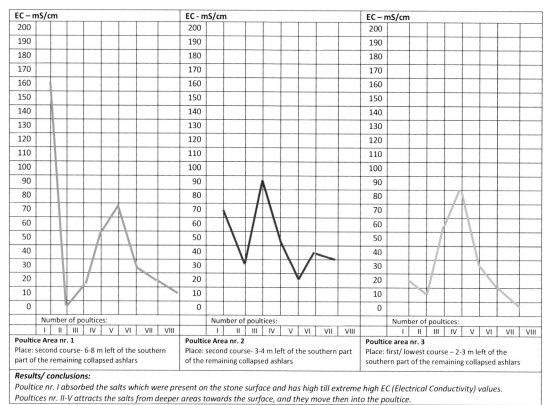

EC – mS/cm								EC - mS/cm								EC – mS/cm							
200								200								200							
190								190								190							
180								180								180							
170								170								170							
160								160								160							
150								150								150							
140								140								140							
130								130								130							
120								120								120							
110								110								110							
100								100								100							
90								90								90							
80								80								80							
70								70								70							
60								60								60							
50								50								50							
40								40								40							
30								30								30							
20								20								20							
10								10								10							
0								0								0							
Number of poultices:								Number of poultices:								Number of poultices:							
I	II	III	IV	V	VI	VII	VIII	I	II	III	IV	V	VI	VII	VIII	I	II	III	IV	V	VI	VII	VIII

Poultice Area nr. 1	**Poultice Area nr. 2**	**Poultice area nr. 3**
Place: second course- 6-8 m left of the southern part of the remaining collapsed ashlars	Place: second course- 3-4 m left of the southern part of the remaining collapsed ashlars	Place: first/ lowest course – 2-3 m left of the southern part of the remaining collapsed ashlars

Results/ conclusions:
Poultice nr. I absorbed the salts which were present on the stone surface and has high till extreme high EC (Electrical Conductivity) values. Poultices nr. II-V attracts the salts from deeper areas towards the surface, and they move then into the poultice.

Table 36.7: Grout and Mortar Recipes (by Volume Parts)

Grout (ratio lime: aggregates as 1:1)		**Lime mortar for repointing or filling cracks (ratio lime: aggregates as 1:3 or 1:3,5)**	
1	Slaked lime	1	Slaked lime
0.25	Ceramic powder	1.50	Arad sand
0.25	Tuff powder	0.50–0.75	Ceramic powder
0.50	Wood ash powder*	0.50–0.75	Tuff powder
		0.50–0.75	Wood ash powder

*Wood ash powder is added as an emulsifier, preventing sinking of the other aggregates

To conclude the conservation efforts between 1996–1998, parts of the remaining ancient Early Roman walls were exposed to weather conditions during hundreds of years, presumably without proper copping such as closure of top of the wall with a roof, floor or fieldstones and mortar (Fig. 36.1). The material in the core of the wall, behind the ashlars, is unknown and could range from soil, arches, stone rubble, mortar—all of which might have absorbed rain, and if present, sewage. During conservation work in 1996–1998, frequent flooding was noticed over the stone surface, from the top to the bottom of the wall. Heavy salt deterioration was observed in the lower courses, behind the southern part of the remaining collapse of the ashlars. The salts converted the hard *meleke* and *mizzi hilu* limestone into a very porous, soft and chalk-like stone.

The Waqf's repointing in October 1997 of a vast area at the top of the Wall with a non-porous and impermeable white cement (Fig. 36.4c) created a "water sper" on a huge area and caused water from the leakages from the top of the wall to percolate down. Cement normally contains harmful sodium and sulfate salts. In this case, the impermeable character of the cement is much more problematic than those of the salts themselves.

Salt contamination was observed and tested on the Western and Southern retaining Wall (southwest corner) of the Temple Mount. The salt tests were performed on soil from the ground, soil in the wall (found in the joints between ashlars) and on the stones. It is possible to conclude that the salt contamination was not due to ancient or modern building materials. The main cause of deterioration was past and present leakage and past and present flooding. The irrigation system in the garden north of the Islamic Museum is one possible source; another might be the absence of a sewage system at the Islamic Museum and the Al-Aqsa Mosque. The possibility of (leaking) cisterns (Schiller 1989; Bahat 2000) on top of the southwest corner of the Temple Mount should be checked in order to verify possible sources of leakage and flooding, which are a source of salts.

Conservation Efforts Between 2018 and 2020

On July 23, 2018, a piece of an ancient ashlar, weighing some 100 kilos, became detached from the Western Wall in the Robinson's Arch portion of the Davidson Archaeological Park and fell from a height of 11–12 m (not excavated until 1970) into the Ezrat Yisrael Prayer Area (Fig. 36.13). The fallen stone, associated with the original construction of the Western Wall, was located next to a water channel from a later period, detached from the wall, behind a negative of the detached area showing roots and salts. Conservation efforts included examining the original materials surrounding the detached stone, in order to understand why it had become detached, and examining potential mortar materials that could be used to secure the stone back in place.

Analytical methods are currently available that enable measurements to be taken in the field. The instrumentation we used assesses chemical (based on X-ray fluorescence spectrometer—XRF) and mineralogical (based on Fourier Transform Infrared Spectroscopy—FTIR) information. This information coupled the quantitative composition of the salts (relative quantity) to the molecular phase in which they are found. This showed that sulfur (S) was present as a gypsum phase ($CaSO_4$), which is soluble and destructive, and not as barium sulfate ($BaSO_4$), which is an insoluble salt, that poses no threat to the cultural remains.

XRF measurements were taken using a Bruker Tracer 5i portable XRF spectrometer. These are surface measurements, so two spots were measured to test for surface degradation and chemical composition. A wide aperture with a spot size of ~8 mm was used for averaging the elemental composition, due to the large variability in the μm scale. The XRF can detect elements from magnesium (Mg) to uranium (U) in the periodic table of elements. The instrument is equipped with a Rh-anode, miniaturized X-ray tube and a Peltier-cooled high-resolution silicon drift detector (SDD). Each acquisition ran for 60 seconds at 15 kV for major elements (Mg to Ca) and additional 15 seconds at 40 kV with an Al-Ti filter for trace elements (Ti to U). An internal calibration by Bruker, "Mudrock dual," based on the work of Rowe *et al.* (2012), was used to quantify elements expected in rocks (including trace amounts). FTIR was done using a Nicolet iS5 spectrometer at 4 cm^{-1} resolution. In order to create the infrared spectra, a gram of sample was homogenized in an agate mortar and approximately 0.2 mg were ground to a fine powder and then mixed with

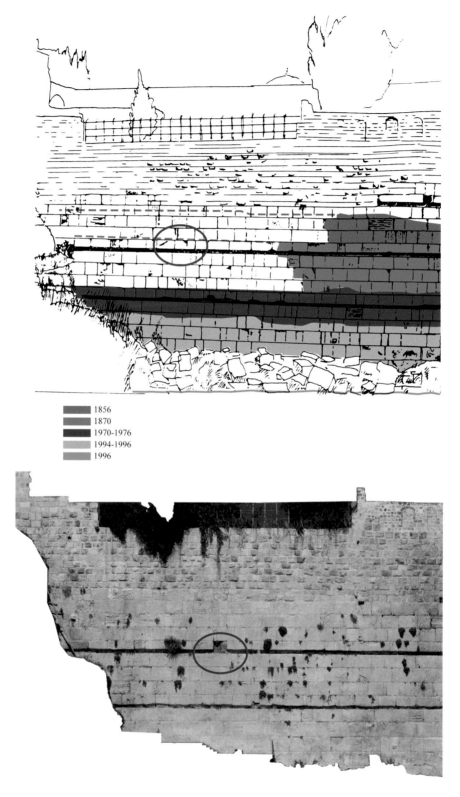

Figure 36.13: Location (a red circle) of the collapsed stone in Ezrat Yisrael Prayer Area. Above: illustration of the level not excavated until 1970. Below: Location today.

approximately 20 mg of KBr (FTIR-grade). Samples were then pressed into a 7 mm pellet using a hand press (PIKE Technologies).

THE COLLAPSED STONE

Salt deposits and roots infiltration were found in different locations where part of the ashlar was detached (Fig 36.14). This emphasized the extent of biological and chemical degradation processes, which presumably caused the stone to fall (Fig. 36.14a insert 1). It also shows the composite materials that were found in joints between the stones, which could have functioned as mortars. These mortars are a mixture of gray and white materials (Fig. 36.14a insert 2). A row below the detached stone, plasters were seen adhered to the wall, and inside the water channel, showing a different composition, including pottery fragments (Fig. 36.14b insert). Stone, mortar and plaster fragments were found and collected for further analysis. Fig. 36.15 shows the different locations of the samples for mineralogical analysis (Red) and the location of non-invasive chemical examinations by XRF (Yellow).

Mineralogical results based on FTIR show that there are two major mineral types: calcite ($CaCO_3$) and gypsum ($CaSO_4$) (Fig. 36.16). Calcite references show FTIR peaks at 1421, 875 and 712 cm^{-1}, while gypsum shows different peaks at 3540, 3405, 1619, 1143, 1116, 671 and 601 cm^{-1}, making them distinguishable based on FTIR peaks (Weiner 2010). The gypsum was found covering the inner core of the stones (Sample 1 inner core vs outer core), suggesting the gypsum was deposited there, and not acting as a binder of the stones. Samples 4 and 5 are adhered to the adjacent stone and may act as binders of mortars, but it is unlikely. These samples show peaks that are similar to that of the mineral calcite, as is found in the inner core of the local stone (Sample 1 in Fig. 36.15). The mortar from the row below (the sample is shown in Fig. 36.14B insert), associated with a later period, is made of calcite and silica (SiO_2), suggesting it is a lime-based mortar with silica additives (main peak of silica is located at 1033 cm^{-1}). Interestingly, the parts of the ashlar that were left behind after the detachment show the presence of gypsum (Samples 3, 6, and the outer part of Samples 1 and 2). This shows gypsum is a product of salt deposition and was not intentionally used as a binder. Therefore, mapping its presence will lead to understanding the rate of degradation, based on salts deposition.

Chemical composition results based on XRF show that the materials in the area of the detached stone were showing high values of calcium (Ca) and sulfur (S), with minor elements of aluminium (Al), silicon (Si) and iron (Fe) (Fig. 17 and Table 36.8). A single sample showed the presence of chlorine (Cl), a component of soluble salts. Argon (Ar) is an element that is present in the air and detected by the device. Chemical observations of high sulfur components on the surface of the detached stone (Samples 7–9), while the stones outside the detached area (Samples 10 and 12) show no sulfur, support degradation processes that occur in cracks. The presence of salts, such as chlorine and sulfur, was shown in cracks and on degraded surfaces and was formed through the processes of dissolution and precipitation (present on the surfaces of the stone fragments 7–9 that were left behind on the detached stone; see locations in Fig. 36.15). This is in agreement with the observations from FTIR, showing the mineral gypsum. The stones adjacent to the collapsed stone (Samples 10 and 12 in Fig. 36.15), show no salts present, i.e., only the exposed surfaces in cracks contained sulfur and gypsum.

To conclude, gypsum is a major component that relates to the detached area of the collapsed stone, showing that (1) it is found in cracks and is connected to the detachment process, and (2) it is not connected to the function of mortars as this gypsum is not found in joints between ashlars. The mechanism of dissolution and precipitation of gypsum with changing relative humidity would

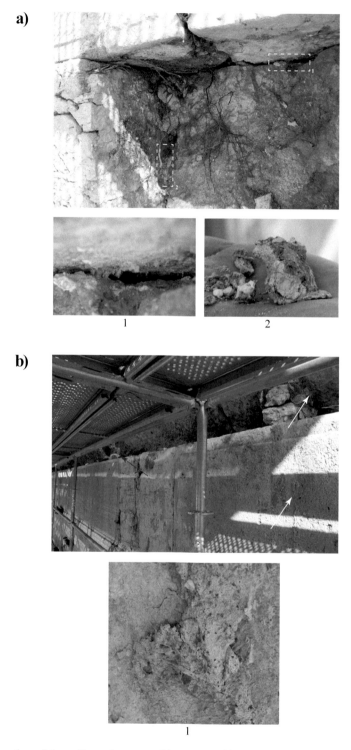

Figure 36.14: Location of the collapsed stone and its surroundings. (a) Image of salt deposits (1) and roots that were found in the location of the collapsed stone, and the location of the materials that were found between stones, that could have been used for mortars (2). (b) Image of the row of stones below the collapsed stone, showing the relative location of the collapsed stone (red arrow), and locations of mortars that were found in the channel and adhered to the stones (white arrows).

Figure 36.15: Location of samples at the collapsed stone. Yellow indicates place of sampling for chemical analysis (via XRF) and red for mineralogical analysis (via FTIR).

cause instability and enlargement of cracks in the Western Wall stones. The sources of the sulfates could be derived by sewage in the former Mughrabi neighborhood, airborne pollution that contains sulfur dioxide, irrigation systems that transport water from the upper to the lower areas, which contain sulfates from either the fill in the back of the wall, or from the top gardens. Mapping indicators such as plants, moisture and salts in July 2020 (Figs. 36.5c and 36.8c) show a correlation between the leakage of water with salts and plant activities (found between the Ezrat Yisrael Prayer Area and Robinson's Arch area). In addition, these indicators are mainly around the joints of ashlars, suggesting that the water came from inside the wall toward the surface, via the joints. Wide open joints with badly deteriorated edges and with a width of 5–12 cm, were noticed in the upper courses (Fig. 36.4b), right under the Ottoman reconstructed part, which was repointed with an impermeable cement in 10.1997 (Fig. 36.4c). In addition, plants and birds were found in the joints, suggesting that the soil from within these joints, and from behind the wall, is a major contributor to salts in the Western Wall.

ANALYTICAL INVESTIGATIONS OF SALTS IN ANCIENT MORTARS IN 2020

Mortars are pyrotechnological materials, composed of a binder and aggregates (additives), aimed at consolidating and maintaining stones and ashlars, installations and masonry. These materials are relatively porous and may include among other materials gypsum and lime-based binders (Artioli 2010). Mortars of different periods were found in association with the Western Wall, dated to post-Herodian periods. The retaining wall itself is built in a dry building technique (Varshevski and Peretz 1992; Hagbi and Van Zuiden 2019). During a conservation survey in 2020, 36 mortar and

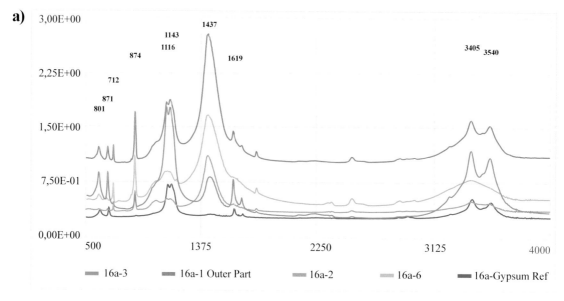

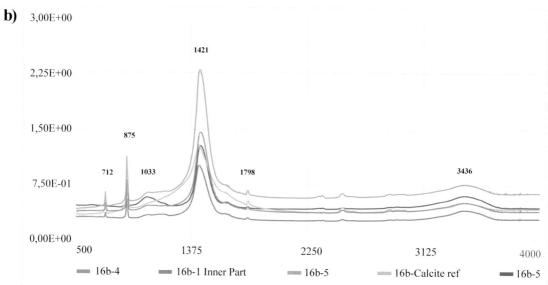

Figure 36.16: FTIR spectra of the different materials from the Western Wall. (a) Gypsum is present in Samples 3, 6, the outer part of Samples 1 and 2. Calcite is also present in Samples 3, 6, the outer part of Samples 1 and 2 as the construction stones are made of limestone. (b) Calcite is present in dominant in Samples 4, 5, the inner core of Sample 1. The mortar from the row below is also composed mainly of calcite.

plaster samples were collected from the Ezrat Yisrael Prayer Area, Robinson's Arch area and the Main Prayer Plaza (Fig. 36.18).

The evolution of techniques and instrumentation through time shows the development from basic tests in the 1990s to high-resolution analytical instrumentations in 2020. In the 1990s, visual observations were used to construct maps of the distribution of salts, illustrating deterioration. In 2020, X-ray Fluorescence (XRF) and Fourier Transform Infrared Spectroscopy (FTIR) were used to construct point analysis with high-resolution analytical data that enabled (1) the quantification of the salts; (2) determining their mineralogical nature; and (3) mapping their distribution.

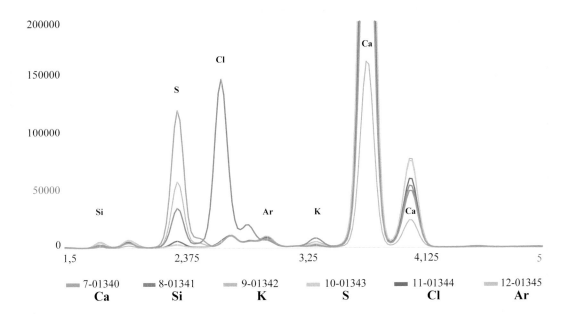

Figure 36.17: X-ray fluorescence spectra, showing the elemental composition of the materials. The main elements are sulfur and calcium, and one sample shows the presence of chlorine (Sample 2). Two modern mortars (microsilica cast and repointing mortar), candidates for conservation efforts, show different amounts of silica components, on a calcium-based binder.

Salts were characterized mineralogically using FTIR, following peaks of gypsum (located at 3540, 3405, 1619, 1143, 1116, 671 and 601 cm[-1]) and potassium nitrate (located at 1384 cm[-1]), which are clearly visible in IR spectra. In addition, chlorine (Cl), potassium (K) and sulfur (S) were monitored chemically on the same samples, using XRF, enabling the quantification of sodium chloride (NaCl, i.e., table salt), potassium nitrate (KNO_3) and gypsum ($CaSO_4$), respectively (Table 37.7). These components are typical for salt efflorescence, with different solubility properties. Sodium chloride and potassium nitrate are highly soluble, and usually remain in solution during the humidity cycles throughout the day. Gypsum is less soluble, so it may recrystallize during these humid cycles. Dissolution and recrystallization cycles enlarge cracks and deform the pores in which they are found, causing degradation to the stone and mortars.

In general, all the mortars show calcite as the main component, associating them to lime-based mortars and not gypsum-based mortars (Artioli 2010). The salts that were found include chlorides, nitrates and sulfates, based on chemistry and structure. Chemical measurements based on XRF show high amounts of chlorine and sulfur in mortars compared to the stones they were associated with. Mineralogical measurements based on FTIR show the presence of sodium nitrate and calcium sulfate (gypsum), which are not found naturally in the associated stones. Salt concentrations vary greatly, but around the stone that fell in the Ezrat Yisrael Prayer Area, (Samples 10–12 in the Ezrat Yisrael Prayer Area, the collapsed stone in Table 36.7), there are between 1.5–13.5% (gypsum was found as the main mineral), while the natural stones shove below 0.4%.

Salts above 1.5% were found to be concentrated in two major locations: surrounding the collapsed stone in the Ezrat Yisrael Prayer Area (mainly along the Early Islamic drainage pipe) and surrounding the arch at Robinson's Arch area (Fig. 36.19A). These salts were found by coupling chemical information (XRF) and mineralogical information (FTIR). While XRF provides

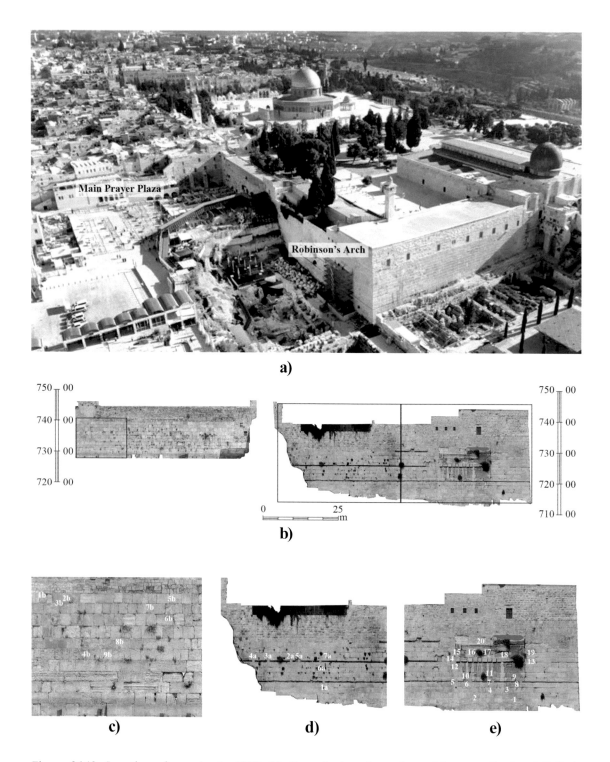

Figure 36.18: Location of samples in 2020. (a) General view from above (photo credit: Israel Police). (b) Locations of study. (c) Main Prayer Plaza. (d) Ezrat Yisrael Prayer Area. (e) Robinson's Arch area.

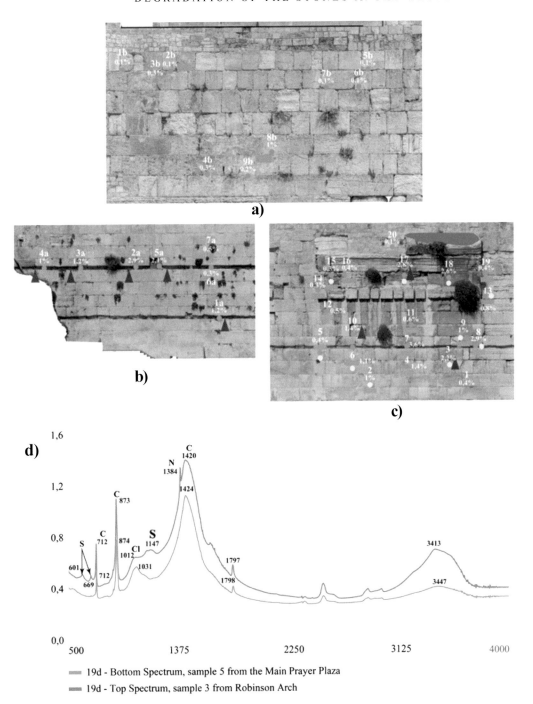

Figure 36.19: Salts distribution in 2020. Salts concentrations (%) are marked below the sample number, based on XRF internal calibration (Rowe *et al.* 2012). FTIR peaks mark the presence of gypsum or nitrates in the spectra: red triangles mark sulfates, when they are a major component and orange squares when they are are only traces. Nitrate presence is marked with a yellow circle. (a) Main Prayer Plaza. (b) Ezrat Yisrael Prayer area. (c) Robinson's Arch area. (d) IR spectra of lime-mortar with sulfates as a major component, marked by red triangles, and nitrates, marked with orange squares (top spectrum, Sample 3 from Robinson's Arch), and clean lime-mortar with no salts (bottom spectrum, Sample 5 from the Main Prayer Plaza).

quantitative numbers (Fig. 36.19A), FTIR provides semi-quantitative estimations based on peak positions (Fig. 36.19B). Mortar samples could not be sampled from in between Robinson's Arch and the Ezrat Yisrael Prayer Area due to the location of scaffolding (Fig. 36.11). The analytical maps complement visual observation by adding characterization to the observed salts, distinguishing between highly soluble salts (nitrates, chlorides) and sulfates with limited solubility. Interestingly, visual observations did not allocate high moisture content, plants or salts in the Ezrat Yisrael Prayer Area and Robinson's Arch area (Fig. 36.5). This implies that the salts in these areas are in their soluble phases or could not be identified visually. Moreover, the fact that the salts are found in the Ezrat Yisrael Prayer Area and Robinson's Arch area, which is in the perimeter of the moisture area, suggests that the majority of the salts are still in their soluble phase.

It is hard to assess the source of the salts, but they could derive from (1) the soil and leakages behind the Western Wall, (2) sewage from the urban Mughrabi settlement along the northern part of the wall in the 16–20th centuries), (3) airborne pollution that contains sulfur dioxide, and (4) sulfates from the irrigation systems that transport water from the upper areas to the bottom parts. Soil EC was found to be high and channeling the water irrigation did change salts efflorescence patterns, which means that probably the source of salts is a combination of all the options.

CONCLUSIONS

Conservation studies in the 1990s and 2020 allowed monitoring the degradation of stones in the Western Wall. The initial degradation started in the Roman destruction of 70 CE, showing cracks in the stones, but since excavations exposed new areas, plants, moisture and salts accelerated growth of the cracks. One proof is that a part of an ashlar fell, leaving behind only salts. Analytical instrumentation, such as Electrical Conductivity, chemical and mineralogical characterization based on XRF and FTIR, respectively, show that soil can contain large amounts of salts, and that salts can be quantified to assess the degradation state in different areas. Results from the Main Prayer Plaza, the Ezrat Yisrael Prayer Area and Robinson's Arch area show that coupling visual observations of salts distribution and quantified chemical and mineralogical analysis of these salts can highlight areas at higher risk. Salt concentrations that are comparable to the location where the stone fell were found in the Ezrat Yisrael Prayer Area and Robinson's Arch area. Conservation efforts should take this input into account and design modern materials that are compatible with changing environments of moisture and salt quantity near these areas, preventing another collapse of stones from the Western Wall.

Table 36.8: Visual Description of Mortar Samples Collected from the Ezrat Yisrael Prayer Area, Robinson's Arch Area and the Main Prayer Plaza*

Location	Sample	Mineralogical analysis (FTIR)	Chemical analysis (XRF) (Cl % / K % / S % / total %)	Comments
Ezrat Yisrael Prayer Area	1A	Calcite, gypsum, silicates	0.18 / 0.03 / 1.02 / 1.24	Lime binder + 1.2% salts
	2A	Calcite, gypsum, silicates	0.9 / 0.09 / 1.95 / 2.94	Lime binder + 2.9% salts
	3A	Calcite, gypsum, silicates	0.2 / <LOD / 1.03 / 1.23	Lime binder + 1.2% salts
	4A	Calcite, gypsum, silicates	0.5 / 0.14 / 0.38 / 1.01	Lime binder + 1% salts
	5A	Calcite, gypsum, silicates	0.3 / <LOD / 1.8 / 2.12	Lime binder + 2.1% salts
	6A	Calcite, silicates	0.16 / 0.17 / <LOD / 0.34	Lime binder + 0.3% salts
	7A	Calcite, silicates	0.14 / 0.17 / 0.08 / 0.51	Lime binder + 0.5% salts
Ezrat Yisrael Prayer Area—The collapsed ashlar (samples in Fig. 36.15)	1 inner	Calcite	N.A.	Limestone
	1 outer	Calcite, gypsum	N.A. / <LOD / 13.57 / 13.57	Limestone + 13.5 % salts
	2	Calcite, gypsum	0.23 / 0.13 / <LOD / 0.36	Limestone + 0.3 % salts
	3	Calcite, gypsum	0.69 / 0.13 / 7.18 / 8.01	Limestone + 8 % salts
	4	Calcite	1.64 / 0.43 / 1.31 / 3.38	Limestone + 3.3 % salts
	5	Calcite	2.03 / 0.48 / 1.21 / 3.74	Limestone + 3.7 % salts
	6	Calcite, gypsum	0.61 / 0.16 / 0.74 / 1.52	Limestone + 1.5 % salts
	8	N.A.	N.A. / 0.13 / 4.04 / 4.17	Limestone + 4 % salts

*Mineralogical interpretation is based on FTIR peak shape positions (Weiner 2010). Chemical analysis is based on XRF measurements, calibrated using internal calibration (Rowe et al. 2012). <LOD is below limit of detection, and information not available is N.A., and errors are typically 5%

Location	Sample	Mineralogical analysis (FTIR)	Chemical analysis (XRF) (Cl % / K % / S % / total %)	Comments
	9	N.A.	N.A. / <LOD / 5.75 / 5.75	Limestone + 5.7 % salts
	10	N.A.	N.A. / <LOD / <LOD / <LOD	Limestone
	11	N.A.	N.A. / <LOD / 0.38 / 0.38	Limestone + 0.38 % salts
	12	N.A.	N.A. / <LOD / <LOD / <LOD	Limestone
Robinson's Arch area	1	Calcite, silicates	0.23 / 0.02 / 0.21 / 0.46	Lime binder + 0.4% salts
	2	Calcite, silicates, nitrates	0.75 / 0.17 / 0.1 / 1.02	Lime binder + 1% salts
	3	Calcite, gypsum, silicates, nitrates	0.86 / 0.45 / 0.93 / 2.25	Lime binder + 2.2% salts
	4	Calcite, silicates	1.3 / 0.13 / 0.01 / 1.45	Lime binder + 1.4% salts
	5	Calcite, silicates, nitrates	0.45 / 0.01 / <LOD / 0.47	Lime binder + 0.4% salts
	6	Calcite, silicates, nitrates	0.53 / 0.58 / <LOD / 1.11	Lime binder + 1.1% salts
	7	Calcite, silicates, nitrates	1.85 / 1.25 / 0.56 / 3.65	Lime binder + 3.6% salts
	8	Calcite, silicates, nitrates	1.54 / 0.73 / 0.70 / 2.98	Lime binder + 2.9% salts
	9	Calcite, nitrates	0.9 / 0.1 / <LOD / 1	Lime binder + 1% salts
	10	Calcite, gypsum, silicates, nitrates	0.8 / 0.22 / 0.41 / 1.43	Lime binder + 1.4% salts
	11	Calcite	0.56 / 0.05 / <LOD / 0.6	Lime binder + 0.6% salts
	12	Calcite, silicates	0.25 / 0.10 / <LOD / 0.35	Lime binder + 0.3% salts
	13	Calcite, aragonite, silicates, nitrates	0.68 / 0.10 / 0.08 / 0.87	Lime binder + 0.8% salts
	14	Calcite, quartz	0.15 / 0.08 / 0.03 / 0.26	Lime binder + 0.2% salts
	15	Calcite, silicates, nitrates	0.32 / <LOD / <LOD / 0.3	Lime binder + 0.3% salts
	16	Calcite, silicates	0.29 / <LOD / 0.16 / 0.46	Lime binder + 0.4% salts

Location	Sample	Mineralogical analysis (FTIR)	Chemical analysis (XRF) (Cl % / K % / S % / total %)	Comments
	17	Calcite, gypsum, silicates, nitrates	1.6 / 0.32 / 0.95 / 2.88	Lime binder + 2.8% salts
	18	Calcite, silicates, nitrates	2.07 / 0.47 / 0.11 / 2.66	Lime binder + 2.6% salts
	19	Calcite, aragonite, silicates	0.32 / 0.04 / 0.09 / 0.47	Lime binder + 0.4% salts
	20	Calcite, aragonite, silicates	0.11 / <LOD / <LOD / 0.1	Lime binder + 0.1% salts
The Main Prayer Plaza	1B	Calcite, silicates	0.13 / <LOD / <LOD / 0.1	Lime binder + 0.1% salts
	2B	Calcite, silicates	0.13 / <LOD / <LOD / 0.1	Lime binder + 0.1% salts
	3B	Calcite, silicates	0.10 / 0.16 / 0.04 / 0.3	Lime binder + 0.3% salts
	4B	Calcite, silicates	0.15 / 0.16 / 0.16 / 0.3	Lime binder + 0.3% salts
	5B	Calcite, silicates	0.04 / 0.11 / <LOD / 0.16	Lime binder + 0.1% salts
	6B	Calcite	0.19 / <LOD / <LOD / 0.19	Lime binder + 0.1% salts
	7B	Calcite	0.14 / <LOD / <LOD / 0.14	Lime binder + 0.1% salts
	8B	Calcite, silicates	0.31 / 0.28 / 0.39 / 1	Lime binder + 1% salts
	9B	Calcite, silicates	0.18 / 0.06 / <LOD / 0.25	Lime binder + 0.2% salts

REFERENCES

Arnold, A. 1981. Nature and Reactions of Saline Minerals in Walls. In: Rossi-Manaresi, R., ed. *The Conservation of Stone II: Preprints of the Contributions to the International Symposium Bologna.* Rome.

Artioli, G. 2010. *Scientific Methods and Cultural Heritage: An Introduction to the Application of Materials Science to Archaeometry and Conservation Science.* Oxford.

Ashurst, J. and Ashurst, N. 1989. *Practical Building Conservation, an English Heritage Technical Handbook,* Vol. 3: *Mortars Plasters and Renders.* Aldershot.

Bahat, D. 2000. *Carta's Great Historical Atlas of Jerusalem.* Jerusalem (Hebrew).

Bahat, D. 2013. *The Jerusalem Western Wall Tunnel.* Jerusalem.

Bradley, S.M. and Hanna, S.B. 1986. The Effect of Soluble Salt Movements on the Conservation of an Egyptian Limestone Standing Figure. In: Brommelle, N.S. and Smith, P., eds. *Case Studies in the Conservation of Stone and Wall Paintings: Preprints of the Contributions to the Bologna Congress.* London.

Doehne, E. and Price, C.A. 2010. *Stone Conservation: An Overview of Current Research* (2nd edition). Los Angeles.

Gill, D. 1996. The Geology of the City of David and Its Ancient Subterranean Waterworks. In: Ariel, D.T. and De Groot, A., eds. *Excavations at the City of David 1978–1985, Directed by Yigal Shiloh,* Vol. 4 (Qedem 35). Jerusalem.

Gill, D. 2019. Bedrock Geology and Building Stones in the Western Wall Plaza Excavations and the Jerusalem Area, Appendix 1. In: Weksler-Bdolah, S. and Onn, A., eds. *Jerusalem: Western Wall Plaza Excavations,* Vol. 1: *The Roman and Byzantine Remains: Architecture and Stratigraphy* (IAA Reports 63). Jerusalem.

Hagbi, M. and Van Zuiden, A. 2019. "Shaping the Stones"—Technical Aspects in the Endeavor to Lay the Foundation Stones of the Western Wall. In: Meiron, E., ed. *City of David: Studies of Ancient Jerusalem* 14. Jerusalem: 42–59 (Hebrew).

Hanna, S.B. 1984. The Use of Organo-Silanes for the Treatment of Limestone in an Advanced State of Deterioration. In: Brommelle, N.S., Pye, E., Smith, P. and Thomson, G., eds. *Adhesives and Consolidants: Preprints of the Contributions to the Paris Congress.* London.

Hillenbrand, R. 2000. *Ottoman Jerusalem: The Living City, 1517–1917.* London: 479–491.

Mazar, B. 1971. The Excavations in the Old City of Jerusalem near the Temple Mount—Second Preliminary Report, 1969–70 Seasons. *Eretz-Israel* 10: 1–34 (Hebrew).

Mazar, B. 1976. The Archaeological Excavations near the Temple Mount. In: Yadin, Y., ed. *Jerusalem Revealed: Archaeology in the Holy City 1968–1974.* New Haven and London.

Mazar, E. 2011. *The Walls of the Temple Mount.* Jerusalem.

Patrich, J. and Edelcopp, M. 2015. The Stages in the Evolution of the Temple Mount—a Reassessment. *Eretz-Israel* 31: 305–325.

Price, C.A. 1984. The Consolidation of Limestone using a Lime Poultice and Lime Water. In: Brommelle, N.S., Pye, E., Smith, P. and Thomson, G., eds. *Adhesives and Consolidants: Preprints of the Contributions to the Paris Congress.* London.

Price, C.A. 1996. *Stone Conservation: An Overview of Current Research.* Santa Monica.

Reich, R. and Baruch, Y. 2016. On Expansion of the Temple Mount in the Late Second Temple Period. *Cathedra* 164: 7–24 (Hebrew).

Reich, R. and Billig, Y. 2000. Excavations near the Temple Mount and Robinson's Arch, 1994–1996. In: Geva, H., ed. *Ancient Jerusalem Revealed, Reprinted and Expanded Edition.* Jerusalem.

Ritmeyer, L. 2006. *The Quest: Revealing the Temple Mount in Jerusalem.* Jerusalem.

Rowe, H., Hughes, N. and Robinson, K. 2012. The Quantification and Application of Handheld Energy-Dispersive X-Ray Fluorescence (ED-XRF) in Mudrock Chemostratigraphy and Geochemistry. *Chemical Geology* 324: 122–131.

Schiller, E. 1989. *The Temple Mount and Its Sites,* Vol. 64–65 (Ariel: Journal for Knowledge on the Land of Israel 64–65). Jerusalem (Hebrew).

Van Bommel, B., Ex, N. and Scholten, F., eds. 2001. *The Prince and the Caesar—Restoration and History of the Sepulchral Monument of William of Orange.* Holland (Dutch).

Warzawski, A. and Peretz, A. 1992. Building the Temple Mount: Organization and Execution. *Cathedra* 66:
  3–46 (Hebrew).
Weiner, S. 2010. *Microarchaeology: Beyond the Visible Archaeological Record*. New York.
Wihr, R. 1980. *Restoration of Stone Monuments.* Munich (German).

CHAPTER 37

CONSERVATION PHILOSOPHY AND WORK ON THE BASE OF THE WESTERN WALL

Aliza Van Zuiden

During the past decade, a new approach has developed in the relationship between public and ancient sites. "The right of the public to know" and "the right of the public to visit" have become focal points in the exposure and maintenance of ancient sites and buildings. This has been a result of the approach of the Israel Antiquities Authority, under the direction of the late Yehoshua (Shuka) Dorfman, who believed in strengthening the link between the public and the antiquities that surround them (Dorfman 2015). He maintained that this link should not be thought of merely in terms of an emotional connection to one's history, but as a physical link with the ability of people to actually see the past.

However, interaction between antiquities and the public can be hazardous. Before any site can be allowed to become vulnerable to such exposure, conservators must prevent damage caused by the two major enemies of ancient sites: vegetation, which can break apart mighty walls, and above all, human activity (like climbing on unstable walls, graffiti and dismantling walls for reuse of the stones). The task of a conservator is to minimize damage and prevent the collapse of ancient structures.

A case in point is the Western Wall of the Temple Mount. Once tourists leave the drainage channel (the ancient sewer *cloaca maxima* of the Herodian city), that leads up from the City of David, they approach the base of the Western Wall face-to-face. Here, people are able to touch the ashlars. Possible damage due to human intervention is rendered even greater as a result of the custom, sanctioned and even encouraged, of inserting notes with prayers and wishes, personal photographs or even checks in the cracks of the ashlars, which often causes detachment of large stone scales and leads to the loss of precious information on ancient chiseling techniques (Figs. 37.1, 37.2).

In order to prevent such damage, a major conservation activity was undertaken by the Conservation Department of the IAA on the base of the southern part of the Western Wall. The cracks, regardless of size, have been sealed with specially prepared hydraulic lime-based mixtures that were applied with syringes ("mini-grouting") and/or spatulas ("support edges" Figs. 37.3, 37.4).

Joints between the ashlars were not sealed, so as not to lose the information that the wall is "dry-built." The insertion of notes between the stones or in a joint does not cause damage to the ashlars and was therefore not prevented. While the work conducted was aimed at conservation, it was approached with the understanding that during the conservation work, observations could be made, which might be important for understanding the structure and the manner in which it was built. The following report presents the documentation and observations made in this light during the conservation work.

RESEARCH AND DOCUMENTATION

Before any conservation work was executed, the ashlars were carefully examined by the author and measured and drawn to scale by the surveyor and draftsman K. Attoun of the Conservation Department

Figure 37.1: Sample of a stone scale partly detached, prior to conservation. Next to the stone scale, part of the ashlar has completely disappeared.

Figure 37.2: Sample, prior to conservation, of cracks and thin scales that can easily be detached when notes are inserted in the cracks.

Figure 37.3: Conservation: injection of a lime-based grout using syringes.

Figure 37.4: One of the ashlars after conservation: 1.5 liter of a lime-based grout was injected between the stone scales and the cracks, running parallel to the stone surface and supporting edges were applied along the cracks.

of the IAA. Building technology was observed as well. During these observations, a few factors became clear and were important in our understanding of the construction of the Western Wall.

THE WESTERN WALL FOUNDATIONS

The foundation of the Western Wall consists of 7–8 courses of large ashlars (only the first 3–4 courses of which were excavated and are visible). These courses were always below the street and shop level of the Second Temple. The bedrock was partially leveled and the first row was placed directly on the bedrock without any addition of lime mortar. Large formations of unremoved bedrock are still visible to the west of the Western Wall.

DRY CONSTRUCTION

No building mortar, whether lime-based mortar or lime-soil mortar ("hot mix," consisting of quick lime and soil) was found in the joints between the ashlars of the Western Wall. In two or three cases where the lower side of the ashlars is not completely straight, some filling material was noted. This material consisted of stone chips and soil, but no signs of lime (Fig. 37.5).

CHISEL MARKS

The base of the Western Wall, which, as mentioned above, was always beneath ground level, is built of huge ashlars. The middle part of each stone is embossed and coarsely or moderately coarsely chiseled, displaying signs of up to five different chiseling techniques and tools (axe, pick, point chisel, gouge or small flat chisel and a claw tool or tooth chisel) on a single ashlar (Fig. 37.6; Hill 1999). This, in all likelihood, signifies the arrival of a new group of craftsmen to the quarry, each mason having to practice different techniques and tools on one or two stones (Hagbi and Van Zuiden 2019).

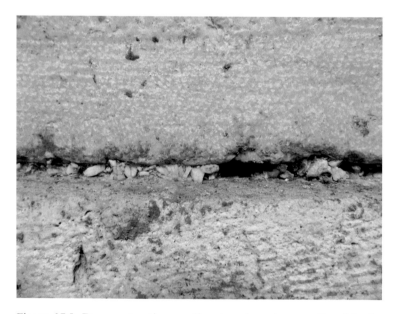

Figure 37.5: Dry construction: no lime-based mortar was found in the joints between the ashlars. In this (rare) case stone chips and local soil were noted between the ashlars.

The margins were, however, all finely chiseled with a tooth chisel or claw tool in typical Herodian style, in order to arrive at an aesthetic, straight, flat edge, which enabled the dry construction, with a joint width of 0–1 mm, without the use of any lime-based mortar.

STRUCTURAL CRACKS

The observation and mapping of the directions and width of the cracks enabled a conservator and engineer to understand the nature of the building and its state of preservation. Cracks can indicate former earthquakes, sinking of foundations or problems with tensile or compressive strength (Fig. 37.7). On the Western Wall Foundations, all structural cracks are vertically orientated,

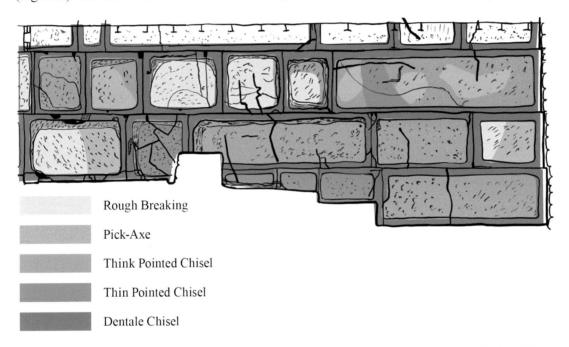

Rough Breaking

Pick-Axe

Think Pointed Chisel

Thin Pointed Chisel

Dentale Chisel

Figure 37.6: Plan of the Western Wall Foundations, exposed in the current excavation with five different chiseling techniques indicated. Often 3-4 types can be found on one ashlar.

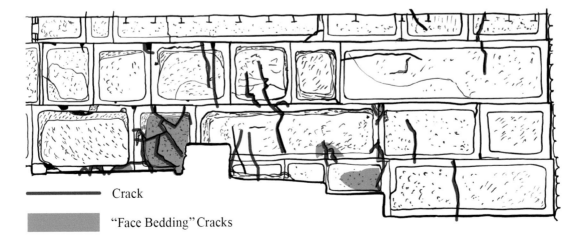

Crack

"Face Bedding" Cracks

Figure 37.7: Structural, vertical cracks along the Western Wall Foundations.

demonstrating that there may have been problems, albeit minor, with compressive strength. Small or medium-sized stone chips in the thin joints are capable of breaking the ashlars. One can observe fine cracks at a 90° angle to the stone surface, sometimes continuing over 2–3 ashlars.

A special phenomenon is that of cracks running parallel to the stone surface (which are less visible). Once a stone block is quarried, it can be used in different positions in the wall. In most cases, it was preferable to insert the ashlar in the same position in the wall as it was in the quarry, described as "horizontal bedding." Once the stone was turned 90° in the direction of the stone mason, it was defined as "face bedding." All cracks and thin separation layers between the bedding layers were now at the face or façade of the Wall (Figs. 37.8–37.9). The stone scales can easily be detached, especially when paper notes are inserted into the cracks. Mini-grouting and support edges are compulsory treatments.

ANCIENT REPAIRS

During examination of the ashlars, many ancient stone repairs consisting of a fine lime mortar were found (Fig. 37.10). Once the mortar was partially hardened, the repairs were finely chiseled with a claw tool or tooth chisel, resembling the chiseling technique on the stone itself. Most of the ancient repairs were executed on a very high, professional level (Fig. 37.11).

Ninety percent or more of all repairs are situated at the corners or edges of the stone, indicating the likelihood that the ashlars were chiseled at the quarry and then transported to the building site. During transport or installation, many corners and edges were probably damaged and had to be repaired on-site (Fig. 37.12).

Once the ashlars for the Western Wall itself (building above ground level) were prepared, it seems that the work strategy changed. The ashlars were coarsely chiseled at the quarry, transported to the building site, and the final chiseling was performed next to the Wall or on the Wall itself in order to minimize damage from transport or installation.

During the years 1996–1999, not a single ancient repair was found on the above-ground-level lower 3–4 course ashlars during the conservation work performed by the author. The mortar of

Figure 37.8: "Face-bedding"—cracks parallel to the stone surface.

Figure 37.9: "Face-bedding"—cracks parallel to the stone surface.

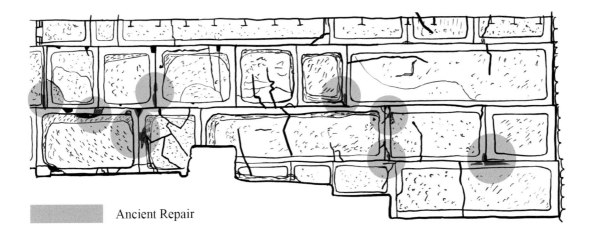

Ancient Repair

Figure 37.10: Distribution of ancient repairs along the Western Wall Foundations.

Figure 37.11: Ancient repair with quick lime and stone powder. Once the mortar started to harden, fine chiseling, similar to that on the stone surface was performed.

Figure 37.12: Ancient stone repair with quick lime and stone powder. Note the incisions in the mortar to mark the original joint.

the ancient repairs was examined by the author under a stereo microscope with a magnification of 10–60 times. It showed a fine mixture of quick lime and stone powder/fine stone chips with a rather hard consistency. Further analysis of the mortar using a petrographic, polarizing microscope (e.g., Franzini *et al.* 1999; Elsen 2006) or other advanced methods (e.g., XRF analysis. See Chapter 36) may help shed additional light on the nature and composition of the materials used in the construction projects of Herodian and post-Herodian Jerusalem.

REFERENCES

Dorfman, Y. 2015. *Under the Surface.* Tel Aviv (Hebrew).

Elsen, J. 2006. Microscopy of Historic Mortars—A Review. *Cement and Concrete Research* 36: 1416–1424.

Franzini, M., Leoni, L., Lezzerini, M. and Satori, F. 1999. On the Binder of Some Ancient Mortars. *Minerology and Petrology* 67: 59–69.

Hagbi, M. and Van Zuiden, A. 2019. "Shaping the Stones"—Technical Aspects of the Endeavor to Lay the Foundation Stones of the Western Wall. In: Meiron, E., ed. *City of David: Studies of Ancient Jerusalem.* The 20th Conference. Megalim Institute, City of David 14. Jerusalem: 42–59 (Hebrew).

Hill, P. 1999. Traditional Hand Working of Stone: Methods and Recognition. In: Dimes, G. and Ashurst, J., eds. *Conservation of Building and Decorative Stone.* Oxford: 97–106.

PART V:
SYNTHESIS
AND
SUMMARY

CHAPTER 38

PAST, PRESENT AND FUTURE

Yuval Baruch and Ronny Reich

This book contains excavation reports and studies that relate to the Southern Wall of the Herodian Temple Mount complex and its southeastern and southwestern corners. These reports and studies discuss the multi-faceted archaeological, historical, architectural and artistic aspects of the Wall. They delve into the magnificent feats of ancient construction and engineering and the modern triumphs of conservation and reclamation.

The Southern Wall is the most researched and archaeologically rich of all the Temple Mount walls and the expeditions presented in this volume are not the first to study them. But we fervently believe that now, after spending over 20 years investigating, observing and inquiring into the whys and wherefores of this mass of holy stones, the scientific and other information we have collected and collated into the current volume has the potential to contribute to a greater understanding of the Southern Wall and the roads leading to it than was ever possible previously.

With this volume, we have attempted to characterize this magnificent agregation of stones as it relates to the urban topography of an ancient place and especially as it relates as an essential element of a sacred space. While we have focused mainly on its exterior, we have not ignored the importance of its construction from within: the Double Gate and the Triple Gate, the underground system of Solomon's Stables, the cisterns and water channels, the series of constructed cells and compartments. These are all below the level of today's Temple Mount esplanade, and unlike other sites on the Mount, they allow a direct examination of architectural evolvement from the days of Herod to the present. Archaeology has enabled us to delineate the story of the Southern Wall in a chronological continuum, from earliest times to the present.

While the book focuses on our work, it recognizes the extraordinary contributions of the researchers who preceded us, beginning with Charles Warren's pioneering excavations and research, continuing with the extensive excavations conducted on almost the entire length of the Southern Wall by Benjamin Mazar and Meir Ben-Dov, followed by the documentation project of the Wall by Eilat Mazar. The importance of these excavations is detailed for us by Shimon Gibson, who reviews the history of research and documentation along the Southern Wall and its two corners

We divided our report into three parts: past, present and future. The bulk of the material deals with the past and includes the excavation reports of limited-area excavations conducted in relation to the Southern Wall—that of Baruch and Reich near the southeastern corner of the Temple Mount; Hagbi and Uziel's excavations near the southwestern corner and Reich and Billig's 1994 excavation at the Western Wall, adjacent and under Robinson's Arch, which provides insight on the last period of settlement in this area. The architectural observations refer to data that transpired as a result of all the above excavations combined, together with evidence that came from previous excavations

Our observations from these excavations can be summed up in the following chronological summary:

IRON II (LATE FIRST TEMPLE PERIOD)

The Temple Mount complex is located on the northern half of the Eastern Hill. The southern sector and the sector near the Gihon Spring, where ancient Jerusalem developed, is known in the Bible as the "City of David" (2 Sam 5:6–9; 1 Chron 11:4–9). The sacred area of the city was in the northern, higher part of the hill, where the Temple of Solomon and the Temples that came later were built.

In archaeological excavations (ours, and those that preceded them) conducted at the foot of the Temple Mount walls, along the foundations, evidence was uncovered indicating that in the late First Temple period (early 8th century BCE), the boundaries of the inhabited area of Jerusalem's Eastern Hill extended northward, as far as the Temple Mount complex, as well as along the slopes of the Tyropoeon Valley, in addition to the city's expansion to the Western Hill (Avigad 1980: 31–60). These remains indicate the existence of an urban continuum that included the City of David in the southern part of the Eastern Hill, the northern part of the "Ophel" area, the slopes of the Tyropoeon Valley and the Western Hill (see Fig. 3.1).

We suggest, however, that a certain urban separation was maintained between the sacred space of the Temple Mount complex and the residential buildings, as implied in Ezekiel 43:8: "in their setting of their threshold by My threshold, and their doorpost beside My doorpost, and there was but the wall between Me and them; and they have defiled My holy name." In all likelihood, even in the Iron II, the period of the First Temple, roads were constructed between the built-up areas and the sacred complex, some of which may have been hallowed paths. An allusion to such a sacred artery in the days of the First Temple can be found in the words of Isaiah: "And a highway shall be there, and a way, and it shall be called the way of holiness; the unclean shall not pass over it" (35:8).

There is insufficient archaeological data to establish the development of the Temple Mount as a sacred complex from its beginnings to the days of Herod; the exception is the Eastern Wall of the complex, which is a remnant of the pre-Herodian complex and remains, discovered during the archaeological survey carried out near the southeastern corner of the upper part of the Temple Mount (Baruch, Reich and Sandhaus 2018). On the other hand, the expansion of the sacred complex in the days of Herod can clearly be seen and studied. By adding to this the data from our excavations, we have been able to deduce that Herod's Temple Mount expansion project, especially to the west and south, necessitated the evacuation of residents of these areas from their homes. Houses in these areas were demolished and the lands on which the walls of the future complex were to be built were cleared of all constructions and leveled.

We unearthed segments of walls and mainly rock-hewn installations preceding the Herodian expansion project. Most of the installations from this period were hewn cisterns used to store water. It is not yet possible, however, from the scant remains that survived, to ascertain the character of these residential areas (Table 38.1).

THE HASMONEAN OR PRE-HERODIAN PERIOD

No remains of buildings, levels or installations of any kind dated from the 6th to the 3rd century BCE were discovered, nor were any found in the excavations that preceded those detailed in this book.

Excavations in the areas near the Triple Gate and the southeastern corner revealed data relating to the Second Temple period, including the period that preceded Herod's Temple Mount expansion project. Admittedly, these sections of wall and segments of installations are few, but they are sufficient to indicate that they are from this period. Moreover, they suggest that the extensive

Table 38.1: Archeological Remains from the Late Iron II Discovered at the Feet of the Southern and Western Walls

Number	Type of remains	Date	Excavators
1	Layer of soil; pottery, including complete juglet under Ophel Wall and east of it	8th–7th centuries BCE	Warren 1884, Pls. 19, 20
2	Remains of walls and installations near southeastern corner of Temple Mount complex	7th century BCE	Baruch and Reich, this volume, Chapter 4
3	Hewn and plastered pit (below Triple Gate), containing rich assemblage of pottery vessels	8th century BCE	E. Mazar and B. Mazar 1989: 56–57, Locus 15013
4	Circular cisterns at foot of Robinson's Arch (later traversed by Herodian drainage channel)	8th century BCE	Warren 1884: Pl. XVIII; Chapter 27 Reich and Shukron 2011b: illustrations 1, 15, 16.
5	Cistern hewn in rock and plastered slightly to north of Robinson's Arch. The foundation of Western Wall intersects cistern.	8th–6th centuries BCE	Shukron 2012: 29–30; Chapter 33

residential neighborhood, the houses of which were evacuated and demolished for the purpose of the expansion project, extended from the Western Wall area of the Temple Mount to the eastern fringes of the city. Beyond the stratigraphic data, as was discerned in the excavations, these remains preceded the expansion project, which is evident from another feature: the orientation of the sections of walls and installations, especially the *miqwa᾿ot* (ritual baths), which differ from the clear east–west axis orientation of the Southern Wall of the Temple Mount. In contrast, the direction of the wall segments are different and correspond to the orientation of the local ridge, which is northwest–southeast.

Here, too, as observed in the Iron Age, it is difficult to establish the character of the residential areas that developed south of the Temple Mount and along its slopes. One fact is particularly striking, namely the existence of numerous *miqwa᾿ot* in this area, including those which predate the Herodian expansion. This seems to indicate that the observance of the Jewish *Halakha* (religious code of law) was common as early as the rise of the Hasmonean dynasty in the late 2nd century BCE (Reich 2013: 103–113).

Another important relic we found worth noting in this context was a drainage channel that runs through the base of the Tyropoeon Valley; it apparently drained parts of the city that were later covered up during Herod's expansion of the Temple Mount complex, and hence fell into disuse during the expansion (Warren 1884: Pl V). This channel was replaced by a new main sewer drainage that runs under the Herodian Street at the foot of Robinson's Arch and bypasses the southwestern corner.

Noteworthy, too, is the location of the entrance gates at the Southern Wall—the Double Gate and the Triple Gate. It is accepted that these gates were built in the Southern Wall of the extended complex to the south and on the same axis as the gates of the pre-Herodian complex, known as the Hulda Gates. It can thus be estimated that similar to the extended Herodian complex, a road also led to the pre-Herodian Hulda Gates. The large number of pre-Herodian *miqwa᾿ot* in the area, including a possible pair of *miqwa᾿ot* that were constructed in relation to the western Hulda Gates, also points to the importance of the area in relation to pilgrimages (Reich 1989).

THE HERODIAN PERIOD

More than a century ago, Warren documented marks and letters on the foundation stones of both the southeastern and northeastern corners. We discovered additional letters, with a similar interpretation, on the cornerstones of the southwestern corner. Deciphering the letters anew—those discovered by Warren as well as additional letters presented here—brought us to suggest that they carried a unique significance when seen as acronyms (*Kof, Het, Tav*), and had a religious and perhaps even a ceremonial significance (Reich and Baruch 2016). Therefore, the corners of the Temple Mount are of particular importance in establishing the building process of the Temple Mount extension, as is said: "The stone which the builders rejected has become the chief corner-stone" (Psalms 118:22), i.e., the cornerstones were probably the first to be laid down in a ceremony during the construction of the extension.

Entrance gates to the sacred complex (the Double Gate and Triple Gate) were built in the immense Southern Wall. Monumental staircases leading to the gates were installed from the south, in front of them. A road, built as a sloping ramp, extended from the southeastern corner westward toward the Triple Gate. The excavations near the southeastern corner concentrated on both ends of this ramp. It was proved that previous reconstructions of this road as a stepped street, similar to its western counterpart, were incorrect. Although there was a stone-paved street here, the data indicate that what had been thought to be a stepped street was in actuality a sloping ramp. Moreover, the rate of the gradient implies that the ramp was used for conveying sacrificial animals (thousands of sheep before the festival of Pesach) toward the Triple Gate and into the underground spaces below the Temple Mount. This, too, may explain the unusual size of the gate—the Triple Gate (with three openings), compared to its western counterpart (with only two openings) and to the other gates of the Temple Mount. This ramp may also have been used to lead the scapegoat, and on rare occasions the red heifer, down from the Temple Mount.

Another stepped road was installed adjacent to and abutting the Southern Wall. It starts near the southwestern corner and continues from there toward the Double Gate, where it joins the plaza in front of the gate. This road was designed for pedestrians. To the south of this road, on a lower level, an additional large plaza was constructed, paved with huge flagstones. At the southwestern corner of the Temple Mount, the stepped street connects to the main street, which ascends from the Siloam Pool in the south, along the Tyropoeon Valley and along the Western Wall of the Temple Mount. It turns out that the part of the street that runs along the Temple Mount is supported on a system of built and sealed cells filled with earth.

A segment of the support system built along the Western Wall, to support the street and structures along its eastern side, was exposed in the excavations conducted by Hagbi and Uziel. The excavations exposed three compartments filled with a layer of stone chips, likely related to the final carving of the Western Wall's ashlars, sealed by layers of earth fill used to raise the life level in the area. The excavation exposed the lower ca. 2.5 m of the compartments, yielding a rich collection of finds, including pottery, glass, coins, stone vessels, charcoal and fauna. The finds from the excavation can be securely dated to the 1st century CE, with the numismatic evidence suggesting the fills were deposited in the first third of that century. The exposure of the Western Wall ashlars also brought to light interesting data regarding its construction, including the possibility that the area was used by stone carvers to practice their craft on courses that would be buried beneath the surface, in order to master their skills that would be applied to the upper, exposed courses.

The excavation of the structural system exposed in Hagbi and Uziel's excavations presented in this volume continue the earlier excavations further to the north and directly beneath Robinson's

Arch. The finds from these excavations date the construction of the Western Wall, notably the part bearing Robinson's Arch, to the period following the procuratorship of Valerius Gratus (17/18 CE); and the paving of the main street following the procuratorship of Pontius Pilatus (26–36 CE)—i.e., several decades after Herod's death (4 BCE; Reich and Shukron 2011b; Szanton *et al.* 2019). It should be noted that Ariel, in his excavation dates these coins to a few years later (see Chapter 11). However, this post-dating does not create an essential change. It simply puts the construction of this particular part of the Western Wall of the Temple Mount a few years later in the 1st century CE.[1]

Our research of the Southern Wall of the Temple Mount complex revealed that building the approach roads from the south was undertaken as an integral part of the construction of the entire complex during the expansion; it included adaptation of the rock to the expansion plan. Therefore, the late dating of the construction of the road system indicates that the duration of the construction of the entire complex, in effect, lasted almost through to the end of the Second Temple period. This supports Josephus's comment that it was Agrippa II who permitted the people to pave the city streets with stones (*Ant.* 20.219–223; *War* 5.36–38).

In addition, non-intrusive tests using ground-penetrating radar, were conducted in the Temple Mount Western Wall, where Robinson's Arch is located. These revealed important data regarding the engineering of the wall that bore the arch. New methods have enabled us to re-examine some of the engineering phenomena, especially the use of long stones. It seems that for the sake of expanding the Temple Mount complex to the south, the project engineers were required to come up with exceptional solutions. Clearly, the Eastern and Western Walls of the Temple Mount posed particular construction challenges for the engineers. It is worth re-reading Flavius Josephus's impressions of the entire construction project:

> Now in the western quarters of the enclosure of the temple there were four gates. The first led to the King's palace and went to a passage over the intermediate valley. Two more led to the suburbs of the city: and the last led to the other city, where the road descended down into the valley by a great number of steps, and thence up again by the ascent. For the city lay over against the temple, in the manner of a theatre; and was encompassed with a deep valley, along the entire south quarter. But the fourth front of the temple, which was southward, had indeed itself 19 gates in its middle: as also it had the royal cloisters, with three walks: which reached in length from the east valley, unto that on the west: for it was impossible it should reach any farther. And this cloister deserves to be mentioned better than any other under the sun (*Ant.* 15.411).

It appears that Josephus's description refers to the expansion of the complex to the south and not just to one particular structure; and in our opinion, this is reliable and consistent with the archaeological reality.

Evidence of Destruction

A close examination of the complex shows that large parts of the Southern Herodian Wall were destroyed. At one point, between the Double Gate and the Triple Gate, save for a single layer of stones, the walls were almost completely demolished. The wall in the southeastern corner, however, was preserved in its entirety, up to a horizontal protruding cornice that served as the coping. The

---

[1] The excavations near the southwestern corner of the compound (led by Yuval Baruch, Hélène Machline, Navot Rom and Ayala Zilberstein) continue as of May 2022 and will add additional technical data on how the streets were built and established along the Temple Mount walls and other archeological aspects.

remains of the cornice, both of the exterior façade and interior walls, were preserved and today they are located in a small room in the pinnacle, known as the "Cradle of Jesus," of the southeast corner of the Temple Mount (Baruch *et al.* forthcoming). Although we do not include exploration of the room in this book, we nevertheless present a Hebrew inscription engraved on one of the Herodian stones documented in its eastern wall.

Several dozen stones were discovered collapsed in excavations conducted near the southeastern corner of the complex. This assemblage, which was cataloged and researched by O. Peleg-Barkat, included stone fragments such as column drums, architectural fragments and decorated stones, joining the assemblage of the finds documented elsewhere along the Southern Wall. Such a large concentration of decorated architectural items leads to the conclusion that the fallen stones originated in magnificent buildings built on top of and within the Temple Mount: the Royal Portico and possibly stones incorporated into the Triple Gate, similar to those known from the Double Gate, which has survived and remained almost intact and is thus an extraordinary example of the splendor of the Herodian buildings that were on the Temple Mount.

THE LATE ROMAN PERIOD

To a great extent, the history of the Temple Mount complex following the destruction of the city in 70 CE is unclear. The most prominent find we have is related to the days of the Roman city, Aelia Capitolina, at the Southern Wall of the Temple Mount complex. A formal Latin inscription placed upside down above the Double Gate lintel, after the restoration and reconstruction of the front of the gate (CIIP No. 718), mentions the name of Emperor Antoninus Pius. Beyond that, there is no other evidence that might contribute to previous proposals that the Southern Wall was restored in Roman times as part of a plan to rejuvenate the Temple Mount complex and construct a temple to the Roman god Jupiter in place of the demolished Jewish Temple.

The excavations near the southeastern corner contribute significantly to our understanding of this area in the Late Roman period, despite the limited excavation. A large number of pottery fragments, clay bricks, square clay tubes (*tubuli*) and terracotta tiles with imprints of the Tenth Roman Legion, indicate that this was an area of activity in the Late Roman period. The square clay pipes used specifically in bathhouses indicate that such a structure existed nearby. Since a bathhouse requires a constant supply of running water, one possibility is that it had been built along an extension of the low-level aqueduct that, in the Second Temple period, reached as far as the center of the Temple Mount complex, and that an extension of it southward supplied the suggested bathhouse with water.

The Baruch and Reich excavation re-examined the section of the wall that abuts the southeastern corner of the Temple Mount complex. Up to the present study, it had been accepted that this section of wall was a remnant of an ancient Roman wall that was later incorporated into the Byzantine fortification system that became known as the Ophel Wall. Beyond the architectural analysis, the proposal is based on the fact that earth fills dating to the Late Roman period abut this section of wall from the west. These fills were considered as a leveled and open surface in the area adjacent to the wall. Until now it was considered a Byzantine Ophel wall; now it is considered an ancient Roman wall that was later incorporated into the Byzantine fortification system that later became known as the Ophel Wall.

THE BYZANTINE PERIOD

During the Byzantine period, the Ophel area up to the Southern Wall itself enjoyed a development boom. Dozens of buildings shot up throughout the area, most of them dwellings built according to a standard plan that included central courtyards and wings of various rooms and facilities. Some were built against the Temple Mount walls. Monumental buildings, their purpose unclear, were constructed west of the Ophel, and subsequently served as the foundations for the construction of Umayyad buildings (Reich and Baruch 2016). The entire area was surrounded to the east and southeast by a system of fortifications that included a massive ashlar wall with towers all along the Ophel Wall.

As part of the research of the system of sealed compartments that carry the sloping ramp that ascends to the Triple Gate from the east, we suggested that the wall that abuts the southeastern corner of the Temple Mount complex from the southwest and which was incorporated into the fortification system of the city in the Byzantine period, is actually founded on one of the walls of the sealed compartments from the Second Temple period.

Next to the southeastern corner of the Temple Mount complex, a multi-roomed building was built (Mazar and Mazar 2003). In the excavation next to the southeast corner, the area along one of the outer walls of the building was exposed. It was re-documented, and its foundation trench was excavated. North of this multi-room building a narrow road or alley was exposed that passes between the building itself and the Southern Wall of the Temple Mount. This road may have led to a gate that was incorporated into the northernmost tower of the Ophel Wall.

Our research did not provide sufficient information regarding the wall itself, and therefore there is insufficient data that contributes to the character of the Temple Mount complex in the Byzantine period. However, historical evidence of Byzantine Christian activity that took place in the southern part of the complex cannot be overlooked, especially within the southeastern part of the underground system of Solomon's Stables. It is possible that there was even a convent of nuns established there.[2]

As mentioned above, this part of the complex is the one that has survived to the tallest height of all the ruined sections of the Temple Mount, which is why sacred traditions identified this place with the turret, or Pinnacle, of the Temple, the place where Satan tempted Jesus (Matthew 4:5–7; Luke 4:9–12).

THE EARLY ISLAMIC PERIOD

The early Islamic period, certainly since the reign of the Umayyad Caliphs, is characterized by monumental construction activities in the area south of the Temple Mount and within the Temple Mount itself (Ben-Dov 1973).

No remains from the early Islamic period were uncovered in the excavations and especially from those conducted near the southeastern corner; however, we attribute this to the removal of the strata of the post-Byzantine settlement by the archaeologists who preceded us. On the other hand, a thorough examination of the walls of the Temple Mount, including its gates, suggested that the restoration of the ruined walls was a systematic measure undertaken by the Umayyad rulers as part of their transformation of the Temple Mount complex into a sacred Islamic compound (see Mazar 1971: 4).

The style of the restoration of the gaps in the wall was different from the typical Herodian construction; different stones were used, and it was therefore easy to distinguish. A thorough survey of the Double Gate façade, which was carried out as part of the documentation of the walls, also led to a similar conclusion, although it created doubts, because the front of the gate is built according to Byzantine artistic standards. There is no doubt, however, that the restoration of the walls was part of the process of transforming the Temple Mount complex into a sacred Islamic compound.

---

[2] On the existence of the monastery of the Pure Women, see Eliav 2005: 145, note 50.

Other constructions were added as well, mainly four monumental buildings, built at the foot of the complex to the south and southwest of the Mount, with a road system between them (Ben-Dov 1973; 1982: 293–321). Some of the structures were built on the remains of previous Byzantine buildings. It seems that as part of these construction operations, the Double Gate structure was also rebuilt, while maintaining the details of its plan and decorations.

In 1994 a cemetery was excavated to the west of the Temple Mount complex, under Robinson's Arch. It is unusual to find a cemetery within city walls, and moreover, one in which, as it turned out, people of different faiths were buried. This discovery may point to the victims of an earthquake, attributed to the 11th century, or perhaps to another traumatic event that preceded the Crusader conquest. It is possible to link the Arabic inscriptions engraved on the Western Wall stones that were documented during the conservation work at the site to this cemetery. The Hebrew inscription from Isaiah 66:14, discovered and published previously, is shown here to be connected to this cemetery and thus receives a dating, which is later than that attributed to it by those who discovered it.

THE MIDDLE AGES

Medium-sized ashlars (*mizi ahmar* type) were discerned in two segments along the Southern Wall, one west of the Triple Gate and the other east of it. These ashlars have margins that surround bulging bosses typical of the Frankish style of building. These segments surround the underground compound known as Solomon's Stables. Similar types of stones were used in Crusader buildings in Jerusalem, such as the Citadel. We have suggested, as opposed to previous opinions,[3] that this is a characteristic of Crusader construction.

There is a gate with a single blocked opening and a pointed arch in the eastern part of the Southern Wall. The gate's threshold represents the floor level of Solomon's Stables. Warren documented an opening at the end of a built tunnel, about 30 m long and 3 m below the level of the Single Gate (1884: Pl. 24). At the inner end of the tunnel is an opening leading to the level of Solomon's Stables. Today the opening of the tunnel is blocked.

At the Southern Wall, south of the Double Gate, Mazar and Ben-Dov uncovered a line of a wall that they dated to the Middle Ages.[4] It seems that after the Crusaders established themselves on the Temple Mount and in order to fortify this vulnerable area, a wall was erected parallel to the Southern Wall, which extended eastward, up to the Single Gate. This fortification system also included the remains exposed near the Khatiniyya complex, which was built in front of the blocked Double Gate. We estimate that the Khatiniyya complex, located in the middle of the Southern Wall, was built—or renovated—by the Knights Templar, to facilitate, among other things, the access to the Temple Mount from the south; hence, this structure also served as a gatehouse for visitors to the Temple Mount complex, in place of the blocked Double Gate.

THE PRESENT AND FUTURE

In this section, we assembled several studies that, among others, included Hebrew and Arabic inscriptions discovered in the past and not necessarily the result of the excavations reported here,

---

[3]   E. Mazar suggested that this was a pre-Crusader Fatimid construction (E. Mazar 2011: 266 and Southern Wall map), while others saw it as an Ayyubid and even Mamluk construction (Seligman 2007).

[4]   This wall was dismantled at an early stage of the Mazar and Ben-Dov excavations, so that documentation regarding it is missing (a photograph and schematic plan of the wall were provided by Ben-Dov (1983: 70–71).

although they relate to them. Of the short Hebrew inscriptions (a single word or even a single letter), we discuss the one found in Jesus' Cradle. It is in fact the first Hebrew/Aramaic inscription of the late Second Temple period detected within the premises of the Herodian Temple Mount. We observed that the extremely long and high wall of the Herodian enclosure bore a relatively small number of inscriptions and markings, and that some of these, as attested by another inscription we discovered, was most probably inscribed before the stones were set in place.

The Arabic inscriptions from the Umayyad period found on the ashlars of the southwestern corner of the Temple Mount wall, prove the spirit of the time: piety, and the Caliph's policy of emphasizing the centrality of the Islamic revival.

In an attempt to understand some of the characteristics of the Herodian architecture, we recreated a modern scaffolding of Robinson's Arch. We found "architectural seams" on both sides of the arch and these prove without a doubt that the arch itself was inserted into an existing constructed part of the Western Wall of the Temple Mount. We believe this is an important contribution to the architectural history of the construction of the Temple Mount.

The process of restoring the walls and their dates and two archaeoscientific studies that enable a reassessment of the Double Gate façade—a [14]Carbon study and a Ground Penetrating Radar (GPR) survey, conducted on the Herodian masonry of the Western Wall executed not on a particular stone, but across a considerable section of Herodian construction, to its full length and height—establish conclusively the thickness of the Herodian masonry and that the space behind the masonry is not a void but a fill of unknown nature, piled upon the inner side of the Herodian stonework.

Archaeological excavation, as is well known, damages the ground, destroys and disrupts remains from ancient periods and obscures information embedded and preserved in the ground. Therefore, archaeological excavations are carried out only under certain conditions by permit from the State. A main condition is that the excavation must conclude in a suitable scientific publication.

However, with the exposure of ancient walls and antiquities to the elements and other weathering factors, archaeological excavation also starts an inevitable process of erosion. This process has been slowed down by soot and soil for hundreds and thousands of years, and exposure not only brings about revelation but intensifies its possible deterioration. Even though scientists may have collected the data that the excavations had to offer and have written studies to their satisfaction, the tasks of the archaeological excavation are incomplete. Walls from various periods exposed in the area must be re-covered with earth after exposure, or alternatively need conservation and attention.

Conservation of antiquities requires raising awareness, research on the destructive processes of natural and man-made factors on remaining finds, and practical actions to preserve them. The main component unearthed in excavations in the area discussed in this volume are the Herodian Walls to the west and the south of the Temple Mount. Despite their great strength that is clearly visible to even the untrained eye, the chemical and physical weathering of the modern world is harmful to them as well.

Three components of conservation are addressed in this report. They include a discussion of the "philosophy" of conservation, research into the chemical processes that damage the Western Wall stones, and a detailed report of the use made of several sections of the Southern Wall, and the southern section of the Western Wall—which is, in itself, a considerable section (ca. 70 m out of the 490 m long Western Wall). But compared to the enormous size of the structure and the length of the walls, it is clear that this operation will have to be continued in the years to come. The research and reports presented here, therefore, constitute appropriate preparation for such actions. Our studies, which represent various aspects of conservation of architectural remains, are recommended for present and future preservation of other architectural remains.

In conclusion, this report, which deals with small-scale excavations and a diverse series of studies, brings to the general public and certainly to the scholarly community, new raw data, new scientific insights on antiquity, and practical reference to important cultural assets in Israel and around the world.

REFERENCES

Avigad, N. 1980. *Discovering Jerusalem*. Nashville.

Baruch, Y., Czitron, D., Peleg-Barkat, O. and Reich, R. Forthcoming. The Cradle of Jesus in the Temple Mount Jerusalem: Architectural and Artistic Aspects. *Eretz-Israel*. Jerusalem.

Baruch, Y., Reich, R. and Sandhaus, D. 2018. A Decade of Archaeological Exploration on the Temple Mount. *Tel Aviv* 45(1): 3–22.

Ben-Dov, M. 1973. Building Techniques in the Omayyad Palaces near the Temple Mount, Jerusalem. *Eretz-Israel* 11: 75–91 (Hebrew).

Ben-Dov, M. 1982. *In the Shadow of the Temple: The Discovery of Ancient Jerusalem*. New York.

CIIP: Cotton, H.M., Di Segni, L., Eck, W., Isaac, B., Kushnir-Stein, A., Misgav, H., Price, J., Roll, I. and Yardeni, A. 2010. *Corpus Inscriptionum Iudaeae/Palaestinae*, Vol. 1: *Jerusalem*, Part 1: 1–704. Berlin and New York.

Mazar, E. 2003. *The Temple Mount Excavations in Jerusalem 1968–1978 Directed by Benjamin Mazar, Final Reports*, Vol. 2: *The Byzantine and Early Islamic Periods* (Qedem 43). Jerusalem.

Mazar, E. and Mazar, B. 1989. *Excavations in the South of the Temple Mount: The Ophel of Biblical Jerusalem* (Qedem 29). Jerusalem.

Peleg-Barkat, O. 2017. Herodian Architectural Decoration and King Herod's Royal Portico. In: *The Temple Mount Excavations in Jerusalem 1968–1978 Directed by Benjamin Mazar*, Vol. 5. (Qedem 57). Jerusalem.

Reich, R. 1989. Two Possible *Miqwaʾot* on the Temple Mount. *Israel Exploration Journal* 39: 63–65.

Reich, R. 2013. *Miqwaʾot (Jewish Ritual Baths) in Eretz-Israel in the Second Temple and Mishna and Talmud Periods*. Jerusalem (Hebrew).

Reich, R. and Baruch, Y. 2016. The Meaning of the Inscribed Stones at the Corners of the Herodian Temple Mount. *Revue Biblique* 123(1): 118–124.

Reich, R. and Shukron, E. 2011a. Excavations at Robinson's Arch 2011: From the Paved Street to Natural Rock. In: Baruch, E., Levi-Reifer, A. and Faust, A., eds. *New Studies on Jerusalem* 17. Ramat Gan: 219–238 (Hebrew, with English abstract: 56–57).

Reich, R. and Shukron, E. 2011b. Excavations in Jerusalem Beneath the Paved Street and in the Sewage Channel next to Robinson's Arch. *Qadmoniot* 142: 66–73 (Hebrew).

Seligman, J. 2007. Solomon's Stables, the Temple Mount, Jerusalem: The Events Concerning the Destruction of Antiquities 1999. *ʿAtiqot* 56: 33–53.

Shukron, E. 2012. A Public Reservoir from the First Temple Period near the Western Wall. In: Baruch, E., Levin, Y. and Levy-Reifer, A., eds. *New Studies on Jerusalem* 18. Ramat Gan: 29–30 (Hebrew).

Szanton, N., Hagbi, M., Uziel, J. and Ariel, D.T. 2019. Monumental Building Projects in Jerusalem at the Days of Pontius Pilate—A View from the Stepped Street. *Tel Aviv* 46: 147–166.

Warren, C. 1884. *Plans, Elevations, Sections, etc. Shewing the Results of the Excavations at Jerusalem, 1867–70, Executed for the Committee of the Palestine Exploration Fund*. London.

Weksler-Bdolah, S. 2020. *Aelia Capitolina—Jerusalem in the Roman Period in Light of Archaeological Research* (Mnemosyne Supplements 432). Leiden and Boston.